EMBERS OF WAR

EMBERS OF WAR

THE FALL OF AN EMPIRE AND THE
MAKING OF AMERICA'S VIETNAM

FREDRIK LOGEVALL

Published in the United States by Random House,
an imprint of The Random House Publishing Group,
a division of Random House, Inc., New York.

RANDOM HOUSE and colophon are registered
trademarks of Random House, Inc.

Illustration credits are located on page 803.

LIBRARY OF CONGRESS CATALOGING-IN-PUBLICATION DATA
Logevall, Fredrik
Embers of war: the fall of an empire and the making of
America's Vietnam / Fredrik Logevall.
p. cm.
Includes bibliographical references and index.
ISBN 978-0-375-50442-6 (acid-free paper)
ISBN 978-0-679-64519-1 (eBook)
1. Indochinese War, 1946–1954. 2. Indochinese War,
1946–1954—Diplomatic history. 3. France—Colonies—
Asia. 4. Vietnam—Colonization. 5. Vietnam—Politics
and government—1945–1975. 6. United States—Foreign
relations—France. 7. France—Foreign relations—United
States. 8. United States—Foreign relations—Vietnam.
9. Vietnam—Foreign relations—United States. 10. Vietnam
War, 1961–1975—Causes. I. Title.
DS553.1.L64 2012
959.704'1—dc23

Printed in the United States of America on acid-free paper

Maps by Mapping Specialists, Ltd.

www.atrandom.com

2 4 6 8 9 7 5 3 1

FIRST EDITION

Title page photos: Fox Photos/Getty Images (left) and
ECPAD (right)
Book design by Barbara Bachman

CONTENTS

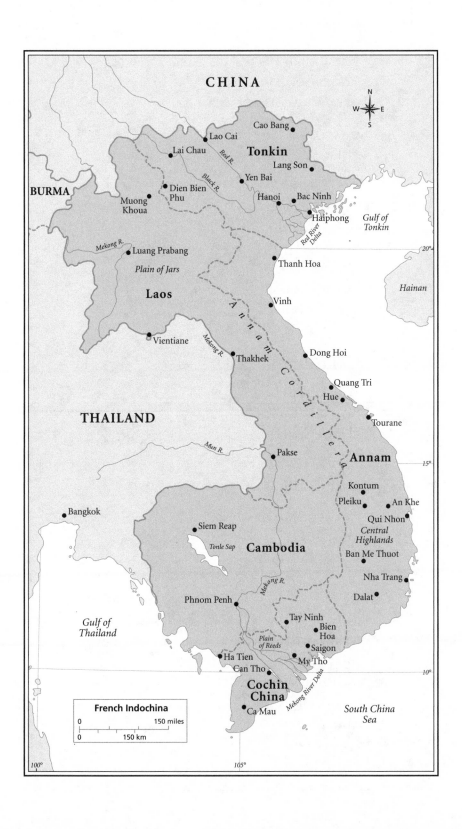

CHINA

N
W — E
S

Cao Bang

Lao Cai

Lai Chau

Red R.

Tonkin

Lang Son

Yen Bai

Black R.

Hanoi

Bac Ninh

Dien Bien
Phu

Muong
Khoua

Haiphong

Gulf of
Tonkin

BURMA

Mekong R.

Luang Prabang

Plain of Jars

Red River
Delta

20°

Thanh Hoa

Hainan

Laos

Vinh

Vientiane

Mekong R.

Thakhek

Annam
Cordillera

Dong Hoi

Quang Tri

Hue

THAILAND

Tourane

Mun R.

Pakse

Annam

15°

Kontum

Pleiku

An Khe

Qui Nhon

Bangkok

Siem Reap

Central
Highlands

Tonle Sap

Cambodia

Ban Me Thuot

Nha Trang

Phnom Penh

Mekong R.

Dalat

Gulf of
Thailand

Tay Ninh

Bien
Hoa

Plain
of Reeds

Saigon

Ha Tien

Can Tho

My Tho

10°

Cochin
China

Mekong River Delta

South China
Sea

Ca Mau

French Indochina

0   150 miles

0   150 km

100°

105°

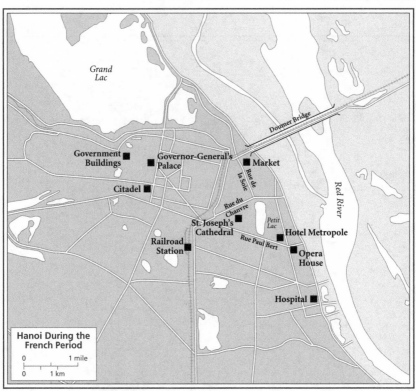

Government
Buildings

Governor-General's
Palace

Market

*Grand
Lac*

Doumer Bridge

Red River

Citadel

Rue de
la Soie

Rue du
Chanvre

St. Joseph's
Cathedral

*Petit
Lac*

Hotel Metropole

Railroad
Station

Rue Paul Bert

Opera
House

Hospital

**Hanoi During the
French Period**

0   1 mile

0   1 km

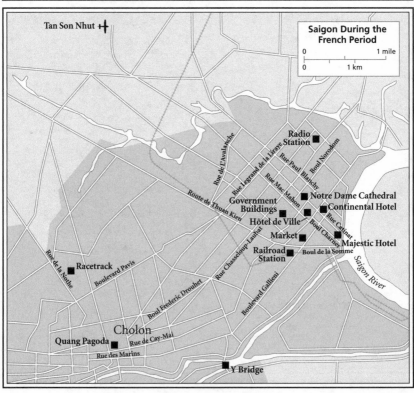

Tan Son Nhut

**Saigon During the
French Period**

0   1 mile

0   1 km

Radio
Station

Boul Norodom

Rue de l'Avalanche

Rue Legrand de la Liraye

Rue Paul Blanchy

Rue Mac Mahon

Route de Thuan Kieu

Government
Buildings

Notre Dame Cathedral

Continental Hotel

Rue Catinat

Hôtel de Ville

Boul Charner

Market

Majestic Hotel

Railroad
Station

Boul de la Somme

Saigon River

Rue de la Nothe

Racetrack

Boulevard Pavis

Rue Chasseloup-Laubat

Boulevard Galliéni

Boul Frederic Drouhet

Cholon

Quang Pagoda

Rue de Cay-Mai

Rue des Marins

Y Bridge

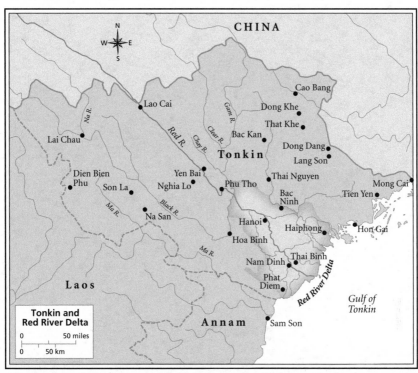

Tonkin and Red River Delta

0   50 miles
0   50 km

CHINA

Cao Bang
Dong Khe
That Khe
Lao Cai
Gam R.
Bac Kan
Clear R.
Dong Dang
Lai Chau
Na R.
Red R.
Chay R.
Tonkin
Lang Son
Mong Cai
Dien Bien Phu
Yen Bai
Thai Nguyen
Tien Yen
Son La
Nghia Lo
Phu Tho
Bac Ninh
Ma R.
Black R.
Na San
Hanoi
Haiphong
Hon Gai
Hoa Binh
Thai Binh
Ma R.
Nam Dinh
Laos
Phat Diem
Red River Delta
Gulf of Tonkin
Annam
Sam Son

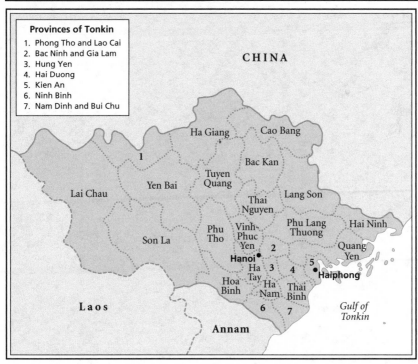

Provinces of Tonkin
1. Phong Tho and Lao Cai
2. Bac Ninh and Gia Lam
3. Hung Yen
4. Hai Duong
5. Kien An
6. Ninh Binh
7. Nam Dinh and Bui Chu

CHINA

Ha Giang
Cao Bang
Bac Kan
1
Tuyen Quang
Yen Bai
Lang Son
Lai Chau
Thai Nguyen
Phu Lang Thuong
Hai Ninh
Vinh Phuc Yen
Son La
Phu Tho
2
Quang Yen
Hanoi
Ha Tay
3
4
5
Haiphong
Hoa Binh
Ha Nam
Thai Binh
Laos
6
7
Gulf of Tonkin
Annam

PREFACE

IT IS SAIGON, IN SOUTHERN VIETNAM, IN THE HEART OF COLONIAL
French Indochina, on a brilliantly sunny autumn day in October 1951. A
young congressman from Massachusetts, John Fitzgerald Kennedy, age
thirty-four, arrives by plane at the city's Tan Son Nhut airport, accompanied by his younger siblings Robert and Patricia. Pale and thin, and suffering from a secret illness—Addison's disease—that will almost kill him
later in the trip, he is on a seven-week, twenty-five-thousand-mile tour of
Asia and the Middle East designed to burnish his foreign-policy credentials in advance of a Senate run the following year.[1] Besides Indochina,
other stops include Israel, Iran, Pakistan, India, Singapore, Thailand,
Malaya, Korea, and Japan.

Kennedy views this stop on the journey with special anticipation.
Indochina, he knows, is in the midst of a violent struggle, pitting colonial France and her Indochinese allies, supported by the United States,
against the Ho Chi Minh–led Viet Minh, who have the backing of China
and the Soviet Union. For almost five years, the fighting has raged, with
no end in sight. Originally it had been largely a Franco-Vietnamese affair,
resulting from Paris leaders' attempt to rebuild the colonial state and international order that had existed before World War II, and Vietnamese
nationalists' determination to redefine that state in a new postcolonial
order. Now the crisis is moving steadily toward the epicenter of Asian
Cold War politics, and the congressman understands it could loom ever
larger in U.S. foreign policy and by extension in his own political career.

Hardly have the Kennedys landed and disembarked when there is a
sudden outburst of gunfire nearby. "What was that?" asks JFK. "Small-

arms fire," comes the reply. "Another attack by the Viet Minh." The three siblings soon realize that the bustling facade that Saigon (the "Paris of the Orient," in the hoary cliché of travel writers) always presents to the visitor is a thin disguise for tension and insecurity. The cafés are packed, the bakeries loaded with French baguettes, and the shopkeepers along the fashionable rue Catinat do brisk business. But the restaurants have anti-grenade netting over their terraces, and palpable nervousness hangs in the air. There's a war on, and though the main action is in Tonkin to the north, Saigon lies in a war-dominated countryside. The Viet Minh have base areas less than twenty-five miles away, and they conduct frequent—and often brazen—attacks on villages right next to the city.[2]

The Kennedys are told they cannot venture outside Saigon by car. Though the French rule the roads during daylight hours, at twilight control shifts to the insurgents, and there's always the danger of getting stuck in the countryside as the sun sets. So the siblings stay put, conscious of the fact that even in the heart of town, there are occasional grenade attacks, kidnappings, and assassinations. They spend the first evening on the fourth-floor rooftop bar of the waterfront Majestic Hotel, glimpsing gun flashes as French artillery fires across the Saigon River, hoping to hit Viet Minh mortar sites. (The novelist Graham Greene, who will immortalize the war with his classic work *The Quiet American,* and who will enter our narrative in due course, is also a guest at the hotel.) "Cannot go outside city because of guerrillas," the twenty-six-year-old Robert writes in his diary. "Could hear shooting as evening wore on."[3]

The next afternoon Jack ventures off alone, making for the small flat on the nearby Boulevard Charner occupied by Seymour Topping, the Associated Press bureau chief. "I'll only be a few minutes," Kennedy says at the door. He stays more than two hours, peppering the journalist with questions about every aspect of the war. The answers are sobering. The French are losing and likely can't recover, Topping tells him, for the simple reason that Ho Chi Minh has captured the leadership of the Vietnamese nationalist movement and has a seemingly inexhaustible supply of recruits for his army. He also controls the mountain passes to China, whose leader, Mao Zedong, is supplying the Viet Minh with weapons and training. Kennedy asks what the Vietnamese think of the United States. Not much, Topping replies. At the end of the Pacific War in 1945, Americans had stood supreme, immensely popular throughout Southeast Asia for their vanquishing of Japan and for the steadfast anticolonialism of the just-deceased Franklin Delano Roosevelt. Their esteem grew when they followed through on a pledge to grant independence to the Philippines. But that was then. Now the United States is resented and even hated by many Vietnamese for her vigorous backing of the French colonial war effort.[4]

Topping's grim analysis impresses Kennedy, and he is further convinced after a conversation with Edmund Gullion, the young counselor at the American legation, who speaks in similar terms. Kennedy poses tough questions during briefings with the U.S. minister, Donald Heath, and the French high commissioner and military commander, General Jean de Lattre de Tassigny. Why, he asks Heath, should the mass of the Vietnamese people be expected to join the struggle to keep their country a part of the French empire? What would be their motivation? The questions irritate Heath, a Francophile of the first order, and de Lattre is no happier after his session with the lawmaker. The Frenchman, a blazingly charismatic figure who earlier in the year demonstrated his strategic and tactical sagacity in turning back three major Viet Minh offensives, has just returned from a triumphant visit to the United States, where journalists lauded him as the "French MacArthur" and senior officials proclaimed the vital importance of his mission to the broader Cold War. He vows to take the fight to the enemy now that the rainy season is drawing to a close, and he assures Kennedy that France will see the struggle through to the end. The American is skeptical, having heard differently from both Topping and Gullion. De Lattre, sensing his guest's doubt, sends a formal letter of complaint to Heath but nevertheless arranges for the Kennedy brothers to visit Hanoi in the north and tour the fortifications guarding the Red River Delta approaches to the city.[5]

"We are more and more becoming colonialists in the minds of the people," Kennedy writes in a trip diary. "Because everyone believes that we control the U.N. [and] because our wealth is supposedly inexhaustible, we will be damned if we don't do what they [the emerging nations] want." The United States should avoid the path trod by the declining British and French empires and instead show that the enemy is not merely Communism but "poverty and want," "sickness and disease," and "injustice and inequality," all of which are the daily lot of millions of Asians and Arabs.

Upon returning to Boston in late November, Kennedy continues the theme in a radio address and in a speech before the Boston Chamber of Commerce. "In Indochina we have allied ourselves to the desperate effort of the French regime to hang on to the remnants of an empire," he declares. "There is no broad general support of the native Vietnam Government among the people of that area," for it "is a puppet government." Every neutral observer believes "a free election . . . would go in favor of Ho and his Communists."[6]

Bobby Kennedy's perspective is much the same. The French, he writes to his father, are "greatly hated," and America's aid has made her unpopular by association. "Our mistake has been not to insist on definite political reforms by the French toward the natives as prerequisites to any aid. As it stands now we are becoming more & more involved in the war to a point where we can't back out." He concludes: "It doesn't seem to be a picture with a very bright future."[7]

Indeed. After the Kennedys' departure, despite ever-rising levels of U.S. assistance, France's fortunes continued to spiral downward, until by mid-1954 she had lost the war, following a spectacular defeat in the Battle of Dien Bien Phu, one of the great military engagements of modern times. The Eisenhower administration, by then far more committed to the war effort than were the French themselves, actively considered intervening with military force—perhaps with tactical nuclear weapons, in a heatedly debated secret plan ominously code-named Operation Vulture—to try to save the French position, and came closer to doing so than is generally believed. Neither President Dwight D. Eisenhower nor the U.S. Congress wanted to proceed without allied and especially British involvement, however, and the Winston Churchill government in London resisted strong administration pressure to go along. A peace agreement signed in Geneva divided Vietnam at the seventeenth parallel pending nationwide elections in 1956. Ho's Communist nationalist government took control north of the parallel, its capital in Hanoi, while the southern portion came under the rule of the Catholic nationalist Ngo Dinh Diem. Diem gradually solidified his authority in South Vietnam and, with Washington's staunch support, bypassed the elections. For a time he seemed to prosper, and U.S. officials—Senator John F. Kennedy among them—crowed about a "Diem miracle." But the appearances deceived. In the late 1950s, an insurgency, supported by Hanoi (at first hesitantly), took root in the south.

By 1959, a new war for Vietnam had begun, a war the Vietnamese would come to call "the American war." That July, two American servicemen, Major Dale Buis and Master Sergeant Chester Ovnand, were killed in an insurgent attack on a base near Bien Hoa, twenty miles north of Saigon. Theirs would be the first of more than 58,000 names carved into the black granite wall of the Vietnam Veterans Memorial in Washington.

FEW TOPICS IN CONTEMPORARY HISTORY have been studied and analyzed and debated more than the Vietnam War. The long and bloody struggle, which killed in excess of three million Vietnamese and wreaked destruction on huge portions of Vietnam, Laos, and Cambodia, has inspired a vast outpouring of books, articles, television documentaries, and Hollywood movies, as well as scholarly conferences and college courses. Nor is there any reason to believe the torrent of words will slow anytime soon, given the war's immense human and material toll and given its deep—and persisting—resonance in American politics and culture. Yet remarkably, we still do not have a full-fledged international account of how the whole saga began, a book that takes us from the end of World War I, when the future of the European colonial empires still seemed secure, through World War II and then the Franco–Viet Minh War and its dramatic climax, to the fateful American decision to build up and defend South Vietnam.[8] *Embers of War* is an attempt at such a history. It is the story of one Western power's demise in Indochina and the arrival of another, of a revolutionary army's stunning victory in 1954 in the face of immense challenges, and of the failure of that victory to bring lasting peace to Vietnam.[9] To put it a different way, it is the story of how Dale Buis and Chester Ovnand came to be stationed and meet their fates in a far-off land that many of their compatriots barely knew existed.

But it's not merely as a prelude to America's Vietnam debacle that the earlier period merits our attention. Straddling as it did the twentieth century's midpoint, the French Indochina War sat at the intersection of the grand political forces that drove world affairs during the century.[10] Thus Indochina's experience between 1945 and 1954 is intimately bound up with the transformative effects of the Second World War and the outbreak and escalation of the Cold War, and in particular with the emergence of the United States as the predominant power in Asian and world affairs. And thus the struggle is also part of the story of European colonialism and its encounter with anticolonial nationalists—who drew their inspiration in part from European and American ideas and promises. In this way, the Franco–Viet Minh War was simultaneously an East-West and North-South conflict, pitting European imperialism in its autumn phase against the two main competitors that gained momentum by midcentury—Communist-inspired revolutionary nationalism and U.S.-backed liberal internationalism. If similar processes played out across much of the globe after 1945, Vietnam deserves special study because it was one of the first places where this destructive dynamic could be seen. It was also where the dynamic remained in place, decade after bloody decade.[11]

My goal in this book is to help a new generation of readers relive this extraordinary story: a twentieth-century epic featuring life-and-death decisions made under profound pressure, a vast mobilization of men and resources, and a remarkable cast of larger-than-life characters ranging from Ho Chi Minh to Charles de Gaulle to Dean Acheson to Zhou Enlai, from Bao Dai to Anthony Eden to Edward Lansdale to Ngo Dinh Diem, as well as half a dozen U.S. presidents. Throughout, the focus is on the political and diplomatic dimensions of the struggle, but I also devote considerable space to the military campaigns that, I maintain, were crucial to the outcome.[12] Laos and Cambodia enter the narrative at various points, but I give pride of place to developments in Vietnam, far more populous and politically important than her Indochinese neighbors.

In retrospect, given the broader historical context, there is an air of inevitability about the flow of events in this story, as there is about a great river. A prostrate France, having been overrun by Nazi Germany in a mere six weeks in 1940 and further humiliated in meekly ceding Indochina to the advancing Japanese, sought after 1945 to reestablish colonial control, at a time when the whole edifice of the European imperial system was crumbling; how could she possibly hope to succeed? Add to this the ruthless discipline, tenacity, and fighting skill of the Viet Minh, and the comparative weakness of non-Communist Vietnamese nationalists—before and after 1954—and it becomes seemingly all but impossible to imagine a different result than the one that occurred.

Yet the story of the French Indochina War and its aftermath is a contingent one, full of alternative political choices, major and minor, considered and taken, reconsidered and altered, in Paris and Saigon, in Washington and Beijing, and in the Viet Minh's headquarters in the jungles of Tonkin. It's a reminder to us that to the decision makers of the past, the future was merely a set of possibilities. If the decolonization of Indochina was bound to occur, the process could have played out in a variety of ways, as the experience of European colonies in other parts of South and Southeast Asia shows.[13] Moreover, difficult though it may be to remember now, in the early going the odds were against the Viet Minh. They were weak and vulnerable in military and diplomatic terms, a reality not lost on Ho Chi Minh, a political pragmatist who labored diligently and in vain both to head off war with France and to get official American backing for his cause. Nor could Ho get meaningful assistance from Soviet dictator Joseph Stalin, who was preoccupied with European concerns and in any event deemed the Vietnamese leader too independent-minded to be trusted. Even the French Communist Party, anxious to appear patriotic and moderate before the metropolitan electorate, repeatedly refused his pleas for support, and indeed connived in the venture of reconquest.

And so the Viet Minh for a long time fought alone, largely isolated in non-Asian world opinion. The French had a massive superiority in weapons and could take and hold any area they really wanted. Even after Chinese aid started to flow to the Viet Minh in early 1950, the outlook remained uncertain, as France could now claim a still-more-powerful patron of her own, in the form of the United States. Throughout the struggle, Vietnamese sources show, Viet Minh units under General Vo Nguyen Giap endured unfathomable hardships, including acute food shortages and logistical difficulties and, after 1950, the terrifying effects of a new U.S.-produced industrial weapon of the age: napalm. In May 1954, at the moment of the glorious Dien Bien Phu triumph, Giap's army was exhausted, a spent force with sagging morale, in desperate need of a respite.

Politically too, Ho, for all his deep and broad popular support and charismatic appeal, always faced domestic challenges to his authority. Beginning in 1947, the French tried to rally to the anti–Viet Minh cause Vietnamese nationalists who so far had stayed neutral, and to peel away from Ho those anti-Communists who to that point had endorsed him. Ho himself saw the danger: What if Paris made far-reaching concessions to a rival Vietnamese regime, involving the transfer of genuine executive and legislative authority and a commitment to eventual independence? It could be a disaster. Later, after the partition in mid-1954, another worry: What if the South Vietnamese government—with a leader, Diem, whose nationalist credentials were almost as sterling as his own—could strengthen its authority to the point that it could doom forever his dream of a unified Vietnam under Viet Minh control? These were live possibilities, much discussed and debated in the Viet Minh inner councils and among informed analysts elsewhere.

Which is not to say they were ever close to being realized. To argue for contingency and the inherent plausibility of alternative outcomes is not to say all were equally probable. This is the advantage that hindsight affords. Though many senior French officials understood that in Vietnamese nationalism they faced a very potent entity, one made immeasurably stronger by the nature and outcome of the Pacific War, they could never bring themselves to grant the concessions necessary to have a hope of mollifying this force. An independent Vietnamese nation-state wholly or even mostly free of French control remained outside their imaginations; they could not make the mental leap required.[14] Even Pierre Mendès France, a heroic figure to many for his longtime advocacy of negotiations with Ho and his key role as prime minister in ending the fighting in 1954, did not embrace decolonization, not fully, and not until after the game was up. American officials, who pressed Paris hard to grant full independence *and* continue the war against the Viet Minh, did not comprehend the basic problem: Why should France fight a dangerous, bloody, inconclusive war that would end in the abandonment of French interests in Asia?

As for Diem's prospects after 1954, these were never as hopeless as most early histories claimed or as rosy as some later authors asserted.

An intelligent and courageous patriot, Diem was the only major non-Communist political figure to emerge in Vietnam from 1945 to 1975 even remotely able to think disinterestedly of his country's future, of constructing a political framework, or of challenging the Communist leadership in the north on something approaching competitive grounds. Given the indifference among the great powers—including North Vietnam's allies China and the Soviet Union—about following through with the elections for reunification called for at Geneva, it's not impossible to imagine a scenario in which Diem's South Vietnam survives, South Korea–style, into the indefinite future. But neither is it easy to imagine such an outcome. Over time, Diem's shortcomings as a leader—his rigidity, his limited conception of leadership, his easy resort to political repression—became more and more obvious. U.S. officials, well aware of these weaknesses but seeing no viable alternative leader on the horizon, stayed with him, their leverage declining with each passing year despite the regime's utter dependence on American aid. Contrary to common wisdom, it was Diem, not the United States, who possessed the dominant voice in South Vietnamese politics. Washington never had as much influence over Vietnamese affairs after 1954 as France had had before.

The Saigon regime faced difficult odds for another reason too. Many thousands of Vietnamese who might otherwise have wanted no part of Communism joined the Viet Minh against the French, motivated by a deep desire to achieve national independence. Among them were many of the most able and dedicated patriots in the country. Other nationalist groups, meanwhile, had either withered because they refused to choose sides or had thrown in their lot with the French against the Communists, hoping to achieve independence through incremental political reform, but instead losing all credibility with their compatriots for partnering with the hated colonial overlord. As a result, the human resources available to build a viable state in southern Vietnam after 1954 constituted, in author Neil Sheehan's words, "a mere residue," diminished by years of vacillation, compromise, and collaboration, riven by dissension and intrigue.[15]

Readers familiar with the American war in Vietnam—and with the debates surrounding more recent U.S. military interventions—may experience feelings of déjà vu at points in this book. The soldierly complaints about the difficulty of telling friend from foe, and about the poor fighting spirit among "our" as compared to "their" indigenous troops; the gripes by commanders about timorous and meddling politicians back home; the solemn warnings against disengagement, as this would dishonor the soldiers who had already fallen (the "sunk-cost fallacy," social psychologists would call it); the stubborn insistence that "premature" negotiations should be avoided—all these refrains, ubiquitous in 1966 and 1967 (and in 2004 and 2005), could be heard also in 1948 and 1949. The same was true of the tactical and strategic "innovations" U.S. planners offered up; most of these, including the concept of "counterinsurgency" (as the Americans would call it), had been tried also under the French. And always, there were the promises of imminent success, of corners about to be turned. When U.S. commanding general William Westmoreland in late 1967 exulted that "we have reached an important point when the end begins to come into view," he was repeating a prediction made by French commander Henri Navarre a decade and a half earlier, in May 1953.[16]

Civilian leaders, meanwhile, in Paris as much as in Washington, boxed themselves in with their constant public affirmations of the conflict's importance and of the certainty of ultimate success. To order a halt and reverse course would be to call into question their own and their country's judgment and to threaten their careers, their reputations. Far better in the short term—always the term that matters most to the ambitious politician—to forge ahead and hope for the best, to ignore the warning signs and the contrary intelligence and diplomatic reports. With each passing year after 1949, the struggle for senior French policy makers became less about the future of Indochina, less about grand geopolitical concerns, and more about domestic political strategizing, careerism, and satiating powerful interest groups at home.[17] The main objective now was to avoid embarrassment and hang on, to muddle through, to avoid outright defeat, at least until the next vote of confidence or the next election. "The stalemate machine," Daniel Ellsberg would call it with reference to the American war; it was fully operational also during the French struggle.[18] Sophistry and vapid argumentation became the order of the day, as leaders sought to save face—or, as they would put it, to achieve an "honorable peace"—while treasure and lives were being lost. That the general public was for a long time apathetic about the war—most French voters, like most Americans later, were too preoccupied with their own lives to become interested in a small Asian country thousands of miles away—did not lessen this imperative, even if in theory it should have; it merely made it easier for officials to offer rote affirmations in favor of the status quo.

Journalist David Halberstam, asked by a British colleague to comment on his wartime reporting in Vietnam, remarked, "The problem was trying to cover something every day as news when in fact the real key was that it was all derivative of the French Indochina war, which is history. So you really should have had a third paragraph in each story which should have said, 'All of this is shit and none of this means anything because we are in the same footsteps as the French and we are prisoners of their experience.' " America's intervention, Halberstam said on a later occasion, occurred "in the embers of another colonial war."[19]

Somehow, American leaders for a long time convinced themselves that the remarkable similarities between the French experience and their own were not really there. What mattered, they maintained, was that the French were a decadent people trying vainly to prop up a colonial empire, their army a hidebound, intellectually bankrupt enterprise. They had fought badly in Indochina and deserved to lose. Americans, on the other hand, were the good guys, militarily invincible, who selflessly had come to help the Vietnamese in their hour of need and would then go home. "We have a clean base there now, without a taint of colonialism," Secretary of State John Foster Dulles crowed to a friend as France pulled the last of her soldiers out of Vietnam. "Dien Bien Phu was a blessing in disguise."[20]

It was, for the most part, self-delusion. For one thing, the French Expeditionary Corps usually fought with bravery and determination and skill, as we shall see. For another, France's war was also America's war—Washington footed much of the bill, supplied most of the weaponry, and pressed Paris leaders to hang tough when their will faltered. Well before the climax at Dien Bien Phu, Viet Minh leaders considered the United States, not France, their principal foe. Furthermore, what Dulles and other U.S. officials for a long time didn't fathom, and then refused to acknowledge after they did, was that colonialism is often in the eyes of the beholder: To a great many Vietnamese after 1954, the United States was just another big white Western power, as responsible as the French for the suffering of the first war and now there to impose her will on them, to tell them how to conduct their affairs, with guns at the ready.[21] The other side, led by the venerable "Uncle Ho," had opposed the Japanese and driven out the French and thereby secured a nationalist legitimacy that was, in a fundamental way, fixed for all time—whatever their later governing misdeeds. They, much more than the succession of governments in South Vietnam, were the heirs of an anticolonial revolution.

Ironically, Ho Chi Minh had been among those who for a long time resisted drawing this conclusion about America and her role. For thirty years, from the 1910s until 1948–49, he clung to the hope that the United States *was* different—a new kind of world power that had been born out of an anticolonial reaction and was an advocate of self-determination for all nations, large and small. Like many deeply held beliefs, this one had taken root early, when the twenty-something Ho visited Boston and New York in 1912–13 and a few years later read Woodrow Wilson's Fourteen Points. The United States, he came fervently to believe, could be the champion of his cause. (In the French nightmare, he was right.)[22] In 1919, at the end of the Great War, with Wilson due in Paris to negotiate a peace "to end all wars," the unknown young nationalist set out to make his case. It's here that our story begins.

EMBERS OF WAR

A VIETNAMESE IN PARIS

IN JUNE 1919, AS WORLD LEADERS GATHERED IN PARIS TO SHAPE the peace following "the war to end all wars," a young man from Vietnam set out to present them with a petition called "The Demands of the Vietnamese People." He hoped in particular to reach Woodrow Wilson, the American president who stood at center stage in Paris and whose Fourteen Points seemed to promise self-determination for all peoples. "All subject peoples," the petition read, "are filled with hope by the prospect that an era of right and justice is opening to them . . . in the struggle of civilization against barbarism." It then listed eight demands for the French overlords of Vietnam, including Vietnamese representation in the French parliament, freedom of the press and the right of free association in Vietnam, freedom of emigration and foreign travel, and the establishment of rule of law instead of rule by decree. The petition was signed, "For the Group of Vietnamese Patriots, Nguyen Ai Quoc."[1]

To better his chances of winning an audience with Wilson, Quoc had rented a morning coat for the occasion. But he never got anywhere near the American president—or any of the other principal players. Thin and frail, with gaunt facial features and piercing black eyes, his unimposing figure was lost among the other nationalist representatives from Asia and Africa who also clamored to meet the American president. Wilson probably never even saw the petition; he certainly did not reply to it.[2] Throughout the war, he had framed his principles in sweeping, universal terms, but it's clear that when he spoke of self-determination he had Europeans primarily in mind—in particular the peoples dominated by the defeated Central Powers of Germany and Austria-Hungary. If he did not explicitly exclude non-European peoples from the right to self-rule, neither did he expect the peace conference to grapple with colonial questions beyond those arising from the war itself. Colonial peoples might achieve independence, Wilson evidently believed, but not right away and not without the tutelage of a "civilized" power that would prepare them for self-government.[3]

One group that did pay attention to Nguyen Ai Quoc's appeal was the Sûreté Générale, the French security police. They soon began tailing him and confiscating letters and articles he wrote, and they appealed for information to the colonial administration in Hanoi. Who was this mystery agitator? Where did he come from? Why did his name not show up in the immigration records for Indochinese entering into France? Gradually that autumn, a picture took form. He hailed from Nghe An province on the narrow and mountainous coast of north-central Vietnam, but had apparently been abroad for several years, spending much of his time in London. He had a wide circle of acquaintances among the disparate community of Vietnamese in Paris—intellectuals as well as workers and soldiers conscripted during the war—and appeared to have broad support among them. He maintained contacts with Irish and Korean nationalists who had come to Paris to lobby the great powers for independence. To pay the bills, he worked as a photo retoucher and took whatever freelance journalism assignments he could find. His age was uncertain, but Sûreté officials took him to be about thirty. By the start of 1920, they had staked out his apartment at 6 Villa des Gobelins, a quiet, residential cul-de-sac in the thirteenth arrondissement in southeastern Paris.[4]

Little did anyone know that this wraithlike and penniless scribe would in time become one of the great revolutionaries of the twentieth century, his face more recognizable to more people than those of the great statesmen who snubbed him in 1919. He would lead his people into total war against not one but two Western powers, first France and then the United States, in a struggle lasting three decades and costing millions of lives. His name then would no longer be Nguyen Ai Quoc (He Who Loves His Country). It would be Ho Chi Minh (He Who Enlightens).[5]

II

VIETNAM UNDER FRENCH DOMINATION WAS ALL HO CHI MINH HAD ever known, but this was not saying a great deal: He was still a young man in 1919. Compared to the Dutch in the East Indies, or the British in India, the French were neophyte imperialists in this part of the world, having gained full colonial control of Vietnam only a few years before Ho's birth.[6] Their initial arrival had come much earlier—already in the mid-seventeenth century Paris had established missionary and trade organizations in Vietnam—but only in 1850, under the pretext of protecting Vietnamese Catholics, did they begin their conquest. By 1884, they had achieved colonial domination of Vietnam, and in short order they added neighboring Cambodia and Laos to what now became the Indochinese fold.

It was a long trip from home for the young Frenchmen sent to take up colonial posts. The journey covered some 8,500 miles and might take weeks, with stops along the way in places such as Port Said, Aden, and Singapore. Upon arrival in Vietnam—or Annam, as the French called it—some adjusted quickly, some did not, but a great many in both categories expressed stupefied wonder at the extraordinary biodiversity they encountered. Even those who saw only a part of the country witnessed so much that was new to them—the vast deltas, the astonishingly eroded limestone peaks, the sand-dune coastal forests, the forest mosaics and savannalike grassland. Many wrote home with vivid descriptions of the flora and fauna, the countless species they had never seen before. Many commented on the sheer luster of the place, of the seemingly infinite number of shades of green, in the rice paddies, the grasses, the palms, the rubber trees with their green oval leaves, the pine trees on faraway hills. And they wrote of the challenge of enduring the heavy rains of the monsoon (which were to have a profound impact on the fighting to come) and the soaring temperatures of the dry season.

From early on, the lure of profit was the engine that drove French colonial policy. Commercial interests and government officials sought economic gain by exploiting the area's natural resources and opening up new markets for the manufactured goods of metropolitan France. Indochina, in this regard, held special appeal, offering an entry point into the (theoretically) immense market of China.[7]

But colonies were not merely a hedge against the vicissitudes of the capitalist economic cycle; they were also a potential source of military strength, grandeur, and national security. The colonial venture in Southeast Asia would, so the argument went, enhance French power and increase its credibility on the world stage. It would also prevent rival world powers, notably Great Britain, from staking a claim on the territory. "The political interest in this expedition," the Commission de la Cochinchine (Special Commission for Indochina) noted in 1857, "arises from the force of circumstances propelling the Western nations toward the Far East. Are we to be the only ones who possess nothing in the area, while the English, the Dutch, the Spanish, and even the Russians establish themselves there?" With the British holding a dominant position in eastern China along the coast, French planners turned their focus southward, to the Vietnamese shore of the South China Sea. In the words of the Marseille Chamber of Commerce in 1865, the goal was "to make Saigon a French Singapore."[8]

To the metropolitan populace, officials offered a different justification. France, they proclaimed, was engaged in a noble "civilizing mission" (*mission civilisatrice*), dispensing the benefits of modern civilization to the primitive peoples of Asia and Africa: the "white man's burden," Rudyard Kipling had called it in his famous poem of 1899. In earlier times, this sentiment had usually been cloaked in religious terms—to bring the word of God to the heathen—but by the 1880s and 1890s, the civilizing mission of French colonialism could be couched in secular language: Commercial development would integrate Asian societies into the world market. This would lead not only to their economic development but to a modern society based on representative government, the rule of law, and individual freedom.[9]

There were contradictions in these objectives, as perceptive observers quickly saw. The publicized goal of the civilizing mission rested uneasily alongside the pragmatic objective of exploiting the economic resources of the colonial territories for the benefit of the home country. As a result, the colonial government was never prepared to support the development of an indigenous manufacturing and commercial sector in Indochina that might compete against manufactured goods imported from France. The industrialization of colonial Indochina thus never occurred. Nor could Paris sincerely promote democratic institutions in Indochina when, in the end, such a society would inevitably wish to reclaim its independence. The first elected political entities in Indochina, which took the form of municipal councils in the larger cities and assemblies at the provincial level, lacked meaningful decision-making power and were composed mostly of Europeans or of wealthy local elites prepared to work within the colonial system. Unlike in India, where the emergence of the Indian Congress Party allowed nationalists to pursue their quest for independence partly through constitutional means, Ho Chi Minh and his colleagues were forced down revolutionary roads.

All the while, the message of the *mission civilisatrice* continued to be preached and even to animate the private discussions of some colonial officials, who believed they were bringing modernity and civilization to the Indochinese people, even when their actions often suggested something else. This ambiguity at the heart of French colonial policy would never go away; ultimately, it would bring the whole enterprise crashing down.

Equally portentous for the future was the division of Vietnam into three separate regions: Cochin China in the south (Nam Bo), a formal colony, along with the "protectorates" of Annam in the center (Trung Bo) and Tonkin in the north (Bac Bo). This division generated a welter of administrative arrangements that were in reality less complex than they seemed, for Annam and Tonkin were really colonies too. From 1887, a single ruler, the Paris-appointed governor-general of the "French Indochinese Union," dominated all three sections of Vietnam, along with Laos and Cambodia, from his palace in Hanoi.[10]

Yet the three sections of Vietnam developed differently, in part because the topography dictated as much. With her curved, hourglass shape, measuring some 127,000 square miles (about three-quarters the size of California, or slightly smaller than Japan), she bedeviled French administrators, and it didn't help that the two deltas where most of the population lived, one in the north and one in the south, were seven hundred miles apart, connected via a long and narrow central region that at one point tapered to just thirty miles in width. Annam and Tonkin, poor in natural resources, attracted relatively little direct French economic penetration and were from the start somewhat peripheral in the colonial system. Cochin China, by contrast, experienced intensive efforts at economic exploitation and cultural transformation. Boasting a tropical climate and fertile soil, Cochin China became the principal base of French capitalism in Vietnam and the destination of choice for the French nationals who emigrated there. Many settled in the rich Mekong Delta, built up from a shallow marine bottom by alluvial deposits of the mighty Mekong River that terminates its meandering course here. Saigon, the colony's capital and commercial center, became known variously as the "Pearl of the Far East" and the "Paris of the Orient."

Early governors-general devoted much energy to economic development, using various forms of direct and indirect taxation to finance much of the work. These taxes placed a heavy burden on the majority-peasant populace, arousing widespread resentment, but the achievements were considerable: the creation of a road and railway network; the development of rubber plantations, many of them along the Cambodian border, and mining operations; the establishment of irrigation systems that vastly increased the area of cultivable rice paddies in the Mekong Delta; the combating of malaria; the construction of hospitals and schools; and the creation of a Pasteur Institute in Hanoi, as well as a university.

In relatively short order, there emerged an affluent Vietnamese bourgeoisie centered in Saigon, its wealth based on commerce and absentee landlordism. Frequently its members grew to admire French culture and institutions, eating the same food and wearing the same clothes as the settlers, or *colons*. (Sometimes more than admiration was at work: They hoped that by so doing, they could establish civilizational parity on the cultural front.) But they were often scorned by these same *colons*, and many of them resented the economic domination of the Europeans and the absence of genuine political autonomy. Nevertheless, when these Vietnamese agitated for increased political influence and economic benefits, they generally did so within the confines of the French colonial system.

Others were not so constrained. Beginning in the first decade of the twentieth century, the colonial system came under challenge from the first generation of nationalists, who were inspired in part by the very educational system that the French had imposed, which sought to elevate

French teachings and models over Confucian ones. Some of these teachings were, to say the least, unhelpful to the colonial enterprise. Voltaire's condemnation of tyranny, Rousseau's embrace of popular sovereignty, and Victor Hugo's advocacy of liberty and defense of workers' uprisings turned some Vietnamese into that curious creature found also elsewhere in the empire: the Francophile anticolonialist. These early nationalists also drew encouragement from Japan's victory in the Russo-Japanese War of 1904–5, which showed conclusively that Asians could triumph over European power. By 1907, alarmed colonial military officials could report the existence of "revolutionary and subversive theories" among indigenous troops, and in the succeeding years exiled leaders, many of them in Japan, flooded their homeland with anti-French pamphlets and poems. In colonial prisons, meanwhile, squalid conditions and overcrowding in common rooms fueled nationalist agitation. For a time, French authorities kept a lid on the agitation, and by the outbreak of World War I in 1914 they felt sufficiently secure to leave only 2,500 European military personnel in Indochina.[11]

Scarcely did they realize that the war, a global struggle with an important colonial dimension, would be a major catalyst for nationalist movements throughout Asia and Africa. Hundreds of thousands of Chinese, Vietnamese, Indians, and Africans fought on the Western Front, with some 200,000 perishing on the French side alone. A new generation of Vietnamese expected something in return for this massive sacrifice and were not impressed by the sentimental imperialism that extolled the participation of people of all colors and religions in saving "eternal France." In particular, these Vietnamese counted on French authorities to adopt a reformist policy in Indochina, greatly increasing local autonomy, and they were emboldened by several powerful forces emerging at the same global conjuncture: Wilsonianism, with its promise of self-determination; Bolshevism and the birth of the Third International (Comintern), created to support and guide Communists throughout the world and preaching anti-imperialism; and the example of Sun Yat-sen's Nationalist Party in China, which preached a tripartite message of nationalism, democracy, and socialism.

III

FOR HO CHI MINH, CERTAINLY, THE GREAT WAR WOULD HAVE THIS kind of transformative impact, even if his nationalist agitation predated the outbreak of hostilities. Christened Nguyen Sinh Cung at his birth in Nghe An in 1890, he took the name Nguyen Tat Thanh (Nguyen Who Will Succeed) at age ten.[12] Under his father's tutelage, Ho studied classical Confucian texts but also the writings of leading Vietnamese nationalists such as Phan Boi Chau and Phan Chu Trinh. These left a deep impression, and when Ho enrolled at the prestigious National Academy in Hue in 1907, he had already committed himself to the great task of reclaiming Vietnam for the Vietnamese people. The following year he was expelled for lending support to peasants protesting high agricultural taxes and corvée labor. Pursued by the French secret police, Ho made his way south, taking jobs where he could. In early 1911, at age twenty-one, intent on saving his country and learning more about European civilization, he left Vietnam, signing on as an assistant cook on a steamer bound for France, under the pseudonym Van Ba—the first of some seventy aliases he would use. He would not see Vietnam again for thirty years.

Ho Chi Minh's travels would take him over the next several years to ports in Asia and Africa, to Mexico and South America, to the United States and Britain. He first reached French soil in September 1911, disembarking in Marseille. His views were complex, mixing opposition to colonialism with a fascination with French culture and a respect for the French ideas of *liberté, égalité, et fraternité* that he would never reject. France, he realized, was not exclusively a nation of policemen and colonial officials, and he hardly came off as radical in his first communication with the authorities, an application for admission to a government school training bureaucrats for service in the colonies. "I am eager to learn and hope to serve France among my compatriots," he wrote.[13] Skeptics will say he was merely being careful with his words, and that he sought admission to this academy merely so he would learn from France how to fight France. Possibly, but there's no doubt he possessed in these years conflicting feelings about the colonial overlord and about how swiftly independence for Vietnam must come. Like many colonial subjects, Ho then still believed, in that prewar moment, that the "modernization" of his country might be best achieved working *with* the colonizers, not against them, and that Republican France would in fact live up to the ideals she professed to hold dear.[14]

In late 1912, he crossed the Atlantic aboard a French vessel, visiting Boston before taking a job as a laborer in New York City. Manhattan's skyline astonished him, and he was impressed that Chinese immigrants in the United States could claim legal protection even though they were ineligible for U.S. citizenship. He expressed admiration for Abraham Lincoln's leadership in ending slavery and preserving the Union. But Ho also saw the grim realities of America's current race relations as he mingled with blacks in Harlem. It dismayed him that America could espouse such idealistic principles yet subject blacks to segregation, to blatant discrimination in all areas of public life, to lynching.

Ho Chi Minh stayed in the United States several months, whereupon he decamped for London, finding work as a pastry chef under the renowned chef Auguste Escoffier at the luxurious Carlton Hotel. Always thirsty for knowledge—it was one of his distinctive personal attributes—he spent his free time reading and writing and improving his English. (He eventually spoke it almost fluently, along with French, Russian, and Chinese.)[15] The Irish struggle for independence moved him deeply, and he later wrote that he cried upon learning of the death in 1920 of the mayor of Cork, Terence MacSwiney, who had been sentenced to two years in prison by the British and who suffered in anguish for seventy-four days during a hunger strike.[16] Here again, as in New York, Ho witnessed the disconnect between theory and practice, saw the willingness of even liberal democracies to tolerate discrimination and colonialism.

All the while, Paris beckoned. At the end of the Great War, Ho crossed the English Channel and immediately immersed himself in the political activities of anticolonial nationalists living in the French capital.[17] Soon he became one of their leaders, working first from shabby apartments at 10 rue de Stockholm and 56 rue M. le Prince, then from the flat at Villa des Gobelins. In the spring of 1919, together with fellow nationalists Phan Chu Trinh and Phan Van Truong, he drafted the petition for the Allied leaders at the Paris Peace Conference. To be more precise, Ho and Trinh came up with the basic points, and Truong—the ablest stylist of the three, at least in French—wrote them down, over the signature Nguyen Ai Quoc.

As Ho himself perhaps understood, his appearance at the Peace Conference marked the start of a new chapter of his life, and it would have done so irrespective of how the Allied statesmen reacted to his modest plea. In the months thereafter, he became more radicalized, more certain that his cause must be the full independence of peoples subjected to colonialism of any sort. He couldn't count on Woodrow Wilson, he knew—he had read into Wilson's message a universal liberating agenda that the American never intended. Accordingly, Ho made connections with Koreans fighting for independence from Japan, and Irish activists who sought the same from Britain. When the governor-general of Indochina, Albert Sarraut, late in 1919 proposed a set of reforms to colonial policy in Indochina, Ho rejected them as inadequate. The reforms, he charged, would have little or no impact on ordinary Vietnamese, who lived lives of scorn and humiliation. His activism now drew the attention of French Socialists such as Léon Blum and Jean Longuet, who invited him to join them. He did, attending the party's congress in the provincial capital of Tours in December 1920.

A striking photograph taken at the meeting shows a slender and intense Ho addressing a group of well-fed and mustachioed Frenchmen, appealing to them for support, "in the name of all Socialists, right wing or left wing."

It is impossible for me in just a few minutes to demonstrate to you all the atrocities committed in Indochina by the bandits of capitalism. There are more prisons than schools and the prisons are always terribly overcrowded. . . . Freedom of the press and opinion does not exist for us, nor does the freedom to unite or associate. We don't have the right to emigrate or travel abroad. We live in the blackest ignorance because we don't have the freedom of instruction. In Indochina, they do their best to intoxicate us with opium and brutalize us with alcohol. They kill many thousands of [Vietnamese] and massacre thousands of others to defend interests that are not theirs. That, comrades, is how twenty million [Vietnam-

ese], who represent more than half the population of France, are
treated.[18]

The speech, twelve minutes in length and delivered without notes,
won warm applause but little more. Ho quickly realized that colonialism
ranked low for a party focused on the struggle between capitalism and
socialism within France. When a group of socialists broke off to form
the French Communist Party, Ho went with them. He had read Lenin's
"Theses on the National and Colonial Questions," a document that, in
his own words, attracted him as a means of liberating Vietnam and other
oppressed countries from colonial rule. Other Marxist writers whose
work he knew seemed concerned only with how to achieve a classless
utopia, a subject that left him cold. Only Lenin spoke powerfully about
the connection between capitalism and imperialism and about the potential for nationalist movements in Africa and Asia. Only he offered a
cogent explanation for colonialist rule and a viable blueprint for national
liberation and for modernizing a poor agricultural society such as Vietnam's. Communism could be applied to Asia, Ho Chi Minh assured his

NGUYEN AI QUOC AT THE CONGRESS OF THE
FRENCH SOCIALIST PARTY, TOURS, DECEMBER 29, 1920.

Vietnamese allies in Paris; more than that, it was in keeping with Asian traditions based on notions of social equality and community. Moreover, Lenin had pledged Soviet support, through the Comintern, for nationalist uprisings throughout the colonial world as a key first step in fomenting worldwide socialist revolution against the capitalist order. What could be more relevant to Indochina's situation?[19]

"What emotion, enthusiasm, clear-sightedness and confidence it instilled in me," he recalled, years later, of reading Lenin's pamphlet. "I was overjoyed to tears. Though sitting alone in my room, I shouted aloud as if addressing large crowds: 'Dear martyrs, compatriots! This is what we need, this is our path to liberation.' "[20]

One is tempted to draw a straight line between the failure of the great powers to address the colonial question seriously in 1919 and this decision by Ho Chi Minh—and many other Asian nationalists—to turn to more aggressive means to achieve independent nation-states. There's something to the notion. Lenin's position on colonialism and self-determination was substantially formed by the time the peace conference got under way, but he was very much in Wilson's shadow that year, his words far less influential in the colonial world. The American president had set the terms of the armistice and appeared ready to do the same for the peace settlement. Upon arrival in Europe, he was showered with adulation everywhere he went, greeted as a conquering hero, a savior of the world. Lenin's Bolsheviks, meanwhile, were struggling to maintain power in Russia, engaged in a bloody civil war whose outcome was anything but certain. Only later, after the collapse of what historian Erez Manela has aptly called "the Wilsonian Moment" and the stabilization of Soviet rule in Russia, did Lenin's influence in the colonial world begin to surpass Wilson's. For Ho Chi Minh, the turn had been made by the early weeks of 1921.[21]

Thus began for Ho a frenetic period of writing and of attending conferences and lectures. He cofounded a journal, *La Paria* (*The Outcast*), and churned out articles for publications such as *Le Journal du peuple*, *L'Humanité*, and *La revue communiste*. He wrote and staged a play, *Le Dragon de bambou*, a scathing portrayal of an imaginary Asian king; the audience response was apparently underwhelming, and the play closed after a brief run. He found time to attend art exhibitions and concerts, to read Hugo and Voltaire and Shakespeare, and to hang out in the cafés of Montmartre, where everyone debated everything. In May 1922 he even wrote an article for the movie magazine *Cinégraph* that showed again his complex view of the colonial metropole. The French boxer Georges Carpentier had just defeated the British champion Ted Lewis, and Ho, writing under the pseudonym Guy N'Qua, waxed indignant that French sportswriters had resorted to Franglais in their coverage with phrases such as "le manager," "le knockout," "le round." He urged Prime Minister Raymond Poincaré to ban the use of foreign words by newspapers. France, he grandly proclaimed in a letter written during this period, was the land of Voltaire and Hugo, who personified "the spirit of brotherhood and noble love of peace" that permeated French society.[22]

In these years, as he would all his life, Ho made a deep and winning impression on those he encountered. Many remarked on his humor, sensitivity, and sentimentality, on his extraordinary ability to charm. Recalled Léo Poldès, a member of the French Socialist Party who founded the Club de Faubourg, the setting for many debates Ho attended:

> It was at one of our weekly meetings that I noticed this thin, almost anemic indigene in the rear. He had a Chaplinesque aura about him—simultaneously sad and comic, *vous savez*. I was instantly struck by his piercing dark eyes. He posed a provocative question; it eludes me now. I encouraged him to return. He did, and I grew more and more affectionate toward him. He was *très sympathique*—reserved but not shy, intense but not fanatical, and extremely clever. I especially liked his ironic way of deprecating everyone while, at the same time, deprecating himself.[23]

Later many of these traits would appear also in his public utterances and his diplomatic negotiations, which some interpreted as posturing intended merely to mislead his interlocutors and enemies. Perhaps, but if Ho was always a tactician, the evidence is strong that he also had his spontaneous side. A marvelous example of this comes from Jacques Sternel, a union organizer who offered words of support for Vietnamese workers in France. Ho came up to thank him. "He asked my permission to kiss me on both cheeks," Sternel remembered. "And it was certainly not an exceptional gesture on his part. There were only three of us there: him, my wife, and I. That's just the kind of emotional impulses he always had."[24]

IV

THE CHARM AND THE CLEVER DEBATING POINTS WENT ONLY SO far. Over the course of 1922 and the first part of 1923, Ho Chi Minh came to the depressing realization—and not for the last time—that the French Communist Party attached barely more priority to the colonial question than had the Socialists. For both parties, European issues were what truly mattered. No doubt this recognition played into Ho's decision in 1923 to leave Paris for Moscow. The move would put him closer to home, and he hoped also to meet Lenin and other Soviet leaders. On June 13, 1923, in an elaborately prepared plan to elude police surveillance, he made his way to Gare du Nord and boarded a train for Berlin, posing as a Chinese businessman. From there he continued to Hamburg, then by boat to Petrograd (later Leningrad, now St. Petersburg), finally reaching Moscow at the start of July.

Here too there would be disappointment. Lenin was ill and dying, and passed away in January 1924. Ho Chi Minh took the news hard: "Lenin was our father, our teacher, our comrade, our representative. Now, he is a shining star showing us the way to Socialism." Ho joined the crowds waiting hours in −30°C temperatures to view the dead leader, and suffered frostbite to his fingers and nose. He participated in meetings of the Comintern, wrote articles for various publications, and, it seems, enrolled at the newly founded School for the Oppressed People of the East (also known as the Stalin School), which trained Communist cadres and helped organize revolutionary movements in Asia. But Ho found relatively little interest for his message—which he articulated in meetings both of the Comintern and of the Peasant International, or Cresintern—that the agrarian societies of Asia had nationalist aspirations and revolutionary potential that must be nurtured. Eurocentrism reigned supreme here just as it did in the French Communist Party, and just as it did among American champions of "self-determination." He was, he later said, a "voice crying in the wilderness."[25]

Still, the Moscow interlude must have been a heady time for Ho, as he communed with what he called "the great Socialist family." No longer did he have to fear that the French police were watching his every move, ready to arrest him and charge him with treason. He was seen in Red Square in the company of senior Soviet leaders Gregory Zinoviev and Kliment Voroshilov and became known as a specialist on colonial affairs and also on Asia. In the autumn of 1924, the Soviets sent him to southern China, ostensibly to act as an interpreter for the Comintern's advisory mission to Sun Yat-sen's Nationalist government in Canton but in reality to organize the first Marxist revolutionary organization in Indochina. To that end, he published a journal, created the Vietnamese Revolutionary Youth League in 1925, and set up a training institute that attracted students from all over Vietnam. Along with Marxism-Leninism, he taught his own brand of revolutionary ethics: thrift, prudence, respect for learning, modesty, and generosity—virtues that, as biographer William J. Duiker notes, had more to do with Confucian morality than with Leninism.[26]

In 1927, when Chiang Kai-shek began to crack down on the Chinese left, the institute was disbanded and Ho, pursued by the police, fled to Hong Kong and from there to Moscow. The Comintern sent him to France and then, at his request, to Thailand, where he spent two years organizing Vietnamese expatriates. Then, early in 1930, Ho Chi Minh presided over the creation of the Vietnamese Communist Party in Hong Kong. Eight months later, in October, on Moscow's instructions, it was renamed the Indochinese Communist Party (ICP), with responsibility for spurring revolutionary activity throughout French Indochina.

Initially, the ICP was but one of a plethora of entities within the Vietnamese nationalist movement. The more Francophile reformist groups advocated nonviolent reformism and were centered in Cochin China. Most sought to change colonial policy without alienating France and vowed to keep Vietnam firmly within the French Union. Of greater lasting significance, however, were more revolutionary approaches, especially in Annam and Tonkin. In the cities of Hanoi and Hue, and in provincial and district capitals scattered throughout Vietnam, anticolonial elements began to form clandestine political organizations dedicated to the eviction of the French and the restoration of national independence. The Vietnamese Nationalist Party—or VNQDD, the Viet Nam

Quoc Dan Dang—was the most important of these groups, and by 1929 it had some fifteen hundred members, most of them organized into small groups in the Red River Delta in Tonkin. Formed on the model of Sun Yat-sen's Nationalist Party, the VNQDD saw armed revolution as the lone means of gaining freedom for Vietnam, and in early 1930, it tried to foment a general uprising by Vietnamese serving in the French Army. On February 9, Vietnamese infantrymen massacred their French officers in Yen Bai. The French swiftly crushed the revolt, and the VNQDD's leaders were executed, were jailed, or fled to China. The party ceased to be a threat to colonial control.[27]

Other non-Communist nationalist groups fared no better. Despite the intensity of the Vietnamese national identity, these parties were plagued almost from the beginning with deep factional splits and the absence of a mass base. To be sure, internal divisions were a common feature in anticolonial movements throughout the Third World and had many causes, including personality clashes and disputes over strategy. In some places, such as India and Malaya, leaders overcame the differences and established a broad alliance against the colonial power. Not so in Vietnam. Here the regional and tactical differences proved too deep, or the personality disputes too severe, for nationalist parties to band together. To compound the problem, anti-Communist political parties in Vietnam showed scant interest in forming close ties with the mass of the population. With their urban roots and middle-class concerns, party leaders tended to adopt a nonchalant attitude toward the issues vital to Vietnamese peasants, such as land hunger, government corruption, and high taxes.

All this created an opening for Ho Chi Minh and the ICP. French security services soon singled the party out as the most serious threat to colonial authority and devoted most of their resources to identifying the leadership. But Ho and his top lieutenants survived all French efforts to eliminate them—Ho kept constantly on the move in the 1930s, spending one year in Moscow, then in China, then in the USSR again, using different pseudonyms, his health often poor. In the mid-1930s, the party benefited from changes in the international scene. From 1936 to 1939, pressure from French authorities eased as a Popular Front government in Paris allowed Communist parties in the colonies an increased measure of freedom, the result of increased cooperation between the Soviet Union and the Western democracies against the common threat of global fascism. In late 1939, however, after Moscow signed a nonaggression pact with Nazi Germany, French authorities outlawed the ICP and forced its leaders into hiding. Other party members were arrested and sent to Poulo Condore (Con Dao), the notorious island prison camp in the South China Sea, where they endured wretched conditions and defiantly plotted for the future.[28]

The relative ease with which the French carried out this crackdown was a sign of the continuing weakness of nationalist opposition within Indochina—and by extension, of the continuing ability of the colonial master to have his way. A few thousand French officials could maintain effective control over some twenty-five million Indochinese, a reality that casts doubt on the claim by some historians that colonial control (not merely in Indochina but all over the empire) was in the interwar period already drastically undermined.[29] Perhaps the seeds of the empire's ultimate collapse were already planted, its racist foundation more and more contrary to the spirit of the times, but as the 1930s drew to a close, only the most optimistic Vietnamese revolutionary—or pessimistic colonial administrator—could believe that France would soon be made to part with this Pearl of the Far East, this jewel of the imperial crown.

But a tidal wave was coming, one that would sweep over Southeast Asia and leave behind a new configuration of power—and more than that, a crucial undermining of the legitimacy (and practicality) of the entire colonialist enterprise. In September 1939, a new war broke out, and by mid-June 1940, France stood on the brink of defeat at the hands of invading Nazi German forces. Japan, on friendly terms with Germany and sensing an opportunity to expand southward, prepared to seize French Indochina. And Ho Chi Minh, meeting with associates in southern China, said he saw "a very favorable opportunity for the Vietnamese revolution. We must seek every means to return home to take advantage of it."[30]

PART ONE

LIBERATIONS, 1940–1945

CHAPTER 1

"THE EMPIRE IS WITH US!"

IN THE LATE AFTERNOON OF JUNE 18, 1940, THE TALL, STIFF-BACKED Frenchman walked into the BBC studios in London. His country stood on the brink of defeat. German columns were sweeping through France and had entered Paris. The French government under Marshal Philippe Pétain had fled for Bordeaux and had asked the Germans to state their terms for an armistice. These were the darkest days in the country's history, but General Charles de Gaulle, who had arrived in London the day before, was convinced that France could rise again—provided that her people did not lose heart. De Gaulle had met earlier in the day with Prime Minister Winston Churchill and had secured permission to make a broadcast to France.[1]

He was pale, recalled one of those present, with a brown forelock stuck to his forehead. "He stared at the microphone as though it were France and as though he wanted to hypnotize it. His voice was clear, firm, and rather loud, the voice of a man speaking to his troops before battle. He did not seem nervous but extremely tense, as though he were concentrating all his power in one single moment."[2]

De Gaulle's thoughts that day were on the French Empire, whose resources, he sensed, could keep France in the war and fighting. And they were with Britain and the United States, great powers with whom he could ally. "Believe what I tell you," de Gaulle intoned into the microphone, "for I know of what I speak, and I say that nothing is lost for France." Then, like a cleric chanting a litany, he declared: "For France is not alone. She is not alone. She is not alone. She has a vast Empire behind her. She can unite with the British Empire that rules the seas and is continuing the fight. Like Britain, she can make unlimited use of the immense industrial resources of the United States."[3]

The broadcast, which lasted barely four minutes, has gone down in French history as *L'Appel du 18 Juin*. At the time, however, few heard it and few knew who de Gaulle was. Alexander Cadogan, the permanent undersecretary at the British Foreign Office, knew only that de Gaulle had a "head like a pineapple and hips like a woman's."[4] Robert Murphy, the counselor at the U.S. embassy in Paris, could not recall ever having heard of him before that day. The same was true of most of de Gaulle's compatriots. Although he was notorious within French military circles for his advocacy of the mechanization of the army and the offensive deployment of tanks, few outside that select group would have recognized his name, much less known the essentials of his biography: the birth in Lille in 1890; the diploma from the military academy at Saint-Cyr; the five failed (in part because of his conspicuous height) escape attempts from German prison camps in World War I; the postwar military career initially under the wing of Pétain.

De Gaulle had been promoted to the rank of brigadier general only a few weeks before, in the midst of the Battle of France (thus making him, at forty-nine, the youngest general in the army). He then joined Premier Paul Reynaud's government on June 5 as undersecretary of state for war. Reynaud sought to carry on the fight, but twelve days later, with the French war effort collapsing wholesale, as German armies were well south of Dijon and pressing down the Atlantic coast, he resigned. De Gaulle, certain that Pétain would seek an armistice, escaped to London, determined to continue the resistance from there.

The basis for de Gaulle's speech that fateful day was his conviction that the conflict was not limited to Europe. It was a "world war," he declared, one "not bound by the Battle of France." He would be proven correct. Likewise, Britain and the United States would become critical to the ultimate victory of de Gaulle's "Free French" organization, though not in the way he imagined. Even his deep faith in the empire's importance to his cause would in time find a certain degree of vindication.[5]

A vast empire it was. In 1940, it ranked in size second only to the British, extending some six million square miles and with an overseas population of eighty million. The island of Madagascar alone was bigger than metropolitan France. The colonies of Equatorial and West Africa together were as large as the United States. In the Middle East, the French were a major presence, and they had holdings as well in the Caribbean and the Pacific. And of course, there was Indochina, the Pearl of the Empire, rich in rubber plantations and rice fields. As the farthest-flung of the key French possessions, it along with Algeria (administered as part of France proper) conferred great power status on France and, it was thought, gave her an important voice in global affairs. As a whole, the empire took more than a third of all French trade in the 1930s (a figure inflated by the fact that the Depression caused business leaders to fall back on colonial markets); colonial troops made up 11 percent of mobilized men in 1939.[6]

In his memoirs of the war, de Gaulle recalled his feelings as he sat in London in 1940 and watched the deterioration of the French position in the Far East, at the expense of the encroaching Japanese. "To me, steering a very small boat on the ocean of war, Indochina seemed like a great ship out of control, to which I could give no aid until I had slowly got together the means of rescue," he wrote. "As I saw her move away into the mist, I swore to myself that I would one day bring her back."[7]

It was an immense task, de Gaulle knew. The journey would be as long as it was treacherous. It would take time to win French loyalty and French territory and so to establish his legitimacy as the authentic representative of the French nation. In those early days, hardly anyone answered his call. Not only did few people come from France to join him, but most leading French figures already in London decided to return home to support the Pétain government, which negotiated an armistice with Germany on June 22 and set up a collaborationist regime in Vichy, a damp, gloomy spa town best known for its foul-smelling waters.[8] Even many of those who wanted to go on fighting rejected de Gaulle's call. Some went instead to the United States, while others, including the imperial proconsuls in North Africa and other territories (under the terms of the armistice, the empire was left in French hands), were unprepared to reject the authority of the eighty-four-year-old Pétain, savior of France at Verdun in 1916. The only exceptions in the early months were French Equatorial Africa (Chad, French Congo, and Oubangui-Chari, but not Gabon) and the Cameroons, which declared for de Gaulle in August

1940. That same month a French military court sentenced de Gaulle to death in absentia, for treason against the Vichy regime.[9]

"You are alone," Churchill told de Gaulle, "I shall recognize you alone." On June 28, the British government voiced its backing of de Gaulle as "leader of all the Free French, wherever they are to be found, who rally to him in support of the Allied cause."[10]

The phrasing was important: The British were endorsing de Gaulle the man rather than his organization. Whereas the general saw his outfit as a proto-government rivaling that in Vichy, most London officials hoped Free France could be restricted to the role of a *légion combattante,* a group of French citizens fighting as a unit within the Allied armies. For them, the only French government was that headed by Marshal Pétain. Still, limited though it was, the British pronouncement was a critical early endorsement of de Gaulle, arguably as important as any he would ever receive. His bold action on June 18 made an impression on Churchill, one that would never quite dissipate even during the tensest moments—and there would be many in the years to come—in their relationship. The romantic in Churchill admired de Gaulle's epic adventure, his self-importance, his claim to speak for *la France éternelle.* He saw a certain nobility in the Frenchman's bravado and shared with him a love of drama and a deep sense of history. When in September the two men joined together in a scheme to try to win French West Africa away from Vichy with an operation against Dakar, de Gaulle rose in Churchill's esteem despite the fact that the plan ended in humiliating failure. To the House of Commons, the prime minister extolled de Gaulle's calm and authoritative bearing throughout the engagement and said he had more confidence in the general than ever.[11]

"I had continuous difficulties and many sharp antagonisms with him," Churchill would write of his relationship with de Gaulle. "I knew he was no friend of England. But I always recognized in him the spirit and conception which, across the pages of history, the word 'France' would ever proclaim. I understood and admired, while I resented, his arrogant demeanor. Here he was—a refugee, an exile from his country under sentence of death, in a position entirely dependent upon the good will of Britain, and now of the United States. The Germans had conquered his country. He had no real foothold anywhere. Never mind; he defied all."[12]

A very different attitude prevailed in Washington, where President Franklin Delano Roosevelt and his advisers from the start kept their distance from de Gaulle and his cause. Shocked and appalled by France's swift collapse against the Germans, despite having what on paper was arguably Europe's strongest army, Roosevelt concluded that France had essentially ceased to exist. Thenceforth, during moments of pessimism (and not infrequently in happier times as well), he believed the worst about France and concluded she would never again regain her status as a leading power. Investing military might and diplomatic aid in trying to defend her was therefore pointless. Following the armistice, Washington chose a policy of expedience, maintaining diplomatic relations with Vichy in the hope that the French fleet and the Pétain government would not be driven totally into the arms of the Nazis. As for de Gaulle, he was as yet largely a nonentity for Roosevelt. In time, as we shall see, the American president would adopt toward the general an attitude of unremitting hostility.

II

IN INDOCHINA, WORD OF THE FRENCH DEFEAT HIT LIKE A BOLT FROM the blue. Already in 1939, after Germany's attack on Poland, there had been murmurings in Saigon and Hanoi, among *colons* as well as literate Vietnamese, about whether Hitler could be stopped, and if he couldn't, what it would mean for them. A 1938 French film shown on local screens asked *Are We Defended?* and left the answer disconcertingly open. Still, no one had imagined that the defeat of *la belle France* could ever occur so swiftly, so completely. The turn of events may have seemed especially dizzying in Indochina and elsewhere in the empire, for certain key details—that French forces fought hard and suffered huge losses at Sedan and elsewhere along the river Meuse, for example, or that the greater part of the French army was taken prisoner—emerged only slowly in the colonies.[13]

"Overnight, our world had changed," recalled Bui Diem, a young French-educated Vietnamese in Hanoi who had breathlessly followed news accounts of the fighting. "Mine was the third generation for whom the universe had been bounded by France, her language, her culture, and her stultifying colonial apparatus. Now, in a moment, the larger world had intruded itself on our perceptions. Our ears were opened wide, straining to pick up signals from the outside that would give us some hint as to what this might mean."[14]

In the governor-general's residence in Hanoi, speculation was rife. General Georges Catroux, only a year into the job, was devoted to the empire and to keeping France in the fight against Hitler; for both reasons he was drawn immediately to de Gaulle's cause. The two men went way back, having been prisoners of war together in a high-security camp in Ingolstadt, Germany, in World War I, and they maintained deep mutual respect. But Catroux, an intelligent and highly literate five-star general who as a young man had been an aide-de-camp in Hanoi but whose recent postings had been in North Africa, was powerless; his Indochina, isolated from the metropole by thousands of miles of ocean, faced growing pressure from Japan.[15] For Tokyo authorities, the fall of France represented a perfect opportunity to remove several obstacles to their New Order in East Asia. Three years into a war with Chiang Kai-shek's Republican China, the Japanese had long been bothered about American weapons and other Western supplies reaching beleaguered Chinese armies via the railway that ran from Haiphong to Kunming. The amounts were significant: An estimated 48 percent of all supplies came by this route. Catroux succumbed to Japanese pressure to sharply limit shipments of weapons, but food and other supplies continued to arrive, and the Japanese began to think that only by seizing Indochina could they stop the flow. Moreover, Indochina could provide imperial Japan with significant supplies of rubber, tin, coal, and rice—all important in ending her dependence upon foreign sources of vital strategic raw materials. Geostrategically, meanwhile, Indochina could serve as an advanced base for operations against the Far Eastern possessions of the other Western colonial powers. For senior Japanese leaders, in short, the events in Europe opened up glorious new possibilities. Hitler's victories, American ambassador to Tokyo Joseph Grew noted, "like strong wine, have gone to their heads."[16]

In Hanoi, Catroux moved cautiously, aware that he had few cards to play. In previous months, as Japanese gains in China brought them ever closer to Indochina, he realized how inadequate Indochina's defenses were. He had only about 50,000 troops at his disposal, of which some 38,000 were native forces of suspect loyalty. The air force had only twenty-five modern aircraft in all of Indochina, while the navy possessed only a light cruiser, two gunboats, two sloops, and two auxiliary patrol craft. Munitions and other military supplies were negligently low. The Paris government, reeling under the Nazi onslaught, could offer no tangible assistance, he knew, and neither could Britain, focused as she was on the German menace and the defense of Singapore and Malaya. In April and again in May and June, British officials cautioned Catroux against taking any action that might risk war with Japan. Even if His Majesty's government wanted to provide military assistance, Sir Percy Noble, commander of the British Far Eastern Fleet, told Catroux in late April, it could not; it had no resources to give. The same message was reiterated repeatedly in the weeks thereafter.[17]

The United States was Catroux's last hope. On June 19, the day after de Gaulle's speech, René de Saint-Quentin, the French ambassador in Washington, put two questions to Undersecretary of State Sumner Welles. What would the United States do if Indochina came under Japanese attack? And in the meantime, would Washington provide immediate military assistance to Indochina, in the form of 120 aircraft as well as antiaircraft guns? Welles's reply echoed that of the British. The United States, he said, would do nothing that might provoke the outbreak of hostilities with Japan and therefore would not act to thwart an attack on Indochina. She would provide no planes or weapons. In that case, asked Saint-Quentin, what choice did Saigon have but to accept the Japanese demands? "I will not answer you officially," Welles said, "but that is what I would do in your place."[18]

Saint-Quentin and Welles didn't know it, but hours earlier Japan had issued an ultimatum to Catroux. The Tokyo government demanded an end to the shipment through Tonkin of trucks, gasoline, or other goods of military use to China, as well as the establishment of a Japanese control commission in Indochina to supervise the implementation of the agreement. Catroux ordered Saint-Quentin to make one more appeal to the Americans; when that too failed, he decided to accept the Japanese terms, hoping to forestall a Japanese invasion and preserve French control over Indochina. Already by June 29, Japanese checkpoints had been established in Tonkin at Haiphong, Ha Giang, Lao Cai, Cao Bang, and

Lang Son. Perhaps, Catroux reasoned, Tokyo leaders hoped to avoid a costly—in yen and men—occupation of Indochina; perhaps he could temporize and hold on, waiting for a more favorable turn in the war. He cabled his government on June 26: "When one is beaten, when one has few planes and little anti-aircraft defense, no submarines, one tries to keep one's property without having to fight and one negotiates. That is what I have done."[19]

Who could blame him? His regime was isolated, his defenses hope-lessly inadequate. Moreover, Catroux's reading of the Japanese inten-tions proved correct, at least in the short term. Tokyo officials had a full-fledged colonial project, dating to the late nineteenth century and revived in the early 1930s, but in Indochina they were happy to practice the type of informal imperialism that the United States and other world powers had on occasion embraced—they were content, that is to say, to move patiently into Indochina with the consent of the French. Had the Japanese merely wanted to stop the transfer traffic to China, they could have conquered Tonkin, taken over railroad traffic, and used Vietnamese air bases to bomb transport routes like the Burma Road, linking Burma and China. Had they wanted to take outright colonial control over all of Indochina, they probably had the means to do that as well (though at the risk of a major depletion of manpower). But their chief aim was to use the country's installations for future military projects and to get at Indochi-na's coal, rubber, tin, and, above all, food supplies. These the Japanese could most easily and efficiently secure if they left the French nominally in charge and avoided taking on the complicated task of day-to-day gov-erning. "The Japanese government," foreign minister Yosuke Matsuoka informed the Vichy ambassador to Tokyo, "has every intention of re-specting the rights and interests of France in the Far East, particularly the territorial integrity of Indochina and the sovereignty of France over the entire area of the Indochinese Union."[20]

If Catroux thought he had little choice but to accept Japan's demand, his superiors in France felt differently. On their knees before Hitler, barely settled in Vichy amid extraordinary confusion, they were deeply attached to the empire as one remaining manifestation of French great-ness, as proof positive that Vichy was more than a mouthpiece of a de-feated nation. They frowned dismissively on Catroux's surrender and summarily sacked him. In his place they appointed Vice Admiral Jean Decoux, commander in chief of French naval forces in the Far East, who had the virtue of already being on the scene in Indochina. Decoux could also be expected to be reliably pro-Vichy, unlike Catroux, whom many officials around Pétain thought dangerously pro-British and pro-de Gaulle. Outraged by his dismissal, Catroux pretended not to receive the order to step down and blithely continued governing and negotiating with the Japanese. It took a second order from Vichy for him to relinquish power, and not until July 20 did Decoux assume control. Catroux promptly joined de Gaulle and the Free French in London, the first high-profile official to do so.[21]

Why, it may be asked, given these Gaullist sympathies, did Catroux not try harder to rally Indochina to the Gaullist side in those final days of June and early July, while he still held power? It is difficult to be sure, but he appears to have suspected that most of the *colons* in Indochina would not in the end defy Vichy, particularly when neither Britain nor the United States was likely to come to their aid. More important, Catroux was convinced that an open commitment to the British and the Free French would merely provide Japan with a pretext to seize the colony. Sympathetic though he was to the Free French cause, Catroux attached the highest importance to keeping Indochina under French control.

That became Decoux's chief objective. After he arrived in Vietnam to assume leadership, he maintained Catroux's policy of playing for time. Though unswervingly loyal to Pétain, Decoux was no friend of the Axis powers, and he worked tenaciously to limit Japanese gains. In August 1940, when Tokyo demanded use of Tonkin's airports and seaports, as well as transit rights to the Chinese border, the admiral calculated that a U.S. pledge of diplomatic support for the French position might enable Vichy to resist. Some in Vichy agreed, notably Jean Chauvel, head of the Far Eastern Division in the Foreign Ministry. The Roosevelt administration, Chauvel pointed out, had been "surprised and mortified" by the French collapse in Europe, but saw little that could be done in that arena in the short term. In the Far East, however, Washington could be expected to assert its interests. French resistance in Indochina might induce Roosevelt to take a firmer line against Japan. Chauvel insisted that the European war and the Asian crisis were part of one global struggle, and that the United States would eventually become a belligerent, via the Pacific. If additional concessions to Japan became absolutely essential, he concluded, "we must on each occasion drive the United States into a corner, to lead them to recognize their impotence to help us, to make them admit that the maintenance of a French presence . . . was preferable to an eviction which had left all freedom to their adversary."[22]

Other officials saw little hope in playing the American card. Foreign Minister Paul Baudouin, a former manager of the Bank of Indochina who was married to a Vietnamese, argued that France would be powerless if Japan opted to invade. "The position is unhappily very simple," he wrote in his diary. "If we refuse Japan she will attack Indo-China which is incapable of being defended. Indo-China will be a hundred percent lost. If we negotiate with Japan, if we avoid the worst, that is to say the total loss of the colony, we preserve the chances that the future may perhaps bring us." Meaningful American assistance was simply not a realistic proposition, Baudouin insisted. That was the message given him by Washington's chargé d'affaires in Vichy, Robert Murphy, and the line articulated by senior officials in Washington. On August 22, Sumner Welles told Ambassador Saint-Quentin that the United States could not come to Indochina's assistance but that she "appreciated the difficulties with which the French Government was faced and did not consider that it would be justified in reproaching France if certain military facilities were accorded Japan." In other words, if you know what's good for you, make concessions.[23]

Wartime calculations drove this U.S. decision, but no doubt it also mattered that few Americans in 1940 had any experience with Indochina. The peninsula was on the periphery of the periphery of interwar American foreign relations, and neither businessmen nor diplomats took much interest in Indochinese affairs. For the public, Indochina entered their consciousness only through articles in *National Geographic,* or old newsreels, showing exotic but dutiful natives in colorful dress. Fewer than a hundred Americans lived in Indochina before World War II, and most of them were missionaries seeking to spread God's word from small missions scattered about Vietnam. Until 1940, a single consul based in Saigon represented U.S. interests in the colony, and even he found himself with a good deal of leisure time on his hands.[24]

On August 29, Vichy concluded an agreement with Japan that recognized Japan's "preeminent position" in the Far East and granted Tokyo special economic privileges in Indochina. Japan also received transit facilities in Tonkin, subject to agreement between the military officials on the spot. In exchange, Japan recognized the "permanent French interests in Indochina." Negotiations continued in Hanoi in September and went slowly, as French negotiator General Maurice Martin held out hope for an American naval intervention that would cause Japan to scale down her demands. Increasingly impatient, the Japanese warned Martin that Japanese troops from the Twenty-second Army, based in Nanning, would enter Indochina at 10 P.M. on September 22, whatever the outcome of the negotiations. At 2:30 P.M. on the twenty-second, the negotiators signed an agreement authorizing the Japanese to station 6,000 troops in Tonkin north of the Red River; to use three Tonkin airfields; and to send up to 25,000 men through Tonkin into Yunnan in southern China.[25]

The agreement stipulated that the first Japanese units would arrive by sea. But the Twenty-second Army was intent on moving its elite Fifth Infantry Division across the Chinese border near Lang Son at precisely 10 P.M. Not long after crossing the frontier, the Japanese units became engaged in a fierce firefight near the French position at Dong Dang. Almost immediately, skirmishing also began at other frontier posts. For two days the battle raged, with the key French position of Lang Son falling on the twenty-fifth. The French forces had suffered a major defeat—two posts were gone, casualties were significant (estimates run to 150 dead on the French side), and hundreds of Indochinese riflemen deserted in the course of the battle. It might have been much worse had not Decoux and Baudouin appealed directly to Tokyo and had not the emperor personally ordered his troops to halt their advance. The Japanese apologized for the incident and termed it a "dreadful mistake," but they had made their point: Governor-General Decoux and the French might still be the rulers of Indochina, but they operated at the mercy of Japan.[26]

Decoux did his best to pretend otherwise. To anyone who would listen, he claimed that the Japanese were not an occupying force but were merely *stationed* in the country; that the French administration functioned freely and without impediment; and that the police and security services were solely in French hands. The tricolor, he noted, continued to fly over his headquarters in Hanoi. And indeed, French authority in Indochina remained formidable, as Ho Chi Minh and the Indochinese Communist Party learned firsthand in the fall of 1940. Sensing opportunity with the fall of France in June, the ICP in the autumn launched uprisings in both Tonkin and Cochin China against French authorities, only to be brutally crushed. In Cochin China, the French used their few aircraft as well as armored units and artillery to destroy whole villages, killing hundreds in the process. Up to eight thousand people were detained, and more than one hundred ICP cadres were executed. Not until early 1945 would the party's southern branch recover from this defeat.[27]

III

YET IN THIS GLOOMIEST OF HOURS FOR THE VIETNAMESE COMMU-nists would occur one of the key developments in the thirty-five-year struggle for Vietnam. Ho Chi Minh had objected to the uprisings, considering them premature, but he was convinced that, with international events moving fast and Decoux's government isolated from metropolitan France, the potential for revolution in Vietnam was much enhanced. Along with other party leaders, he determined that there should be a plenary meeting of the party's Central Committee in the spring of 1941. For symbolic reasons, they agreed, the meeting should occur on Vietnamese soil. In the early weeks of that year, Ho Chi Minh slipped across the frontier from China by sampan and set up headquarters in a cave near the hamlet of Pac Bo, in Cao Bang province. It was the first time in three decades he had set foot in his native country. And it was not far inside either—Pac Bo, which Ho reached by traversing forty miles through thick jungle growth and over steep mountains, was less than a mile from the Chinese frontier. Near the cave ran a small stream that Ho named for his hero Lenin and a massive outgrowth that he dubbed Karl Marx Peak.

The living conditions were austere: The group slept on planks of wood in the cold and damp cave and had only one small oil lamp among them. The diet was meager, mostly soup of corn and bamboo shoots, fortified by fish caught in the stream. Each morning Ho woke up early to do calisthenics and then swim in the stream before sitting down to work at a flat rock he used as a desk. He spent long hours reading, writing—on his trusted Hermès typewriter—and conducting meetings, all for the purpose of setting up a new Communist-dominated united front and outlining a strategy for liberating Vietnam from foreign rule. Ho and his colleagues formalized their plans at what would become known as the Eighth Plenum of the Indochinese Communist Party, which convened at the Pac Bo camp for nine days in mid-May 1941. The delegates sat on simple wood blocks around a bamboo table, and out of their discussions a new party came into being. Its official title was Viet Nam Doc Lap Dong Minh Hoi, or the Revolutionary League for the Independence of Vietnam—or, for history, the Viet Minh. Dang Xuan Khu, alias Truong Chinh ("Long March" in Vietnamese), an intellectual who had been with the ICP since its creation and had edited a party journal, became acting general secretary.[28]

Led by Ho Chi Minh, the delegates set a basic policy that would in time enable this small minority to capture the seething nationalism of Vietnam and make it theirs, and to bring disaster upon first France and then the United States. The longing to be free from foreign domination was the most potent force in Vietnam, Ho reminded his colleagues, which meant that the Viet Minh had to be a patriotic, broad-based movement, directed against both French colonial rule and the growing Japanese presence in the country. Women would play a vital role in the effort, and should be given equal rights. The result, notes historian Huynh Kim Khanh, was a "radical redefinition of the nature and tasks of the Vietnamese revolution," away from the class struggle and toward national liberation. This emphasis on patriotism can be seen in the organization's name, which not only stressed the issue of independence but replaced the word *Indochina* with the singular *Vietnam*.[29]

"National Salvation is the common cause to the whole of our people," Ho declared in a widely circulated letter in June 1941. "Every Vietnamese must take a part in it. He who has money will contribute his money, he who has strength will contribute his strength, he who has talent will contribute his talent. I pledge to use all my modest abilities to follow you, and am ready for the last sacrifice."[30] He elaborated on these points in myriad publications, including a "History of Our Country" that extolled Vietnam's glorious and heroic past and her valiant struggles against Chinese invasions. He also churned out articles for a journal titled *Viet Nam*

Doc lap (*Independent Vietnam*), more than 150 issues of which were distributed in northern Tonkin. The contents of a typical issue could be strikingly diverse, including, say, an article attacking Pétain and Decoux, a fable for children, and a short poem such as "Song of the Soldier" or "Song of the Guerrilla," to be sung in a round.[31]

Was there a contradiction between this emphasis on patriotism and national unity, and the internationalism of the Comintern? Some authors have said so, but it's really a false dichotomy. True, the Comintern generally frowned on overt expressions of nationalism and emphasized the primacy of the class struggle. But the Comintern did not deny colonized peoples the right to celebrate their past or to try to throw off their oppressors. Lenin, as we have seen, expressly offered Soviet backing for anticolonial nationalism. Ho Chi Minh and his five colleagues around that table in the cave in Pac Bo were Communists, convinced that Marxism-Leninism represented the best path of development for their country. But it was their country. They saw no contradiction between their Communism and their fervent desire to make Vietnam Vietnamese again. "By founding the Viet Minh," historian Pierre Brocheux writes in denying any contradiction, "Ho Chi Minh brought together—or at least into synergy—the dynamism of nationalism and that of international communism."[32]

As the Pac Bo meeting broke up, the delegates knew their principal task: to create a movement for independence that would generate mass support among the Vietnamese people as well as win the sympathy of the Allied powers. Victory over the French and Japanese imperialists would mean national liberation and would bring to power a broad-based government dominated by the ICP but including other nationalist elements. Once that core objective was established, work could begin to usher in the proletarian or socialist stage of the revolution.

IV

IT WOULD TAKE FOUR YEARS FOR THE VIET MINH TO FULLY ASSERT themselves, but both French and Japanese authorities understood early on that Vietnamese nationalism was a potentially powerful adversary. (Long before this point, indeed, French security officials had been tracking Vietnamese nationalists across Vietnam and Southeast Asia and beyond.) They responded by at once colluding to keep that nationalism in check and competing with each other for the hearts and minds of the Vietnamese. The Japanese tried to impress the Vietnamese with propaganda and cultural events about their "Greater East Asia Co-Prosperity Sphere" and touted their slogan "Asia for the Asians." They organized judo classes and distributed Tokyo movies and magazines. Decoux countered with the "Indochinese Federation," a mutually beneficial organization of different peoples, each with separate traditions, held together and directed by France. He also promoted Vietnamese language and culture, established an ambitious program of public works, and ordered salaries of native functionaries to be brought closer to those of their French counterparts. He even authorized the use of the until-then-forbidden name "Vietnam."[33]

ADMIRAL JEAN DECOUX (LEFT) LEADS A JAPANESE
COMMANDER PAST A LINE OF FRENCH TROOPS IN 1941.

Decoux took special pride in his innovations on behalf of the colony's youth. He increased the number of Vietnamese children enrolled in school, raising the total from 450,000 in 1939 to 700,000 in 1944 (although this still only constituted 14 percent of the school-age population). He built new schools and hired new teachers. The Youth and Sports organization, meanwhile, led by Maurice Ducuroy, sought to draw students away from the Japanese and nationalist influence through organized athletics and cultural events. The French constructed sports stadiums, swimming pools, and libraries all over Indochina. By 1944,

Ducuroy could claim more than a thousand new sports instructors and 86,000 registered members of sports societies. He organized swimming meets and track-and-field competitions, as well as an annual Tour d'Indochine bicycle race extending 4,100 kilometers across all five parts of Indochina—and modeled closely on its metropolitan prototype, the Tour de France, down to the yellow jersey worn by the overall race leader. When Japanese officials asked if Japanese athletes might compete in these sporting events, Ducuroy allowed them to sign up for cycling and the ball game pelota but not for swimming and track and field, where they were known to excel.[34]

"Throughout four dramatic years," Decoux would write later of the Youth and Sports program, "all these young people, who were not our blood, and most often did not speak our language, gave the 25 million Indochinese a moving example of fidelity and obedience to our devastated fatherland."[35] The remark gives insight into Decoux's attitude regarding his own position and the people of Indochina. Patterning his administration on Marshal Pétain's authoritarian Vichy regime, which liquidated France's democratic institutions and persecuted Communists, Freemasons, and Jews, he expected obedience and gratitude, in equal measure, from the Vietnamese, and he tolerated no nationalist agitation.

The main instrument of French rule remained the Sûreté Générale, the all-powerful French police. Decoux gave the Sûreté more personnel and expanded its powers, and he applauded its plan to recruit a "Legion of Combatants" to hunt down Vietnamese nationalists as well as *colons* who might be a threat to the regime. On the authority of Decoux and in the name of Vichy, Sûreté agents also pursued Jews, liberals, and Freemasons. Dossiers were opened on people suspected of associating with the Japanese, and the Sûreté could intern anyone deemed "dangerous" without trial and force them to labor in "special working groups." This included Gaullists, who by some estimates suffered more repression in Indochina than anywhere else in the empire. Newspapers and periodicals were suppressed—at least seventeen were shut down between 1940 and 1943. At the Indochinese University in Hanoi, a special commission was set up to enforce quotas on the number of Jewish students—a straightforward task, it would seem, as there were only some eighty Jews in all of Tonkin, forty-nine of whom were in the military.[36]

This, then, was Decoux's master plan: to show one and all that, despite defeat in France and acquiescence to Japanese occupation, his government was still firmly in control and capable of subduing challenges to its authority. For a time, the strategy worked. In the countryside, where the Japanese rarely ventured and 90 percent of the Vietnamese people lived, life went on pretty much as before; the French in control, the routine of life more or less unchanged. In urban areas, though, among educated Vietnamese as well as French settlers, no demonstration of French authority could hide the plain fact that Japan had established her presence with singular ease. Decoux understood this as clearly as anyone, but he hoped—and hope is all it could have been—that Japan's appetite for expansion in Indochina had been satiated.

It was not to be. In 1941, Japanese attention turned southward again. In September 1940, Tokyo had officially joined the Axis by signing the Tripartite Pact with Germany and Italy. In the months thereafter, army minister and then prime minister Hideki Tojo and his colleagues plotted their next move. To facilitate good relations with Thailand, Tokyo officials consented to a Thai plan to attack Indochina in order to regain territory on the right bank of the Mekong River ceded to Laos and Cambodia at the turn of the century. A series of Franco-Thai skirmishes ensued, with no clear victor except in a naval battle that the French won handily. Yet even though Thailand got the worst of the encounter, Japan, eager to have Thai cooperation for a planned drive toward Singapore and Burma, forced upon France a settlement that granted Thailand many of her claims. Once again, the hollowness of independent French colonial rule over Indochina was exposed.[37]

In April 1941, Japan signed a nonaggression pact with the Soviet Union, then watched with satisfaction as Hitler's forces invaded Russia in June. The Japanese might have used this occasion of Soviet weakness to conquer parts of Siberia—a plan they actively considered—but instead they concentrated on expanding the empire to the south. On July 14, only ten months after signing its agreement with France, Tokyo presented Vichy with a new ultimatum that would allow the establishment of Japanese bases and troops in southern Indochina. Vichy consented, and on July 25 Japanese troops landed in Saigon to occupy strategic areas in the south, including the key port of Cam Ranh Bay and airfields at Da

Areas of Japanese control,
December 1941

0   500 miles
0   500 km

U.S.S.R.

MANCHURIA

Harbin

Sakhalin

Kuril Islands

Amur R.

Sea of Japan

MONGOLIA

INNER MONGOLIA

Mukden

KOREA

JAPAN

Kweisui   Peking

Port Arthur

Yellow R.

Kaifeng

East China
Sea

CHINA

Hankow,
1938

Shanghai

Hangchow

Ichang,
1940

Yangtze R.

Nachang, 1939

Foochow,
1941

Amoy,
1938

Formosa

Ryukyu Islands

Kunming   Pearl R.   Canton,
1938

Swatow,
1938

Nanning,
1941

Hong Kong,
1941

PACIFIC
OCEAN

BURMA   Hanoi

Hainan,
1939

FRENCH INDOCHINA,
1941

Mekong R.

South China
Sea

THAILAND

PHILIPPINES

Saigon

BRITISH
NORTH BORNEO

BRUNEI

MALAYA   SARAWAK

DUTCH EAST INDIES

Nang and Bien Hoa. This gave the Japanese a forward vantage point from which to move quickly against Malaya, Singapore, the Dutch East Indies (today's Indonesia), and the Philippines. There was jubilation in Tokyo, where nobody seemed to remember the cautionary words a few weeks before of Foreign Minister Yosuke Matsuoka, who worried that such an operation would bring innumerable logistical difficulties and risk war with the United States. "A military operation in the Southern Seas," Matsuoka had warned, "will court disaster for our country."[38]

V

AND INDEED, THE MIKADO'S MOVE INTO COCHIN CHINA LAUNCHED a series of actions and reactions that put Japan and the United States on a collision course, culminating in the outbreak of war five months later. Events in Vietnam, so much a concern of a succession of postwar American presidents, and arguably the undoing of two of them, proved decisive here as well, in the last half of 1941, in making the United States a belligerent, and in joining the Asian and European conflicts into one *world* war.

Early on July 24, the White House received word that Japanese warships had appeared off Cam Ranh Bay, and that a dozen troop transports were on the way. American analysts were stunned, even though cables from the Paris embassy and MAGIC intercepts[39]—decoded Japanese communications—had told them for days to expect such a southward thrust. They grasped immediately the threat posed to the U.S. position in the Philippines and the British posture in Malaya and Singapore. That afternoon President Roosevelt summoned Japan's special envoy, Admiral Kichisaburo Nomura, to the Oval Office and proposed a neutralization of Indochina. In return for the withdrawal of all Japanese forces, Washington would seek an international agreement to regard Indochina as a neutral country in which the existing French government would remain in control. The president must have known the proposal would find little favor in Tokyo, for he did not wait for a response before taking a much more forceful step: On the twenty-fifth, the administration froze all Japanese assets in the United States, imposed an embargo, and ended the export of petroleum to Japan.

Just what Roosevelt and his aides sought to achieve by this aggressive response has divided historians for more than half a century, but it seems most likely that the president himself did not intend to cut off all petroleum exports or mean for the freezing of assets to be permanent. He wanted to create uncertainty in Tokyo, not provoke a U.S.-Japanese war. Contrary to FDR's intention, however, second-echelon officials in the State Department—among them Dean Acheson, later to be secretary of state under Harry Truman and an important player in our story—imposed a total embargo while the president was meeting with Winston Churchill at Placentia Bay, off the coast of Newfoundland. By the time Roosevelt returned to the capital on August 16, it was deemed too late to step back, for reasons political and diplomatic. The embargo received strong popular support, and polls showed that a majority of Americans now preferred to risk war rather than allow Japan to become more powerful. Furthermore, U.S. officials feared that the Japanese would see any modification as a sign of American weakness.[40]

For Japan, so poor in natural resources, the implications were dire. The country consumed roughly twelve thousand tons of oil each day, 90 percent of it imported, and also imported most of her zinc, iron ore, bauxite, manganese, cotton, and wheat. She could not survive a year of a thorough embargo—unless she seized British and Dutch possessions in Asia. Prime Minister Fumimaro Konoe, a moderate among hard-liners, proposed a summit meeting with FDR and indicated a willingness to withdraw from Indochina as soon as the war with China was settled. Roosevelt was tempted by this offer, but his secretary of state, Cordell Hull, persuaded him to insist on Japanese abandonment of China as a precondition for such a meeting. The proposal collapsed, and Konoe was ousted as prime minister in mid-October. Tojo replaced him. Diplomatic maneuverings continued, and in November Tojo offered to move troops out of Indochina immediately, and out of China once general peace was restored, in return for a million tons of aviation gasoline. Hull rejected the offer and repeated the American insistence on Japanese withdrawal from China and abandonment of the Southeast Asian adventure. On December 7, Japan's main carrier force, seeking to destroy the American fleet and thereby purchase time to complete its southward expansion, struck Pearl Harbor.

The news rocked world capitals. No one doubted that American involvement changed the equation, not merely in the Asian conflict but in the European war—this even before Japan's Axis partner Germany declared war on the United States on December 11. For Charles de Gaulle, the end result was now assured. "Of course, there will be military operations, battles, conflicts, but the war is finished since the outcome is known from now on," he remarked. "In this industrial war, nothing will be able to resist American power."[41]

Since his June 1940 *appel*, de Gaulle had worked to establish the legitimacy of the Free French as authentic representatives of the nation in the eyes of the Allies, on whom he depended for both economic and military support. The colonies that backed him played an essential part in this endeavor, because with their support de Gaulle could claim for the Free French a status analogous to the other governments-in-exile that were then active in London, even though both Britain and the United States maintained relations with Vichy and recognized it as the legitimate successor to the Third Republic. Although the effort to rally colonial support had met with only limited success—in late 1941, Vichy still controlled the most important areas of the empire—de Gaulle hoped Pearl Harbor would change the equation. On December 8, he proclaimed common cause with Washington and declared war on Japan.

CHAPTER 2

THE ANTI-IMPERIALIST

D E GAULLE'S MOMENT OF HOPE DID NOT LAST LONG. PEARL HARBOR and the American entry into the war, it soon became clear, had failed to improve his organization's standing in Washington. In the eyes of President Franklin Roosevelt and Secretary of State Cordell Hull, the Free French continued to be an illegitimate and potentially dangerous group, with which limited agreements might be negotiated on matters of pressing concern but which was in no way representative. It certainly did not have to be consulted when French interests were at stake. Both men believed that Franco-German disputes lay at the root of much of Europe's inability to maintain the peace. Both doubted that France could be a stabilizing force in world affairs after the war, given what they saw as her weak political system and the failure of her armed forces to put up more of a fight against the Wehrmacht. France was a fading power, Roosevelt believed. Her people, he told aides, would have to undergo a fundamental transformation in order to have a workable society.[1]

Roosevelt had not yet met de Gaulle, but he knew enough to dislike him. Basic personality differences played a role. In social interaction, de Gaulle was as austere and pompous as FDR was relaxed and jovial. For months, Roosevelt had heard Hull and other advisers rail against the general's egotism and haughty style, his serene confidence that he represented the destiny of the French people. Roosevelt, with his preference for the complicated, the ambiguous, and the devious, would get irritated just listening to these aides. In Kenneth S. Davis's perceptive formulation, the president was often contemptuous of "men who pursued their objectives in uncompromisingly straight lines, men who disdainfully eschewed the tactics of . . . cajolery and concealment and misdirection, which were for Roosevelt part and parcel of the art, or the game, of elective politics."[2]

That the two men sought to convey fundamentally different images exacerbated the problem. Successful American presidents project a populist image. They do not place themselves above their compatriots but strive whenever possible to show qualities typical of "average" Americans. If they have an intellectual bent, they do their best to hide it. To be likable, smiling, and unpretentious is all-important; to express the values of middle America an essential prerequisite for greatness. In France, great leaders historically do exactly the opposite: They stand above the masses, remote figures embodying France's *gloire* and *grandeur.* They don't try to be folksy or common in speech. No one cultivated this image more assiduously than de Gaulle. The general was not shy about invoking *Notre Dame de France*—Our Lady of France—or about identifying himself with national heroes such as Jeanne d'Arc and Clemenceau. Roosevelt, though reasonably familiar with the French language and culture, did not comprehend this French mythmaking, while de Gaulle, in his general ignorance of American ways, viewed FDR's geniality as a guise for hypocrisy and artifice.[3]

Relations between de Gaulle and Roosevelt suffered a major blow on Christmas Eve 1941, when Free French troops, acting on de Gaulle's orders, occupied St. Pierre and Miquelon, two tiny Vichy-controlled islands off Newfoundland with a population of five thousand. Roosevelt opposed anything liable to alienate Vichy, and Cordell Hull, already convinced that de Gaulle was a fascist and an enemy of the United States, condemned this "arbitrary action" by the "so-called Free French." Residents of the islands, however, held a plebiscite resulting in a near-unanimous vote for affiliation with de Gaulle's organization. And the American media, led by *The New York Times,* lauded the general's initiative and attacked Hull. The St. Pierre–Miquelon affair infuriated and embarrassed Roosevelt, who emerged from it with the strong suspicion that the leader of Free France was not himself committed to human freedom and would, if given the chance, establish a dictatorship in postwar France.[4]

II

THAT DE GAULLE FULLY SHARED VICHY'S DESIRE TO PRESERVE THE French Empire only enhanced Roosevelt's disdain.[5] By the time of Pearl Harbor, he had become a committed anticolonialist. European colonialism had helped bring on both the First World War and the current one, he was convinced, and the continued existence of empires would in all likelihood result in future conflagrations. Western sway over much of Asia and Africa was no less threatening to world stability than German expansionism, he went so far as to say. Therefore all colonies should be given their independence. The president's son Elliott records FDR as saying, some months after U.S. entry into the war: "Don't think for a moment, Elliott, that Americans would be dying in the Pacific tonight, if it hadn't been for the shortsighted greed of the French and the British and the Dutch. Shall we allow them to do it all, all over again [after the war]?" Although the reliability of Elliott's direct quotation may be questioned, there is little doubt he captured his father's basic conviction. Earlier, in March 1941, FDR had told the White House Correspondents' Association: "There has never been, there isn't now, and there never will be, any race of people on earth fit to serve as masters over their fellow men. . . . We believe that any nationality, no matter how small, has the inherent right to its own nationhood."[6]

One can imagine the assembled journalists nodding vigorously in affirmation. A general distaste for colonialism, after all, came with being an American: Other U.S. leaders could have spoken in identical language about all nationalities having the right to their own nationhood. But it is also true that Roosevelt's views on colonialism had undergone a dramatic change, and that he now was more insistent on the matter than many in official Washington who were never as willing to sacrifice European interests on anticolonial grounds. In his early years of public life, he had been a proponent of imperial control. Echoing very much the French *mission civilisatrice,* FDR thought it justifiable and necessary for the United States to impose the blessings of her civilization on the more backward and less fortunate peoples, by force if necessary. Nor was his motive solely humanitarian: Like his cousin Theodore Roosevelt, he believed geopolitical imperatives demanded that the United States control whatever land or water was necessary to ensure the protection of the Panama Canal and the water approaches to the United States. Later, as assistant secretary of the navy in the Wilson administration, Roosevelt held a paternalistic attitude toward existing American colonies, and at least in the Caribbean he would have supported further territorial acquisitions.[7]

At the same time, and somewhat incongruously, Roosevelt came out early in favor of the Wilsonian program of collective security. As the Democratic vice-presidential nominee in 1920, he campaigned vigorously for American entry into the League of Nations, and in the years thereafter he embraced the Wilsonian view that active U.S. involvement in international affairs was essential to securing the nation's peace and prosperity.[8] What is more, like Wilson he emerged from World War I convinced that the scramble for empire not only had set the European powers against one another and created the conditions that led to war, but also worked against securing a negotiated settlement during the fighting. French and British war aims regarding territory and influence, particularly in the Middle East, had made effective mediation impossible.

In the mid-1920s, Roosevelt began urging a more cooperative U.S. policy in Latin America, and he strongly opposed intervention when instability threatened in Nicaragua. He had not lost his missionary zeal to improve the lot of less fortunate peoples, but the methods U.S. officials used increasingly troubled him. American imperialism in Latin America had achieved important humanitarian achievements, he acknowledged, but at what cost? Might there be a better way? Gingerly at first, and then more strongly, Roosevelt began in the late 1920s to urge that Latin American countries be treated as independent sovereign states and that territories like the Philippines be pushed more rapidly toward full independence.[9] In 1933, shortly after entering the White House, Roosevelt announced that the United States would thenceforth act as a "good neighbor" in her dealings with Latin America. The phrase promised more than it delivered—his administration continued to support and bolster dictators in the region, believing that they would promote stability and preserve U.S. economic interests—but the Good Neighbor Policy nevertheless marked a real departure in hemispheric relations, and it stood in sharp contrast to the colonialism of the Europeans. In his first term FDR also approved the granting of "commonwealth" status to the Philippines, with the expectation that full independence would come in 1946. These policies, journalist Walter Lippmann enthused during World War II, showed that great powers did not need to impose formal colonial controls on weaker countries within their "orbit." As such, Roosevelt's approach was "the only true substitute for empire."[10]

To be sure, neither Lippmann nor Roosevelt advocated immediate self-rule for all parts of the colonial world. Neither doubted that immediate independence for many colonies would cause widespread disorder and conflict. Roosevelt fully shared prevailing views regarding white and Western superiority, and his anticolonialism came with all the burdens of paternalism and ignorance. The important point here, however, is that even before the start of World War II, he had reached the conclusion that, for good or ill, complete independence was foreordained for all or almost all the European colonies.[11]

III

BY THE START OF 1941, ROOSEVELT, PRESSURED BY JAPANESE ANTI-colonial propaganda and smug about having set the proper example by promising independence for the Philippines, began pressing Britain on the issue. At his meeting with Churchill in August at Placentia Bay, he insisted that achieving a stable peace required a commitment to develop "backward countries." "I can't believe," FDR reportedly said, "that we can fight a war against fascist slavery, and at the same time not work to free people all over the world from a backward colonial policy." Churchill, so devoted to the British Empire, objected to this line of reasoning, but in muted tones, desperate as he was to gain U.S. assistance in the war in Europe. The meeting's most publicized accomplishment, a statement of broad war aims that became known as the Atlantic Charter, included a clause respecting "the right of all peoples to choose the form of government under which they will live." Going further than Wilson in 1919, Roosevelt would make clear he considered this declaration to have universal applications, applying not only to the German and Japanese empires but to all colonial holdings everywhere. Churchill, however, assured Parliament that it referred only to the sovereignty of previously self-governing European peoples conquered by Germany—"quite a separate problem from the progressive evolution of self-governing institutions in the regions and peoples which owe allegiance to the British Crown." To Leo Amery, Britain's secretary of state for India, Churchill said the pledge could be invoked "only . . . in such cases when the transference of territory or sovereignty arose."[12]

FRANKLIN ROOSEVELT AND WINSTON CHURCHILL CONFER DURING THEIR MEETING AT PLACENTIA BAY NEAR NEWFOUNDLAND IN AUGUST 1941.

But the prime minister had allowed FDR to outmaneuver him. A "Rooseveltian moment" was in the making: Nationalist leaders in colonies all over the globe, not least Indochina, interpreted the charter as an unambiguous commitment to independence, as the president intended. For many of them, Roosevelt became a hero. Moreover, the wide attention given to the Atlantic Charter in the American press meant that public opinion was now focused on the issue, and it would remain near the forefront of popular attitudes for the rest of the war. Editorial writers and columnists generally applauded the self-determination clause, while among nationalist leaders overseas the United States now occupied the moral high ground.[13]

In the short term, though, Churchill got his way. When the two leaders met again a few weeks after Pearl Harbor, this time in Washington, Roosevelt suggested that Britain commit herself publicly to granting independence to India. Churchill, taken aback, rejected the idea strongly—"so strongly and at such length," he later wrote, "that [Roosevelt] never raised it verbally again."[14] Churchill said he would rather resign than "desert" the Indian people. Roosevelt got the message. He continued in 1942 to tell aides that London should promote self-government for India, and he had intermediaries make the same case to London, but he more or less ceased pressing the matter personally with Churchill. With Japan making rapid imperial and military gains in Asia—Hong Kong fell in December 1941, Singapore in February 1942, Rangoon in March, the Philippines in May—and with German forces in control of huge swaths of Europe, FDR worried that continued pressure on the intransigent British leader could endanger Allied unity at a critical time. South Asia, relatively unimportant in geopolitical terms, would have to wait.

Here as elsewhere during the war, Roosevelt showed a propensity to let short-term, pragmatic concerns drive his actions in foreign affairs. His fundamental anticolonialism had not dissipated, however—he remained steadfast in the belief that Indian independence was inevitable—and in 1943 he shifted his attack to a colonial power that did not have Britain's geopolitical importance, namely France. Indochina, in particular, became for him a near obsession. Early in the war, U.S. officials had on several occasions expressly endorsed the return of Indochina to French control at the end of hostilities, but these statements lacked conviction. Roosevelt, still contemptuous of the French performance in the Battle of France three years earlier, grew more and more convinced that Indochina had been the springboard for the Japanese attack on the Philippines, Malaya, and the Dutch East Indies, and he blamed Vichy authorities for repeatedly giving in to Tokyo's demands in 1940–41 without first consulting Washington. This was a dubious reading of history—American officials, as we have seen, had been consulted at most points and had tacitly encouraged first Catroux's and then Decoux's concessions—but the president clung to it nonetheless. He also held up Indochina as an example of colonial mismanagement, a place where exploitation and indifference had left the indigenous people in a terrible condition—an argument that tracked closely with that proffered by Ho Chi Minh in various writings, notably *Le procès de la colonisation française* (translated into English as *French Colonialism on Trial*).

French officials, Vichyite as well as Gaullist, despaired at this presidential message, but it didn't surprise them. "The American people, born of an anticolonial revolution, are hostile to colonies by tradition," read one typical Foreign Ministry report, noting that the hostility cut across party lines and class lines. As such, it was that rare issue "on which American opinion is not divided." Moreover, the study continued, Roosevelt's policy played into the American public's "penchant for crusades"—his Wilsonian rhetoric allowed Americans to endow the sacrifices on the battlefield with ennobling purpose, in this case bringing self-determination to oppressed peoples. Then too, less lofty principles were involved. The report charged that American businessmen favored decolonization mostly in order to gain access to raw materials and markets, so as to maximize profits and to maintain production after the war. The basic aim seemed to be "an open door for merchandise as well as capital," the authors claimed, and there could be no doubt who would emerge on top: "The open door would favor powerful Americans over European competitors."[15]

Not coincidentally, Roosevelt's hostility to a French return to Indochina increased as Charles de Gaulle's position strengthened. His animus against the general was deep and unrelenting—bizarrely so, in hindsight. When the Allies attacked North Africa in November 1942, they sought Free French involvement, in order to convince French commanders in Algeria and Morocco not to resist the invasion. But Roosevelt ruled out including de Gaulle in the operation. Instead, he and Churchill placed their bets on Henri Giraud, a stiff and formal French general whose most compelling calling card appeared to be that he had escaped from German prison camps in both world wars. Giraud, it soon became clear, had movie-star looks but not much else; he had neither the brainpower nor the charisma to be effective. The Allied landings resulted in Germany's occupation of Vichy-governed territory in southern France and to Vichy's diplomatic break with the United States. Even after Washington's

Vichy strategy had lost its usefulness, and Giraud's attempt to wrest control of the Free French had collapsed, the administration remained stubbornly skeptical of de Gaulle and his movement. FDR and several of his top aides questioned the extent of de Gaulle's support among the French people and ruled out making commitments that might be "harmful" to postliberation France.[16]

But if Indochina and potentially other colonies should not be returned to the colonial powers after the war, what should happen to them? Roosevelt proposed a trusteeship formula by which the colonies would be raised to independence through several stages. Those not ready for independence—which in FDR's view included all of France's possessions—would be placed under a nonexploitive international trusteeship formed by the United Nations. In laying out this plan to British foreign secretary Anthony Eden in March 1943, the president singled out Indochina as an area that should be controlled by this new system. Eden, destined to play a leading role in Britain's Indochina policy for the next dozen years, questioned whether FDR was being too harsh on the French, but the president waved the query away. France, he said, should be prepared to place part of her overseas territory under the authority of the United Nations. But what about the American pledges to restore to France her possessions? Undersecretary of State Sumner Welles interjected. Those pledges applied only to North Africa, Roosevelt replied.[17]

Welles needed little convincing. A key presidential adviser—he often enjoyed closer access to the president than did his boss Cordell Hull, a fact that did not go unnoticed by Hull—the urbane and articulate undersecretary spoke frequently of the surging nationalism in the colonial world and of the folly of attempting to deny Asian peoples' demands for independence. "In various parts of the world," Welles said in extolling the trusteeship idea, "there are many peoples who are clamoring for freedom from the colonial powers. Unless some system can be worked out to help these peoples, we shall be encountering trouble. It would be like failing to install a safety valve and then waiting for the boiler to blow up."[18]

The trusteeship concept bore a close relationship to Woodrow Wilson's post–World War I mandate system. Roosevelt conceded that very few nations had actually evolved from the mandate system, but he insisted on its essential soundness. Under his plan, the mandate name was dropped in favor of trusteeship, so as to not have the stigma of the moribund League of Nations; this time the enforcement mechanism would be a greater degree of international accountability. As before, the core principle was that a colonial territory is not the exclusive preserve of the power that controls it but constitutes a "sacred trust" over which the international community has certain responsibilities.[19]

Eden grasped that this was old wine in new bottles, and he didn't like the taste. He and others in the Foreign Office suspected the Americans of seeking to use trusteeships to their own economic advantage—the "international supervision of colonies" would simply be a smoke screen by which America could facilitate access to the economic resources of the colonies and spread her influence globally. What really frightened the British, though, was the president's insistence on international control over the trusteeships. However ill-defined the details of his plan, trusteeship would surely compel the ruling state to follow international regulations, probably as laid down by the United Nations, and to commit to a timetable for the colony's independence. This was anathema to Eden and his colleagues, who promptly set about trying to modify the trusteeship formula. They said they would accept an *advisory* role for other nations but no more. When FDR proved unbending, they switched to a policy of avoidance, eluding U.S. attempts to take up the issue.[20]

IV

MUCH TO CHURCHILL'S ANNOYANCE, ROOSEVELT SOUGHT TO RE-cruit Chinese leader Chiang Kai-shek to the anticolonialist cause. In the president's mind, China would serve as a counterweight to Britain and the other European colonial powers in postwar Asia, and would join with Washington in a kind of Sino-American axis dominating much of Asia and the Pacific. Chiang was a willing recruit. He shared FDR's view that colonialism in Asia played into the hands of Japan, and he had vague notions—encouraged by Roosevelt—of participating in the departure of the British from India. He welcomed the president's plan to make China one of the four major powers after the war, with significant responsibilities in keeping peace and stability in Asia.[21]

But the budding Sino-American romance did not last. The two leaders failed to hit it off at their only wartime meeting, in Cairo in November 1943. At the Mena House Hotel, in the shadow of the pyramids, Roosevelt sought Chiang's support for his trusteeship scheme, but Chiang resisted, expressing a preference for outright independence for Indochina and other Asian colonies. To FDR's claim that he supported the return of Hong Kong to Chinese rule, Chiang said he would have no reply until the president first discussed the colony's future with the British.

Roosevelt did convince Chiang—as well as Churchill (who also attended the meeting) and Stalin (who did not)—to issue a joint press release on Allied Pacific war aims. The "Cairo Declaration" called for Japan's unconditional surrender and her expulsion from territories "taken by violence and greed." All Chinese territory "stolen" by Japan would be returned. Overall, though, Roosevelt found the Chinese leader weak and indecisive, and he left Cairo less confident that Chiang could play his assigned role after the war. No doubt the president's judgment was affected by the growing drumbeat of despair among American observers in China, who in late 1943 grew steadily more critical of the Chiang Kai-shek regime. They spoke of widespread governmental corruption and venality, low morale, and a general unwillingness among military leaders to fight the Japanese. Meanwhile, the Chinese Communists under Mao Zedong, who had been waging an intermittent struggle against Chiang's Nationalist (Guomindang) government since the late 1920s, were gaining strength in the north.[22]

On Indochina, Roosevelt remained undaunted. From Cairo, he traveled to Tehran for meetings with Churchill and, for the first time, Stalin. During their initial get-together, FDR stressed to Stalin the importance of preparing the people of Indochina for self-government along the lines of what the United States had done in the Philippines. Stalin concurred that Indochina should not be returned to France and said he supported independence for all colonial subjects. "The president," wrote a note taker, "remarked that after 100 years of French rule in Indochina, the inhabitants were worse off than they had been before." When Roosevelt turned the discussion to his trusteeship scheme, implying that Chiang Kai-shek agreed, Stalin expressed support. As the meeting drew to a close, they agreed there was no point in discussing the India matter with Churchill.[23]

Over dinner that same day, with Churchill also in attendance, Stalin again said he opposed a French return to Indochina. Roosevelt seized the opening to extol international accountability through trusteeships, carefully limiting his examples to French territories (New Caledonia in the Pacific, and Dakar on the west coast of Africa) so as to avoid offending the prime minister. Churchill was unimpressed. He pledged that Britain would seek no new territory after the war, but since the Big Four would be charged with maintaining postwar stability, they should be given individual control over certain strategically valuable areas. After Roosevelt took ill and retired for the night, Stalin continued to press Churchill on the need to keep France from reclaiming her empire. His concern was not the Indochinese people per se: He cared little about Southeast Asia, and his mistrust of Ho Chi Minh, dating back to their encounters in the 1920s, had not disappeared. Rather, he saw his stance as a means to weaken the European colonial empires more generally, and to ensure that the France that emerged from the war was a minor player on the world stage.[24]

After his return from Iran, Roosevelt maintained the pressure. The French were again in the forefront of his thinking in mid-December, when he told the ambassadors of Great Britain, the USSR, Turkey, Egypt, and Iran of his plan for Indochina. The Indochinese people had not been adequately prepared for immediate independence, the president acknowledged, but this was no reason to allow the French to wander in and reclaim colonial control. Rather, the best solution would be a trusteeship that would enable Indochina to develop along the Philippines model. The Soviet government supported this idea, FDR cheerfully reminded the British ambassador in a White House meeting in January 1944, adding that he had made his feelings known in twenty-five discussions with Prime Minister Churchill—"or perhaps *discussed* is the wrong word. I have spoken about it 25 times, but the Prime Minister has never said anything."[25]

That Roosevelt and Stalin seemed to propose a piecemeal attack on colonial empire was scant comfort to Churchill and other British officials. It was a slippery slope, they were convinced—or, if you will, a dangerous game of dominoes: If Indochina was allowed to fall from colonial control, what would keep Burma, Malaya, India, and other parts of the British Empire from being next? "We'd better look out," Alexander Cadogan, permanent undersecretary of the Foreign Office, warned in early 1944 after learning of another Roosevelt attack on the "hopeless" French record in Indochina. "Were the French any more 'hopeless' than we in Malaya or the Dutch in the East Indies?"[26]

It annoyed London strategists that the American president seemed so oblivious both to Indochina's geostrategic importance and to the need to have a strong and stable France in postwar Europe. For them, Indochina was the linchpin of all Southeast Asia, a barrier between China to the north and a string of prized British possessions to the south. Japan had used it as a forward base for her operations against Malaya and Burma, and this could not be allowed to happen again. Postwar Indochina thus needed to be kept peaceful and stable, and France was in a better position than anyone else to ensure that happened. In Europe, meanwhile, Britain would need to be able to work well with France, whatever scenario played out on the continent—German revival, Soviet expansion, U.S. withdrawal, general social and economic collapse.[27]

How to secure such a cooperative France? Partly, London planners determined, by supporting Charles de Gaulle's determination to retain the French colonies, including Indochina, and partly by avoiding arguments with Washington on the issue. "Roosevelt has been more outspoken to me on that subject than any other colonial matter," Churchill reminded Eden in mid-1944, "and I imagine it is one of his principal war aims to liberate Indochina from France. . . . Do you really want to go and stir all this up at such a time as this?"[28] Quietly, London officials stonewalled American efforts in early and mid-1944 to negotiate on the colonial issue. Roosevelt continued to push his trusteeship plan and his opposition to a French return to Indochina, but with less urgency as 1944 progressed.

Military developments help explain the shift. As battlefield fortunes shifted decisively in the Allies' favor and victory in both Europe and Asia could be perceived, Roosevelt had to confront a dilemma that had existed just beneath the surface since the war began: how to square a desire for a new global order based on self-determination and free trade with a need for postwar cooperation among the great powers. Had colonialism been the only thing at stake, FDR might well have continued to press the British and the French, and to insist on a specific timetable by which all the European colonial powers—including also the Dutch and Portuguese—would grant independence to their colonies. But in 1944, he thought more and more about what would happen once the fighting stopped. Some of his assumptions regarding the Four Policemen—the United States, the United Kingdom, the Soviet Union, and China, who would maintain order in their respective spheres—he realized, would require revision.

China, for example, now seemed unlikely to be able to assume her position as one of the four. That spring a full-scale Chinese civil war seemed increasingly probable, as Chiang allocated more and more of his forces to combating the Communists rather than the Japanese. In May, Roosevelt told his cabinet that he was "apprehensive for the first time as to China holding together for the duration of the war." Infighting among Guomindang officials had become endemic, and foreign observers reported widespread government corruption. Even *Life* magazine, long a champion of Chiang, published a report by Theodore White warning that "we are being played for suckers" by Chinese leaders who were hoarding American supplies to use in the "inevitable civil war." Meanwhile China's strategic importance in the war as a whole declined rapidly in 1944. Originally American planners believed that air bases in northeastern China would have to be established in order to defeat Japan, but in 1944 it became apparent that an "island-hopping" campaign across the Pacific would provide a quicker and easier route to the Japanese homeland—and that route was fully under U.S. control, obviating the need to deal with allies. The China theater, once vital in American military strategy, was fast becoming peripheral.[29]

Simultaneously, Roosevelt heard arguments that another of the policemen, the Soviet Union, might be less than cooperative after the war. As the Red Army advanced westward, crushing whole Nazi divisions in its path, senior U.S. analysts expressed concerns about Stalin's ambitions, not merely in Europe but in Asia as well. "Our relations with the Soviets have taken a startling turn evident during the last two months," U.S. ambassador to Moscow W. Averell Harriman reported in mid-

September. "They have held up our requests with complete indifference to our interests and have shown an unwillingness even to discuss the pressing problems." Harriman warned that the Russians were becoming "a world bully wherever their interests are involved. This policy will reach into China and the Pacific as well when they can turn their attention in that direction."[30]

V

THE TURMOIL IN CHINA AND THE UNCERTAINTY ABOUT SOVIET INTENtions strengthened the hand of those in the foreign policy bureaucracy in Washington who argued for allowing Britain and France to retain their Asian territories after the armistice. For the better part of a year, these "conservatives" had been waging a campaign against "progressive" colleagues who shared FDR's hostility toward a French return to Indochina and sought to promote Indochina's development toward independence under a degree of international supervision. Many of the conservatives shared the president's antipathy toward de Gaulle and his disdain toward France's lackluster performance against German and Japanese aggression, but they rejected his claim that France should not play a major role in world affairs for many years to come. On the contrary, they argued, the United States would need a strong France immediately after the war in order to bring stability to Europe and to the larger world system.[31]

French authorities picked up on this schism in U.S. decision making and sought to exploit it. All too aware of the Americans' preponderant power in the Western Pacific—"Nothing will or can be done in Indochina without their agreement, at least tacit," one senior official reminded his colleagues—they stepped up their efforts in 1944 to reestablish France's claim to Indochina, and to do so before Washington settled on firm policy. Most important, de Gaulle reasoned, would be to get French troops involved in the campaign to liberate Indochina. He recalled candidly in his memoir: "I regarded it as essential that the conflict not come to an end without our participation. Otherwise, every policy, every army, every aspect of public opinion would certainly insist upon our abdication in Indochina. On the other hand, if we took part in the battle—even though the latter were near its conclusion—French blood shed on the soil of Indochina would constitute an impressive claim."[32]

Accordingly, de Gaulle and his aides set about organizing a force capable of fighting the Japanese. Beginning in mid-1944, Free French agents parachuted into Indochina to make contact with Gaullist sympathizers and to coordinate resistance. French diplomats also worked to get Allied assistance in sending fresh troops to Indochina and to convince the U.S. government to allow regular French units to participate in the broader Pacific War. Washington proved resistant, but the French kept pressing. In a series of midlevel bilateral meetings devoted to Indochina, they stressed their benevolent intentions toward the Indochinese population and their determination to grant them greater autonomy after the war. Indochina, they vowed, would enjoy "a new political status" involving new governing arrangements of a "liberal character." For good measure, they also stressed the metropole's success in promoting Indochina's economic development earlier in the century, and they insisted that the *indigènes* were deeply grateful as a result. "The population of our colonies has always had confidence in us," Minister of Colonies René Pleven told foreign journalists in October.[33]

The urgings of the conservatives in Washington, combined with the pressure from the British and French, chipped away at FDR's resolve. But only partly. His dislike of French imperialism and of de Gaulle personally were undiminished, and he clung to the belief—or at least the hope—that the general would soon be a spent force. It mattered not that a growing chorus of voices in Congress and the press loudly proclaimed otherwise, insisting that de Gaulle was now the leader of the French nation and was not going away. Already in 1943, these observers reminded the White House, de Gaulle had assumed leadership of an Algiers-based Comité français de la Libération nationale (CFLN) to administer the liberated territories and coordinate military action; now, in the spring of 1944, the committee had assumed the functions and legitimacy of a Provisional Government of the French Republic.

When de Gaulle arrived in Washington in July 1944 for three days of meetings, Roosevelt made an outward show of respect and admiration, but behind closed doors he stuck to his position. In the postwar world, he told de Gaulle, France would be reduced to the status of a spectator. The Big Four of the United States, the Soviet Union, Great Britain, and China would be predominant, and Western Europe would recede in comparison to other parts of the world. The new United Nations organization would help contain Soviet ambitions, while on the Western side the United States would be supreme. De Gaulle cautioned against relying on China as an effective ally and said a regenerated France would again be a leading world power. To FDR's claim that self-determination would be a guiding principle of America's postwar policy, de Gaulle replied that France would be prepared to discuss the form of colonial relationships—dependent territories could thenceforth receive more autonomy—but would not surrender any part of her empire. Their conversations were, as the wonderful French expression has it, *dialogues de sourds* (dialogues of the deaf).³⁴

De Gaulle, nevertheless, was impressed by what he saw on the trip. It was his first exposure to the great power center of official America, and he came away acutely conscious of the overwhelming self-confidence of the elite, and the dynamism of American society. From Washington, he traveled to New York City and was awed by what he saw. "*C'est énorme,*" he remarked while looking out the window of his suite at the Waldorf Astoria at the cars streaming by below. "This country has not built automobiles for three years and look at all the cars . . . what a capital they represent . . . and what a powerful country." The United States was predominant among all countries, he went on, and would remain so for years to come: Her industrial might and her agricultural production gave her an enormous advantage over all others. "She will be the wealthiest and best-equipped country after the war is over," he concluded, and she "is already trying to rule the world."³⁵

Shortly before his return flight to Algiers, de Gaulle told a packed room of reporters that his visit had been a success. "I am sure that, henceforth, the settlement of all the common problems we face, and will face . . . will be easier because we now understand each other better." A reporter asked whether de Gaulle expected the French Empire to be returned whole. Yes, he replied, France "will find everything intact that belongs to her," though France "is also certain that the form of French organization in the world will not be the same." Did France regard herself as a great power? someone else asked. Too ridiculous a notion even to consider, he replied. As for the prospect of formal U.S. recognition of the committee in Algiers as the Provisional Government of France, de Gaulle said it had not been the purpose of his trip to gain such recognition but he hoped it would come.[36]

It was, an observer remarked, a serenely confident performance. And no wonder: De Gaulle knew he had British backing, both for his leadership of France and for the retention of the empire. He knew he had eclipsed all potential rivals for leadership of the French nation. It was a nation, moreover, that could expect to be liberated. The massive Allied cross-channel invasion of France had commenced a month earlier, and though it very nearly ended in disaster, the Normandy beachhead became the center of a massive buildup over the ensuing weeks. By the end of July, close to 1.5 million troops had been transported across the English Channel and were beginning to break out of the coastal perimeter. Even then Roosevelt half-expected some unknown leader to emerge from the liberated territories and claim the legitimacy of the government of the republic. But it was de Gaulle the French people wanted. General Dwight D. Eisenhower, Supreme Allied Commander, grasped this reality and moreover had none of Roosevelt's personal dislike of the general. To FDR's consternation, Eisenhower allowed de Gaulle's Free French forces the honor of entering Paris first. On August 25, 1944, de Gaulle announced the liberation of Paris to an ecstatic crowd at the city's Hôtel de Ville.

He had seen his astonishing claim of June 1940 vindicated by Allied forces and by resistance inside and outside France: The war had not been lost. The humiliating defeat of 1940 had been retrieved. The following day the general led a triumphant, solemn promenade up the Champs-Élysées, the procession reaching Notre Dame at four-thirty in the afternoon. "The effect was fantastic," Malcolm Muggeridge, then a British intelligence official, recalled of the scene. "The huge congregation who had all been standing suddenly fell flat on their faces. . . . There was a single exception: one solitary figure, like a lonely giant. It was, of course, de Gaulle. Thenceforth, that was how I always saw him—towering and alone; the rest, prostrate."[37]

Eisenhower would not have put it in those words, but he grasped the

CHARLES DE GAULLE WALKS DOWN THE CHAMPS-ÉLYSÉES, FROM THE ARC DE TRIOMPHE TO NOTRE DAME, AUGUST 26, 1944. ON HIS IMMEDIATE LEFT ONE STEP BEHIND IS GENERAL PHILIPPE LECLERC, WHO WILL LATER COMMAND FRENCH UNION FORCES IN INDOCHINA AND CONCLUDE THAT MILITARY VICTORY IS UNACHIEVABLE.

essential point: This was de Gaulle's moment. But if the Allied commander's tact and diplomatic skill in handling the Frenchman won him admiration from observers at the time and historians since, this also placed Roosevelt in an embarrassing position. The new secretary of state, Edward Stettinius, along with army generals Eisenhower and George C. Marshall, told the president there was only one way to go: He had to accept de Gaulle as president of the Provisional Government of France. The State Department drew up plans for formal recognition. Roosevelt let them sit on his desk for several weeks before finally relenting and signing on October 23.

VI

BY MIDAUTUMN OF 1944, THEN, ROOSEVELT'S PLAN FOR POSTWAR Indochina was in trouble. The turmoil in China and the growing weakness of the Chiang regime, the mounting concerns about Soviet ambitions in Europe and elsewhere, and the ascendancy of de Gaulle with his commitment to maintaining the empire—all these served to diminish the chances that France would be kept from reclaiming control of her Southeast Asian territories.

Roosevelt had begun to lose control of events. In August, London officials had helped Gaullist agents to enter Indochina. Some weeks later Churchill allowed French military personnel to participate in activities of South East Asia Command (SEAC); he should have sought Roosevelt's approval before doing so but was content to merely get the okay of American military officials.[38] Although FDR disavowed Churchill's action when he learned of it, and also rejected a plan to provide materials to resistance groups inside Indochina, the mere presence of the French personnel had great symbolic importance. SEAC commander Lord Louis Mountbatten provided extensive air support for Free French operatives in Indochina in late 1944 and encouraged cooperation between Britain's intelligence apparatus in the Far East and its Gaullist counterpart, the Direction générale des études et recherches. In December alone, British forces carried out forty-six air operations and succeeded in establishing a radio network among resistance cells in Indochina, building up stores of military equipment for use in a possible future campaign against Japan and occasionally transporting French agents into and out of the region. "I do not think the Americans realize anything like the extent to which our penetration of French Indo-China jointly with the French has already progressed," one diplomat exulted to the Foreign Office in January 1945.[39]

Perhaps not, but some of Roosevelt's senior advisers had begun singing a new song on Indochina, one with a decidedly British sound. That same month Harry Hopkins told Stettinius and the secretary of war, Henry Stimson, that there was a need "for a complete review not only of the Indochina situation but of our entire French approach," for the French felt "we were opposing their regrowth." Stimson indicated his support by observing that "France has become a great military base." The same month Joseph Grew of the State Department told Australian officials that he believed Indochina would stay French.[40]

These officials may have taken their cue from the president. Over the final weeks of 1944, his steadfastness on the issue of France's return to Indochina had begun to falter, due mostly to British intransigence and perhaps also to his own rapidly failing health. London officials wanted explicit presidential approval for a new plan to use French commandos for an operation inside Indochina aimed at destroying Japanese communications. Roosevelt at first denied the request, but on January 4, 1945, he agreed to look the other way while the saboteurs were deployed. He may have believed that the operation would yield a significant payoff in the war effort, and that the French deployment was too small to make a meaningful difference to the French effort to reclaim control over Indochina. But it's also possible he had shifted his position and was now prepared to entertain the possibility that France could return to Indochina if she promised to implement sweeping reforms and set a firm timetable for independence. He strenuously denied any such change—in the first half of January, he told both a State Department official and a British diplomat that Indochina must not be turned back to the French—but some softening likely took place.[41] At the Yalta conference in the Crimea in February 1945, Roosevelt backed off his insistence on enforcing an international trusteeship over colonial areas; except in the case of Japanese-mandated territories, he now said, such internationalization would happen only with the consent of the colonial power. At Yalta, he informed Stalin that he would not allow U.S. ships to be used to carry French troops to Indochina, but he also recommended to the Soviet leader that they not raise the Indochina matter with Churchill. "It would only make the British mad," FDR rationalized. "Better to keep quiet just now."[42]

Yet it would be a mistake to conclude from this, as some historians have done, that the start of 1945 was some kind of watershed moment in which the United States abandoned her anticolonial impulses and supported a French return to Indochina.[43] Roosevelt had not slackened in his belief that the imperialist system was bankrupt and decolonization inevitable, and that the United States needed to be on the right side of history. In October 1944, he told a visiting French admiral that following Japan's defeat, the situation of the Western powers in the Pacific would be perilous. "The ideas of independence have become more familiar to the populations so far submitted to the authority of European countries," the president said. "I believe if we do not wish to be thrown out by these people, we must find a general formula to resolve the relations between the White and Yellow races." The nature of the formula could vary from country to country, but "within a given time span" all the colonies would have to become independent.[44]

At Yalta, FDR was contradictory, backing off on international trusteeships but telling Stalin he still "had in mind" some such solution for Indochina. On his return trip from the conference, in an off-the-record session with reporters aboard the USS *Quincy,* he condemned the British and French empires, comparing them unfavorably to the successful U.S. record in the Philippines and the commitment Washington had made to give the colony its independence. Roosevelt remained uncomfortable with the idea of French forces operating in Indochina, and he ruled out proposals for a greater French involvement in the anti-Japanese campaign there. He had retreated from the notion of *international* trusteeships, but the colonial powers would still act as trustees, remaining in control only long enough to prepare the colony for independence. Concluded a British official after Yalta: " 'Colonial trusteeship' is still very much alive as part of the U.S. [government's] policy."[45]

The means had changed, but not the goal. On March 8, upon his return from Yalta and from several days of rest in Hyde Park, the president held separate White House meetings with his ambassador to China, Patrick Hurley, and the commander of the China theater forces, General Albert C. Wedemeyer. Hurley tried to engage Roosevelt on the emerging civil war in China, but the president's attention was elsewhere. He listened with apparent attention to what Hurley had to say but then changed the subject to Indochina. Wedemeyer too found it impossible to get the president to stay focused on China. FDR remarked that he and Stalin had agreed that trusteeship, not colonization, was required in Indochina, and he ordered Wedemeyer not to provide any supplies whatsoever to French forces operating in Asia. National independence was the wave of the future, he said, not empires or spheres of influence.[46]

It was a frail man who uttered these words. Roosevelt was dying. Both Hurley and Wedemeyer were shocked by his appearance that day, and close aides such as Harry Hopkins knew the end was near. He hung on for another month; then, in the early afternoon of April 12, he suffered a massive cerebral hemorrhage and died.

Charles de Gaulle, notwithstanding the frosty interpersonal relationship, offered a moving tribute: "I am more shocked than I can say. It is
a terrible loss not only for our country and me personally but for all humankind." On his order, France observed a national day of mourning, an
honor never before accorded a foreigner.[47]

Roosevelt left an Indochina policy that was in flux, for global developments in 1944 had complicated his easy anti-French pronouncements of
1942 and 1943. He never succeeded in reconciling his deep opposition
to European colonialism with his equally heartfelt commitment to securing postwar cooperation among the great powers. In his final months he
moderated his Indochina policy in important ways, but he never retreated
from his belief that the continued existence of European colonial empires
undermined the peace of the world. In mid-March, he told State Department colonial expert Charles Taussig that France could return to Indochina, but only if Paris accepted the obligations of a trustee, including
setting a date for independence. On April 5 in Warm Springs, Georgia,
at what turned out to be his last press conference, Roosevelt appeared
with Philippine president Sergio Osmeña beside him. Once Japan was
defeated, FDR told the assembled reporters, the Philippines would be
given more or less immediate independence. Such action would send a
clear message to the European powers that the colonial age had passed.[48]

For four years, European colonial officials had heard this Rooseveltian message and had fretted about it, had schemed to thwart the president's designs. (Significantly, few of *them* thought FDR altered his policy
in a meaningful way in the final months.)[49] The question before them
now was whether the new man in the White House, Harry Truman,
would follow in his predecessor's footsteps or chart a new course. Indochina would present an early test, these European leaders understood.
For there, an event had occurred that would have profound implications
for the Anglo-French effort to reclaim French control and for Vietnamese
nationalists' determination to resist them.

CHAPTER 3

CROSSROADS

Shortly after six p.m. on march 9, 1945, a visitor arrived at the opulent Saigon offices of the French governor-general, Admiral Jean Decoux. It was Shunichi Matsumoto, Japan's ambassador to Indochina, there ostensibly for the purpose of signing a previously worked-out agreement concerning rice supplies and French financial support for Japanese troops. As the signing ceremony ended, Matsumoto asked Decoux to linger for a private conversation. Matsumoto appeared nervous, the Frenchman later recalled, "something rare in an Asiatic." It soon became clear why: Tokyo had ordered the ambassador to present an ultimatum, which required unconditional French acceptance no later than nine o'clock that same evening. The entire colonial administration, including army, navy, police, and banks, were to be placed under Japanese command.[1]

For almost five years, Decoux had dreaded the arrival of this moment. Ever since he took office, in July 1940, his overriding objective had been to preserve French sovereignty over Indochina, at least in a nominal sense, so that after the armistice the colony could still be a jewel in the empire. Now Tokyo had issued a demand that, if agreed to, would abolish French colonial control over Indochina. Decoux played for time, but Matsumoto did not budge—the deadline was firm. The Frenchman consulted with several associates, and at 8:45 sent a letter via messenger urging a continuation of the discussions beyond the nine o'clock deadline. The letter carrier went to the wrong building, and it was not until 9:25 that he could at last present the letter to Matsumoto. By then, reports of fighting in Hanoi and Haiphong had already come in. Matsumoto scanned the document, declared, "This is doubtless a rejection," and ordered the Japanese military machine into action.[2]

It was a carefully planned campaign, code-named Operation Bright Moon. Ever since October 1944, when U.S. forces began their reconquest of the Philippine Islands, the Japanese Military Command had feared that the Allies would use the islands to invade Indochina in order to cut off Japan from her forces in Southeast Asia. And indeed, South East Asia Command (SEAC), based in Kandy, Ceylon, under British admiral Lord Louis Mountbatten, viewed Indochina as an increasingly important theater of operations. Bombers of the U.S. Fourteenth Air Force under Major General Claire L. Chennault operating from South China regularly attacked Japanese targets in Vietnam, sometimes ranging as far south as Saigon to hit ports and rail centers. To add to Tokyo's concerns, French resistance inside Indochina appeared to be growing, and the Decoux regime seemed clearly to be switching its allegiance from Vichy to de Gaulle's Free France. The concerns grew in January 1945, when American forces attacked Luzon in the Philippines. In conjunction with this attack, Admiral William F. Halsey, commander of the U.S. Third Fleet, launched a brief but devastating naval raid along the Indochina coast between Cam Ranh Bay and Qui Nhon, in order to deflect Japanese attention from Admiral Nimitz's advance on Iwo Jima and Okinawa. The Japanese Thirty-eighth Army responded with a major reinforcement of garrisons in Indochina, especially in Tonkin, Annam, and Laos.

Through MAGIC intercepts Washington officials were able to follow closely Tokyo's preparations for Bright Moon. A Japanese Navy message intercepted on January 17, for example, stated categorically that "landings in Indo-China by Allied forces are imminent." A summary of intercepts on February 11 said that "the Japanese have become increasingly concerned over the possibility of Allied landings in Indo-China and have been taking various measures—and thinking about others." On March 3, Japan's foreign minister informed Tokyo's diplomats abroad that "we have decided to resort to force of arms" in French Indochina. By March 5, this decision was known in Washington (it took about forty-eight hours for raw intercepts to be processed and translated), and U.S. analysts now also had a good estimate of the balance of forces on the ground: roughly

JAPAN'S OIL SUPPLIES BURNING ALONG THE WATERFRONT IN SAIGON
AFTER AN AIR RAID BY THE U.S. NAVY'S THIRD FLEET, JANUARY 12, 1945.

65,000 Japanese troops versus about 60,000 French Indochina Army forces (of whom approximately 12,000 were Europeans).[3]

Viewed in totality, the available evidence—including the MAGIC intercepts—suggests strongly that Tokyo officials, increasingly resigned to the inevitability of defeat in the war, saw a takeover in Indochina as giving them a stronger position either for negotiation or for fanatic resistance. It's also clear that their task was made easier by the chronic inability of French Resistance forces to keep their activities and plans secret. Many *colons* openly expressed their support for the Resistance, and French soldiers collected arms dropped in the countryside and deposited them in arsenals in full view of the Japanese. Portraits of de Gaulle even hung in the public offices of the French High Command. On top of all that, the Japanese had cracked the French codes and were reading all the French ciphers. Their surveillance of French activities was child's play, and on the evening of March 9 they had their troops ready in strategic positions to negate the anticipated French moves.[4]

Certainly the French were taken by surprise, even though they had drawn up plans to counter just this kind of Japanese thrust and even though intelligence reports had warned that an attack might be imminent. One by one that evening their garrisons fell. Almost without exception, the senior French commanders were captured in their homes or in those of Japanese officers with whom they were dining (the meal invitations being part of the ruse). In Saigon, Japanese forces moved immediately on Decoux's palace and seized him as well as several other high-ranking French ministers. Throughout Indochina, they took over administrative buildings and public utilities and seized radio stations, banks, and industries. Public beatings and executions of colonial officials occurred in numerous locales, and there were widespread reports of French women being raped by Japanese soldiers—including in Bac Giang province, where the province *résident*'s wife was gang-raped.[5]

Some senior French officials put personal safety before military duty. General Eugène Mordant, former commander of the French Indochina Army and covert leader of the Gaullist Resistance in Indochina, made his way to the Citadel in Hanoi after the shooting began, where he told officers not to waste their ammunition. He then went by foot to the private home of a friend and in the morning dispatched a note to the Japanese, indicating where they could find him. Accused later of cowardice, Mordant would claim he had hurt his leg in climbing over the wall to the Citadel and would not long have eluded the Japanese by foot, and that he intended to offer the Japanese his life so they might spare the lives of others. There is no evidence he made any such offer.[6]

A few French units resisted. Ignoring Mordant's advice, the Citadel in Hanoi held out for several hours, even after the capture of General Georges Aymé, Mordant's successor as commander of the French Indochina Army, and even after a captured French trumpeter blew "*Cessez le feu!*" The Japanese finally gained control of the Citadel on the afternoon of the tenth, but after fierce fighting: 87 Europeans and about 100 Vietnamese were killed on the one side, 115 Japanese on the other. In Lang Son, the French garrison held out until noon on the tenth, whereupon the Japanese beheaded or bayoneted to death the survivors. One French commander, a Colonel Robert, was offered a pistol to commit "honorable" suicide; he refused and was beheaded.[7]

Only a small fraction of the Tonkin army managed to avoid early capture. One force of two thousand men, under General Marcel Alessandri, escaped to Dien Bien Phu in the remote northwestern part of Tonkin, near the Laotian border. Alessandri was soon joined by General Gabriel Sabattier, who had the presence of mind to leave Hanoi before the shooting started. Soon after arriving in Dien Bien Phu, Sabattier learned that General de Gaulle had appointed him commander of all French forces in Indochina and, further, that he was to maintain a presence in northern Indochina at any cost, to signify the continued French presence in the colony. It proved an impossible task, in the face of relentless Japanese pursuit, severe supply shortages, and plummeting troop morale. Paris sent no money, and Sabattier's store of piasters and opium was almost gone. With the Americans offering only medicines, he saw no option but to seek sanctuary in southern China. In April and May, about 5,700 Indochina Army soldiers, including 2,400 Europeans, straggled across the frontier at various points, in wretched condition. They were promptly disarmed by the disdainful Chinese.[8]

II

THIS WAS A PIVOTAL MOMENT FOR FRANCE IN INDOCHINA. THE MARCH coup dealt a blow to imperial authority from which it would never fully recover. Colonial rule had been based on the notion of European cultural and military supremacy, and though France had offered little more than token resistance to Japan in 1940, only now did most Vietnamese fully grasp how hollow was the French basis of power. The Japanese diplomatic victories in 1940–41, important though they were in many respects, had not appreciably altered everyday sociopolitical relations in Indochina—French officials thereafter still governed in the countryside and the villages, where Japanese officials seldom if ever set foot. Now, however, in the space of a few days, French colonial authority had disappeared, in plain view of Vietnamese in both urban and rural areas. Even de Gaulle's modest hope that a token French military presence could be kept in northwestern Tonkin—he quite logically reasoned that such a presence would make it much easier to reassert French authority once the Pacific War was over—had been dashed. Nor did he have any means of sending troops to the Far East without access to Allied shipping. To add insult to injury, the Japanese prevailed on Bao Dai, the titular emperor of Vietnam, to proclaim his country's "independence" and to appoint a new anti-French administration under Tran Trong Kim, a retired history teacher, to be based in Hue.[9] The monarchs in Cambodia and Laos soon followed suit. Indochina seemed to be disappearing overnight.

The implications were profound, not least for the cause of Vietnamese nationalism. In the absence of colonial restraint, the latent political forces in Vietnam, which had been stymied or given only narrow lanes of expression before March 9, now received a new lease on life. Before World War II, French control over some twenty-three million Vietnamese could be maintained by twelve thousand French soldiers plus perhaps three or four times as many native troops, assisted by a very efficient secret police. Very soon after the *coup de force,* it became clear that such minimal numbers would thenceforth be insufficient, that any French attempt to reclaim control would demand vastly larger numbers. The woeful response to the coup made that abundantly clear. Although few Vietnamese felt any kinship toward Japan, they had expected the Americans, not the French, to liberate them. American prestige in Vietnam had risen dramatically since U.S. forces began the reconquest of the Philippines some months before and affirmed that Filipinos would soon achieve their independence. Many Vietnamese believed that the sounds of gunfire and explosions on March 9 meant that the Americans had arrived. The reality was otherwise, but a key point remained: In the hour of extreme danger, the French had shown themselves wholly outclassed by an adversary that was itself perilously close to defeat in the larger world war.[10]

France, all independent observers could agree, had experienced a severe decline in power, in both absolute and relative terms, as indeed had all the European colonial powers—Britain, certainly, but also the Netherlands, Belgium, and Portugal. If an Allied victory in most theaters seemed all but certain in March 1945 and highly likely even in the Far East, for Ho Chi Minh—and for other nationalist leaders in Asia and Africa—the continued viability of the colonial empires was anything but assured, committed though Europe's leaders might be to that objective. France, after fighting to liberate herself from Axis tyranny, could not now easily deny that liberty to others in her fold, especially given the high hopes they invested in the new French nation that emerged from the Resistance. The stage was set for a collision of nationalisms.[11]

In Paris, though, these myriad problems concerning the colonial enterprise were ignored, or at least unacknowledged, by politicians who found it easy to assume that France's five-year nightmare was over and that things could once again be more or less as they were. For the Paris government, indeed, the March coup in Indochina, however disastrous militarily, was something of a political godsend, since it allowed de Gaulle and other leaders to say that France had spilled blood in the defense of her own territory. What's more, the coup removed the political embarrassment that was the collaborationist Decoux regime; thenceforth Indochina would be squarely in the fight against Japan. On March 14, de Gaulle delivered a heartfelt broadcast in which he promised to reverse the effects of the coup and criticized the Allies for not doing more to help the French in Indochina or to transport French troops to the Far East. "Not for a single hour did France lose the hope and the will to recover Free Indochina," he intoned. He made clear that, in his mind at least, it was *French* Indochina that battled the Japanese, and that *French* Indochina it would remain: "By the trials of all and the blood of the soldiers at this moment a solemn pact is sealed between France and the peoples of the Indochinese Union."[12]

Time and again during these weeks, de Gaulle spoke of the cohesion, the unbreakable bond, between metropolitan France and her overseas territories. Like so many in the Free French movement, he failed to grasp that the colonial peoples might consider liberation from foreign rule as important as he did. The bloody events in Indochina were a cause for concern, de Gaulle told the French Provisional Government's Consultative Assembly on March 20, but France could and would prevail. He read a cable from one of the besieged French garrisons in Indochina praising the morale of the troops, pleading for immediate aid, and concluding with a patriotic flourish: *Vive la France!*[13]

The chamber erupted in shouts of support. Some assembly members were seen wiping away tears. For them, as for most of their compatriots in 1945, it was self-evident that the colonies were essential to the pressing task that lay ahead: restoring France to her central place on the international stage. The debates in the Consultative Assembly that spring made starkly clear that a consensus existed around the proposition that France's future grandeur depended on the preservation of the empire. "Either we want France to resume her place as a great nation or we don't," assembly rapporteur Hettier de Boislambert declared in one session. "If that is not what we want, then there is nothing else for any of us to do here." Or as Gaston Monnerville, an assimilated black from French Guiana who was president of the Assembly Committee on Overseas France, put it: "France must make a choice: to remain a second-rank nation or instead, thanks to the contribution of her overseas territories, to become once again a great power. . . . France is at a crossroads. Let her hesitate no longer."[14]

Jean-Paul Sartre put the matter more simply: "In the space of five years," he wrote that spring, "we have acquired a formidable inferiority complex."[15] A vigorous defense of the empire would be necessary to overcome it.

There were other motivations too. French business enterprises were keen to reestablish themselves in Indochina. The Michelin Tire and Rubber Company, for example, owned large rubber plantations in the interior areas of Cochin China, and numerous French firms profited from deposits of bauxite, manganese, and other minerals. In terms of security too, Indochina could be an asset, assembly members reminded one another. In World War I, France had drawn on an enormous reservoir of soldiers from the empire to help defend her against the Central Powers. Though the defeat in 1940 happened too quickly for colonial troops to be put to use, in a future war the imperial holdings could once again be critical to victory.

And yet, French officials understood, on some level at least, that times *had* changed; that in Indochina and elsewhere, it would no longer do to simply assert French sovereignty. Special inducements would have to be dangled to persuade the Indochinese to return to the French fold, in view of Japan's offer for independence. Moreover, Franklin Roosevelt's anti-colonial pronouncements over the past several years had left their mark on Paris authorities. The fear of FDR-inspired international trusteeship was palpable among them. Nor was it simply the Americans that were a source of concern in this regard; both Stalin and Chiang Kai-shek had indicated general support for the trusteeship idea.[16]

Hence the issuance on March 24 of a carefully crafted declaration on Indochina that pledged a new imperial relationship, one based on federalism but rejecting independence.[17] The ideas contained therein were not new. Already a year earlier, in January 1944, representatives of Free France had met in Brazzaville, the capital of Free French Equatorial Africa, to discuss postwar colonial policies. Though Indochina was not on the agenda, the Brazzaville conferees vowed to "elevate" native peoples in the empire through ideals of wider citizenship and constitutional reforms that would give birth to a form of federalism of "associated peoples." The colonies would not be mere appendages of metropolitan France but would be developed in accordance with their own interests. Self-government would not happen, however—federalism was indeed designed to head it off—and the international community would have no say in how France conducted her colonial affairs. Any changes would be made within the family, much as the United States might decide to alter the status of Puerto Rico or the Virgin Islands.[18]

The Indochina declaration, already drafted when the Japanese takeover occurred, built on this Brazzaville foundation. Its principal authors were Henri Laurentie, director of political affairs in the Ministry of Colonies, and his top Indochina expert, Léon Pignon. The declaration announced the formation of an "Indochinese Federation" within a larger "French Union." The five "lands" of Indochina—Tonkin, Annam, Cochin China (respectively, northern, central, and southern Vietnam), Cambodia, and Laos—were to be headed by a federal government composed of ministers drawn from both the Indochinese and the French communities in Indochina. The Indochinese population would become eligible for a new form of imperial French citizenship, and would receive new political and electoral rights as well as unprecedented employment opportunities. "Today, Indochina is fighting, and in its army, Indochinese and Frenchmen are striving together for victory, side by side," the declaration said. "All the people, the leading classes as well as the masses who cannot let themselves be misled by the enemy's contrivances, are holding out with courage and gallantry for the triumph of the cause which is that of the entire French community. Thus, Indochina is acquiring further rights to the special position that is its due."[19]

What exactly were these "further rights"? The declaration did not

say, but it promised equal access to jobs for Vietnamese, as well as freedom of the press, of belief, and of association. It pledged the creation of a
"compulsory and effective" primary education system and the expansion
of secondary and further education, and it mandated that the study of
local languages and culture would be closely tied to French culture. Industrialization would be encouraged, and the federation would have economic autonomy. France would retain control over defense and foreign
affairs, and the governor-general would be the arbiter of local differences.
The French Constituent Assembly would determine the final shape of
political participation.[20]

"A decisive turning point in French colonial policy," one French official jubilantly said of the declaration as it was issued. In reality, it was
anachronistic even before the ink on it had dried. Drafted largely before
the Japanese takeover, it seemed blind to the new realities on the ground
in Indochina. Thus while the French press—including Communist and
Socialist newspapers—praised the proclamation, Indochinese groups in
France excoriated it for its vagueness on the all-important matter of Indochinese autonomy and freedom. The Japanese had declared Cambodia
and Annam independent; why was Paris not doing the same? To these
skeptics, the declaration seemed to exist uneasily between two contradictory principles: increased autonomy for Indochina and closer imperial
unity. Even more egregious, the declaration's demand that the tripartite
division of Vietnam be kept defied growing clamor among virtually all
politically conscious Vietnamese—from the most conservative mandarin
to the most radical Marxist—for national unity, and it indicated that Paris
intended to adhere to its prewar policy of "divide and rule." The French,
Joseph Buttinger would later write, "were preparing to destroy the independence of Vietnam at the very moment when it was about to become a
reality."[21]

III

IF ALL VIETNAMESE NATIONALISTS WERE IN ACCORD ON THIS POINT,
one group was particularly well situated to articulate it and present an alternative: the Indochinese Communist Party, led by Ho Chi Minh. For
Ho and the ICP, the March coup represented a glorious opportunity,

one they moved swiftly to seize. In 1941, the party had been in disarray, its members dead or incarcerated or living precariously in the jungles and swamps of the Vietnamese interior. Gradually, however, its fortunes revived, for several reasons. Most important, perhaps, the Vichy-Japan modus vivendi of 1940–45 over time grievously undermined those Vietnamese nationalist groups that had tied their fortunes to either the French or the Japanese; all were mortally wounded by the association. At the same time, the Vichy-Japan détente allowed the ICP-dominated Viet Minh to launch attacks on France's colonial rule without being labeled as profascist or hostile to the Allied cause. Elsewhere in Southeast Asia where such agreements between Tokyo and the colonial power did not exist—notably in Malaya, Indonesia, and the Philippines—Communist parties were not so lucky.[22]

By early 1943, the Viet Minh had gained a considerable amount of control in northern Tonkin—specifically in the provinces of Cao Bang, Bac Kan, and Lang Son. This border region, peopled substantially by ethnic minorities (notably Tai, Nung, Dao, and Hmong) living in a clan-based social system, had never been brought fully under French control. The Viet Minh too encountered resistance but gradually gained the trust and participation of the population in several districts. On July 8, 1944, the French police discovered a Viet Minh base near Soc Giang in Cao Bang containing a sizable cache of arms, tracts, and clothing, and warned of the immediate need to "re-establish authority." The following month two village chiefs were assassinated and several Viet Minh hideouts were discovered, confirming, the Sûreté reported, "some voluntary support" by the population. Louis Arnoux, the head of the Sûreté, had by then already identified the leader of the movement. In a letter to Decoux, he noted the effectiveness of "the guerrilla tactics advocated by the propaganda leaflets printed in China by the anti-French parties—whose leader now seems to be Ho Chi Minh, alias Nguyen Ai Quoc."[23]

And indeed, Ho Chi Minh's importance to the revolutionary cause in this period would be hard to exaggerate. He had been arrested in China in August 1942 by local authorities suspicious of his political activities; by his own estimate he then passed through eighteen prisons before winning his release in August 1943. During his incarceration, he kept in touch with his closest colleagues via letters written in disappearing ink, and upon his release, he stepped up his efforts to form a broad united front to drive the French and the Japanese from Indochina. In 1944, he helped put together a precarious coalition—known as the Vietnam Revolutionary League, or Viet Nam Cach Menh Dong Minh Hoi—with several non-Communist groups operating from exile in southern China. The ICP was from the start the central force in this coalition, and Ho the leading personality. He took care to downplay his background as an agent of the Comintern and talked up the need for nationalist unity. "I am a communist but what is important to me now is the independence and the freedom of my country, not communism," he told a Chinese general at the close of the congress establishing the league. "I personally guarantee you that communism will not become a reality in Vietnam for another fifty years."[24]

By late 1944, Ho Chi Minh, now back in Tonkin, could see the endgame. He predicted that Japan would lose the Pacific War, France would seek to regain Indochina, and before that Tokyo would overthrow the Decoux regime in order to protect its army. The result would be a power vacuum the Viet Minh could fill.[25] But he cautioned his more militant comrades to move carefully and to avoid launching a premature insurrection. Japan's defeat was inevitable, he told them; why not wait until the fruit was ripe to be picked? Even in Tonkin, Ho knew, the Viet Minh controlled only a small part of the territory, while in the rest of the country—especially in Cochin China in the south—its presence was spotty at best. (Some provinces remained devoid of Viet Minh organizing until well into 1945.) "The hour of peaceful revolution has passed," Ho said, "but the hour of the more general insurrections has not yet sounded."[26]

Then came March 9, the auspicious moment. The removal of the French secret police after the coup, together with Japan concentrating her presence in the urban areas of Vietnam in preparation for a possible Allied invasion, gave the Viet Minh considerable advantages in their underground work and propaganda efforts. The Japanese, having chased French troops out of Vietnam, did not think it vital to keep a troop presence in the northern provinces of Tonkin in light of more pressing concerns, and thus the Viet Minh had the region largely to themselves. Slowly, in the late spring and summer months, the Viet Minh began to spread southward toward the Red River Delta.[27]

For Ho and other members of the ICP Central Committee, the much-anticipated revolutionary conditions were now fast approaching. Shortly after the coup, the Central Committee convened under the direction of acting general secretary Truong Chinh to make preparations for a general uprising leading to a seizure of power at the end of the Pacific War. As reflected in the directive issued at the meeting's end, the committee agreed on the danger of moving too fast: Though the Japanese action would not produce a truly independent Vietnam, it would take time for the public to come down from its postcoup euphoria. Hence the party should bide its time and work to expand its base of support and introduce the Viet Minh flag and doctrine to the people. Eventually these efforts would culminate in a general uprising, "for example, when the Japanese Army surrenders to the Allies or when the Allies are decisively engaged in Indochina." The Viet Minh should be the main force working with the Allies, the directive said, and Viet Minh representatives should greet Allied units as they entered each village. These instructions would stay in place right up to the time of Japan's surrender.[28]

One other factor assisted the Viet Minh cause: the terrible famine that ravaged parts of Vietnam, and especially Tonkin and northern Annam, in 1944–45. These areas, less agriculturally blessed than Cochin China, had long depended on rice shipped from the south to survive. In the 1920s and 1930s, output in Tonkin declined due to reductions in acreage, even as the population expanded by more than 30 percent. Starting in 1941, bad weather and the requisition policies of the French and Japanese caused supplies to decline, and drought and insects caused the spring 1944 rice crop to decline by 19 percent compared to the previous year. That autumn, major flooding destroyed a large part of the October crop in the north, but the colonial government nevertheless increased the quantity of rice the peasants had to deliver. At the same time, Allied bombing of roads and railways dramatically reduced shipments from the Mekong Delta, as did colonial policies that made it unprofitable to ship grain to the north.[29]

By February 1945, a catastrophe loomed. Still, the French and the Japanese continued to stockpile rice for their own future use, and after the March 9 takeover the Japanese seized control of the French stocks. Meanwhile poor villagers in the north were succumbing by the thousands. In many areas, streets were littered with dying peasants, and oxcarts filled with corpses were a common sight. Families roamed from village to village, hoping to find grain. Or they retreated to their homes, shared the few remaining morsels, and died quietly, one by one. Some people, having consumed everything that could be eaten—bark, roots, leaves, dogs, and rats—resorted to cannibalism, causing parents to fear that their children would be stolen and eaten. Some parents sold their children for a few cups of rice. Duong Thieu Chi, a provincial official in Nam Dinh, made sure to avoid eating in restaurants or stalls when he traveled during these months, for fear that the meat served might be rat or human flesh.[30]

A French observer, perhaps aware of his country's failure over the previous decades to develop an effective system for the prevention and relief of famine, despite pleas for them after each crisis, had this to say: "From looking at these bodies, which are shriveled up on roadsides with only a handful of straw for clothes as well as for the burial garment, one feels ashamed of being human."[31]

It is impossible to know how many people perished in the famine, but the scale is clear enough. In May 1945, as the crisis eased, officials used statistics from various provinces in Tonkin to declare that to that point,

VICTIMS OF THE MASS FAMINE IN NORTHERN VIETNAM IN 1944–45.

precisely 380,969 people had died by starvation. A year later, using more complete figures, analysts estimated that one million people had died in Tonkin, and another 300,000 in Annam. In later years, the estimates would climb higher still, to two million deaths in a five-month period in 1945. Even if one adopts the lower figure of one million for Tonkin, the implications are appalling: 10 percent of the population in the affected region died of starvation in less than half a year. Particularly hard-hit were the provinces of Nam Dinh, Thai Binh, Hai Duong, and Kien An. In these provinces, and indeed throughout Tonkin and Annam, the perception became widespread that the Japanese and especially the French were to blame for the disaster with their inhumane policies, and that Bao Dai and his ministers had been feckless in responding to the crisis.[32]

The Viet Minh, however, benefited from the widespread popular perception that they alone had tried hard to reduce the suffering. As desperate peasants stormed granaries to take rice, Viet Minh operatives often assumed leadership of the revolt, directing "rice struggles" to break open warehouses and distribute food to the hungry. These efforts, though growing out of grassroots popular protest more than Viet Minh initiative per se, left a lasting impression on many peasants and undoubtedly aided the efforts of Viet Minh forces operating in the mountain regions around the Red River Delta to seize control over rural areas and recruit followers from villages under their control. The tiny elite forces under Vo Nguyen Giap were now combined with other units in the country into a new Vietnamese Liberation Army (Viet Nam Giai Phong Quan). By May, the VLA's trained forces had reached five thousand, although many lacked weapons.[33]

The Kim government in Hue, meanwhile, was completely ineffectual. Widely perceived to be a vassal of the Japanese, its leading members were competent professionals—doctors, lawyers, professors—who faced near-impossible odds. Not only did they have to heed the wishes of the army of occupation; they also had to deal with the sorry state of the country's infrastructure after years of war. Allied bombing had caused major damage to the railroads and halted most shipping. Even the basic task of getting governmental messages out from Hue to the provincial towns proved difficult and largely dependent on the goodwill of the Japanese, who controlled many of the roads. As for money, the government had no finances to speak of, and whatever revenues it managed to bring in, it had to turn over to the Japanese. As spring turned into summer and the certainty of Japan's defeat in the war became more and more apparent, many members of Kim's cabinet grasped the essential futility of their situation: The government was irrevocably linked to a hated occupier whose days were numbered.

IV

THE GROWING PRESENCE OF THE VIET MINH IN TONKIN WAS NOT lost on American officials in the Pacific theater, who saw important implications for the war effort. The Japanese takeover had eradicated the French intelligence network in Indochina, these analysts knew, and also disrupted the activities of the Americans' so-called GBT espionage unit (named after the last names of its three leaders), which during 1944 had produced a wealth of useful intelligence information.[34] Hence the potential utility of using the Viet Minh to assist Allied actions. New directives from Washington gave these U.S. units more flexibility, allowing them to seek cooperation with any and all resistance groups provided that such actions did not interfere with planned operations.[35]

Thus it was that Captain Charles Fenn of the Office of Strategic Services (OSS), the principal U.S. wartime intelligence agency, sought out meetings with Ho Chi Minh in Kunming in southern China. Fenn, a London-born former Marine Corps officer who would go on to write plays and novels as well as a respected biography of Ho, headed OSS operations for Indochina from headquarters in Kunming. There he heard about Ho's organization and about Ho's role in helping locate downed American pilots and providing intelligence on Japanese troop movements. Moreover, Fenn knew, Ho sometimes dropped by the Office of War Information facility in the city to read the *Encyclopedia Americana* and *Time* magazine. A face-to-face encounter seemed in order, Fenn determined.

Ho was eager to oblige. He had indeed come to Kunming expressly for the purpose of making contact with American officials. No Allied power loomed larger in his mind than the United States. Much as he had pinned his nationalist hopes at the end of the First World War on the

Americans, pressing his case for Vietnamese independence on Woodrow Wilson at the Versailles Peace Conference, so he now looked to Washington for help as the Second World War drew to a close. He continued to believe that, by the circumstances of her birth, the United States was uniquely able among the great powers to grasp the nature of the "colonial problem." The British might have cosigned the Atlantic Charter with its embrace of self-determination, but the document was wholly an American creation. Even the Soviet Union's leadership did not possess this understanding. With everything in the Pacific War going the Americans' way, and with Washington certain to dominate world politics in the years to come, Ho saw every reason to see what this Fenn fellow wanted.[36]

They met on March 17 at the Dragon's Gate Café. Ho Chi Minh was accompanied by a close Viet Minh associate, Pham Van Dong. "His silvery wisp of beard suggests age," Fenn wrote of Ho in his diary that day, "but his face is vigorous and his eyes bright and gleaming." The three conversed in French. Fenn asked what Ho wanted from the United States. Only recognition for the Viet Minh, came the reply. But what about the rumors that it was a Communist organization? Fenn asked. The French label Communist all Annamites who want independence, Ho said, neatly evading a direct answer. When Fenn suggested the possibility of mutual assistance, Ho readily agreed.

"I already felt sure he was our man," Fenn recalled, noting the "clear-cut talk [and] Buddha-like composure" of his correspondent. "Baudelaire felt the wings of insanity touch his mind; but that morning I felt the wings of genius touch mine."[37]

Fenn, who had studied graphology, also provided an analysis of Ho's handwriting, from which he concluded:

The essential features are simplicity, desire to make everything clear, remarkable self-control. Knows how to keep a secret. Neat, orderly, unassuming, no interest in dress or outward show. Self-confident and dignified. Gentle but firm. Loyal, sincere, and generous, would make a good friend. Outgoing, gets along with anyone. Keen analytical mind, difficult to deceive. Shows readiness to ask questions. Good judge of character. Full of enthusiasm, energy, initiative. Conscientious; painstaking attention to detail. Imaginative, interested in aesthetics, particularly literature. Good sense of humor.

Faults: diplomatic to the point of contriving. Could be moody and obstinate.[38]

At a second meeting three days later—this one at the Indochina Café, where they sipped strong coffee filtered in the French style—the two men made a deal whereby the OSS would provide radio equipment and a limited amount of arms and ammunition in exchange for Viet Minh assistance in intelligence gathering, sabotaging Japanese installations, and rescuing American pilots. But Ho Chi Minh also had something else on his mind that day: He asked if he could meet Claire Chennault, adviser to Chiang Kai-shek, founder of the famed "Flying Tigers," and commander of the Fourteenth Air Force. Fenn said he'd do his best, and ten days later the two men presented themselves at Chennault's outer office for a late-morning meeting, Fenn in a gabardine bush jacket and Ho in a simple cotton tunic and sandals. Chennault, for his part, cut an imposing figure in his perfectly pressed uniform. (He had that effect on people: Winston Churchill, upon seeing Chennault make his entrance at a conference earlier in the war and learning of his identity, whispered to an aide, "Well, thank God he's on our side.")[39]

Chennault thanked Ho for his efforts to save U.S. pilots, and Ho responded by expressing his admiration for Chennault and the Flying Tigers. Neither man spoke about the French, or about politics, but as the meeting ended, Ho asked for a favor: Could he have the general's photograph? In an instant, a young female assistant appeared with a folder of eight-by-ten glossies. "Take your pick," Chennault said. Ho selected one and asked the general to sign it. The assistant produced a Parker 51, and Chennault scrawled across the bottom: "Yours Sincerely, Claire L. Chennault."[40]

Ho Chi Minh had his prized possession. In the weeks and months thereafter, he waved the photograph like a magic wand on his travels throughout the region, the better to prove that his movement had official recognition from the Allies and in particular from the United States. And he had some justification for making that claim. In April, the OSS provided Ho Chi Minh with air transportation to Jiangxi, not far from the Vietnam border, and later OSS personnel joined the Viet Minh at Ho's headquarters at Pac Bo. One of them, radio operator Mac Shinn, an Asian-American, established radio contact with Kunming, and the OSS began to air-drop supplies, including medicine, a radio set, and a few weapons for training. In return, the Viet Minh provided the United States with intelligence reports and rescued several U.S. airmen.[41]

The OSS called its Vietnam operation the Deer Mission. On July 16, a Deer Team led by Colonel Allison Thomas parachuted into Ho's new forward base, a tiny village in the jungle called Tan Trao, not far from the Thai Nguyen provincial capital. After disentangling himself from the banyan tree into which his parachute had slammed him, Thomas spoke a "few flowery sentences" to two hundred Viet Minh soldiers assembled near a banner proclaiming "Welcome to Our American Friends." Ho Chi Minh, speaking in good idiomatic English, cordially greeted the OSS team and offered supper, but it was clear to the Americans that he was ill, "shaking like a leaf and obviously running a high fever." The next day Ho denounced the French but remarked that "we welcome 10 million Americans." Thomas was impressed by what he heard. "Forget the Communist Bogy," he radioed OSS headquarters in Kunming. "Viet Minh League is not Communist. Stands for freedom and reforms against French harshness."[42]

Thomas's analysis was wrong, or at least incomplete. If the Viet Minh stood for independence and against French repression, their core leadership that summer also remained staunchly Communist. But Ho in particular among top strategists wore the ideology lightly, so much so that even Soviet officials questioned his Communist credentials. In Mao Zedong's Chinese Communist Party too, analysts wondered where the Viet Minh, should they win the right to rule a free Vietnam, would take the country.

Other OSS personnel soon parachuted into Pac Bo, including a medic who diagnosed Ho Chi Minh's ailments as malaria and dysentery. Quinine and sulfa drugs restored his health, but Ho remained frail. To a remarkable degree, he made a winning impression on these Americans, who invariably described him as warm, intelligent, and keen to cooperate with the United States.[43] As a sign of friendship, they named him "OSS Agent 19." Everywhere the Americans went, impoverished villagers thanked them with gifts of food and clothing, no doubt especially welcome after the devastating famine of that spring. The villagers inter-

HO CHI MINH WITH MEMBERS OF THE U.S. DEER TEAM IN PAC BO. ON HO'S IMMEDIATE RIGHT IS ALLISON THOMAS, AND THEN RENÉ DÉFOURNEAUX, ANOTHER MEMBER OF THE U.S. TEAM. NEXT TO DÉFOURNEAUX IS VO NGU-YEN GIAP.

preted the foreigners' presence as a sign of U.S. anticolonial and anti-Japanese sentiments.

In early August the Deer Team began to give Viet Minh soldiers weapons training. During many conversations with the OSS members, Ho said that he hoped young Vietnamese could study in the United States and that American technicians could help build an independent Vietnam. Citing history, Ho remarked that "your statesmen make eloquent speeches about . . . self-determination. We are self-determined. Why not help us? Am I any different from . . . your George Washington?"[44]

V

ONE CAN IMAGINE HOW MUCH HO RELISHED THESE CONTACTS WITH the mighty Americans. His Viet Minh had endured years of isolation, receiving no aid from his ideological allies in the Soviet Union; now the world's most powerful nation seemed to be throwing her support behind his nation's long quest for liberation. Surely he understood that the road ahead would be a difficult one for him, even treacherous, but with the Japanese facing total defeat and the Americans making welcome noises, he had reason to feel a measure of confidence.

"You've got to judge someone on the basis of what he wants," wrote one American who was with Ho at his jungle headquarters during this time. "Ho couldn't be French, and he knew he could fight the French on his terms. He was afraid of the Chinese, and he couldn't deal with them because they'd always demand their pound of flesh. Moscow, so far away, was good at blowing up bridges, but not much good at building them up again. If it weren't for the war, of course, Ho wouldn't have had a chance against the long background of French colonialism. But now he was in the saddle, although it wasn't clear what horse he was riding. For the moment, surely, he was helping us, on the ground. We and the French were in a position to help him in the future. I think he was ready to remain pro-West."[45]

Away from Tonkin, however, and away from the freewheeling atmosphere in Kunming, American policy was moving in a very different direction. Roosevelt's death on April 12 had brought to power a new administration, one with a markedly different assessment of what ought to happen in Indochina and in the colonial world generally. Harry S. Truman, thrust into the presidency at a time of global war, had almost no international experience. An unsuccessful haberdasher and former U.S. senator from Missouri, Truman had been selected as FDR's running mate in 1944 because he was the second choice of each faction of the Democratic Party, and the only candidate all of them could accept. Whereas Roosevelt seldom made a decision until forced to do so, Truman often acted on impulse; while FDR could be described by associates as "sphinxlike," Truman tended to tell people precisely what he thought; whereas Roosevelt saw the world in various shades of gray, for his successor it was often black-and-white.

Truman had none of FDR's personal interest in French Indochina's future, and his administration from the start focused its energies on the pressing tasks of securing the victory over the reeling Germans and delivering a knockout blow to Japan. Precisely for those reasons, however, astute observers quickly saw a change in Washington's position on what ought to happen in postwar Indochina. Truman probably knew little or nothing of Roosevelt's trusteeship scheme, and neither he nor his top foreign policy aide, James F. Byrnes, the former Supreme Court justice and director of war mobilization, gave much thought to the broader issue of colonial nationalism. Sensing an opening, pro-French voices in the State Department immediately pushed for a reevaluation of policy toward Indochina. On the day following Roosevelt's death, the State-War-Navy Coordinating Committee, the interagency forerunner to the National Security Council, took up the matter with the aim of making a recommendation to the new president.

Thus came to the fore sharp internal differences among U.S. analysts, differences that had been kept muted so long as Roosevelt was alive. Support for FDR's anticolonialist agitation came, as before, chiefly from some Asia specialists, such as John Carter Vincent, head of the Office of Far Eastern Affairs, and Abbot Low Moffat, chief of the newly established Southwest Pacific Affairs Division (later the Southeast Asian Affairs Division), who felt certain that the United States had to come down on the side of the anticolonial movement sweeping through Southeast Asia. General Albert Wedemeyer, the U.S. commander in Chungking, likewise clung to the Rooseveltian position and squabbled with SEAC's Mountbatten over which commander held responsibility for military operations in Indochina, and over how much assistance should be given to French efforts to reclaim colonial control. When Mountbatten, whose superiors in London supported a French return, informed Wedemeyer that he intended to fly twenty-six sorties into Indochina to support French guerrilla actions, the American objected strongly, on the grounds that Indochina was properly part of Chiang Kai-shek's theater rather than Mountbatten's responsibility. Wedemeyer suspected that any SEAC missions would merely serve as a cover to enhance French power over postwar developments.[46]

But such voices were a minority. Most U.S. analysts had their primary attention on Europe, and on making sure that Franco-American relations remained stable. Cooperation from Paris, these observers argued, would be needed to check possible Soviet expansionism, a specter made more real by Moscow's tightening grip in early 1945 over Poland, Romania, and Bulgaria. Moreover, the French Communists were destined to emerge out of the war as the most powerful political party in France and thus had to be handled carefully. Blocking French efforts to recover Indochina would probably enhance the Communists' advantage by discouraging partnership with the West.[47]

The interagency discussion yielded, in late April, a State Department recommendation that the United States not oppose a French return to Indochina but merely seek assurances from Paris that it would grant more self-government and increased local autonomy to the Indochinese people. Though termed a compromise, the recommendation in fact marked a sharp departure from previous U.S. policy. As such, it stands as a pivotal moment in the long history of American involvement in Vietnam. "The recommendation," historian Ronald Spector has written, "was a long step away from Roosevelt's unwavering insistence on creating a trusteeship."[48]

The differences, to be sure, did not go away. As we shall see, there were still those in Washington who were convinced that the United States was on the wrong side of history in supporting French colonial ambitions in Southeast Asia. At the field level in Indochina itself, that conviction was even more widely held. But the thrust of high-level policy was now plainly going in a new direction, which is evident in hindsight but was perceived as well by many at the time. When world leaders convened in San Francisco in late April and May to form the United Nations, senior U.S. officials did not raise the issue of trusteeship for Indochina. On the contrary, U.S. secretary of state Edward Stettinius assured French foreign minister Georges Bidault with remarkable aplomb that "the record is entirely innocent of any official statement of the U.S. government questioning, even by implication, French sovereignty over Indochina." James Dunn of the State Department's European desk, a deeply conservative man whom Eleanor Roosevelt once called a "fascist" for his views on colonial matters, spoke in similar terms in San Francisco and worked hard behind the scenes to create a pro-French consensus. A report prepared for Harry Truman on June 2 acknowledged that "independence sentiment in the area is believed to be increasingly strong" but declared that "the United States recognizes French sovereignty over Indochina." When Truman met Chiang Kai-shek in Washington some weeks later, he dismissed any notion of trusteeship for Indochina.[49]

All this brought smiles to French lips. Paris officials had come to San Francisco in an aggressive mood and had worked hard, both there and in other meetings with U.S. officials in Washington and Paris, to induce the Truman administration to abandon formally any notion of an international trusteeship for Indochina. As Georges Bidault insisted at every opportunity during these weeks, the decision regarding Indochina's future rested with France alone. Now U.S. leaders were in effect saying they agreed. Perceptive French analysts understood that they still faced potential problems with the Americans—Washington had not indicated any active *support* for French efforts in the Far East, and even the new administration seemed annoyingly sympathetic to the pleas of nationalists throughout the colonial world—but they were relieved nonetheless.

The general thrust of U.S. policy on Indochina was confirmed when American, British, and Soviet leaders convened in the Berlin suburb of Potsdam in July. Nazi Germany had surrendered in May, and the Allies now gathered to determine the postwar order and to clarify and implement agreements made previously at Yalta. De Gaulle was not invited, despite his persistent efforts to gain representation. He had earned Washington's and London's ire for sending French troops to the former French mandates of Syria and Lebanon, both of which had recently established their independence, and for proceeding with plans to make territorial "adjustments" in the Val d'Aosta area of northwestern Italy. U.S. officials, embarrassed by this defiance at a time when Truman was lecturing the Soviets about their heavy-handed actions in Eastern Europe, left de Gaulle off the Potsdam guest list.[50]

Notwithstanding de Gaulle's absence from the meeting, or because of it, French interests regarding Indochina fared well—in the short term, at least. The long-standing dispute between Mountbatten and Wedemeyer over theater boundaries was resolved in a way that benefited French aims. Mountbatten's SEAC operations would thenceforth include Indochina south of the sixteenth parallel (just below Tourane), while China would be in charge north of that line. American resources and attention could thus be focused on preparing for the final thrust against the Japanese home islands, but it also opened the door to Franco-British cooperation in securing French control over the colony. U.S. officials also agreed to let French officials participate in surrender ceremonies throughout Indochina (that is, even in the Chinese-controlled north) and to involve French forces in the Far East in order to hasten that surrender.[51]

Yet in a different sense the Potsdam agreement worked against French aims and in favor of Ho Chi Minh's, though this would become clear only in time. The Chinese occupation of the northern half of Vietnam looked likely to complicate Paris's plan to rebuild the colonial state. And so indeed it would. The Viet Minh would be given vital time to build up their forces and cement their authority in Tonkin, with hugely important implications for the war to come. Among many Vietnamese intellectuals, meanwhile, the conviction would take hold that France's exclusion from the conference constituted further proof that she had become a second-rate, expendable power.

For now, however, de Gaulle delighted in the fact that he could dispatch to the region an Expeditionary Corps for the Far East. As leader of the mission, de Gaulle selected General Philippe Leclerc, the celebrated commander of the French Second Armored Division that had liberated Paris the previous year. Leclerc indicated a preference for a Moroccan assignment, but the general prevailed on him to go to Asia. Indochina, he told Leclerc, presented a vital and difficult challenge, but one that it was well within France's power to meet.

The Pacific War ended before Leclerc's force had a chance to intervene. On August 15, after the Hiroshima and Nagasaki atomic bombings and the Soviet Union's declaration of war against Japan, Emperor Hirohito announced Japan's surrender. The Japanese, whose actions since 1940 had done so much to transform French Indochina, now promised to create more upheaval, this time by leaving the scene. There would be a vacuum of power, all informed observers could see, and the question was who would fill it. Charles de Gaulle, for one, seemingly had little doubt. On August 15, he sent a message from "the Mother Country to the Indochinese Union," expressing France's "joy, solicitude, and gratitude" for Indochina's "loyalty to France" and her resistance to the Japanese. Even as he uttered those words, however, in the jungles of Tonkin, Ho Chi Minh and his Viet Minh readied to make a triumphant entry into Hanoi. Their message to the crowds awaiting them: With Japan defeated and France prostrate, the moment of liberation was at hand.[52]

CHAPTER 4

"ALL MEN ARE CREATED EQUAL"

Hanoi would be the epicenter of the upheaval, the place where Ho Chi Minh, on a stifling-hot September day in 1945, in front of hundreds of thousands, would proclaim Vietnamese independence: Hanoi, with its wide boulevards, shady trees, and formal gardens, its ornate pastel-colored buildings erected to the glory of France at the turn of the century and in the interwar years. Physically compact, contained by the Red River to the north and the east, and surrounded by paddy fields on the other sides, its many lakes were a reminder to the visitor that the site was once little more than a swamp.

From the start, the French had invested the city's architecture with important symbolic power, to signify colonial authority. Major buildings constructed in the French neoclassical style included the Governor-General's Palace, the Opera House, St. Joseph's Cathedral, and the Hanoi railway station. The Paul Doumer (later Long Bien) bridge, built around the turn of the century on a design by the company of Gustave Eiffel, was a major engineering feat, being 1.7 kilometers long and spanning a Red River that shifted from year to year. Along the fashionable rue Paul Bert, French shops sprang up as the century turned, as did innumerable sidewalk cafés.[1]

An American visitor to the city, Henry G. Bryant, president of the Geographical Society of Philadelphia, liked what he saw. Hanoi, he commented in 1909, "is indeed a creditable creation of the French colonizing spirit, with its broad avenues, stately government buildings, sunny parks, and good hotel. . . . Should fate decree that I be exiled to the French colonies of Asia, Hanoi would be my choice as an abiding place." Another American, Harry Franck, said after a visit in the mid-1920s: "It is quite a city, with expensive modern buildings, electric street-cars—found nowhere else in the colony—railways in four directions, many automobiles, both of the taxi-cab and private limousine variety, several excellent hotels; in short, it is a little Paris of the tropics, with some advantages that even Paris does not have."[2]

Many Vietnamese too were attracted by the city's bright lights. "Perhaps on nights when there are no moon and stars, the peasants in Nam Dinh, Thai Binh, Hai Duong, Bac Ninh, Son Tay, and Hoa Binh go out into their courtyards and see a shining halo," the author Vu Trong Phung said. "There, hovering over a thousand years of culture and glowing with easy riches, what the peasants see is the halo over Hanoi, and they are still leaving their villages for it!" Once there, some became willing collaborators with the colonizers; others became disillusioned and returned to their villages; most sought merely to eke out an existence for themselves and their families. Over time, however, as we've seen, many joined the movement for independence, which took a great many forms but which was always centered in the urban areas of Vietnam. More than any place, it came to be centered in Hanoi.[3]

When Ho entered the city on August 26, it was for the first time. He had risen from his provincial Nghe An upbringing to travel to the far reaches of the globe—to Paris, to London, to New York City—and to become a nationalist leader, yet only now, at age fifty-five, did he set foot in his country's cultural and political center. Almost four decades the journey had taken. In the immediate sense, the trip had started four days earlier, when Ho left Tan Trao by foot and by boat, bound for the capital. Still weak from his illness, he had to be carried part of the way on a stretcher, and after crossing the Red River on the twenty-fifth, the entourage halted in the northern suburbs of Hanoi. The next day, accompanied by Party Secretary Truong Chinh in a commandeered car, Ho crossed the Doumer Bridge and made for a three-story row house on Hang Nhang Street, in the Chinese section of town.[4]

It was a heady time for Ho Chi Minh and his comrades, the critical stage of what would become known as the August Revolution. Things had moved rapidly since news reached Tonkin of the atomic bombings and Japan's collapse. Already on August 11, as rumors circulated that Tokyo was about to surrender, members of the Indochinese Communist Party regional committee began to prepare for an insurrection to seize Hanoi from the Japanese. Two days later Viet Minh leaders from many parts of the country met in Tan Trao to the north for a previously scheduled party conference (to be known in history as the Ninth Plenum) and reached a resolution that a nationwide insurrection should occur immediately to bring about an independent republic under the leadership of the Viet Minh. Using the name Nguyen Ai Quoc for the last time, Ho issued an "appeal to the people." "Dear fellow countrymen!" he declared. "The decisive hour has struck for the destiny of our people. Let all of us stand up and rely on our own strength to free ourselves. Many oppressed peoples the world over are vying with each other in wresting back independence. We should not lag behind. Forward! Forward! Under the banner of the Viet Minh, let us valiantly march forward!"[5]

Much more than they would later acknowledge, Viet Minh leaders rode to power on the wave of suffering in the north, caused by the famine that had hit earlier in the year and further strengthened by the overthrow of the French and the defeat of the Japanese.[6] In official Vietnamese historiography, this dimension is largely absent; Ho and his colleagues are depicted as the masters of events, directing developments from the top. Their decisions and actions were important, but there is no question that they were beneficiaries of an upswell of protest from below.

Throughout the third week of August, Viet Minh forces took control in towns and villages in various parts of Annam and Tonkin. Resistance was usually minimal, as local authorities simply handed over power to the insurgents and as Japanese forces, now part of a defeated empire, stayed neutral. In Hanoi on August 19, Viet Minh forces seized control of all important public buildings except the Japanese-guarded Bank of Indochina, and announced their seizure of power from a balcony of what was then and remains today the Hanoi Opera House. For the first time since Francis Garnier seized it for France in 1873, the city was in Vietnamese hands. In Hue, Emperor Bao Dai announced he would support a government led by Ho Chi Minh, but a mass rally in Hanoi demanded that he abdicate his throne. He did so on August 25, declaring his support for the Viet Minh regime and handing over the imperial sword to the new national government, with all the legitimacy that that symbolic act conferred.[7]

A young female medical student observed the scene:

The Royal Family was grouped on the left-hand side of the court-yard. The crowd was thronging on the right. Suddenly, a man's voice cried out: "From this day on, royalty is abolished in Vietnam. Bao Dai is from here on the simple citizen Vinh Thuy. And now, citizen Vinh Thuy has permission to speak." Next, Emperor Bao Dai, who looked very young, stepped forward. He addressed the crowd: "Citizens, let me be understood. I prefer to be a free citizen than an enslaved king."[8]

"The Vietnamese people do not want, and cannot abide foreign domination or administration any longer," Bao Dai wrote in a letter to Charles de Gaulle in Paris. "I implore you to understand that the only way to safeguard French interests and the spiritual influence of France in Indochina is to openly recognize Vietnam's independence and to disavow any idea of reestablishing sovereignty or a French administration here in any form. We could understand each other so well and become friends if you would stop pretending that you are still our masters."[9]

One can imagine Ho's feelings of anticipation as he and Truong Chinh entered the city that first day, passing through streets festooned with Viet Minh flags and banners. Here he was, in the city that had so long fired his imagination, and his revolutionary forces were already in control! Yet Ho knew that dangers lurked around every corner. To associates he quoted Lenin's famous warning: "Seizing power is difficult, but keeping it is even harder." The food problem would require immediate attention, as widespread starvation remained a major threat. (Farmers had taken to eating the seed rice earmarked for the next season's planting.) Rival nationalist groups such as the Viet Nam Quoc Dan Dang (Vietnamese Nationalist Party, or VNQDD) and the formerly pro-Japanese Dai Viet were reeling from the Viet Minh's bold assertion of strength and superior organization but might yet rise again. Most serious of all, Ho knew, the French were determined to restore colonial control, and it was not yet clear how the other victorious Allies would react. Hence the importance, in the minds

A WOMEN'S DETACHMENT OF THE LIBERATION ARMY, CARRYING
WEAPONS AND THE VIET MINH FLAG, IN HANOI, LATE AUGUST 1945.

of all party leaders, of announcing the formation of a provisional government, and of doing so before the arrival of Allied occupation forces. On
August 29, Ho Chi Minh quietly formed his first government.[10]

Then on September 2—the same day that Japan signed the instruments of surrender on the deck of the U.S. battleship *Missouri* in Tokyo
Bay—he presented the government to the country and, at a rally before
hundreds of thousands, proclaimed Vietnamese independence. Thus
came into being the Democratic Republic of Vietnam (DRV). The rally
took place in Ba Dinh Square, a spacious grassy field not far from the
Governor-General's Palace in Hanoi. A sense of anticipation permeated
the city that morning. Young Vietnamese had worked through the night
bedecking nearby buildings with flowers, banners, and, notably, the Viet
Minh flag—a lone gold star on a field of red. On some banners were nationalist slogans proclaiming in English, Vietnamese, French, Chinese, and
Russian: "Vietnam for the Vietnamese"; "Long Live Vietnamese Independence"; "Independence or Death"; "Welcome to the Allies"; "Death
to French Imperialism." Peasants made the trek from nearby villages and
now mingled with merchants and mandarins. Schools were closed for the
occasion, and teachers armed with whistles walked at the head of bands
of children singing revolutionary songs. Scouts who had been mobilized
by the French and the Japanese now enthusiastically supported the new

national government. Ethnic minority groups from the hills were present as well, clothed in their distinctively colored headgear, skirts, and sashes. One contingent that could not be present was allowed to participate vicariously: Inmates at the Central Prison were given three pigs to slaughter, cook, and eat "in celebration of Vietnam's independence day."[11]

Ho Chi Minh arrived in a prewar American automobile with outriders on bicycles. He strode to a hastily built platform decked out with white and red cloth; with him were members of the new government's cabinet. More than strode, he bounded, to the surprise of onlookers who expected rulers to walk in a careful, stately manner. While almost everyone on the stage wore Western suits and ties, Ho chose a high-collared faded khaki jacket and white rubber sandals—his standard uniform as head of state for the next twenty-four years—and an old hat. His address, hammered out on his old portable typewriter over the previous days, was preceded by loud, prearranged chants of "Independence! Independence!"

He began slowly, spoke a few sentences, then stopped and asked his listeners, "Compatriots, can you hear me?" The crowd roared back, "Yes, we hear you!" At that moment, some who were present later said, a special bond was struck. Tran Trung Thanh, a young self-defense cadre, recalled that, although he didn't yet know who Ho Chi Minh was exactly, this exchange of words moved him to tears, and led him to take one particular slogan on a banner as his personal motto: "Independence or death!" Said another observer, Dr. Tran Duy Hung: "We did not just shout with our mouths but with all our hearts, the hearts of over 400,000 people standing in the square then."[12]

To the few Americans in the audience, Ho's next words were stunning. "All men are created equal. They are endowed by their Creator with certain inalienable rights; among these are Life, Liberty, and the pursuit of Happiness. . . . All the peoples on the earth are equal from birth, all the peoples have a right to live and to be happy and free." These were "undeniable truths," Ho continued, and had been accepted as such by the French people themselves since the time of the French Revolution. Yet for eighty years, France had abused these truths in her treatment of the Vietnamese people—Ho singled out the division of Vietnam into three administrative units, the killing or imprisonment of patriots, the expropriation of raw materials and land, and the levying of "hundreds of unfair taxes." France referred to herself as the "protector" of Vietnam, yet twice in the past five years she had sold the territory to Japan. Well, no more: "Today we are determined to oppose the wicked schemes of the French imperialists, and we call upon the victorious Allies to recognize our freedom and independence."[13]

The reference to the American Declaration of Independence and the "victorious Allies" was deliberate and was echoed by Vo Nguyen Giap, the former history teacher who now commanded the Viet Minh "Liberation Army," who took the podium after Ho finished. Giap appealed specifically to the United States and China for support (interestingly, neither he nor Ho mentioned the socialist Soviet Union), claiming that the "Vietnamese masses had eagerly risen to fight Japan," whereas the French colonialists had joined forces with the fascist Japanese for the duration of the war. Now the French readied to return, and the world community should work to stop them; if it didn't, Vietnam would struggle alone. "Following in the steps of our forefathers," Giap exclaimed, "the present generation will fight a final battle, so that generations to follow will forever be able to live in independence, freedom, and happiness."[14]

In between the two speeches, Tran Duy Hung recalled, "an airplane, a small plane, circled over us. We did not know whose plane it was. We thought that it was a Vietnamese plane. But when it swooped down over us, we recognized the American flag. The crowd cheered enthusiastically."[15]

II

IT IS A STARTLING ASPECT OF VIET MINH THINKING IN THESE CRITICAL weeks, the degree to which Ho Chi Minh and his colleagues looked to Washington for support in their struggle. They understood what every other observer of the international scene understood: that the United States was emerging from the war as by far the strongest nation in the world, as the only real superpower, and therefore uniquely able to affect the course of events in the developing world. In the Asia-Pacific, in particular, America stood supreme. At Tan Trao, Ho had pressed members of the OSS Deer Team on the question of whether Washington would intercede in Indochina or leave matters to the French and perhaps Chinese. The question suggested uncertainty, and the evidence is considerable that he held in this period a dual vision of the United States. On the one hand, as a bastion of capitalism, America could be an opponent of the future world revolution; on the other hand, her leader for most of World War II had been Franklin Roosevelt, a major world voice for the liberation of colonial peoples in Asia and Africa and the principal figure behind the Atlantic Charter. As a foe of European colonialism, the United States could thus be of enormous help to the Viet Minh cause, but not if serious tensions arose between the capitalist powers and the USSR; in such an eventuality, Washington could choose to, in effect, strike a bargain with France, supporting her efforts in Indochina in exchange for help in countering Moscow.[16]

At times, the uncertainty regarding U.S. plans slid into pessimism. Not long before his arrival in Hanoi, Ho wrote his friend Charles Fenn a plaintive letter, expressing his satisfaction that the war had ended but disappointment that "our American friends" would be leaving him soon. "And their leaving," he wrote, "means that relations between you and us will be more difficult." At other times, hopes must have soared. When on August 15 word reached Tan Trao (on an OSS-supplied radio) that Japan's Emperor Hirohito had instructed his subjects to capitulate, Americans and Vietnamese broke out in raucous celebration. Flares were launched into the sky, songs were sung, and liquor flowed. The Vietnamese shouted joyously that independence was at hand, and the Americans responded with cheers of "Hip-hip-hooray!"[17]

In other parts of Vietnam too, nationalists of all stripes hoped for American support. To a degree difficult to appreciate today, with our knowledge of the bloodshed and animosity that was to follow, admiration for the United States was intense and near universal that summer. It was a Rooseveltian moment. The United States, recalled Bui Diem, later a top official in the South Vietnamese government, was the "shining giant" whose commitment to freedom was real, who would end forever colonial control. These nationalists viewed with apprehension the impending arrival of the Chinese and the British (who were given the task at Potsdam, it will be recalled, of disarming the Japanese in northern and southern Vietnam, respectively, at the conclusion of hostilities), which made them all the more attached to the image of America as savior. Bui Diem again:

"We could not understand why they had agreed to let the British and Chinese in, but the Americans themselves had representatives in Vietnam, and their presence sparked a wild hope that the United States was interested. And if they were interested, they might yet be prevailed upon to act."[18]

The most important of those representatives was Archimedes L. Patti, an intelligence veteran who had led covert operations in North Africa, Sicily, and Salerno. Born in New York to poor Italian immigrants, Patti had been appointed after Tokyo's surrender to head a team to fly to Hanoi in order to secure the release of Allied POWs held in Japanese camps, and also to provide intelligence on conditions in Indochina. He arrived on August 22, accompanied by twelve other OSS members and a smaller French delegation headed by Jean Sainteny, the head of French intelligence operations in China, whose ostensible mission was to administer to the needs of French POWs. Sainteny was a former banker in Hanoi and the son-in-law of Albert Sarraut, the former governor of Indochina and a leading French colonial thinker.

Both groups took up residence at the stylish (then and now) Metropole Hotel in the city's center. From there, Patti opened negotiations with Japanese occupation authorities and established contact with local Viet Minh leaders. On Sunday, September 26, these Viet Minh officials held a quasi-parade in Patti's honor (complete with a band playing "The Star-Spangled Banner") and that same day the newly arrived Ho Chi Minh invited him to lunch—sure signs of the importance they attached to courting the young American. After a meal of fish soup, braised chicken, and pork, the two men appraised the fluid situation. Ho expressed displeasure that Sainteny was now in Hanoi through the good offices of the Americans, and he warned Patti that the French team's aims went well beyond looking after prisoners of war. France sought to reclaim control and would get support in this goal from Great Britain, Ho told him. The Chinese, meanwhile, would sell out Vietnamese interests to achieve objectives of their own.[19]

Patti listened intently. He had met with Ho Chi Minh once before, in April 1945, in southern China, on the subject of potential OSS–Viet Minh cooperation in the struggle against Japan. The two had talked then late into the night, smoking Patti's Chesterfields and sipping tea.

Patti came away "indelibly" impressed with Ho's patriotism and social acumen. Now they were face-to-face again, and Patti couldn't help but reflect on the Viet Minh leader's appearance, so emaciated in comparison with the earlier encounter. But Patti again found himself charmed by Ho's political sophistication, by his grace, and by his grasp of current world developments. And as in April, Ho left no doubt that he desperately wanted Allied, and especially American, backing. At a subsequent meeting, Ho solicited Patti's input in the drafting of the proclamation of independence. "Ho called for me to see him urgently," Patti recalled. "He presented me with these sheets of paper. I looked at them and I said, 'What do I do with them? I can't read them.' He started to translate. So I just listened carefully and I was shocked. I was shocked to hear the first words of our own Declaration of Independence, especially in making reference to the Creator. He had the words life and liberty kind of transposed and I worked it out for him a little bit and said 'I think this is the way it should be.' "[20]

One is struck in retrospect by the bond that seemed to develop between the two men, and by the extent to which Ho Chi Minh and his colleagues devoted their energies during these crucial days to Patti. At each encounter, Viet Minh officials pressed Patti regarding U.S. plans for Indochina. The list of tasks they faced as the leaders of a new government was as long as it was daunting—to build a legitimate army; to bring food to a populace still suffering from the effects of the famine; to neutralize competing Vietnamese nationalist groups—but none loomed as large as securing international help in thwarting French and perhaps Chinese designs on their country. By his own account Patti responded cautiously, promising merely to pass on messages to his higher-ups, and to refrain from revealing Ho's whereabouts to either the French or the Chinese. But more than once he also referenced Franklin Roosevelt's staunch commitment to Vietnamese self-determination, an assertion that surely raised Vietnamese hopes but oversimplified FDR's thinking and in any event ignored the change under Truman.[21]

Like Roosevelt, Patti could on occasion succumb to a patronizing and cryptoracist view of the Vietnamese, doubting in some (but not all) reports to Kunming that the "Annamites" had the requisite political maturity either to hold their own in negotiations with the French or to

ARCHIMEDES PATTI, WHO REVELED IN THE ATTENTION, IS IN THE SEAT OF
HONOR AS HE MEETS WITH VIET MINH OFFICIALS IN HANOI IN LATE
AUGUST 1945. ON HIS RIGHT IS VO NGUYEN GIAP.

govern effectively. But too much should not be made of this attitude, for
he nevertheless favored an American policy that had as its aim keeping
France from reclaiming control. The Viet Minh's dedication and fervor,
as demonstrated throughout the summer and especially in the heady
days of late August, impressed Patti enormously, as did the broad support the front seemed to enjoy from the population. On the evening of
September 2, after witnessing the extraordinary events that day in Ba
Dinh Square, Patti reported by radio to Kunming, "From what I have
seen these people mean business and I am afraid the French will have to
deal with them. For that matter we will all have to deal with them." The
French, he concluded in another dispatch, had little chance of reasserting
lasting control. "Political situation critical . . . Viet Minh strong and belligerent and definitely anti-French. Suggest no more French be permitted
to enter French Indo-China and especially not armed."[22]

France, however, was already on her way, and with tacit American
blessing. At almost the same moment that Archimedes Patti's airplane
touched down in Hanoi, Charles de Gaulle, leader of the French Provisional Government, arrived in Washington, D.C., for a much-anticipated
set of meetings with administration officials. No less than his nationalist
rival in Vietnam, Ho Chi Minh, de Gaulle considered the United States

the single most important player in the emerging Indochina drama, the main potential obstacle to his plan to once again tie the tricolor to the mast in Saigon and Hanoi. He had been encouraged, in this regard, by the U.S. positions at the San Francisco and Potsdam meetings, which he took to say that Truman would not stand in his way. But the Washington meetings nevertheless carried great importance for de Gaulle, and he made a studied effort to please. Upon landing in the American capital, he offered a glowing tribute to the United States in halting but tolerable English, and speaking in French at a state dinner at the White House that evening, he hailed America and France as *"les deux piliers de la civilisation."* A whirlwind of activity followed, including visits to both the U.S. Naval and Military Academies, to FDR's grave at Hyde Park, and to the vast new airport under construction in Idlewild, Queens (later JFK). In Manhattan, de Gaulle toured the city perched precariously on top of the backseat of a convertible, cheered by hundreds of thousands.[23]

Behind the scenes, though, tensions simmered. There was no hiding the fact that, in the eyes of official America, France had suffered a dramatic loss in prestige. And though Truman did not share FDR's deep personal dislike of de Gaulle, he questioned whether the general was the man for the job of pulling France together. De Gaulle took himself and his ideas far too seriously, the president told British officials in advance of the visit, and, "to use a saying that we have away back in Missouri," was something of a "pinhead." Truman said he intended to speak to the Frenchman "like a Dutch uncle" and make clear that Washington expected France to do its full part in her recovery. Whether France could ever recover fully was doubtful: To aides, the president said the French showed none of the "bulldog" tenacity exhibited by the British during the war. To the British ambassador, he said that whereas the rural people in Belgium were getting down to the work of recovery, their French counterparts were listless and content to wait for outside assistance to save them.[24]

Yet there could be no question on providing that assistance, Truman believed. France might have fallen out of the ranks of great powers, but Washington needed a stable and friendly France in order to fully secure in peacetime the hard-fought victories of the battlefield. In Europe, this meant providing economic assistance of various kinds to the Paris government and working to smooth out Franco-American differences over the future of defeated Germany; outside Europe, it meant giving assurances that the French empire was, at least for the foreseeable future, secure.[25]

On Indochina, administration officials sought to dispel any apprehensions on de Gaulle's part regarding French sovereignty over the area. They did not object when, at a press conference on the twenty-fourth, he said that "the position of France in Indochina is very simple: France means to recover its sovereignty over Indochina." And when de Gaulle remarked privately—and ambiguously—that Paris would be prepared to discuss eventual independence for the colonies, Truman replied that his administration would not oppose a return to French authority in Indochina.[26]

On August 30, Patti forwarded a message from Ho Chi Minh to President Truman, via American authorities in Kunming, that asked for the Viet Minh to be involved in any Allied discussion regarding Vietnam's postwar status. Truman did not reply.

III

THERE WOULD BE MORE SUCH LETTERS IN THE WEEKS AND MONTHS ahead; these too would go unanswered. Yet it is this first nonreply that lingers in the mind. August 1945 was the open moment, when so much hung in the balance, when the future course of the French imperial enterprise in Indochina was anyone's guess. The energies of Truman and his top foreign policy aides may have been directed elsewhere that month—to the paramount tasks in postwar Europe, and to securing Japan's formal surrender—but savvy French and Vietnamese leaders were not wrong to attach so much importance to American thinking. For at the occasion of Japan's surrender, the United States had an extraordinary political power in Asia of a kind never seen before (or since). For tens of millions of Asians that summer, the very remoteness of America added to her allure, to her perceived omnipotence. In the words of journalist Harold Isaacs, who traveled in Vietnam and other parts of Asia for *Newsweek* in the fall of 1945 and wrote a book about the experience, the United States was "a shining temple of virtue of righteousness, where men were like gods amid unending poverty." It was a country of awesome might, a country that could endure a string of defeats against a seemingly unstoppable foe, roar back to deliver a crushing and emphatic blow, and thereby stand astride all of Asia. Yet amazingly enough, America did not seek to use this power to engage in a colonial power grab; on the contrary, she sought to relinquish territorial control, as evidenced by her formal commitment to granting independence to the Philippines.[27]

These were partial truths at best, Isaacs acknowledged, but tens of millions of Asians, many of them possessing scant knowledge of the outside world, believed them. For them, the United States could be "both altruistic and wise: altruistic enough to side with the cause of freedom for its own sake, wise enough to see that continued imperialism in the British, Dutch, French, and Japanese style would bring no peace anywhere." For self-interested reasons, Washington leaders ought to be on the side of change in Asia. The recent war, after all, had exposed the crippling weaknesses of the old system. During Japan's wave of attacks in the first half of 1942, the British, Dutch, and American colonies had collapsed one by one, like so many houses of cards. In Indochina, military action had proved unnecessary, as coercive diplomacy had been enough to beat down the French. In each of these places, the indigenous populations, with rare exceptions, had either welcomed the invaders, or stood by passively, or cleverly sought to exploit for their own gain the rupture between the colonialists. Everywhere Tokyo officials had proved unable to consolidate whatever initial support they received, thereby underscoring—in the minds of nationalists all over Asia—the degree to which colonial or colonial-type control would thenceforth be unsustainable.[28]

Surely the United States would see all this, nationalists in the region told themselves and one another. Surely she would see that her postwar aims dovetailed perfectly with theirs. The United States, after all, was not like the other great powers, or at least it differed from them in key respects; whereas the British, the French, and the Dutch were wholly to be mistrusted, Americans could be believed, if not completely, then at least substantially. Ho Chi Minh, being more farsighted than most, had his suspicions on this score, as he revealed in his August letter to Charles

Fenn, but even Ho held to what he thought was a well-founded hope that the Atlantic Charter's principles would animate the postwar world. Archimedes Patti seemed to think they would; didn't that mean something?

Not really, no. With his assurances to de Gaulle in Washington, Truman had indicated the course his administration would follow on Indochina, at least in the short term. Washington would not act to prevent a French return to Indochina. There were voices in the State Department who objected to this policy, who believed firmly that the United States had to stand for change, for a new order of things, a decolonization of the international system, but they had lost out to those in Washington who stood, in effect, for the old order of things, and who moreover had their eyes firmly fixed on Soviet moves in postwar Europe. French pleas would get their due attention and would be answered; Viet Minh pleas would not.

In historical terms, it was a monumental decision by Truman, and like so many that U.S. presidents would make in the decades to come, it had little to do with Vietnam herself—it was all about American priorities on the world stage. France had made her intentions clear, and the administration did not dare defy a European ally that it deemed crucial to world order, for the mere sake of honoring the principles of the Atlantic Charter.

But even on its own terms there are reasons to question the logic of the administration's policy. Was it in fact logical, given the unquestioned importance of ensuring a strong France in Europe, to support her hard-line posture against a formidable nationalist movement in the far reaches of Southeast Asia? The looming conflict in Vietnam was sure to drain French strength away from Europe, to consume resources that all Paris officials knew were scarce to begin with, perhaps ultimately compelling Washington to in effect pay twice—once to bolster France in Europe, once to strengthen her in Indochina.[29]

How things might have gone had Truman chosen differently is a tantalizing "What if?" question. There is scarce evidence that Ho Chi Minh would have allied himself with the United States in the emerging East-West divide, or that a reunified Vietnam under his leadership would have chosen a non-Communist path in the future. But neither should we assume that Ho necessarily would have aligned his nation closely with the Soviet Union in the Cold War; he might well have opted for an independent Communist course of the type Yugoslav leader Josip Broz Tito would follow. And certainly this much seems clear: A decision by the Truman administration to support Vietnamese independence in the late summer and fall of 1945 would have gone a long way toward averting the mass bloodshed and destruction that was to follow.

IV

ONE CAN IMAGINE THE SENSE OF RELIEF WITH WHICH INDOCHINA planners in Paris greeted the news of Truman's assurances during the Washington meetings. But these same officials knew that serious obstacles remained to the goal of achieving a swift assumption of control in the colony. Jean Sainteny, having arrived in Hanoi on board Patti's plane, had found himself a virtual prisoner of Japanese forces and snubbed by Viet Minh officials. "Political situation in Hanoi worse than we could have foreseen," Sainteny cabled Paris not long after arriving, acknowledging that Ho Chi Minh was the most popular figure in all the land. "Have found Hanoi solely decked out with [Viet Minh] flags." In another missive he warned of a "concerted Allied maneuver aimed at eliminating the French from Indochina," and in a third he spoke of a "total loss of face for France."[30]

Sainteny's frustration built as his team's isolation continued, but he took comfort from the boisterous greeting he received whenever he came into contact with French civilians, who at this point numbered about twenty thousand in Hanoi. Though his relationship with Patti was marked by mutual suspicion, the two got on reasonably well and dined together on several occasions in those early days. They had, it turned out, a good deal in common. Both were in their thirties; both were veterans of their country's intelligence services. Patti had fought in Europe alongside agents of the Deuxième Bureau (French military intelligence) as well as Britain's MI5 and still felt, he later remarked, "a certain amount of allegiance."[31]

On one occasion, Patti and Sainteny had just completed lunch at the Governor-General's Palace when they saw three young French women walking by on the street, one dressed in blue, the middle one in white, and the other one in red. Tears welled up in Sainteny's eyes at this imaginative act of patriotism, so similar in spirit to what he recalled from the German occupation in France. Patti commented that this was probably the first French flag they had seen since arriving in Hanoi, to which the Frenchman shot back, "Yes, but I give you my word that it is not the last."[32]

The problem for France was how to get sizable numbers of French forces to Indochina in short order. The Pacific War had in effect ended too quickly, before Paris could dispatch forces to the region. A mere 979 men and seventeen vehicles were available in Ceylon (where the Fifth Colonial Regiment was stationed) for inclusion with the British and Indian contingents that would take charge of disarming the Japanese south of the sixteenth parallel. Another 2,300 in Madagascar could be ready to board ships within two weeks, while the 17,000-strong Ninth Colonial Division in France could embark by the middle of September. General Leclerc, newly arrived in Ceylon, requested an increase in the number of American-made C-47 Dakota transport aircraft allocated to Indochina. Without them, he said, or without shallow-draft landing craft, there would be no way to get French troops into Indochina north of the sixteenth parallel. The request was granted, and Paris also got permission from Washington to use Lend-Lease supplies, originally earmarked for operations against Germany and Japan, to equip the troops bound for Indochina.[33]

The fact remained, though, that France would not be able to exert meaningful influence on the ground in Indochina for several more weeks, during which time she would be at the mercy of the arriving Chinese and British forces. In the final days of August, the first advance units of a 150,000-strong Chinese army under Lu Han, a warlord of Yunnan province, crossed the frontier into Indochina. With them were an American military advisory team, under the command of Brigadier General Philip E. Gallagher. On September 9, the main force entered Hanoi. They looked haggard and malnourished, their yellow uniforms tattered— a marked contrast to the spit and polish of the Japanese troops. One Vietnamese observer of the scene that day recalled: "The Chinese looked as if they would steal anything not tied down. Almost immediately, they began to live up to the worst suspicions of them. They settled into the country like a swarm of locusts, grabbing up everything in sight." Said Archimedes Patti: "Sidewalks, doorways, and side streets were cluttered with [Chinese] soldiers and camp followers hovering over bundles of personal belongings, with household furnishings and military gear strewn everywhere. Many had staked claims in private gardens and courtyards and settled down to brew tea, do household chores and start the laundry."[34]

A detachment of about fifty Chinese soldiers marched into the home of Duong Van Mai Elliott's family. "They herded us upstairs and took over the ground floor," she remembered. "The peasant soldiers were not used to urban amenities and at first [her brother] Giu had to teach them how to turn on the electric lights and ceiling fans. They were so pleased that they would stand by the switches, turning them off and on and staring in wonder at the effect."[35]

For Ho Chi Minh, the ragged appearance of the Chinese troops was less important than their ultimate aims. Officially they were there, as per the Potsdam agreement, to oversee the surrender of Japanese troops and preserve law and order north of the sixteenth parallel until a new administration could assume control. But what kind of government did Chongqing want? Over the years, Chiang Kai-shek had voiced periodic support for Roosevelt's trusteeship idea and had offered assurances that China had no desire to seize Indochina for herself. Ho and other Viet Minh leaders, however, had little doubt that Chongqing would try to manipulate events to its own advantage, which could involve seeking a compromise with Paris. Viet Minh concerns on this score increased when Chinese foreign minister T. V. Soong told French authorities in August and again in September that his government did not oppose a French return to the peninsula.[36]

To complicate matters further for Ho and his allies, the Chinese troops were accompanied by sizable numbers of Vietnamese nationalists who had spent the war years in China and now were returning home intent on playing key political roles. None posed an immediate threat to the Viet Minh's position in Tonkin—except in a few provincial towns in the north—but their mere presence added to Ho's conviction that he had to move gingerly vis-à-vis the Chinese occupation authorities. He accordingly told Lu Han's political adviser, as well as General Gallagher, that his government would cooperate with the Chinese, and he instructed

Giap to place his small band of armed troops in such a way as to avoid a confrontation with the occupying force. He also dropped the emotive title of Liberation Army in favor of the blander National Guard (Ve Quoc Doan).[37]

Nor did Ho raise objections when Lu Han, upon arriving in Hanoi on September 14, unceremoniously took over the Governor-General's Palace from the Sainteny team. (The Frenchmen, embarrassed and angry in equal measure, were forced to relocate to a much smaller villa downtown.) Lu Han responded by acting cordially, for the most part, toward Viet Minh officials and instructing the Vietnamese nationalists in his entourage to do the same. As the weeks passed, his occupation policy revealed a strong anti-French bias. French *colons* in Hanoi were stripped of their weapons while Vietnamese were allowed to keep theirs, and government buildings, communications, and almost the whole of the civil administration were kept in Viet Minh hands. The Chinese rejected repeated French requests to bring in French troops and administrators.[38]

V

HAD THIS SITUATION PREVAILED IN THE WHOLE OF VIETNAM, THE long and bloody struggle for Vietnam, so injurious to all who took part, might have been over before it began. In the southern part of the country, however, which the Chinese soldiers did not enter, the situation was more fluid and much more favorable to French prospects. At the moment of Ho's proclamation of independence in Hanoi, Cochin China was fractious, divided. A multiplicity of rival political and religious groups, some of which had collaborated with the Japanese or the French, competed with the Viet Minh for supremacy. In the aftermath of the abortive revolt in 1940, the French had decimated the Communists in the south, who were still in the process of rebuilding at the time of Japan's surrender. They faced stiff challenges from the Cao Dai and Hoa Hao religious sects (the former an exotic mixture of spiritualism, Confucianism, Buddhism, and Catholicism; the latter a fundamentalist Buddhist splinter group) that had achieved popularity in various parts of Cochin China since the prewar period. And they had to confront several Trotskyite groups, who had a sizable presence in the south. As well, the Viet Minh found few supporters among those southerners who had profiteered in the period of colonial rule and who planned for a return of the French.[39]

Saigon, as always, was the locus of the agitation. Under the French it had become a metropolis, much bigger than Hanoi, with a population in mid-1945 of well over a million, including the twin ethnic Chinese city of Cholon. Most Western visitors, however, saw only the tightly confined center of Saigon, which seemed to many a piece of France transplanted into a tropical and Far Eastern setting, complete with handsome boulevards and squares, cream-colored rococo administration buildings, gracious villas, and intimate sidewalk cafés and pâtisseries. Here many of the tree-lined streets were named for Frenchmen who had helped conquer Cochin China (Bonard, Charner, de la Grandière) or for famous World War I battles (La Marne, Verdun, De La Somme). And here stood Notre Dame Cathedral, built by the French in 1883 in neo-Romanesque style and featuring modest twin steeples. A statue of the Virgin Mary graced the entrance to the church, looking down rue Catinat (now Dong Khoi), Saigon's legendary thoroughfare bearing the name of the French battleship that had steamed into Tourane (Da Nang) harbor in 1856 and opened fire on the harbor forts. The commercial stretch of rue Catinat ran no more than three hundred yards and was bounded by two hotels: on one end the Continental and on the other, overlooking the left bank of the dark and sullen Saigon River, the Majestic. In between them were shops displaying perfumes, cheeses, and frogs' legs from Paris, and innumerable restaurants and bars, many of them packed deep into the night and offering every French dish from crêpes suzette to escargot. In daytime, there was the aroma of freshly baked baguettes and the *maisons de coiffeur,* where French women went to have their hair styled and set—a vain hope in this humid climate.[40]

Rue Catinat's reputation had taken hold early. Visiting in 1893, the Frenchman Pierre Barrelon would write of walking down a street "famous for its splendid boutiques, decorated pubs, and unending movement of carriages. . . . The rue Catinat is remarkably animated. . . . Here the liveliness is entirely European, and I was going to say Parisian; long before me it has been said Saigon is the 'Paris of the East.' "[41]

Now, though, fifty-two years later, Saigon and rue Catinat were becoming animated for a different reason. Although an ICP-dominated

"Committee of the South," led by Tran Van Giau, had seized control of the city and other parts of Cochin China, its control was precarious. Until early September, order was maintained, despite grumbling from the Cao Dai, the Hoa Hao, and the Trotskyites over Tran Van Giau's decision to negotiate with French representative Jean Cédile (the latter having parachuted into Cochin China on August 22). As the futility of the talks became widely known—the Viet Minh would discuss the country's future ties to France only on condition that the French first recognize Vietnam's independence, which Cédile refused to do—the frustration boiled over. French residents, afraid of losing their colonial privileges, braced for a struggle, while political skirmishing among the rival Vietnamese groups increased. In short order, Giau and the committee lost control of events.[42]

Even worse, they did so precisely at the moment when Allied troops were about to arrive in Saigon. The first contingent of British troops, largely comprising Nepalese Gurkhas and Muslims from the Punjab and Hyderabad in the Twentieth Indian Division, entered the city on September 12. On every street hung large banners: "Vive les Alliés," "Down with French Imperialism," "Long Live Liberty and Independence." The troops' orders were to disarm the Japanese and to maintain law and order. More broadly, though, British officials, in London as well as in Saigon, saw their task as facilitating a French return. Unlike in the Middle East, where France was a rival to British interests, in Southeast Asia she was a de facto ally, a partner in preserving European colonial control in the region.[43]

As ever, London strategists had to tread carefully, so as not to offend anticolonial sentiment in the United States or complicate relations with China. "We should avoid at all costs laying ourselves open to the accusation that we are assisting the West to suppress the East," one junior official observed. "Such an accusation will rise readily to the lips of the Americans and Chinese and would be likely to create an unfavorable impression throughout Asia." Other British analysts expressed similar concerns. But the course to be traveled was never in doubt. A failure to bolster the French in Vietnam could cause chaos in the country and also spur dissidence in Britain's possessions—two very frightening prospects indeed. Hence the fundamental British objective: to get French troops into Indochina as quickly as possible, and then withdraw British forces with dispatch.[44]

The man assigned to this task, Major General Douglas Gracey, commander of the Twentieth, has been described by historians as miscast for his role, in view of his pro-French bias and his paternalistic philosophy that "natives" should not defy Europeans. An unreconstructed colonialist, born in and of the empire, Gracey had spent his whole career with the Indian Army. "The question of the government of Indochina is exclusively French," he said before leaving for Vietnam. "Civil and military control by the French is only a matter of weeks." But if Gracey was unusual for his forthrightness, his thinking was fully within the mainstream of British official thinking in the period. Thus Foreign Secretary Ernest Bevin could tell the Chinese ambassador in September: "We naturally assumed that Indo-China would return to France." And thus Anthony Eden could recall that "an Anglo-Indian force under General Gracey occupied the southern half of the country until the French were able to resume control."[45]

Still, it cannot be denied that Gracey by his initial actions in Saigon exacerbated an already-tense situation. His nickname was "Bruiser," and it fit. When he arrived at Tan Son Nhut airfield aboard an American C-47 on September 13, he walked straight past the Viet Minh delegation waiting patiently by the tarmac and departed in the company of a group of Japanese soldiers. Gracey refused to meet Viet Minh leaders in the days thereafter, and indeed ordered that they be evicted from the former Governor-General's Palace. "They came to see me and said 'welcome' and all that sort of thing," he later said. "It was an unpleasant situation and I promptly kicked them out. They were obviously communists."[46]

On the twenty-first, following more unrest, Gracey proclaimed martial law. He banned public meetings and demonstrations, imposed a curfew, and closed down the Vietnamese press—even as he allowed French newspapers to continue to publish. Looters and saboteurs, he said, would be summarily shot. In effect the nationalist government was being shut down. The next day, encouraged by Cédile, Gracey released and rearmed more than a thousand excitable French soldiers. The soldiers, their ranks swollen by angry French civilians, promptly set about terrorizing any Vietnamese they encountered. Hundreds were beaten and jailed, and some Committee of the South members were hanged. One French woman who sympathized with the Viet Minh had her hair shaved off like those who collaborated with the Germans in metropolitan France. By midmorning on the twenty-third, the French flag was once more flying from most important buildings.

It was, in the words of one Briton on the scene, a coup d'état:

> As clocks chimed 0300 a ragtag grim silent army of 300 men, armed to the teeth, padded silently along the deserted streets. The Coup d'Etat was beginning and Saigon was about to become French again. This was the culmination of an incredible week of turbulent rumours and imminent uprisings. Who would strike first? Would it be the Annamese, angry, confident, truculent? Or the French? "Three o'clock Sunday morning," the word went round; and 300 tough men went out to take the city.[47]

Another observer, the Paris-based photojournalist Germaine Krull, who had arrived with the first contingent of Gurkhas on September 12,

FRENCH TROOPS ROUND UP VIETNAMESE NATIONALISTS
IN SAIGON, SEPTEMBER 1945.

noted with disgust in her diary the sight of "these men, who were supposed to be the soldiers of France, this undisciplined horde whose laughing and singing I could hear from my window, corrupted by too many years in the tropics, too many women, too much opium and too many months of inactivity in the camp," and who were now wandering through the streets "as if celebrating 14 July, their guns slung over their shoulders, cigarettes dangling from their lips." On the rue Catinat she observed "soldiers driving before them a group of Annamites bound, slave-fashion to a long rope. Women spat in their faces. They were on the verge of being lynched." That night Krull "realized only too well what a serious mistake we had made and how grave the consequences would be. . . . Instead of regaining our prestige we had lost it forever, and, worse still, we had lost the trust of the few remaining Annamites who believe in us. We had showed them that the new France was even more to be feared than the old one."[48]

Gracey, angered by the brutality of these "tough men," ordered the former detainees back to barracks as punishment, but the damage was done: Viet Minh leaders on the twenty-fourth mobilized a massive general strike that paralyzed Saigon. French civilians barricaded their houses or sought refuge in the old Continental Hotel. Bursts of gunfire and the thuds of mortar rounds could be heard throughout the city, as Viet Minh squads attacked the airport and stormed the local jail to liberate hundreds of Vietnamese prisoners. At dawn on the twenty-fifth, Vietnamese bands of various political stripes slipped past Japanese guards in the Cité Herault section of town and massacred scores of French and Eurasian civilians, among them many women and children.[49]

Thus began, it could be argued, the Vietnamese war of liberation against France. It would take several more months before the struggle would extend to the entire south, and more than a year before it also engulfed Hanoi and the north, which is why historians typically date the start of the war as late 1946. But this date, September 23, 1945, may be as plausible a start date as any.[50]

"But why," Gracey's chief political spokesman was asked, "why would you not talk with the Viet Minh before the shooting started?"

"Because you cannot negotiate when a pistol is held at your head," the Briton replied.

"You mean you can negotiate only when you hold a pistol at the other party's head?"

He shrugged.[51]

To Lieutenant Colonel Peter A. Dewey, Patti's OSS counterpart in the south, the situation was desperate. The son of a Republican congressman and a graduate of Yale, Dewey was a remarkably accomplished young man. He had been a correspondent for the *Chicago Daily News* and had enlisted in the Polish Army before the United States became involved in the war. In 1943, he had joined the OSS and led a paratroop unit that parachuted into southern France and helped organize the French underground. Along the way, he developed a reputation for uncommon physical daring. In 1944, he was a member of one of the legendary Jedburgh teams that parachuted into occupied France to conduct sabotage and guerrilla warfare, at great personal peril. Fluent in French, disdainful of autocracy, he had also found time to author two books, including one on the French defeat in 1940. Now, at the ripe old age of twenty-eight, he found himself heading the small OSS contingent in Cochin China to find POWs and gather intelligence.

Dewey fully shared Patti's anticolonial predilections and had helped facilitate the earlier failed negotiations between Cédile and the Viet Minh. He had sought an early audience with Gracey, but the Englishman rebuffed him. To Gracey, indeed, the troubles in Saigon could be blamed partly on Dewey and his OSS detachment, whom he declared persona non grata and labeled "blatantly subversive" for supposedly conniving with the Viet Minh.[52] He demanded that Dewey leave Indochina as soon as possible. Dewey duly packed his bags and, on the morning of September 26, headed for the airport in a jeep. The plane sent from Bangkok to fetch him had not arrived, so Dewey got back in the jeep and made for the mission headquarters to have lunch. He took a shortcut past the Saigon golf course and found the road blocked by logs and branches. Slowing to swerve around the obstacle, he saw some Vietnamese in the ditch and cursed at them in French. Perhaps mistaking him for a Frenchman, they opened fire, hitting him in the back of the head and killing him instantly. Dewey's fellow passenger, Captain Herbert Bluechel, a former movie chain operator from San Francisco, escaped unharmed, a bullet knocking off his cap as he ran, the Vietnamese in hot pursuit.[53]

Peter Dewey was the first of nearly sixty thousand Americans to be killed in Vietnam. His body was never found, and the French and Viet Minh accused each other of being responsible for the murder. Washington reacted to the killing by scaling back the OSS presence and activities in Saigon. Before he left for the airport on that final day, Dewey had summarized his thinking in a report: "Cochinchina is burning, the French and British are finished here, and we [the United States] ought to clear out of Southeast Asia."[54]

VI

IN THE DAYS FOLLOWING THE CITÉ HERAULT MASSACRE, GENERAL Gracey managed to calm Saigon, but not before additional skirmishes caused the deaths of some two hundred Vietnamese and several dozen French civilians. The general persuaded French and Vietnamese representatives to resume talks and made preparations for the arrival of the rest of this division, as well as the first troops from France. He also supervised the establishment of a base for his troops, which in due course would feature a bagpipe band, theaters, and a brothel with separate facilities for Indians and Europeans. In facilitating Franco-Vietnamese talks, Gracey acted on the instructions of Lord Mountbatten, SEAC commander, who had rebuked him for his failure to deal with Vietnamese authorities and who said a political settlement should be secured immediately. But the negotiations got nowhere; neither the French nor the Vietnamese were willing to make the concessions on sovereignty that the other side demanded. A fragile truce nevertheless took hold, and it was still in place when the French battleship *Richelieu* and the light cruiser *Triomphant* arrived on October 3 and began to debark Leclerc's Fifth Colonial Regiment. The commander himself arrived two days later and, with Gracey, began to penetrate pockets of resistance. The killings began again, by both sides, inside and outside Saigon. The shops along the rue Catinat were shuttered, cafés were empty, and there were no *cyclos* in the streets.[55]

Major Jacques Philippe de Hautecloque, an aristocratic cavalryman and graduate of Saint-Cyr, had taken the pseudonym "Leclerc" to protect his family in France when he declared for de Gaulle in 1940. Dashing, charismatic, and deeply religious—every day of his adult life, when circumstances permitted, he received the Eucharist—Leclerc achieved his first distinction when he led 2,500 mostly African troops across 1,500 miles of the Sahara Desert in 1942 to join the British Eighth Army in its campaign against Rommel. In 1944, he led the Second French Armored Division in the liberation of Paris, formally entering the city in triumph alongside de Gaulle on August 26 (see photo on p. 62). Later he took Strasbourg, personally hoisting the tricolor over the cathedral. His selection, a year later, as commander of the Indochina effort was greeted with jubilation by *colons* throughout Cochin China, and they gave him a hero's welcome as he entered Saigon. French flags flew everywhere, and portraits of de Gaulle hung in shop windows.

De Gaulle's instructions to Leclerc had been plain: Be firm, and don't compromise. Beginning on October 12, Leclerc and Gracey used their forces—augmented by sizable numbers of Japanese troops, who were ordered to take part—to push outward from Saigon, taking the suburbs of Go Vap and Gia Dinh, then moving northwestward to Bien Hoa on the twenty-third and to Thu Dau Mot on the twenty-fifth. Also on the twenty-fifth, the French captured control of My Tho in the south, the gateway to the Mekong Delta, using both a naval force attacking from the river estuary and land troops moving by road from Saigon. Vinh Long and Can Tho, both important trading and communications centers in the delta, fell on October 29 and November 1, respectively. Many of these engagements were hard fought, however, as the nationalists proved resilient, showing themselves adept at withdrawing and regrouping, then, under the cover of night, striking back. Casualties were significant on both sides: The British Indian Division, for example, suffered nineteen killed and sixty-eight wounded by early November, while the Japanese lost fifty-four dead and seventy-nine wounded. This latter figure did not include a sizable number of Japanese—somewhere between one thousand and three thousand—who deserted their units and fought on the side of the Vietnamese (meaning that in some engagements Japanese fought Japanese).[56]

In his initial public statements, Leclerc expressed confidence that absolute French control could be established quickly, within a few weeks. With the arrival of his first full division of French regulars, the Second Armored Division, in late October, his optimism increased as his troop count reached 4,500 men. Then the Ninth Colonial Division arrived aboard eight American ships (the first significant act, it may be said, of U.S. aid). Many of the troops wore uniforms of American issue and carried American equipment. Leclerc now thought he had enough men to undertake operations even in distant parts of Cochin China. It marked an important shift in the balance of armed forces. By the middle of December, most of the towns in Vietnam south of the sixteenth parallel had come under French control. It all seemed to be going according to plan.

But close observers saw ominous signs of trouble. George Wickes, an American with the OSS who spent much of the fall in Saigon, thought the French would be hard-pressed to win a lasting victory. "The French are not quite so confident as they were at the start that this would be cleared up a in few weeks," Wickes wrote his parents in late November after a visit to the countryside north of Saigon. "And I believe that, unless they always keep large garrisons and patrols everywhere, they will not be able to keep the country submissive as it was before. The Annamite's great advantage lies in the fact that he is everywhere, that he does not need to fight pitched battles or organize troops to be a threat and that no amount of reprisal can completely defeat him. I cannot say how it will end, but at least it will be a long time before Frenchmen can roam about the country with peace of mind."[57]

Leclerc himself began to suffer nagging doubts or at least an awareness that the task ahead was complex. He reflected on something Mountbatten had told him in Ceylon, where Leclerc had stopped en route to Indochina: that postwar Asia was very different from the prewar variety, and there was no going back. Leclerc soon came to agree. "One does not kill ideas with bullets," he told aides, and he warned superiors that France must avoid a large-scale war. Military action was necessary—troops had to be used to hold cities and lines of communication—but there could be no long-term military solution. Any hope of imposing such a solution would require a vastly larger French fighting force, which Paris was in no position to provide, now or in the foreseeable future. The task of French forces, therefore, would be to reassert French control and thereby give negotiators a base from which to proceed to a generalized political settlement involving mutual concessions.[58]

It was a prescient assessment but it fell on deaf ears. As 1945—the year historian David Marr has called the most important in modern

Vietnamese history—drew to a close, most French officials concerned with Indochina, far from seeing major obstacles ahead for the objective of reclaiming control of the colony, saw reasons for optimism.[59] Didn't Leclerc's own actions, after all, show that things were moving in the right direction? His troops had gained control of much of Cochin China and were poised to move north. In Cambodia, meanwhile, French efforts to reestablish authority were proceeding well. Diplomatically too, the signs seemed to point in the right direction and not merely with respect to the welcome support from the British. Negotiations had begun with the Chinese that, French officials hoped, would in short order result in an agreement allowing for the withdrawal of Lu Han's forces from Tonkin. The Americans, though not to be trusted—in both Paris and Saigon, French observers suspected Washington of seeking to undermine French interests in Indochina—were for the moment sticking to a neutral policy that tilted to France.

More than anything, though, it was the presence of one man, a brand-new arrival in Vietnam, that ensured the failure of any French move to an early political settlement. That was Leclerc's civilian counterpart, Georges Thierry d'Argenlieu, the high commissioner, who like the general had been instructed by de Gaulle to brook no defiance from any Vietnamese and who was determined to live up to that instruction. He was a man of the cloth, a former monk, whose appointment had been criticized by some *colons* on the grounds that as a cleric he might be too liberal, that he might give away the store. They need not have worried. For the high commissioner who set foot in Saigon on October 31, 1945, quickly showed himself to be a warrior monk. His policy decisions in the year that followed would set the conditions and the course for the outbreak of a full-scale war.

PART TWO

COLONIAL STRUGGLE, 1946–1949

CHAPTER 5

THE WARRIOR MONK

H E WAS BORN IN BREST, IN BRITTANY, ON AUGUST 7, 1889, THE third of six children of Olivier Thierry d'Argenlieu, an aristocratic naval officer. Following in his father's career path, the young Georges Thierry entered the École Navale in Brest in 1906 and, upon graduation, followed the typical career of a naval officer. After World War I, however, he resigned his commission at the rank of lieutenant in order to join the Carmelite Order, a Catholic religious body noted for dogmatic severity and strict moral views. D'Argenlieu, known as Father Louis of the Trinity among his brethren, rose rapidly in his calling and by the late 1930s had become the Carmelites' provincial in France.[1]

With the outbreak of World War II, he returned to his previous career. Captured by the Germans after the fall of France, he escaped and joined de Gaulle in London in 1940 as a *capitaine de corvette,* later rising to become an admiral and, successively, high commissioner for France in the Pacific, commander in chief of Free French naval forces based in Britain, and assistant chief of the Free French General Staff. D'Argenlieu's devotion to de Gaulle and Free France puzzled many who saw him as a natural Pétainist, in view of his royalist birth, his Carmelite training, and his adherence to the extreme right political views so favored by French naval men. Whatever its source, his Gaullism was genuine and unshakable, and he took up his new charge with determination, fully sharing the general's uncompromising ideas about maintaining the empire for the glory of France.[2]

Of average height and with a thin, angular face, Thierry d'Argenlieu was fifty-six years old when he arrived in Saigon, on the final day of October 1945, to take up his post as high commissioner for Indochina. He immediately installed himself in the Norodom Palace, symbol of colonial pomp and splendor, and set about meeting his charge from de Gaulle to reestablish French authority. "It is the sacred duty of France to reestablish order, respect for law, freedom to work, and security for all wherever she extends her authority," he declared at an early point. France, he said, was coming to liberate the Vietnamese. On some occasions in the early weeks, d'Argenlieu sounded notes of conciliation, but over time his pronouncements became harsher, perhaps as a result of pressure placed on him by many *colons* in Saigon—administrators, planters, professionals, military officials—virtually all of whom pushed a hard-line policy. Or perhaps this increased toughness resulted more from the success of Gracey and Leclerc in extending military control over Cochin China in late 1945 and early 1946.[3]

Whatever the cause, by the early weeks of the new year, the high commissioner had a well-earned reputation for unwavering firmness in his dealings with Vietnamese nationalists. Aloof, haughty, and bitingly sarcastic, he terrified his underlings and was known to reduce bureaucrats to quivering compliance. An autocrat to the core, d'Argenlieu also sought to project an air of mysticism and almost religious veneration. Largely unemotional up to a certain point, he could then launch into passionate oratory and bring himself to tears. His worldview was Manichean, black-and-white with few shades of gray. Good had to prevail over evil. Far-reaching compromise was out of the question. As 1946 progressed, more than a few observers, including some who shared the desire to reclaim French control over Indochina, would comment on this rigidity of mind, this lack of intellectual dexterity. As one wag on his staff quietly put it, d'Argenlieu had "the most brilliant mind of the twelfth century." The problem was that he was about to be faced with one of the most delicate political and historical problems of the twentieth—decolonization—and he didn't have the breadth of mind to understand the forces against him.[4]

This matters enormously in the story of 1946 in Vietnam, because as the year began, Ho Chi Minh in Hanoi had reached a sobering conclusion: He had no option but to seek a negotiated settlement with France.

ADMIRAL D'ARGENLIEU
INSPECTS TROOPS AT
SAIGON'S TAN SON NHUT
AIRPORT, JUNE 1946.

Always conscious, even during the glorious days of August 1945, of the obstacles that lay in the way of real independence for Vietnam, the veteran nationalist knew full well that the first essential task of any revolutionary party is to establish power throughout the country and to create the machinery that will solidify that power and ensure that it is accepted by, if not the whole population, at least the vast majority of it. Equally important, Ho believed, the Democratic Republic of Vietnam (DRV) had to create her own laws and schedule elections. Hence his government's early efforts, beginning already in September, to strengthen its position. It moved quickly, for example, to abolish an iniquitous head tax and the land taxes on small landowners, while carefully avoiding a general redistribution of land that might antagonize Vietnamese landlords. Some landholdings of the French, however, along with those of "traitors," were confiscated and given to landless peasants. Forced labor was outlawed, and the eight-hour workday became law. An ambitious literacy campaign was launched.

The government also announced that general elections based on universal suffrage would be held, in order to elect a national assembly that would be the supreme political body representing the will of the people. Women candidates would be encouraged to run. To attract moderate elements and to avoid alienating the Chinese occupying army, Ho declared that the new government would include all "patriotic elements" in the society, not merely workers and peasants. Later, in November, he formally dissolved the Indochinese Communist Party (which continued to operate behind the scenes). This action too was designed to reassure the Chinese occupiers, who in their own country were engaged in open warfare against Communists, but Ho said nothing of that motivation, or of the related one of easing U.S. concerns about his ideological convictions. The ICP, he merely said, was no longer needed. His country was his party.[5]

Not everyone embraced these measures. Ho Chi Minh personally had broad support, not merely in Tonkin and Annam but in the south as well, and the army won widespread devotion for its perceived discipline and for its stated willingness to fight wherever and whenever ordered. But many were warily skeptical regarding the new government in Hanoi as well as the local administrative committees. Among the substantial Catholic minority, roughly 10 percent of the population, some leaders supported the DRV, but many Catholics worried about being harassed for their faith and for their historical links to the French. As evidence, they pointed to the government's use of military tribunals to punish hundreds of "counterrevolutionaries" by jailing or even executing them (the latter at the hands of specially formed "honor squads for the elimination of traitors"). Though Ho proved quite skillful in alleviating these fears, partly through conciliatory statements directed at the Catholic clergy, suspicions remained, particularly given the penchant of local committees for ignoring central directives and seizing land, harassing property owners, and outlawing numerous traditional customs.[6]

But severe weaknesses in the economy and in military preparedness, more than anything, pushed Ho toward seeking some kind of deal with the French. Late in the year, another terrible famine in the north was barely averted by a range of short-term measures; thousands nevertheless starved to death. The Hanoi government's revenues remained meager, partly because, in keeping with Viet Minh promises, various taxes had been abolished. The government had to resort to a public appeal for contributions to the treasury, a scheme that brought a pittance until Ho personally asked for the people's help. All over Tonkin in late September, during what was called "Gold Week," individuals appeared at collection points with offerings of gold and silver family heirlooms, necklaces and weddings bands, wristwatches, and precious gems. One eighty-year-old woman secured a place in the national mythology by donating her life savings: a gold ingot wrapped in red silk. According to Vo Nguyen Giap's recollection, in a few days the government collected twenty million piasters and 370 kilograms of gold.[7]

A significant sum, but hardly more than a fraction of what the new government needed, particularly given the monumental task of creating a national army. From the moment of the DRV's founding, her leaders determined that they would have to build a modern regular army capable of defending the entire territory of Vietnam, from the Chinese border in the north to the Ca Mau peninsula in the south. Recruitment for this National Defense Guard (the renamed Vietnamese Liberation Army) in the fall of 1945 went well—by the end of the year, Giap had some fifty thousand soldiers, a tenfold increase from August. In addition, major efforts were made in these months to organize self-defense and guerrilla units throughout the northern and central provinces. In Hanoi, the self-defense militia (*tu ve*) comprised virtually all the young men in the city and numbered in the tens of thousands.[8]

But how to supply these various units with weapons and ammunition? The problem was acute, perhaps even insoluble. The government had managed to accumulate some firearms from various sources, including the surrendering Japanese troops, but not nearly enough. Many units had to train only with sticks, spears, and primitive flintlocks turned out by local blacksmiths. With reluctance, Ho agreed to use proceeds from Gold Week to purchase thirty thousand rifles and two thousand machine guns from the Chinese. Giap also sent underlings to Hong Kong and Bangkok to barter gold, opium, and rice shipments for weapons. All of it helped, but Ho and Giap understood that critical shortages remained, particularly with respect to ammunition. The rapid gains made by Gracey and Leclerc in Cochin China against the underequipped units of Tran Van Giau made clear how formidable the military test would be.[9]

Another fact weighed on Ho Chi Minh's mind: His Viet Minh, though already an inspiration to nationalists all over the colonial world, stood alone where it counted, among the big players on the international stage.

Stalin's Soviet Union was not merely uninterested but had been prepared to accept the future of Southeast Asia in Chiang Kai-shek's hands. The French Communist Party, though the largest in France, followed the Stalinist line and counseled patience and moderation; its leader, Maurice Thorez, vice president in de Gaulle's government, said he did not intend "to liquidate the French position in Indochina." Stalin raised no objection. He moreover continued to suspect Ho of being too independent, too much the nationalist, and too desirous of American support. (Stalin had been told of the Viet Minh–OSS cooperation in 1945.) The British, for their part, were actively helping the French reclaim Cochin China, while the Americans seemed to have settled on a neutral policy that—in effect if not in intention—leaned toward France. Ho continued to send letters to the White House asking for support; with each nonreply, he lost a bit more faith.[10]

Add to all this Ho's concern about Chinese occupation forces north of the sixteenth parallel, and it's easy to understand his resort to diplomacy. He told anxious comrades not to forget that the last time the Chinese came, they had stayed a thousand years. Moreover, he added, Lu Han's forces had given aid and comfort to Ho's main nationalist rivals, the Viet Nam Quoc Dan Dang (VNQDD, or Vietnamese Nationalist Party) and the Dai Viet, who had been thrown on the defensive by the Viet Minh's superior organization and boldness but who might yet rebound. Better by far to put up with the French for a time. True, it meant delaying full national independence for some time to come, and retarding the progress of the revolution in the south, but what real alternative was there?

II

THE TALKS BEGAN IN MID-OCTOBER 1945, WITH THE FIRST SUB-stantial session occurring on December 1. Ho's interlocutor was Jean Sainteny, who had remained in Hanoi after his frustrating experience in August and been appointed French commissioner for Tonkin and northern Annam (above the sixteenth parallel). The two men would form, in the months that followed, if not a genuine bond as is sometimes claimed, at least a smooth working relationship. Ho Chi Minh came to trust Sainteny more than other Paris officials with whom he met, and to like him more. He came to see what others saw in the Frenchman (in addition, that is, to his matinee-idol looks): a deep intelligence that was matched by a personal modesty and capacity to listen. No doubt it helped that Sainteny also possessed a thorough knowledge of Indochina, having been a colonial official in the interwar period. For his part, Sainteny found Ho to be a "strong and honorable personality" who was "not basically anti-French." In his book *Histoire d'une paix manquée* (*Story of a Lost Peace*), published in 1953, Sainteny would speak of "his vast culture, his intelligence, his incredible energy, his asceticism," and the incomparable prestige this gave him among the Vietnamese people. But Ho was also patient, Sainteny stressed, willing to maintain an association with France for some specified period: "He had struggled towards [independence] for 35 years; he could certainly wait a few years more."[11]

Léon Pignon, a brilliant career colonial officer with a Machiavellian cast of mind who accompanied Sainteny to many of the negotiating sessions, was more skeptical of Ho's sincerity and more determined to reclaim full French sovereignty over Indochina. To him, Ho was "a great actor" who possessed a "Communist face" and would not long stomach a close association with France; Paris therefore should seek to build up other nationalists rather than work with Ho. But even Pignon, a graduate of the French École Coloniale who had served his first stint in Indochina in 1933–36 and whose sister taught at the Lycée Albert Sarraut in Hanoi, developed a grudging respect for the Viet Minh leader and did not dispute Sainteny's characterization of Ho as a man of moderation who favored compromise over violence. Where Sainteny and Pignon perhaps most differed was in the relative weight they gave to Ho's humility and pride: Sainteny emphasized the former, Pignon the latter.[12]

From the start the negotiations were complicated by the ongoing Viet Minh–sponsored resistance movement in Cochin China, and by Ho's insistence on the inclusion of the term *independence* (*doc lap*) in any final agreement. Sainteny, meanwhile, was instructed to gain Viet Minh assent to the entry of French troops into Tonkin, where about twenty thousand French nationals still lived, in exchange for a French vow to bring about the departure of the Chinese occupation force under Lu Han. Regarding the future status of Cochin China, Paris ordered Sainteny to insist that it be viewed as distinct from Tonkin and Annam, and that its people be allowed to choose their own destiny. The talks soon settled into a pattern, with the two men pressing their respective positions in a smoke-filled meeting room in a villa on Paul Bert Square in Hanoi. Sainteny would puff on his pipe, and Ho would smoke whatever cigarettes (Chinese, American, French) were available. Back and forth they would go, two men with considerable mutual respect and even affection, debating the meaning of particular French and Vietnamese words and phrases. They made little headway.[13]

Gradually, though, as 1945 turned into 1946, both sides softened their position. The outcome of the Vietnamese national elections on January 6 bolstered Ho Chi Minh's legitimacy—the Viet Minh fielded the vast majority of candidates and won a decisive victory. At the same time, however, General Leclerc continued to strengthen the French military position in Cochin China, to the point that by February he seemed poised to turn his attention northward. Diplomatically too, Ho had reason to worry, as the parallel Sino-French negotiations to secure a Chinese withdrawal from Tonkin were beginning to show real promise. The French, it now seemed clear, were advancing north, come what might. Yet to fight them on the battlefield was quite out of the question: Giap's forces were too ill equipped and too undertrained. To remain intransigent in the talks, on the other hand, and if necessary withdraw the DRV government from Hanoi as the French advanced, risked losing the initiative to the anti–Viet Minh and pro-French Vietnamese groups in Hanoi.

Ho, aware that a conciliatory posture included risks of its own—it would threaten popular support for the DRV among many nationalists, some of whom were more anti-French than he was—chose to press harder for a deal. He truly wanted a negotiated solution. No doubt he was also motivated by the abrupt resignation, on January 20, 1946, of Charles de Gaulle as head of the French government. De Gaulle's departure, unrelated to the empire and caused by his frustration with parliamentary squabbling in Paris, removed what Ho took to be a major obstacle to an acceptable deal, and he had some reason to believe that the new government under Socialist Félix Gouin would be less intransigent.

On the French side, General Leclerc had the same hope. He did not advocate wholesale concessions to the Vietnamese, and he continued to affirm the righteousness of the French cause. (Leclerc was never as conciliatory, never as moderate, as many historians have suggested.)[14] But he grasped that the military means at his disposal were limited and that he faced not one but two potential foes in Tonkin—the Viet Minh as well as the Chinese occupying forces under Lu Han. This necessitated some kind of agreement with the DRV, the general believed, though from his perspective the accord need not necessarily come before French troops landed in the north. It might indeed be preferable to sign the deal *after* that landing, since this could prevent Ho Chi Minh and his government from leaving the capital and taking to the hinterland to commence an interminable guerrilla war in both north and south. Such a war, Leclerc believed, would be a disaster for France.

Publicly Leclerc conveyed confidence, telling the press on February 5 that "the pacification of Cochin China and southern Annam is all over." The following month he estimated that his troops controlled not just the cities but the vast majority of villages as well. Inside, however, he feared that the task in the north would be infinitely larger and that even in the south his success could prove fleeting. He needed no reminder that he had benefited from the presence of Japanese as well as British forces in the early clashes, and that this assistance was now ending. Nor did he need anyone to tell him that relative strength of non–Viet Minh elements in Cochin China—notably the Hoa Hao and Cao Dai religious sects with their backing in the countryside, and the Trotskyites with their urban supporters—could in time dissipate. The very ease of the military victories thus far achieved worried Leclerc. Few real battles had taken place, as the guerrillas simply vanished into the jungle, perhaps with the intention to return to fight another day. Leclerc would not have quibbled seriously with historian Bernard Fall's later assertion that in early 1946, France gained control of Cochin China—but only "to the extent of 100 yards on either side of all major roads."[15]

For Leclerc, then, military force had to be coupled with subtle diplomatic maneuvering if France was to reclaim—as he very much wanted—her predominant position in Indochina. Accordingly, taking advantage of d'Argenlieu's temporary absence from Saigon (he had returned to Paris to report on his policies), Leclerc in mid-February appealed to Paris to agree to concessions, including use of the word *in-dependence,* which both de Gaulle and d'Argenlieu had vehemently opposed. The restoration of substantial French control over the south, the general contended, meant that France could now agree to mutual concessions, the better to limit Viet Minh ambitions. Paris might well have accepted this line of argument had not Sainteny reported from one of his meetings with Ho that the DRV leader might accept something less than "independence." Sainteny accordingly received instructions—drafted by d'Argenlieu—to offer Ho "self-government" within the framework of the Indochinese Federation and the French Union. In return, Ho must accept the stationing of French troops in Tonkin and agree to various cultural and economic privileges for France. On the pesky question of Cochin China's future, Sainteny should offer a compromise: A plebiscite would be held in all three regions of Vietnam to determine whether the population wished to affiliate with the new state or make a separate deal with France.[16]

Ho was in a tough spot, facing pressure from several quarters—from Sainteny and the French, from his Chinese occupiers who counseled moderation, and from Vietnamese nationalist parties (notably the VNQDD and the Dai Viet) who accused him of preparing to sell out to France. The signing of a Sino-French agreement in Chongqing on February 28, in which the Chinese agreed to return home in exchange for significant economic concessions from France, reduced his maneuverability further—the agreement, Ho knew, paved the way for a French invasion of Tonkin.

And indeed, the French were about to launch Operation Bentré, a secret plan for the reoccupation of Indochina north of the sixteenth parallel. Hatched in Leclerc's headquarters some months earlier (and named for a town and province at the mouth of the Mekong River), the plan had several elements but centered on landing a sizable force at the port city of Haiphong and, in coordination with a smaller force arriving by plane, proceeding to capture Hanoi. Over a period of three days starting on February 27, the French Ninth Division of Colonial Infantry and Second Armored Division—a total force of some twenty-one thousand men, most of them wearing American helmets, packs, fatigues, and boots—boarded warships, and on March 1, a fleet of thirty-five ships sailed from Saigon north along the coast. Because of the movement of the tide, the landing would have to occur on either March 4, 5, or 6, or it could not occur again until the sixteenth. An early objective: to rearm three thousand French soldiers who remained interned at the Hanoi Citadel—and who, Bentré planners surely knew, would be in a vengeance-seeking mood.[17]

The French hoped that the arrival of the troops, following fast on the heels of the Chongqing agreement, would compel Ho to agree to a deal on French terms. But the risks were huge. What if the Vietnamese chose instead to stand and fight? And of more pressing concern, what if the Chinese refused to offer their support to the troop landing? That is what occurred. French general Raoul Salan secured permission from the Chinese to have the vessels "present" themselves in Haiphong's harbor on March 6 but not to disembark any troops. Chinese leader Chiang Kai-shek, anxious to secure his southern flank at a time when his struggle against Mao Zedong's Communists was heating up in north-eastern China, had no wish to become embroiled in a Vietnamese war of liberation. When the French ships entered the Haiphong harbor on the morning of March 6, the Chinese batteries in the cities began firing. The ships returned fire, and the fighting continued until eleven A.M., with both sides suffering casualties. Chinese negotiators, meanwhile, leaned hard on both the French and the Vietnamese to come to an accord. Strike a bargain, they in effect ordered, or you may find yourselves fighting us as well as your main adversary.

The blackmail tactic worked. In the afternoon of March 6, the two sides, under intense Chinese pressure, signed a "Preliminary Convention," wherein the French recognized the "Republic of Vietnam" as a "free state" (état libre) within the Indochinese Federation and French Union; the Vietnamese agreed to welcome twenty-five thousand French troops for five years to relieve departing Chinese forces; and France in turn agreed to accept the results of a future popular referendum on the issue of unifying the three regions.[18] The new National Assembly in Hanoi, which had been elected in January, approved the deal, with the understanding that it was preliminary and that additional negotiations would follow in short order. Some Vietnamese militants condemned the accord as a sellout, but Ho reiterated his conviction that the first order of business was to be rid of the dread Chinese. "As for me," he told aides, "I prefer to sniff French shit for five years than eat Chinese shit for the rest of my life."[19]

Not an appealing notion either way. The Ho-Sainteny deal was hardly what Viet Minh leaders had anticipated in the glorious days of the August Revolution, or what any close Indochina observer could have predicted one year earlier, in March 1945, at the time of the Japanese *coup de force*. That action, after all, had formally ended French dominion over Indochina and had revealed just how hollow colonial control had become. French forces had put up embarrassingly little resistance. Yet now, twelve months later, France was back, well on the way to reclaiming control south of the sixteenth parallel and seemingly ready to do the same north of the line. Little wonder that when Sainteny, after the signing ceremony, raised a glass and exulted to Ho that they had ended the possibility of major war, the veteran revolutionary demurred. "We are not yet satisfied because we have not yet won complete independence." He paused, then added, "But we will achieve it."[20]

To Western visitors, Ho Chi Minh in this period offered both conciliation and determination. He told American intelligence officers Frank White and George Wickes of his fond memories of living in Boston and New York and of his admiration for American principles as enshrined in the Declaration of Independence, then asked the two men to convey to Washington his high hopes for U.S. support for his nation's quest for independence. And to a senior British diplomat, Ho condemned what he saw as d'Argenlieu's effort to create a separatist movement in Cochin China (80 percent of southerners wanted union with the north, he insisted, notwithstanding some age-old regional frictions) but admitted that his people were as yet unprepared to assume their full duties of citizenship. That was why Vietnam was eager to get advice and counsel from France, from Britain, from the United States—provided it was granted in a spirit of cooperation and not in the form of "master" to "slave." The French seemed to want to retain their full sovereignty over Vietnam, and this, Ho vowed, nationalists in his country would never accept.

The visitors came away impressed. "When you talk to him he strikes you as quite above the ordinary run of mortals," Wickes wrote in a letter home. "Perhaps it is the spirit that great patriots are supposed to have. Surely he has that—long struggling has left him mild and resigned, still sustaining some small idealism and hope [that war can be avoided]. But I think it is particularly his kindliness, his simplicity, his down-to-earthness. I think Abraham Lincoln must have been such a man, calm, sane, and humble." To the Briton, meanwhile, Ho was an "outstanding character" with "excellent idiomatic English." "I came away with the impression that I had been talking to a sincere patriot though obviously imbued with all the characteristics of a convinced revolutionary. . . . There is no doubt in my mind that he is prepared to go to any lengths to attain his object."[21]

III

WHICH TELLS US SOMETHING ABOUT HOW THE MARCH 6 ACCORDS should be interpreted in history: as a mere pause in a struggle that had already begun. The agreement raised hopes in some quarters that a peaceful resolution was at hand—notably in Washington, where numerous officials saw it as proof that France had come to embrace the need for far-reaching, fundamental changes in the Franco-Vietnamese relationship—but it may in fact have had the opposite effect, making large-scale fighting more likely. For while Paris recognized Vietnam's "independence," it also won entry for French troops into the north, which gave it the means to revoke what it had promised. The Viet Minh, meanwhile, secured precious time to build up their military strength. No less important, through her recognition of the "free state" of Vietnam, France in effect made the DRV the sole legitimate Vietnamese voice in the entire country.[22]

Sainteny, to be sure, was sincere—if perhaps naïve—in his toast on March 6. He hoped the deal might be the basis for a genuine settlement. Nor was he alone among French analysts in expressing this view. Indeed, one finds in the internal French record in early 1946 a fascinating fluidity in official thinking about the best course of action in Indochina—though fascinating in part because it remained circumscribed, with virtually all analysts holding to the view that Indochina ought to remain within the empire. The January resignation of Charles de Gaulle, it's clear, gave a boost to those, like veteran colonial official Henri Laurentie, who believed that the old colonial order could not be restored in toto, that the world had changed, that it was now essential to give substance to the vague promises of liberalization made during the war. The decision made around this time to give the Colonial Ministry a new name—the

Ministry of Overseas France (Ministère de l'Outre-mer)—is one sign of the changed atmosphere. In the military, meanwhile, it was no longer anathema to argue that negotiations involving mutual concessions had to be part of French strategy. A growing number of officers thought there were simply not enough boots on the ground to stake everything on a military solution, and little prospect that more could be found.[23]

The shakeup in French domestic politics following de Gaulle's departure also gave a boost to the forces for reform and diplomacy, at least temporarily. Though the empire was a low priority for both the public and politicians in this period, all three political parties that dominated the scene voiced at least rhetorical backing for greater autonomy to Indochina and other parts of this reconstituted "Overseas France." The Socialists (Section française de l'Internationale ouvrière, or SFIO) professed support for greater self-rule for imperial territories but were split internally on how quickly changes should occur. The Communist Party (Parti communiste français, or PCF), as we have seen, counseled moderation and generally sought to steer clear of colonial issues but claimed to stand for far-reaching reform in Indochina and elsewhere. Even the Mouvement républicain populaire (MRP), the centrist Catholic party that was destined to dominate Indochina policy during much of the decade that followed, and that would in short order adopt a hard-line stance, made noises in February seeking a revamped French Union that would allow more autonomy for the Indochinese and other colonial peoples.[24]

But whatever fluidity existed in Paris did not exist where it may have mattered most: in the high commissioner's office in Saigon. Here, paradoxically, de Gaulle's departure may have had the effect not of boosting the forces of reform, but of thwarting them. Admiral d'Argenlieu and his staff had considerable freedom to maneuver in implementing policy directives from Paris, and that freedom now increased, as political maneuvering preoccupied many officials in the metropole. What's more, d'Argenlieu, ever the loyal Gaullist, very likely took the general's departure as a license to clamp down harder in Indochina, in order to affirm the Gaullist line until such a time as de Gaulle could return to power. D'Argenlieu initially professed to support the March 6 convention, but privately he grumbled, with clear reference to Leclerc: "I marvel at France having such a fine expeditionary force in Indochina, and that her commanders prefer to talk rather than fight."[25]

Little by little the admiral set about retracting the concessions France had made. In mid-April, in talks with Vo Nguyen Giap at Dalat—a mountain resort known for its elegant villas and its comparatively cool weather—he refused to discuss a provision in the March 6 Accords calling for joint Franco-Vietnamese efforts to end hostilities in the south (skirmishes there continued, despite an official cease-fire), or to act on the matter of the referendum regarding whether Cochin China would reunite with the north. D'Argenlieu and Giap also clashed on the future status of Vietnam as a "free state." For Giap, the DRV's position in the French Union would be as an essentially sovereign state, but the Frenchman countered that the French Union was a federation, which meant that each free state within it must relinquish part of its sovereignty to the central authority and specifically to the high commissioner appointed in Paris, that is, himself.[26]

It all set an ominous tone for the next round of negotiations, set to take place in France later in the spring. On June 1, a mere twenty-four hours after Ho left Vietnam bound for Paris, d'Argenlieu, in clear violation of the March 6 Accords and without informing Paris, "recognized" the autonomous "Republic of Cochin China" in the name of France. The idea was to present both Ho Chi Minh and the Paris government with a fait accompli, for if there was an autonomous republic in the south, there could be no question of holding a referendum on territorial unity. Never mind that d'Argenlieu had no authority to recognize a Cochin Chinese republic even if it had been legitimate; and never mind that the scheme had minimal support among the southern populace.[27] Ho, upon receiving the news, said there must be a misunderstanding—surely the high commissioner would not do such a thing—but there was none.

Upon arriving in France, Ho spent two weeks at the beach resort of Biarritz, in the southwest, while some in his delegation went ahead to Paris. Sainteny was sent to keep him company. Ho fumed at d'Argenlieu's antics and threatened to return to Hanoi at once, but the Frenchman convinced him to give the upcoming talks a chance—and to try to enjoy himself while he waited. The two men attended a bullfight and a pelota

HO CHI MINH AND JEAN SAINTENY WITH OTHER MEMBERS OF THE
VIETNAMESE DELEGATION IN BIARRITZ, FRANCE, IN JUNE 1946

tournament across the border in Spain, went fishing, and visited the
Catholic sanctuary at Lourdes. Ho asked people what it was like to live
under German occupation and attended a commemoration of de Gaulle's
June 18, 1940, call to resistance, held at the memorial to the dead of the
Biarritz resistance. After one festive meal at a restaurant in the small fishing village of Biriatou, Ho signed the guest book with the words, "Seas
and oceans do not separate brothers who love each other."[28]

Whenever he ventured out among people, whether in Biarritz or in
Paris, Ho enjoyed a warm reception. He charmed most everyone, not
least the press corps. Reporter after reporter found him engaging, witty,
and winningly self-deprecating. To women journalists, he presented
flowers. "As soon as one approaches this frail man," commented one
scribe, "one shares the admiration of all men around him, over whom he
towers with his serenity acquired from wide experience." Other observers compared him to Confucius, to Saint John the Baptist, to the Bud-
dha. Everywhere people commented on his savoir faire, his open love of
children, his asceticism—he refused to drink—and his attire: the simple,
high-buttoned linen suit that he wore on all occasions, formal and informal. Ho won praise as well from the France-Vietnam Association, which

included among its members Emmanuel Mounier, Pablo Picasso, Paul Rivet, and François Mauriac.[29]

No one was more smitten than Jacques Dumaine, director of protocol at the Ministry of Foreign Affairs. When Ho was invited to sit at the official podium during a ceremony on July 14, Bastille Day, Georges Bidault, the newly invested president of the Provisional Government, instructed Dumaine to place Ho's chair a little bit behind his own. Dumaine did as told, but grudgingly. "Ho is playing the role of Mahatma," he noted admiringly, "and his simplicity is quite genuine." Dumaine subsequently invited Ho to lunch and wrote of the encounter: "We had an intimate lunch with Ho Chi Minh. One has to admire the mastery of this self-taught man, his language skills, his ability to make his views accessible, to make his intentions seem moderate, and his politeness. His entourage is nervous, fanatical, and reckless, while he plays the wise and insightful one."[30]

To those concerned about his Marxism, Ho offered soothing words. Maybe in fifty years, Vietnam would be ready for Communism, he told a group of journalists in Paris the week before, "but not now." Any change to the economic system would be gradual, and the Vietnamese constitution—modeled, he emphasized, on the American one—contained safeguards for private property. "If the capitalists come to our country, it will be a good thing for them," he added. "They will make money, but not as it was made in the old days. From now on it is fifty-fifty."[31]

Ho knew that this personal success and his reassuring rhetoric would count for little in the end. The bilateral negotiations were what truly mattered. When at last the talks were set to begin, southeast of Paris at the famed palace in the forest of Fontainebleau, playground for generations of French royals, he was dismayed to see no prominent figures in the French delegation, merely midlevel colonial officials and three obscure politicians, all of them unsympathetic to the Vietnamese position. The roster reflected the results of an election in France in early June, which shifted the balance in the Assembly to the right and, generally, to those who shared d'Argenlieu's views. The new government, under the MRP's Bidault, saw no reason to compromise with the Vietnamese, and it took this firm position in part because of a letter to MRP chairman Maurice Schumann, dated June 8, from none other than Philippe Leclerc. The general, it seems, had shifted his position dramatically. France, he now wrote, had practically won in Indochina, having in the spring months secured most of the vital points. She therefore should not concede much at Fontainebleau, particularly to Ho Chi Minh, a man who sought only to throw the French out of Vietnam altogether. "I think, under these conditions, that it would be very dangerous for the French representatives at the negotiations to let themselves be fooled by the deceptive language (democracy, resistance, the new France) that Ho Chi Minh and his team utilize to perfection," Leclerc wrote.[32]

IV

AND SO LECLERC, NEVER AS FAR FROM D'ARGENLIEU'S HARD-LINE position as some authors have claimed, now stood more or less right beside him. The French move into Tonkin following the March 6 Accords had gone reasonably well, Leclerc reasoned, with the first units coming ashore at Haiphong on March 8. The French population of Hanoi and Haiphong was giddy with joy at the arrival of its long-awaited army, and at the French forces' occupation—over the vociferous objections of the Vietnamese—of the Governor-General's Palace in Hanoi two weeks later. ("It seemed the return of Vietnam's colonial enslavement," recalled Bui Diem of watching the French troops reenter Hanoi.) In subsequent weeks, the French strengthened their posture in various spots north of the sixteenth parallel, and though huge tasks remained and fighting continued in the south, the French commander may have noted the progress made and opted to see the glass as half full.[33]

Whatever its source, Leclerc's perspective meshed well with that of Bidault. A former history teacher who had studied at the Sorbonne, Bidault had been active in the Resistance during the Nazi occupation, then had served as foreign minister in de Gaulle's Provisional Government beginning in August 1944. He founded the MRP and served as foreign minister in Félix Gouin's government in early 1946 before now taking the presidency himself. To Bidault, who would be at the front line of French policy on Indochina for much of the next eight years, and to many of his ministers, war was unthinkable, but the alternative, giving away in-

FRENCH TROOPS ENTER HANOI AS MASSES OF *COLONS*
TURN OUT TO CHEER, MARCH 1946.

dependence to the "yellow men" (*les jaunes*), who in the past had been so easily dominated, was even more unimaginable. Bidault accordingly instructed the team at Fontainebleau, led by Max André, a die-hard believer in the empire with close ties to the Bank of Indochina, to adhere to a firm posture in the talks, which got under way on July 6. The head of the Vietnamese delegation, Pham Van Dong, meanwhile, was less inclined to compromise than the Giap delegation at Dalat in April had been.[34]

To no one's surprise, therefore, the old problems immediately resurfaced as the discussions began. The Vietnamese wanted independence and a weak form of association with France. France sought guided *self-government* (the English word was used in internal documents) within the French Union, with France controlling the sovereignty of Vietnam—in other words, the French would hold the crucial ministries. On Cochin China, the Vietnamese held steadfast to the line that it was part of their country, but the French refused to budge. According to Pham Van Dong,

André said to him: "We only need an ordinary police operation for eight days to clean all of you out." France, in other words, had no need to compromise.[35]

Days and weeks passed, and the gap between the Vietnamese and the French never seemed to narrow. The French had given Ho a giant red carpet at his hotel when he first arrived, as was the custom with visiting heads of state. David Ben-Gurion, the Israeli leader, who was in Paris at the time, remarked that "Ho's descending fortunes could be measured by the progressive shrinking of the protocolary carpet. On Ho's arrival it had extended from the sidewalk to his room. As the summer wore on, it was limited to the lobby, then to the staircase, and finally simply to the corridor in front of Ho's suite."[36]

Ho seriously exaggerated the weight of left-wing opinion in France. The hoped-for support from the Socialists and Communists never materialized, notwithstanding the gushing praise that the respective party newspapers heaped on the Vietnamese. Marius Moutet, the beleaguered minister of Overseas France, whose socialist party had lost ground in the recent election, proved unwilling to champion independence for Vietnam, and Communist leader Thorez was likewise equivocal. Over lunch in July, the veteran socialist leader Léon Blum assured Ho, "I will be there at difficult moments. Count on me." That too would turn out to be false.[37]

In Saigon, meanwhile, Thierry d'Argenlieu continued his efforts at sabotage. Leclerc had by now left Indochina—in July he was reassigned to North Africa and was succeeded in Indochina by General Jean Étienne Valluy—which made the subversion easier. He declared that the future relationship between France and Indochina could not be decided solely by delegates representing the Hanoi government and that, accordingly, another conference would be convened, this one at Dalat, on August 1. Its purpose would be to discuss an "Indochinese Federation" comprising Cochin China, Laos, and Cambodia, as well as southern Annam and the Central Highlands. Hanoi would not be represented at all. When word of this Dalat plan reached Fontainebleau, Pham Van Dong reacted with fury and broke off negotiations, much to d'Argenlieu's delight. The two sides eventually returned to the table, but the deep divisions remained. Provisional agreements were drawn up on a range of economic issues, but the stubborn refusal of the French to discuss political issues—notably the status of Cochin China—rendered these agreements worthless to the Vietnamese delegation. Eight weeks of talks, Pham Van Dong concluded on September 10, as the conference drew to a close, had shown only that no basis for serious negotiations existed.[38]

Ho Chi Minh, not yet willing to abandon all hope, sent his delegation back to Vietnam while he stayed behind in Paris to make one last push for a deal. To reporters he emphasized the DRV's need for allies and her willingness to go it alone if necessary. The United States, as always, loomed large in his mind. "Your country," he told American journalist David Schoenbrun on September 11, "can play a vital role for peace in Southeast Asia. The memory of Roosevelt is still strong. You never had an empire, never exploited the Asian peoples. The example you set in the Philippines was an inspiration to all of us. Your ties with France are strong and durable and you have great influence in this country. I urge you to report to your people the need there is to swing the balance toward peace and independence before it is too late for all of us. Do not be blinded by this issue of Communism."

To Schoenbrun's reply that Americans did not think Communism was compatible with freedom, Ho nodded in understanding but said the Vietnamese people would not rest until true independence had been won. "If men you call Communists are the only men who lead the fight for independence, then Vietnam will be Communist. Independence is the motivating force, not Communism. . . . On the issue of independence and the unity of North and South we are all in agreement, Communists, Catholics, Republicans, peasants, workers. If we must, we will fight together for those aims."

Schoenbrun marveled at the self-assured language. "But, President Ho, this is extraordinary. How can you hope to wage war against the French? You have no army, you have no modern weapons. Why, such a war would seem hopeless to you!"

"No, it would not be hopeless. It would be hard, desperate, but we could win." History offered many examples of ragged bands defeating modern armies—think of the Yugoslav partisans against the Germans or, further back, simple American farmers taking on the mighty British Empire! "The spirit of man is more powerful than his own machines." The Viet Minh, Ho stressed, would make full use of the swamps, the thick jungles, the mountains and caves, the terrain they knew so well. "It will be a war between an elephant and a tiger. If the tiger ever stands still the elephant will crush him with his mighty tusks. But the tiger does not stand still. He lurks in the jungle by day and emerges only at night. He will leap upon the back of the elephant, tearing huge chunks from his hide, and then he will leap back into the dark jungle. And slowly the elephant will bleed to death. That will be the war of Indochina."[39]

The confident words masked deep private doubts. "Don't leave me this way," Ho despaired to Sainteny and Moutet on the same day as the Schoenbrun interview. "Arm me against those who would seek to displace me. You will not regret it." Ho feared that radical elements among the Viet Minh would resort to force prematurely; perhaps he also feared for his own position of authority, should he return with nothing to show for two months of haggling. He assured the two Frenchmen that his government would respect a meaningful agreement but also warned them: "If we have to fight, we will fight. You will kill ten of us, and we will kill one of you, and in the end it is you who will be exhausted."[40]

At midnight on the fourteenth, Ho slipped out of the Hotel Royal Monceau and made his way along the Avenue Hoche to Moutet's apartment. The Frenchman was already in bed. Ho sat down beside him. One imagines the scene: the gaunt and goateed revolutionary and the portly and gray Moutet discussing the fate of Vietnam in a Paris bedroom in the dead of night. Before long, the two men have attached their initials to a partial agreement, which they call a Modus Vivendi. It seemingly safeguards most of the rights in Indochina that the French have sought, both at Dalat in April and at Fontainebleau, while offering little to the Vietnamese. As for the difficult political questions, it postpones these for future negotiations, which are to start no later than January 1947. Also included is a cease-fire between French and Vietnamese forces in the south, to take effect on October 30. No mention is made of ultimate independence for Vietnam.

Sainteny would later refer to the Modus Vivendi as a "pathetic" agreement that gave Ho "far less than he had hoped for when he came to France." Just why the veteran revolutionary chose to sign is somewhat of a mystery. Perhaps he simply sought to buy time, both to prepare for war and to see if the November elections in France might produce a government dependent on Communist and Socialist support and more likely to make concessions. He told young supporters on September 15, thinking back to Blum's promise in July: "Have confidence in Léon Blum, whatever may happen."[41]

Later that day Ho left Paris, for the last time. Never again would he set foot in the city he knew so well—better, perhaps, than any other. Despite the numerous frustrations of the previous weeks, he had enjoyed his stay in key respects. He had taken time to visit many of his old Paris haunts, had mingled frequently with French intellectuals and politicians, and had devoured any and all newspapers, and overall the city and its culture undoubtedly stirred something deep in his soul. An intangible but real connection to the colonial overlord remained, despite his decades-long campaign to win independence for his country, and despite his sense that all-out war was drawing ever closer. Nor was he alone in this feeling. It's a fascinating thing about many Vietnamese nationalists of the period, the degree to which they possessed complex and conflicting feelings about France. Said Ho to author Jean Lacouture earlier in the year: "A race such as yours which has given the world the literature of freedom will always find us friends. . . . If you only knew, monsieur, how passionately I reread Victor Hugo and Michelet year after year."[42]

The same sense comes through in Ho's notebook of the trip, a fascinating account not initially meant for public release. There are entries on international developments that matter to him, including the declaration of independence in the Philippines early in July and the U.S. atomic tests at Bikini Atoll (but curiously not France's evacuation of Syria and Lebanon, marking the effective end of her colonialist claims in the Middle East), and on the stakes in the negotiations. But it is his admiration for France and the French that leaves the strongest impression. He records that on June 30 he wanted to take a walk in Monceau Park at six o'clock in the morning, only to find the gate locked. When the guard learned that he was a foreigner who had recently arrived in France, he let him in without knowing Ho Chi Minh's identity: "It is just a small anecdote but it is enough to show that the French, in France, are courteous and respectful of foreigners." Another section, titled "The Beautiful Qualities of the French," comments on their attachment to lofty principles such as liberty and fraternity and their passion for intellectual argument and debate. Of the generally welcoming reception given him, he writes that "it was not because I was the president of a nation that they behaved that way; they just naturally showed friendship toward us."[43]

The question looms: Did Ho's Paris sojourn in mid-1946 represent the great lost chance for a genuine and far-reaching accord, one that could have defused the growing crisis before it devolved into large-scale war, one that could have prevented thirty years of indescribably bloody and destructive war on the Indochinese peninsula? What if the French had really put Ho's conciliatory words to the test? He was not staking out a maximalist position, after all—he was not demanding full and complete independence. He sought compromise and indicated a willingness—maybe even a desire—to maintain an association with France. The French could have retained every important commercial, cultural, and political tie, losing only the outer trappings of colonial rule. In the event, his hosts couldn't bring themselves to explore the proposition, certainly not at the highest levels. The opportunity was missed, but it was never close to being seized. Instead, the failure of the Fontainebleau talks allowed hard-liners on both sides to dig in, rendering a compromise settlement more remote than ever.

As Ho Chi Minh departed this country he loved, he had no illusions: The war clouds were gathering fast.

CHAPTER 6

THE SPARK

IT WOULD BE LATE OCTOBER 1946 BEFORE HO CHI MINH ARRIVED
back in Hanoi. For reasons that remain murky, he chose to travel home
not by airplane but by a French ship whose leisurely passage from Toulon
to Haiphong took several weeks.[1] He was away more than four months,
during which time Vo Nguyen Giap led the Democratic Republic of Vietnam and worked feverishly to prepare for war.

It was an awesome responsibility for the young Giap, but he proved
equal to the task. Of medium height and with prominent cheekbones
and deep-set eyes, he had about him a reserved and unassuming air that
masked a steely determination. Not yet thirty-five when Ho departed for
France, he would become a profoundly important factor in the revolution's success—a largely self-taught military commander who oversaw
the forces that took on first the mighty French and then the even might-
ier Americans. Only Ho himself was more responsible for the ultimate
success of the revolution. Over the years, Giap would make his share of
mistakes on the battlefield, but his record as a logistician, strategist, and
organizer is nevertheless extraordinary and ranks him with the finest
military leaders of modern history—with Wellington, Grant, Lee, and
Rommel. He proved spectacularly adept, in particular, at using the often-
limited means at his disposal as well as the terrain, which he knew better
than his adversaries because it was his own.

He was born into modest circumstances, on August 21, 1911, in
Quang Binh province in the narrow waist of central Vietnam, near the
seventeenth parallel. The name Giap meant "armor." His father, who in-

stilled in the young boy a respect for education, died in a French prison after being arrested for subversion; an older sister died the same way. These tragedies fostered in Giap a hatred of the French, and he was further inspired to fight colonial rule after reading, at age fourteen, Ho Chi Minh's *French Colonialism on Trial*. In short order, Giap became active in nationalist politics, and the French Sûreté opened a file on him. Imprisoned briefly at age eighteen for organizing a student demonstration, Giap was given permission to enroll at the French-run Lycée Albert Sarraut in Hanoi. He proved an exceptionally able and diligent student and continued on for a law degree at the University of Hanoi, another French institution, refusing a scholarship to study for a doctorate in Paris.

During this time he married and, in order to support his wife and their young daughter, took a position teaching history at a private school in Hanoi. His lectures could be intoxicating. On the first day of class, one student recalled, Giap announced that he would depart from the usual curriculum, which covered France from 1789 to the mid-nineteenth century. "Look, there are a lot of books about this stuff," he declared as he paced at the front of the room. "If you want to know about it, you can look it up. I'm going to tell you about two things—the French Revolution and Napoleon." The students sat transfixed as Giap expounded on Marie Antoinette's indulgences, on Robespierre's life and Danton's death, and—most of all—on Napoleon's military campaigns. Right down to individual minor battles he would go, his admiration for Napoleon palpable, the students hanging on every word.[2]

All the while he continued to immerse himself in nationalist literature, including that of Ho Chi Minh. In 1937, he joined the Indochinese Communist Party, and in 1938, he wrote a book, *The Question of National Liberation in Indochina*. ICP leaders took notice of this smart and educated comrade, who seemed to possess boundless energy. In 1940, they sent Giap and another young party member, Pham Van Dong, to China to make contact with Ho. (Giap's wife wept as he bade her farewell; arrested soon thereafter by the French, she died in Hanoi's Hoa Lo prison, though Giap would not learn the news for three years.) The encounter occurred in Kunming. At fifty, Ho was frail and hunched over, but Giap immediately noticed the piercing eyes. The three men launched into a lively discussion as they walked along the waterfront, and a bond was struck.[3] On Ho's orders, Giap went to Yan'an, in northern China, to take part in military training with Mao Zedong's Communist forces, then returned south in time to be present at the historic founding of the Viet Minh in the cave near Pac Bo in Cao Bang in May 1941.[4]

"Political action should precede military action," Ho frequently proclaimed in these years. But armed struggle would surely come in the end, and preparations must be made. Giap was made head of the Military Committee for the Viet Minh's General Directorate, in charge of building up and training the movement's armed forces. On December 12, 1944, he presided over the creation of the National Liberation Army of Vietnam—thirty-one men and three women at the start, who between them reportedly had one light machine gun, seventeen modern rifles, two revolvers, and fourteen additional firearms of various kinds. Gradually the army's ranks swelled, and it began to clear whole districts in the mountainous areas of Tonkin. By the time of the Japanese coup of 1945, the Viet Minh had a genuine base area.

Giap by now was one of Ho's principal lieutenants, seldom leaving his side for long. He was there at Tan Trao in August 1945, when the party created the National Committee for the Liberation of Vietnam. Giap ran its military subgroup and signed the order to begin the general uprising. This committee effectively became the provisional government of the DRV on September 2, 1945. Giap served as minister of the interior in Ho's first government and over time made himself more and more the indispensable man—capable and efficient and ruthless in equal measure. It surprised no one when he assumed leadership of the DRV during Ho's sojourn to France.

Historian Stein Tønnesson notes an important difference between the deputy and the chief. Giap was the more cold and calculating of the two, a man who stirred awe and admiration in his underlings but not the kind of devotion Ho generated. When Giap speaks in his memoirs of the fabulously persuasive force of his master, Tønnesson remarks, he does not see the importance of Ho's sincerity. "Uncle Ho had an extraordinary flair for detecting the thoughts and feelings of the enemy," Giap writes. "With great shrewdness, he worked out a concrete treatment for each type and each individual. . . . Even his enemies, men who were notoriously anticommunist, showed respect for him. They seemed to lose some of their aggressiveness when they were in his presence." Concludes Tønnesson: "In Giap's rational brain, Ho's charm is reduced to a tool."[5]

II

SOMEHOW GIAP HAD TO DEVISE A STRATEGY FOR VICTORY. FRENCH firepower would initially be vastly greater than his own, he knew, and he turned for guidance to his Yan'an experience and in particular to the theories of Mao Zedong, who in a succession of essays published in the late 1930s had maintained that successful revolutionary war strategy must pass through three phases: withdrawal, equilibrium, and general offensive. During the first phase, insurgents, facing a foe of superior power, avoid major engagements and rely on small-scale guerrilla tactics to sap the will and strength of government forces. They raid when possible and fall back when necessary. As the guerrillas build up their strength and achieve rough parity, they enter the second phase of the struggle, launching a mix of guerrilla and conventional operations to keep the enemy off balance. In this phase, a sense of futility begins to permeate the thinking of the government's troops as casualties and costs mount, with no decision in sight. As the stalemate causes the enemy's morale to plummet, the insurgents launch the general offensive, using conventional attacks with regular army units. Their goal in this third phase is to defeat government forces and exercise political control over territory.

Beginning already in the spring of 1946, Giap had sought to create two large military base areas from which to wage the first phase of the struggle. To these bases, he could withdraw his principal forces as necessary for rest and refitting, and recruit new troops to be trained. The more important of the two would be the area of northern Tonkin known as the Viet Bac, comprising the provinces of Bac Kan, Cao Bang, Lang Son, Ha Giang, Tuyen Quang, and Thai Nguyen. Giap and his aides knew this region well: It had been a main area of operations for them in 1944 and 1945. Its many limestone caves could be used as offices and workshops; its terrain—for the most part heavily forested and mountainous, and poorly suited to food growing—was relatively easy to defend; and its sparse population was broadly sympathetic to the Viet Minh cause. The second base area was more problematic, Giap acknowledged. This was the region made up of the provinces of Thanh Hoa, Nghe An, and Ha Tinh, to the south of the Red River Delta. It was far less well prepared, far more exposed to enemy attack. The attraction here was the greater proximity to Hanoi and Haiphong, and to the sea.[6]

In other respects too, Vo Nguyen Giap used the spring and summer months to strengthen the Viet Minh position. In May the Chinese forces under Lu Han began to withdraw across the Sino-Vietnamese frontier. The French sought to move in quickly but were for the most part stymied. It was the wet season, and Giap's troops were nimbler at navigating the difficult conditions and establishing control of the evacuated areas. Adept at sabotaging roads and bridges, they continually frustrated the road-bound French, delaying them long enough to take scores of important towns and villages out of play. Inevitably, there were military clashes. At Bac Ninh, a village nineteen miles northwest of Hanoi, for example, a Viet Minh unit's ambush of a French truck convoy on August 4 led to a fierce nine-hour battle involving machine guns, mortars, and grenades. Casualties were heavy on both sides, with the French suffering 12 men killed and 41 wounded. Tensions rose.[7]

Meanwhile, those rival nationalist groups that had depended on Chinese support—notably the VNQDD and Dai Viet—now found themselves squeezed by both the Viet Minh and the French. Giap, seizing the opportunity, used scattered guerrilla outbreaks as an excuse to mercilessly crush these groups, often with French blessing. Hundreds, perhaps thousands, of non-Communist rivals were killed. More and more the Viet Minh, who had previously had genuine legitimacy in calling themselves a broad-based nationalist front, was synonymous with the Communist movement. Northern Vietnam, recalled one Dai Viet member of this period, was being transformed into a police state. Many non-Communist Vietnamese suddenly felt squeezed: There seemed to be no real way of resisting Communism except by the unpalatable means of accepting French control or the formation of a government inspired by and beholden to the Paris master.[8]

All the while Giap sought to maintain the official cease-fire with the French. Notwithstanding periodic clashes that continued to occur in the early autumn, he still wanted to delay the outbreak of major hostilities. The cease-fire still held as Ho Chi Minh reentered Hanoi in late October, but neither he nor any other close observer could mistake the heightening animosity. Both sides girded for war. In the north a DRV government continued to sit in Hanoi, and the Viet Minh held effective control in much of Tonkin and northern Annam, while the French, though they had occupation forces in Hanoi, Haiphong, and other garrisons in the north, still sought a toehold. In many northern municipalities, French-language shop and street signs were replaced by Vietnamese ones. (The few exceptions were, interestingly, in English, such as the large sign for a "Pork Butcher Specialist" that hung in a window on a busy Hanoi street.) In the south, meanwhile, France had solidified her hold on major urban areas, and in Saigon there now operated a French-installed government that showed some semblance of authority, at least intermittently. In the countryside of Cochin China, however, this government had minimal power, and French military control generally extended no farther than the rifle range of the units on patrol.[9]

Indeed, the French position in the south looked increasingly tenuous as the autumn began. No longer were British and Japanese forces there to help quell the dissent, and moreover the best French troops had gone north, leaving less experienced units to control the entire area of Cochin China and southern Annam. The leader of the guerrilla forces in the south, Nguyen Binh, a native northerner who had made a name for himself during World War II as an organizer of anti-Japanese and then anti-French activities in the Red River Delta, had been appointed the DRV's military commander in the south the previous fall. Initially he focused his energies on unifying various bandit groups, sects, and religious forces into an organized armed force in order to fight the returning French. But in April and May 1946, as the new provisional French-sanctioned Cochin Chinese government was established and the main French units ventured north, he stepped up guerrilla activities, ordering political assassinations and the harassing of French forces. On April 10, Nguyen Binh announced the formation of a National United Front, including elements of the Cao Dai and Hoa Hao religious sects, dedicated to fighting French colonialism, and in the summer months the guerrilla war in the south increased in intensity, its leader taking time in June to join the Indochinese Communist Party.[10]

Nguyen Binh's effectiveness as a guerrilla leader came in part because he was confident enough to act on his own initiative when necessary. But he also received general instructions from party leaders in the north. Tran Huy Lieu, minister of communications and propaganda in Ho's first government and a longtime acquaintance of Nguyen Binh, signed many of the missives. In one set of instructions, penned in September 1946, Tran captured core elements of what would become the Viet Minh way of war. "The guerrillas," he wrote, "operate in a familiar atmosphere. Secrecy and surprise are the general conditions for their success in confrontations with a clumsy adversary who is badly informed and operates in an unfavorable climate."

> The miracle of the guerrilla is that the whole population contributes. The soldier is the inhabitant, and the inhabitant is the soldier. . . . The tactics consist of avoiding well guarded positions, attacking posts where the garrison is weak, advancing if the enemy retreats and retreating if the enemy advances, organizing ambushes where the enemy will be overcome by numbers in spite of his value. . . . One of the guerrilla tactics consists in making the enemy "blind." Our soldiers do not wear uniforms, they don't concentrate in barracks, and they slip through the crowds that hide them if necessary. In that way, the French soldiers are incapable of detecting their presence.[11]

Already now, well before the outbreak of major war, the Viet Minh leadership understood the principles of guerrilla warfare.

In September and October, French officials in Saigon reported a growing number of clashes with "rebel" forces. To help cope with these altercations, High Commissioner Georges Thierry d'Argenlieu strove to create an army of "partisans," that is, Vietnamese fighting on the side of the French. In mid-September, he asked Paris to provide weapons and supplies for 9,300 partisans in Cochin China and another 1,200 operating in southern Annam. The request was granted, but the materials could not be delivered quickly. Though the telegrams flowing into Paris invariably reported that the "rebels" were suffering the vast bulk of the casualties in the clashes, taken in aggregate the reports show a gradual strengthening of the Viet Minh position in the south. By late October the French controlled no more than a quarter of Cochin China.[12]

Politically too, the French position in the south grew steadily weaker. In August 1946, Dr. Nguyen Van Thinh, the avowedly anti-Communist president of the French-backed Cochin Chinese Republic, complained privately that d'Argenlieu's administration seemed hell-bent on making him look like a puppet. What kind of entity did he lead, he asked bitterly, a colony or a republic with genuine authority? The French claimed the latter but acted otherwise. Thinh's frustration continued to grow in the weeks that followed. On November 10, his body was found hanging from the latch of his window. D'Argenlieu spun the news of the suicide as best he could, informing Paris that Thinh must have been motivated by a desire to publicize the injustices done to him by backers of Ho Chi Minh's government. The admiral may have been unaware of a chilling analogue: Eighty years earlier, at the time of France's colonization of Cochin China, the mandarin Phan Thanh Gian, having chosen to collaborate with the new foreign masters, likewise ended his predicament by taking his own life.[13]

III

D'ARGENLIEU AND HIS COLLEAGUES NEEDED SOMETHING NEW AND dramatic, a game changer. Their hope of securing firm control of Cochin China as a means of forcing Ho Chi Minh's regime to come to terms had plainly come to naught—an honest appraisal would have to conclude that the French position in Cochin China was slipping away, while in Tonkin, Ho's administration retained a powerful grip on much of the populace. Moreover, the cease-fire in the south agreed to in the Ho-Moutet Modus Vivendi would only make things worse over time, by giving the Viet Minh a free hand to quietly expand their control in the countryside. Only one possibility remained: to strike at the heart of Viet Minh power in the north. "Instead of contenting ourselves with controlling rebel attacks in the south," General Jean Étienne Valluy, the commander for French forces, recommended in mid-October, "we should put serious pressure on the rebels by taking large-scale initiatives in Hanoi and Annam. This seems to me to be the inevitable recourse to the ultima ratio." D'Argenlieu concurred and asked Paris for reinforcements in the form of a light armored division of ten thousand troops. The request was approved on October 23.[14]

Haiphong was the scene of the first major clash. The port city was key to French hopes in the north, as its harbor serviced the needs of the Red River Delta—and, d'Argenlieu suspected, brought crucial contraband (weapons, motor oil, gasoline) from China to Giap's forces, in exchange for rice. In Paul Mus's apt phrase, Haiphong was "the lungs of Tonkin."[15] That French and Viet Minh troops controlled different sections of the city added to the tension, and the two sides also squabbled over the right to collect customs duties. By the end of October, rumors were rife in the city of a coming French attack on Viet Minh–held sectors, and the local French commander issued secret orders for the use of tanks and artillery should hostilities erupt. By holding Haiphong and other ports, Valluy optimistically declared in his war plans submitted to d'Argenlieu on November 9, France would "put the Tonkinese authorities and populace at our mercy through the asphyxiation of the country's economy."[16]

But what if Haiphong could not be held? Valluy shuddered at the thought. All other goals must be subordinated to the task of securing the city. To facilitate the objective, Valluy, long convinced that his forces were too dispersed, advocated the evacuation of French garrisons in several important towns—Nam Dinh, Lang Son, Bac Ninh, and Phu Lang Thuong. He even floated the idea of abandoning Hanoi but quickly backed off, acknowledging that it would send a powerful psychological message, signaling a French retreat. Yet a purely military solution would not be possible, the general continued, and thus it would be essential to carry out, in the first phase of the operation, a series of coups d'état in cities throughout Tonkin, the better to neutralize Ho Chi Minh's government.[17]

D'Argenlieu, whose sense of urgency was strengthened by Thinh's suicide as well as by the outcome of parliamentary elections in France, in which the Communists made major gains (thereby threatening the medium- and long-term prospects for an unyielding French posture on Indochina, and perhaps the admiral's own job), did not reject wholesale Valluy's plan but overall considered it too cautious. Evacuations of the type the general wanted were neither wise nor necessary, he determined, and there could certainly be no question of withdrawing from Hanoi.

Above all, France must gird for battle: "If, in spite of the efforts of the French government to arrive at a satisfactory agreement with the Hanoi Government," the admiral instructed Valluy on November 12, just before departing for Paris, "hostilities should resume on the various operational theaters in Indochina, it matters that our troops are capable of not just enduring a sudden attack from the adversary, but in addition responding by decisive forceful action. . . . We must hence foresee the hypothesis under which the French Government, after having exhausted all of its conciliatory resources, views itself obliged, in order to retaliate against a resumption of hostilities, to resort to a forceful action against the Hanoi Government."[18]

The admiral received full-throated backing for his view from Léon Pignon, federal commissioner for political affairs within the Saigon administration. Pignon, widely respected in Paris for his knowledge of Indochinese history and society, warned the metropolitan government's Indochina Committee (Comité interministériel de l'Indochine, or COMININDO) that decisive action against the Viet Minh in Tonkin was imperative to bolster the morale of *colons* throughout Indochina and particularly in Saigon. Only by dealing forcefully with Ho Chi Minh's regime could France stem the rapid decline that had occurred since the Japanese coup of March 1945. A failure to act swiftly, Pignon added, would allow the United States to gradually increase her economic penetration in the colony.[19]

D'Argenlieu expected to be back in Vietnam before things came to a head, but events would not wait for him. On the thirteenth, the very day he left for France, the Vietnamese command in Haiphong reported an "extremely provocative" French attitude and cautioned its troops to prepare for potential hostilities. The following day the DRV Interior Ministry instructed "all cities and Haiphong" to compel French soldiers to return to the French sector if they ventured out of their designated zones without a Vietnamese permit.[20]

Then, on November 20, the combustible mix ignited. A French patrol ship seized a Chinese junk carrying a load of gasoline. Viet Minh troops intercepted the French craft and arrested its crew members. In the ensuing attempts to rescue the French personnel, shots were fired, and the fighting soon spread to other parts of the city. At the Opera House, a troupe of Vietnamese actors beat back the French with antique muskets. By nightfall, 240 Vietnamese and seven Frenchmen lay dead.[21]

The following day the two sides agreed to a cease-fire. There the matter might have ended had French officers not sought to exploit the incident to secure a strategic advantage. On the twenty-second, General Valluy ordered the volatile local commander, Colonel Pierre-Louis Dèbes, a forty-six-year-old World War II veteran who harbored a deep dislike of the Vietnamese, to "take maximum advantage of this incident in order to improve our position in Haiphong. It seems clear that we are facing premeditated aggression, carefully planned by the regular Vietnamese army which seems no longer to be following its Government's orders. . . . The moment has arrived to teach a hard lesson to those who have so treacherously attacked us. By every possible means you must take complete control of Haiphong and force the Vietnamese government and army into submission."[22]

Valluy issued this directive despite a warning from his cautious senior subordinate, General Louis Morlière, commander of French forces in Northern Indochina, that any effort to take the city while minimizing French casualties would involve massive destruction and Vietnamese loss of life and would be a wholesale violation of both the March 6 Accords and the Modus Vivendi. At six A.M. on the twenty-third, Dèbes demanded a full Vietnamese withdrawal from the Chinese quarter of Haiphong and the nearby village of Lac Vien, and further that all Vietnamese civilians in these areas be disarmed. Claiming the authority of the high commissioner for these demands, he gave the Vietnamese until nine A.M. to accept these conditions. The Vietnamese refused to comply, whereupon Dèbes ordered a general attack, supported by artillery.

At 10:05 A.M. it began, a prolonged naval and aerial bombardment that, over two days, reduced much of the Vietnamese and Chinese quarters of Haiphong to rubble. How many Vietnamese died has never been firmly established, but certainly the number is in the thousands. According to credible reports, civilians attempting to flee the town were strafed by Spitfires. A French officer, Henri Martin, said years later: "When we visited Haiphong afterwards, all the Vietnamese neighborhoods were completely wiped out. There were dead buried under debris. . . . It is difficult to know the exact figure. But the larger part of the city, it seemed to us from what we saw, [that is] almost the entire Vietnamese part of the city, had been destroyed."[23]

Strikingly, Valluy did not get prior approval from Paris for the bombardment. Not for the first time and not for the last, Saigon made a major policy decision without so much as consulting metropolitan officials. Even d'Argenlieu, then in Paris for meetings with Georges Bidault, leader of the Provisional Government of France, and others, learned of Valluy's order only after it had been issued. Then again, there's no doubt Valluy acted in full confidence that the high commissioner would approve his action. So he did. On November 24, d'Argenlieu cabled his congratulations from Paris and added: "We will never retreat or surrender." He even quoted an instruction from Bidault (likely meant only for Cochin China) "to use all means to ensure law and order are respected." By the twenty-eighth, the French were in control of Haiphong, and also of Lang Son, the frontier garrison town where fighting had broken out the previous week.[24]

Ho Chi Minh, fast losing hope for an accommodation, told a French reporter that neither France nor Vietnam "can afford the luxury of a bloody war." But, he added, the Vietnamese would endure an "atrocious struggle," no matter how lengthy, rather than "renounce their liberty." He also appealed to the French parliament to honor the agreements of the previous months, insisting on the "sincere desire of the Vietnamese Government and people to collaborate fraternally with the French people" and on "the desire of Viet Nam to be part of the French Union." In early December, Jean Sainteny arrived for a last-ditch (as it turned out) attempt at averting a conflagration. His instructions: to back Ho and his supposed moderate allies against hard-liners, while offering no new substantive concessions. Nothing came of his efforts, as Valluy insisted on an aggressive posture and Viet Minh troops strengthened their positions in and around Hanoi. Haiphong was virtually isolated by Viet Minh roadblocks. Ho, meanwhile, played for time, hoping for U.S. mediation or the formation of a government in Paris more favorable to the Vietnamese cause.[25]

The first hope was in vain; the Truman administration ruled out a mediating role. In early December, the administration had dispatched Abbot Low Moffat to Hanoi to reassure the Viet Minh leader of U.S.

support for greater Vietnamese "autonomy within the framework of democratic institutions," and to warn him against using force to achieve that objective—and not incidentally, to assess the degree to which Ho's government was dominated by Communists and loyal to Moscow. Ho, suffering from illness during the meeting, assured Moffat that national independence, not Communism, was his first objective. Maybe in fifty years things would be different, he said, repeating the line he had used in Paris during the summer, but fifty years was a long time off. He asked for U.S. assistance and in exchange offered the use of Cam Ranh Bay as a naval base. To convey his seriousness of purpose, Ho dispatched General Giap to a cocktail party hosted by the U.S. consulate in Moffat's honor. "To everyone's surprise," a British observer noted, Giap stayed a long time.[26]

Moffat was noncommittal. He reported to Washington that Communists were indeed in control of the Vietnamese government and that for now a French presence would be required, so as to ward off both Soviet and possible Chinese encroachment. Moffat's superiors took that as evidence that they should reject Ho's overtures and steer clear of any formal role. They paid less attention to the other part of Moffat's report, in which he expressed sympathy for the nationalist cause and a conviction that France had no option but to compromise. On December 17, the State Department issued a circular to missions abroad that made note of the Viet Minh's Communist character and said a continued French presence in Indochina was imperative, "not only as [an] antidote to Soviet influence, but to protect Vietnam and Southeast Asia from future Chinese imperialism."[27]

Some observers despaired at this policy decision, seeing it as a missed opportunity to avert major conflict. Lauriston Sharp, a Cornell University anthropologist who had served in the region during the war and who still consulted for the State Department, complained bitterly that by its feckless lack of leadership Washington had helped create the present "vacuum" in Vietnam. After all, most Americans concerned with foreign affairs understood that the colonial era was over and that its revival was an exercise in putting Humpty Dumpty back on the wall; why not act on that basis? One firmly worded telegram from the Truman administration, reminding Paris of its obligations under the March 6 Accords—in particular to recognize the Viet Minh as a legitimate authority—could have headed off the crisis, Sharp told a colleague.[28]

Ho Chi Minh had better luck with his second wish, that for new leadership in Paris. On December 17, Léon Blum became premier of France at the head of an all-Socialist cabinet—the same Blum who, earlier in the summer, had assured Ho, "I will be there at difficult moments. Count on me." Could this be the development that the advocates of a political solution needed? There were grounds for hope. Just a week earlier Blum had written in the Socialist paper *Le Populaire* that French policy in Vietnam was bankrupt. "There is one way, and one way only," he wrote, "to maintain in Indochina the prestige of our civilization, of our political and spiritual influence, and of our legitimate interests: We must reach agreement on the basis of independence, we must keep confidence and preserve friendship." A leader of France had, at long last, uttered the magic word: *independence.*

But it was too little, too late. Blum presided over a weak government, a kind of stopgap regime meant to serve out the final weeks of the Provisional Government until the constitution of the Fourth Republic would go into effect. He was in no position to quickly reverse the aggressive Indochina policy that had taken shape over the previous months. Even had he been able to implement a reversal in Paris, in Vietnam the momentum for major war was now too great. Hanoi had become a checkerboard of areas controlled by the French and the Viet Minh, and the tension was enormous. Tens of thousands of residents fled for the countryside. The Viet Minh plan was to compel the French to fight house by house, block by block. This would enable the Viet Minh government and key army units to evacuate the city for a base in the mountains. Accordingly, militia and army units dug up streets, built roadblocks, and cut holes through neighboring houses to facilitate troop movement.[29]

On December 17, after Valluy ordered the removal of the Viet Minh barricades, *tu ve* militiamen and French troops clashed at various spots in Hanoi. Both sides suffered significant casualties. "If those gooks want a fight, they'll get it," Valluy declared. Legionnaires lined the streets from the Citadel to the Paul Doumer Bridge, and French armored cars began demolishing the Viet Minh roadblocks. The next day Valluy issued an ultimatum that no additional obstructions be erected in Hanoi, and he further announced that, beginning two days thence, French units would assume control of public security in the city. In response, Ho Chi Minh ordered preparations for an assault on French installations the following day, December 19.[30]

IV

THE ATTACK WAS SCHEDULED FOR SEVEN P.M., BUT THE HOUR passed without incident. Throughout the day, there had been rumors of possible eleventh-hour peace moves, and the DRV Central Committee, meeting early in the afternoon, appeared hesitant. At eight P.M., however, there was an explosion, and the streets were plunged into darkness. This was the signal for *tu ve* units to strike. Their few pieces of artillery opened up on French installations just as many French troops were returning to their barracks after a special movie screening. Bursts of gunfire and the explosions of grenades and mortar shells could be heard through the night, and trucks and armored vehicles roared through the darkened streets. An early casualty was Sainteny, who was seriously hurt when his armored car hit a mine. Vo Nguyen Giap had withdrawn many of his regular forces to the mountain fastnesses to the north, but he had three divisions near the racecourse in the suburbs to the southwest and beside Le Grand Lac (now West Lake, or Ho Tay); he did not, however, use them that first night.[31]

The following day, December 20, as the fighting spread to various parts of the country—to Bac Ninh and Nam Dinh in the north, to Hue and Tourane (Da Nang) on the central coast, to Saigon in the south—Ho Chi Minh issued an appeal for national resistance, vowing that though the struggle would be long and difficult, victory would come in the end. The Vietnamese people responded. Hundreds of thousands of them, north and south, declared their commitment to the cause, the ouster of the French and the creation of a Vietnam for the Vietnamese. Youths volunteered in droves for the military. "The flame of nationalism never burned as bright in the hearts of the people, and the Vietnamese never united as strongly behind the Viet Minh, as in those first days and months of the resistance," recalled Mai Elliott, who resided in Hanoi with her family that December.[32]

The French soon swept into Elliott's neighborhood, with shouts of *"En avant!"* and accompanied by German shepherds, searching for Viet Minh soldiers or collaborators. "The streets echoed with the furious barking of the dogs, the crunching of French boots, and the angry voices of the soldiers, who were spoiling for retaliation." Her brother Giu, a member of the Vietnamese militia, surrendered rather than risk being shot. Narrowly escaping death at the hands of a bare-chested French soldier, Giu was taken away to a makeshift POW camp at Hoa Lo prison, where he witnessed acts of extreme brutality by some French guards and unexpected acts of kindness by others. One prisoner, a Viet Minh security officer, interrogated just moments before Giu's turn came, was led away, shoved against a wall, and shot in the mouth. Giu himself won release a few months later. He would survive both the French and the American wars and later settle in France and then California.[33]

In short order, French units moved to seize control of key installations but usually found, to their frustration, that the Viet Minh leadership had quietly slipped away. Even then, house-to-house fighting proved laborious and dangerous, despite the fact that the enemy was composed largely of a hodgepodge of lightly armed militia and police-

DEAD BODIES BEING REMOVED FROM A HANOI STREET DURING THE
BATTLE OF HANOI, DECEMBER 20, 1946.

men, who would fire on the French—with ancient French muskets, old American rifles, Japanese carbines, and British Bren automatics—and then disappear inside the labyrinth of homes whose walls had been pierced to allow easy movement. The French were further slowed by the proliferation of hastily built barricades on Hanoi's streets, many of them rigged with crude mines.

It all portended trouble for French officials, who had expected to seal off and destroy Viet Minh forces in Hanoi within a matter of days. Two months it would take before the Viet Minh units, under the cover of darkness, withdrew from the city, their primary mission accomplished. They had succeeded in pinning down French forces in the capital, thereby buying the necessary time to move the government and main military force to their mountain base.

Whatever date one chooses for the start of the First Vietnam War— September 1945, with the outbreak of fighting in Cochin China, or November–December 1946, with the conflagration in Tonkin—by the start of 1947 there was fighting throughout Vietnam.[34] Both sides had taken the necessary steps toward war, and in hindsight it's tempting to see the whole thing as inevitable, especially after the failure of the Fontainebleau talks. But wars are never inevitable; they depend on the actions of individual leaders who could have chosen differently, who had, if not a menu of options, then at least an alternative to large-scale violence.

Yet if it takes actions by two sides to make a war, both sides are not always equally culpable. And if it's true that the Vietnamese fired the first shots on December 19, ultimately France bears primary responsibility for precipitating the conflict. D'Argenlieu, dubbed the "Bloody Monk" by the left-wing press in Paris, had enormous power to formulate policy, often without consulting Paris, and as we have seen, he thwarted the prospects for a negotiated solution at several junctures in 1946; he seemed determined to provoke the Hanoi government into full-scale hostilities. D'Argenlieu, upon returning from a brief visit to France in late December 1946, vowed that France would never relinquish her hold on Indochina. The granting of independence, he declared, "would only be a fiction deeply prejudicial to the interests of the two parties."[35]

It would be too much, however, to call this "D'Argenlieu's War." The high commissioner's core objective—to keep Indochina French—was broadly shared among officials in Paris as well as *colons* in Saigon and Hanoi. It is striking, the degree to which all parts of the political spectrum in France in 1945–46 shared the conviction that Indochina ought to remain within the French colonial empire. The left, to be sure, favored bona fide negotiations with Hanoi, but both the SFIO and the PCF were adamant that they did not want to see France reduced to what the Communist newspaper *L'Humanité* called "her own small metropolitan community." Both attached importance to reclaiming and maintaining French prestige and saw the preservation of the empire as essential to that task. The Socialists, who dominated French politics in the crucial early postwar years, professed opposition to d'Argenlieu's efforts to sabotage the March 6 Accords, but in practice they tolerated his actions, just as they tolerated Valluy's provocations in Haiphong and Hanoi; at the Fontainebleau talks, the Socialist representatives were as intransigent as any on the French side. PCF leaders, meanwhile, despite becoming the largest party in the November 1946 elections (taking 28 percent and 170 deputies), kept a low profile on Indochina in the critical weeks thereafter, anxious as they were to appear a moderate and patriotic force.[36]

Even Léon Blum, a broad-thinking humanist and fundamentally decent man who genuinely despaired at the onset of war, could say at once on December 23, less than a week into the Battle of Hanoi, that the old colonial system was finished *and* that renewed negotiations were possible only once "order" was restored. Minister of Overseas France Marius Moutet likewise said there could be no talks without an "end to terrorism."[37]

Most important of all in this constellation of voices on the French political scene was the MRP under Georges Bidault, which opposed not only negotiations with Ho but the granting of independence to *any* Vietnamese regime. Thrust into the heart of government not long after liberation, the MRP would maintain a tight hold on foreign and colonial policy for years to come and as such would hold extraordinary sway over the speed and complexion of imperial reform. As a group, the party's leaders lacked experience in colonial affairs, and its senior figures—Bidault, Robert Schuman, and René Pleven—adhered to a rigid and intransigent colonial policy that stood in marked contrast to their often supple and forward-thinking approach to European affairs.[38]

French public opinion, meanwhile, did not register significant opposition to the use of military force in Indochina. Information, for one thing, was hard to come by. In 1946, French newspapers did not have their own correspondents in Indochina, which left journalists dependent on the Associated Press and Agence France-Presse (AFP) for news. D'Argenlieu, deeply suspicious of independent journalism, maintained strict control over the AFP, making it in essence a government propaganda arm. Not surprisingly, therefore, the six main Paris dailies did little in-depth reporting in November and December and generally blamed the Vietnamese for the outbreak of violence. On November 28, after the French bombardment of Haiphong had leveled parts of the city and killed thousands, *Le Monde*'s Rémy Roure assured readers that, from the French side, "not a single shot had been fired, except in defense."[39]

Looming large over the entire process was one man: Charles de Gaulle. Though technically absent from the political stage after January 1946, his influence remained enormous, as historian Frédéric Turpin's careful research makes clear. As leader of the Free French, he had possessed the power in 1944–45 to foil the plans of his country's colonial lobby; he did not do so. Indeed, the general's policy during and after World War II had been to reclaim Indochina for France, on the grounds that French grandeur demanded it. The choice of Admiral d'Argenlieu for high commissioner had been his. He, no one else, instructed d'Argenlieu and Leclerc to be uncompromising in their dealings with Vietnamese nationalists and to prepare to use force. During the conference at Fontainebleau, de Gaulle pressed Bidault to resist giving in to Vietnamese demands, and he announced publicly his conviction that France must remain "united with the territories which she opened to civilization," lest she lose her great power status. Throughout the autumn, he stuck firmly to this position, and in the November-December crisis, he maintained staunch backing for d'Argenlieu's uncompromising posture. On December 17, de Gaulle hosted the admiral for more than three hours at his home in Colombey-les-Deux-Églises and assured him that as far as Indochina was concerned, it was d'Argenlieu and not the government that represented France.[40]

A week later d'Argenlieu, now back in Saigon, expressed satisfaction with the turn of events. "Personally," he wrote in his diary, "I have since September 1945 loyally executed the policy of agreement in Indochina. It has borne fruit everywhere, except with the Hanoi government. *It's over.*"[41]

It was anything but.

CHAPTER 7

WAR WITHOUT FRONTS

THE FIGHTING WAS FIERCE FROM THE START. BY THE MIDDLE OF January 1947, less than a month into the hostilities, large portions of Hanoi were reduced to rubble, and public buildings such as the Pasteur Institute and numerous hospitals suffered major damage. Elsewhere in the Red River Delta the clashes were likewise intense, notably in Nam Dinh, forty-five miles southeast of Hanoi, and Bac Ninh, nineteen miles to the northeast. The Vietnamese used artillery and mortars as well as sabotage—they repeatedly cut vital roads, including that between Haiphong and Hanoi, and they set off bombs to sever rail lines and destroy bridges. The French responded with tanks and Spitfires. Food supplies grew scarce, especially in Hanoi. By early February, after six weeks of combat, the French reported 1,855 men killed or severely wounded. Vietnamese casualties are harder to determine but were far higher.[1]

Bit by bit, the superior French arms forced the Vietnamese back. By late February 1947, the French Expeditionary Corps had taken control of Hanoi, Haiphong, Hon Gai, and Hue, and by March it had gained a tenuous hold over the Red River Delta. By the start of April, the French controlled most of the main towns in Tonkin and Annam. The lightly armed local militia and regional fighting units, charged by Vo Nguyen Giap with the defense of key areas, were no match for General Valluy's then-still-fast-moving mechanized columns. Ho Chi Minh was forced to withdraw his government to a shifting series of jungle headquarters in its long-standing stronghold in the region of Thai Nguyen–Bac Kan–Tuyen Quang.

In Cochin China, meanwhile, guerrilla activity increased in the weeks following December 19 and was effective enough to reduce the amount of territory the French controlled. In the urban areas, however, the French retained the upper hand; in these weeks, the region as a whole saw a lot less large-scale fighting than occurred in the north. Hopeful French commanders described a pesky but tolerable level of insecurity in the south and hoped to maintain it as they devoted primary attention and resources to the north.

Jean Étienne Valluy was the first in a long line of French generals who would take the battle to Giap; like all the rest, he possessed formidable credentials. Forty-six years old, a highly decorated officer who had joined the military as a private in 1917 at the age of seventeen, his courage and skill in the Great War had won him both a Croix de Guerre for valor and an appointment to Saint-Cyr, the French military academy. Following the war, he rose through the ranks, assuming a number of staff and command jobs, and at the outbreak of war in 1940 he was a major and operations officer with the French XXI Corps. Taken prisoner by the Germans in 1940, Valluy was repatriated in 1941 and by 1944 had become a brigadier general and chief of staff of General Jean de Lattre de Tassigny's First French Army in Europe. In 1945 he assumed command of the Ninth Colonial Infantry Division and earned praise for his hard-driving command against stubborn German resistance.[2]

Like Leclerc before him, Valluy understood that he did not have the military capability to fight a long and costly guerrilla war against the Viet Minh. His problem was manpower. He knew he would not get any conscripts from France—no Paris government was deemed likely to survive a decision to send draftees (in part because of the tradition of using specialized corps of professional volunteers in colonial conflicts). So he had to rely on volunteers as well as colonial troops from Africa—Moroccan, Algerian, Tunisian, and Senegalese—and from Indochina herself (Vietnamese, Cambodians, and Laotians, as well as assorted ethnic minority groups). Also available were a variety of paramilitary forces and an assortment of local militias and self-defense groups.

African troops were as yet few in number. In May 1945 Charles de Gaulle had prohibited their use in Indochina on the grounds that they might be unduly influenced by Vietnamese nationalist discourse and might seek to implement these ideas upon their return home. He also worried that their presence could sharpen American anticolonialist critiques of French imperalism. Now, however, the acute need for fighting men compelled a change in the policy, and during the course of 1947 more and more African conscripts were deployed.

In addition, Valluy had units of the French Foreign Legion, about which so much has been written, and which included within it a sizable number of ex-Nazis.[3] Most legionnaires in Indochina in 1947 were indeed Germans in their midtwenties who had gone into the Wehrmacht young and knew no occupation but war, who had helped conquer France in 1940, and who bore scars from wounds suffered in Russia, Poland, or Romania. The majority took a five-year enlistment as means to escape the French prison system; partly as a result of their experience with that system, they had no special love for the French. In most cases, the legionnaires assembled at Marseille for the long journey ahead, having already passed through security screenings in recruiting centers in Paris or Lyon or Lille. Fiercely jealous of its record as a stronghold against Marxism-Leninism, the Legion's security officers took special care to weed out not just murderers, sexual offenders, and other felons but Communists as well.[4]

Occasionally a legionnaire with a more surprising nationality would turn up. One evening U.S. journalist Seymour Topping, during a tour of French installations in northern Tonkin, dined in the Foreign Legion officers' club in Lang Son near the Chinese frontier; he bumped into a tall and slim lieutenant whose accent sounded familiar. He was Robert Fleet, a captain in the U.S. Army during World War II and a lover of arms and uniforms and battle. Drawn to the Legion for the chance to experience again the thrill of the fight, Fleet prevailed upon Topping not to reveal his name because of the U.S. law banning service by Americans in foreign armies.[5]

The French nationals in the Expeditionary Corps, meanwhile, numbered in the tens of thousands, but they essentially composed the officer corps for the colonial and Legion troops as well as the staffs of headquarters and administrative units. They trickled in at regular intervals in the early months of the year but never in the numbers that Valluy wanted to see.

This manpower shortage left the general with limited options, and his predicament worsened in March 1947, when an additional division of French colonial troops had to be diverted en route to Indochina to quell an insurgency in Madagascar. Yet there could be no question of turning back, not in his mind or that of other senior French officials. "It is impossible to negotiate with those people," Overseas Minister Marius Moutet declared of the Viet Minh during a visit to Saigon in January. "They have fallen to the lowest levels of barbarity." A few days later, after his entourage had been fired upon during a stop in Hanoi, Moutet added: "Before there is any negotiation it will be necessary to get a military decision."[6]

Valluy expressed confidence that his troops could build on their early successes and complete the task. He hoped that a series of pincer movements combining air, land, and river-borne forces could finish off the enemy swiftly, before Giap had time to build up his forces. By cementing French control of the Red River Delta and Route Coloniale 4 (RC4), which ran close to the Chinese border in the far north, Valluy planned to contain the Viet Minh maquis, cut them off from all contact with the outside, and then exterminate them.[7]

II

IT DIDN'T WORK OUT THAT WAY. GIAP GRASPED RIGHT AWAY THAT he must deny the French the quick victory they sought. But he also understood that he had to avoid open and large-scale engagements if at all possible; his forces were simply too weak. He in effect ceded the major towns and lines of communication in Tonkin and Annam as he withdrew the bulk of his army to the Viet Bac. Patience would be his main weapon as he plotted for a protracted war based roughly on Mao's three-phase model of withdrawal (from major towns and cities), equilibrium, and general offensive. Already on December 22, 1946, a mere three days into the fighting, the DRV issued a proclamation stating that the war would be fought along these lines.[8]

The declaration was drafted by theoretician Truong Chinh, who elaborated on the essentials of this Maoist strategy in a publication titled *The Resistance Will Win*, which appeared in February 1947. Secretary-general of the Indochinese Communist Party until its ostensible dissolution in November 1945, Truong Chinh became head of the "Marxist

Study Group" that formally took the party's place, and he later led the Vietnamese Workers Party (VWP, or Lao Dong), as the Communist Party was called after its revival in 1951. In *Resistance,* he cautioned that the timing of the transition from one of Mao's phases to the next could not be determined in advance; it depended on the relative strength of revolutionary forces, the degree of support for the insurgency in the general population, and the extent of demoralization among enemy forces. The struggle would certainly be long and difficult and would require maintaining solidarity with the Cambodian and Lao peoples and indeed with all those who suffered under the French Union. More than Mao, Truong Chinh stressed the importance of international powers—in this case, principally the United States, the Soviet Union, and China—to the success of the insurgency, and he emphasized that French public opinion could ultimately prove decisive. Over time, declining morale and increasing public opposition to the fighting would seriously impair the French war effort.[9]

By relying on this three-phase approach, Giap hoped to retain the strategic initiative and control the tempo of the war. Not a major theoretician himself, he would nevertheless over the years leave his own mark on the Maoist strategy, as we shall see. Now, in early 1947, he set about following the strictures of the first phase: to preserve his forces, to withdraw into protected territory, and to be content with harassing the enemy's convoys and bases. To skeptical subordinates who wanted to go right away to large-scale engagements, Giap offered a firm reply: Such an approach promised only defeat at the hands of the infinitely more powerful French. The Battle of Hanoi in December–January had shown the foolishness of trying to go at them directly.[10]

And so, 1947 would be a year of strategic defense from the Viet Minh perspective. The main force regulars—the *chu luc,* who numbered roughly thirty thousand early in the year—would bide their time in their Viet Bac strongholds, which were mostly remote, cloaked by forest, and largely inaccessible to the French. These main units lacked a ready arms supply and moreover needed to undergo additional training. On Giap's orders, they were not to be committed to military action if it could possibly be avoided, leaving the task of harassing French Union troops to the regional forces. To build up support in the countryside, the Indochinese Communist Party—which, though supposedly dissolved by Ho Chi Minh in late 1945, continued to operate at the district level and below, and to control the corresponding Viet Minh government administration—created village committees and militias and established a comprehensive and popular literacy program. Indoctrination was carried out at evening meetings held two or three times per week, during which cadres expounded the Viet Minh philosophy and anticolonial propaganda. To support the armed forces, the party collected taxes—cash extortion in the towns and rice levies in the villages—and recruited porters to serve in the clandestine logistical network. When the situation demanded, the cadres reinforced education and propaganda with terror tactics, including assassination of village leaders.[11]

The terror had to be carefully calibrated, Giap understood, for it was a double-edged sword. There were just so many bombs you could toss into homes and theaters, only so many throats you could cut. If you went too far, if you killed too many village notables, you risked a vigilante reaction, in which people rose up and declared, "To hell with it. We're going to get killed regardless; we might as well band together and take a few of the gangsters with us." Terror would be a part of the Viet Minh arsenal, used when it suited their operations, but always handled with precision. It would be utilized selectively, not only in the military sense but in the sociological sense, targeting only those people who by virtue of their positions or their extensive landholdings weren't very popular anyway.[12]

In time it would become clear that Giap had formidable advantages that the French, in seven years of war, would never overcome. One was the physical environment. Vietnam is a vast and varied country, running from the rugged and mountainous north to the populous rice lands along the coast, to the jungles and grasslands of the south, like the marshy Plain of Reeds (Plaine des Joncs), which creeps from the Cambodian frontier to the very outskirts of Saigon. Though the Viet Minh would face their own difficulties adapting to this diversity, they nevertheless proved far more adept at doing so than the French. Valluy had hoped in the spring of 1947 to continue his gains from the early months, but the arrival of the monsoon season, which runs from May to October and typically sees at least sixty inches of rain, ruined this possibility and forced him to call a halt. During the monsoon, valley floors turn into swamps, hillsides be-

A FRENCH UNION TRUCK BOGGING DOWN IN THE MUD ON ROUTE
COLONIALE 4 IN NORTHERN TONKIN ON THE CHINESE BORDER.

come saturated and treacherous, and many single-track roads turn into
rivers.[13]

Even in dry weather, as Valluy would discover to his sorrow, the
road network was primitive, an object of neglect by a succession of colonial administrators. In the Viet Bac, which for the duration of the war
would remain the main headquarters, supply base, and training ground
of the Viet Minh, to speak of *roads* was really a euphemism. Cart paths
and trails were numerous, but even the grandly named Route Coloniale
3 (RC3), the main thoroughfare in the area, which appeared as a thick
line on the map, was a one-lane dirt road, seldom more than twelve feet
across, with weak bridges and countless ambush sites. Such was its state
of repair most of the time that the fastest-moving convoy could not average more than eight miles per hour. The same was true of Route Coloniale 4 from Cao Bang to Tien Yen, and the road from Tien Yen to Hon
Gai. The "highway" linking Hanoi and Haiphong consisted of little more
than a series of ruts, though it did permit two-way traffic. Nor were the
bridges and causeways elsewhere in the country much better—with some
exceptions, such as the Paul Doumer Bridge in Hanoi, few were built to

allow passage by heavy trucks and armored vehicles. As for passage off the roads by wheeled vehicles, this was usually impossible. Tanks and half-tracks frequently bogged down in the saturated earth of the deltas, and even amphibious tractors often were halted by vegetation clogging their tracks.[14]

Already in 1945–46, in the early fighting in Cochin China, French Union officers learned that they were prisoners of the roads. They learned it again when hostilities commenced in the north. Theirs was a European army, whose great advantage was in its heavy weapons but that needed roads and bridges to bring those weapons to the battlefield. Very quickly the guerrillas and regional forces proved adept at sabotage, often by digging "piano-key" ditches from alternate sides of the road. Crews would be sent out to repair them, whereupon they were dug up again; inevitably, some of the villagers recruited by the French to refill the trenches were those who, come nightfall, returned to dig them up again. The process repeated itself endlessly, but the overall effect was to seriously hamper French mobility—and, of course, leave convoys dangerously exposed to ambush. Typically the guerrillas would establish themselves on both sides of a narrow pass and then drop grenades onto the slow-moving convoy almost directly beneath them. Simultaneously they would open up with machine-gun fire from close range. When one truck was forced to halt, blocking the road for the vehicles behind, the guerrillas would charge down the hillside, using more grenades and more gunfire. Antivehicle mines, fashioned from unexploded French shells and bombs that were ingeniously (and courageously) re-fused, were another constant danger to the convoys, as were snipers hiding in the often dense brush along the roadways. Bridges, so vital to French mobility, were subject to frequent sabotage and would often be booby-trapped to explode when French engineers arrived to rebuild them.[15]

Even when no ambushers were present, travel along many roads in Tonkin was treacherous. North of Lang Son, the notorious RC4, destined to bring nightmares to a succession of French commanders, became hair-raisingly difficult. At Dong Dang it passed within 750 yards of the Chinese frontier, then climbed over narrow passes and snaked along mountain ledges and innumerable hairpin bends, before plunging down steeply to more tight turns. Drivers, often alone in the cabin—manpower was too short for two-man crews—had to navigate the road in old beat-up American-made GMC trucks, many lacking spare tires or functioning springs. Usually the cabin would be baking hot, and the driver, swinging the steering wheel from lock to lock on the hairpins, had to strain to see through the mist to make sure he was a safe distance from the truck in front of him. Breakdowns were common and could halt the entire convoy for long, nerve-racking hours.[16]

Much of the Viet Minh activity occurred at night, giving rise to one of the leitmotifs of the war: Areas controlled by the French during the day would become guerrilla territory after sundown. But this truism is also misleading, for even in daylight hours the Viet Minh in mid-1947 controlled as much as half the territory of Vietnam. The French were lords of the towns and the main roads; the Viet Minh of the countryside, the remote villages, and the walking trails. In Tonkin, Giap's forces controlled the whole area northeast and east of the Red River and Hanoi, as well as the fertile provinces south of the Red River Delta down to northern Annam, including the towns of Thanh Hoa and Vinh. In northern and central Annam, between the towns of Vinh and Qui Nhon, the French held only a narrow coastal strip beginning just north of Quang Tri and ending slightly south of Tourane (Da Nang), in addition to part of the thinly populated highland; the rest of the territory, perhaps 80 percent of the total, was from the start of the conflict in Viet Minh hands. In southern Annam and in Cochin China, French control was more extensive. They held all the cities, including the distant highland towns of Pleiku and Kontum, and they had at least nominal control (though not at night) of the major roads. Even here, though, guerrilla action was frequent, and a few areas were under Viet Minh control—including Ca Mau in the extreme south, and the region around Ha Tien on the Cambodian border. Saigon, meanwhile, featured regular grenade attacks on cafés and bars frequented by *colons,* and French authorities felt compelled to maintain a strict curfew of eleven P.M.[17]

Which points to a more fundamental problem confronting the colonial power: the strong anti-French and nationalist feelings among the vast majority of Vietnamese. Seven years earlier, in 1940, France had been able to control all of Indochina with a few thousand troops; now Valluy had upward of a hundred thousand, and it was not nearly enough. The presence of Vietnamese regional forces and smaller guerrilla units (in addition to the regular army), many of whose members lacked uniforms and were peasants and laborers when not fighting, is evidence of the broad participation in the war against the French (though not necessarily of affection for the Viet Minh). The pervasive anti-French animus enabled Viet Minh forces to assemble undetected, to withdraw when the enemy appeared in force, to hide their weapons, to expand their ranks, and to gather excellent intelligence concerning the strength, the maneuvers, and often even the plans of the French. And when the enemy, unable to determine who was a fighter and who was not, reacted to the guerrilla attacks by killing civilians, the main effect was to deepen the hatred for the French and to bring new guerrillas into the fold.[18]

Women, children, the elderly—all contributed to the common cause. The author Le Ly Hayslip recalls a song her mother sang to her during her childhood in a village in Central Vietnam:

> *In our village today*
> *A big battle was fought,*
> *French kill and arrest the people;*
> *The fields and villages burn,*
> *The people, they run to the winds;*
> *To the north, to the south,*
> *To Xam Ho, to Ky La.*
> *When they run, they look back;*
> *They see houses in flames.*[19]

For the French, the problem was in part one of intelligence, though not in the way one might think. French military intelligence services in Indochina were generally highly competent and professional. Most of the time the French High Command could read, on charts and maps prepared by its various intelligence sections, the full order of battle of Viet Minh units, with an accuracy that was often greater than, and rarely less than, 80 percent. Almost never did the Viet Minh initiate an operation of major significance that had not been anticipated by these services. At the lower levels, however, battalion commanders and detachment commanders were often victims of the most brutal surprises—in the form of road mines, ambushes, and grenade attacks. When a French Union patrol would enter a village, it lacked the information that would have allowed it to screen the inhabitants and identify nonuniformed Viet Minh. "It is clear," a postwar French study would conclude, "that a distinction must be made here between the precise, deep intelligence which was always available to the High Command, and the immediate and local intelligence that was almost never obtained by subordinate units. Thus it was written: 'It was the Commander in Chief who kept the battalion commander informed while the latter was never able to reciprocate.' "[20]

The issue for these battalion commanders was in large part the political character of the war. To gather information by technical means—signal intelligence, aerial photography, and other technical collection systems—was a relatively straightforward task: The French had the means and the expertise to do it. Human intelligence, or "humint," was another matter. It didn't take French commanders long to realize that many Vietnamese agents had contacts with both sides; one could never be assured of their loyalty. At times, an agent might seem a little too eager to spout whatever information the French wanted to hear, particularly if he or she sensed that payment might follow. Prisoners, likewise, often were so anxious to please their interrogator that their information was unreliable, or they deliberately provided false information. Even in those instances when the information from an agent or prisoner seemed legitimate, it was often out of date before it could be confirmed.

To try to improve the quality of the humint, French officers sometimes resorted to coercive interrogation methods, including torture. (Their DRV opposite numbers did the same.) Just how often they did so remains impossible to know in the absence of methodologically reliable studies of the issue, but Vietnamese memoirs and histories of the war leave no doubt that the army and the security services used torture from an early point in the fighting and at various points thereafter. As for the efficacy of the practice, a postwar internal study by the Deuxième Bureau was unambiguous: The use of torture during interrogations of Viet Minh prisoners did not improve the quality of the intelligence provided.

For the Expeditionary Corps, as for the Americans two decades later, it was all intensely frustrating—the enemy's elusiveness, his capacity for surprise and for striking at any moment, and the impossibility much of the time of telling friend from foe. It was a war without fronts, where the enemy was everywhere and nowhere at the same time. Time and again French units would move into a target area in force, only to find no one there; the adversary had vanished, as if vaporized. So the French would pull out—for they had not nearly enough troops to occupy permanently the sites they had taken—and the Viet Minh would return, as swiftly as they had left. Whenever a French commander did choose to occupy a locale, he invariably found it isolated and hard to supply, his troops doomed to defensive action or to no action at all, and limited in their control to the small area immediately surrounding their base. Not only that, each soldier used for such occupations was one fewer combatant available for large-scale action against the main centers of Viet Minh power.

The numbers just didn't add up. General Leclerc, who went to Indochina on a brief inspection tour at the start of 1947, returned to the metropole filled with foreboding, telling associates that France would need a minimum of five hundred thousand troops to subjugate a people so committed to their independence. Such a figure being utterly impossible, for logistical as well as political reasons, the general concluded that "the major problem from now on is political." A French Foreign Legion officer who refused to be identified told *The New York Times* in the same week that France faced an unwinnable war against an elusive adversary. He echoed Leclerc's claim that Paris had far too few boots on the ground in Vietnam, and he noted that "the Annamese are better organized than is the French Army for war in Indo-China." The same sentiments were expressed by midlevel British and American officials. Abbot Low Moffat of the U.S. State Department, for example, told a senior British diplomat over dinner in Singapore that France was headed for disaster.[21]

No doubt the foregoing litany of obstacles in the path of success stands out more sharply in retrospect than it did at the time. Hindsight can distort; prophets become prophets only in time. Alongside the gloomy prognostications of Abbot Low Moffat and other skeptics could be placed other contemporaneous judgments, also plausible, that emphasized the precariousness of the Viet Minh's position. Ho Chi Minh himself succumbed to such concern on occasion, as did Giap. The French, after all, had scored big victories in the first months of 1947, and they could conceivably have had more, had not the monsoon season intervened and compelled Valluy to lie low for the summer months. Their firepower vastly exceeded that of the Viet Minh, who also lacked supplies and medicines, and whose commanders had woefully little battlefield experience. Internationally, the sympathy that many felt for the Vietnamese revolutionary cause had not translated into tangible—whether material or diplomatic—support.

Even in domestic political terms, there were questions. It was not yet certain that Ho and his colleagues would be able to fully harness the seething anti-French opinion prevalent among large majorities of Vietnamese and turn it into deep and lasting support for the DRV. The embryonic state launched in 1945 remained in many respects just that: embryonic. How to create a state apparatus that would enable the center to direct and coordinate regional affairs remained, in many ways, a problem to be solved.

III

CERTAINLY, FEW IN METROPOLITAN FRANCE IN EARLY 1947 BE-lieved their country was heading over a cliff in Indochina. For one thing, the newspapers they read each day tended to present a very different picture of developments on the ground. None of the Parisian dailies had a correspondent anywhere in Indochina in those early months, and colonial officials in Hanoi and Saigon therefore found it easy to transmit only an official version of events—one that emphasized Viet Minh perfidy and French restraint, and that blamed Ho Chi Minh both for the outbreak of fighting and for the failure of diplomacy. And anyway, hadn't Valluy racked up victory after victory in the early fighting? Though a few publications geared to the intelligentsia, such as Jean-Paul Sartre's *Les Temps Modernes,* condemned the government's resort to war in Indochina, public opinion surveys showed little support for early withdrawal. Most politicians too were united around the proposition that France must not quit Indochina—such a course, many parliamentarians declared, would only cause the Americans to come in and establish an economic stranglehold over the territory. France, many on both the left and the right declared, still had a *mission civilisatrice* to play in the region.[22]

Stirrings of unrest in various parts of the empire also caused officials to wish to clamp down in Indochina. The Ministry of Overseas France became convinced that North African, Malagasy, and Vietnamese nationalists planned to foment rebellions to throw off the colonial state. In this "atmosphere of imperial paranoia" (as historian Martin Thomas calls it), local administrations acquired increased latitude to suppress any dissent.[23] Often they took full advantage. In the Madagascar rebellion, for example, French authorities depicted the leaders of the Mouvement démocratique de la rénovation malgache (MDRM) in the most sinister terms possible and ordered a staggeringly brutal military retribution, much of it administered by the Expeditionary Force bound for Indochina. The massacre, combined with extreme deprivation, killed an estimated one hundred thousand Madagascans, a figure acknowledged and then withdrawn by French officials in 1949.

And yet in March 1947, as the National Assembly took up the issue of military expenditures, one could detect the beginnings of a serious rift over Indochina. In January, Premier Paul Ramadier, a Socialist whose government inaugurated the Fourth Republic, had received almost unanimous support in the Assembly for his policy of establishing security and order before entering talks with "representative" Vietnamese; now that support was splintering. The Communists (PCF), having moved in previous weeks to a confrontationist posture on a range of domestic and foreign policy issues, called for immediate and serious negotiations—involving mutual concessions—with the Viet Minh. The desire on the part of the Vietnamese for independence was completely understandable, party spokesmen declared, and they blasted High Commissioner d'Argenlieu for contributing to the outbreak of warfare with his various violations of the March 6 Accords. On the right the MRP, led by Maurice Schumann, pointed to Valluy's success in securing control of the major population centers and communication links in Tonkin and called for a continued application of a *politique de force*. The Viet Minh should be crushed, Schumann declared, and there could be no compromise agreement with Ho Chi Minh.

In between these extremes, the Socialists groped for a middle way but in effect endorsed the MRP line. Ramadier pledged to seek a negotiated settlement and to end the war swiftly, but he heaped scorn on the traitorous Viet Minh and their "criminal" leader. Overseas Minister Moutet vigorously asserted France's right to be in Indochina and continued to blame the Viet Minh for the failure to achieve a political solution. France, he thundered on the floor of the Assembly chamber, would never accept a settlement imposed by violence. Or, it seemed, any settlement involving Ho Chi Minh: When the Viet Minh leader proposed reopening talks on the basis of the restoration of the status quo ante bellum, Ramadier offered an immediate and categorical no. Paul Reynaud, the prime minister at the time of the defeat in 1940 who now sat as an Independent, won broad backing for his claim that if France left this "admirable balcony on the Pacific," she would cease to be a great power.[24]

So stormy did some of the sessions get that blows were exchanged, not only in the corridors but on one occasion in the chamber itself. The Socialist reformer Maurice Viollette, having advocated broad concessions to the Viet Minh, was punched to the ground by angry deputies from the opposition benches. On three separate occasions, the Communists walked out. Tensions reached a fever pitch when Reynaud, reading from a document purportedly showing that one of Ho Chi Minh's representatives in Paris, Duong Bach Mai, was responsible for atrocities committed against Frenchmen in Indochina, was told by a deputy that this man was present in the public gallery at that very moment. Amid cries of "This is the criminal!" and "Arrest him!" the session had to be suspended. Duong Bach Mai was soon detained and deported to Vietnam.[25]

The government's aggressive posture prevailed in the March parliamentary debate in good part because hard-liners occupied the key positions in the French policy-making structure—as they would for much of the war. Though a dozen prime ministers came and went between September 1944 and mid-1950, only two men—Georges Bidault and Robert Schuman, both of them militant on Indochina—presided over the Foreign Ministry. Likewise, the two most important ambassadors, Henri Bonnet in Washington and René Massigli in London, hewed close to the MRP line on foreign policy in general and on Indochina in particular. The same was true of the Socialist Moutet at the Ministry of Overseas France, as well as his successor (in November 1947) Paul Coste-Floret of the MRP.[26]

The real problem for the government, in terms of managing opinion on Indochina in 1947, was not at home but abroad. Neither the Soviet Union nor Great Britain nor the United States had tried hard to prevent the outbreak of war in late 1946; in 1947, all three continued to tread warily, a reality that worked to the general advantage of France. To the relief of Paris leaders—and to Ho Chi Minh's intense disappointment—Joseph Stalin remained primarily concerned with keeping Soviet relations with France on a smooth plane, and he avoided expressing any open support for the DRV. The British too could be counted on to continue to affirm French sovereignty over Indochina; London officials might urge restraint, might recommend that Paris avoid undue provocations and work toward a "political solution," but they would not do more, concerned as they were with maintaining dominion over their own colonial holdings. They indeed faced growing turmoil of their own in the region: In Malaya, postwar economic and political dislocation had generated labor unrest and a deep sense of alienation among the Chinese community.

The United States was another story. French mistrust of American intentions ran deep, both among *colons* and among officials in the metropole. There was the suspicion, expressed in the March parliamentary debate and in the press, that Washington sought to displace France and incorporate Indochina within its growing economic empire. There was the persistent fear that the U.S. military would tighten restrictions on the Paris government's ability to transfer American-built military equipment to the Far East. And most of all there was the worry that American leaders would act on their deeply held anticolonial instincts and promote a settlement of the war that would force a French departure from Indochina. Already, it seemed, the Truman administration was moving to oppose any effort by the Dutch to use military means to restore control in Java; could Indochina be next? From Washington, Bonnet said that the Truman administration would likely stick to its policy of noninterference in Indochina in the short term, but he warned darkly that "circumstances could change," on account of Americans' innate "Puritanism" and overbearing sense of "superior moral duty." Or as Reynaud put it on the floor of the Chamber: The task of "the colonizing peoples" of the world was now more difficult, on account of Americans' hostility to the enterprise.[27]

IV

THE OLD MAN KNEW WHEREOF HE SPOKE: A BROAD CONSENSUS existed in American officialdom that colonialism was a spent force in world affairs. But the divisions of old—between conservatives (many of them Europeanists in the State Department), who thought it essential to preserve close ties to France, if necessary by tacitly supporting her policy in Indochina, and liberals (predominantly Asianists), who believed that war would only radicalize Vietnamese nationalists and make compromise more difficult—had not gone away. More than many histories of the period have suggested, planners were divided about the proper American course of action.[28] But just as in France, albeit for different reasons, the conservatives ultimately triumphed, in large measure because of senior officials' growing tendency in early 1947 to see Indochina in the context of the deepening confrontation with the Soviet Union. "The Cold War," as Walter Lippmann would christen this conflict that year, would continue to shape U.S. policy choices on Vietnam for the next quarter-century (and not merely in geopolitical terms; the domestic political Cold War, as we shall see, mattered enormously).

Soviet-American relations had deteriorated sharply by mid-1946; the wartime Grand Alliance was but a fading memory. Few close observers were all that surprised. Even before World War II had ended, perceptive analysts anticipated that the United States and the Soviet Union would seek to fill the power vacuum sure to follow the armistice, and that friction would result. The two countries had a history of hostility and tension, and both were militarily powerful. Most of all, they were divided by sharply differing political economies with widely divergent needs, and by a deep ideological chasm. Sure enough, in 1946 and early 1947, Moscow and Washington clashed over a range of issues: over European reconstruction, over the division of Germany, over Iran, and over the civil war in Greece. Harry Truman, warned by leading GOP senator Arthur Vandenberg that he would have to "scare the hell out of the American people" to gain congressional approval for a $400 million aid package for Greece and Turkey, delivered an alarmist speech in March 1947 intended to stake out the American role in the postwar

world. Communism, the president declared, fed on economic dislocation and imperiled the world. "If Greece should fall under the control
of an armed minority," he gravely concluded in an early version of the
domino theory, "the effect upon its neighbor Turkey, would be immediate and serious. Confusion and disorder might well spread throughout
the entire Middle East."[29]

Then the key sentence in what came to be called the Truman Doctrine: "I believe it must be the policy of the United States to support free
peoples who are resisting attempted subjugation by armed minorities or
by outside pressures." Never mind that the Soviet Union was little involved in the Greek civil war, that the Communists in Greece were more
pro-Tito than pro-Stalin, and that the resistance movement had non-
Communist as well as Communist members. And never mind that the
Soviets were not threatening Turkey at the time. Congress approved the
funds, and the United States was launched on the construction of an international economic and defensive network to protect American prosperity and security and to advance U.S. hegemony.

Truman's globalism encountered prominent critics, among them former vice president Henry Wallace, isolationist senator Robert A. Taft,
and columnist Walter Lippmann, who warned variously that the policy
would bankrupt the Treasury and that it marked a misreading of both
Soviet capabilities and intentions.[30] The critique failed to find traction
in the halls of power in Washington, for by spring 1947, Soviet hostility
was a staple of both policy documents and much journalistic reporting.
Equally important in historical terms and for Vietnam policy in particular, by then there was no mistaking the growing salience of apocalyptic
anti-Communism in American political discourse. In March, Truman
created the Federal Employee Loyalty Program, which gave government
security officials authorization to screen two million employees of the
federal government for any hint of political deviance. It marked the beginning of an anti-Communist crusade inside the United States that par-
alleled the Cold War abroad and had no real likeness anywhere else in the
Western world, in either scope or intensity.[31] More and more, a staunch
and undifferentiated anti-Communism became the required posture
of all aspiring politicians, whether Republican or Democrat; more and

more, alternative visions for relations with Moscow were deemed illegitimate.

In response to this emerging U.S.-Soviet confrontation and this changing American mood, French leaders shifted their public diplomacy on Indochina. In Vietnam, Admiral Thierry d'Argenlieu early in the year moved what was then still a localized and strictly Franco-Vietnamese conflict to the highest international level, that of East versus West, Communism versus anti-Communism. Long convinced that Washington and Moscow would clash on the world stage, the admiral now told anyone who would listen that Ho and the Viet Minh were mere pawns in Stalin's struggle for world supremacy. France, he vowed, would never allow the Sovietization of a people it had nurtured and defended for decades, and he called Indochina a key battle in the West's emerging struggle with Moscow.[32]

That basic message, articulated also by other French officials—though not by all; General Leclerc said in January that "anticommunism will be a useless tool as long as the problem of nationalism remains unresolved"—found a receptive audience in Washington. Despite the fact that the State Department saw no evidence of mass popular support for Communism within Vietnam, and further that it was not ideology but a desire for independence and a hatred of the French that drove the unrest, the principals in U.S. decision making proceeded on the basis of worst-case assumptions. Dean Acheson, the undersecretary of state and a figure of growing influence at Foggy Bottom, said that while the Viet Minh had never acknowledged any connection to the Kremlin, neither had they explicitly denied such a tie. Other U.S. analysts noted Ho Chi Minh's training in Moscow in the 1920s and speculated that the Soviet government was cleverly concealing its involvement in Southeast Asian nationalist movements. Here again the lack of evidence for such involvement did not seem to matter, as skeptics were given the impossible task of proving a negative, of proving Soviet noninvolvement. Even liberals, who surmised (correctly) that France was using the Communist bogey to justify a war undertaken for other reasons, feared that Moscow would seek to exploit the situation if the fighting grew more bloody; hence their push for a serious U.S. effort at facilitating a negotiated settlement. Such a settlement would undercut the appeal of radicalism within Vietnam and at the same time deny the Soviets a propaganda advantage.[33]

As before, American strategists also feared the effects in France herself of a French defeat in Indochina. To oppose Dutch efforts to use military force to subdue nationalists in Java was one thing—the Netherlands was a minor player on the European stage. France was different. Might a defeat cause Western-oriented moderates to lose their grip on power in Paris and enhance the prestige of the Soviet-supported PCF, maybe even bring that party to power? The thought gave the Truman team heartburn and made them reluctant to quibble with Paris over its pursuit of a military solution in far-off Southeast Asia. True, these men acknowledged, Stalin was not actively engaged in fomenting revolution in France and indeed kept the PCF at arm's length, but this was only because he sought to avoid an international crisis while the future of Germany remained an open question; once that issue was resolved, he would surely turn his focus to France.

But senior officials were loath to simply throw U.S. support behind Valluy's war effort. They ruled out direct assistance to the military campaign and told Paris planners that any attempt to reconquer Vietnam by force of arms would be wrongheaded. At the same time, they knew full well that a sizable chunk of the unrestricted U.S. economic assistance to France ($1.9 billion between July 1945 and July 1948) was being used to pay war costs. General George C. Marshall, the new secretary of state and a man attuned to the complexities of Asian revolutionary wars (he had recently been a mediator between the Chinese Nationalists and Communists), showed this high-level ambivalence in a cable to ambassador to France Jefferson Caffery in February, in which he instructed the diplomat to discuss Indochina with French leaders. "On the one hand," Marshall wrote, "we have only the friendliest feelings toward France and we are anxious in every way we can to support France in her fight to regain her economic, political, and military strength and to restore herself as in fact one of [the] major powers of [the] world." In spite of any misunderstanding that might have arisen in the minds of the French in regard to the U.S. position concerning Indochina, "they must appreciate that we have fully recognized France's sovereign position in that area and we do not wish to have it appear that we are in any way endeavoring [to] undermine that position."

On the other hand, Caffery was not one to shy away from criticizing French policy: "We cannot shut our eyes to the fact that there are two sides to this problem and that our reports indicate both a lack of French understanding of [the] other side (more in Saigon than in Paris) and continued existence of a dangerously outmoded colonial outlook and methods in the area. Furthermore, there is no escape from the fact that the trend of the times is to the effect that colonial empires in the XIX century sense are rapidly becom[ing] a thing of the past."

Marshall acknowledged the French claim that Ho Chi Minh had "direct Communist connections" and further that Washington did not wish to see a colonial administration supplanted by one controlled by the Kremlin. But he insisted—along with State Department liberals such as Moffat and Kenneth Landon—that the Vietnamese nationalists were motivated not by Marxist ideology but by a thirst for national independence. Should another government make a push for a UN diplomatic initiative, the general said, the United States would therefore have no option but to grant her support.

What, then, should be Caffery's final recommendation to his French interlocutors? There was none. Marshall could only throw up his hands as he concluded, in a startling admission of impotence: "Frankly, we have no solution [to the] problem to suggest."[34]

Washington's continuing indecision left the initiative to the French. But Paris leaders knew they had merely dodged a bullet, and that they still had a job to do in overcoming opposition to their policy within the British and especially the American policy-making establishments. "It appears that the Indochina affair must now be dealt with not so much on its actual merits but even more so by taking account of the likely international impacts and consequences," Jean Chauvel of the Foreign Ministry wrote in February.[35]

Ho Chi Minh would not have put it much differently. From the start, the veteran revolutionary had understood the importance of gaining foreign support for his cause; now, with the military situation developing into an uneasy stalemate and with the enemy still holding the advantage by many indices of power, he thought it more vital still. Thus far France had played her political hand better than his DRV, he knew—Paris had secured a hands-off policy from all the major powers and the tacit backing of some of them, while his government fought alone. This, he determined, had to change.

Diplomacy, that is to say, was about to assume new importance, for both sides. It would do so, however, in the context of a deepening rift in the global arena between East and West, this new thing called the Cold War.

CHAPTER 8

"IF I ACCEPTED THESE TERMS I'D BE A COWARD"

"WOULD YOU ACCEPT THESE TERMS IF YOU WERE IN MY PLACE?" Ho Chi Minh asked the Frenchman who had come to talk peace with him at his headquarters in Thai Nguyen, forty-five miles north of Hanoi. It was near midnight on May 14, 1947, and the visitor had just arrived after a two-day trek through the threatening Viet Minh–controlled terrain, armed with a new French proposal for a diplomatic settlement of the war.

He had been sent by Émile Bollaert, who some weeks earlier had replaced the notorious Admiral Georges Thierry d'Argenlieu as high commissioner in Indochina. The "bloody monk," widely believed to have sparked the war with his aggressive actions in 1946, had become a liability in France's efforts to create international legitimacy for her actions against the Viet Minh. His bombastic pronouncements, his rigid views, his thinly veiled anti-Americanism—it all proved too much for planners in Paris, not to mention American and British diplomats in Vietnam. Bollaert, a civilian with minimal background in foreign affairs, would be different, French officials promised, much more subtle and "constructive" than his predecessor had been. Hardly a revealing assertion, skeptics replied. Who wouldn't be?[1]

Bollaert's first charge: to reopen talks with the Viet Minh. The move was undertaken partly for domestic political reasons—the Ramadier government wanted to show its Socialist members that contact with Ho was being maintained—and partly in order to show Americans and others in the world community that France really desired a political settlement. Bollaert assured U.S. ambassador Jefferson Caffery even before leaving for Vietnam that there could be no return to "previous colonial practices" and that Paris was committed to finding a peaceful resolution to the struggle. He repeated the vow when Ho Chi Minh in April formally proposed peace talks with a view to a cease-fire. But in fact few French policy makers were willing to compromise or to abandon the essence of "previous colonial practices." Victory, after all, was within grasp. "There is no military problem any longer in Indochina," Paul Coste-Floret, the minister of war, boasted in May. "The success of French arms is complete." (But didn't the Viet Minh control huge swaths of territory in Tonkin and Annam? a skeptical reporter asked. Yes, Coste-Floret allowed, but the territory in question was sparsely populated and would count for little in the end.) "Talks" with Ho Chi Minh were fine, he and others believed, so long as they concerned the modalities of the Viet Minh's surrender.[2]

For the mission to Ho's jungle headquarters, Bollaert selected one of his most knowledgeable political advisers, a scholar and teacher who enjoyed considerable respect among many Vietnamese for his knowledge of the country and who ranks as one of the most extraordinary figures in our story. Paul Léon Joseph Mus was born at his parents' home in Bourges in central France on June 1, 1902. He came of age in World War I–era Hanoi, his father having been in charge of establishing a Western education system to impart French technical expertise and traditions to elite Vietnamese youths. In 1907, the elder Mus opened the Collège du protectorat, later known as the École normale, from which a dozen years later his son would graduate. A child of empire, Paul was then an unquestioning believer in France's civilizing mission, and through the 1930s, he wrote nothing critical of colonialism in Indochina or the empire—nothing, for example, about the bloody repression of the peasant uprisings in Nghe Tinh province in 1930–31, which occurred while he was in Vietnam as an officer-reservist in the Indochinese colonial army.[3]

The Second World War, however, changed him. When the Nazis invaded, he was back in France, commanding a platoon of colonial machine gunners and peasant-soldiers at Valvin and Sully-sur-Loire. His actions earned him the Croix de Guerre. When he joined de Gaulle's Free French movement in 1942, Mus's Indochina expertise made him a prime candidate to conduct clandestine activities in Indochina. And so, in January 1945 he parachuted into Tonkin to contact the resistance and rally Vietnamese to the Free French cause. He was in Hanoi on the night of March 9, when the Japanese launched their *coup de force*. Under disguise, Mus managed to escape the city and make his way through two hundred and fifty miles of hostile territory—all of it on foot, and having to rely on Vietnamese villagers for shelter and travel guidance—before linking up with French colonial troops retreating into southern China. That September he accompanied General Leclerc's delegation to the Japanese surrender ceremony in Tokyo Bay, and then in the autumn participated in Leclerc's reoccupation of Cochin China.[4]

Already in 1945, in a remarkable report he titled "Note sur la crise morale franco-indochinoise," Mus emphasized the profound sense of patriotism and national identity animating the Vietnamese. This moral fervor, he plainly implied, was as deep as that felt by Frenchmen living under the yoke of the Nazi occupation, and it had moved Vietnamese to resist foreign occupation throughout their history. "In short, what the Vietnamese have preserved, through all the vicissitudes of their history, is a community of blood, of language, of sentiment," Mus wrote. "One can say that this is their essential milieu and one from which the Annamite never willingly distances himself for any length of time. For anyone who is familiar with this people, the background to this state of things, the model that is more or less unconscious, yet a concrete manifestation of this communitarian ideal, is the village. This is the form in which the Annamite lives as a social being, and the basis of his patriotism."[5]

For Mus, it was no longer possible by war's end to hold easy assumptions concerning the French Empire and its legitimacy. How, he wondered, could one justify a colonial system that placed some men above others, particularly when those others resisted it? More specifically, how could one support a French effort to reclaim control over Indochina—by force if necessary—in view of the nationalist fervor sweeping the land? The questions gnawed at Mus's sensibility. Though he was not yet prepared to advocate an immediate and unilateral French withdrawal from Indochina, he began to imagine a new, postcolonial order, in which all men would have to be seen as equals, in which the Vietnamese demand for independence would be met.

By early 1947, when Mus agreed to become Bollaert's political adviser, he hoped there might yet be time to avert an all-out war. But even before he set out for Ho Chi Minh's headquarters in the second week of May—as in March 1945, he traveled on foot, this time some forty miles over narrow paths and through Viet Minh–controlled territory—that hope must have been largely dashed, in view of the talking points he had been given. He was to inform Ho that France would agree to a cease-fire if the Viet Minh laid down their weapons, allowed French troops to circulate freely in areas they presently held, and arranged for the handover of numerous Foreign Legion deserters.

Mus had ample time to contemplate these terms on his trek and also to decide how he should begin the encounter. He opted to greet Ho with a simple *"Comment allez-vous?"* (How are you?) and to see how the Viet Minh leader answered. At three A.M. on May 12, he was brought into Ho Chi Minh's presence and offered his greeting. *"Suffisament bien"* (Well enough) came the reply, which Mus thought was hardly the word choice of a man inclined to bow to a French ultimatum. Sure enough, as Mus laid out the specifics of the French proposal, he could see he was getting nowhere. "In the French Union there is no place for cowards," Ho said after he had finished. "If I accepted these conditions I would be one." Mus did not disagree. When Ho asked if Mus would accept the terms if the positions were reversed, he could only answer no. And with that, the session ended. The champagne bottle that Ho Chi Minh had set aside in the event of a successful meeting remained unopened, and Mus soon set off on the long walk back to Hanoi. He was despondent but could not help but admire the veteran revolutionary's unshakable determination. The mission, he later recalled, taught him "more than in thirty years elsewhere about what a people could wish for and accomplish."[6]

After Paul Mus's visit, no non-Communist Westerner is believed to have seen Ho Chi Minh in the jungle until midway through 1954. By then the French war had ended in defeat and Paul Mus had published a classic study of contemporary Vietnam, a dense, convoluted, mesmerizing work titled *Viêt-Nam: sociologie d'une guerre* (1952).[7] His stature in Vietnamese studies would be enormous, perhaps unmatched anywhere in the Western world, and he would hold joint professorial appointments at the Collège de France and Yale University (alternating semesters between the two institutions). But long before that, indeed already now in the spring of 1947, Mus had drawn three major conclusions: that Ho was the undisputed leader of the Viet Minh; that Ho had an almost serene confidence in the Viet Minh's revolutionary program; and that this program had already accomplished an enormous amount in the countryside through which Mus was passing. French forces might be able to reoccupy these regions, the Frenchman reasoned, but they could never achieve lasting control over them. Why? Because France had already lost the battle that counted most: the battle for the support of the local population. Peasants by the tens of thousands were innocently working their fields by day, then turning into guerrillas after dark, engaging in sabotage and bolstering the fortunes of Viet Minh regular forces. How could France prevail in such a struggle? She could not. Already in 1947, Mus believed that it would be a war for people rather than for territory, and that the Viet Minh would be supreme.[8]

II

IRONICALLY, MUS FELT MORE CONFIDENCE ON THESE POINTS THAN did Ho Chi Minh himself. The onetime playwright had shown again that he was a pretty fair actor—but his steely determination in the Frenchman's presence that night masked deep trepidations about the road ahead. No doubt Mus was right that politics would win out, that people mattered more than territory, and that the revolutionary forces had inherent advantages at the local level, where the mass of Vietnamese lived, that the colonials could never hope to match. But would it be enough? What about the colossal French superiority in military firepower, so transparent in the fighting to this point? To overcome this element, Ho Chi Minh believed he would need political strength of a very different kind. He would need support abroad, in France and among the great powers on the world stage.

Yet here too the enemy was stronger. Ever since 1940, France had shown remarkable diplomatic prowess amid geopolitical weakness, first by maintaining day-to-day sovereignty in Indochina and then, after Japan's defeat, gaining broad international backing to reclaim full colonial control. Most recently, during the fall crisis and the outbreak of war, she had convinced the great powers to maintain a hands-off posture.

The revolutionary government, by stark contrast, had achieved precious little. It fought alone, militarily and politically, isolated from potential allies in the Communist and non-Communist world. In the late summer of 1945, when Ho Chi Minh declared Vietnamese independence, his movement had no substantial contact with the Communist parties in Europe and Moscow or even with Mao Zedong's forces, then holed up in far-off Yan'an and Manchuria. The situation was much the same two years later. From time to time, the Soviet Union meekly advised Paris against reestablishing old-style colonialism in Indochina and urged the two sides to find "common ground," but she would go no further. Stalin remained suspicious of Ho Chi Minh's ideological bona fides—especially following Ho's tactical decision in late 1945 to dissolve the Indochinese Communist Party—and he was in any event much more interested in Europe, the heart of the emerging Cold War, where he hoped to see the French Communist Party take power and help block American expansion. Stalin needed no convincing by PCF leaders that they had to tread carefully on the Indochinese war, lest they be accused of treason for undermining the army's efforts to restore *La plus grande France*. Only with the PCF's expulsion from the ruling coalition in the spring of 1947 did party leaders begin to hum a different tune; but even then they could offer little more than internal party resolutions in favor of early negotiations and the withdrawal of French troops. The Chinese Communists, meanwhile, were too busy fighting Chiang Kai-shek's government forces in northern China and Manchuria in early 1947 to offer the DRV much tangible support.[9]

Nor could Ho claim meaningful support from the non-Communist world. Nationalist leaders in India and Southeast Asia offered pledges of moral support, but these affirmations, though welcome, carried little practical import. Hardly anyone in the major world capitals paid attention in January 1947 when Pandit Nehru, then vice president of the self-declared Indian interim government and its minister for external affairs, publicly appealed to France to "revert to peaceful methods in Indo-China." Fewer still took note of Burmese nationalist leader Aung San's declaration, also in January, that it was "necessary for all the states of Asia to assist" the Vietnamese in their fight. In London, where officials *did* make note of these pronouncements by two colonial subjects, the response was distinctly cool. The new anticolonial agitation sweeping Asia had to be delicately handled, these planners agreed, and made impossible any large-scale British support for the French war effort. But their bedrock outlook had not changed: Britain still had a strong interest in propping up French rule in Indochina. Quietly, British authorities in Malaya squashed an attempt to organize a volunteer force to fight alongside the Viet Minh, while in India they successfully discouraged the dispatch of a joint Indo-Burmese force.

That left the United States. No nation mattered more in the international arena, in Ho Chi Minh's eyes; none had more power to thwart French designs and to facilitate a settlement leading to Vietnamese independence. For that matter, his government probably had more anticolonialist sympathy in American circles than elsewhere, at least among the big players. But sympathy gets you only so far. What matters in the end is active support, and here Washington had offered almost nothing since those heady days in Pac Bo in the summer of 1945, when Americans and Vietnamese seemed to be in full accord, marching together for the cause of Vietnamese independence. Back then Franklin Roosevelt's anticolonial fervor, and in particular his aversion to any French attempt to reclaim Indochina, still seemed to animate U.S. policy. No longer.

But perhaps there was still hope. The French were plainly still nervous about the depth and extent of America's support, and maybe with good reason: Americans still seemed to adhere, on some level, to a reflexive egalitarianism in world affairs, to an opposition to imperialism. Perhaps this could be exploited, Ho and his lieutenants believed. In the spring of 1947, while Paul Mus readied to make his trek to Ho's headquarters, the Viet Minh leader sent his personal envoy, Pham Ngoc Thach, a physician who would later serve as Ho's personal doctor, to Bangkok to stress to American diplomats stationed there the moderate nature of the Vietnamese revolution and the opportunities that would be available to U.S. investors following independence. Vietnam would not be Communist for decades, Thach assured these men, and even then the government would be a moderate, inclusive, nationally oriented one. Communism in Vietnam, as it had existed since the early 1930s, he even said at one point, "is nothing more than a means of arriving at independence." And Americans could feel confident about the DRV's economic program: "The communist ministers . . . favor the development of capitalist autonomy and call on foreign capital for the reconstruction of the country." U.S. firms could expect to get special privileges, Thach went on, including tax and other concessions, and American tourists would find postcolonial Vietnam "an ideal place" to visit.[10]

In July, having failed to elicit the desired American response, Thach turned still more pragmatic. "We recognize the world-politics of the U.S. at this time does not permit taking a position against the French," he now acknowledged. But the Truman administration could nevertheless help by providing economic and cultural assistance to Vietnam, and by endeavoring to mediate the conflict either through tripartite discussions or through having the newly independent Philippines take the Vietnamese case before the United Nations. That same month Ho Chi Minh made a further gesture designed partly to conciliate Americans and other non-Communist observers abroad: He reshuffled his government, replacing three Communist ministers (including Giap as defense minister, though he remained battlefield commander) with non-Communists who supported his policies.[11]

The efforts were for naught—once again. What for Ho constituted an urgent need ranked far down on the list of priorities for an American administration confronting a deepening Cold War in Europe. The top foreign policy minds in Washington that summer were focused on winning congressional approval for and then implementing the Marshall Plan (formally the European Recovery Program), a massive loan program designed to help resuscitate the war-ravaged economies of Western Europe and thereby check Soviet expansion. France occupied a key place in the plan, and U.S. planners were as disinclined as ever to potentially destabilize French politics by taking an aggressively anticolonial position vis-à-vis Indochina. When Secretary of State George Marshall in July asked Vietnam- and France-based diplomats for an assessment of the DRV, should Paris be compelled to recognize Ho's government as the legitimate ruling body in Vietnam, he got a range of appraisals. Some argued for taking Pham Ngoc Thach at his word and denied that the DRV was squarely in the Soviet camp. Others maintained just as strongly that Ho Chi Minh was wholly committed to the Kremlin's cause and could not be trusted.

U.S. policy did not change. There would be no American-led mediation, no congressional aid package, no talks to discuss future trade concessions for American companies. As summer turned into fall, the

Truman administration chose to remain where it had been when the fighting began: on the sidelines, torn between a desire to buck up a crucial ally in Europe and a conviction that it must not associate itself closely with that ally's colonial war. Paris officials, eager as always to head off any American "meddling" on Indochina, breathed a sigh of relief.

It was a bitter pill for Ho to swallow, not least because he knew the taste so well. He responded by redoubling his efforts to strengthen contacts with the French Communists and with Moscow. In September, the indefatigable Pham Ngoc Thach, fresh off his efforts with the Americans in Bangkok, traveled to Europe as Ho's special envoy. He met with PCF leaders Jacques Duclos and Maurice Thorez, but he appears to have made no headway—Duclos impressed upon him the importance of Vietnam doing her utmost in the struggle for liberation, to which Thach replied that it was a shame the PCF had done so little to try to prevent the war. The Soviets too were more or less unresponsive. A measure of the importance they attached to Thach's mission is that they chose not to bring him to the Kremlin to meet with senior officials; he got only an audience in Bern, with the Soviet ambassador to Switzerland. When Thach asked the ambassador if a later visit to Moscow might be possible, he received a noncommittal reply. No invitation ever came.[12]

III

THE DANGER FOR HO IN THESE CONTINUING DIPLOMATIC FAILURES was not merely that they perpetuated the Viet Minh's international isolation, ensuring that the war would continue and that Giap's forces would be fighting alone. They also risked undermining his personal as well as his government's authority at home. If he could not convince most audiences abroad that the DRV was the sole and legitimate government of Vietnam, over time more and more domestic voices would have their own doubts on that score. Ho knew it, and his Vietnamese rivals knew it.

The French knew it too. More and more, as 1947 progressed, they pondered a tantalizing question: What if you could win the people's allegiance away from the Viet Minh? Many Vietnamese, after all, northern as well as southern, did not support Ho's revolution, were anti-Communist, and loathed Vo Nguyen Giap's capacity for ruthlessness and repression. Could they be persuaded to coalesce around another Vietnamese leader who, if not exactly pro-French, would be less hostile to France's aims? Senior strategists, led by Léon Pignon, thought so. Even as they rejected genuine negotiations with the Viet Minh and disavowed full independence for Vietnam, they cast about for such a figure, who would simultaneously draw support away from Ho Chi Minh and win favor with the Americans, and in the process win greater support for the war effort in the French Assembly, where many Socialists and all Communists were clamoring for an end to the fighting through negotiations with Ho. The move could also alter views elsewhere in Asia, where many national leaders condemned France for engaging in what they saw as naked colonial aggression.[13]

One name stood out: Bao Dai, the portly, fleshy thirty-four-year-old former emperor who had abdicated during the August Revolution in 1945. If he could unite all anti-Communist nationalists behind him, the Viet Minh, reduced to a mere "faction," would be forced to come to an agreement with France on French terms, or face defeat by the joint forces of the French and the Bao Dai government. If Ho refused to go along and kept fighting, the war would thenceforth not be a colonial struggle; it would be Vietnamese civil war, a war between Communism and anti-Communism, with France on the side of virtue, fighting for the Vietnamese and for the West against the Red Terror.

Thus came to the fore a rhetorical strategy from which the French would not deviate for the remainder of the war. It was disingenuous in the extreme, an ex post facto justification for a war initiated and fought on other grounds. Paris had no intention of granting the full independence that most every nationalist in Vietnam sought. But as a public rationale, the new approach was a kind of masterstroke, for it bought increased support for French aims in Vietnam and in the international community, most important in the United States. It was indeed tailor-made for American audiences. As the astute observer Philippe Devillers later said, through this "Bao Dai Solution," Paris would use anti-Communism to neutralize America's anticolonialism. An ostensibly nationalist regime would be the means by which the war against the Viet Minh would be redefined for Americans as part of the emerging struggle against Communism. And no longer would doves in Washington be able to claim that Ho Chi Minh alone represented legitimate Vietnamese nationalism.[14]

Why Bao Dai? Because he enjoyed considerable influence among Vietnamese, and because the French thought he had the attributes they particularly valued: In their eyes, he was weak and malleable, concerned principally with indulging his passions for gambling, sport, and womanizing. It didn't hurt that a number of other Vietnamese nationalists, including members of the Dai Viet and the VNQDD, expressed their support for Bao Dai against the Viet Minh, and that some leaders of the Cao Dai and Hoa Hao religious sects did the same. Ngo Dinh Diem, a prominent Catholic nationalist and later America's "miracle man" in South Vietnam, asserted that Bao Dai could produce Vietnamese independence without the "Red Terror."[15]

Bao Dai's biography allowed for these varying assessments. He had been crowned emperor upon the death of his father in 1925, at the age of twelve, whereupon he was sent to Paris for several years of schooling. He had studied music and literature, practiced tennis with French champion Henri Cochet, learned Ping-Pong and bridge, dressed in tweeds and flannels, and generally showed little inclination to return to his homeland. But return he did, formally becoming the thirteenth emperor of the Nguyen dynasty in 1932. Later he married the beautiful Mariette-Jeanne Nguyen Hui Tai Lan, the Catholic daughter of a wealthy Cochin Chinese merchant. They produced five children. To the surprise of some, Bao Dai quickly championed reforms in the judicial and educational systems and attempted to put an end to the more outdated trappings of Vietnamese royalty. He ended, for example, the ancient custom (*lay*) whereby mandarins would prostrate themselves before him with their foreheads touching the ground; thenceforth, a bow would be sufficient.[16]

But the French swiftly made clear who held the real power, and the young sovereign gave more and more attention to his leisure activities. He devoted weeks at a time to hunting expeditions in the jungle highlands, reportedly bagging single-handedly a sizable percentage of Vietnam's tigers. (He preferred to track the tigers into their dens, with a lamp attached to his head and a rifle at his side. One time, legend had it, he killed one with his bare hands.) Upon his abdication in August 1945, he became a "supreme counselor" to Ho Chi Minh, but by March 1946 he had disassociated himself from the Viet Minh and relocated to Hong Kong. A steady stream of messengers and old collaborators of the French now

BAO DAI AS A YOUNG BOY IN
PARIS, WHERE THE FRENCH
SENT HIM TO BE EDUCATED.

arrived in the British colony to urge Bao Dai to head a French-sponsored anti–Viet Minh government. Mus stopped by after his encounter with Ho, and Bollaert himself came in June. Bao Dai reacted cautiously and said he would demand of France as much as Ho demanded: the dissolution of the Cochin China government, the reunification of Vietnam under one government, and full independence.

The ex-emperor's firmness surprised Frenchmen who looked upon him as nothing more than an indolent playboy. Lazy he was, and a pleasure seeker of the first order, but he was also an intelligent man whose bland, expressionless face hid a keen political sense, a quick study who perceived immediately that Paris officials sought to use him as a means to preserve colonial control. In July 1947, he announced that he was neither for nor against Ho Chi Minh's DRV but above partisan squabbles, and he vowed that he would not return home unless his people wanted him. At the same time, a new National Union Front, composed of various anti–Viet Minh nationalist groups, urged all political, religious, and social groups to unite under Bao Dai. It exhorted the ex-emperor to lead the struggle for Vietnamese independence and unity and to fight the Communist menace.[17]

In the months that followed, Bao Dai softened his stance and moved gradually closer to the French. Bollaert, admonished during meetings in Paris not to enter negotiations with Ho, gave a major speech at Ha Dong near Hanoi in September in which he offered not independence for Vietnam but a qualified form of "liberty" within the French Union. The Vietnamese could run their own internal affairs and decide "for themselves" whether Cochin China should join the Republic of Vietnam, but France would maintain control of military, diplomatic, and economic relations. There was no room for negotiation on these points, the high commissioner added; the offer "must be rejected or accepted as a whole."[18] The Viet Minh dismissed the offer immediately, and various non-Communist nationalists denounced the speech for failing utterly to provide a rallying point for the anti–Viet Minh cause.[19] But Bao Dai—whose self-confidence always sagged at moments of crisis—indicated a willingness to deal with the French on this basis. It was a first step on the slippery road to surrender.

IV

IN RETROSPECT, WITH KNOWLEDGE OF WHAT WAS TO COME, FRANCE'S unyielding diplomatic posture in 1947 seems difficult to comprehend. But in the context of the time, it was hardly so strange. Ho Chi Minh, after all, was having minimal success winning broad international support for his cause, and French arms had scored numerous victories early in the year, before the arrival of the monsoon. Throughout the summer, many top officials continued to believe that a military solution was at hand—once General Valluy launched his fall offensive, they proclaimed, he would finish off the Viet Minh once and for all. The general did all he could to stoke this belief, and he received firm backing from War Minister Coste-Floret and Foreign Minister Bidault. On October 7, after months of careful planning and preparation, Valluy launched Operation Léa, a large-scale attack involving seventeen battalions and all the heavy equipment and modern arms the French possessed. (Almost certainly it was the largest military action in French colonial history to that point.) The principal aim was to capture the Viet Minh leadership at its headquarters in the Viet Bac and in the process destroy a sizable chunk of the Viet Minh army. In addition, Valluy hoped to isolate the Viet Minh and cut off their trading routes to southern China. In a single stroke, the war could be won, the French commander told superiors in Paris.

Immediately there were problems. Valluy's plan called for a concentric attack involving airborne, amphibious, and overland columns. But the key initial phase, involving the dropping of paratroops near the Viet Minh headquarters at Bac Kan, foundered on the inability to get the troops in place quickly enough. It took three trips and many hours to get a mere 950 parachutists to the target area, forfeiting the advantages of surprise. Even then Viet Minh leaders were initially caught flat-footed and suffered heavy casualties: Though the DRV intelligence network had gotten wind of the operation two days earlier, a communication snafu meant that the information reached Bac Kan just as the French were launching the attack. Ho and Giap managed to get away, but with only minutes to spare. They were forced to leave behind arms and munitions caches as well as stacks of secret documents. One senior DRV official, the well-known scholar Nguyen Van To, was killed by paratroopers as he tried to escape.[20]

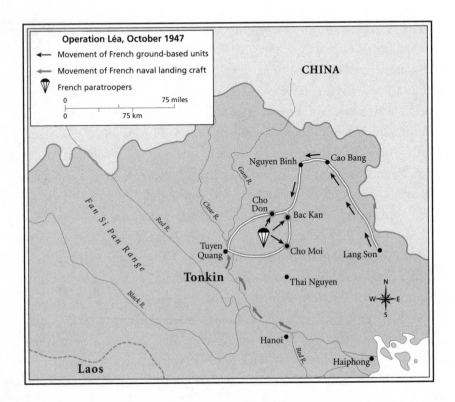

Within a day, Giap had rallied the Viet Minh troops, and they battled the airborne troops on even terms. Meanwhile, the French northern pincer—ten battalions moving by road from Lang Son to Cao Bang and from there west to Nguyen Binh and south to Bac Kan, for a total of 140 miles—bogged down on account of ambushes, blown bridges, and piano-key ditches on the roads. Not until October 13 did the task force reach the vicinity of Bac Kan, and there the Viet Minh put up fierce resistance. Only on the sixteenth did the mechanized Moroccan Colonial Infantry Regiment break through to relieve the battered and encircled paratroopers. As for the southern pincer, consisting of four battalions moving by naval landing craft up the Clear and Gam rivers, it never reached the battle zone at all; on the nineteenth, its units, having been forced by sand-bars and other obstructions to move to a land route, stumbled onto the northern task force moving south. On November 8, one month after it began, Operation Léa was called off.[21]

Valluy then launched Operation Ceinture (Belt), which was designed to squeeze—hence the name—enemy forces at the southern edge of the Viet Bac between Thai Nguyen and Tuyen Quang. Eighteen battalions, eighteen navy landing craft, and paratroops were committed to the task of crushing some of Giap's best units. The French cleared a sizable chunk of the territory and captured large stocks of supplies, but the major set-piece battle never occurred. Giap wanted no part of such an encounter. As would happen countless times over the next quarter-century—to the French and to the Americans—the enemy slipped through the lines, secure in the knowledge that he could fight another day. On December 22, the French pulled back to the lowlands except for a string of isolated border forts along the Chinese border. The Viet Minh immediately moved back into the abandoned areas.[22]

The French took comfort from the fact that they had captured the Viet Minh headquarters and killed—so they claimed—nine thousand enemy combatants. This figure was almost certainly inflated, and in any event it missed the larger point: that at the end of 1947, the position of the French outside the delta was again roughly what it had been a year before. Valluy had failed in his aim of destroying the Viet Minh with one giant stroke. It would be more accurate to say that the enemy had managed a draw, which in the circumstances was the same as a victory. Valluy now faced the reality of a long war and a Paris government that was not about to order national conscription for this faraway Asian colony.

All of which added to the French sense of urgency regarding the political sphere. Through the fall, analysts in the Colonial Ministry, led by Léon Pignon, worked feverishly to implement the Bao Dai policy. Since Bollaert's speech at Ha Dong, the courtship of Bao Dai had not yielded much in the way of results, and the French feared he might yet slip out of their reach. At times, he seemed alarmingly solicitous of the Viet Minh, speaking of them as the most vital force in the country (Ho reciprocated by saying of Bao Dai that "he may be far from us in distance, but not in our thoughts"); at other times, he seemed too chummy with the Americans—perhaps, the French worried, because he sought to use Washington to back up his demands for Vietnamese independence. After much coming and going of emissaries between Vietnam and Hong Kong, Bao Dai was persuaded to confer again with Bollaert. They met on December 7 aboard a French ship anchored in the Baie d'Along, north of Haiphong, where spectacular greenish-gray limestone cliffs rim the water. Bao Dai sought a firm French commitment to independence, but he got nothing of the kind. Unaccountably, he agreed to put his name to a "protocol" that did contain the magic word but so hedged it with qualifications that it lost all meaning.[23]

Bao Dai knew he had been had. Facing criticism from Vietnamese intellectuals of all stripes, and seeking to escape his commitment to resume his imperial duties, he fled to Europe—to Geneva, to Cannes, to Paris—where he spent his days at the bridge table (he had become an expert player) and on the tennis court and his nights at the cabaret. Whenever French officials tracked him down, he showed himself to be at once diffident and uncompromising, expressing support for negotiations but also reluctance to commit himself further without more solid guarantees. His reading of the French political scene hardly left him reassured—on the one side, the MRP as well as supporters of General de Gaulle declared the Baie d'Along deal to be too generous and independence for Vietnam out of the question; on the other, the Communists and many Socialists called for resumption of negotiations with Ho Chi Minh. None of the successive French governments—four in 1948—dared to try to force the issue.[24]

But Bollaert continued to champion the protocol, and Bao Dai eventually agreed to attend a follow-up meeting in the Baie d'Along. There, on June 8, 1948, with the ex-emperor present, Bollaert signed an accord with General Nguyen Van Xuan, former head of the "Republic of Cochin China" and now chief of the new French-sponsored Vietnamese national government. France "solemnly" recognized the independence of Vietnam within the French Union, and her right to bring about the union of the three sections of the country, but retained control over its army, finances, and foreign relations. Again Bao Dai suffered buyer's remorse and promptly turned up his nose at the new agreement. He left again for the French Riviera, declaring that he would not wear the crown until "true unity and real independence" had been achieved.

The new government's lack of credibility was starkly evident at its "grand" inaugural ceremony in Hanoi. Fewer than fifty Vietnamese were on hand—not including police and soldiers—and the event lacked any semblance of organization. General Xuan appeared in court dress and looked uncomfortable throughout. Masses of schoolchildren were herded in to wave flags and shout slogans, but this served only to accentuate the farcical nature of the event. Various receptions and dinner followed, but the air of unreality never dissipated. A British observer who took in the scene marveled at the total lack of enthusiasm, not least among the local "Annamites."[25]

Still, the moment was not without significance. The French had publicly recognized Bao Dai as a potential head of state and had explicitly promised "independence"—a pledge Ho Chi Minh had failed to extract from them at Fontainebleau two years before. In the Xuan government, moreover, Vietnam now had her first formal opposition to the Viet Minh. Might Ho Chi Minh's hold over the non-Communist nationalists now be broken, or at least seriously weakened? Ho feared as much, and he wasted no time in branding Bao Dai and those who constituted the new government as traitors. He needn't have worried. The agreement soon generated more support for the DRV than for the ex-emperor, as the *colons* in Vietnam immediately denounced Bollaert's "surrender" and said real power was and would remain in French hands, and as Paris leaders dithered over whether to extend formal ratification to the agreement. Weeks went by without even a debate in the National Assembly, and Bollaert, his frustration building by the day, eventually flew back to Vietnam without an explicit vote of confidence. Only a sense of sheer loyalty to his party kept him from staying put in France. At the end of September, he announced that he would not accept the prolongation of his appointment.[26]

The Xuan government, meanwhile, was without funds and without an army—and, in a real sense, without a leader. Nguyen Van Xuan had been educated at the prestigious École polytechnique in Paris and spent most of his life in France; French was now his language of choice. As head of Admiral d'Argenlieu's pet project, the Republic of Cochin China, he had actively worked against Vietnamese unity, and he developed a reputation for utter untrustworthiness. Charming and articulate, he devoted most of his time to scheming and conniving and developed no mass following among the Vietnamese. For many anti–Viet Minh nationalists, the Bao Dai solution in which they had put so much faith and effort now seemed like no solution at all. They grasped the obvious point: The French government, by pushing this solution without at the same time moving on decolonization, had grievously undermined their cause.

So little seemed to have changed. Wage and salary scales for French and Vietnamese remained different. A Vietnamese working for the government earned only 60 percent of the salary of a Frenchman in the same position with the same qualifications and seniority. At Le Cercle Sportif, Saigon's swank athletic club, membership was still restricted to "Europeans and assimilated," the latter being the Eurasians and the small group of Vietnamese who had become French citizens. And the leading French-language newspaper, *L'Union Française,* still carried on the top of its front page a decades-old quotation from France's great imperialist, Marshal Hubert Lyautey: "Claim the fine title of colonialist, at this time above all when a whole school seems to deny the grandeur and effectiveness of France's colonial effort."[27]

V

IN THE AUTUMN OF 1948 CAME A DEVELOPMENT THAT WOULD ALTER the calculations on all sides in both France and Vietnam and, in due course, profoundly affect the nature of the Indochina War: In China's long-running civil war, the fortunes swung sharply in favor of Mao Zedong's Communists. With the fall of Jinzhou in October, the remaining Nationalist positions in Manchuria collapsed. The following month Mao's forces prevailed in the crucial Huaihai battle in east-central China, despite the commitment of half a million Guomindang troops. By early December, Beijing and Tianjin were within reach.[28] For French war planners, the implications were obvious: A victory by Mao would inevitably strengthen Ho Chi Minh and thereby perhaps doom forever their hope of splitting the Vietnamese nationalist movement. Time was against them, they understood, and the Bao Dai solution must either be applied without delay or be overtaken by events. The new high commissioner, Léon Pignon, who unlike Bollaert was a genuine Indochina expert, had been a hard-liner on the war but now was given the pressing task of following this policy through.[29]

Adding to the French concern in 1948 were the meager economic figures and the state of the military campaign. The two were of course connected. Production in rice, rubber, coal, and cement in Indochina as a whole rose above the 1947 totals but was still far below prewar levels, chiefly owing to labor difficulties and lack of security. Chaotic and hazardous communications made it difficult to bring goods down to the ports. Consequently, Indochina still experienced a large adverse balance of trade. Whereas in 1938 rice exports had totaled 1.5 million tons, in 1948 the figure was a mere 170,000 tons. Meanwhile a French plan for the reconstruction and re-equipping of Indochina remained at an early blueprint stage.[30]

On the military side, 1948 saw no major operations of the type General Valluy attempted in the fall of 1947. The size of the Expeditionary Corps remained static at roughly one hundred thousand, which was far too few to allow large-scale engagements, or even significant penetrations into Viet Minh areas. So Valluy focused instead on holding what he had taken the previous year, including the string of frontier forts in northern Tonkin along Route Coloniale 4, which snaked along the Chinese frontier for 150 miles from Tien Yen to Cao Bang. Even this proved difficult, owing to the vulnerable lines of communication. Many posts had to be supplied by air, and road convoys were repeatedly attacked. On February 28, 1948, for example, a Foreign Legion company inching its way along the RC4 was ambushed and took 22 dead and 33 wounded—about

40 percent casualties. A few weeks later there was another such attack, and then another—by year's end, French forces suffered close to three dozen major ambushes along the RC4 alone.[31]

French commanders spent endless hours trying to find a way to thwart the ambushers. No alternative existed, they determined, but to work to open all important routes using infantry forces, and to try—at least for long convoys—to hold all hills from which fire could be brought to bear on the road. Major convoys involving two hundred or more vehicles would also be backed by several infantry battalions and artillery groups and by two squadrons of armored cars. These measures helped, but only at the margins. The attacks kept coming.

Bac Kan was a case in point. Though the French attack on the town in Operation Léa the previous fall had failed to capture the Viet Minh leadership, French commanders had noisily announced their capture of the seat of Ho's government. Bollaert boasted that the tricolor would forever fly in the town. What a difference a year made. Through the first half of 1948, the road to the garrison, covering mostly dangerous mountainous territory from Cao Bang, had been open to military convoys, though at a cost of many French lives lost and weapons captured. In August, Viet Minh forces gained control of the road; thereafter the garrison of three hundred men and a roughly equal number of civilians had to be resupplied entirely by air. And the enemy kept closing in. French outposts near Bac Kan faced frequent attacks in September and October; one of them claimed the lives of thirty legionnaires and three French officers and wounded fifty more. Bac Kan had no strategic value, but the French would lose face if they ever gave up Ho Chi Minh's former headquarters. So they grimly hung on.[32]

In the Red River Delta too, the Viet Minh maintained the pressure in 1948, launching pinprick attacks on Hanoi and its environs and doing everything possible to disrupt the flow of supplies along the vital Hanoi-Haiphong corridor. In a single three-day stretch in mid-September, four trains running from the port city to the capital were blown up using mines, causing numerous deaths and injuries, and forty-five trucks were destroyed. By October, not a drop of gasoline was available for civilians in Hanoi.[33]

In Cochin China, the security situation seemed better, at least in the major towns. The cafés along Saigon's fashionable rue Catinat remained packed with *colons* and other Westerners, with Foreign Legion officers and their women, as white-clad Vietnamese waiters hurried among the tables with glasses of cognac and Pernod. The French still lounged by the pool and played tennis at Le Cercle Sportif, still gathered at fashionable La Pagode to sip coffee and people-watch, still dined lavishly at Au Chalet. But appearances were deceptive. A midnight curfew was in effect for the city, and military trucks rumbled through the streets. Each night the sounds of fighting on Saigon's outskirts—rifle, machine gun, mortar, artillery—could be heard, and only a foolish foreigner ventured outside the city limits after nightfall. (During the day, the prudent did so only in armed convoy.) Even within the limits, the war could intrude with sudden and deadly ferocity—through a grenade attack on a café, or a roadside bombing of a French truck, or a shooting in broad daylight of a French man or woman.

"Every night the explosions, coming one after another like a stick of bombs, formed the background of the city's noise," the journalist Lucien Bodard, who was in Vietnam for much of the war, would write of the grenade attacks, which usually took place in the twilight, just after sunset. "Each outburst lasted only a few seconds; each grenade was a sharp bang, a few shrieks from those who had been hit, one or two flying shadows, and then several minutes later the klaxon of an ambulance and a police car."[34] In retaliation, French agents assassinated Viet Minh suspects and dumped their bodies on street corners as a warning to the insurgents to desist.

A young Canadian who would go on to become prime minister of his country was traveling through Asia that fall and winter. Handsome and cosmopolitan at age twenty-nine, Pierre Elliott Trudeau arrived from Thailand to find in Saigon "hate, strife, and inevitable waste of men, money, and morals." Once again, he wrote his mother, the youth of France were in uniform, fighting a war that was going "nowhere fast." Soldiers filled the streets, and people could travel only in convoys. The French held the towns and main roads while the insurgents ruled the countryside, and "nobody holds the peace, though on both sides men die, [are] wounded, suffer and atrocities are committed in the name of elusive righteousness and honor." After a brief visit to Angkor Wat,

Trudeau returned to Saigon, where he managed to get admission to Le Cercle Sportif and saw women whose "bathing suits have gone one better than those in France."[35]

Elsewhere in the south, the Viet Minh were strongly entrenched in the Plain of Reeds west of Saigon and in the Ca Mau peninsula in the far south. In 1948, they regularly ventured outside these areas to stage numerous successful attacks, not all of them under the cover of darkness—in one daytime assault, on a convoy of seventy vehicles traveling between Saigon and Dalat on May 1, a Viet Minh battalion killed 82 persons and took 150 civilians hostage. (The hostages were freed by a Moroccan unit following an intense firefight.)[36] The French countered with an impressive security sweep in the Mekong Delta in the second half of the year. With Vo Nguyen Giap content to rely on guerrilla attacks and the French unable to mount major operations, the war settled into an uneasy stalemate in all three regions of the country. And a stalemate, while ideal to neither side, suited Giap's purposes much more than they suited Valluy's, not least because Giap's troop count was increasing much more rapidly than his opposite number's—by year's end, Viet Minh forces numbered some 250,000 men. By then, more than half the population of the country lived in territory controlled by the Viet Minh.[37]

Casualties, meanwhile, continued to mount. When a British officer visited the French military hospital in Saigon at the end of the year, he found that the number of wounded was much increased over the previous December. The total was now almost eight hundred men, roughly a quarter of whom had serious injuries—the loss of one or more limbs, head wounds, lungs pierced by shrapnel. During the officer's two-hour visit, twenty-four serious operation cases were received. Nearly all were the result of road mines.[38]

VI

BAO DAI TOO SAW THE IMPLICATIONS OF THE VIET MINH'S MILItary success and of Mao's gains in China. They gave him increased leverage but also reduced his options. The French, with one eye on Mao's advancing armies and the other on their own stalemated war, might now give him more of what he wanted, but they might also abandon him if he dithered; they could opt simply to back Xuan and start a new Cochin China experiment with a puppet government run from Paris. He decided to take the plunge, hopeful also that the Americans—who were always at the forefront of his calculations—would now be more inclined to get involved. The reasoning went like this: To contain the Chinese Communists, the Truman administration would step up assistance to France in Indochina, but only if U.S. officials were persuaded that the French cause was vital to the West. This, however, presupposed that the Vietnam that was to be "saved" from Communism was not a mere colonial entity but an independent nation, one headed not by a French puppet but by a genuine nationalist with broad popular support. Paris leaders would balk initially, but they too needed to stay in America's good graces. If Washington stood firm, the prospects were good for far-reaching French concessions to anti-Communist nationalism.[39]

On March 8, 1949, Bao Dai and French president Vincent Auriol concluded, by an exchange of letters, the Élysée Accords, so named for the grand presidential palace in Paris at which the ceremony took place. The accord reconfirmed Vietnam's autonomy and her status as an "Associated State" within the French Union (Laos received the same status that July, and Cambodia in November), and it spelled out how the liquidation of Cochin Chinese separatism would occur. This new "State of Vietnam" also was promised her own army for internal security reasons, but with the crucial proviso that this army would be equipped and, in effect, directed by France. Many Vietnamese already serving in the Expeditionary Corps (some thirty-eight thousand in early 1949) resisted transfer to the new army, and there was from the start an acute shortage of officers. More important, under the Élysée Accords, Vietnam's foreign and defense relations would remain under French control, and in various other ways too the accord showed that Paris retained ultimate sovereignty. Vietnam under Bao Dai, that is to say, would become independent only when French leaders decided she was good and ready.

To no one's surprise, the announcement of the agreement aroused scant enthusiasm in Vietnam. The DRV leadership immediately denounced the deal, and Ho Chi Minh went on the radio to declare he would continue the struggle until complete independence was won. In April, the Viet Minh issued a warrant for Bao Dai's arrest on the charge of high treason. French efforts to drum up excitement among other Vietnamese, meanwhile, foundered on the widespread feelings of apathy ("it means no improvement in my life") or cynicism ("the so-called independence is a sham") or both.[40]

Still, the French had their Bao Dai solution. They now turned to what had been a principal motive behind the plan in the first place: securing increased American material and diplomatic backing. Barely had the ink on the accord dried than the Ministry of Overseas France showed the text to U.S. diplomats. Not even the National Assembly got to see it sooner. In the weeks that followed, officials took every chance to try to convince Americans of the liberality of French policy and of Bao Dai's stature as the only thing standing in the way of a Communist takeover. The tactic worked. It did so despite the fact that Washington had long held doubts about Bao Dai's viability as a nationalist leader. Already in December 1947 the Central Intelligence Agency had concluded that any government under the emperor would be fatally harmed by association with France and would never pose a serious threat to the "fanatical loyalty" inspired by Ho. Thirteen months later, in January 1949, a State Department analysis predicted that a Bao Dai administration "might become virtually a puppet government separated from the people and existing only by the presence of French military forces." Should that happen, an April 1949 memo warned, "we must then follow blindly down a dead-end alley, expending our limited resources . . . in a fight that would be hopeless."[41]

It might be a dead-end alley, others in the administration said, or it might not be. What swung the Truman administration in favor of the Élysée Accords was the possibility, distant though it might be, that Bao Dai really was a viable moderate nationalist alternative to Ho Chi Minh, and moreover that the risks of committing to him and to the French were smaller than the risks of doing nothing. Mao's forces were pressing forward to victory in China, and global Communism seemed to be on the march. Something had to be done.

It mattered too that powerful voices in American society were pressing the argument. In 1949, Henry R. Luce's *Time* and its sister publication, *Life,* insisted—more and more loudly as the year progressed—that France was fighting for the West in Indochina and therefore must have robust U.S. support. A great many people heard the message. *Time* was for many Americans at midcentury more than a magazine: It was a kind of unofficial but authoritative version of America's noble cause in the Cold War. *Life*, for its part, was read by an astonishing 44.4 percent of college-educated males. Though few Americans had heard of Luce, they lapped up the news as filtered through his prism. "If the U.S. goes into Asia," *Time* declared in October 1949, then she will have to "go in with both feet, with money and authority, with the will to help Asians build their own strong, free societies and with the result of preventing them from committing national suicide under the strains of that painful process." The magazine left no doubt that the effort must be made. Syndicated columnist Joseph Alsop argued likewise, notably in a quartet of columns he penned during a stay in Saigon in June, in which he excoriated the French for dragging their feet in the negotiations with Bao Dai.[42]

For Ho too, 1949 would prove to be pivotal. The astonishing developments in world politics during that year would influence his cause no less than the French. After years of diplomatic failure, of international isolation, his Democratic Republic of Vietnam would taste her first real success, though with implications that he could not foresee. The war was about to change. Up to now largely a Franco-Vietnamese affair, resulting from Paris leaders' attempt to reclaim colonial control and Vietnamese nationalistic determination to thwart them and define a new postcolonial order, it would become something else, something more.

The great powers were coming to Vietnam.

PART THREE

EAST MEETS WEST, 1949–1953

CHAPTER 9

"THE CENTER OF THE COLD WAR"

"HAVING PUT OUR HAND TO THE PLOW, WE WOULD NOT LOOK back."[1] Such was Dean Acheson's characterization of the American decision to effectively abandon her neutral policy and back the French war effort with substantial economic and military aid. It was an apt characterization, not only for 1949 but for many years to come. For the better part of twenty years, it would be the mantra of American administrations on Vietnam: Don't look back; keep pressing ahead. Not until 1968, when Lyndon Baines Johnson curtailed the bombing, agreed to negotiations with Hanoi, and announced he would not seek reelection, did the direction change. Even then, the war had another five years to run.

Acheson's words come from his memoir, which appeared at about the time the beleaguered LBJ fled Washington in 1969, a man broken by the war. The year before, Acheson had been among the "Wise Men" who had counseled Johnson that there was no light at the end of the tunnel in Vietnam, that he had no choice but to reduce U.S. involvement. Acheson was in a position to know, for he had been there at the start two decades prior. Hardly one to be accused of excessive modesty, Acheson titled his memoir *Present at the Creation,* and indeed he was. He was a central player, arguably *the* central player, in the drama of the late 1940s and early 1950s that saw the United States become a global hegemon, the self-appointed defender of Western civilization. As one account has it, he was more responsible for the Truman Doctrine than Truman, more the architect of the Marshall Plan than Marshall. Later, he was instrumental in frightening the Senate into ratifying the North Atlantic Treaty Organization, America's first-ever peacetime military alliance. More than any other presidential adviser, arguably more than President Truman himself, Acheson shaped the nation's postwar role on the world stage.[2]

Including in Southeast Asia. Though the latter-day Acheson wasn't keen to underscore the fact, he was also "present at the creation" of his country's long and difficult commitment to Vietnam. The State Department dominated decision making on Indochina in the second half of the 1940s, and Acheson, by virtue of his role as secretary of state after January 1949—and a forceful and decisive one at that—was the man in charge when the big decisions of 1949–50 had to be made.

His rise in government had been rapid. Born in Middletown, Connecticut, on April 11, 1893, the son of an Episcopal bishop, Acheson attended Groton and Yale, followed by Harvard Law School. After a period with the Washington law firm of Covington & Burling, he entered the federal government as undersecretary of the treasury in 1933. During the Second World War, he served as assistant secretary of state, and in 1945 he became undersecretary (the second-ranking position in the department), quickly earning a reputation for being orderly, efficient, savvy, and discreet. In January 1949, after a period away from government, he was summoned back by Truman to assume the top job.

Truman chose him because of his loyalty and his qualifications, and his formidable intelligence, but it didn't hurt that he so much looked and sounded the part. He strode forth as the quintessence of the striped-pants diplomat, with his Savile Row suits, his erect bearing, his astonishing mustache, his manners, his precision, and his dry Anglo wit. "He looked more like a British foreign secretary than any British foreign secretary I ever saw," said the longtime *New York Times* Washington bureau chief James "Scotty" Reston, who saw a few. And in fact, Acheson was an Anglophile of the first order, who could be outspoken in his admiration for the British Empire. He was also a staunch anti-Communist and was often brusquely impatient with, and suspicious of, the nationalist leaders of the colonial world. When a State Department analyst in February 1949 noted the general absence of anti-American propaganda coming out of Viet Minh headquarters, and suggested that Ho Chi Minh still hoped for U.S. backing for—or at least noninterference in—his cause, Acheson was unmoved. The question, he said some weeks later, of whether Ho Chi

Minh was as much a "nationalist as a Commie is irrelevant. All Stalinists in colonial areas are nationalists." Ho, he said, was an "outright Commie."[3]

To acknowledge the possibility of national Communism was to acknowledge that the world was a complex place, and this Acheson and Truman and other American leaders were loath to do. If, for example, Yugoslav leader Josip Broz Tito (whose break with Moscow had become public the previous year) really was a nationalist as well as a Communist, and if Mao Zedong and Ho Chi Minh were the same, then the world was altogether more complicated than most Americans—including educated, erudite ones like Acheson—preferred to believe. It was far easier to see these leaders as mere pawns of a hyperpowerful superstate emanating from the Kremlin—regardless of what the evidence showed.[4]

All of which would suggest that Acheson was a godsend for the men hunkered down in the French defense ministry. In actuality, though, he was torn in his early months in office about which way to go on Vietnam. In February 1949, he commented acidly, "Over the past three years," the French "have shown no impressively sincere intention or desire to make the concessions which seem necessary to solve the Indochina question." In the early spring, Acheson resisted pressure from State Department conservatives to throw full U.S. support behind France and the Bao Dai solution. He couldn't get away from the notion that Bao Dai was a weak leader with no hope of winning broad popular support, couldn't get away from the suspicion that France sought merely to continue her colonial war under a new guise. In this respect Acheson endorsed the views of the liberal voices at Foggy Bottom, Asian specialists such as Charles Reed, the former consul general in Saigon who had penned the "dead-end alley" memo in January and who continued in the spring to voice deep pessimism regarding the prospects in Indochina. Far better, Reed advised, for the United States to make her stand against Communism in a more hospitable environment such as Thailand.[5]

Ultimately, however, Acheson couldn't bring himself to act on this knowledge and instead sided with the conservatives. When he visited Paris for a foreign ministers' meeting in June, he listened sympathetically as the new U.S. ambassador, David Bruce, laid out why a failure to back France in Indochina could have disastrous effects in French politics.

The centrist governments comprised of the MRP, the Socialists, and the Radical Socialists, Bruce noted, faced ever-mounting pressure from the Communists on the left and the Gaullists on the right. With the NATO treaty close to signing, any policy that harmed the centrists—whose credibility, after all, was most on the line in Indochina—risked harming U.S. strategic interests. Granting full independence to the Vietnamese would compel Paris to make similar pledges to other colonies, notably Morocco and Tunisia. The French public would oppose a swift loss of the empire, and therefore the government would fall, thereby endangering French policies with respect to German sovereignty and European security. And besides, the ambassador tossed in, the Vietnamese were not ready to assume the responsibilities of independence in any case.[6] As for Bao Dai and his chances against the Viet Minh, Acheson in the end backed the argument put forth by the new consul general in Saigon, George M. Abbott. "Our support will not insure Bao Dai's success," Abbott acknowledged, "but the lack of it will probably make certain his failure." Acheson concurred, though even in accepting the point, he continued through the end of 1949 to withhold formal recognition of the Bao Dai regime, at least pending the French National Assembly's explicit endorsement of the Élysée Accords.[7]

And Ho Chi Minh? Acheson's view of him grew more and more dim in 1949. In radio interviews with Western journalists, Ho steadfastly denied that he was a Russian puppet and insisted that his government was not Communist but was composed of many elements. *Newsweek* concluded that Ho might be "more of a Vietnamese nationalist right now than a Communist stooge," but Acheson wasn't buying. When French analyst Paul Mus told midlevel State Department officials in April that Ho had the full support of the Vietnamese except for a tiny minority in Cochin China, Acheson no doubt heard or read a recap of the conversation but again refused to budge. He and his colleagues chose instead to believe that support for the Viet Minh would plummet once France gave real and meaningful authority to an "independent" Bao Dai regime.[8] The obvious questions that followed—What if Bao Dai was not granted such powers? Why should France continue the fight if Vietnam was to be independent?—were not discussed.

EAST MEETS WEST, 1949-1953 | 221

II

BROADER INTERNATIONAL DEVELOPMENTS ALSO SHAPED ACHESON'S thinking on Vietnam in 1949. He began to pay more attention to Southeast Asia's economic potential, particularly in terms of facilitating Japan's recovery. Given the instability in China, Washington planners deemed it absolutely essential to secure a stable, prosperous Japan under U.S. control. Southeast Asia, rich in rice, tin, oil, and minerals, and with a population of 170 million (bigger than the United States), could play a principal role in this endeavor. George F. Kennan, head of the Policy Planning Staff, influenced Acheson in this direction, as did the young Dean Rusk, deputy undersecretary of state and a man Acheson asked to take on a larger role in Asian policy. The maintenance of a pro-Western Southeast Asia, they and other government analysts argued, would provide the markets and resources necessary for Japan's economic revival—and help the recovery of Western Europe (by then well under way, but showing signs of a slowdown) as well. According to Rusk, the importation of rice from Indochina, for example, could be a terrific boon in securing Japan's revitalization.[9]

Then, in the second half of the year, came two momentous developments: In August, the Soviet Union for the first time detonated an atomic device; and in September, Mao Zedong's forces completed their rout of Chiang Kai-shek's Guomindang. Specialists had known that it was only a matter of time before Stalin got the bomb, but most thought the time would be the early or mid-1950s, not August 1949. The implications were huge (if not quite as enormous as some doomsayers in Washington proclaimed). It meant the end of the U.S. atomic monopoly and immediately raised fears that Stalin might embark on an aggressive course to expand his global reach. That worrisome thought only gained more currency the next month, when Mao Zedong consolidated his victory in China. Here neither the event nor the timing was a surprise to specialists—Nanjing had fallen in April, Shanghai in May, and Changsha in August—but for ordinary Americans it was sobering to hear Mao dramatically declare, from the Gate of Heavenly Peace in Beijing, the founding of the People's

Republic of China (PRC). Chiang and the remnants of his army fled to Formosa (now Taiwan).

Though some senior U.S. officials, Acheson among them, believed that the USSR and Mao's government would ultimately experience a rift, in the short term the dangers seemed all too real. Instantly, the number of major Communist foes had doubled. As a report by the National Security Council (NSC) had put it in June, "the extension of Communist authority in China represents a grievous political defeat for us. . . . If Southeast Asia is also swept by Communism, we shall have suffered a major political rout the repercussions of which will be felt throughout the rest of the world, especially in the Middle East and in a then critically exposed Australia. . . . The colonial-nationalist conflict provides a fertile field for subversive Communist movements, and it is now clear that Southeast Asia is the target for a coordinated offensive directed by the Kremlin."[10]

There was in fact no such coordinated offensive. Stalin's interest in Southeast Asia remained minimal, it was soon clear, and his feelings about the Chinese developments were decidedly mixed. Still, U.S. leaders could be forgiven for thinking that Communism was on the march in the region. In addition to Mao in China and Ho in Vietnam, there were Communist-led rebellions in Indonesia, in newly independent Burma, in Malaya, and in the Philippines. All four rebellions would fail in due course, but in late 1949 their mere existence fueled American fears. Did the historical momentum now lie with the Communists? Even if it didn't in objective terms, might the perception gain hold that it did, producing a bandwagon effect that could have a pernicious impact on American national security interests? It seemed all too possible.

The NSC report, with its warnings of the far-reaching consequences—the Middle East! Australia!—of a loss of Southeast Asia, was an early version of what would come to be known as the domino theory. Knock over one game piece, and the rest would inevitably topple. For the next twenty-five years, high U.S. officials, on both the civilian and the military sides, in both Republican and Democratic administrations, linked the outcome in Vietnam to a chain reaction of regional and global effects, arguing that defeat in Vietnam would have calamitous consequences not merely for that country but for the rest of Southeast Asia and perhaps beyond. Though the nature and cogency of the domino theory shifted over time, the core claim remained the same: If Vietnam was allowed to "fall," other countries would inevitably follow suit.

It was always an odd theory, and it became more so with the passage of time, as we shall see. Most egregiously, it posited that the countries of East and Southeast Asia had no individuality, no history of their own, no unique circumstances in social, political, and economic life that differentiated them from their neighbors. Yet the theory had a certain plausibility at the outset in 1949–50, while the regional implications of Mao's triumph were unclear. Its simple imagery also perfectly suited the charged political atmosphere in the United States in the period. Apocalyptic anti-Communism was the order of the day, and the assaults on the Truman administration were ferocious. Tapping into the solipsism that can course through the American body politic, Republicans (and some conservative Democrats) said that only Americans could have been responsible for the Soviet bomb and the China debacle. Soviet spies, working with American accomplices, must have speeded Stalin's atomic timetable by stealing U.S. secrets (they did). Truman must have "lost" China, must have allowed Chiang Kai-shek to be defeated when it was well within his power—with American assistance—to prevail (it wasn't). Now all of Asia was ripe for Communist plucking (not exactly). Said a young California congressman named Richard M. Nixon, in reference to China, "The deck was stacked on the communist side of the table."[11]

Acheson was an early target of the Red-baiters. At his 1949 confirmation hearing, he refused to criticize Alger Hiss, the former State Department official accused of espionage; a year later, after two sensational trials ended in a conviction for perjury, Acheson grandly announced to reporters, "I do not intend to turn my back on Alger Hiss." For the Republican right, already disdainful of Acheson for what they saw as his superciliousness and arrogance (he talks, said one, "as if a piece of fish had got stuck in his mustache"), it was an irresistible opening. Senator Joseph McCarthy of Wisconsin interrupted a Senate hearing to report the "fantastic statement the Secretary of State has made in the last few minutes." McCarthy asked aloud if this meant that Acheson would not turn his back on other Communists in Washington as well. Richard Nixon called Acheson's remarks "disgusting," and later referred to him as the "Red Dean of the College of Cowardly Containment," in a choice bit of alliteration. Senator William Jenner, Republican of Indiana, chimed in that Acheson was a Communist whose treachery had caused China to fall. Later, in his memoirs, Nixon elaborated that Acheson had presented a perfect target to Republicans seeking a symbol of the effete Eastern establishment. His "clipped mustache, his British tweeds, and his haughty manner made him the perfect foil for the snobbish kind of foreign service personality and mentality that had been taken in hook, line, and sinker by the Communists."[12]

These were absurd charges against a principal architect of America's Cold War strategy, a man whose aversion to Communism went down to his very bones. But in the context of 1949–50, such attacks on the administration left their mark, and the decision to aid France in Vietnam cannot be understood without consideration of the charged domestic political milieu out of which it emerged. Especially with the defeat in China, Acheson and Truman felt compelled to show America's mettle *somewhere,* especially in that region, in part to insulate the administration against Republican charges that it was too soft on Moscow—and now Beijing too. Southeast Asia was the logical place.

III

BY THE START OF 1950, THEN, THE WORLD'S MOST POWERFUL NAtion seemed poised to throw her full support behind the French war effort. No official action, however, had yet been taken, and there matters might have rested for some time but for dramatic news out of the east: On January 18, the People's Republic of China extended formal recognition to Ho Chi Minh's government, and on January 30 the Soviet Union did likewise. In the weeks thereafter, Moscow's Eastern European satellites followed suit, as did North Korea. Viet Minh diplomacy, so dismally unsuccessful for so long, had scored a colossal victory (if one with a hefty price tag, as we shall see), one that Ho desperately needed even as he also feared its implications.[13]

His efforts had centered initially on the Soviet Union. But he had a tricky path to walk, given his determination (strongly held through much of 1949) to avoid spurring the Americans into full and open support of France and her counterrevolutionary Bao Dai–led state. In 1948, the ICP reminded party functionaries to refrain from criticizing Washington in their pronouncements and to adopt a neutral line:

> The foreign policy of our government towards the United States of America for the actual period and for as long as the United States of America does not betray us, will not have the intention either to turn [our government] against them or to act in any way so as to incur their animosity. . . . Nevertheless, when it comes to public matters, it is formally prohibited to write, in any document, newspaper or book, one single word or one single line capable of incurring harmful repercussions on the foreign policy of our government in terms of its relations with the United States of America.[14]

Such a posture was unlikely to score points with a Soviet leadership already questioning Ho Chi Minh's socialist bona fides. Nor was this declaration exceptional for the period—in his interviews in 1945–50, when asked about the broader international situation and the growing rift between East and West, Ho always took care to strike a neutral pose. Even as party leaders took great satisfaction in the successes of Mao's Communist forces to the north, therefore, they rejoiced quietly; even as they sought to win recognition as well as assistance from Moscow, they also continued to meet with American diplomats in Bangkok, among them Lieutenant William H. Hunter, an assistant naval attaché who had traveled widely in Indochina and knew players on both sides personally. Stalin, at odds with independent-minded Yugoslavian leader Josip Broz Tito since 1948, couldn't abide Communists who showed anything less than complete fidelity to the Kremlin line.[15]

When French Communist Party leader Maurice Thorez tried to convince Stalin that he could trust Ho's commitment to the cause, Stalin demurred. Ho had collaborated too much with the Americans in World War II, he replied, and failed to solicit advice from the Kremlin before making key decisions. Case in point: Ho's decision to dissolve the ICP in 1945. Thorez tried to say that the dissolution had been merely tactical, but the Soviet dictator would not hear it. A Soviet Foreign Ministry memo dated January 14, 1950, spoke of "ambiguity" in Ho Chi Minh's interviews. "Speaking about the Vietnam government's attitude towards the U.S., Ho Chi Minh evades the issue of U.S. expansionist policy towards Vietnam. . . . Until now Ho Chi Minh abstained from the assessment of [the] Imperialist nature of the North Atlantic Pact and of the U.S. attempt to establish a Pacific bloc as a branch of this pact."[16]

And yet before that month was out, the USSR had taken the important step of extending diplomatic recognition to the Democratic Republic of Vietnam. Why? In large part because Stalin felt compelled to follow Mao's lead. And for the Chinese, the decision was, by all accounts, a relatively easy one. Contacts between Ho's government and Mao's forces, for a long time modest because of geographic separation and because the Chinese Communist Party (CCP) had been too preoccupied fighting its own war to provide direct and substantial support, increased markedly beginning in late 1948. In January 1949, Truong Chinh told the Sixth Plenum of the ICP that Mao's army might soon conquer all of China and that "we must be ready to welcome it." In April, Chiang Kai-shek's Guomindang forces fled Nanjing and the Red Army crossed the Yangtze, and in midyear the Vietnamese dispatched about a thousand men to southern China to attack Guomindang units in collaboration with local CCP troops. To senior CCP leaders, never as bothered as Stalin had been by Ho's dissolution of the party in 1945, it was a welcome sign of the Viet Minh's internationalist commitment.

In mid-1949, as the Chinese Communists publicly proclaimed their determination to "lean to one side" in the Cold War and their rejection of Titoism, Liu Shaoqi, the CCP's second in command, traveled to Moscow for secret meetings with Kremlin leaders, including Stalin.[17] A key item of discussion was the Vietnamese revolution and how to respond to it. Stalin, showing again his lack of interest in Southeast Asia, expressed his desire to see the CCP take primary responsibility for providing support for the Viet Minh. Liu Shaoqi agreed, and he promised a skeptical Stalin that Ho Chi Minh was a true internationalist at heart. Mao Zedong offered the same assurance when he held talks with Stalin in Moscow on Christmas Eve. That same day Liu Shaoqi, now back in Beijing, chaired a Politburo meeting to discuss Indochina policy. Any decision to assist the Viet Minh would exact a price, he told his colleagues, since the French government had not yet decided whether to grant diplomatic recognition to the new China and would obviously be offended should Beijing opt to recognize the DRV. Nevertheless the Politburo decided to invite a Viet Minh delegation to the Chinese capital for consultations, and to send a senior commander of the People's Liberation Army (PLA), Luo Guibo, to Vietnam as the CCP's general representative.

The following week Ho Chi Minh set out on foot for the Chinese frontier, dressed in his now-familiar khaki suit. He traveled under the name Ding. For seventeen days he walked, arriving at Guangxi on about January 20, 1950. On January 30, he arrived in Beijing. Mao was still in Moscow, but Liu Shaoqi assured Ho that major assistance would be forthcoming, including diplomatic recognition.[18]

From Beijing, Ho continued on to Moscow, arriving in the Soviet capital by train on February 10. Mao was still there, having himself gotten his fill of both the bitterly cold Russian winter and Stalin's vast reservoir of distrust. The Kremlin leader had long thought Mao unreliable, an ersatz Communist whose motives were always to be questioned. As early as 1940, Stalin had complained that the CCP was largely a peasant organization that gave far too little role to the working class. He referred to Mao as that "cave-dweller-like Marxist," whose ideas were primitive and who—like Ho Chi Minh—was probably, underneath it all, much more nationalist than internationalist. It mattered not that the CCP had supported Moscow in excluding Tito from the Cominform in 1948; Stalin still considered Mao and Ho both to be closet Titos. "He mistrusted us," Mao later complained, speaking of Stalin's view of the CCP. "He thought our revolution was a fake."[19]

Of course, Stalin's own nationalism had something to do with his stance, as did his security priorities emerging out of World War II. For much of the Chinese civil war he adhered to a neutral position, calculating that a divided China served the USSR's interests. As late as the beginning of 1949, he had urged Mao not to send his forces across the Yangtze but to be content with holding the northern half of the country. This was prudent, he said, to avoid provoking the United States. But as Communist troops continued to advance and victory became assured, Stalin shifted his rhetoric. He now praised Mao as a "true Marxist leader" and during Mao's visit agreed—though only after a delay of several weeks, during which the Chinese leader was left to seethe, half prisoner, half pampered guest, in Stalin's personal dacha—to rescind the Sino-Soviet friendship treaty that Stalin had concluded with Chiang Kai-shek in favor of a new one with the PRC.[20]

At Mao's urging, Stalin agreed to meet with Ho Chi Minh. Still focused on European concerns and still distrustful of Ho, the Soviet leader affirmed his government's recognition of the DRV but ruled out direct Soviet involvement in the war against the French. "There must be a division of labor between China and the Soviet Union," Stalin said. As his government had to meet its commitments in Eastern Europe, it would be up to China to give Vietnam what she needed. "China won't lose in this deal," the Soviet leader added, "because even if it provides Vietnam with second-hand articles, it will be given new ones by the Soviet Union." Ho Chi Minh pressed the issue, urging Stalin to sign the same treaty of alliance with the DRV that he had just signed publicly with Mao. Impossible, came the reply; Ho, after all, was in Moscow on a secret mission. Ho responded—perhaps in jest—that he could be flown around Moscow in a helicopter and then land with suitable publicity, to which Stalin replied: "Oh, you orientals. You have such rich imaginations."[21]

It was hardly the reception Ho had hoped for, but Mao promised him (both there and in Beijing, to which the two leaders returned on March 3) that the PRC would do her best "to offer all the military assistance Vietnam needed in its struggle against France." He soon set about making good on his word. For Mao, the Vietnamese struggle represented an opportunity to promote the Chinese model for revolution and also served his country's national security interests. Like so many Chinese rulers before him, he sought to keep neighboring areas from being in hostile hands, and he worried in particular that the United States might become more involved—whether in Indochina, in the Taiwan strait, or in the increasingly tense Korean peninsula.[22]

Personal ties between Ho and senior Chinese Communists may have made a difference too. Already in the early 1920s, while in Paris, Ho had met CCP leaders such as Zhou Enlai, Wang Ruofi, and Li Fuchun; later, it will be recalled, he spent time in Canton (Guangzhou) assisting Mikhail Borodin, the Comintern representative to the new Chinese revolutionary government led by the Nationalist Party. In Canton he had also engaged in various anticolonial activities, including teaching a political training class for Vietnamese youth. Among the guest speakers he invited in: Zhou Enlai and Liu Shaoqi. Fluent in Chinese, Ho later translated Mao's study "On Protracted War" from Chinese into French.[23]

Now, a quarter of a century later, Ho could board the train for the trip home secure in the knowledge that he had Chinese backing for his cause. But he also must have had feelings of ambivalence as he looked out the window of his train car, contemplating what lay ahead. The Sino-Soviet recognition of his government, however necessary, was certain to alienate a lot of Vietnamese moderates, after all, and limit Vietnam's room for maneuver with respect to non-Communist Asia. It also would isolate the DRV from the United States, Britain, and Japan and drastically increase the danger of a major American intervention on the side of Bao Dai and the French. A certain degree of independence had been lost. At various points in 1949, Ho had denied publicly that his government was about to identify itself with either the CCP or Stalin's Russia. In a radio interview with American journalist Harold Isaacs, for example, he ridiculed the notion of the Viet Minh falling under Soviet or Chinese domination and vowed that independence would come through the DRV's own efforts. For that matter, could the Chinese Communists really be trusted? Notwithstanding the toasts and vows of eternal friendship in Beijing, mutual suspicions remained, including on Ho's part.[24]

IV

AND THERE WAS ONE MORE REASON FOR HO CHI MINH TO FEEL APprehension on that long journey home: His fervent hope of bringing American support for his cause, held with varying degrees of conviction since World War I, since he had tried to get an audience with Woodrow Wilson at Versailles, was now definitively and probably permanently dashed. For on February 7, while Ho had still been en route to the Soviet capital, Dean Acheson had announced formal U.S. recognition of the Bao Dai government and its sister regimes in Laos and Cambodia. As neither security, democracy, nor independence could exist in any area "dominated by Soviet imperialism," the United States, Acheson had declared, would extend economic and military aid to France and her allied governments in Indochina.[25]

At last, French officials had what they had so long sought. They were further pleased to see recognition come also from Britain, Australia, and New Zealand, and in short order from a range of other governments: Belgium, Luxembourg, the Netherlands, Greece, Italy, Spain, South Korea, Thailand, Argentina, Bolivia, Chile, Costa Rica, Cuba, Honduras, Brazil, Venezuela, Jordan, and South Africa. That only two Asian countries—South Korea and Thailand—were on the list was a concern, but Paris analysts nevertheless thought a corner had been turned. "The situation has had the effect of internationalizing a problem which before this was a French problem," one Foreign Ministry cable enthused.[26]

Truer words were never spoken by a *fonctionnaire*. Paris officials had made the sale: They had brought the Cold War to Vietnam. Just like the Viet Minh, they retained their age-old ambivalence about opening Indochina to foreign influence; and, like the Viet Minh, they had nevertheless chosen to bet on the internationalization of the war, to take the struggle to the diplomatic front. France had convinced her principal Western allies that she was bearing the brunt of an international struggle between East and West, between the forces of Communism and the forces of freedom. French colonial power was no longer the only thing at stake in Indochina, each of these governments in effect now agreed, and because France was fighting her allies' battle, she was entitled to a generous measure of military and political assistance.[27]

Which meant, ultimately, American assistance. Pleased though Paris officials were by the large number of countries that opened relations with the Associated States, only one really mattered. (It's telling that all the others moved only after Washington did.) Yet even after the glorious news of February 7, the French worried that they might still lose the prize. Specifically, they feared that the Truman administration might, as a means to boost its influence in Vietnam and also avoid the taint of colonialism, choose to bypass France and give the aid directly to Bao Dai. And indeed, American decision makers gave the idea consideration, especially after Bao Dai's defense minister Phan Huy Quat proposed to U.S. consular official Edmund Gullion in Saigon in March that the United States assume direct responsibility for training and equipping a Vietnamese army.[28]

To which the French replied: no, never, not a chance. General Marcel Carpentier, the new French commander in Vietnam, told *The New York Times* that if military equipment went directly to Bao Dai, "I would resign

within twenty-four hours." The Vietnamese "have no military organization which could effectively utilize the equipment. It would be wasted,
as in China, and the United States has had enough of that." Carpentier's
civilian counterpart, High Commissioner Léon Pignon, echoed these
sentiments, patiently telling a reporter that only France had the technical capability to accept and distribute weapons and other equipment.
Bao Dai was lazy and had few followers, Pignon confided to a British
diplomat, and though Vietnamese troops fought reasonably well when
brigaded with French forces, they were apathetic and undisciplined
when left to their own devices. Lest there be any ambiguity regarding
their position, the French also brought out their trump card: They might
quit Indochina altogether if Washington failed to come up with aid or
demanded too many concessions to Bao Dai. "My country might cut her
losses" in such an eventuality, Foreign Ministry secretary Alexandre Parodi told Ambassador David Bruce, and other Paris diplomats issued
that same warning elsewhere.[29]

A mere bluff? Possibly, but the Truman team was not willing to call
it. In March, Secretary of State Acheson, with customary candor, told the
Senate Foreign Relations Committee: "We do not want to get into a position where the French say, 'You take over; we aren't able to go ahead with
this.' We want the French to stay there. . . . The French have got to carry
[the burden] in Indochina, and we are willing to help, but not to substitute for them." Acheson cautioned the lawmakers that "the thing we want
to be careful about is that we do not press the French to the point where
they say, 'All right, take over the damned country. We don't want it,' and
put their soldiers on ships and send them back to France."[30]

Acheson had more on his mind than Indochina in making these remarks. He also sought to avoid destabilizing the Paris government as
it was preparing to make concessions to the administration over allied
policy toward Germany. It all combined to limit Washington's leverage
over France, and it frustrated the secretary. On May 1, President Truman formally approved an aid program of $23.3 million for the Indochi-
nese states. He did so on Acheson's recommendation, yet the secretary
was frustrated, telling associates that the French seemed "paralyzed, in a
state of moving neither forward nor backward." The only thing to do was
to press on, in the hope that Carpentier and his Expeditionary Corps

A TECHNICIAN APPLIES A QUICK PAINT JOB TO A U.S.-SUPPLIED C-119
TRANSPORT PLANE AT HAIPHONG AIR BASE, CHANGING THE WHITE STAR
OF THE U.S. AIR FORCE INTO THE FRENCH TRICOLOR.

could turn things around and bring Ho Chi Minh to his knees. A few
weeks later Dean Rusk, the newly appointed assistant secretary of state
for Far Eastern affairs, summarized the policy in testimony before the
Senate Foreign Relations Committee. The United States must support
France in Indochina, he said, because without the French presence, the
Communists would win. How long would the disorder last? a senator
asked. Rusk replied that he did not know but added that he personally
was not pessimistic. Asia, he said, was waiting to see who won.[31]

Rusk may not have been pessimistic, but others in Washington were.
As had been the case ever since Franklin Roosevelt vowed during the
Second World War to keep the French from returning to Indochina, there
were those who envisioned disaster ahead should America join the war
against Ho. Some were in the State Department—for example, Charlton
Ogburn, head of the Southeast Asia division, who doubted that the introduction of U.S. military aid would make any real difference to what
was a futile colonial effort—and some were outside the executive branch.

Some were not in government at all. Walter Lippmann, the most influential columnist in the land, had tried some weeks earlier, in early April, to nudge the administration away from doing what in fact it seemed about to do. "We shall not be able to reverse our whole position in Asia and to support a colonial war against national independence," he wrote. "That would shatter our prestige in the rest of Asia. And even if we were willing to do that, there is no way that this Congress would or could promise enough money and enough military aid to enable the French army to plan a campaign of pacification which would last for many years."[32]

One can imagine Acheson nodding solemnly as he read Lippmann's words; he very likely disagreed with none of them. Yet he gambled that the United States would be able to keep that prestige—by continuing to pressure Paris to grant more rights and freedoms to the Associated States—even as she threw her lot behind France's four-year-old war.

A new day had dawned. At the time Acheson announced the recognition of Bao Dai, there were perhaps a dozen Americans living in Saigon, and not all that many more elsewhere in Vietnam. The French had resisted U.S. business ventures, and the majority of Americans in Indochina were missionaries, numbering perhaps 120, mostly from the Christian and Missionary Alliance along with a small contingent of Seventh-Day Adventists. Now, though, the U.S. presence grew markedly, as the Truman administration began to assemble what journalist Seymour Topping, who arrived in Saigon in February to take up his post as Associated Press bureau chief and thus saw it firsthand, called "the usual panoply of intervention": large diplomatic and information staffs as well as economic and military aid missions. American warships called at the city's port as "a sign of friendship for Vietnam."[33]

The liberal *New Republic* summarized the new reality: "Southeast Asia is the center of the cold war. Indo-China is the center of Southeast Asia. America is late with a program to save Indo-China. But we are on our way."[34]

V

AT VIET MINH HEADQUARTERS, LEADERS UNDERSTOOD THAT THEY now faced the very real prospect of a major increase in U.S. support for the French war effort. The possibility worried them, especially as the balance between the two sides in the war remained so delicate. But most senior officials also felt certain that they had achieved a monumental victory. They had won formal recognition from the world's two leading socialist states and the promise of significant assistance from one of them. Vietnam was back on the map of nations and part of the internationalist Communist world now stretching, in ICP general secretary Truong Chinh's words, from the Elbe to the Mekong. The humiliation of the colonial past seemed as if it could finally be swept away. In early February 1950, while Ho was still away, the party resolved that it would follow Mao Zedong's lead and lean to the Soviet-led Communist side in the Cold War. Fighting a war of national liberation would not be enough, Truong Chinh told his colleagues; Vietnam must do her part in the internationalist struggle against the imperialist bloc led by the United States:

> When it comes to the struggle of the democratic camp against the imperialists, Indochina is an outpost, a fortress on the anti-imperialist defense perimeter in Southeast Asia. . . . In Indochina, not only are the interests of our people and the French colonialists in conflict, but in reality the interests of the two camps, the imperialist and democratic ones, are also in conflict at the world level. The Indochina problem has become an entirely international problem.[35]

The new Sino-Vietnamese arrangement soon had tangible effects. In short order, Beijing created a Chinese Military Advisory Group (CMAG) and sent senior PLA officers south to assist in the training of Viet Minh units and plot strategy. The Fourth Field Army of the PLA set up a military school for the Vietnamese. Sizable amounts of Chinese military and nonmilitary equipment followed, though it paled next to what the Americans were providing the French. The outbreak of the Korean War in late June, and the announcement by the United States that she would intervene militarily on behalf of South Korea, only strengthened these Sino-Vietnamese ties. With the arrival of the U.S. Seventh Fleet in the Taiwan Straits, Beijing leaders felt certain that Washington was embarked on a course of aggression aimed at China, North Korea, and Vietnam. In July, the CMAG, led by General Wei Guoqing, was formally established, its seventy-nine officers instructed that they had a "glorious internationalist duty" to carry out in Vietnam. By August, group members were in place in Vietnam.[36]

French installations in northern Tonkin were now extremely vulnerable. Long before August 1950, in fact already in early 1949, as PLA units became more active along the border and on a few occasions joined in operations with Viet Minh forces, French commanders fretted about the extension of Mao's power into South China. In May 1949, Paris sent the ominously named General Georges Revers (*Revers* means "setback" or "reverse" in French), chief of the general staff, to Vietnam to examine the military situation and make his recommendation in the light of the probability of a Communist win in China. The first months of the year had not produced a change in the overall nature of the war; it remained a stalemate, which as before was to the disadvantage of the French. The Viet Minh did not have the capacity to wage major attacks on the deltas, but they continued to infiltrate behind the lines, and to reduce the number of villages under Bao Dai's administration. In Tonkin, the all-important line of communication between Hanoi and Haiphong was still subject to frequent guerrilla attacks, and meanwhile the French had too few troops to consolidate gains made during operations. The same was true in Annam. In Cochin China, the French efforts at pacification achieved some successes, but the Viet Minh remained strongly rooted in the Plain of Reeds and in the Ca Mau peninsula. In a measure of that strength, the Viet Minh under commanding general Nguyen Binh were able to mount numerous large operations, involving hundreds of troops, in and around the Mekong Delta in the latter part of 1949; the French were obliged to send major reinforcements and were able to prevail only at considerable cost.[37]

A Viet Minh attack could come anywhere. Edmund Gullion of the U.S. embassy recalled witnessing the assassination of the head of the French Sûreté in late April 1950:

It was in the morning but I hadn't come from my flat, and I just walked by the square and I saw Bazin [the Sûreté chief] just about to get in his car, and he was carrying this leather folder. And in front of him was another parked car with some Vietnamese in it. As he started to get into it, this other Vietnamese jumped out of the parked car right in front of him, holding an enormous revolver in both hands, the way they do in American movies now, two-handed, and pumped shots into his belly. I was right across the street from him, a narrow street, and I ducked behind a barber's chair [in the open]. The assassin got in the car and drove away. The irony of it was that they were expecting some kind of ceremony and there was a French squad rehearsing for it, and I remember seeing this fellow go right past them—and he was never found.

Just prior to his death, Bazin had told a French reporter: "Every day the Viet Minh radio says, 'Bazin, you are going to die.'" He said he hoped he would get them before they got him.[38]

More and more, the French High Command found itself committing valuable manpower to the basic task of keeping a minimum number of road and river axes of communications open, if only during daylight hours. It established a chain of military posts along specified routes, whose task was to maintain visual surveillance over key sections and extend security over more distant sections by calling in mortar and artillery fire. Watchtowers began dotting the landscape in Cochin China in 1948 and were extended to central Vietnam the following year; generally, these fieldworks were within sight of one another, at an interval of approximately one kilometer, and were manned by five or six men, usually auxiliaries. The system achieved some success but tied down a lot of troops in static positions, and the posts often proved vulnerable to nighttime Viet Minh attacks.

Revers in his report catalogued many of these problems and drew sobering conclusions. No military solution favoring France was possible, he argued, not in the long run. All actions must proceed from this basis, and ultimately Paris leaders would need to seek a "peace of the brave" with Ho Chi Minh's Democratic Republic of Vietnam. Bao Dai was a poor leader whose government had minimal support, and France did not have enough manpower in Indochina to impose her will on the population. Since the Viet Minh were bound, sooner or later, to gain significant assistance from the Chinese Communists, France could not realistically hope to hold the whole of Tonkin (at least not without the introduction of American ground forces); instead, she should withdraw from all of Tonkin except a rough quadrilateral around the Red River Delta anchored on Haiphong, Hoa Binh, Viet Tri, Thai Nguyen, and Mong Cai. The fortresses on the Chinese frontier along Route Coloniale 4, already suffering from the relentless attacks on the convoys, would become indefensible if the PLA reached the border and decided to aid the Viet Minh. They were, moreover, strategically unimportant and were tying down troops badly needed in the Red River Delta.[39]

The Revers report was top secret and was made for the private information of senior French policy makers. It thus caused an uproar when excerpts from it were broadcast on Viet Minh radio and when, following a fight between a French soldier and a Vietnamese student on a Paris bus, a copy of the report was discovered in the latter's briefcase. The student, Do Dai Phuoc, led French counterespionage agents to another Vietnamese student's apartment, where they found seventy-two additional copies. Subsequent investigation revealed that the document had circulated widely within the French capital's large Vietnamese community. A major political scandal—"The Generals' Affair"—erupted, preoccupying the chattering classes for months and delaying a final decision on Revers's call for an evacuation of the northern forts.[40] The months went by. In late 1949, Giap stepped up pressure on the convoys along the RC4, and the consolidation of PLA control in South China increased his determination to subject the French installations to a major assault. He grasped what the new French commander in chief, Marcel Carpentier—a wunderkind who had gone from major in 1940 to lieutenant general in 1946, but who knew little about Indochina—also grasped: that these posts were forlorn islands in a Viet Minh sea.

CHAPTER 10

ATTACK ON THE RC4

A<small>T 6:45 IN THE MORNING OF MAY 25, 1950, A VIOLENT FUSIL-</small>lade suddenly rained down on the small French garrison (eight hundred men, mostly Moroccan) at Dong Khe, a post situated between Cao Bang and That Khe along the RC4. The post was a bastion in the French military system where convoys could stop to rest in the shelter of the French flag. Giap's aim: to take and hold Dong Khe, thereby isolating Cao Bang from its links with That Khe. In the days prior, four Viet Minh infantry battalions succeeded in hoisting five 75mm cannons onto the heights surrounding the town without being detected by the garrison, and then proceeded to unleash barrage after barrage on the post. It was a preview of the technique they would use at Dien Bien Phu. For forty-eight hours the shelling continued, whereupon the Viet Minh overran Dong Khe in a human-wave assault.

The French responded quickly, dispatching thirty-four aircraft to drop a battalion of paratroops upon the town. They caught the Viet Minh units completely off guard and after intense fighting forced them to flee for the jungle. Giap had reinforcements he could have called in, but the monsoon was fast approaching, and he chose to call it a day. The French congratulated themselves on their quick deployment of the paratroops rather than face the deeper truth of their extreme vulnerability in the Viet Bac. They chose not to take this last great chance to evacuate the frontier posts while time remained.[1]

Giap, having seen what his forces could do in a major engagement, believed the time had come to shift to the strategic offensive. With China as a secure rear base, a sanctuary where his troops could be trained, re-organized, and equipped for more conventional operations, he could prepare to strike the first hammer blow against the French Union. By the late spring, the Viet Minh had grown to a force of about a quarter of a million troops, organized into three components: a regular army (*chu luc*), regional units, and guerrilla-militia forces. The regular forces, with an estimated strength of 120,000, Giap organized into six divisions, on European lines—the 304th, 308th, 312th, 316th, 320th, and 325th; five were rooted in Tonkin, and the sixth (the 325th) was based in central Vietnam. Each had three infantry regiments, an artillery battalion, and an antiaircraft battalion, as well as staff and support elements. The task of these regular forces was to conduct a war of maneuver, aimed at drawing French units into combat in locales and under conditions in which French advantages in firepower and air support would be neutralized. The isolated French garrison in an outlying area was thus always a tempting target, and if the attack could occur during the *crachin,* or misty season in Tonkin, when the low cloud cover inhibited French aerial bombardment and resupply, so much the better.[2]

To keep these new formations fighting in the field required complex logistical planning. For example, senior Viet Minh planners determined that maintaining an infantry division in action away from its base required the use of roughly fifty thousand local peasants as porters, each carrying about forty-five pounds in supplies. These numbers could be reduced when bicycles were available—when pushed along roads and tracks by the rider, these specially outfitted vehicles could carry up to two hundred pounds during the dry season—but even then the figure was huge. The porter had to carry his own rations with him, which usually took the form of rice in a cloth bandolier. As a general rule, a porter was not to be away from home for more than two weeks, meaning that he would spend "seven carrying days" with the army unit and then could commence the return journey to his village. Fresh porters would be conscripted as the division continued its journey.[3]

The regional and guerrilla-militia forces had vital tasks of their own, mostly related to defensive and security matters but also including small-scale guerrilla operations against static enemy positions. Giap's early writings stress the importance of these roles. Each province and district had

VIET MINH SOLDIERS CROSS A BAMBOO PONTOON BRIDGE IN BAC KAN PROVINCE IN NORTHERN VIETNAM, IN 1950. THIS CONSTRUCTION TECHNIQUE WOULD BE USED FREQUENTLY IN THE WAR AND AGAIN LATER IN THE STRUGGLE AGAINST THE UNITED STATES.

responsibility for raising and equipping its own units of regional troops, who on occasion served as a general reserve for the regular army. At the province level, battalions sometimes comprised several rifle companies and a support company equipped with light machine guns and mortars. Ammunition was often in short supply, but these battalions could take on French units effectively for brief periods of time. Often they also had the task of training the guerrilla-militia forces, who tended to be unarmed or lightly armed and were usually part-timers. Their chief duties included intelligence gathering, transport, and sabotage. A better-armed element of the guerrilla-militia forces, so-called elite irregulars, was equipped with grenades, rifles, and mines, and sometimes even a few automatic weapons. It frequently joined with the regional forces in local operations.

Women took on key roles in the war effort. Though barred from enlisting in the regular army, they served by the thousands in the DRV bureaucracy—though almost never in senior positions—and as nurses and doctors. Many also carried out dangerous undercover sabotage, espionage, and assassination missions in the urban areas of Vietnam, or signed up for duty in the guerrilla-militia forces. At one point in Hung Yen province, for example, 6,700 women served in these forces, taking part in 680 guerrilla operations. A considerable number of them paid with their lives or were seriously wounded.

Giap spent the rainy season preparing for a large-scale autumn offensive. There was in effect a truce in the fighting from July to September, as the war came to a stop in the wet. The rain fell almost continuously, and the rivers overflowed. The spongy, saturated jungles were virtually impassable by French troops—and, for that matter, by Viet Minh units—and the going was not much easier in the watery surfaces of the deltas. Recalled one French observer: "The soldiers were overwhelmed and blinded by the forces of nature, by the soaking vegetation, the mountains that vanished in the clouds, the rivers swirling with turbid, dangerously rapid water, by the mud, the heat, by everything. It was a formless, green-gray world, devoid of outline, inimical, a world in which every movement, even eating was an effort."[4]

Resourceful commanders take advantage of such intermissions. Giap and his subordinates engaged in meticulous preparations during the summer months, even going so far as to construct elaborate models of the

French posts of That Khe, Dong Khe, and Cao Bang, which their troops then practiced taking, day after day after day. They sabotaged roads and bridges, hoping to slow the advance of French motorized forces. They also used propaganda to wage a war of nerves against the French and the Bao Dai government, playing up the theme of a forthcoming offensive.

Most critical of all, Giap received considerable assistance from the Chinese, as pledged by Mao Zedong to Ho Chi Minh in Moscow and Beijing earlier in the year. On June 18, Liu Shaoqi, vice chairman of the Chinese Communist Party, instructed Chen Geng, commander of the PLA's Twentieth Army Corps and a longtime acquaintance of Ho Chi Minh, to "work out a generally practical plan based on Vietnam's conditions (including military establishments, politics, economy, topography, and transportation) and on the limits of our assistance (including, in particular, our shipping supplies)." Upon receiving this plan, Beijing could "implement various aid programs, including making a priority list of materials to be shipped, training cadres, and rectifying troops, expanding recruits, organizing logistical work, and conducting battles."[5]

In short order, Chinese advisers were assigned to numerous Viet Minh units at battalion level and above, and the PRC also provided a large amount of weaponry and other matériel—by one authoritative account more than 14,000 guns, 1,700 machine guns, about 150 pieces of varying kinds of cannons, 2,800 tons of grain, and large amounts of ammunition, uniforms, medicine, and communication equipment. Some 200 heavy Molotova trucks stocked with supplies ran continuously from Canton and across South China, crossing into Vietnam in the gaps in the French defense line northeast of Cao Bang, the western anchor on the RC4. If the amounts in these truck beds still did not come close to matching what Washington gave to the French Union—by early 1951, the French would receive some 7,200 tons of military equipment per month on average—it nevertheless had a highly significant impact. Meanwhile, Viet Minh forces were sent to China's Yunnan province for training by PLA officers, including in the use of explosives. By early September, they were back in Vietnam, gathered on the lines of penetration, using the jungle to keep themselves hidden.[6]

The result was a Viet Minh main battle force in Tonkin whose firepower was roughly equal to that of the French Expeditionary Corps and

THE FORBIDDING TERRAIN OF CAO BANG NEAR THE CHINESE
BORDER, THROUGH WHICH CHINESE AID TO THE VIET MINH
BEGAN TO FLOW IN 1950.

in some respects superior. In certain heavy weapons, for example, such
as bazookas and mortars, a Viet Minh battalion could now outgun its
French counterpart. The French retained total superiority in naval vessels, aircraft, armored vehicles, and—with some exceptions—artillery,
but overall Giap, by the early autumn of 1950, possessed a fighting force
that could accomplish what it had never been able to do before: Go toe-
to-toe with the adversary.[7]

II

FRENCH INTELLIGENCE CODE BREAKERS PICKED UP SIGNS THAT
Giap was preparing a major operation in the north along the frontier
ridge. By the end of the first week of September, analysts knew that an attack was imminent, but not where. Some French posts had by then been
evacuated—the truly impossible positions beyond Cao Bang, notably Tra
Linh and Nguyen Binh (not to be confused with the Viet Minh leader

of the same name)—but many were still occupied, for prestige reasons largely, and to guard the cemeteries (for the French could not bear the thought of the Vietnamese taking the burial sites and their white crosses). Both Dong Khe and That Khe were thought to be targets, and Lang Son perhaps as well, but hard evidence was elusive. Moreover, the French grossly underestimated the size of the attacking force: Instead of eighteen to twenty battalions as predicted, Giap was readying thirty to thirty-two battalions, including six heavy battalions and numerous artillery. Meanwhile, the vagaries of French domestic politics hurt Carpentier's planning, as the cabinet in Paris turned down his request for reinforcements and instead in August *reduced* the number of French soldiers in Indochina by nine thousand, on grounds of cost. The increased American aid had yet to really manifest itself, and the war was a major drain on French resources. Pleas from Hanoi to consider using conscripts in Vietnam also met with deaf ears in Paris; no politician wanted to go anywhere near the notion.[8]

Overall, the French land forces in Indochina totaled some 250,000. About 40 percent of these were regular French forces (metropolitan, Foreign Legion, colonial); the remainder was about equally divided between Vietnamese army forces (under French command) and irregular *supplétifs,* plus a few thousand Laotian and Cambodian troops. On the support side, French women were a growing presence, as part of the *Personnel féminin de l'armée de terre* (PFAT). Many were secretaries, but sizable numbers also served in combat areas as ambulance drivers, nurses, surgeons, and helicopter pilots. Among the latter were several women who flew into high-danger battle situations to evacuate wounded soldiers and provide vital first aid. One pilot, Paule Dupont d'Isigny, by war's end had logged some four thousand hours in Indochina and conducted more than thirty missions to rescue wounded soldiers from combat zones. Still other women worked as parachute riggers for the airborne units. (An experienced crew of two could fold one parachute in seven minutes.) Before the war was over, more than a hundred PFAT members would be killed in action.

In Tonkin, where the immediate threat loomed, Carpentier had some 53,000 troops at his disposal. Practically all of them, however, were engaged in internal security duties, and although thirteen battalions were earmarked as a mobile reserve, they were not in fact readily available to meet an external threat. The Expeditionary Corps still maintained its superiority in equipment, but much of the equipment was obsolete, and there were deficiencies, particularly in aircraft, so crucial to the French in maintaining their lines of communication. Though the general morale of the individual French officer and soldier was reasonably high, there were unsettling reports flowing to Paris of a slackening will and a "defensive-mindedness" among high officers, some of whom voiced despair at the rising number of French Union casualties—some 100,000 to this point in the war, including 25,000 dead or captured. Some colonial troops, meanwhile, notably the Moroccans, were reportedly beginning to question what they were doing, waging war against a people whose nationalistic effort they admired and themselves sought to emulate.[9]

The picture was not all bad, to be sure. An intensive pacification effort in the first half of the year, commanded by Major General Marcel Alessandri and designed to clear the Red River Delta and thereby deny the Viet Minh a major source of rice, had achieved considerable success—the flow of rice was cut almost in half. This was a severe problem for the DRV not merely in nutritional terms but also because rice was the medium of exchange of the Viet Minh economy. Troops were paid in rice; services and supplies were purchased with rice. Through the middle months of the year, rice rations for Giap's forces were cut again and again. In addition, pressure on the Hanoi-Haiphong corridor had eased somewhat, to the point that in April the French opened the road to mostly unrestricted traffic by day, whereas before it was restricted to armed convoy travel three days per week. In Cochin China, Viet Minh southern commander Nguyen Binh's attacks on French posts—around Tra Vinh, Vinh Long, Bien Hoa, Thu Dau Mot, Than Son, Can Tho, Soc Trang, and Sa Dec—diminished markedly in both frequency and intensity in the spring, after he suffered crushing losses in the face of French artillery and airpower, and *colons* in Saigon spoke of a palpable easing of tension in the city. Thenceforth the war would play out mostly in Tonkin and northern Annam.[10]

Carpentier, recognizing his position of weakness in the far north, in early September ordered that Cao Bang be evacuated and that Thai Nguyen be captured immediately beforehand. Though the two operations were not militarily connected, Carpentier reasoned that the easy capture of Thai Nguyen—and there was no reason to believe Giap would put up a major effort to defend it—would deflect press attention away from the abandonment of Cao Bang. Carpentier ordered that both actions be completed by mid-October, just before the end of the rainy season. He figured Giap's forces would not be in position to attack before then.

He figured wrong. At dawn on September 16, after months of careful preparation, the Viet Minh leader threw five battalions with artillery and mortar support against Dong Khe. Two companies of legionnaires put up furious resistance and initially held their own, even though heavy cloud cover precluded air support. Nervous tension enveloped Giap's command headquarters nearby, particularly after news arrived that a key Viet Minh regiment had lost its way and been unable to join in the attack. There were reports of heavy Viet Minh casualties. Ho Chi Minh, who had arrived at the headquarters the week before, sunburned after a weeklong journey on foot, urged calm. The operation should continue, he said. Giap and Chen Geng agreed. For two days, the fighting raged, until at ten A.M. on September 18, fifty-two hours after the first shots were fired, the Dong Khe post fell. One officer and thirty-one legionnaires managed to get away at the last minute, emerging out of the jungle near That Khe a week later.[11]

The garrison at Cao Bang, fifteen miles to the north, was now cut off, and the French determined they had no choice but to attempt a fighting retreat southward before the Viet Minh could encircle them. Instead of moving down Route Coloniale 3 toward French units moving northward from Thai Nguyen, however, Carpentier foolishly elected to use the RC4. He reinforced Cao Bang by air with a battalion of North Africans and assembled a force of 3,500 mostly Moroccan troops and a crack paratroop battalion at That Khe, fourteen miles south of Dong Khe. This force, code-named Task Force Bayard, would camouflage the move of the Cao Bang column, meet it halfway, and then escort it back to That Khe. But its commander, Lieutenant General Marcel Le Page, his orders sketchy, vacillated and did not move out of That Khe until September 30. A rumor floated among the soldiers that Le Page's parting words were "We shall never come back."[12]

In Cao Bang, meanwhile, Lieutenant Colonel Pierre Charton, a squat,

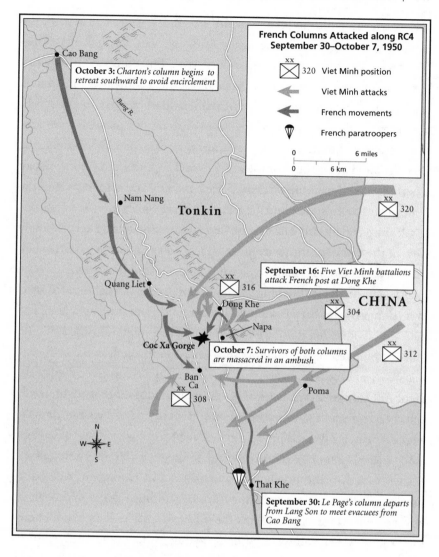

French Columns Attacked along RC4
September 30–October 7, 1950

⊠ xx 320	Viet Minh position
←	Viet Minh attacks
←	French movements
⛱	French paratroopers

0 ————— 6 miles
0 ————— 6 km

Cao Bang

October 3: *Charton's column begins to retreat southward to avoid encirclement*

Bang R.

Nam Nang

Tonkin

⊠ xx 320

Quang Liet

⊠ xx 316

September 16: *Five Viet Minh battalions attack French post at Dong Khe*

Dong Khe

⊠ xx 304

CHINA

Napa

Coc Xa Gorge

⊠ xx 312

October 7: *Survivors of both columns are massacred in an ambush*

Ban Ca

⊠ xx 308

Poma

N W E S

⛱ That Khe

September 30: *Le Page's column departs from Lang Son to meet evacuees from Cao Bang*

no-nonsense commander much loved by his men for his personal courage and his foul mouth, ignored orders to leave his equipment behind and move south on foot. Instead he loaded his personnel into trucks and took with him his artillery pieces as well. On October 3, in this way, 2,600 soldiers—including almost a thousand Moroccans and six hundred legionnaires—and five hundred civilians (including the town's prostitutes) began to move the thirty-three miles to Dong Khe. The column, like a giant caterpillar with metallic bristles, stretched for miles; almost immediately it ran into ambushes and blown-up bridges. By early the next morning, having covered only nine miles, it was blocked. To the south, the Le Page relief force, which had advanced to a few miles from Dong Khe, had also been halted in its tracks. The numerically superior Viet Minh closed in from both sides of the dense forested hills, using roadside bombs, machine guns, and artillery. Bad weather and low-lying mist prevented air support for the French Union troops, who were now completely at the mercy of the attackers. On Carpentier's orders, the French commanders burned their trucks and supplies and (in the case of Charton) abandoned the artillery pieces, then moved off the RC4 in the hope of outflanking the blocking forces. The new plan was to rendezvous at a feature called Hill 477 east of Coc Xa. Progress was excruciatingly slow in the thick brush, as scouts used machetes to hack a path through the dense growth, and many men were simply lost in the forest.[13]

Alessandri, upon learning of the order, wired Carpentier: "Cancel everything. If you carry it out it will be a crime." But it was too late. The message, at once threatening and insubordinate, went unheeded.[14]

"We plunged into the mountains, on a 'trail' which was a trail only in name," a Hungarian legionnaire in the Le Page column recalled of the night of October 3–4. "Several of our wounded died that night. They could not take falling every ten or twenty yards with their porters. We were all beat, for we had practically not slept since we left our base [four days earlier]. Climb, descend several times each day on these abrupt slopes loaded to the maximum with packs and equipment was back-breaking." Always, both columns feared an ambush that could come at any moment and, even worse, felt the incomparable anxiety of not know-ing exactly where you were, of being astray in the natural labyrinth of monstrous vegetation, with no guides or detailed maps, with food and water and ammunition running out, and with the enemy all around you.[15]

Viet Minh troops too were exhausted, having pursued their prey for six days and nights, but there would be no rest on the seventh day. "Why do we need to rest now?" Ho Chi Minh declared. "We are tired but the enemy is ten times more so. A runner on the point of reaching his finishing-line cannot rest." Giap followed with a short message to the troops via telephone on October 6: "I am sure that the enemy is hun-grier and colder than you. He has suffered heavier losses and his morale has been undermined as he is a defeated invaders' army. Therefore, you must put more effort into your work in order to annihilate most of the enemy troops. Rainy and foggy weather is all the more favorable to us. . . . Forward!"[16]

By the time Charton and Le Page linked up on October 7, both columns had taken huge casualties and were low on water, food, and ammunition. And the worst was yet to come. The two commands had filed into an enormous ambush: Fifteen Viet Minh battalions had closed in. Panic set in among the Moroccans, who had a well-earned reputation for extraordinary courage and resilience; all of a sudden, many of them fled down the cliff faces screaming *"Allah-Akbar! Allah-Akbar!"* The French force was disintegrating into a mob. Charton and Le Page and the remaining battalion commanders decided to divide the survivors into small parties and flee through the jungle toward That Khe, twenty miles away. Some of the groups made it; many did not. Charton was wounded and taken prisoner by the Viet Minh. The forest was swarming with Viet Minh shouting *"Rendez-vous, soldats français! Rendez-vous, vous êtes perdus!"* ("Give yourselves up, French soldiers, you are lost!")[17]

Some French units dropped their rifles and surrendered, too exhausted and hungry to go on. "They all stretched out their hands to ask for food," a Viet Minh officer recalled. "But we were not much better off as far as food was concerned. Our rice rations, which we carried in sausage cloth sacks around our shoulders, had been considerably depleted by many days of fighting. . . . At first we gave them each a ball of cooked rice. Later we had to halve the ball, then divide again into three parts. They gobbled it in the twinkling of an eye, then obediently followed our orders to move toward the POW camp along the forest tracks."[18]

Ultimately, only some 600 men from the two columns made it back to French lines. The Expeditionary Corps had suffered 6,000 casualties, of whom no fewer than 4,800 were listed as dead or missing. Charton's column alone lost 75 officers, 295 NCOs, and 2,939 from other ranks. Other combined losses included more than 100 mortars and some 950 machine guns, 8,000 rifles, and 450 trucks. "The disaster of RC4" was by far the most devastating defeat of the war to this point. General Carpentier, stunned and shattered, facing the prospect of informing Paris that the Charton and Le Page columns had been wiped out, flew over the scene and could only say mysteriously, "Everything that could happen has happened."[19]

In author Bernard Fall's later estimation, it was the greatest French colonial defeat since the loss of Montcalm at Quebec in 1759. General Giap wouldn't have put it in those words, but he found his own way to register the magnitude of his achievement: He joined his Chinese advisers in a celebratory feast and got drunk for the first time in his life.[20]

The engagement also showed something else: that the war had entered a new, intensive, deadly phase, as the Cold War not only internationalized the diplomatic nature of the conflict but militarized it in unprecedented ways.

To compound the calamity, French posts far from the fighting were simply abandoned. Most important among these was Lang Son, a pleasant town of ten thousand constructed in the French provincial style with wide streets and low yellow-brown houses, and the main post at the eastern edge of the ridge. It was evacuated on Carpentier's orders on October 17–18. Large stocks of arms, ammunitions, stores, and vehicles were left behind for the Viet Minh to claim—enough to supply Giap's army for many months.

By the nineteenth, the French had been driven out of northern Tonkin, from the sea to the Red River. The border to China was completely open, from Lao Cai to coastal Mong Cai. The French fell back on a 375-mile northern perimeter, with Hanoi at its core. Panic swept the French communities in Hanoi and elsewhere in the delta, and there was open talk of abandoning Tonkin entirely. Officials scoffed at the notion, but they quietly made preparations to evacuate all women and children from Hanoi, until ordered to stop by High Commissioner Léon Pignon, who vowed the city would be defended house by house. Some firms nevertheless moved their surplus stocks and archives to Haiphong or Saigon.[21] For Carpentier and his underlings in Saigon, most distressing for the future was that the Viet Minh had shown themselves to be so much more than the ragtag, primitive bandit gang of French imagination (or at least rhetoric); they were a serious fighting force, disciplined and courageous, able to move rapidly and maneuver, and willing to take major battlefield losses.

And indeed, Viet Minh casualties in the Border Campaign (as it came to be called, or *bien gioi* to the Vietnamese) were extremely heavy—much heavier than was known at the time. Of the 30,000 troops Giap threw into the fight, as many as 9,000, or 30 percent, may have been killed. Not all died on the battlefield. Because of the rough terrain and distances, porters could evacuate only about 6 percent of the wounded to hospitals within six hours; the rest arrived only later, some of them as late as twelve or eighteen hours after going down. Even then, their ordeal was far from over, as they typically had to endure excruciating waits to go into surgery. Many never made it to the operating table. Nor had the DRV's medical services factored in that they would need also to take care of hundreds of wounded European, African, and North African troops captured in the battle. Many of these soldiers also succumbed, whether from inadequate treatment of their injuries or from illness contracted in the malaria-infested jungles of Cao Bang.[22]

Giap's success was due in large measure to his preponderance of manpower and to atmospheric conditions. At all times he had at least a 3 to 1 superiority in numbers, and at Dong Khe it was more like 8 to 1. Communication between Viet Minh units was excellent throughout, and Giap could move units precisely where they were needed within the battle zone. After some early mistakes, his officers used coordinated artillery fire effectively, and their staff work was efficient. Intelligence agents in the villages used transmitting sets to give precise information on French movements, which allowed Giap to attack at times and places of his choosing. The ground mist so common at that time of year, as the rains were ending, helped as well: It prevented the French from using airpower to assist the two columns. The French Union command arrangements, meanwhile, were vague, and it was never clear who commanded whom. Marcel Le Page, who commanded the Lang Son column, was the wrong man for the job, an artilleryman with little experience in jungle warfare and a tendency toward indecision and self-doubt (qualities duly noted by his men).[23]

And, of course, the human and material aid provided by the Chinese, both before and during the campaign, mattered enormously. Measuring exactly how this assistance influenced the course of events remains to this day difficult, however, and care should be taken to avoid exaggeration—it's worth recalling that the French garrisons along the RC4 were isolated and highly vulnerable even before the PLA's arrival, with each convoy completely at the mercy of guerrillas lurking in the hills and gorges along the road. Giap in later years would acknowledge the important material and training assistance provided by the Chinese in 1950, while insisting that he and Ho Chi Minh were the chief decision makers. They and they alone chose where and when to attack, and they hung tough when Chen Geng urged caution or delay.[24] Maybe, but Giap would not have been able to strike remotely as hard, or leave the French nearly as bloodied, without the support provided by his northern neighbor.

In late November, Carpentier ordered several operations to try to regain the initiative. Little was accomplished. In one action, commanded by Charton and designed to encircle and destroy several Viet Minh battalions thought to be operating around two villages in Thai Binh province southeast of Hanoi, bad weather delayed the drop of paratroopers by two hours, which meant the planned encirclement of the villages was not completed. When Charton's men arrived, the villages were deserted. The next day the French searched seven or eight other villages in the same area; these too were more or less empty, as residents could be seen running away at the approach of troops. Even people working in the fields disappeared without a trace. No enemy soldiers were ever spotted, and no weapons uncovered. French troops did note, though, that most of the villages had pro–Viet Minh posters and pictures of Ho Chi Minh.[25]

III

THE FRENCH FACED A STARK NEW REALITY. THE CAO BANG DISASter, beyond the enormous loss of blood and treasure, beyond the immediate humiliation of having been out-generaled and out-fought by a supposedly inferior enemy, showed that in this war, time was not on France's side. The strategy of isolating the Viet Bac and of reducing the areas under Viet Minh control had not succeeded; to the contrary, Ho Chi Minh's government now had firm control over a huge swath of Tonkin and threatened the rest; it also remained a formidable presence in many parts of Annam and Cochin China. French commanders might not wish to admit it, at least not without a few drinks in them, but an outright defeat of the enemy was now almost impossible to imagine. He had solidified his hold on the Viet Bac and had at least tacit support of the mass of the population there, and he had a powerful neighbor to the north, ready and willing to help his cause.

Which is not to say Ho was invincible. The Viet Minh had scored a stunning victory, but their strength in late 1950 should not be overestimated. Giap's army, now formally named the People's Army of Vietnam (PAVN), had long and difficult supply lines, and it still lacked much of the equipment, including airplanes, of a modern army. Its food supplies were, as almost always, a source of concern. Nor were the Viet Minh yet in a position to make a serious play for the big prize, the Red River Delta, and it's doubtful that Giap at this stage would have been able to rapidly and immediately dispatch from one place to another the troops required to reinforce a success or avert a disaster. French Union forces, meanwhile, were about to be bolstered by an infusion of aircraft and other materials from the United States.[26]

French officials were quick to remind themselves and one another of these points. Maybe too quick. Certainly, there could be no talk of quitting, of seeking a fig-leaf diplomatic settlement with Ho that would allow an exit from the morass. France's credibility was on the line, as was the personal credibility of her leaders. And one could speak as well of partisan credibility being at stake. France from 1947 to 1951 had a string of coalition governments, each one standing to the ideological right of its predecessor. Indochina was one reason for this rightward drift. Unbending resolve to tackle the Viet Minh became pivotal to the MRP, the dominant party in these coalitions, which feared a disastrous hemorrhage of support to the Gaullist Rassemblement du peuple français (RPF) if it bowed to Socialist and Communist demands for negotiation with Ho Chi Minh. The declining influence of the French left in colonial and defense policy was critical to the French choices in Indochina that resulted in adherence to the Bao Dai solution, refusal to pursue direct negotiation with the Viet Minh leadership, and greater attachment to U.S. Cold War imperatives, as American military aid became fundamental to the continuation of the French war effort from this point on.[27]

Broader public opinion in France played little part in determining this firm posture. The country paid attention to Indochina because of the French troops engaged there, and there was despair at the immense loss of life in the October defeats, but one could still speak in late 1950 of a general indifference to questions affecting Southeast Asia and the Far East. On foreign affairs, most voters were far more concerned about Germany, about France's eastern frontiers, and about building up the armed forces to resist yet another invasion across the Rhine. Many expressed opposition to the Indochina War on the narrow grounds that the expenditures of manpower and money there took away from this preparation at home. But the unpopularity of the war did not yet translate into mass active opposition, and thus politicians could act with a considerable degree of impunity.

And so, in the fall of 1950, with one notable exception, no new voices were raised in French governmental circles in favor of immediate negotiations leading to withdrawal. The exception was Pierre Mendès France, an articulate leader of the Radical Party (which, despite the name, was a party of the center-left). Decrying the government's inertia, Mendès France called the war an exercise in futility, one that moreover was exacting a huge cost in blood and treasure. "It is the entire conception of our action in Indochina that is false," he declared from the rostrum in the Assembly, "for it is based on a military effort that is insufficient . . . to bring about a solution by force and on a policy that is incapable of assuring us the support of the people."

> Things cannot continue like this. . . . There are only two solutions. The first consists in realizing our objectives in Indochina by means of military force. If we choose that, let us at least avoid illusions and pious lies. To achieve decisive military successes rapidly we need three times as many troops in the field and a tripling of appropriations, and we need them very quickly. . . . The military solution is a massive new effort, sufficiently massive and sufficiently rapid to anticipate the already considerable development of the forces opposed to us.

Mendès France went on to enumerate the sacrifices that would be required in order to give this option a realistic chance: new taxes, conscription, a reduction of defenses in Europe, a slowdown in productive investment, and the impossibility ultimately of opposing the German rearmament sought by the United States. Would it not be better, he asked, to choose the second option, involving a negotiated settlement with Ho Chi Minh? "An agreement involves concessions, broad concessions, without doubt more significant than those that would have been sufficient in the past. One may reject this solution. It is difficult to apply. But then we must speak the truth to the country. We must inform it of the price that will have to be paid to bring the other solution about."[28]

The plea fell on deaf ears in the corridors of power. Disengagement short of victory would insult the memory of the Frenchmen who had died defending the cause, top civilian and military leaders insisted, a stock argument they would use time and time again in the months to come (as would, beginning in the mid-1960s, their American successors). It would simply be necessary to try harder, to perform better—and to do so under new French leadership in Hanoi. Carpentier, commander in chief of the French Expeditionary Corps and thus ultimately responsible for the Cao Bang disaster, was recalled, as was High Commissioner Pignon, who had vacillated before endorsing the decision to withdraw completely from the border region. In their place, Paris sent General Jean de Lattre de Tassigny, a World War II hero who was given both titles: commander in chief and high commissioner. He would turn out to be an inspired choice, as we shall see, at least with respect to the former title.

French leaders also now committed themselves to something they had hitherto resisted: the formation of a Vietnamese national army. They had made a few halfhearted moves in this direction in 1948 and 1949, but the French High Command held sole responsibility for the conduct of operations and for Vietnam's internal security. In November 1950, the existing Vietnamese forces, all of which served under French officers, totaled only eight battalions. None was at full strength, and all were underequipped. But the autumn calamity called into question all previous assumptions; for many French officials, it became glaringly obvious that an increase in trained Indochinese manpower would be essential to turn the tide against the Viet Minh—for political and economic no less than military reasons. More manpower was essential, yet it could not come from France or elsewhere in the empire. Accordingly, in November

1950, a Vietnamese Military Academy was opened, its mission to train one hundred and fifty Vietnamese officers per year. Its leaders announced plans to form four Vietnamese divisions during 1951, partly from newly enlisted recruits and partly from existing French-officered units.[29]

The announcement was of course an admission of weakness, tacit acknowledgment that the Expeditionary Corps as presently constituted was not up to the job. But the move gave desperate war planners in Paris a reason to hope both that their great and growing military manpower needs could be met and that Bao Dai's anemic government could, by fielding its own army, enhance its popular support. The ordinary villager was weary of the war, French analysts believed, and wished for nothing more than peace and security. If Bao Dai could exploit this desire, if he could convince the peasantry that he would provide that security, he might be able to swing public opinion in his favor. But for that argument to have any chance of working, he needed to be his own man. And to be his own man, he needed Vietnamese troops. Far too many villagers were reluctant to enter areas held by the Expeditionary Corps. Many of them chose instead to back the Viet Minh, not out of ideological conviction but because they were Vietnamese.

It was a disingenuous argument, of course, inasmuch as France was still unwilling to *let* Bao Dai be his own man, still unwilling to grant his government real independence. But certainly Paris officials were right to see a Vietnamese national army as essential; without it, there could be no hope of weaning significant non-Communist Vietnamese support away from Ho Chi Minh's cause. And if the creation of such a force could cause the Americans, who had long favored the proposition, to boost their military and other assistance to the war effort, so much the better.

On that score too, many French officials saw some reasons for hope in the midst of their late-autumn gloom.[30] The pivotal U.S. decision to provide aid to the French military effort had preceded the outbreak of fighting in Korea, but the war there shaped the nature of the U.S. aid program in key ways. On the first day of the North Korean attack, June 25, 1950, President Truman ordered that assistance to Indochina be increased and accelerated; on the thirtieth, the day U.S. troops were committed to combat in Korea (as part of a UN force), eight C-47 transport planes arrived in Saigon with the first shipments of American matériel for the French.

The Korean fighting also formed the backdrop for a July mission to Indochina headed by John Melby of the State Department and Major General Graves B. Erskine of the Marine Corps. Their report, though critical of what Erskine in particular saw as the defensive posture and mind-set of the French, concluded that the war could be won with an infusion of American material assistance. (It was a standard feature of such U.S. "survey missions" during the war: They almost always returned with a "can-do" recommendation for positive action, no matter how intractable the problem might seem to outside observers.) By early August, military supplies sufficient to equip twelve infantry battalions were en route by ship to Vietnam. To oversee the delivery of this expanded American assistance, and to "evaluate French tactical efficiency in the use of U.S. equipment," the administration created the Military Assistance Advisory Group (MAAG), whose first contingent of officers and enlisted men arrived in Saigon in September, and the Special Mission for Technical and Economic Assistance (STEM), which began its work the same month. Significantly, the French ruled out any kind of training role for MAAG and made clear they would allow no American interference in the conduct of the war.[31]

UN forces in Korea reeled under the onslaught in those early weeks. But General Douglas MacArthur's bold landing at Inchon in mid-September stopped the North Korean advance, and his counterattack in the following weeks drove them back almost to the Chinese frontier. In mid-October, however, the first Chinese units crossed into Korea, and on November 25 they began a vigorous offensive, driving U.S. troops before them. For Truman and his advisers, Chinese entry was a body blow. It raised the stakes in all of Asia. Mao's China had to be contained, not merely on the Korean peninsula but anywhere it seemed to threaten. Sniping at the French for their colonial policy in Indochina, though it did not cease entirely, suddenly seemed to many in Washington a self-indulgent luxury. As one high-level internal document put it, the military situation in Vietnam "is so grave as to require the very highest priority of the United States." In October, a shipment of forty Hellcat fighter aircraft arrived in Vietnam, and in November, the administration accelerated deliveries to Indochina of ninety Bearcat fighters and forty-one B-26 bombers, as well as transportation equipment and bulldozers. These commitments made the size of the military assistance program for Indochina second only to the support for U.S. combat forces in Korea.[32]

A subtle but crucial shift in American thinking had occurred. Washington strategists still emphasized the need for a successful political response to blunt Ho Chi Minh's nationalist appeal, but they now connected this ambition more closely to the military struggle. Hence their vociferous support for the French plans for a new Vietnamese national army; it would, after all, serve both ends. Was there a risk that this new army could be "turned against us"? Yes, a joint State-Defense report acknowledged in early December. But that possibility had to be considered alongside the prospect of ultimate defeat if things continued on their present course. "The former is a risk, the latter well-nigh a certainty. . . . Much of the stigma of colonialism can be removed if, where necessary, yellow men will be killed by yellow men rather than by white men alone." The inclusion of the word *alone* was telling, for the report's conclusion left no doubt that a French presence was vital for the foreseeable future and that the Paris government should get the military assistance it needed. For France's cause in Indochina was also America's. "America without Asia will have been reduced to the Western Hemisphere and a precarious foothold on the western fringe of the Eurasian continent," the authors concluded, but "success will vindicate and give added meaning to America and the American way of life."[33]

In time, as we shall see, French leaders would have second thoughts about this internationalization of the war effort. Inevitably, the growth in U.S. involvement gave Washington officials increased leverage in the decision making and lessened France's freedom of maneuver. For now, though, only one thing mattered: The struggle demanded an infusion of resources, which only the Americans could provide.

Vietnamese non-Communists likewise saw their leverage reduced with the Americans' arrival. Whereas in Indonesia non-Communist nationalists under Sukarno won U.S. backing in their struggle against the Netherlands and secured independence via an international negotiated settlement in 1949, in Vietnam a different dynamic prevailed. Here the non-Communists were allied with the French against the Viet Minh and thus had far less chance to play the Americans—who saw this as a Cold War struggle first and foremost—against the colonial overlord. With each passing month, it seemed, non-Communist nationalist groups such as the Dai Viet and VNQDD saw their influence recede.

At Ho Chi Minh's headquarters in the Viet Bac, the hope as 1950 drew to a close was that the hour had passed for the new measures to affect the course of events. It was too late now for the enemy to raise a legitimate Vietnamese fighting force, too late for the mighty Americans to make a meaningful difference on the ground. Following the glorious victory in the Border Campaign, red bunting appeared in villages all over Tonkin to welcome the victorious soldiers. Resistance committees proliferated throughout the north. By midautumn, recalled one Viet Minh soldier who took part in the Cao Bang fighting, army political officers were assuring troops that they would be "in Hanoi for Tet," and there was a pervasive sense that "the general counteroffensive had begun." The soldier described a typical mass rally that he and his unit came across as they marched from the frontier ridge to the delta: "The propaganda sections were already in place and had installed an information room where a phonograph played military tunes. A propagandist on a box decorated by the red flag with the yellow star harangued the crowd and the young people. 'The People's Army will be in Hanoi for Tet. This is the present that the army will give President Ho for the new year.' "[34]

Ho Chi Minh would get no such gift for the Tet holiday. Unbeknownst to the party propagandists who made their pitch, and to the cheering crowds who heard them, change was coming to Vietnam, in the form of a new French commander with a different conception of how to wage the struggle and the strength to realize that vision. And unbeknownst to them, Vo Nguyen Giap was about to make his biggest blunder of the war.

CHAPTER 11

KING JEAN

FOR ONE YOUNG FRENCH LIEUTENANT, THE SITUATION IN VIETNAM in autumn 1950, following the disaster on the RC4, approached the point of no return. Bernard de Lattre de Tassigny, age twenty-three, an infantry lieutenant in the French Expeditionary Corps, had been in Indochina for a year, commanding a post some twenty miles southeast of Hanoi. He was a remarkable young man. At fifteen, he had helped his father escape from a wartime prison in daring fashion, then had joined the Free French Army and become the youngest soldier to be decorated with the Médaille militaire. Still a teenager in the campaigns of 1944–45, he was wounded in battle and received commendations for his bravery and dedication. In Indochina, he quickly won praise from his superiors, one of whom wrote, "He is one of the few officers who has really given thought to the problem of our presence here, and he has resolved it in a concrete manner."[1]

Specifically, de Lattre had determined that the key to success lay in capturing the active support of the rural population; in the phrase of a later era, French soldiers and officers had to win the "hearts and minds" of the peasantry. The war had to be won politically if it was to be won at all, and that meant striving to meet the needs of people where they lived, whether in the form of providing security, or building schoolhouses or athletic fields, or improving sanitation. If killing had to be done—and the young lieutenant didn't doubt it—it should be done as quietly as possible, with a knife or rifle, not with heavy artillery or aerial bombardment.

From the start, de Lattre immersed himself in the often-mundane tasks of pacification. Judging from his letters home and the reports of his superiors, he had success: One report exulted that de Lattre "has captured the hearts of the local population."[2] Over time, though, his letters began to take on lugubrious tones, especially as news reached him of the calamity in Cao Bang. He despaired at the "fear psychosis" gripping some fellow officers, and at the louche lifestyle led by others, and he complained of the absence of firm, purposeful command. "Tell Father we need him, without him it will go wrong," he wrote his mother on October 23.[3]

The son got his wish. In early December, Jean de Lattre de Tassigny was appointed commander in chief of the Expeditionary Corps and high commissioner for Indochina, with complete control over the conduct of military operations as well as governmental affairs. Paris authorities, convinced that the conflicts of authority had impeded essential action at critical moments, chose to give both military and civilian powers to one individual. The elder de Lattre's appointment did not come as a surprise, but neither was it entirely expected. Bernard was overjoyed. "What we need," he wrote his father after the appointment was made, "is a leader who leads, fresh blood and new machinery, and no more niggling, no more small-time warfare; and then, with the morale that we still have in spite of it all, we could save everything."[4]

We could save everything. Those words would resound often in the months ahead. A savior had come, or so for a time it seemed. Jean de Lattre, one of France's great military leaders of the twentieth century, with a string of accomplishments already under his belt, would have perhaps his biggest success in Vietnam. Born in 1889 in Mouilleron-en-Pareds, a village in the Vendée whose other famous son was Georges Clemenceau, young Jean went to Saint-Cyr and from there to the trenches of World War I. Five different times he was wounded, swiftly earning a reputation for courage and calmness under fire. Once, during a German cavalry charge, an enemy lance pierced de Lattre's chest; unmounted but undaunted, he killed two of the enemy with his sword, then escaped.

Between the wars de Lattre served under France's famed Marshal Lyautey in Morocco and at the outbreak of the Battle of France led the Fourteenth Infantry Division as it tried valiantly to hold the German Panzers near Rheims. Later jailed by the Vichy regime for defying orders to keep his troops in barracks rather than fight the Germans, he escaped with the help of his wife and the young Bernard, who smuggled into his cell a small saw hidden in a bouquet of flowers and a ten-yard rope stuffed in a bag of laundry. De Lattre joined the Free French and in 1944–45 led the First French Army (which landed with the Americans in Provence on August 15, 1944) in its glorious march from the southern coast to the Rhine and the Danube. Among his prizes after crossing the Rhine were Karlsruhe, Stuttgart, and Freudenstadt. At one time, his command included 125,000 American troops.[5]

Even then, de Lattre's temperament was the stuff of legend. Like Douglas MacArthur, to whom he bore a strong physical resemblance and was often compared, he could be impatient with superiors' instructions; like MacArthur, he was vain and had a flair for the intensely dramatic. "General de Théatre," some called him. A brilliant mimic, he was excellent company, and even detractors acknowledged his extraordinary personal magnetism. More than one observer compared him to Churchill for his singular ability to dominate any room he entered, to attract all attention to himself, and to keep listeners enthralled with his magnetism, his self-deprecating wit, his eloquence.

But there was also a dark side. Egocentric to the point of megalomania, de Lattre was prone to moodiness and to volcanic expressions of anger toward underlings. Meticulous in his personal appearance—he wore uniforms tailored by Lanvin, the stylish Paris couturier—he demanded that subordinates be likewise, and he bristled when on inspections his hosts failed to welcome him with the ceremonial he considered his due (hence a second nickname: *Le Roi Jean*, or King Jean). Always he was notoriously touchy about honor—both his own and his country's. On one occasion, during a dinner for Allied commanders, de Lattre refused to touch his food and wine because Marshal Zhukov of the Red Army neglected to mention France in a toast praising Allied armies. Informed of his mistake, Zhukov offered a separate toast to France. A mollified de Lattre began to eat and drink.[6]

At the conclusion of the war, General de Gaulle sent de Lattre to Berlin to participate in the Armistice ceremony, even though France hadn't been invited. De Lattre signed as a witness and exulted: "Victory has arrived . . . radiant victory of springtime, which gives back to our France her youth, her strength and her hope." This was not mere rhetoric. De

Lattre believed in his country, believed in the empire, and in the postwar years did everything he could to restore France to what he considered her rightful place among the leading powers. Beginning in late 1945, he served as inspector general and chief of staff of the French Army and then as commander of Western Union (the precursor to NATO) ground forces—in effect, Western Europe's top general.

His acceptance in late 1950 of the Indochina posting surprised some who saw it as a step down in professional terms, but for de Lattre there could be no question of declining. A gambler by nature, he had always trained his troops to embrace the need to take risks; now he had to live up to his teaching. More important, his country was at war, and the war was going badly, with his only son in the heart of the action. An outright defeat seemed all too possible. In this hour of maximum need, he had to answer the call. "I have nothing to gain and doubtless much to lose," de Lattre replied when Prime Minister René Pleven asked him to take up the post. "All the more reason for accepting, and, as a good soldier, I shall do so without hesitation."[7]

De Lattre saw as his foremost aim keeping Indochina firmly within the French Union, but his initial utterances emphasized the menace posed by the forces of international Communism. He told the American journalist Robert Shaplen that France was in Vietnam "to save it from Peking and Moscow." Paris might have acted out of colonialist motives in the past, but no more. "We have abandoned all colonial positions completely," he assured a skeptical Shaplen. "The work we are doing is for the salvation of the Vietnamese people"—and the security of the Western world. The Vietnam struggle, he insisted at every opportunity, was another front in the war that the West was waging in Korea. The stakes were huge: "Tonkin is the keystone of the defense of Southeast Asia. If Tonkin falls, Siam falls with Burma, and Malaya is dangerously compromised. Without Tonkin the rest of Indochina is soon lost."[8]

Did de Lattre really believe it was so simple? It's hard to be sure. His hatred of Communism knew no bounds, and he was convinced that his actions in Indochina ultimately mattered as much to the West's defense as did MacArthur's in Korea. But he also knew that the imagery of countries falling one by one, like bowling pins—or, as it were, dominoes—resonated in the halls of power in Washington, among both civilians and military men. And on this point de Lattre needed no schooling: The success or failure of the daunting task that confronted him, he knew, depended in large measure on the attitudes and policies of the Truman White House.

II

HE SET OUT FROM ORLY AIRPORT AT MIDNIGHT ON DECEMBER 13. Some two thousand old comrades of the First French Army turned out to see him off, their banners fluttering in the nighttime breeze. It was a moving moment for de Lattre, proof, he said, that *les gars* (the boys, as he called his men) still trusted him, that the spirit of the First Army still lived. Five days later his plane touched down in Saigon. It was December 19, four years to the day since the outbreak of major war.

"His plane came in and de Lattre stood at the top of a flight of stairs, on the platform, the gangplank, and he turned his profile this way," Edmund Gullion, second in command at the American legation, recalled of the scene. "He had a magnificent profile (something like MacArthur), and watching him arrive, he seemed seven foot tall, stiff and straight and he took white gloves and pulled them carefully on his hands, like that—a very symbolic gesture, symbolizing in the honor of the corps [that] a gentleman aristocrat was in office. But the symbolism of pulling on the gloves was lost on no one. . . . He was coming down to clean up this mess."[9]

Immediately he made clear that spit and polish, flourish and ceremony, would be the order of the day. The Guard of Honor presented arms, and the band played "The Marseillaise." To de Lattre, however, the guard appeared slovenly, and in front of bystanders he ripped into the colonel in charge, a terrifying treatment known in French slang as the "shampoo." He then unleashed a torrent of abuse on the bandleader, on the grounds that one instrument was out of tune. To all assembled, there could be no doubt: King Jean had arrived.[10]

Later that day the general addressed a gathering of French officers, telling them he couldn't guarantee any easy victories or early improvement in the battlefield situation. What he could promise was firm command: "From now on, you will be led." He promptly canceled the order for the evacuation of women and children from Hanoi—"As long as women and children are here, the men won't dare let go"—and announced that his wife would soon join him from Paris. He vowed that Tonkin would be held, rejecting claims by some French officers that a concentration on southern Annam and Cochin China was unavoidable. These statements immediately bolstered morale among civilians and troops, as did his announcement that he would fly immediately to Tonkin. (At this departure too there was a ceremony, and again de Lattre went on a tirade: He ordered twenty-five days' confinement for the pilot of his plane, for failing to put the new commander's insignia on the fuselage. To a bearded copilot, de Lattre snapped: "You've got five minutes to shave yourself clean!")[11]

In Tonkin, there was no denying the gravity of the situation. French Union garrisons on the northern and northeastern frontiers had been forced, due to the Viet Minh assaults in the Border Campaign, to withdraw to the Red River Delta, the possession of which de Lattre deemed

DE LATTRE AND BAO DAI DURING AN AWARDS
CEREMONY IN EARLY 1951.

essential to the defense of Indochina as a whole. Upon arriving in Hanoi, he reaffirmed that dependents would stay and again said he would not allow Tonkin to fall.

In the days thereafter, he shuttled all over the delta in his small Morane spotter plane, showing scant regard for his own physical safety—more than once his entourage came under enemy fire—and a level of energy that left aides utterly exhausted. Everywhere he touched dormant chords of national pride and brought forth cheers from the assembled French troops; everywhere he ruthlessly weeded out the incompetent and the (by his standards) lackadaisical. His mantra at each stop: There will be no quitting Indochina until the Communists have been defeated.

But de Lattre knew that bucking up the fighting spirit of his soldiers, essential though it was, wouldn't be enough. He consequently undertook a regrouping of French forces and reorganized the system of defense in Tonkin. Relying on the Armée d'Afrique tactics he had learned under Marshal Lyautey in Morocco in the 1920s, de Lattre emphasized the need for mobility, even in terrain that limited rapid movement to roads, with the accompanying dangers of ambush. Accordingly, he organized *groupes mobiles* (striking groups), each consisting essentially of a headquarters with sufficient command and communication facilities, to which could be assigned three or more infantry battalions and supporting troops. These *groupes mobiles* would move quickly to engage Viet Minh units and relieve besieged posts; when attacked, they would use the Armée d'Afrique tactic of simultaneous assault from at least two, and sometimes three or more, different encircling directions. The artillery, firing from the road deep into the jungle, would be dispersed throughout the length of a column and thus could not all be lost in a single ambush.[12]

To enhance mobility and protect the delta, de Lattre ordered the construction of a series of self-contained and mutually supporting defense works, or blockhouses, all around the area. This chain of fortified concrete positions—built in groups of five or six, one or two miles apart, and designed to accommodate between three and ten soldiers—which became known as the "De Lattre Line," had been recommended in the Revers Report of May 1949, but nothing had been done. Until now. De Lattre supervised much of the construction personally and drove the crews mercilessly; by the end of 1951, more than a thousand of the posts had been created, on a line that stretched in a rough semicircle from the sea near the Baie d'Along, along the northern edge of the delta to Vinh Yen, and then southeast to the sea again near Phat Diem, enclosing protectively both Hanoi and Haiphong. (See map on p. 269.) Supported by these positions, the *groupes mobiles* could set forth in search of enemy units, and also—in theory, at least—protect against rice smuggling as well as major Viet Minh assaults.

Two problems remained, however: finding enough bodies to man these many hundreds of strongpoints, and making sure the troops were adequately supplied. To meet the first objective, de Lattre sought and received reinforcements of North African units and Foreign Legionnaires. He knew, though, that Paris would never authorize sufficient numbers of troops for Indochina to do more than hold the line. The money wasn't there.[13] He therefore accelerated what the French were now calling the *jaunissement* (literally "yellowing"), the building up of the still-embryonic Vietnamese National Army (VNA). At the time of de Lattre's arrival, these comprised eleven battalions and nine gendarmerie units, and he swiftly ordered the creation of an additional twenty-five battalions, four armored squadrons, and eight artillery batteries. This Vietnamese force would perform the task, so the argument went, of pacifying and defending areas not under effective Viet Minh control, thereby freeing the Expeditionary Corps for offensive action. Many of the best officers and NCOs of the French Army, among them Bernard, volunteered to serve as the necessary initial cadres for these Vietnamese units.[14]

For equipment, de Lattre turned to the United States. He took satisfaction from that fact that Washington's aid had begun flowing more freely, and in particular he welcomed the dispatch of dozens of Bearcat fighters and B-26 bombers, as well as transportation equipment and bulldozers. American artillery shells were also arriving in much larger quantities, as were vital 105mm howitzers. But much more would be needed. From the U.S. liaison office in Indochina, de Lattre requested urgently needed materials. Among the items was an American weapon designed for jungle fighting: napalm. His predecessors had made scant use of this jellied petroleum that ignites on contact, but de Lattre determined at once that it could have enormous utility.[15]

III

IN HIS JUNGLE HEADQUARTERS NEAR THAI NGUYEN, FIFTY MILES north of Hanoi, General Vo Nguyen Giap greeted the news of de Lattre's appointment with satisfaction, even delight. Always fascinated by military laurels and recognition, Giap viewed the selection of such an illustrious figure as a compliment to himself and to his troops, and he eagerly took up the challenge. "The French are sending against the People's Army a foe worthy of its steel," he declared. "We will defeat him on his own ground."[16] Brimming with confidence following his victories in northern Tonkin, Giap now set his sights upon the Red River Delta and Hanoi. His Chinese advisers, flush with excitement about the success of the Border Campaign and of their human-wave attacks against the Americans in Korea, now urged Giap to use the same tactics against the French in Vietnam.

For some months, a debate had been raging in high Viet Minh councils about whether the time had come to shift to the third and final stage of Maoist people's war, the general offensive. Did the success in the autumn offensive suggest that conditions were now ripe? Was a "preponderance of forces" in just one area sufficient, or did one need to have it all over the country? How vulnerable were the French in the delta, and would a Viet Minh victory there presage the crumbling of the entire colonial edifice? Senior officials went around and around on these questions; Giap was among those who argued that his forces could move to the third stage before they held absolute material superiority on the battlefield. Others disagreed, but Giap's advocacy received a boost from the growing rice shortage in Viet Minh–held areas; unless revolutionary forces could expand their presence in the delta, he and others insisted, the food situation would become desperate. (Already the government had ordered people to drastically curtail their consumption of rice so that sufficient amounts would be available to the armed forces.) A fragile consensus emerged to launch the opening stages of what seemed likely to be a protracted and complex offensive. The first stage: a major assault on the delta from the northwest.[17]

Giap prided himself on his meticulous preparation for battle, but here he miscalculated—his hubris got the better of him. He gave insufficient thought to his great advantage in the Border Campaign: The French were dispersed and had few lines of communication or transport. But that advantage did not apply in the delta: Here the French were much better placed. While Viet Minh forces moved into position north of Hanoi—sixty-five infantry, twelve artillery, and eight engineer battalions, from the 308th and 312th Divisions, together with civilian porters who brought five thousand tons of rice, ammunition, and weapons—Viet Minh propagandists began posting leaflets around the delta bearing the inscription, "Ho Chi Minh in Hanoi for Tet." (Tet is the Chinese lunar new year, falling usually in February.) French commanders girded for battle, and their intelligence analysts (especially those of the Service de documentation extérieure et de contre-espionnage, or SDECE) identified the general whereabouts of the enemy's concentration and the probable attack date.

The first target in what would become known as the Day River Battles was Vinh Yen, some thirty miles northwest of Hanoi on the north side of the Red River, near where it debouched from the highlands. The town was one of Hanoi's protective bastions; if it fell, the road to the capital

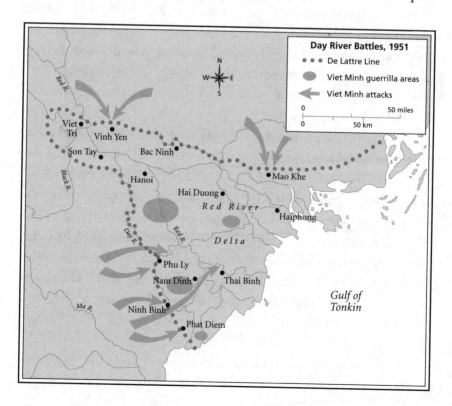

would be open. Giap planned to use his two divisions to breach Vinh Yen's defenses and force a gap, through which his forces could make a dash for Hanoi. On the evening of January 13, two regiments of the 308th assaulted Bao Chuc, a small post near the town held by about fifty Senegalese and Vietnamese who fought to the last man and succumbed after two bayonet counterattacks. A *groupe mobile* sent to relieve the post was surrounded and likewise assailed by enemy units that had taken up positions on the surrounding hills. It looked like the leaflet vow would be made good.

De Lattre now took personal charge of the battle. On the fourteenth, he flew right into Vinh Yen in his spotter plane and from there ordered the mobilization of all available reserves and the transfer of troops from Cochin China to the north. On the fifteenth, he sent a *groupe mobile* of crack North African troops to seize the heights around Vinh Yen. The effort appeared to have succeeded, but suddenly at sundown on the sixteenth, there came wave upon wave of Viet Minh infantry to conquer the hastily dug defenses of the hill line. Merciless hand-to-hand combat ensued, with grenades and tommy guns; casualties were heavy on both sides. De Lattre, returning to Vinh Yen for a second time, realized the gravity of the situation and ordered all available aircraft—both fighter-bombers and transport planes capable of dumping American-made napalm canisters—into what would be the heaviest aerial bombardment of the entire war.[18]

Relentlessly, the napalm bombs rained down on the Viet Minh troops, literally roasting thousands of them. Early on January 17, the 312th Division tried a final mass attack; it badly mauled a battalion under Colonel Paul Vanuxem but was blocked by a curtain of roaring napalm. After that, the attacks became spasmodic, then died away completely. The air grew silent. The French looked around in stunned disbelief: They had prevailed; they remained lords of the battlefield. Giap had lost 6,000 dead and 8,000 wounded and had been defeated in the open field. French airpower, using a terrifying new weapon, had proved decisive. A Viet Minh officer wrote in his diary:

All of a sudden a sound can be heard in the sky and strange birds appear, getting larger and larger. Airplanes. I order my men to take cover from the bombs and machine-gun bullets. But the planes dive upon us without firing their guns. However, all of a sudden, hell opens in front of my eyes. Hell comes in the form of large, egg-shaped containers, dropping from the first plane, followed by other eggs from the second and third plane. Immense sheets of flames, extending over hundreds of meters, it seems, strike terror in the ranks of my soldiers. This is *napalm,* the fire that falls from the skies.

Another plane swoops down behind us and again drops a na-palm bomb. The bomb falls closely behind us and I feel its fiery breath touching my whole body. The men are now fleeing in all directions and I cannot hold them back. There is no way of hold-ing out under this torrent of fire that flows in all directions and burns everything in its passage. On all sides, flames surround us now. In addition, French artillery and mortars now have our range and transform into a fiery tomb what had been, ten minutes ago, a quiet part of the forest.[19]

As de Lattre well understood, the victory at Vinh Yen would have been impossible without the timely arrival of American airplanes, weap-ons, and ammunition. The napalm bombs and howitzers were partic-ularly important, but de Lattre also knew that virtually all the aircraft employed were of U.S. origin, as was much of the artillery. At a trium-phant press conference in Saigon on January 23, he lauded the United States for her assistance in the battle. Describing the visit U.S. minister Donald R. Heath had made with him to the combat area a few days be-fore, the French commander said that French officers had "eagerly seized the occasion to voice their gratitude for American supplies." To Heath privately, he said that the napalm had been crucial.[20]

Giap too grasped the importance of the stepped-up American aid to the enemy's cause. But he was unwilling to admit that Vinh Yen repre-sented a serious defeat, or that it showed his forces unready for a major battle of maneuver. The operation was a close-run thing, he reasoned; the result could easily have gone the other way. Twice more that spring Giap tried to break into the delta; both times he failed. In late March, he sent twenty-one battalions against the French garrison around Mao

Khe, a coastal village some twenty miles northwest of Haiphong. The French, undermanned by a ratio of three to one, repulsed the attack, thanks again largely to their command of the air and their superior artillery. Napalm was again used to devastating effect. Losses were high on both sides. The French sustained casualties of roughly 25 percent, and the Viet Minh left more than four hundred bodies on the battlefield. A week later the Viet Minh attacked again at nearby Dong Trieu; again they were beaten back.[21]

The third attempt came in late May. This time Giap moved from the south, in a classical maneuver against the French defenses in the southeast along the Day River. The objective was twofold: to capture the rice crops in the area, then ripe for harvesting, and to take the strongly Catholic area around Ninh Binh and Phat Diem, which to this point had proved stubbornly resistant to Viet Minh infiltration. It took the Viet Minh two months to move—mostly by night, to avoid detection—troops and porters and supplies all the way around the delta, and the monsoon rains started before the operation could begin. But Giap was confident, in part because one regiment of the 320th Division had managed to infiltrate behind enemy lines near Thai Binh, where it joined up with regional units in order to attack the French from the rear.

The assault began on May 29 as Viet Minh units crossed the Day River. They achieved the element of surprise and made initial gains, but de Lattre swiftly organized eight motorized brigades. Heavy fighting ensued, and for days the outcome was in doubt. Some positions around Ninh Binh changed hands several times. But the Catholic militia proved adept at interior defense, and French riverine forces finally cut Giap's supply lines across the river. By June 6, the French had gained the initiative. Four days later Giap ordered a withdrawal. He left some 9,000 dead and 1,000 captured.[22]

He had been outclassed, had shown his inexperience as a general. Cocksure by nature, he had failed to heed what the Vinh Yen defeat had taught about the difficulty of penetrating the delta. Neither he nor his staff yet understood adequately how to move large units or how to handle them in battle. He had sent them into action in open terrain during daylight, which made them easy targets for superior French firepower. He had failed to leave himself with reserve units and thus had no way to exploit sudden opportunities, and his withdrawals from all three operations had been chaotic and slow, causing further Viet Minh casualties. Only belatedly did he grasp what napalm could do to massed formations. Senior party leaders, notably theoretician Truong Chinh, accused Giap of causing needless massacres and of selecting the wrong commanders; even Ho Chi Minh, whose own leadership was called into question, expressed distress at the heavy battle losses. DRV radio broadcasts obliquely criticized the offensives by praising the guerrilla techniques used early in the war, and there were reports of increased desertions from Viet Minh ranks. Even the Chinese, now facing a prolonged fight against the Americans in Korea, sang a different tune than at the start of the year, emphasizing the need for caution. Giap didn't lose his position, but his authority was undermined. He resolved to steer clear of large set-piece engagements for the foreseeable future and to return to guerrilla warfare.[23]

A captured order of the day signed by Giap following the defeats put the matter plainly: "Our troops, who have shown their superiority as guerrillas, should, from now on, not seek massive battle. The general counteroffensive is called off. Regional elements will enter by small groups into towns and reinforce the urban networks. The prize of revolutionary warfare remains the population."[24]

IV

THEN TOO, IT MATTERED THAT GIAP HAD COME UP AGAINST A FORMIDable opposing commander. With each successive victory in early 1951 de Lattre's prestige rose. His expressions of vanity and his explosions of anger at underlings did not cease—he fired one stenographer with the words, "You don't know how to dress, Miss, and your hair is dirty"—and in the officer corps murmurings could be heard about the "reckless prima donna" who led them.[25] But de Lattre showed again that he was a man of action and courage who feared nobody, and even those who disliked him took their hats off to him. Some journalists likened his Vinh Yen victory to the miracle of the Marne in 1914. Admittedly, he hadn't gained one inch of new territory, but without him, many were convinced, Hanoi would have fallen to the Viet Minh. To the *colons* in both Hanoi and Saigon, he was the hero they had long sought; to the politicians and much of the press in Paris, he was the general who might yet save French Indochina. He was *Le Roi Jean*.

He was also the proud father. In early May, he had personally decorated Bernard with the Croix de Guerre, and he never hesitated to wax lyrical before reporters and others about the young man's exploits in the field. In one such session, with a Belgian journalist on May 30, in the midst of the fighting in Ninh Binh, the general discussed the battlefield situation and referred with particular pride to the role being played by Bernard, who was leading a platoon of Vietnamese troops. The interview was nearing its end when an assistant burst into the room, his face ashen. De Lattre took one look at him and, before the aide could open his mouth, exclaimed: "Bernard is dead!"[26]

It was true. Bernard had been killed earlier that day, on the banks of the Day River near Nam Dinh. His company had been ordered to hold a rocky hillock, and during the night Bernard had taken up a position on the summit, along with a Vietnamese corporal and a French lieutenant named Mercier. Sometime after one o'clock, the corporal was wounded in a small-arms firefight, and soon thereafter Viet Minh troops could be seen advancing in the plain below. At about three o'clock, mortar shells began to fall near the rock; one found its mark, mortally wounding Mercier and instantly killing Bernard. The wounded corporal helped carry the bodies to a cave at the foot of the rock, then returned to his post to continue the fight.[27]

De Lattre was shattered. To his wife, then in Paris, he telegraphed: "Forgive me for not having been able to protect him." A few days later he flew back to France with the casket containing his only son. A funeral followed at the Chapel Saint-Louis, at the Invalides, and at the request of Madame de Lattre, the service also honored all Frenchmen who had fallen in Indochina. The next day Bernard was buried at his father's birthplace, Mouilleron-en-Pareds.

In time, the devastating effect of the son's death on the general's outlook would become clear for all to see. Initially, though, he masked his despair, stressing at every opportunity that both his Christian faith and his faith in the importance of France's mission in Indochina were undiminished. Bernard had given his life for the most noble of causes, he insisted—perhaps, some thought, a bit too insistently.

Upon his return from France, he threw himself into his tasks with even more energy than before, driving his aides to exhaustion. (There were subtle hints too that his own physical stamina was suffering—a sign, perhaps, that the cancer that would claim his life was already at work within. He still toiled deep into the night, but his vigor slackened in the later hours.) Dissatisfied with the pace of construction of the De Lattre Line, he committed more manpower to the task. Concerned about the level of Viet Minh infiltration inside the delta, he ordered stepped-up efforts aimed at "cleaning" the interior. These "*nettoyage*" sweeps achieved considerable success but did not attain the full effect because of the absence of any civil organization capable of taking control of "cleansed" areas. De Lattre blamed Bao Dai's government, headed by Prime Minister Tran Van Huu, for this absence, for not doing enough to build up an effective administrative structure, and for failing to arouse broad popular support. He demanded the immediate firing of ministers he considered ineffectual; Huu, widely regarded as among the most pro-French of officials, resisted.[28]

The old Franco-Vietnamese political problems had in fact not gone away. From his very first speech in Vietnam, on December 19, and at all points thereafter, de Lattre had stressed that Vietnam was free and that his mission was merely to help it protect that freedom. Imperial control was no more. As he told Huu and other Vietnamese ministers during a tour of the Vinh Yen battlefield in mid-April: "Some of you may look upon these blockhouses as the outward sign of the permanence of the French occupation. On the contrary, Mr. Prime Minister, they are the ramparts behind which the independence of Vietnam will be built up."[29] Huu was skeptical, as were others in his entourage. For them, as for a great many non-Communist Vietnamese that spring, France still showed scant signs of granting Vietnam anything that looked like real independence. The French had ceded control of the treasury and the customs service to the Bao Dai administration, but the high commissioner's office plainly exercised ultimate control on key issues, not least those pertaining to the war effort. His dictatorial methods also had begun to grate. Many Vietnamese accordingly still took a wait-and-see attitude—not least Bao Dai himself, who spent much of the first half of the year on the French Riviera, polishing his tennis game. For his part, Huu, a competent administrator who lacked charisma, had little following among the people and seemed largely unperturbed by the fact.

De Lattre called them *attentistes* (literally, "those who wait," or fence sitters), the Vietnamese who refused to make the necessary effort. By the middle of the year, he used the term more and more often, against more and more people. Bitter, he said he had come to Vietnam to assist the Associated States (the euphemistic term now increasingly in use, referring to the pseudogovernments of Vietnam, Laos, and Cambodia) cement their already-granted independence within the French Union and to crush those who sought to impose a Communist system on a freedom-loving people. And what help did the Vietnamese provide? Precious little. They were not doing their share, were not all that interested in the struggle against Ho Chi Minh; they were even, he charged, stabbing him in the back. Huu's government was apathetic and weak, and middle-class Vietnamese—the very people who had the most stake in the outcome of the war—were not signing up for the army. Despite a desperate shortage of medics, for example, not a single doctor could be induced to sign up.[30]

It was his standard refrain in the summer months, and there's no doubt Bernard's death played a role in both the nature and frequency of his outbursts. Already in June, he began to assert that the Viet Minh attacks on the Day River—those that killed Bernard—were made possible by the treachery of the Catholic bishops at Phat Diem. He offered little evidence for the charge. More generally, de Lattre now declared that French officers and soldiers had sacrificed themselves needlessly to defend and protect a selfish and mistrustful Vietnamese people. "If this constant sacrificing of our youths' flower does not prove us sincere in our desire to give Vietnam independence," he asked, with scarcely disguised contempt, "what further is necessary to drive the point home?" In a "bona fide war," he would at least have the consolation that his son had died a heroic death. Instead, Bernard had been "offered up on behalf of an ungrateful people," who not only had failed to warn the French troops that there were Viet Minh in the vicinity, but had "booed and hissed 'vendus' ['sell-out'] at the Vietnamese soldiers accompanying them."[31]

Maybe the general deep down inside felt some personal responsibility for the death. Rumors circulated quietly that he himself had assigned his son to that particular battalion, in order to break up Bernard's affair with a Vietnamese woman who once had been a mistress of Emperor Bao Dai.[32]

To remind all and sundry of the sacrifices being made by the French Union for the defense of Vietnam, de Lattre ordered a series of commemorative services be held for his fallen son, at various points around the country. On July 5, for example, there was a solemn mass in St. Joseph's Cathedral in Hanoi. Reluctant Vietnamese ministers were compelled to fly to Tonkin—how could one decline such an invitation?—as were equally reluctant members of the diplomatic community, most of whom weren't informed of the event until eight o'clock the night before. Hasty arrangements were made, and the aircraft left Saigon at four-thirty A.M. in order to make it in time for the service. After everyone else in the cathedral had been seated, and following an imposing silence, the general made a dramatic entrance and took his place next to the bishop. A Trappist monk delivered an eloquent address built on the theme of Bernard as a symbol of France's contribution to the preservation of liberty.[33]

The next week de Lattre returned to the theme, this time at an awards ceremony at a school for privileged Vietnamese boys—none of whom, experience had taught him, could be expected to join the army. Prime Minister Huu was in attendance. De Lattre reminded the students that Frenchmen were dying on their behalf (he left out the fact that most of those dying were legionnaires and imperial troops) and said there could be no room in this struggle for *attentistes*—"those miserable persons who want independence without war." This was the war for Vietnam's future, he declared, and France would carry the fight only if Vietnamese elites joined with her. "Certain people pretend that Vietnam cannot be independent because it is part of the French Union. Not true! In our universe, and in our world of today, there can be no nations absolutely independent. There are only fruitful interdependencies and harmful dependencies. . . . Young men of Vietnam, to whom I feel as close as I do to the youth of my native land, the moment has come for you to defend your country."[34]

It was a stirring message by a supremely talented orator. A standing ovation and raucous applause followed. But de Lattre knew that occasional speeches were not enough. That same month he prevailed upon Bao Dai and Huu to decree a "general mobilization" to conscript sixty thousand men for two months of training. This decree and de Lattre's continual pronouncements were not without effect—recruitment into the Vietnamese National Army continued to move upward through the summer and fall—but the fundamental problem remained: Altogether too many privileged Vietnamese were unwilling to fight and die for Bao Dai's government. Many sought to avoid military service completely; others pulled every available string to steer clear of combat duty. Only half the five hundred student-reserve officer candidates selected by the Ministry of Defense for the first increment of the mobilization ever reported for duty at the officer training centers in Thu Duc and Nam Dinh.[35] Government bureaucrats too operated with what the French saw as a maddening diffidence and a tendency to focus their energies on political intrigue rather than on fighting the challenge posed by Ho Chi Minh's forces.

V

IF IN DE LATTRE'S VIEW THE VIETNAMESE WERE UNGRATEFUL, IN-sincere, and even treacherous, he had hardly better things to say about the Americans. The latter, indeed, in his mind were in good measure responsible for the *attentisme* problem. Repeatedly he criticized American journalists for questioning France's commitment to granting the Vietnamese full independence, and it irritated him that the Truman administration sought to administer its aid directly to the Vietnamese and not through the French. Still more annoying was the U.S. legation's constant trumpeting of American economic assistance, which made France seem "like a poor cousin in Viet eyes." De Lattre banned any mention of U.S. economic aid in the French-language newspapers in Vietnam, and he lashed out at the self-congratulatory pronouncements of the Economic Aid Mission (STEM), which he said was engaging in propaganda and political work in addition to producing economic reports. American representatives sought to undermine his authority, he charged, and to implant themselves in Vietnam in place of France. When an American embassy official protested that this was Communist propaganda, de Lattre replied that even Communists were sometimes right.[36]

Most upsetting of all to de Lattre and his staff were the activities of the U.S. Information Service (USIS), a State Department program charged with the conduct of public diplomacy—that is, propaganda.

It outraged the French that so many Vietnamese were enrolling in the USIS's English-language classes, particularly when so few of them had adequate command of French. Was this one more sign that the United States sought to supplant France in Vietnam? French officials thought so. And why was it that the USIS's first translation effort was a history of the United States? "This seems either absurd or offensive to most French who have found that even literate Viets know little of [the] history of their own country and almost nothing of [the] history of France," remarked the acting French diplomatic counselor in Saigon. "To expect them to read American history seems [the] height of national egotism on [the] part of Americans."[37]

Secretary of State Dean Acheson scoffed at the French complaints. "If the Viets 'know nothing or little' of their own history or that of France, this is a problem for the Ministry of Education and incidentally one which should have been taken up long ago," the secretary of state commented acidly. It was not America's problem.[38] De Lattre, however, was undaunted. At the opening of the USIS's new reading room on July 23, he took the opportunity to warn that there was no room in Vietnam for American political or cultural or economic competition. "Because of this . . . simple fact—war—there can no longer be any struggle for influence any more than there can be rivalry of interests," he said.

> There is only one struggle in Asia just as there is only one defense in Europe. Every action of the free peoples must combine in that struggle; and America's influence in Indochina is exercised within the framework of the efforts made against the common enemy. This necessary framework, without which there can be neither organization nor dynamic cohesion nor success, is at the present time furnished by the structure of the French Union. Nothing must weaken that structure, for if it should disappear there would arise—as all admit—a situation and a regime the first effects of which would be the elimination of every American influence as of every French influence.

As always, he sought also to connect the two Asian wars: "America and France are today giving the world examples of enterprises which

he needed, and the VNA was not ready to make up the difference—and wouldn't be ready for a long time to come, if ever. U.S. aid, crucial to the enterprise, had been stepped up since the start of the year, which was good, but the Americans' penchant for sticking their noses into everything was less than helpful. In other words, went this line of argument, de Lattre had determined he could not get enough from the two players that mattered most to him: the Bao Dai administration and the U.S. government.

This interpretation of his mood seems correct. In support of it there is also this: The general's health was now in steep decline, the cancer cells advancing rapidly inside his body. Did he know he was gravely ill? It's hard to be sure—the formal diagnosis wouldn't come until October—but associates could see that all was not well. Surely his illness added to his frustrations, to his feelings of resentment, to his ill temper. Never a patient man, he now seemed intolerant of even minor delays and setbacks. Yet the old personal magnetism hadn't disappeared, at least not among those who saw him only intermittently or met him for the first time. For them, he could still radiate charm and sincerity. When Thomas E. Dewey, governor of New York and the Republican presidential nominee in 1948, visited Saigon in July, he fell under the general's spell. "He is the most exciting personality I have met in many years," Dewey enthused afterward.[41]

So impressed was Dewey that he suggested de Lattre visit the United States personally to make the case for the vital importance of France's struggle. De Lattre had been entertaining the idea himself. The road to victory in the war, he was convinced, led through Washington, but the Truman team still needed to be convinced of the full importance of Vietnam in the world picture. He trusted no one else to make the case. In September, accordingly, he left Saigon for the American capital, stopping in France en route. British officials thought he looked tired and worn during a dinner in Paris on the fourth but were impressed by the case he laid out, by his passionate defense of French policy. Also impressed were two prominent Americans he saw in the French capital, General Dwight Eisenhower, who had succeeded him as Western Europe's top general and was now NATO commander, and Henry Cabot Lodge, Republican senator from Massachusetts. Both men accepted de Lattre's claim that

France wasn't fighting a selfish colonial war but was defending one of the hinges of the allied front against the East. Both agreed that France deserved greater material and political support in the struggle.[42]

VI

HE ARRIVED BY SHIP, ENTERING NEW YORK HARBOR ON SEPTEM-ber 13 aboard the stately *Île de France*. Resplendent in kepi and pigskin gloves, he posed for photos with Humphrey Bogart and Lauren Bacall, who were returning from location filming for *The African Queen*, in which Bogart starred with Katharine Hepburn. De Lattre then asked for a picture of himself with the Statue of Liberty as a backdrop. The massed photographers were quick to oblige, and de Lattre turned his chiseled profile to the lenses and gestured theatrically toward his country's copper gift to America. A fawning cover story in Henry Luce's virulently anti-Communist *Time* called the photo request a "deliberately significant gesture: the general had freedom—and mutual aid—very much in mind." For nine months, the magazine enthused, de Lattre "has been fighting one of freedom's bloodiest and most crucial battles," and he was now coming to the United States to get more aid for Indochina, "the rampart against the Communist surge toward Singapore and the Indies."[43]

That was precisely the message de Lattre wanted to convey during his two-week stay. At every stop, he framed the Indochina struggle in Cold War terms, as a war against "Red colonialism." Just as United Nations forces were fighting the Communist world dictatorship in Korea, so French troops were fighting it in Indochina; these were two fronts in the same struggle. But in Indochina France fought alone. She had willingly assumed the burden of war in Indochina at a tremendous cost to her manpower and financial resources, and while America had provided essential assistance, more must come, in the form of larger and prompter arms deliveries. To assuage American concerns regarding France's ultimate plans, de Lattre insisted that his government had no colonial ambitions in Indochina but was doing everything possible to build up the strength and independence of Vietnam, Laos, and Cambodia.[44]

The message went over well, in large part, both inside and outside the halls of power, but behind the scenes there were tensions. In Washington, where the general got the number one treatment—honor guard, military band, howitzer salute, receptions, dinners—President Truman told him he regarded the Indochina struggle as "the same fight for liberty" as the war in Korea and pledged full support for the French effort. Secretary of State Acheson offered his own assurances: "We shall do all that is possible for you." De Lattre sought clarification: Did this mean that Korea and Indochina would get equal billing in terms of U.S. expenditures? No, came the reply, Indochina's needs, while highly important, would be acted upon only after those in Korea had been fulfilled.[45]

At the Pentagon a few days later, de Lattre tried again. "If you lose Korea," he told Secretary of Defense Robert Lovett and the Joint Chiefs of Staff, "Asia is not lost; but if I lose Indochina, Asia is lost." Tonkin was the key to Southeast Asia, and if Southeast Asia were lost, India would "burn like a match," and there'd be no hindrance to the march of Communism before Suez and Africa. The Muslim world would be engulfed, the Muslims of North Africa would fall in line, and Europe itself would be outflanked. Lovett praised de Lattre's exegesis and said he agreed the stakes in Vietnam were huge, but he added that "the United States has a primary obligation in other theaters, whereas your primary obligation is in your own theater." When de Lattre complained that he felt at times during his visit like a "beggar" and that "your spirit should lead you to send me [greater military aid] without my asking," Lovett said, "We all regard General de Lattre as a comrade in arms and will do everything possible for his theater within our capabilities." The general shot back: "Do not say *my* theater; it is *our* theater."[46]

And so it went, at each stop on the tour. In public, the charismatic Frenchman made a great impression, charming Americans with his heavily accented (but near-fluent) English and winning smiles when he tripped over an idiom. Always he cut a striking figure, whether praying at George Washington's tomb at Mount Vernon, or visiting the naval and military academies as well as Fort Benning and Langley Air Force Base, or laying a wreath at the Tomb of the Unknown Soldier, or attending a gala dinner in his honor hosted by Henry Luce at the Union Club in Manhattan. He won praise for his performance on NBC's *Meet the Press*, before an estimated viewing audience of twelve million, and for his address before the National Press Club, where again he pressed the theme that Indochina was the key to saving Asia from the Communist peril: "The loss of Southeast Asia would mean that Communism would have at its disposal essential strategic raw materials, that the Japanese economy would forever be unbalanced, and that the whole of Asia would be threatened." Hanoi was the key to victory, he continued, its importance comparable to Bastogne, where American armies fought off German encirclement in December 1944, and to Berlin, which the Soviets unsuccessfully blockaded some four years later.[47]

From Truman on down, senior U.S. officials publicly affirmed support for the war effort and pledged to speed up military deliveries. In private sessions, though, they refused to accept that Korea and Vietnam were one war, and they pressed the general for more proof that France was sincerely committed to full independence for Indochina, and for greater efforts to build up the Vietnamese fighting forces. *The Washington Post* spoke for much of American officialdom when it editorialized, in the middle of the French general's visit, that "the great problem in increased military aid is to avoid the appearance of propping up colonialism."[48]

Still, when de Lattre and his wife left New York by air shortly before midnight on September 25, bound for Paris, he took satisfaction in the results of the trip. As well he might. The Americans had unambiguously affirmed the critical importance of the fight against Ho Chi Minh and had pledged to bolster their military assistance and to deliver it with more dispatch. In Congress and in the press, and among the general public, awareness of the French war and of French military needs was now much greater than before. As a laudatory *New York Times* editorial put it, the Washington talks made two points plain: "First, we are in basic political agreement with the French. Second, our aid to the Associated States of Indochina will be stepped up. Both are vital."[49]

VII

EVEN BEFORE DE LATTRE'S VISIT, THE AID HAD BEEN SUBSTANtial. He had already received upward of a hundred U.S. fighter planes, fifty bombers and transports, and ground arms for thirty battalions, as well as artillery and naval craft. But other promised deliveries, including trucks and tanks, were months behind schedule. Only 444 of a sched-

DE LATTRE AND A THOROUGHLY SMITTEN GENERAL LAWTON COLLINS
IN HANOI ON OCTOBER 23, 1951.

uled 968 jeeps and 393 of 906 six-by-six trucks, for example, had been
sent in fiscal year 1951. Lovett blamed the slow pace on production problems and a lack of expertise at some plants, but he and other officials
also said the French themselves were partly responsible, chiefly because
of their inadequate maintenance practices. Distribution of matériel already delivered was another problem: Armed convoys were forced to
move slowly—whether by road or water—and were subject to frequent
Viet Minh attacks. Nevertheless, Army Chief of Staff J. Lawton Collins
pledged to de Lattre that U.S. deliveries would be stepped up, and they
were: In the four months following his visit, the French received more
than 130,000 tons of equipment, including 53 million rounds of ammu-

nition, 8,000 general-purpose vehicles, 650 combat vehicles, 200 air-craft, 14,000 automatic weapons, and 3,500 radios.[50]

Collins paid glowing tribute to the success of de Lattre's U.S. trip when he called on the general in Saigon a few weeks later. "You came like a crusader to present the cause for which you were fighting in Indo-China," the American gushed. "You pleaded with all your incomparable ardor and conviction. Few of your campaigns have created enthusiasm that is comparable to that which you raised by your visit to America. No one has ever shown, as you showed, in such simple language, all that is at stake in Indo-China, nor made clear the issues that are possible. To our people you have rendered a great service."[51]

That was one possible view of the Frenchman's mission and cause, but not the only one. Another American, who held a starkly different view, called on de Lattre in Saigon that autumn, a young Democratic congressman who in time would stand at the very apex of America's Vietnam decision making. This was John Fitzgerald Kennedy, whose visit to Indochina in mid-October—accompanied by his brother Robert and sister Patricia, during a tour of Asia and the Middle East—is described at the start of this book. JFK was taken aback by what he saw, it will be recalled—France was engaged in a major colonial war and was plainly losing. The United States, as France's principal ally in the effort, was guilty by association and risked being forced down the same path as the European colonialists. The French-supported Vietnamese government lacked broad popular support, Kennedy determined, and Ho Chi Minh would win any nationwide election.

It was a remarkable message coming from a man who hitherto had sounded every bit the Cold Warrior, blasting the Truman administration, for example, for allowing China to fall to Communism and bragging to constituents about his ties to the rabidly anti-Communist Wisconsin senator Joseph McCarthy. But it's clear that the Asian tour changed JFK's outlook. It convinced him that the United States must align herself with the emerging nations, and that Communism could never be defeated by relying solely or principally on force of arms. His Indochina experience led him to that conclusion, as did a dinner conversation in New Delhi with Jawaharlal Nehru, who called the French war an example of doomed colonialism and said Communism offered the masses "something to die for" whereas the West promised only the status quo. War would not stop Communism, Nehru warned him; it would only enhance it, "for the devastation of war breeds only more poverty and more want." Kennedy agreed, but he wondered if U.S. officials grasped these essential truths. Many of "our representatives abroad seem to be a breed of their own," he said a few weeks later, "moving mainly in their own limited circles not knowing too much of the people to whom they are accredited, unconscious of the fact that their role is not tennis and cocktails, but the interpretation to a foreign country of the meaning of American life and the interpretations to us of that country's aspirations and aims."[52]

Other Americans also held these twin convictions—that the United States was becoming too enmeshed in the war, and that the prospects were nevertheless bleak. At the CIA and at the State Department, numerous midlevel officials held them, as did some of Kennedy's colleagues on Capitol Hill. Indeed, a sizable number of informed Republican and Democratic lawmakers in this period saw the war as resulting primarily from France's determination to preserve her colonial empire; some spoke in language similar to that of JFK.[53] For that matter, even Truman and Acheson themselves agreed on the need for French reforms "toward the natives" and on the danger to American interests of seeming to support colonial control. So did Heath in Saigon, and so did Ambassador David Bruce in Paris. But all four parted company with the Kennedy line in their conviction that the French military effort nevertheless needed America's full support. Cold War imperatives demanded it. Hence the tens of thousands of tons of U.S. military equipment that flowed in to Indochina—that is, to the French, not directly to the VNA—as 1951 turned into 1952.

VIII

DE LATTRE SOUGHT TO PUT SOME OF THAT EQUIPMENT TO IMMEdiate use upon his return to Saigon. He did not have much time left, he knew. He was dying. Doctors had operated on him in Paris in October and had told him his final stay in Vietnam would be brief. Visibly weakened upon landing in Saigon but encouraged by the banners of support along the road as he drove from the airport to the Residency ("Vive le Général de Lattre"), de Lattre sought to show both Paris—where lawmakers prepared to debate the Indochina budget for 1952–53—and Washington that France could regain the ascendancy in the field.

Major military engagements had been few since Giap's return to guerrilla warfare in the summer. Attacks on convoys continued, and there were frequent hit-and-run attacks and assassinations: Most notably, in late July, in a rare example of a suicide bombing, a Viet Minh youth had unloosed from his jacket a grenade that killed himself along with Brigadier General Charles Marie Chanson, the French commander for South Vietnam, and Thai Lap Thanh, a Vietnamese local governor, during a public reception in a town southwest of Saigon. For de Lattre, it was another bitter blow. He considered Chanson—who had earned plaudits for his work in Tonkin in 1946–47 and more recently for getting the better of his Viet Minh counterpart in the south, Nguyen Binh—one of his ablest generals and had watched over and pushed his career for many years.[54]

In the Red River Delta in the north, tension remained high in the late summer and fall, as Giap used regional troops to harass the French to considerable effect. The French answer in the delta was to conduct continual sweeps, using both static battalions and *groupes mobiles*. When these units located a fortified Viet Minh village, its inhabitants were given notice to quit; if they refused to comply, air support was called in to raze the village, usually using napalm. These operations achieved considerable short-term tactical success, and—these being rice-producing areas—caused the DRV's food situation to grow worse. But the old problem remained: The French, undermanned as always, could not long stay in the conquered areas; as soon as they departed, the Viet Minh flowed back in. There existed no civil service organization to stay on the scene to try to work with the peasants, few of whom were in any mood to cooperate with those who had attacked their village.[55]

De Lattre determined that his forces had to take the offensive, to extend their line outward on ground the enemy would have to defend, accepting a pitched battle. He chose the area around Hoa Binh, in the mountains to the west of the delta. An important river and road junction, Hoa Binh was reached by the RC6 from Hanoi and by the Black River, so transport should not be a major problem for French units. Sparsely populated, the area was also likely to suffer few civilian casualties in the fighting. Most important of all, de Lattre reasoned, success at Hoa Binh would cut the main line of communication by which the Viet Minh had drawn rice supplies from the south and sent down Chinese military equipment from the north. An added bonus: Hoa Binh was the capital town of the Muong tribe, whose hostility to the Viet Minh and potential loyalty to the French cause de Lattre sought to cement.[56]

At dawn on November 14, three French paratroop battalions descended on the town, encountering almost no resistance. Simultaneously, some twenty-two infantry and artillery battalions and two armored groups, along with engineering forces to repair sabotaged roads and bridges, began moving up the narrow Black River valley. By the afternoon of the fifteenth, the French had achieved their objectives with virtually no losses and almost no enemy opposition. Giap, sensing he had neither numerical superiority nor an adequate route of withdrawal, had refused battle, pulling his troops back into the forested hills, content to fight another day on his own terms. In December, he was ready. He ordered his 304th, 308th, and 312th Divisions to close in on Hoa Binh and the RC6, while back in the delta he had elements of the 316th and 320th infiltrate from the north and south to harass French rear areas. Although unsuccessful in taking Hoa Binh, the Viet Minh were able to cut first the water and then the land routes into the town. French attempts to reopen communications exacted heavy cost in lives and equipment, and meanwhile the security situation in the delta deteriorated. "We shall never give up Hoa Binh," de Lattre vowed, but he was wrong. In February 1952, General Raoul Salan ordered the post's evacuation.[57] The Viet Minh duly took it and began to push a north-south trail toward central and southern Vietnam, the beginning of what would become the Ho Chi Minh Trail.

The decision was Salan's because by then de Lattre had died. On November 19, 1951, he had left Vietnam, ostensibly for a high-level Paris meeting. On the eve of his departure, there had been a cocktail party in his honor, attended by, among others, Graham Greene, the novelist, who spent the first of several consecutive winters in Saigon in 1951–52. Greene had visited Vietnam briefly early in the year and had been impressed then by de Lattre's fierce dynamism. Now, the novelist observed, "the changes were startling." De Lattre was an altered man, weary and morose, "his rhetoric of hope wearing painfully thin." Even some of his subordinates criticized him, Greene went on, tired as they were of his constant references to his own loss—"others had sacrificed their sons too, and had not been able to fly the bodies home for a Paris funeral."[58]

At the meeting in Paris, de Lattre was lucid and forceful but so weak physically that afterward he had to be carried in a chair up to his apartment. His real reason for coming to France was medical, and on December 18, he underwent major surgery. An additional operation followed on January 5. His condition worsened until his death, confirmation crucifix clutched in his hand, on January 11. In the final days, he confided to General Valluy: "There is only one thing that upsets me: I have never completely understood Indochina." His last words, voiced during a moment of brief consciousness on the ninth, were "Where is Bernard?"[59]

So came to an end *l'année de Lattre.* His year had shown both the power and the limits of individual human agency in issues of war and peace. De Lattre indisputably demonstrated what a decisive contribution to events a leader can make, for without him the war in Tonkin might well have been lost in the early weeks of the year. The Viet Minh might have realized their propaganda claim "Ho Chi Minh in Hanoi by Tet." Critics could reasonably respond that he would have been wiser to concede the north and center and focus instead on strengthening Cochin China, and it's certainly the case that de Lattre faced deep structural problems in his vow to preserve all of Indochina within the French Union. He himself was aware of these problems, not least the lack of broad popular support for the Bao Dai regime and the unwillingness of anti-Communist Vietnamese to fight for the cause. More than his predecessors, he worked to build up the VNA and more broadly to mobilize the population in French-held areas to actively back the war effort.

At the same time, de Lattre's dictatorial methods alienated many Vietnamese, who also found his definition of Vietnamese independence far too restrictive. In one breath, he would say he fully supported Vietnamese nationalist aspirations; in the next, he would demand full popular loyalty to the French Union and to himself as France's representative. He had no patience for the political navigating that independence must involve or for the nationalist who appeared insufficiently grateful. In this way de Lattre, for all his military sagacity and dazzling leadership, for all his daring and élan, was cut from the same cloth as the high commissioners who went before. His parting comment surely is telling: Never did he fully comprehend Indochina.

His determination to keep Indochina within the French Union led him to expend great effort on a second objective: to boost the U.S. military involvement in the war. Here his legacy was of profound importance. De Lattre recognized immediately that only the Americans could supply the material assistance he needed, and over the course of the year he (along with his civilian counterparts in Paris) achieved great success in cementing America's presence. Franco-American tensions remained considerable, but Harry Truman and his top aides bought the general's argument that Korea and Indochina were the same struggle. Of de Lattre's fifty-five weeks as commander in chief, none were more important than the two he spent in the United States. By January 1952 he was gone, but the Americans were more firmly committed to his cause than ever before.

His passing cast a pall over the whole of France. Public mourning was decreed for three days, and for two days the body lay in state in the Invalides while a vast and reverent crowd filed silently past the bier. On January 15, the casket was placed on a tank beneath the Arc de Triomphe, and that evening mounted troops carrying torches escorted it to the Cathedral of Notre Dame, where the president of the republic bestowed upon de Lattre the title of Marshal of France. He was the first in almost three decades to be so honored. The following morning the archbishop of Paris led a solemn mass in the cathedral in the presence of the president, the government, the diplomatic corps, and the top military leadership, together with a large contingent of the general public.[60]

For those who seek symbols, there were several. Charles de Gaulle, so crucial to the initial decision to reclaim Indochina for the empire after World War II, and (even though out of office by then) to wage war there, arrived alone and remained standing solitary for a long time before the coffin. General Eisenhower, soon to begin his campaign for president of the United States, and destined to face his own momentous decisions concerning war and peace in Vietnam, was one of the pallbearers as the casket was conveyed on a gun carriage from the cathedral through the silent crowded streets back to the Place des Invalides. And there was, finally, this: On January 17, the funeral cortège proceeded slowly from Paris to Versailles, Chartres, and Saumur, and on to Mouilleron-en-Pareds, where the coffin was placed in a grave next to that of Bernard, the only son, in the shade of two trees. A nearby windmill was made into a memorial chapel to perpetuate the memory of the father and son who, the citation said, gave their all for France.

CHAPTER 12

THE QUIET ENGLISHMAN

"REDS' TIME BOMBS RIP SAIGON CENTER: MISSILES KILL 2 AND Injure 30 in Spectacular Viet Minh Strike in Indo-China." So blared the headline in *The New York Times* of January 10, 1952. Later newspaper issues raised the dead to eight Vietnamese and two Frenchmen, and thirty-two injured.

Reporter Tillman Durdin had the story: "Agents here of the Viet Minh forces this forenoon staged one of the most spectacular and destructive single incidents in the long history of revolutionary terrorism in Saigon. Two time bombs were exploded at 11 o'clock in the crowded center of two main downtown squares, killing two persons and injuring thirty. Thirteen automobiles were blasted and burned, walls were pitted, windows knocked out, and plaster jarred loose in buildings all around the scene of the explosions."

The bombs had been left in two parked cars, Durdin continued. One blast went off at the Place de Théâtre, which was overlooked by the Opera House, the Continental Hotel, and a complex of shops and offices. The other blast occurred in the square in front of the City Hall, a block away. The two explosions occurred within two minutes of each other, and the police determined that the two automobiles, each bearing false license plates, had been driven up and parked only a short time before the bombs went off. The perpetrators had had time to flee the scene before the explosions occurred.[1]

Life magazine published a photograph of the Place de Théâtre taken immediately after the explosion, and described the scene:

At 11 o'clock . . . a powerful bomb planted by the Viet Minh Communists, exploded in the trunk of an auto parked in the crowded, busy square. The bomb blew the legs from under the man in the foreground and left him bloody and dazed, propped up on the tile sidewalk with his broken left ankle twisted beneath him. It killed the driver of the . . . delivery truck as he sat at the wheel. It riddled and set fire to the truck, made a torch of a cloth-topped jeep, smashed and burned more autos and raked the square with fragments and flame.[2]

Almost immediately doubts emerged that the attacks were the work of the Viet Minh. Their preferred terrorist methods were different: hand grenades thrown from a bicyclist or rolled down a movie aisle, or point-blank shootings, execution-style. To Donald Heath, the U.S. minister, this merely meant the Viet Minh had shifted tactics. "While feat selected is less [an] exhibition of strength than of VM willingness to indulge in cowardly and brutal acts of terrorism," he cabled Washington, "exploit was carried out with grim efficiency and will undoubtedly be heralded as Commie triumph."[3] But veteran journalists thought someone else must be the culprit, as did the French Sûreté. Speculation turned to Colonel Trinh Minh Thé, a flamboyant former Cao Dai chief of staff who had broken with the French in 1951 and, together with twenty-five hundred Cao Dai troops, had set up a headquarters in a swampy area past Tay Ninh near the Cambodian border. His aim: to fight both the French and the Viet Minh, since any authentic nationalism had to oppose both sides. He would be a "Third Force." In radio broadcasts, Thé's operatives took credit for the January 9 blasts, and French officials concluded that he was indeed responsible.[4]

General Thé. The Third Force. A bomb blast in a crowded Saigon square. To readers of Graham Greene's *The Quiet American*—or viewers of Joseph L. Mankiewicz's or Philip Noyce's movie version—it all sounds familiar. Each features prominently in the novel. Greene was away from the city on the day of the explosions but he would soon return, his Vietnam stay now into its third month. He had loved the country—and more particularly, its women—from the start, from his first brief stop in early 1951 on his way home to England from Malaya (which he liked far less).

He had come then at the encouragement of his friend A. G. Trevor-Wilson, the British consul in Hanoi. "I drained a magic potion," Greene later said, "a loving cup which I have shared since with many retired *colons* and officers of the Foreign Legion, whose eyes light up at the mention of Saigon and Hanoi.

"The spell was cast," Greene went on, "by the tall elegant girls in white silk trousers; by the pewter evening light on flat paddy fields, where the water buffaloes trudged fetlock-deep with a slow primeval gait; by the French perfumeries in the rue Catinat, the Chinese gambling houses in Cholon; above all by the feeling of exhilaration which a measure of danger brings to the visitor with a return ticket: the restaurants wired against grenades, the watchtowers striding along the roads of the southern delta with their odd reminders of insecurity: '*Si vous êtes arrêtes ou attaqués en cours de route, prévenez le chef du premier poste important.*'"[5]

Greene would frequently remark on Vietnam's stunning geography, but that wasn't what drew him in. His explanation for his Malaya sojourn applied equally well to Vietnam: "Nature doesn't really interest me—except in so far as it may contain an ambush—that is, something human." As an uncommonly bored schoolboy, Greene is said to have played Russian roulette, to have had a kind of death wish; perhaps he never changed. He was drawn mothlike to "the exciting thing," to physical danger, to societies in the throes of violent upheaval. In *Ways of Escape,* his otherwise reticent autobiography, he acknowledged that he traveled to the revolutions and wars of the colonial world "not to seek material for novels but to regain the sense of insecurity which I had enjoyed in the three blitzes on [wartime] London." To his brother Hugh, he revealingly expressed disappointment in mid-1951 that he had not been present during Vo Nguyen Giap's attack on Phat Diem that spring.[6]

His base of operations was Saigon's best hotel, the luxurious Majestic, built in 1928 according to French design and offering fabulous views of both the rue Catinat and the Saigon River from its fourth-floor rooftop bar. Here he heard the pianist play the latest hits from Paris and saw the sampans floating by on the river below. On occasion, the tracer fire from besieged French posts across the river arced across the evening sky. He also spent time at an apartment a little farther up rue Catinat, at number 109, which today is the Mondial, an unassuming hotel. In between the two stands a building that was the setting for Fowler's apartment in the novel and now occupies the elegant Grand Hotel. Greene liked to take daily walks along this thoroughfare, stopping as the mood struck for a vermouth cassis at the Palais Café (where, in the novel, Fowler plays *quatre-cent-vingt-et-un* with Lieutenant Vigot of the Sûreté), or at Givral's confectionary shop, or at the rooftop café of the Continental Hotel, whose proprietor, Monsieur Franchini, was an affable opium-smoking Corsican known to import prostitutes directly from Paris.[7]

The Pearl of the Far East had begun to lose its luster, to look faded and feel gritty, but that only added to the city's allure for Greene, who reveled in the atmosphere. He stayed out late at restaurants like l'Amiral, a favorite spot of French parachutists and special operations types, and the Arc-en-Ciel on rue des Marins in the Cholon district, with its Chinese food and its upstairs nightclub featuring a Filipino band and floor shows headlined by the likes of Josephine Baker and Charles Trenet, and a bartender whose gin fizz was famous all over the Far East. He developed a taste for opium, boasting in one letter that he managed to smoke five pipes in a night; in later years he would devote many hours during his Vietnam visits to taking the drug.[8] And he sought out prostitutes, notably at Le Parc aux Buffles (Park of Buffalo; in the novel, The House of 500 Girls), reputed to be the world's largest brothel, with four hundred women of various nationalities. The vast complex was surrounded by a wall and contained separate sections for officers and ordinary soldiers.[9]

Greene described a visit in his journal: "After hours. The huge courtyard with the girls sitting in groups. The little lighted rooms. Strolled around. Enormous bonhomie. The Fr. police post inside the brothel. The girl stretched across two pairs of knees. The white elegant legs crossed under the light. Price asked 30 pesetas—8/6d. Then directed to officers' brothel. Much less attractive place, though better girls. To go inside would have made getting out difficult. Price 300 pesetas."[10]

II

GREENE ARRIVED IN VIETNAM IN OCTOBER 1951, SOON AFTER THE publication of one of his masterpieces, *The End of the Affair,* and having just that week graced the cover of *Time.* ("The next Dostoevsky," the magazine called him.)[11] He had not come with the intention of writing a novel on the war. He was on assignment from *Time*'s sister publication, *Life,* whose publisher, Henry Luce, and editor Emmet John Hughes had been impressed with an evocative—and staunchly anti-Communist— piece Greene had written for the magazine on the insurgency in Malaya. They commissioned him to write one also on the Indochina struggle. He wasted no time getting into the action, joining a French bombing squadron on an operation in Tonkin mere days after his arrival. "I went on two missions," he wrote his son Francis.

The first was to bomb & machine gun round a town which the Communists had captured. My aircraft went alone. Tiny little cockpit, just room for the pilot (who was also the gunner & bomber), the navigator & me—an hour's flight each way & then three quarters of an hour over the objective. We did 14 dives. It was most uncomfortable, coming rapidly & steeply down from 9000 to 3000 feet. You were pressed forward in your seat & then as you zoomed up again your stomach was pressed in. I began to get used to it after about four dives.

Coming back we went down to about 200 feet & shot up a sampan on the Red River. . . .

It's very hot & difficult to write letters, so would you let Mummy see this one if you think she'd be interested in bombing![12]

Greene returned to the scene in *The Quiet American,* inserting details he spared his son: "Down we went again, away from the gnarled and fissured forest towards the river, flattening out over the neglected rice fields, aimed like a bullet at one small sampan on the yellow stream. The cannon gave a single burst of tracer, and the sampan blew apart in a shower of sparks; we didn't even wait to see our victims struggling to survive, but climbed and made for home." Fowler found the action troubling: "There had been something so shocking in our sudden fortuitous choice of prey—we had just happened to be passing, one burst only was required, there was no one to return our fire, we were gone again, adding our little quota to the world's dead."[13]

Greene also paid an early return visit to Phat Diem, sixty-five miles southeast of Hanoi, not far from the sea, where the Catholic bishop, Le Huu Tu, ruled his diocese like a medieval prince and had his own small army. Himself a Catholic, Greene was fascinated by the bishop and by Phat Diem, with its looming cathedral. Here again his own experience, as recorded in his journal, tracks closely with Fowler's. Like Greene, Fowler accompanies a small group of legionnaires on patrol; like him, he comes across a gruesome scene. "The canal was full of bodies," Fowler narrates. "I am reminded now of an Irish stew containing too much meat. The bodies overlapped: one head, seal-gray, and anonymous as a convict with a shaven scalp, stuck out of the water like a buoy. There was no blood: I suppose it had flowed away a long time ago. I have no idea how many there were: they must have been caught in a cross-fire, trying to get back."[14]

The idea for a novel was already now taking hold in Greene's mind. A key moment was a trip to the province of Ben Tre, forty miles southwest of Saigon. In charge in Ben Tre was Jean Leroy, a Catholic Eurasian (his father was French, his mother Vietnamese) who had taken part in the pacification efforts under Leclerc. Now a colonel in the French Army, Leroy achieved a modest amount of success against the Viet Minh using a

GRAHAM GREENE VISITS PHAT DIEM IN LATE DECEMBER 1951, IN THE COMPANY OF FRENCH UNION TROOPS. IT WAS GREENE'S HABIT TO REFUSE A HELMET ON SUCH MISSIONS.

militia recruited largely among Catholics. His conviction that success in the war effort depended primarily on winning the popular backing of the peasantry impressed Greene, as did the efforts Leroy had made in that direction: He instituted a system of local elections for a consultative assembly, and he cut the land rents for tenants in the province by half. Nor did Greene mind that Leroy had a flair for entertaining: On an island in a lake, he ordered built a bar lit all night by neon lights. To the apparent delight of guests (or at least Greene), he poured brandy down the throats of women and played the theme music from the movie version of Greene's *The Third Man* on the gramophone.[15]

One night in Ben Tre, Greene shared a room with Leo Hochstetter, an American serving as public affairs director for the Economic Aid Mission. By Greene's own telling, Hochstetter was more intelligent and less innocent than the Alden Pyle character in *The Quiet American,* and more gregarious, but there's little doubt that he was a main inspiration for the novel's title character. (Later it would become conventional wisdom that Pyle was modeled on Edward Lansdale, whom we shall encounter in due course and who would become a champion of Trinh Minh Thé, but Greene did not meet Lansdale until after completing much of the novel.) The two men drove together back to Saigon, as Pyle and Fowler do in the novel, and the American lectured Greene on the necessity of creating a Third Force in Vietnam, one beholden neither to the French nor to Ho Chi Minh. Hochstetter even had a candidate in mind: General Thé.[16]

In the novel, which is set in early 1952 and which Greene began writing in March of that year (some of it while ensconced in room 214 at the Continental), Pyle likewise is attached to the Economic Aid Mission. A clean-cut young Bostonian "impregnably armored by his good intentions and his ignorance," he brims with references to *The Challenge to Democracy* and *The Role of the West,* written by his fictional hero York Harding, a political theorist partial to abstractions. "York wrote that what the East needed was a Third Force," Pyle tells Fowler at one point. Later, Fowler hears from his assistant:

"I heard [Pyle] talking the other day at the party the Legation was giving to visiting Congressmen. . . .

"He was talking about the old colonial powers—England and

France, and how you couldn't expect to win the confidence of the Asiatics. That was where America came in with clean hands. . . .

"Then someone asked him some stock question about the chances of the Government here ever beating the Viet Minh and he said a Third Force could do it. There was always a Third Force to be found free from Communism and the taint of colonialism—national democracy he called it; you only had to find a leader and keep him safe from the old colonial powers."[17]

To many readers of the novel, Pyle seems singularly naïve, but his views on the Third Force are not really at odds with what many actual U.S. officials felt at the time. Greene almost certainly heard this line of argument from others besides Hochstetter—including at second hand from bitter French colonial officers. Certainly, we know that Robert Blum, Hochstetter's boss at the Economic Aid Mission, and Edmund Gullion, Heath's young deputy at the legation, were sure that the war effort would fail unless the Vietnamese were convinced they were fighting for genuine independence and democracy. The only way to make them so convinced was to build up a genuine nationalist force that was neither pro-Communist nor obligated to France and that could rally the public to its side. Even those Americans who still insisted on the need to back the French—Heath in Saigon, Bruce in Paris, Acheson and Truman in Washington—fully shared the belief that ultimate success in the struggle depended on the emergence of a Vietnamese government possessing sufficient authority to compete effectively with the Viet Minh for the allegiance of the populace. This, as we've seen, was the motivation behind Washington's embrace of the Bao Dai solution in 1947.

Even the phrase "Third Force" was in currency that winter as Greene began assembling his notes. The previous summer, in July 1951, *The New Republic* had published an article bearing the title "Viet Nam *Has a Third Force.*" The author, Sol Sanders, recently back in the United States after two years in Southeast Asia, excoriated the French and the Viet Minh with equal gusto but said all was not lost: "Beneath the layers of opportunists, French spies, and hangers-on, there is a hard nucleus of patriots who are fighting for a truly independent, libertarian Viet Nam." And later: "Bao Dai's regime, cleansed of the French-supported parasites that now infest it, can still rally to our side the Viet Nam's people [*sic*] who are sick of war and afraid of Stalinism."[18]

III

MORE THAN ANY OTHER OF GREENE'S NOVELS, *THE QUIET AMERICAN* contains firsthand reportage, much of it done on this three-and-a-half-month stay in 1951–52. A comparison of the book with his letters home, his journal, and his articles makes this clear. Much of the time he was in Saigon or Hanoi, but occasionally he accompanied French troops into the field. Tall and unarmed, he was an easy target, but he showed complete disregard for his own physical safety, even when at Phat Diem he found himself in the midst of heavy fighting. (This action too features in the novel.) Greene was not at this point pro-Communist, but the talent and fierce dedication of the Viet Minh impressed him. In his article for *Life,* he acknowledged that many of Ho Chi Minh's supporters were motivated by idealism and were not part of any monolithic Stalinist movement. Even worse from the editors' perspective, Greene saw little chance of stopping Communism in Indochina. The article urged France to prepare herself for retreat from the region and warned Washington that not all social-political problems could be overcome with force. Hughes and Luce, aghast at this message, rejected the piece, despite the fact that Greene also offered up a crude articulation of the domino theory of the type that Fowler ridicules in the novel. ("If Indo-China falls," Greene wrote, "Korea will be isolated, Siam can be invaded in twenty-four hours and Malaya may have to be abandoned.") Thus rebuffed, Greene offered the article to the right-wing *Paris Match,* which published it in July 1952.[19]

Greene concluded the article with a jarringly sentimental tribute to the courage and skill of French soldiers. Maybe he was trying to soften the blow of the impending defeat. But it's also the case that he retained in 1952 a good measure of sympathy for the French cause, and for European colonialism more generally. He had himself been born into the British Empire's administrative class, and its worldview and mores continued to imbue him. He could write movingly of Saigon as the "Paris of the East," and he much enjoyed spending time in the cafés along the rue Catinat in the company of French *colons* and officials. He was indeed in this period something of a Frenchman *manqué*. Castigating the Americans for being "exaggeratedly mistrustful of empires," Greene said the Old World knew better: "We Europeans retain the memory of what we owe Rome, just as Latin America knows what it owes Spain. When the hour of evacuation sounds there will be many Vietnamese who will regret the loss of the language which put them in contact with the art and faith of the West."[20]

Little wonder that Greene and the *colons* got on so well; they spoke in the same terms regarding all that European colonialism had wrought and the damage the Americans could do. It is ironic, therefore, that some leading French officials mistrusted him. General de Lattre, eager to win more American aid and aware that Greene was in Indochina on assignment from an American magazine, initially went out of his way to woo the novelist, inviting him to informal dinners and giving him the use of a military plane. But the general's opinion changed after Greene visited Phat Diem and showed keen interest in Bishop Le Huu Tu. De Lattre hated the bishop's seeming double-dealing, blaming him for his son Bernard's death near Phat Diem the previous year—the bishop, de Lattre believed, had tacitly allowed the Viet Minh to sneak up on the position Bernard's unit was defending. In the general's mind, Greene became a kind of accomplice in the treachery.[21]

The elder de Lattre became convinced that Greene and his friend in Hanoi, the British consul Trevor-Wilson, were in fact spies, working for the British secret service. He blurted out to the head of the Sûreté: "All these English, they're too much! It isn't sufficient that they have a consul who's in the Secret Service, they even send me their novelists as agents and Catholic novelists into the bargain."[22] De Lattre placed both men under Sûreté surveillance and used Vietnamese to assist in the effort. "The French gave us orders to watch Graham Greene very closely," recalled Pham Xuan An, a self-taught English speaker who was tasked with censoring the Englishman's dispatches, and who would later lead an extraordinary double life as a *Time* reporter and Viet Cong spy. "While he was in Asia, smoking opium and pretending to be a journalist, the Deuxième Bureau assured us he was a secret agent in MI6, British Intelligence.

"One day," An continued, "Graham Greene came to the post office to file a story. His report was placed on my desk. It was a long report. 'What do I do with this?' I asked my supervisor. 'You have to be very careful,' he said. 'If there are any words you are not sure about, just cross them out. Your English isn't very good, but there's nothing he can do about it. He can't argue with you. So just go ahead and cross out the words. Mark it up and then give it to the man who types the telegram. They never give him a chance to argue anyway.' "[23]

Greene ridiculed the charge that he was engaged in espionage—the whole episode, he later said, was a comic adventure featuring funny little Frenchmen tailing him, a deluded old general, and a jolly companion (Trevor-Wilson) with an estimable knowledge of Chinese massage parlors. But very likely de Lattre had it right. Trevor-Wilson was not only the consul in Hanoi; he also managed the Secret Intelligence Service's operations in the city. He was, moreover, sympathetic both to the Viet Minh and to fellow Catholic Le Huu Tu's activities. De Lattre declared Trevor-Wilson persona non grata and forced him to leave Indochina in December 1951. As for Greene, he too likely was on dual assignment in Vietnam—for *Life* as well as for the SIS. He had joined the agency in World War II (he and Trevor-Wilson first became acquainted at SIS headquarters at St. Albans in 1943), having been recruited by his sister, and Greene continued the relationship periodically after the war. The Sûreté felt confident Greene was working for the SIS in Indochina, and his own correspondence hints at it. Most likely, the arrangement was informal; he was a kind of "casual spy," passing on observations here and there as the mood struck him.[24]

Greene's sympathetic views toward the French cause in Indochina would in time change, but not his negative assessment of the United States. It was set in stone. Even before he visited the country in 1938, on his way to Mexico, America had become for him a symbol of empty materialism, lack of tradition, political immaturity, and cultural naïveté. In his second novel, *The Name of Action,* published in 1930, we find the stereotype of the bad American, in the form of the arms dealer. Now, two decades later, with the onset of the Cold War and the McCarthyite witch hunts, his view grew darker still. How, he wondered, could a people be at once so smugly self-righteous in their conviction that the American way was best for everyone and so obsessively fearful of the Red menace?[25]

Fowler, the cynical and world-weary English narrator of *The Quiet*

American, boasts at the beginning that he has no politics, but in fact his language is saturated with anti-Americanisms, as he picks up the fight against Pyle's arrogant naïveté. Bitter experience has taught Fowler that the world is not always changeable, that some problems have no solution, and that certain Western abstractions, such as democracy, don't necessarily correspond to how society actually functions. Along comes the Ivy League–educated Pyle, ignorant of the world and full of reforming zeal, "determined to do good, not to any individual person but to a country, a continent, a world." Fowler does not initially see the danger but instead reaches out to shield the American: "That was my first instinct—to protect him. It never occurred to me that there was a greater need to protect myself. Innocence always calls mutely for protection, when we should be so much wiser to guard ourselves against it: innocence is like a dumb leper who has lost his bell, wandering the world meaning no harm."[26]

Innocence in this context does not mean freedom from guilt. This is the paradox on which *The Quiet American* rests. (We shall return to the novel in a later chapter.) Fowler continues to call Pyle "innocent" even after he determines that the American has been supplying plastic explosives to General Thé for use in terrorist attacks. Pyle never suspects that the world is a messy and complicated place and that people's motives, including his own, may be more sinister than they seem. In his mind, there are no limits to what the United States can achieve; he is willing—to use the later Vietnam-era phrase—to destroy a village in order to save it. It's Pyle's very innocence, that is to say, that makes him dangerous.

IV

IN LATER YEARS, GREENE WOULD INSIST THAT HE HAD GOOD REA-son to believe that the CIA was involved in the actual January 9 bomb attacks. Wasn't it a little too convenient, he asked in his memoirs, that *Life* happened to have a photographer right there on the scene? "The *Life* photographer at the moment of the explosion was so well placed that he was able to take an astonishing and horrifying photograph which showed the body of a trishaw driver still upright after his legs had been blown off. This photograph was reproduced in an American propaganda magazine published in Manila over the caption 'The work of Ho Chi Minh,' although General Thé had promptly and proudly claimed the bomb as his own." It seems, though, that the *Life* photos were taken not by a staffer but by an enterprising freelance Vietnamese, who sold copies the next day both to the magazine and to two U.S. officials.[27]

Nor has any other firm evidence for American involvement in the bombing turned up, though it's apparent that among French officials (with whom Greene had close contact) there were strong suspicions to that effect. In mid-February, a few days after Greene departed from Vietnam, Minister Heath informed Washington of a French document that had come into his possession: It advocated French military action against Thé but acknowledged there were risks, as Thé was a genuine nationalist. "It expresses fear," Heath went on, "that reaction would provide U.S. with opportunity [to] strengthen hold on country and . . . it accuses Thé of responsibility for January 9 explosions and claims explosive devices were provided by U.S."[28]

British officials had their own suspicions. Hubert Graves, consul in Saigon, told the Foreign Office of "strong rumours" that "certain American elements" were involved. He noted that the explosives and clockwork devices used were "much too ingenious" to have been manufactured by the Cao Dai-ists themselves, and that another recent bombing by the group, this one of a major bridge, also used unaccountably advanced technology. "It is known," Graves continued, "that members of the American official missions in Saigon make frequent visits to the Tay Ninh area and it is unfortunately now widely stated in Saigon that the Americans are behind General Thé."

Veiled references made by the French to the irresponsible support by the Americans of nationalist groups have, in private conversations with members of my own staff, now become direct accusations that the Americans are providing support to General Thé and his men. Incredible as it may seem, I am afraid that there may be some truth in all this. Members of the American Legation have admitted that their dealings with the sects are bedeviled by their desire to be in a position to use them as the nucleus for guerrilla activity in the event of Indo-China being overrun and it has been suggested that the training and equipment which is being provided for such an eventuality has been put by General Thé to premature use. I conclude this paragraph with considerable reluctance but I can no longer ignore the reports which continue to come in from usually reliable sources.[29]

Trinh Minh Thé himself cultivated the view that he had close ties to the Americans. In early March, after the French Expeditionary Corps attacked his private army's headquarters in Tay Ninh, and some of his soldiers fled, he attempted to boost morale by claiming to have had secret contacts with the Americans that would soon yield a major influx of weapons and cash. He ordered his subordinates to have themselves photographed for the benefit of the U.S. mission in Saigon. When the French attacks resulted in an acute food shortage in the compound, Thé encouraged the rumor that American planes were about to air-drop several tons of rice. He reminded his men that Washington had long supplied the various "sect armies" in Cochin China with money and weapons, using the justification that these armies were officially *supplétifs* of the French military.[30]

The American documentary record is silent on whether there were close U.S. dealings with Trinh Minh Thé in early 1952. American officials certainly paid visits to the Tay Ninh area where Thé had his base, but what actually occurred on those trips remains obscure. No evidence has surfaced that U.S. agents supplied his organization with explosives—though that is not always the type of information that would be recorded on paper. Edmund Gullion subsequently denied any direct American connection with Thé at that time, though he was not quite categorical. "The idea of an independent force springing out of the rice paddies was not something we were really concerned with," he noted. "There were disaffected people, people like [Ngo Dinh] Diem who held themselves aloof from the French for a long time, and we thought they were a more likely independent force [than Thé]." In the same vein, a CIA agent told author Norman Sherry, "To my knowledge, no single agency official was—at that time—in contact with Colonel Thé. And I would know."[31]

The agent's emphasis on the timing is important. A few years thence, as we shall see, at about the time the novel was published, U.S. officials *were* in close contact with Thé and *did* promote him as someone who could play at least a supporting role in a Third Force movement in Vietnam. In 1954–55, none other than Edward Lansdale had contact with Thé and worked to keep him supportive of U.S. policy. In one recently declassified memorandum from the period, Lansdale speaks of Thé's charisma and political strength and calls Thé crucial to achieving America's aims in Vietnam.[32]

That was later. In February 1952, as he readied to leave Saigon and Vietnam, Graham Greene had yet to begin writing his novel. His *Paris Match* article would not appear for another five months. But he had already made certain determinations about the Franco–Viet Minh struggle that are of particular interest here. For one thing, Greene's anti-Communism and sympathy for the French cause did not keep him from appreciating the skill and commitment of the Viet Minh and the corresponding weakness of Bao Dai's regime, with its chronic tendency toward lassitude and incompetence; he grasped already that France faced long odds against success. For another thing, he saw with his own eyes how entrenched the United States was becoming in the anti–Viet Minh effort (he opens *The Quiet American* with Fowler seeing "the lamps burning where they had disembarked the new American planes"), and how much friction existed between the Americans and the French, with whom they were ostensibly allied. Greene spent significant time only with one side in this dispute, which no doubt colored his perceptions, but there's ample additional evidence that in the early months of 1952, relations between French and American officials in Vietnam were more strained than ever.

The seemingly relentless Americanization of South Vietnamese urban culture had something to do with it. More and more, young Saigonese flocked to American films, listened to American popular music, even dressed in the American style they picked up from Hollywood movies— shorts with angled pockets, loose short-sleeved shirts, Bata cotton shoes. Try as colonial officials might to convince themselves and one another that these developments were natural and to be expected, it wasn't always an easy sell, even if there were also continuities: Privileged Vietnamese still preferred French food and French perfume, still used Français as their second (in some cases first) language, and still thought *colons* were more generous tippers than Americans.[33]

Howard Simpson, who arrived in Saigon in January 1952 to take up his post as a press officer for the U.S. Information Service, had barely set foot in the city when he experienced firsthand the French mistrust of all things American. At their first encounter, Jean-Pierre Dannaud, the director of the French Information Service, was cool and condescending toward Simpson and fairly oozed resentment at what he considered American interference in the war effort. Simpson initially brushed this tension off as unrepresentative and as stemming from his own lack of experience in the Far East, but he quickly changed his mind. It dawned on him, he later wrote, that "the two so-called allies saw the future of the Indochinese peninsula from entirely different optics." True, Harry Truman and his top advisers in Washington preached the need to back the anti–Viet Minh struggle, and they matched their rhetoric by sending more and more aid to the French; also true, Donald Heath insisted in his first meeting with Simpson that France was "fighting the good fight" and as such deserved the legation's full support. But neither these high-level convictions nor the diplomatic language and soothing official declarations offered by both sides could mask, Simpson determined, the mutual suspicions and growing rivalry.[34]

He got a fuller taste of that rivalry as soon as he ventured into the field. Although the French High Command had final say on the distribution of American military matériel, a stipulation in the bilateral agreement allowed the U.S. Military Assistance Advisory Group (MAAG) to make suggestions regarding that distribution. In addition, MAAG had the right to conduct "end-use" inspections in the field to determine how the U.S.-supplied equipment was being utilized. Simpson's office, meanwhile, had the task of publicizing the aid program's effectiveness in the United States and abroad. He consequently accompanied the end-use missions—or, as U.S. officials came to call them, "end-use charades." Typically, the visits would take months to schedule, due to "operational requirements" claimed by the French. On the appointed day, French drivers would arrive hours behind schedule and then inexplicably get lost en route to the post. When at last the U.S. officers arrived on scene, they would be told that for "security reasons" the inspection would be limited to service and support units. An elaborate lunch table would be laid for them, with four courses, red and white wine, and cognac toasts offered by the senior French officer present. When Simpson and his colleagues at last emerged into the afternoon sun, it would be too late to visit the outlying posts.[35]

"The flowery mess toasts may have referred to 'our gallant American allies,' Lafayette, and the Normandy landings," Simpson recalled, "but to a majority of the French, both military and civilian, we were '*Les Amerloques*,' a derogatory slang phrase for 'crazy Americans.' They felt we were muscling in on their territory, spreading wild ideas about freedom and independence among the local population, and showing a dangerous tendency toward criminal naïvete in a region we knew little about."[36]

Little wonder Graham Greene in early 1952 found so much to talk about with the French officers in Saigon: "Dangerous" and "criminally naïve" could be Fowler talking about Pyle. Simpson in fact met the novelist on two or three occasions, during which the "aloof and dyspeptic" Greene "made no secret of his basic anti-American feelings" and his misgivings concerning the deepening U.S. involvement in the war. Early on Simpson thought Greene might ask him to help arrange an interview with Donald Heath, but it never happened. The Englishman "remained with his French and Vietnamese contacts, observing the *Amerloques* at a disdainful distance." On a later occasion, Simpson and Greene, both of them hungover from a late night of carousing, found themselves seated side by side on an early morning flight to Laos. They exchanged a cool acknowledgment but, Simpson remembered, "it took no great receptivity to sense Greene's displeasure at being paired with an 'official' American." They passed the flight in silence.[37]

Bemused though he was by the depth of the French mistrust, Simpson acknowledged that the brash behavior of many Americans in Saigon didn't help. The phrase "ugly American" was not yet in use, but the phenomenon could be observed on any given day. Moving through the streets in their large black sedans and new Jeep station wagons, hitting the bars and restaurants en masse sporting crew cuts and aloha shirts that they left untucked, these Yanks never made a pretense of blending in. Even those who were more low-key and subtle tended to separate themselves from everyone but fellow Americans—a point Congressman John F. Kennedy, it will be recalled, had noted on his visit the previous autumn. Each day Simpson and other Americans from USIS and the Aid Mission met for pre-lunch beers at the Continental's terrace café, "a symbol of the old colonial Indochina." He recalled of these sessions: "We were a boisterous group, playing the match game for drinks and laughing loudly at inconsequential jokes, well aware of the disapproving *colons* who left a *cordon sanitaire* of empty tables around us."

"In retrospect," a rueful Simpson concluded, "I can understand some of the French resentment."[38]

Greene, for his part, departed Saigon somewhat sadly on February 9. "I left Saigon yesterday—with certain regrets. I had one or two good friends there. Especially during this last stay. Perhaps I'll write the 'entertainment' I thought of and go back and film it one day. People have been nice to me."[39]

CHAPTER 13

THE TURNING POINT
THAT DIDN'T TURN

D ETERMINED THOUGH THEY WERE TO MAINTAIN A *CORDON SANITAIRE* between themselves and the Americans—not just on the Continental's fabled terrace but everywhere, in figurative as well as literal terms—the French in Indochina in early 1952 understood that they were utterly dependent on U.S. economic and military and diplomatic support. They could work to disrupt the MAAG end-use inspections and thwart all American efforts to cultivate a nationalist, anti-Communist Third Force. They could ignore U.S. recommendations regarding specific military operations and overall strategy, and they could turn a deaf ear to Washington's persistent call for greater efforts at building up the Vietnamese National Army. At the end of the day, however, they needed the United States, needed what only the Truman administration among the West's governments could bring: massive monetary and material support, and international legitimacy.

The lack of leverage went both ways, or so most American officials believed. It didn't matter that the U.S. presence in the war was now growing seemingly on a daily basis, and that Washington's contribution to overall French expenditures in Indochina by the middle of 1952 topped 40 percent; American influence was nevertheless frustratingly limited. The reasons had not merely to do with Southeast Asia. In Europe, the administration sought to bring France firmly into the structure of the fledgling European Defense Community (EDC). Proposed by France's René Pleven in response to Washington's desire for the rearmament of

West Germany, the plan called for a common European army, under joint control, that would help counter the Soviet threat while not re-creating a sovereign German army. U.S. analysts fully understood that the ultimate ratification of the EDC treaty depended inordinately on attitudes in the house of its originator—where Charles de Gaulle, always a force to be reckoned with, immediately denounced it for allowing the dilution of the French army into an intra-European amalgam—and they were loath to do anything in Indochina that could anger Paris officials and journalists and thereby threaten passage.[1]

One fear was that France would be unable to meet her obligations to the EDC and to NATO and at the same time fight a war halfway around the world. Early in 1952, Paris planners calculated that, even with projected American assistance of all kinds, the cost to France of meeting these two requirements would likely rise to over $4 billion—roughly $1 billion for Indochina and the remainder for Europe. Had senior U.S. officials cared only or mostly about the EDC and NATO, they would have insisted that France rid herself of the Indochina burden by promising complete and total independence for Vietnam, and by a specific date. But the Truman administration in 1952 still wanted desperately to keep France in the fight against Ho Chi Minh. As French officials well understood, their military effort in Indochina served American interests at least as much as it served theirs. If U.S. advice became too meddlesome, or if the administration sought to tie strings to its aid, what then? Might the Paris government simply withdraw from Indochina entirely?[2]

It seemed all too possible. Said one American official in Paris in early 1952: "We're approaching now the same situation we faced in the spring of 1947 when things got too much for the British and they dumped Greece and Turkey in our laps. The French can barely hold with what they have here now. . . . If they pull out [of Indochina], the question is put to us." In the same vein, the British ambassador in Paris cautioned: "I fear we may be near a point where the French may turn round and say to us, 'Is this war in the interests of the Western powers, as France can no longer maintain it alone as a French war? Unless you can join us, we shall be obliged to pull out.'"[3]

The possibility of a French withdrawal seemingly grew more real that January, as Paris lawmakers prepared to begin a full-dress debate on Indochina in the National Assembly. De Lattre's death on January 11, just a few days before the start of the debate, set a somber mood for the proceedings, and it was soon clear that a broad cross section of delegates questioned France's continued commitment to the war. Views that a year earlier would have been labeled "defeatist," or "unpatriotic," were openly expressed, and not merely by the left. How could France afford, many delegates asked, to continue a struggle that in 1952 would consume between one-seventh and one-sixth of the entire budget? Answer: She could not, certainly not if she was also to build up a large army in Europe, which alone would enable her to pull her own weight in the organization of Western defense. "I am asking for a change of policy in Indo-China," declared Pierre Mendès France of the Radical Party.

I have never advocated capitulation, but I have asked and am still asking that every avenue be explored for an agreement with the Viet Minh. I am told one cannot negotiate with Communists, with Moscow agents. But what else are the Americans doing in Korea? . . . [A]s long as we go on losing all these officers and men in Indo-China, as long as we go on spending 500 billion francs a year, we shall have no army in Europe, and only 500 billion francs worth of inflation, poverty, and fuel for Communist propaganda.[4]

Influential voices in the French press said in essence the same thing; *Le Monde* and *Le Figaro* both noted that, absent dramatically increased U.S. aid, France would soon have to choose between fulfilling her European responsibilities and seeking a rapid diplomatic solution in Vietnam. At the U.S. embassy in Paris, a despondent David Bruce saw French hopes for victory dashed and the public eager for peace. "A snowball has started to form," the ambassador warned Washington. Absent greater American assistance for the war effort or some kind of "internationalization"—meaning U.S. and British guarantees to defend Indochina militarily—public sentiment for withdrawal would continue to build. The CIA, for its part, said that a full-fledged French reappraisal of Vietnam policy was at hand, with potentially major implications for the United States.[5]

Ultimately, the Pleven government prevailed in the debate, and the

Assembly approved by a wide margin the appropriation of 326 billion francs for land forces in Indochina during 1952. This sum, however, did not cover the air force or navy, and as in previous years a supplemental allocation would be required before long. Pleven declared that the government had secured a fresh mandate for the vigorous prosecution of the war, and he lauded French forces for their "magnificent" performance in the field; a year or eighteen months hence, he predicted, France could secure a negotiated settlement "from positions of strength." His words rang hollow. The dominant mood in the Assembly after the vote, observed one journalist, was that "it couldn't go on like this." If the appropriation passed, "it was only because the French army in Indo-China could not be left high and dry without money or equipment."[6]

Two other factors no doubt shaped the outcome of the vote. One was the growing nationalist restiveness in North Africa, particularly in Morocco and Tunisia. In Rabat, the French faced growing pressure from the sultan, Mohammad Ben Youssef, to grant independence, while in Tunis negotiations had broken down just a few weeks earlier over nationalist demands for home rule. For some Paris officials, the North African tensions were an added reason for withdrawal from Indochina—in the words of Radical leader Édouard Daladier, so long as 7,000 French officers, 32,000 NCOs, and 134,000 soldiers were "marooned" in Vietnam, France would be hopelessly outnumbered in her North African possessions.[7] The alternative view, and the one that won out in the end, was that early disengagement from Vietnam would only intensify nationalist fervor in the Maghreb. (If the Vietnamese can win independence, why can't we?) For the sake of the empire, then, France had to stay the course in Vietnam. Second, Premier Pleven won political points for his announcement, timed perfectly in advance of the Assembly vote, that he had secured agreement for a three-power conference on Indochina, involving Britain, the United States, and France, to take place in Washington later in the month. Pleven assured delegates that France would press for a joint Western policy toward the Far East and direct Anglo-American support in the event of a Chinese Communist move into Indochina.

The prospect of a Chinese military intervention dominated the discussion of Indochina at the tripartite meetings, though there was a divergence of views on the seriousness of the threat. At the start of 1952, the

PRC had about two hundred and fifty thousand troops in the provinces bordering Indochina, many of them ready to cross the frontier on short notice. Both the CIA and the Joint Intelligence Committee of the Joint Chiefs of Staff rejected the likelihood of an invasion, and so did British intelligence. With the Korean War still ongoing and claiming vast Chinese resources, and with the Viet Minh holding their own against the French, these analysts thought Beijing would almost certainly be content to maintain its current level of support—arms and ammunition, technicians and political officers, and the training of Viet Minh NCOs and officers in military centers in southern China.[8] The French, however, insisted on the very real possibility of direct, large-scale Chinese intervention and requested a U.S. commitment to provide air and naval support in that event. The Joint Chiefs of Staff and the National Security Council agreed it was important to decide on a course of action should the Chinese move. But which course?

The question brought to the fore a crucially important difference of opinion among the three Western powers regarding the Cold War in Asia—and, by extension, the ultimate stakes in Vietnam. At the Washington conference and at other meetings that spring, U.S. officials called for responding to a Chinese invasion with air attacks on communications facilities in China proper and a blockade of the China coast. France and Britain disagreed. Partly they did so on narrow selfish grounds—the French wanted no diversion of resources from Indochina, while the British feared that Beijing might retaliate for such an assault by attacking Hong Kong or placing it under economic pressure. But Paris and London also sought to avoid escalating Cold War tensions or doing anything to antagonize unduly Moscow and Beijing. Winston Churchill, again in the prime minister's office following a Tory election victory, questioned the military orientation of America's Cold War strategy and advocated instead a much greater emphasis on East-West negotiations. He and Foreign Secretary Anthony Eden made clear they would not allow Britain to be drawn into a new conflict with China.

For their part, French officials, even as they warned of China's aggressive intentions in Indochina, hinted that they would be open to negotiations involving both Beijing and the Viet Minh. Already a year earlier, in early 1951, Pleven had approached the Truman administration gingerly about the possibility of a diplomatic initiative that would connect the Korean and Vietnamese conflicts and settle both simultaneously; the Americans had dismissed it out of hand. Now Paris leaders raised the matter again. Mendès France's implied question—why was it acceptable for the United States to negotiate with Communist adversaries in Korea but not acceptable for France to do the same in Indochina?—began to resound across the French political spectrum. In April, Christian Pineau of the Socialist Party declared, after a parliamentary mission to Vietnam, that there existed no real solution apart from "international negotiations" involving also the Chinese. Jean Monnet, the architect of postwar French economic planning and a powerful establishment voice ("the power behind the throne," some called him) wanted the war to end because of its impact on France's economic position and her role in Europe. If he had his way, Monnet candidly said, he "would liquidate whatever now remains of French interests in Indochina." At the Foreign Ministry too, there was active consideration of an international agreement including China that would be reached, in effect, over the head of Ho Chi Minh. Such a bargain, many analysts speculated, could salvage something out of the Indochina wreckage and was in any event worth pursuing.[9]

To the Truman administration, negotiations on Vietnam, in whatever form, were anathema—"the forbidden subject," in historian Lloyd Gardner's apt phrase.[10] Harry Truman and Dean Acheson had no love for European colonialism, certainly. But better to have the French there than to face the prospect of a Communist victory, which was sure to follow if France withdrew or negotiated a settlement with Ho Chi Minh. The French, Acheson insisted in June, had to seize the initiative militarily and "think victoriously." Diplomacy should be avoided until such a time as the West could be guaranteed a favorable result.[11]

II

ONE DETECTS SUBTLE BUT IMPORTANT DIFFERENCES HERE IN HOW the French and British on the one hand and the Americans on the other approached the matter of diplomacy with Communist adversaries. Partly the divergence can be chalked up to Washington's hegemonic position—top dogs are seldom much interested in compromise. But other factors were at work as well. European governments, operating in physical proximity to rival powers of comparable strength, had long since determined that the resultant pressures placed a premium on negotiation and give-and-take. Only too familiar with imperfect outcomes, with solutions that were neither black nor white but various shades of gray, most European statesmen in the post–World War II era presumed that national interests were destined to conflict and saw diplomacy as a means of reconciling them. They were prepared to make the best of a bad bargain, to accept the inevitability of failures as well as successes in international affairs.

Americans, on the other hand, shielded from predatory powers for much of their history by two vast oceans, and possessing a very different historical tradition, tended to see things in much less equivocal terms. For them, Old World diplomacy, with its ignoble and complex political choices, had to be rejected, and decisions made on the definite plane of moral principle. The United States, that principle taught, represented the ultimate form of civilization, the source of inspiration for humankind. Her policies were uniquely altruistic, her institutions worthy of special emulation. Any hostility to America was, by definition, hostility to progress and righteousness and therefore was, again by definition, illegitimate.[12]

Privately, to be sure, American officials sometimes spoke in more subtle, less Manichaean terms, and their deep aversion to negotiating with Communists did not prevent them from pursuing that course in Korea. But the aversion conditioned their approach to the Korean talks and helped shape their hard-line posture, as did the fact that they operated in a highly charged domestic political atmosphere. Moreover, 1952 was a presidential election year. Truman and the Democrats knew all too well that GOP critics were ready to pounce on any diplomatic deal, to equate compromise with "appeasement," and to revive support for General Douglas MacArthur's argument that there was "no substitute for victory." Sure enough, when the election campaign geared up in the spring, Republican spokesmen asserted that the White House had been foolish to agree to negotiations on Korea, and that it was compounding the error by continuing them in the face of incontrovertible evidence that the Communists were using the time to build up their forces there.[13]

All of which helps explain Washington's categorical rejection in 1952 of negotiations—whether bilateral between France and the Viet Minh, or multilateral involving also the great powers—over Indochina. Senior French officials themselves were ambivalent about seeking a political solution, and some, such as Defense Minister Georges Bidault, still spoke only in terms of pursuing a military victory. More and more, however, hawks like Bidault were becoming an endangered species in Paris, and to a great many others, even a disadvantageous deal now looked better than continuing a seemingly endless war against a determined foe backed by China.

It's highly revealing in this regard that each time French policy makers inquired to Washington about exploring the possibilities for a diplomatic agreement, they were rebuffed. When Jean Letourneau, the minister for overseas territories who had also taken the job of high commissioner for Indochina, came to Washington in June to discuss a new U.S. aid agreement, he could only offer a gloomy picture of the state of the war. China would never permit the defeat of the Viet Minh, he said publicly, and therefore an armistice should be sought. Negotiations were under way to end the fighting in Korea; why not seek an international agreement for Indochina? The Americans were horrified. They pressured Letourneau to retract his statement, and Acheson assured the National Security Council that the Frenchman had misspoken: He meant to say that France would seek negotiations only after the military situation turned around. The NSC resolved that the United States must "influence the policies of France and the Associated States toward actions consistent with U.S. objectives." More to the point, Acheson elaborated, Washington must "impress upon the French the folly of giving up the offensive strategy so brilliantly launched and carried out by de Lattre in favor of a mere holding operation."[14]

Thus it can be said of the spring of 1952: It was a turning point that didn't turn. French attitudes were undergoing a sea change, as countless observers noted. The war had never been popular, but now, for the first time, one could speak of genuine antiwar agitation. In Ambassador Bruce's words, a snowball had started to form. Yet the Truman administration insisted on pressing forward. De Lattre might be dead, but the example of his "brilliant" offensive strategy lived on and had to be followed. Early negotiations had to be rejected. The French, U.S. policy makers were in effect saying, did not have to choose, did not have to decide between their European and Southeast Asian commitments; they could have both. American assistance would allow it.

A major U.S. policy document, NSC-124, approved by Truman on June 25, summarized the administration's position. The United States, it declared, would oppose negotiations leading to a French withdrawal. Should Paris nevertheless prefer such a course, the United States would seek maximum support from her allies for collective action, including the possibility of air and naval support for the defense of Indochina. Should China intervene, her lines of communication should be interdicted and a naval blockade of the Chinese coast imposed. If these "minimum" measures proved insufficient, the United States should launch "air and naval action in conjunction with at least France and the U.K. against all suitable military targets in China." If France and Britain refused, Washington should consider taking unilateral action.[15]

III

THE SCENARIOS DID NOT MATERIALIZE, NOT THEN. THE FRENCH stayed in, and the Chinese did not invade. In Paris, leaders in mid-1952 affirmed their full commitment to the war effort and, as they always did during the monsoon season, promised great things for the coming fall campaign. In Vietnam, de Lattre's successor as commander in chief, Raoul Salan, had been dealt a blow right from the start, having to order the Hoa Binh evacuation in February and then put the best face on the operation. (He described the retreat as a "tactical maneuver" that would free up more of his troops to tackle the danger in the Red River Delta.)

At least Salan had ample Indochina experience on his side. Born in 1899 and raised in the southern city of Nîmes, he had spent much of the interwar period as a captain in the highlands of northern Vietnam and in a remote part of Laos, developing some proficiency in Laotian and taking a Lao common-law wife along the way, then had directed the intelligence service of the Ministry of Colonies. A division commander in World War II, he had served under de Lattre during the Allied landing in Provence and during the final push into Germany. In October 1945,

Salan went back to Indochina and was named commander for French forces in Tonkin. The following year he attended the abortive Fontaine-bleau conference. When the negotiations failed and the war commenced, he resumed command of French forces in northern Indochina, and in the fall of 1947 he played a central role in the preparation and execution of Operation Léa, which almost captured the Viet Minh leadership at Bac Kan. De Lattre, impressed with Salan's deep experience in Indo-china, and with his belief that France without her empire was not France, named him his deputy in 1950. In that capacity, Salan commanded the battles of Vinh Yen, Nghia Lo, and Hoa Binh in 1951.[16]

Known as *Le Chinois* and *Le Mandarin* for his extensive service in the Far East and for his love of Indochinese artifacts and customs—or because of his fondness for smoking opium, which, it was believed, made your skin turn yellow—Salan was elegant, courteous, and reserved; he had about him an air of mystery. As de Gaulle said of him, "there was something slippery and inscrutable in the character of this capable, clever, and in some respects beguiling figure." Others commented on the mournful, distant quality to his eyes, or his habit of speaking to report-ers while caressing his talisman, a small carved ivory elephant. A tacti-cian more than a strategist, Salan was content in his early weeks to order minor sweeps within the Red River Delta but otherwise to allow things to remain as they were. He looked forward to the rains to give him a pe-riod in which to plan, equip, and prepare.[17]

Vo Nguyen Giap likewise was content to lie low after Hoa Binh. He kept up guerrilla activity inside the northern delta, and Viet Minh units remained active in various areas of the center and the south of Vietnam. Terrorist attacks continued, none more brazen than one in late July on a group of French officers and their families at Cap St. Jacques, a resort town of palms and black sandy beaches at the mouth of the Saigon River. During dinner, while white-clad waiters served the main course, a group of Viet Minh soldiers in stolen Expeditionary Corps uniforms rushed in and hurled grenades and emptied Sten guns into the crowded room. When French soldiers arrived on the scene, they found eight officers, six children, two women, and four Vietnamese servants dead, along with twenty-three wounded. Only a lieutenant who played dead and a small boy who hid behind a chair remained unhurt.[18]

The Viet Minh commander's main concern was the coming fall campaign. Having suffered bloody failures in the delta, he looked for more favorable terrain. He had his eye on the Tai highlands, an almost inaccessible area of mountain gorges, grass-cloaked plateaus, and dense jungle in northwestern Tonkin along the border with Laos. Although far from the delta, these uplands, covering an area the size of Vermont, were dotted with small French posts, and the Viet Minh had thus far failed to generate support for their cause among the roughly three hundred thousand Tai tribal inhabitants. Large-scale operations in this region could plant the necessary infrastructure for political action and moreover would force Salan to choose between abandoning the frontier and exposing northern Laos, or defending it. It would be an agonizing choice for the French, Giap knew: If Salan accepted battle in the northwest, he would draw crucial resources away from the delta to fight in an area desperately short of airfields and passable roads for his motorized troops.[19]

Giap's Chinese advisers helped shape his planning for the Northwest Campaign. It could hardly be otherwise, given China's crucial role in the military effort. Beijing's military aid to the Viet Minh in 1952 increased over the previous year and included some 40,000 rifles, 4,000 submachine guns, 450 mortars, 120 recoilless guns, 45–50 antiaircraft guns, and 30–35 field guns, along with millions of rounds of ammunition and tens of thousands of grenades. The Chinese Military Assistance Group (CMAG), meanwhile, continued to assist Viet Minh generals in the field and to train Viet Minh NCOs and officers at centers in Yunnan province. It all added up to powerful Chinese influence. In early 1952, CMAG officials advocated a major autumn offensive in the northwest, and top Beijing leaders concurred. "It is very important to liberate Laos," said Liu Shaoqi, one of Mao's principal lieutenants.[20]

In September, following the Lao Dong Politburo's decision to formally approve the Northwest Campaign, Ho Chi Minh secretly visited Beijing. He and Mao agreed on a two-stage strategy, whereby Viet Minh forces would focus first on the border region and the "liberation" of Laos, then on moving southward to increase pressure on the Red River Delta. They further agreed that the operation would begin with an attack on the Nghia Lo ridge, a watershed between the Red and Black rivers, along which the French had several small garrisons. Clearing this area would put the Viet

Minh a giant step closer to the Laotian border to the west. Whether Giap had objections to this initial concentration is not clear—certainly he too saw Nghia Lo's importance—but he went along with it.[21]

That same month Giap concentrated the 308th, 312th, and 316th Divisions (at least thirty thousand men) on the east bank of the Red River, between Phu Tho and Yen Bai. The French did not yet know it, but his mission was to take Nghia Lo. As in previous operations, the troops had moved mostly by night and—in view of the French mastery of the air—had put tremendous emphasis on camouflage. In addition to wearing palm-leaf helmets with camouflage nets on them, Viet Minh soldiers carried disks of wire netting on their backs, adorned with the foliage of the terrain through which they passed. When the terrain changed, each soldier had the responsibility of changing the camouflage of the man directly ahead of him. The result: French air reconnaissance failed to pick up more than vague signs of activity. Occasionally, a small group of men advancing single file through the high grass would be identified by French pilots, but by the time the plane made a second sweep, they would be gone, swallowed up by the surrounding foliage. "I just *know* the little bastards are somewhere around here," said one reconnaissance pilot, in a standard gripe. "But go and find them in that mess."[22]

Still, French commanders had the uneasy feeling that something was afoot. The rainy season was ending, and Giap was certain to move. But where? Intelligence reports suggested it would be somewhere west of the Red River, but both the strength and direction of his thrust remained frustratingly unclear. That is, until October 15, when a regiment of the 312th Division surrounded the small French garrison at Gia Hoi, twenty-five miles southeast of Nghia Lo. The French command saw the danger to the posts along the ridgeline and on the following day dropped Major Marcel Bigeard's Sixth Colonial Parachute Battalion into Tu Le, located roughly at the midpoint between Gia Hoi and Nghia Lo. Its mission was to cover the retreat of French forces to forts on the west bank of the Black River.

The following day, October 17, at five P.M., two regiments of the 308th Division attacked Nghia Lo with heavy mortar support. Within an hour, the post fell, as thick cloud cover kept French aircraft away. Sporadic fighting continued through the night, but by sunlight the result was clear:

The French had lost seven hundred men, as well as the anchor of their ridgeline. The entire line now collapsed, as other, smaller posts on either side of it gave way or were abandoned. Covered by the Sixth Parachute Battalion, which fought a furious rearguard action, each French detachment fled for the safety of the Black River forts. Most units made it and were lucky that Giap's logistical difficulties kept him from pressing home his advantage. Low on ammunition and rice, his troops exhausted, he bypassed the fortified French posts and instead sent a force to the northwest, toward the small French garrison at Dien Bien Phu. (It would be overrun in November.)[23]

As for the paratroop battalion, it was given up for lost. Miraculously, though, some members, including Bigeard, survived and were much celebrated when they straggled back behind French lines. They had started out carrying their wounded on bamboo stretchers, but when the litter carriers had grown too exhausted, the wounded were left to their fate. Pro-French partisans who followed the trail of the battalion and its pursuers reported seeing it lined at intervals with the severed heads of paratroopers on bamboo stakes.[24]

In Paris, while the press fumed, Defense Minister René Pleven acknowledged before the National Assembly that the fall of Nghia Lo was "painful for our prestige," but he insisted that neither France's "means to fight" nor her "ability to maneuver" had been lost.[25] Not lost, perhaps, but severely impaired. For the French High Command, the result was reminiscent of the border defeats of October 1950, even if this time the French human and territorial losses were lower. A dispirited French reserve officer summed up the feeling of many: "It looks as though from now on the Indo-Chinese war is to be a permanent nightmare."[26]

In order to reclaim the initiative, or at least divert the Viet Minh from the Black River, Salan launched an offensive along the line of the Red and Clear rivers, northwest of Hanoi. By attacking the enemy base areas around Phu Tho, Phu Doan, and Tuyen Quang, he hoped to cut Giap's lines of supply and communication and destroy his stores, and thereby compel him to draw back from the Tai highlands. Operation Lorraine, launched on October 29, was the largest offensive France ever attempted in Vietnam, involving some thirty thousand men and as many planes, tanks, and artillery as could be scraped together from around the delta.

The operation began well, as the French quickly seized Phu Doan and Phu Yen Binh and found sizable stocks of weapons and ammunition. (They also found proof of Soviet aid, in the form of four Molotova trucks and several Russian-made antiaircraft guns.) But Giap refused to engage. He did not turn his main force back from the Tai country, instead sending mostly regional units to harass the road-bound French. He was convinced that the French would be hampered by their long supply lines, and that Salan would be forced to order a withdrawal.[27]

He was right. On November 14, the French commander, realizing that his salient was too narrow to hold, called a halt to Lorraine. The withdrawal was a precarious operation—as withdrawals typically are—for the Viet Minh now sensed an opportunity. Salan had to rely on his greater speed to carry out the retreat, but he was utterly dependent on a single road, the RC2, parts of which ran through forested country and dangerous defiles vulnerable to ambush. Sure enough, on the seventeenth, a Viet Minh regiment sprang a major ambush on *groupes mobiles* 1 and 4 at the Chan Munong Pass. The column was trapped all day and suffered three hundred casualties. Further fighting ensued at various points along the road, until the column finally hacked its way back into the delta. Operation Lorraine was a miserable failure, costing some 1,200 Expeditionary Corps casualties altogether and failing to draw Giap into major combat. What's more, the Viet Minh commander had taken advantage of the French diversion of resources to the operation to increase infiltration behind the De Lattre Line.[28]

IV

AN EXULTANT GIAP ARTICULATED WHAT HE IMAGINED TO BE SAlan's frustrations: "In such a war, where is the front?" He answered himself by quoting Pascal: *"L'ennemi est partout et nulle part"* ("The enemy is everywhere and nowhere").[29]

That was indeed the feeling of the French Union commanders and the soldiers who fought under them. In the Tai highlands, as in so much of Vietnam, the terrain and vegetation gave the Viet Minh the choice of seeking or refusing combat, of quickly dispersing when danger arose and reassembling later. Masters of night movement and champions of concealment, they seemingly could spring on the French units at any time, in any place. It wasn't true, of course—the highlands area was a vast expanse, and Giap's forces occupied only a tiny fraction at any one time—but the basic uncertainty about the enemy's precise whereabouts (radio intercepts provided general locations) was extremely stressful to Salan's men. That the local tribal population here was much less pro–Viet Minh than elsewhere in Tonkin provided little comfort, for the locals hardly seemed all that pro-French either.

The terrain caused other problems for the Expeditionary Corps. There were few clear landmarks, and maps of the region were approximate, making navigation difficult at best. Usable roads were essentially nonexistent, and French units often found themselves wielding machetes to cut paths through the thick forest vegetation. In the valleys, the bamboo slowed movement, as did the tall elephant grass on the ridges. Although mules were sometimes available for heavy weapons and radios, troops generally had to lug their own food, water, and ammunition. Shortages abounded, not least with respect to rations.

"We lived on rubbish—fish heads and rice," recalled one legionnaire. "We were parachuted in some food once, and we could see that the tins had been painted over. A friend got a hold of a tin and made a hole in it with his bayonet. A sort of green mist flew out. [I] scraped off this painted layer . . . [underneath] it said in French, 'For Arab troops, 1928.'" Some patrols operating in the hills could go weeks without seeing their supplies replenished, during which time they had to worry not merely about the Viet Minh but about countless other enemies as well. There were the fearsome tigers of lore, often heard if not often encountered, and poisonous snakes and scorpions. Stinging insects of various kinds were a constant menace, as were bloodsucking leeches and burrowing ticks. And there were rats, big and savage, that could find their way even into a jungle fort's bunkhouse to bite through a sleeping soldier's boot into his foot. This is what the helplessly wounded and abandoned French soldier most dreaded: not that enemy troops would find him, but that he would be set upon by the rats.[30]

Or if not the rats, the ants. "If you were really wounded badly," the legionnaire observed, "there was an old German saying, 'Magen Schuss, Kopf Schuss—ist Spritzer' (Belly shot, head shot—it's an overdose job).

They'd give you a shot of morphine—that was your lot. . . . We had these collapsible ampoules and we used to stick them in a chap's cheek. You gave them an overdose if they'd got their legs blown off—you're 300km from anywhere—what are you going to do? The chap would be covered in ants in a moment."[31]

The Viet Minh were by no means immune to these terrors. The myth arose among French Union soldiers that the enemy was in his natural element in these highlands, able to move swiftly and easily through even the most difficult terrain and to subsist on the most meager of rations. In fact, most Viet Minh troops were not from the region at all, but from the coastal plains and the two deltas. They too were unfamiliar with much that they encountered and had to adjust to the twilight under the jungle canopy and to the new living conditions. They suffered hardships of their own and had their own nightmares about jungle creatures, about being left wounded and alone in the dense brush. No less than their European foes, the Viet Minh forces were vulnerable to disease—to malaria, dysentery, cholera, and typhoid—which, if it did not kill them, could leave them incapacitated for weeks or months, and could spread from one unit to another. And, like all soldiers at all times, they needed food and equipment; at various times during the Northwest Campaign, they had to endure severe shortages of both.

But endure they did, or at least the vast majority of them. In the first month of the fall campaign, they proved themselves superior to the French at every turn, demolishing them on the Nghia Lo ridge and handily turning back the challenge of Operation Lorraine. When Giap, not long thereafter, hosted an American Communist at his headquarters, he offered his (self-congratulatory) reasons for these Viet Minh victories. "If we have to we can put all our supplies on our back," Giap told Joseph Starobin, a member of the Communist Party USA and foreign editor of the *Daily Worker* who later would publish two slavishly pro–Viet Minh books on his experiences in Indochina. "For short distances, one peasant can carry enough provisions for one soldier." The Northwest Campaign, he went on, was conducted in an area of "relatively vast distances for a country like ours. Two hundred, two hundred and fifty kilometers in width, three rivers to cross—the Clear, the Red, and the Black rivers. We had to move deep into the valleys to hit the heart of the French positions. . . . We had to cross thirty streams, some of them two hundred and fifty yards wide, and make our way over very high mountains." It was brutally difficult, and captured French officers "told us later they could not understand how we could have done it. They did not comprehend how our forces could appear . . . hundreds of kilometers from our bases. One French officer said it was a surprise to see our peasants carrying supplies for the Army, without soldiers guarding them. For the French always have to guard their porters."

The French were in an insoluble dilemma, Giap noted: "Either they try to extend their strong-points once again, with their depleted manpower, in which case they spread themselves thin, or else they move out of their strong-points, which frees territory and population to us."[32]

Conveniently left out of Giap's account—as least as recorded by Starobin—was what occurred after the collapse of Lorraine and the frantic French retreat. In mid-November, his confidence soaring, the Viet Minh commander moved into the second phase of his campaign against the Black River posts. His chief target was Na San, a strongpoint on the west bank of the river, totally cut off from overland supply. Giap reasoned that if he hit the post quickly and hard, it would swiftly collapse, especially given its total dependence on supply by air and its remote location (117 miles west of Hanoi). He underestimated the French, however, who on Salan's orders moved their defensive position from the fort to the dirt airstrip, several miles away, and there constructed an entrenched camp. Mines were laid, barbed wire was hung, and extra reinforcements were flown in, some of them taking up positions in the hilltops surrounding the airstrip. The strip itself was skinned with pierced steel plates to allow the landing of American-made C-47 Dakotas, which soon began arriving at a rate of one every fifteen minutes. Giap's intelligence officers told him that the French had only five weak battalions in place; in reality, they gathered nine full-strength battalions, supported by aircraft. Having constructed what they referred to as a *base aéro-terrestre* (air-ground base), the French girded for battle.[33]

It began on November 23. That morning leading elements of the 308th Division had reached Na San's outer defenses. After nightfall, they attacked, using bazookas, recoilless rifles, grenades, machetes, and wire-busting Bangalore torpedoes. Fierce fighting ensued, and some outposts changed hands several times, but the defenses held and the attackers withdrew. Viet Minh losses were heavy. Giap paused, in order for the rest of his force to arrive. The garrison, meanwhile, saw its position bolstered with the arrival of 105mm howitzer batteries and an additional battalion. Still undervaluing the size of the defending force, Giap launched his second assault after dark on November 30, using thick-packed herds of water buffalo to clear paths through the mines and punch holes in the barbed wire ringing the airstrip. Again he was beaten back with heavy casualties. His blood up, the next night he stubbornly tried yet a third time, throwing two fresh regiments against the French perimeter. Once more the Viet Minh were repulsed, as Bearcats and B-26s arrived from Hanoi to light the scene with flares and strafe the swarming attackers and sear them with napalm. Giap at last gave up and called off the operation.

He had repeated his mistake of early 1951, had given the French what they wanted: a set-piece battle in which they could use their superior firepower to maximum effect. When it was all over, the French counted one thousand enemy corpses on the field since the first assault the previous

RAOUL SALAN, RIGHT, VISITS THE FRENCH FORTIFICATION IN NA SAN, VIETNAM, ON NOVEMBER 28, 1952. HE IS SPEAKING HERE WITH THE COMMANDER OF THE FORT, COLONEL JEAN GILLES.

week, many of them grotesquely rotund on account of being both swollen and clad in Chinese-style padded jackets. Total Viet Minh casualties may have been as high as six thousand, or approximately half the division.[34]

News of the outcome caused jubilation in the French community throughout Indochina. Toasts rang out everywhere to the "Hedgehogs of Na San" (*Hérissons*) and their commander, the one-eyed, bearlike Jean Gilles. The usually frugal French commissary immediately ordered a shipment of Australian beefsteaks, fried potatoes, vegetables, fresh bread, Algerian wine, and three thousand bottles of champagne—one bottle for every four men in the embattled camp. Vietnamese troops got frozen meat, dried fish, and rice, while the North Africans received wine, live sheep, and goats, all brought in by airlift. In the underground mess, Gilles passed out cigars and liquors to his staff and declared, "We've done a nice job here," while in Hanoi officers celebrated by dining sumptuously at La Manoir and the Hotel Metropole or dancing with the taxi-girls at the Ritz and Paramount. The disaster at Nghia Lo and the collapse of Lorraine seemed all but forgotten. An official spokesman declared: "Na San is no longer besieged. . . . [We] have recovered the initiative in the Tai country."[35]

Salan was more circumspect in his evaluation, but he too saw Na San as a great victory. To him, it showed what could be done when he had adequate numbers and equipment at his disposal. He and his lieutenants took particular satisfaction in the failure of the Viet Minh intelligence service, which, when operating away from the Viet Bac or another sympathetic environment, seemingly was as capable of missteps as theirs was. More portentously, in Salan's eyes, the theory of the air-ground base appeared to have been vindicated. Na San, it would turn out, was a dress rehearsal for a bigger battle to come.

V

THROUGHOUT THE FALL CAMPAIGN, HO CHI MINH HAD BEEN LARGELY invisible to the outside world. In the West, rumors were rife that he had died, either from tuberculosis, or an assassin's bullet, or a French bombing raid. Or perhaps he had been done in by an internal party purge. The announcers who spoke in Ho's name were, according to the rumors, imposters. He was, of course, very much alive, as evidenced by his trip (kept a closely guarded secret, even within the DRV zone) to Beijing in September. From there, he had continued on to Moscow, where he attended the Nineteenth Congress of the Communist Party of the Soviet Union. Not until December, after Giap's failure at Na San, did Ho Chi Minh return to Vietnam.

As before, he played a key role in shaping overall Viet Minh strategy and acted as chief recruiter and cheerleader for the revolutionary cause. Early in 1952, a French POW reported, upon being released, that Ho was a highly visible fixture in the area around the headquarters, often seen in the villages, among the farmers in the rice fields, and at cadre gatherings. Dressed in his now-standard simple peasant garb, he exhorted one and all to commit fully to the anti-French struggle and to sacrifice everything for the common goal. To avoid detection or capture by the French, Ho moved residence every three or four days and followed a strict fitness regimen: He rose early to do exercises and, after the workday was over, played volleyball or swam. Though now past the age of sixty, he could still walk thirty miles a day, in difficult mountain terrain, with a pack on his back.[36]

But all was not good for Ho Chi Minh as 1952 drew to a close. Throughout the liberated zone, morale problems were on the rise, as the war entered its seventh year with no end in sight. Most people continued to support the Viet Minh, if only because of their leading role in the independence struggle, but there were worrying signs of disaffection, not least among the peasantry, who formed the backbone of the revolution. The peasants provided the food that kept the government functioning and the People's Army fighting, and the sons that made up the bulk of that military force—a force that now numbered more than a quarter of a million men. Peasants also served as porters, carrying the tons of munitions, weapons, and rice to the battlefield, and the wounded troops away from it.

What had they gained in exchange for this sacrifice? Precious little. The leadership had promised to give them land but had put off implementing land reform, out of fear of alienating the middle class and thereby disrupting the national unity essential to ultimate success in the war effort. With discontent on the rise, the Viet Minh now asked landowners to drastically reduce rents so that tenant farmers could keep a greater percentage of crops and live better. When that voluntary system failed to produce results, leaders tightened the screws, demanding not only that landlords lower the rent but also that they return to the tenant farmers the "excessive" rent that they had charged over the years. Devoted cadres were dispatched to the villages to enforce the new regulations; in many cases, they drummed up false charges against landlords and compelled them to sign papers "confessing" their wrongdoing.[37]

Mai Elliott, in her remarkable account of her family's experience during the long struggle for Vietnam, relates what happened to her uncle Chinh, a landowner, when zealous cadres came to enforce the new policy. Believing that he had done nothing wrong, and that his steadfast support of the Viet Minh would ensure fair treatment, Chinh greeted the cadres calmly. They immediately accused him of cheating his tenants, and, feeling flustered by their threatening attitude and harsh accusations, he signed the papers "confessing" his wrongdoing. She writes: "The cadres told him that over sixteen years—from 1936 to 1952—he had collected a total of about eighty tons of paddy, or unmilled rice—more than his rightful share. Now he had to give all this back to his tenant farmers, each of whom would get a proportionate share depending on the excessive acreage they had rented and the number of years they had worked the land. My uncle felt as though he had been hit by a bolt of lightning."[38]

Among intellectuals too murmurings of discontent could be heard about the food shortages, about the constant demands for sacrifice, about the endless indoctrination sessions and propaganda meetings. On the military side, recruitment was a growing concern. By 1952, the source of manpower from cities had more or less dried up, in part due to French success in disrupting the Viet Minh apparatus in urban areas. The Viet Minh were forced to use more aggressive methods to obtain conscripts in the rural areas, creating further alienation among peasants. There were even widespread reports that some peasants had migrated to other areas to avoid serving.[39]

None of these problems was as yet acute for Ho Chi Minh and other party leaders, but neither was there a sense that they would soon be resolved. Much would depend on how quickly the war against France could be won. Here too, the picture at year's end was cloudy. Up to now, Vo

Nguyen Giap's forces had delivered numerous blows against the enemy and had steadily expanded Viet Minh territorial control throughout Indochina. By most measures, the French were losing the war. But they were not losing quickly, and the ultimate outcome remained unknown. Broadly, the war could still be considered a stalemate, and there was a rough balance of forces on the two sides. Giap had made inroads in the Red River Delta but had not done enough to really test French control there; the same was true in the urban areas to the south. In Saigon, the French position if anything seemed stronger now than in the spring and summer, as evidenced by the drastic reduction in the number of assassinations and bombings in the city in the final months of the year. Meanwhile, the Vietnamese National Army, though still a weak entity, showed at least fleeting signs of becoming a legitimate fighting force. One VNA unit at a small post thirty miles south of Hanoi at the end of December fought off a significant Viet Minh attack, and there were scattered reports of other units showing improved performance in the field. Was it, Ho had to wonder, a sign of things to come?[40]

More worryingly still from Ho's perspective, the enemy's effort at pacification in the south was showing some signs of success. Utilizing the "oil-spot" (*tache d'huile*) technique pioneered in African colonies in the late nineteenth century by Joseph-Simon Gallieni (so named because it resembled an oil spot gradually spreading outward), the French in 1952 worked to extend their control from secure to contested to insecure areas through a mix of military, political, and economic means. This was the approach Bernard de Lattre de Tassigny had called for in 1950, one aimed at winning the hearts and minds of the peasantry and based on the premise—later central to U.S. counterinsurgency doctrine—that although political action alone is insufficient to defeat an insurgency, neither can military force alone achieve decisive results.

The French had made sporadic efforts in this direction since 1948; even now their commitment to it was fitful at best. Smart French planners knew that what worked in the Sahara—where there were obligatory watering points that could be occupied and denied to the rebels—might not work so easily in Indochina. They understood that the oil-spot approach is usually an expensive, time-consuming, chancy proposition, especially for a foreign power—it is always hard for a local population to feel that an army of occupation is its friend. Success is often temporary and tends to come only in areas were revolutionary forces are not already entrenched. Still, the gains, however modest, were a source of concern to Viet Minh officers, one of whom candidly confided to a French counterpart that he had no enemy more dangerous than a doctor who treated the villagers without regard to their political allegiance.[41]

And what about developments outside Vietnam? Always a keen observer of international events, not least those in the United States, Ho Chi Minh knew that a new president had been elected in Washington, a war-hero general whose Republican Party had hammered Democrats for "losing" China and negotiating in Korea, and whose vice-president-elect, Richard Nixon, was a Red-baiter of the first order. What would the new administration do in Indochina? It was too soon to tell, but Ho had ample reason to be worried. When Joseph Starobin interviewed him at a secret location in the mountains of Tonkin early in 1953, Ho used every chance to turn the conversation to things American. He reminisced about seeing the Statue of Liberty and Harlem as a young man and asked Starobin why the supposedly anticolonial Americans would supply bombers to imperial France for use against innocent Vietnamese. Yet again, as 1953 opened, U.S. plans and policies were very much on Ho Chi Minh's mind.

CHAPTER 14

EISENHOWER IN CHARGE

THE NEW AMERICAN PRESIDENT HAD NOT PROVIDED MUCH DETAIL ON his foreign policy plans during the campaign. He didn't have to. For millions of voters, it was enough that he was Ike, supreme commander of the D-day invasion that liberated Nazi-occupied Europe and later chief of staff of the army and supreme commander of NATO. Even many of the delegates at the 1952 Republican convention knew little about his policy stances and didn't care. With his famous grin and soldierly presence, Eisenhower seemed the perfect candidate to restore stability to a troubled land—and to win back the White House after twenty years of Democratic control. Though a Republican, he seemed to much of the electorate somehow above politics, a trusted father figure who could unite a country wracked by division over the Korean War and McCarthyite Red-baiting.

In reality, Eisenhower was a savvy political operator, the possessor of what his vice president, Richard Nixon, termed, with no little admiration, a "devious mind." Well aware of the enormous political advantage that his military pedigree conferred on him, Eisenhower was content to follow what scholars later called a "hidden-hand" political strategy. In the campaign, this meant taking the high road and letting others make the most strident attacks on the Democrats and their candidate Adlai E. Stevenson. It was Nixon—who seemed to relish taking the low road— who saddled Stevenson, an ardent Cold Warrior, with the designation "Adlai the Appeaser," and with having "a PhD from Acheson's College of Cowardly Communist Containment." It was McCarthy who charged

George Marshall, five-star general and secretary of state and then defense under Truman (and a mentor to Eisenhower), with participating in "a [Soviet-led Communist] conspiracy so immense and an infamy so black as to dwarf any previous venture in the history of man."[1]

Eisenhower privately cringed at such rhetoric, but he didn't repudiate it. He frowned on the "purple, prosecuting-attorney style" of the Republican Party platform but didn't disavow it. To the dismay of friends, he did not come to Marshall's defense, even removing, at McCarthy's urging, a passage praising Marshall from a Milwaukee speech.[2] Though Eisenhower didn't entirely trust Nixon, he chose him as his running mate because he believed that Nixon—the man who had "gotten" Alger Hiss— could help him win over Polish American and other ethnic minorities and the Republican Old Guard. When his foreign policy adviser John Foster Dulles got carried away vowing to dump the Democrats' feckless *containment* strategy in favor of one dedicated to the *liberation* of "captive" peoples, Eisenhower reprimanded him, but gingerly, in a way that made him, Eisenhower, seem sensible and prudent but allowed the underlying charge to remain. He himself castigated Truman for "losing" China and for weakening America's posture in the Far East, and he vowed to stop Communist advances elsewhere in the region. In due course, these assertions would come back to haunt him, to box him in and limit his options on Indochina. In the near term, though, they worked: The Stevenson camp had no effective answer, and on election day the Republican ticket rolled to victory.

Foreign policy issues dominated much of the campaign, and no wonder: America was at war in Korea, and no end seemed in sight. Moreover, all signs that autumn pointed to deepening Cold War tensions. Soviet-American relations were marked by intense mutual suspicion, and an atmosphere of hysteria gripped life within both superpowers. In the United States, McCarthy and his allies searched for Communists in the government and in Hollywood, while in the Soviet Union, Stalin unleashed another of his campaigns of "vigilance" against "internal enemies," this one targeting a supposed Jewish "doctor's plot" against the Kremlin leadership. The Americans that fall tested their first thermonuclear weapon, and the Soviets were not far behind. In Asia, the two superpowers jockeyed for supremacy and cast a wary eye on Mao Zedong's China.

It stands to reason that intense speculation surrounded Eisenhower's choice for secretary of state. He named Dulles, a fateful selection that determined the basic coloration of the administration in international affairs, and therefore also the contours of U.S. foreign policy, for the rest of the 1950s. A formidable duo they were. Some early studies exaggerated Dulles's role in policy making, while more recently some historians have unduly minimized it. The truth is that both men were crucial, with Eisenhower ultimately controlling policy but Dulles doing much to shape decisions.[3]

The son of a Presbyterian minister in Watertown, New York, Dulles had been involved in American diplomacy since 1907 when, as an undergraduate, he accompanied the U.S. delegation to the Hague peace conference. Well before that, he took a special interest in foreign affairs, sometimes accompanying his grandfather, the lawyer-diplomat John Watson Foster, who had been secretary of state under President Benjamin Harrison, to dinner parties at the White House. "Foster has been studying to be Secretary of State since he was five years old," Eisenhower joked more than once, and he wasn't that far off. When Dulles was five, his mother wrote of him, "Mentally, he is remarkable for his age. His logical acumen betokens a career as a thinker . . . he reasons with a clearness far beyond his age."[4]

Her judgment would be borne out time and again in the years to come, as her precocious child excelled at every level of education. Upon completing high school at age fifteen, he went to Princeton, where he threw himself into his studies and shunned the eating clubs that were the symbols of the school's social success. He could have been popular at Princeton, he would later say, but it would have consumed too much of his time. Devoutly religious, Dulles opted against following his father's path into the ministry and instead went to law school. Family connections—his uncle, Robert Lansing, was Woodrow Wilson's secretary of state—won him a place on the American delegation to the Paris peace conference in 1919, where he helped draft policy on German reparations and the war guilt question. In the interwar years, Dulles worked his way up the ladder at Sullivan & Cromwell, a prestigious law firm, all the while deepening his interest in politics and public service. By 1927, he was the firm's sole managing partner and one of the highest-paid attorneys in the world.[5]

are as magnanimous and disinterested as the principles and splendor of their cultures," he declared. "It is in a just war, at the head of the United Nations in Korea, that America has thrown the preponderant weight of her power. It is solely to honor her given word, to respect obligations inscribed in the constitution of the French Union, that France has undertaken in Indochina the defense of an area essential to the free world."

Disputable claims, certainly, but hardly evidence of deep Franco-American discord. According to a British onlooker, however, the tension was palpable throughout the ceremony, from the moment early in his speech when de Lattre said: "Can I pay an equal tribute to United States civilization? I must confess that I have had little time to study it." U.S. minister Donald Heath, who in a series of recent speeches had spoken in praise of French culture, made a quick exit after the event. The short-statured American might not have shown up at all had he known de Lattre's private characterization of him: *"ce sacré petit bonhomme d'un petit Consul"* ("this bloody little chap who mistakes himself for a consul").[39]

No one was spared the general's vitriol, it seemed, not even his top deputies. In late July, de Lattre accused his second in command, General Raoul Salan, a seasoned officer with long experience in colonial intelligence work, of being secretly pro-Communist, and of playing poker and smoking opium. Salan admitted to taking opium on occasion to relieve stress but denied the other charges. No leftist poker aficionado he. In hushed tones, Salan told the British consul in Hanoi, A. G. Trevor-Wilson, that de Lattre had become extremely neurotic and sour, with hardly a good word for anyone.[40]

Was de Lattre's bitterness a passing phase? The question was topic A in the diplomatic community in Saigon that summer and among the journalists who gathered daily for drinks at the Continental Hotel's terrace bar—the regulars included Tillman Durdin of *The New York Times* and his wife, Peggy, a freelancer; Lucien Bodard of *France-Soir*; Robert Shaplen of *The New Yorker*; and Max Clos of the Associated Press. He was still grieving, some of them said; give him time. No, others insisted, this went beyond the loss of Bernard. De Lattre despaired at the size of the obstacles that still stood in the way of victory in the war, these analysts believed, notwithstanding his success against Giap's offensives earlier in the year. Paris was not delivering anywhere near the reinforcements

To the outside world, they presented two sharply different styles: Eisenhower was prudent, pragmatic, modest, easygoing; Dulles bombastic, severe, self-important, socially shy, even gauche. In conversation, the president tended to be plainspoken, while Dulles sought refuge in intellectual abstractions. Both men had been raised in deeply religious homes, but whereas Eisenhower wore his faith lightly, the secretary of state came across as inflexibly pious. Still, they developed a close working relationship, based on mutual respect if not perhaps deep affection. Behind closed doors, Dulles sometimes revealed a capacity for flexible and pragmatic thought that would have amazed outsiders, and—even more shocking—a sense of humor. He also showed he knew who was boss. Despite the claims of later detractors, he had no inclination to get ahead of the president on foreign policy, for he understood that his power derived from Eisenhower's confidence in him. He vowed not to repeat the error of his uncle Robert Lansing, who had been dismissed for crossing Wilson. From the start, he and Eisenhower conferred frequently, in person or on the phone or—when the peripatetic secretary of state was abroad—via telegram. Whenever their schedules permitted, they got together privately for a late-afternoon drink at the White House to exchange views.

II

NEITHER EISENHOWER NOR DULLES HAD FOCUSED CLOSE ATTENtion on Indochina in the preceding years, but both were cognizant of the main developments. Eisenhower also possessed his own experience in Southeast Asia to draw upon. In the late 1930s, he served three years under Douglas MacArthur in the Philippines, assisting in the effort to build up a Filipino army to defend the islands against the encroaching Japanese. At that time, he defended America's imperial record, comparing it favorably to that of the European powers; the latter, he wrote in his diary, viewed their overseas possessions as opportunities "for their own economic betterment," whereas Americans believed in "government only by consent of the governed."[9]

As he took the oath of office, Eisenhower's first policy priority was to make good on his campaign promise to end the Korean War as quickly as possible. But his very willingness to discuss peace terms with the North Koreans and the Chinese made him all the more determined to show firmness toward Communism elsewhere in Asia. From the start, he and Dulles sought at all costs to keep France from following their Korea example by negotiating with Ho Chi Minh. Domestic politics was one motivation—McCarthyism was a potent force in American politics that winter, and the two men were eager to avoid giving the Wisconsin senator and his supporters (or for that matter, partisan Democrats) ammunition for the soft-on-Communism charge. But Eisenhower and Dulles also saw Indochina as a key Cold War struggle; if anything, they were more convinced of the point than were their predecessors. Ho Chi Minh had to be defeated, they firmly believed, which meant the French had to stay in the fight.[10]

Which is not to say that they were at all times confident about the prospects. Already two years before, in March 1951, when he commanded Western forces in Europe, Eisenhower had articulated an early version of the domino theory that would later be identified with his name—*and* his skepticism regarding a military solution in Vietnam. He wrote in his diary, after a Paris meeting with Jean de Lattre de Tassigny:

> The French have a knotty problem [in Indochina]—the campaign out there is a draining sore in their side. Yet if they quit and Indochina falls to Commies, it is easily possible that the entire Southeast Asia and Indonesia will go, soon to be followed by India. That prospect makes the whole problem one of interest to us all. I'd favor heavy reinforcement to get the thing over at once; but I'm convinced that no military victory is possible in that kind of theater. Even if Indochina were completely cleared of Communists, right across the border is China with inexhaustible manpower.[11]

How to resolve the contradiction in the penultimate sentence Eisenhower did not explain. Later in 1951, as the de Lattre–directed efforts in Vietnam appeared to bear fruit, his doubts regarding the military outlook seemed to recede, and he now voiced consistent support for increased U.S. backing of the French. The cause was crucial. "General Eisenhower attaches the greatest importance to Indo China—to an extent to which I did not realize at all," U.S. senator Henry Cabot Lodge, a Massachusetts Republican, wrote in his diary after the two men conversed that November.[12]

Dulles felt likewise. At the time a lawyer in private practice, Dulles described Indochina as one of the "most difficult of all" international issues. Supporting the French cause was not pleasant, he conceded—she was a colonial power, after all—but "it seems that, as is so often the case, it is necessary as a practical matter to choose the lesser of two evils because the theoretically ideal solution [an independent, non-Communist Vietnam] is not possible for many reasons."[13]

Here Dulles summarized perfectly the position the Eisenhower administration would take in the all-important (as it turned out) first eighteen months after Inauguration Day. Never mind Eisenhower's conviction that no military victory was possible "in that kind of theater"; never mind the low and sagging support for the war in metropolitan France; never mind that informed observers inside and outside the U.S. government had for years warned that the anti–Viet Minh cause was fraught with peril. For Dulles and Eisenhower both, Vietnam was a vital battle in the larger Cold War, one that had to be waged. A self-professed Francophile, Dulles told the French National Political Science Institute in 1952: "You are there [in Indochina] paying a heavy cost, in lives and money. I am glad that the United States is now helping substantially. I should personally be glad to see us do more, for you have really been left too much alone to discharge a task which is vital to us all."[14]

In its earliest pronouncements, the new administration radiated purpose and resolution on Vietnam. Harry Truman urged them on, telling the president-elect in November that the problem was one of insufficient French aggressiveness in the field and of fence-sitting on the part of the Vietnamese, and that Indochina was an "urgent matter" for the administration to address. From Saigon, the reports were downbeat as the year turned, with Ambassador Donald Heath (his title had been changed from minister in June 1952) expressing newfound pessimism regarding the prospects of the anti–Ho Chi Minh forces. The Viet Minh, he informed Dulles, held the initiative throughout Tonkin and even controlled much of the Red River Delta; should the highlands in the northwest be lost, the Communists would have an open shot at Laos and Thailand. In Saigon, meanwhile, the government under Prime Minister Nguyen Van Tam lacked popular support, and Bao Dai was more and more removed (in every sense of the word) from the struggle.[15]

The only answer was to try harder. Eisenhower's inaugural address drew a direct link between the French soldier killed in Indochina and the American life given in Korea. In early February, in his first State of the Union speech, he characterized the Indochina struggle as part of a worldwide fight against Communist aggression. France in Indochina, he declared in another speech the same month, was "hold[ing] the line of freedom" against "Communist aggression throughout the world." Dulles, meanwhile, said in a nationwide broadcast that "if they [the Soviets] could get this peninsula of Indochina, Siam, Burma, and Malaya, they would have what is called the rice bowl of Asia. . . . And you can see that if the Soviet Union had control of the rice bowl of Asia that would be another weapon which would tend to expand their control into Japan and India."[16]

Privately too, senior officials expressed determination, and a conviction that the stakes were big—bigger even than in Korea. In December 1952, before the inauguration, Eisenhower and top aides discussed Indochina at length aboard the USS *Helena,* en route home from a visit to Korea. The president-elect stressed that the anti–Viet Minh effort was vitally important and would be a major foreign policy issue for his administration. In late January, Dulles told senior U.S. civilian and military officials that defeat in Southeast Asia would lead to the loss of Japan. In March, army chief of staff Joseph Collins produced a memorandum bearing the ominous title "Broadening the Participation of the United States in the Indochina Operation," which called for greater U.S. financial and material support to the French. About the same time, Dulles informed French leaders that the president saw Vietnam and Korea as parts of a single front, and that this distinguished the new administration from its predecessor. Late that month, in his record of a conversation with Eisenhower, Dulles wrote that Indochina was probably the administration's top priority in foreign policy, because unlike Korea its loss could not be localized "but would spread throughout Asia and Europe."[17]

By the time the secretary spoke those words, more than 139,000 metric tons of U.S. equipment had been delivered to the French, including some 900 combat vehicles, 15,000 other vehicles, 2,500 artillery pieces, 24,000 automatic weapons, 75,000 small arms, and almost 9,000 radios. In addition, the French had received 160 F-6F and F-8F fighter planes, 41 B-26 light bombers, and 28 C-47 transports plus 155 aircraft engines and 93,000 bombs.[18] It was a massive amount of matériel, but the new administration offered to do substantially more if Paris would only provide a plan for winning the war.

Britain too preached the need for victory in the struggle. In due course, London and Washington would drift apart in their assessments of what ought to happen in Vietnam, as we shall see; here, however, at the start of 1953, there was little daylight between them. No less than the Eisenhower administration, the Conservative government of Winston Churchill feared the consequences of a French withdrawal and a Viet Minh victory. From Her Majesty's representatives on the scene in Indochina came a steady stream of reports in late 1952 and early 1953 detailing the continuing weaknesses of the Vietnamese National Army and of the French-backed government; at the same time, the embassy in Paris reported flagging support for the war among the metropolitan French populace. Prone to domino theorizing of their own—in particular, they worried that Western defeat in Indochina could render their own posture in Malaya untenable—British officials in this period fully matched the Americans in their desire to stiffen French resolve, and to convince Paris of the need for a more offensive military strategy.[19]

But the French saw their task differently, as was made clear when a delegation headed by new Radical prime minister René Mayer visited Washington a few weeks after the inauguration. Foreign Minister Georges Bidault and High Commissioner for Indochina Jean Letourneau made the trip as well, and in the weeks prior to departure the three men discussed what could be expected of the new American administration, not only with respect to Indochina but also German rearmament, the European Defense Community (EDC), and other issues. Stalin had died suddenly at the beginning of the month, and the trio wondered how that might affect Washington's Soviet policy. Pleased that Eisenhower's early comments described Vietnam not as a colonial war but as a vital Cold War struggle, the French trio acknowledged among themselves that they could not offer Washington merely the "maintenance of a sterile and costly status quo." But they also worried about the new administration's aggressiveness on Indochina and concurred that there could be no thought of increasing the French war effort significantly, no matter how hard the Americans pressed.[20]

What ensued in Washington was another Franco-American dialogue of the deaf. For the French, recalled a U.S. intelligence officer who sat against the wall during one Pentagon session, it was not even a question of *winning* the war:

> Their goal, Letourneau said, was simply to maintain a position of strength from which an honorable settlement could be negotiated. This, he noted, was exactly what the United States was then doing in Korea. This statement seemed to pass right over the heads of the Americans at the table, who suggested that the French seemed not to understand the American proposal. The American spokesman, an assistant secretary of state, restated the American proposition, emphasizing our willingness to provide the means if the French simply provided us with a viable plan for victory. Letourneau, in turn, restated his position, noting that it was "not the policy of his government" to seek a military victory in Indochina, that indeed victory probably was unattainable because of the likelihood that the Chinese would intervene in Indochina to prevent such an outcome, just as they had done in Korea.[21]

Nor did the prime minister offer more assurances. In a conversation aboard the presidential yacht *Williamsburg*, Mayer was evasive on his government's intentions for Indochina, causing Eisenhower to say sharply that there could be no talk of additional U.S. aid if Paris did not produce a plan that, "if it did not lead to complete victory, would, at least, give hope of an ultimate solution." A chastened Mayer promised to drum up something.

Named for Letourneau and largely drafted right there on the spot, while the French team was still on American soil, the core of the plan involved deploying newly raised, U.S.-financed "light" battalions (that is, six hundred men) that would occupy pacified areas in central and southern Vietnam, permitting *groupes mobiles* to be concentrated in

EISENHOWER ENTERTAINS FRENCH LEADERS ON THE *WILLIAMSBURG*,
MARCH 1953. WITH THE PRESIDENT ARE, FROM LEFT, FRENCH
AMBASSADOR HENRI BONNET, RENÉ MAYER, DULLES, AND BIDAULT.

Tonkin. Then, in 1955, Franco-Vietnamese forces would take the offensive against the main Viet Minh units and destroy them. Heavily dependent on a major expansion of the Vietnamese National Army, the plan was criticized by American military analysts who doubted that such an expansion would occur, or that the Viet Minh would oblige by remaining static in the meantime. Trying to clear rear areas before destroying the main Viet Minh forces, Admiral Arthur W. Radford said, would be like "trying to mop up water without turning off the faucet." Some also complained that the proposal avoided the heart of the problem, namely the heavy and growing Viet Minh presence in the Red River Delta. But from Saigon, both Ambassador Heath and MAAG chief General Thomas J. H. Trapnell defended the Letourneau Plan as the best that could be achieved in the circumstances. For want of anything better, Washington officials signed off in April, not expecting much in the way of results.[22]

III

TO ADD TO EISENHOWER'S CONCERNS, IN APRIL THE VIET MINH invaded Laos, until then a backwater in the war. Giap used main-force battalions from three divisions in the attack, hoping to disperse the French across wide stretches of Indochina, and by month's end the quaint royal capital of Luang Prabang was partially surrounded, and the French strongpoints on the Plain of Jars (Plaine des Jarres, so named for the ancient stone burial urns that dotted its landscape) were isolated. In Eisenhower's judgment, the fall of Laos would be no less disastrous than the fall of Vietnam, and probably more so, for Communist control of Laos would permit a hostile drive west as well as south. "If Laos were lost," he warned the National Security Council, the United States would "likely lose the rest of Southeast Asia and Indonesia. The gateway to India, Burma, and Thailand would be open." In fact, however, Giap's objectives in Laos that spring were more limited. He sought primarily to force the French to spread their forces thinner and to plant food depots and a political infrastructure in northern Laos, all for future exploitation. In early May, satisfied that he had achieved these goals and with the monsoon season fast approaching, he withdrew from all but one Laotian province (Sam Neua), leaving the French and their Laotian supporters badly shaken and Americans further convinced that the war effort was foundering.[23]

Eisenhower was particularly distraught. Until the Laos invasion, he told the National Security Council on April 28, he had thought the French would ultimately win the war; now that seemed far less likely. French commanders lacked the requisite aggressiveness and moreover had failed to "instill a desire to hold" among the Vietnamese population. With only limited manpower at their disposal, these commanders moreover had allowed their forces to become separated and divided into isolated pockets, each of which could be supplied only by air. The Viet Minh units, meanwhile, were able to wander around the countryside almost at will. The following week the president returned to the theme, first at a meeting of the NSC, then in a letter to the U.S. ambassador in Paris, C. Douglas Dillon. Only two developments, he said, would really save the situation. The first was an official declaration from the Paris government guaranteeing the independence of the Associated States as soon as the war was concluded. The second was a strong and capable new military commander who would accept battle, not shy away from it.

FRENCH UNION PARATROOPS OPERATING IN THE PLAIN OF JARS IN LAOS,
APRIL 1953, IN ORDER TO TRY TO TURN BACK GIAP'S OFFENSIVE.
THEY ARE CLAD IN SURPLUS U.S. GEAR.

Convinced that the French generals in Vietnam, including current commander Raoul Salan, were generally a "poor lot," Eisenhower called for "a forceful and inspirational leader" in the mold of de Lattre.[24]

The French had heard this message before, but Prime Minister Mayer could do little but swallow hard and smile. He was frustrated by his government's dependence on Washington and by the Eisenhower administration's insistence on a military solution in Indochina at the same time it sought a political settlement in Korea. He fully shared the frustration of President Vincent Auriol, who told Letourneau in late May: "I am more and more worried about the Americans' [overbearing] attitude. Their involvement in the Indochina war is a catastrophe."[25] But the problem was insoluble; the Americans in effect called the shots. Any unilateral move to withdraw from Indochina could lead to an immediate end of U.S. aid, which would expose the Expeditionary Corps and the *colon* community to grave dangers, forcing decolonization. It could also complicate Franco-American relations concerning German rearmament and other issues.

The internationalization of the war, which had looked like such a good idea in 1949–50, when Paris leaders worked so hard to secure allied and especially American backing, had become a crushing burden from which there seemed no real relief.

And yet, Mayer saw no option but to go along, to hope for some tactical victories in the field from which a compromise settlement could, some months down the line, be negotiated. He assured Douglas Dillon that a statement of the type Eisenhower wanted regarding independence would be announced in a future speech (it would happen in July), and he said a new commander would soon be sent to Indochina. But he demurred on Eisenhower's suggestion that he choose either General Augustin Guillaume, commander of French forces in North Africa, or Lieutenant General Jean Valluy, now at Supreme Headquarters, Allied Powers Europe. Guillaume's health was poor, Mayer noted, while Valluy would inflame Vietnamese nationalist opinion in view of his close association with the Haiphong incident of November 1946 and the overall meltdown that had led to the outbreak of full-scale war the following month. Instead, Dillon was told, Paris intended to appoint General Henri Navarre, chief of staff of French NATO forces in Central Europe, who was little known to U.S. officials and had no Indochina experience.[26]

The sense of urgency in Washington was reflected in other ways. In late April, the administration agreed to loan France six C-119 "Flying Boxcars" (with the U.S. insignias painted over) to transport heavy equipment to Laos, and to allow civilian U.S. pilots to fly the planes. The same week the National Security Council approved NSC-149/2, which suggested the possibility of direct American intervention in Indochina in the event of Chinese aggression or, generally, a "basic change" in the situation. Did the Viet Minh invasion of Laos, Special Assistant to the President Robert Cutler asked at a meeting on May 6, constitute such a basic change? In other words, was the United States now prepared to consider a direct military intervention in the conflict? The question was left hanging, suggesting the answer for the moment was no. But that it was raised at all, and that NSC-149/2 won approval, shows how seriously senior policy makers saw the situation.[27]

American pressure contributed to another important decision by the Mayer government that spring: the devaluation of the Indochinese piaster on May 10. The move came in response to increased reports of profiteering in the currency as a result of the artificial maintenance of the exchange rate. The operation, which had gone on for several years, consisted of buying U.S. dollars on the French black market for between 350 and 400 francs for each dollar. The dollars were then sold in Indochina for 50 piasters to the dollar. The piasters in turn were converted back into francs at the official, but highly overvalued, rate of seventeen francs for a piaster, with a consequent profit of as much as 150 percent. (The currency's real value on international markets was eight francs per piaster.) Critics charged that many dollars bought in Paris and sold in Saigon had found their way into the hands of Viet Minh agents, who then used the profits to buy arms with which to kill Frenchmen. Less often mentioned was that this also financed the lavish lifestyles on the Côte d'Azur of Bao Dai and his associates, including the procuring of legions of expensive prostitutes; or that French businessmen and politicians were in on the game.

The costs of the trafficking to the French treasury were considerable: Credible reports put the losses at 500 million francs per day (roughly $1.4 million). The CIA complained that while it had shut down gold smuggling to Bangkok and Singapore, Air France flights on the Paris-Saigon route continued to operate, with gold shipments of the Banque d'Indochine that were then transferred to Macao for sale to the Viet Minh. These were turned over to the Chinese, who purchased weapons for the Viet Minh through Moscow. The agency determined that French bankers were netting a tidy 50 percent profit on the deal, which put roughly five hundred tons of arms in Viet Minh hands every month.[28]

U.S. officials called the situation intolerable and pressed for a devaluation, reminding Paris of their own treasury's major contribution to the Indochina effort. The French press, meanwhile, ran numerous high-profile stories on the issue—notably the left-wing *L'Observateur,* which in early May published documentary evidence against persons profiting from the traffic, citing names and dates. The stories relied in part on the investigations of Jacques Despuech, a disgruntled ex-employee of the Currency Exchange Office, who withstood lawsuits and attempted bribes, even threats on his life and that of his wife, to publish a book-length exposé titled *Le trafic des piastres.*[29] The government responded to this onslaught by announcing a 40 percent devaluation, which disturbed the artificial economic equilibrium in Indochina and generated uproar among *colons,* many of whom had benefited from the inflated rate. More ominously for the future, the action also angered non-Communist nationalists throughout Indochina, including officials in Bao Dai's State of Vietnam government. "Of course we are angry," declared Prime Minister Nguyen Van Tam, who was not known for his nationalist fervor (he had volunteered to serve under General Leclerc early in the war and was a French citizen). The Paris government's failure to consult with him or his ministers prior to the decision was inexcusable, Tam charged, and it suggested that the whole concept of the French Union should be reexamined.[30]

IV

JUST HOW MUCH DELIBERATION WENT INTO THE SELECTION OF Navarre and the piaster devaluation is open to question, for by now Mayer had something bigger on his mind, namely the survival of his three-month-old government. The assaults came from both left and right, and they concerned economic and social policy as well as what critics saw as Mayer's too-favorable view of the EDC and its integrated European army.[31] But the bloody struggle in Indochina also loomed large, particularly as news filtered in of the Viet Minh offensive in Laos. Mayer now faced, according to one close observer, "an unprecedented parliamentary offensive" over the war. The phrase is somewhat misleading, as there was still no mass antiwar movement in the National Assembly, but it does capture the growing domestic pressure on French leaders to find a way out of what many now called *la sale guerre* (the dirty war). In April, a downbeat Bidault complained to Dulles that the government was "caught in a crossfire" between those who opposed the war on moral grounds and those who said it was ruining France economically. That same month former prime minister Edgar Faure proposed a five-power conference to settle the Indochina conflict diplomatically, while in May a public opinion poll commissioned by *Le Monde* found that two-thirds of French voters favored either a unilateral withdrawal of French forces or a negotiated armistice. Only 19 percent advocated stepped-up military action.[32]

Said a Paris-based British diplomat of the popular mood: "A left-wing man-in-the-street will say that it is a dirty war which ought never to have been started and which ought to be brought to an end as quickly as possible for moral reasons quite apart from material ones. If he is not left-wing but averagely cynical he will say that he wants the war to be terminated because it is no concern of his except in so far as it tends to increase the weight of his taxes; his hearth is not menaced by the Viet Minh and the French lives which are lost in Indo-China are those of volunteer soldiers. If he has some finer feelings he may say that the war ought to be brought to an end because it can clearly never be won and that its continuation is meanwhile weakening France."[33]

If this man in the street was a reader of books he could pick up two new authoritative works, Philippe Devillers's *Histoire du Viêt-Nam, de 1940 à 1952* and Paul Mus's *Viêt-Nam: sociologie d'une guerre,* which provided important historical context and implicitly pointed to the giant obstacles in the way of victory.[34] If he opened the influential *Le Monde,* he could read the complaint that while France was exhausting herself in Vietnam, Germany was becoming the leading power in Europe; while in the afternoon paper *Paris-Presse,* he could read Vietnam correspondent Max Harmier declare that France had neither the tactics nor the means to defeat the Viet Minh.[35] And if his curiosity caused him to peruse *L'Express,* a brand-new weekly magazine modeled on *Time,* he would see story after story attacking the war. The magazine came out firing in its first issue, charging that certain political groups, with vested financial interests in Indochina, were "conspiring" to keep the war going. Featured on the cover was Pierre Mendès France of the Radical Party, who declared on page six, in an interview titled "France Can Bear the Truth": "We cannot approach problems of economic recovery without resolving the problem of unproductive costs like rearmament and the Indochina War." No military solution was possible in Vietnam, Mendès France went on, and therefore every effort had to go to gaining a diplomatic settlement, perhaps through direct bilateral negotiations with Ho Chi Minh. "Our negotiating position was better two years ago than it was last year; better last year than it is now; it is probably not as bad now as it will be next year."[36]

More and more, Mendès France was the figure around whom opponents of the war coalesced. *L'Express,* indeed, had come into existence explicitly for the purpose of bringing him into power. When Mayer's government fell on May 21, speculation turned to the prospect of a Mendès France government. He almost succeeded, gaining broad support except among Gaullists and Communists and winning 301 votes, thirteen short of the number required to form a government. Commented Letourneau to the new Indochina commander Navarre: "I am somewhat worried for the future when I see that 300 members of parliament have voted for the nomination of M. Mendès France, thereby practically stating that they are ready to envisage some way of pulling out of Indo-china." In fact, the figure was even higher, as Ambassador Dillon ruefully noted in a cable to Washington: If Communist votes were added, it totaled 406 votes in favor of withdrawal from Indochina.[37]

During lunch with Dillon on June 17, Mendès France elaborated his vision for a political resolution of the war, and his fears for what a stay-the-course policy would bring. France, he began, should guarantee immediate and full independence to the Indochinese states and should set a definite time schedule for the withdrawal of French forces. Together with the Indochinese states, France would then propose an armistice to Ho Chi Minh, subject to nationwide elections for a constituent assembly to establish a constitution for a free and independent Vietnam. The Communists would undoubtedly be the leading entity in that parliament, Mendès France acknowledged, and their subsequent actions would be impossible to know in advance, but those were risks worth taking. Moscow and Beijing, meanwhile, were benefiting from the continuation of the war, since it had the effect of weakening the West; this was added reason to bring it to a swift resolution. The Frenchman concluded with a warning: The only alternative to a policy of the type he had outlined was a political catastrophe in Indochina within the next year.[38]

One wonders: Would it all have been different had he won the vote and become premier? Would he have sought to terminate the war in short order? Probably yes and yes. With hindsight's advantage—and arguably even in the context of the time—it's hard to argue against his claim that the French negotiating position was more favorable in spring 1953 than it would likely be a year thence. Few doubted the depth of his conviction that the war was having a devastating impact on France's financial, diplomatic, and military health. Then again, just what Mendès France would have done as prime minister in 1953—and when he would have done it—is not easy to gauge. To the surprise of many, in his investiture speech he had suddenly turned vague on the war, saying merely that the war was a "crushing burden, which is sapping the strength of France," and promising a "precise plan" in due course.

This ambiguity, some analysts speculated, may have cost Mendès France the necessary votes; it may also have signified uncertainty in his mind about the proper course of action on Indochina. It would be no simple task to bring an end to a long and costly war, he perhaps realized; nor would it be easy to go against the new American administration's aggressive advocacy. Eisenhower had made it unambiguously clear: France had to stay in the fight. Whatever the case, Mendès France had missed his best chance to date to take the reins of power and somehow ease the "crushing burden." In late June, Joseph Laniel, a wealthy, rumpled, and little-known Independent from Normandy with vague foreign policy views, became prime minister, ending a thirty-six-day political crisis. It was the nineteenth French government in the past seven years. Pierre Mendès France was left to ponder what might have been and hope for another chance.

CHAPTER 15

NAVARRE'S AMERICAN PLAN

O N INDOCHINA MATTERS, THE NEW FRENCH LEADER JOSEPH LANIEL
would rely heavily on Georges Bidault, who narrowly failed to become
prime minister himself and who stayed on as foreign minister. Bidault's
personal stake in a successful outcome in Indochina went deeper than
anyone else's, since he had been right there at the center when the crucial early moves were made, first as foreign minister in de Gaulle's Provisional Government in 1944–45, then as president in the summer and fall
of 1946. As foreign minister and then prime minister again in 1947–50,
he had been uncompromising on the war—in the parlance of the later
American war, a hawk among hawks—and he did not waver as defense
minister in 1951–52. It's a remarkable thing, in view of the dizzying turn-
over of governments in the Fourth Republic, that Bidault was seemingly
always there, putting his stamp on the policy, pushing forward, ruling
out compromise. This was Bidault's war if it was anyone's.

Lately, though, the true believer had begun entertaining doubts,
though he kept them mostly private. Still suspicious of negotiations, he
felt pressure from the likes of former prime ministers Paul Reynaud and
Edgar Faure to seek an early end to the war. Both men supported the
proposed European Defense Community and were prepared to offer full
and complete independence to the Indochinese states and leave them
to their fates. France would then be free to concentrate on European issues, which ultimately mattered much more. Easy for them to say, Bidault
thought; they weren't responsible for policy, at least not as he was. (Reynaud was now minister for the Associated States.) Well aware that French

options on Indochina ranged from poor to worse, and that the Eisenhower team was pushing hard—harder than its predecessor—for a more forceful prosecution of the war, he and Laniel moved cautiously at first, avoiding any commitment to direct diplomatic overtures to Ho Chi Minh and affirming their faith in the new commander in chief, Henri Navarre.

Navarre's very lack of experience in Indochina was an asset, Paris leaders insisted. He could approach the issue, they told skeptical Americans, with "an absence of prejudice." A veteran of both world wars and a graduate of Saint-Cyr, Navarre had also spent several years in pacification campaigns in Syria and Morocco and was considered an expert on intelligence matters. When U.S. forces landed in southern France in 1944, Navarre joined them. Later he led an armored regiment in de Lattre's Armée Rhin et Danube. Seven times he was cited for bravery, and he received the Croix de Guerre. Cold and effete in personality, trim and elegant in appearance, Navarre was reputed to have a brilliant analytical mind, and he sought at all times to project an air of authority; in one author's words, "He seemed to have both knowledge and truth, even when he was in doubt."[1] Navarre had not coveted the Indochina appointment, and he made a halfhearted effort to turn it down; once on the scene, however, he threw himself into his task with courage and dedication, ignoring as best he could grumbling from the French officer corps that he was an "arm-chair general" who didn't know Indochina and whose senior appointments had all been in staff and intelligence work.[2]

His task, he knew, was enormous: to lead a war theater larger than metropolitan France, located more than 8,500 miles from home, with a fighting force—approaching half a million men, including the VNA—as large as most combat armies of World War II.[3] Using that force, he had to salvage the war effort, turn things around, and justify the immense sacrifices the Expeditionary Corps had already made—to date, the fighting had killed 3 generals, 8 colonels, 18 lieutenant colonels, 69 majors, 341 captains, 1,140 lieutenants, 3,683 NCOs, and 6,008 soldiers of French nationality; 12,019 legionnaires and Africans; and 14,093 Indochinese troops. These numbers did not include the missing or wounded—about 20,000 and 100,000 respectively.[4]

Publicly, Navarre exuded confidence from the start, insisting before all comers that victory would come in due course. "We will take the offensive," the old cavalryman declared. "We shall give back to our troops the mobility and aggressiveness they have sometimes lacked." If the Associated States applied themselves, he said on another occasion, *"la victoire est certaine."*[5]

This bullishness put Navarre somewhat at odds with his primary mission in Indochina, which was not to destroy the Viet Minh or win an outright victory but merely to create the conditions for an "honorable" exit from the struggle.[6] Nor did it align with some of the reports he received upon arriving in Saigon, such as the one from a Saint-Cyr classmate who greeted him by saying, "Henri, old boy, what have you come to this shithole for? I'm clearing out." Raoul Salan, the outgoing commander, likewise gave him a grim assessment of the prospects in the fighting—General Giap, Salan warned, was organizing his big units effectively and giving them a European character—but Navarre shook it off. Later, he spoke to his staff with macho swagger: "Victory is a woman who gives herself to those who know how to take her."[7]

The remark may help explain why Navarre formed a close working relationship with General John "Iron Mike" O'Daniel, a gruff, cigar-chomping American officer prone to his own rhetorical bluster who had been sent by the Joint Chiefs of Staff to assess French strategy in the war and to dispel any idea of seeking an early diplomatic settlement with Ho Chi Minh. O'Daniel, a veteran of both world wars and Korea, where he had been a corps commander, now served as commander of U.S. Army forces in the Pacific, based at Pearl Harbor. He arrived in Saigon on June 20, 1953, one month after Navarre had assumed command.

Initially, the two men did not see eye to eye. In several early sessions, O'Daniel pressed Navarre—or "Navarrie," as he insisted on calling him—for a plan to win the war, and each time the Frenchman insisted he could not comply. It was for the Paris leadership to make policy, he said; his job as theater commander was merely to execute the mission set for him by the government. Currently, that mission involved maintaining a position of strength from which negotiations could be undertaken at some point in the future. The emphasis would be on holding existing territory and avoiding high-risk operations, of securing, in the first instance, a *coup nul* (a tied game). Frustrated, O'Daniel asked his own subordinates in Bangkok to draw up a plan, one building on the Letourneau Plan from

An ardent believer in American internationalism, Dulles was also deeply anti-Communist and pro-business, and he thought Republicans more trustworthy than Democrats—they were more wealthy, after all, and therefore understood better how the world worked. In 1944 and again in 1948, Dulles advised Thomas E. Dewey's campaigns for president, and he likely would have been the secretary of state in a Dewey administration. A subsequent failed run for the U.S. Senate from New York—Dulles decked his campaign car with a banner proclaiming him "Enemy of the Reds!" which about summarized his platform—convinced him that his political future lay in appointive rather than elective office. Now, in January 1953, at age sixty-five, he would get to run the State Department at last.

Not everyone welcomed his selection. Many Europeans found him too sanctimonious by half and shuddered at his fire-and-brimstone anti-Communism, which they feared would lead to a Soviet-American confrontation and possible nuclear annihilation of the continent. They much preferred the less ideological Dean Acheson. Already in 1942, when Dulles undertook several minor missions to England, one British official found him "the wooliest type of pontificating American. . . . Heaven help us!" Foreign Secretary Anthony Eden, remembering also that Dulles had been equivocal about the Nazi menace in the late 1930s, went so far as to write Eisenhower to express the hope that he would select someone else. Harold Macmillan, like Eden a future Tory prime minister, in his diary that spring referred to the "dunder-headed Dulles" who was "sure to make a 'gaffe' if it is possible to do so."[6]

In the United States, skeptics included Reinhold Niebuhr, the influential theologian, who said of him, "Mr. Dulles's moral universe makes everything quite clear, too clear. . . . Self-righteousness is the inevitable fruit of simple moral judgments."[7] Some Republicans worried that Dulles's propensity for hyperbole and oversimplification could lead also to heightened partisan tensions in Washington. Eisenhower thought so too, but the prospect did not worry him too much. Dulles, he shrewdly determined, could serve as a buffer between him and the Republican right and moreover had enormous experience on his side. Said the president-elect of his choice: "There's only one man I know who has seen more of the world and talked with more people and knows more than he does, and that's me."[8]

into grids and occupied progressively the outside areas and worked *inward*. Both methods required a degree of manpower saturation that the French simply did not have available in Vietnam.

But the bigger problem, as far as some American analysts were concerned, was the growing evidence of disillusion in Paris. On July 3, Laniel pledged publicly that France would "perfect" the independence of the Indochinese states. Washington officials took this as a positive step—recall that Eisenhower had pressed for such a pledge in the spring—but only if it did not signal an intention to bug out of Indochina entirely. Laniel, they noted, had given scant evidence that he intended to fight the war vigorously come the end of the monsoon season. As always, Americans had a hard time grasping the crux of the problem: While granting full independence to Vietnam might be necessary to undermine Ho Chi Minh's nationalist appeal, it also risked making the war irrelevant to French interests.

Nor did Bidault offer more assurances during three days of talks in Washington in July. In the first session, a lengthy affair at Dulles's Georgetown home, he bluntly remarked that French public opinion had turned against the war and that there was broad support in the Assembly for direct talks with Ho Chi Minh. Talk of peace in Korea had a contagious effect in France, and as a result Paris would be forced to seek an early end to the war, by negotiations if necessary. Dulles countered that in Korea the United States had fought her way to a strong bargaining position and that France needed to do the same; only after the military outlook improved should she enter talks with Ho. Bidault nodded in seeming agreement but offered no assurances, beyond the murky promise that France would "liquidate the war with honor."[12]

Privately, most French leaders had given up entirely on the idea of victory but were unwilling to admit it to the Americans. Former prime minister René Mayer was blunt: "It seems evident that among French businessmen and civil servants who know Indochina well, nobody believes any more that it is possible to beat the Viet Minh militarily. Nevertheless, in order to induce Washington to grant France sizable direct assistance, the notion has been propagated that additional efforts might yield decisive results."[13]

II

THE KOREAN ARMISTICE, SIGNED ON JULY 27, HAD A DEVASTATING effect on French thinking, causing a further slackening of the will to continue the fight. Marc Jacquet, the minister for the Associated States, told British officials a few days later that his compatriots were nonplussed: They saw the United States securing a truce in Korea and Britain trading with China and could not understand why their allies should expect them to continue a war in Indochina in which there was no longer a direct French interest. France, he said, wanted the future Korea peace conference extended to cover also Indochina and sought Britain's help in that regard. He added that American aid for the French war effort was insufficient and speculated that Laniel's government was the last that would continue the struggle.[14]

Bernard B. Fall, a French-raised World War II veteran who would in time become one of the most astute analysts of both the French and American wars, and who would be killed while accompanying U.S. Marines on a mission near Hue in early 1967, saw firsthand the effect of the Korean truce as he toured Vietnam in 1953 in order to conduct field research for his Syracuse University doctoral dissertation. Born into a Jewish merchant family in Vienna in 1926, Fall lost both parents at the hands of the Nazis and joined the French underground in November 1942, at age sixteen. As a *maquisard* he soon got a taste of what it meant to fight a guerrilla war against an occupying force. Later, he saw action in the First French Army under de Lattre before being shifted—thanks to his fluency in German—to the French Army's intelligence service. A stint as a researcher for the Nuremberg War Crimes Tribunal followed, whereupon Fall resumed his studies, first at the University of Paris and then in Munich. In 1951 he arrived in the United States, the recipient of a Fulbright fellowship to pursue graduate work at Syracuse. During a summer seminar in Washington in 1952, Fall's instructor encouraged him to pursue research on the Indochina struggle, about which little scholarship had as yet been produced.

Fall took up the challenge with zest. He recalled in an interview in 1966: "By pure accident, one sunny day in Washington, D.C., of all places, in 1952, I got interested in Viet-Nam and it's been sort of a bad love affair ever since."[15]

On May 16, 1953, Fall arrived in Hanoi, carrying a military-style duffel bag and with his precious Leica camera and a new shortwave radio slung over his shoulder. Granted special access as a former French army officer, Fall accompanied units on combat operations, attended lunches and dinners with officers, and kept his eyes and ears open. The signing of the Korean armistice, he later wrote, "brought a wave of exasperation and hopelessness to the senior commanders that—though hidden to outsiders—was nevertheless obvious." For no longer could it be said that France was fighting one front of a two-front war, necessary for the defense of the West. Washington had broken the deal: It had agreed to a separate peace in Asia. And now the Chinese, being no longer preoccupied in Korea, could turn their focus southward. About Navarre, meanwhile, Fall heard mostly complaints—he was timid and uncommunicative, many in the officer corps said, disliked even by his own staff—and few commanders had much good to say about the fighting abilities of Bao Dai's Vietnamese Nationalist Army.[16]

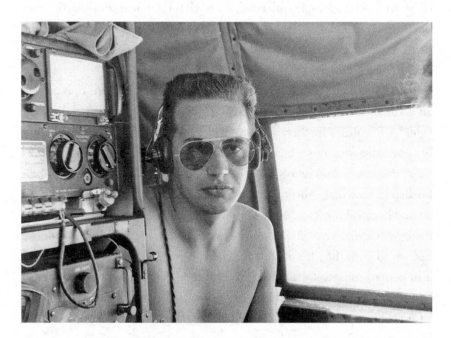

BERNARD FALL ON A SUPPLY DROP MISSION WITH
FRENCH UNION FORCES, 1953.

Fall sought to understand the security situation inside the Red River Delta. A French officer assured him that defenses were strong: "We are going to deny the Communists access to the eight million people in this Delta and the three million tons of rice, and will eventually starve them out and deny them access to the population." Did the Viet Minh hold any areas in the delta? Fall asked. "Yes," the officer replied, pointing to his map, "they hold those little blue blotches, 1, 2, 3, 4, and a little one over here." How did he know? "It is simple, when we go there we get shot at; that's how we know."[17]

Suspicious after hearing Vietnamese friends laugh mockingly at the officer's claims—in their native villages, all the village chiefs were Viet Minh, whatever they told the French—Fall decided to study village tax rolls. These showed conclusively that most of the delta had not paid taxes for years. If the villages were contributing revenues to anyone, it was not to the French-backed government. Equally revealing was the teacher-assignment data: In a school system where teachers were designated by the central government, these same villages were not being assigned teachers from Hanoi. Fall produced his own maps that showed a picture of control "frighteningly different" from what French authorities were reporting. He concluded that the Viet Minh dominated 70 percent of the delta inside the French perimeter—more or less every part of it except Hanoi, Haiphong, and the other large garrison areas.[18]

He wrote home of one excursion in the delta, in which his unit passed an artillery convoy and then passed through an "ominously calm" village. "A few miles further, all of a sudden [we] heard the harsh staccato of automatic weapons, then some more of the same, and a few minutes later, the heavy booms of gunfire. The artillery convoy had been ambushed in the village through which we had passed." Fall's unit had been spared because the Viet Minh were waiting for bigger game. "The whole thing was a matter of sheer, unforeseeable luck, because for a while we had toyed with the idea of staying with the convoy for more protection." The convoy too was fortunate, Fall continued, losing only one dead and a few wounded, but the overall situation was perilous. "In the south today, a train blew up on a bridge and fell into a ravine. . . . Situation is not so hot right now."[19]

A British officer reached a similar conclusion after accompanying a

French unit on a sweep of the delta a few miles south of Hanoi. He wrote of seeing an "innocent looking village" mortared and shelled by tanks and artillery for two hours, and then joining the French troops as they proceeded carefully into the town. A captured villager, presumably Viet Minh, pointed to a pile of debris in the center of the village and said it hid the entrance to a tunnel.

> The large heap is quickly swept away and the Moroccans vigorously set-to with their spades. After a quarter of an hour's digging the tunnel is found far beneath the ground. Two hand grenades are then almost daintily dropped within; after the smoke from the explosion has almost blown away, a tiny head appears above the ground and then another. Seemingly from the depths of the earth ten muddy-looking individuals emerge. They are arrested and a little Moroccan soldier with a cocky smile prepares to descend with a torch to look for the weapons which are bound to be there. But he does not get far. It seems impossible but there are still more communists below. A grenade is hurled at him from the darkness and after an ear-splitting explosion the poor screaming wretch is extracted with both his legs shattered. However, after a few more acts of persuasion the remaining two come up. "Who threw the grenade?" the officer shouts at them. The more timid looking of the two points to his partner who when asked confesses to the deed without the least sign of concern. "Where are the arms?" he is asked but he only shakes his head. The Moroccans gladly shoot him but the prisoners are unmoved by the execution and do not even turn their heads away. And when faced with the same question and the same threat they refuse to answer.

"What is it that they have that we don't have?" the Briton plaintively asked himself, with reference to the villagers and their dedication to Ho Chi Minh. "No doubt [the French] found the weapons but there were plenty of others they did not find. When I left the village all was quiet except for the odd mine going off. Probably the same little drama was going on in all the villages. The following day the troops would leave the area. The Viet Minh would emerge from the many undiscovered tunnels and set to work and rebuild their defences. And next year all these little scenes will be repeated."[20]

A frustrated French intelligence colonel said at about the same time: "As long as the village populations are against us, we'll just be treading water."[21]

III

JOURNALISTS TOO EXPERIENCED THE WAR UP CLOSE, AS THEY HAD since the shooting started seven years earlier, though not all of them got as close to the action as Bernard Fall and the British officer did. The terrace bar at the Continental in Saigon remained the rendezvous point, where they discussed and debated the pressing questions: Would the taciturn Navarre inspire his troops and turn the tide? Would America step up her involvement in the war, perhaps to the point of sending troops? Would China intervene? Would the French (with Washington's help) be able to keep the non-Communist nationalists in Vietnam in check? Would Laniel and Bidault seek direct negotiations with Ho?

No piece of reporting that summer received more attention than a devastating photographic essay in *Life* in August. "Indochina, All But Lost," read the magazine cover, and the article, by Dennis Duncan, depicted a lethargic and fading French war effort. "It is a year when ineffective French tactics, and the ebbing of French will, make it seem that Indochina is lost to the non-communist world," Duncan wrote. "Staff officers keep hours that would delight a banker . . . [and] the troops, following the example of their commanders, take long siestas." U.S. aid, meanwhile, does not reach its intended recipients, because of the French practice of appointing Indochinese officials on the basis of their political affiliations rather than their competence. As a result, "in the background of this war is a society that has become corrupt." Millions cast their lot with the Viet Minh not out of attachment to Communism but out of frustration with the lack of strong nationalist alternatives. An editorial in the same issue endorsed Duncan's findings and accused Paris of pursuing "sophisticated defeatism," even as it called victory "entirely feasible" and advocated more U.S. support in the war. Bidault, well aware of *Life*'s huge circulation in the United States, was outraged by Duncan's claims and threatened to have the magazine pulled from Parisian store shelves. He also instructed officers at the embassy in Washington to register a complaint.[22]

C. D. Jackson, a Time Inc. senior executive and editor who now served as an adviser to Eisenhower on Cold War strategy, fumed that Duncan's spread furnished "invaluable documentation to those who want to pull out" of Indochina. *Life*'s publisher and editor-in-chief, Henry Luce, agreed. He had been away in Rome when a senior editor signed off on the article, and he furiously castigated Duncan as a "Rover Boy" who had "fouled up basic policy."[23] On Luce's orders, the magazine ran a rejoinder in September titled "France Is Fighting the Good Fight." This was the prevailing theme also in Luce's other publication, *Time*. Issue after issue in the spring and summer, while acknowledging setbacks and problems in the war effort, gave readers the impression that the trends pointed in the right direction, that the Franco-American partnership functioned smoothly like a well-oiled machine, and that the "Reds" were on the ropes. Never mind that several of the cables coming in to Time Inc.'s editorial offices from correspondents offered a much different picture, one showing a faltering war effort and expanding Viet Minh reach.[24]

A *Time* cover story on Navarre in September was a perfect counterpoint to the *Life* photographic essay. This one lauded the "quiet but steely, cultured but tough" general's conception of his role and applauded his early actions in the field. (Among them: Operation Hirondelle [Swallow], an airborne raid on enemy supply depots around Lang Son in July that involved two thousand paratroops supported by ten B-26 bombers and fifty-six Bearcat fighters. Numerous depots were destroyed, and the retreat to French lines, covering fifty miles and in crushing heat, took place without incident.) Navarre, the magazine gushed, was "a master of assembling bits and pieces into a pattern and molding the pattern into plans." The article spoke of a "new spirit and optimism" among soldiers "who must fight the ugly war" in Vietnam, and it concluded by quoting an unnamed observer, whose phrasing would come back to haunt both the French and the Americans in later years: "A year ago none of us could see victory. . . . Now we can see it clearly—like light at the end of a tunnel."[25]

The two magazines did have that in common: Victory in Vietnam, both said, was "entirely feasible." *Life* may have been downbeat about the outlook, but it put the blame squarely on French civilian and military leaders for, in effect, giving up just as victory was near. The gulf between the two Luce journals was in this respect much smaller than a quick skimming would suggest. In other press assessments that summer, the same phenomenon could be observed: Some saw the glass as half-full, some as half-empty, but very few saw it as dry or nearly dry. If defeat occurred, principal blame would lie with France, for her unwillingness either to expend more of her human and material resources to fight the war, or to grant the Indochinese people real independence. *The New York Times,* for example, was straightforwardly hawkish, insisting that the defense of Indochina was vital "not merely to France but to the whole of the free world." If Indochina fell, the editors warned, the way would be open to Thailand, Malaya, Burma, and eventually Indonesia, India, and the Philippines.[26]

In the U.S. government too, the range of opinion was narrow, narrower than it had been in previous years. The deep split that had existed among middle-level State Department officials for much of the Truman period—a split that went to the fundamental question of whether the United States should join in the fight against Ho Chi Minh, or remain neutral, or even support him—was to a large extent gone, even if officials still disagreed among themselves about the likely future course of events. The CIA was pessimistic, predicting that the French position was likely to deteriorate progressively and that after mid-1954, "the political and military position could go very rapidly." The Nguyen Van Tam government was "more shadow than substance," the agency noted, and too subservient to Paris to win even the semblance of popular support.[27] In the Pentagon and at State, there were doubts that the Navarre Plan would in fact accomplish what its proponents claimed, while in the Oval Office, Eisenhower expressed frequent frustration with French decision making. But if few Pollyannas walked the corridors of power in Washington, a general consensus nevertheless prevailed among policy makers that the war could ultimately be won—and that, regardless, it was necessary to try.

This was Eisenhower's basic message in remarks before a national governors' conference in Seattle in early August. The Korean armistice had just been signed, and the president took satisfaction in having achieved that primary objective. But he was aware of grumblings within the Republican Party concerning his decision to bargain with godless Communists, and moreover he still believed that Indochina was vital strategically. He set about educating the governors on the importance to U.S. security of the outcome. He began by briefly sketching out the origins of the war, noting that it was variously seen as "an outgrowth of French colonialism" and a struggle "between the communists and the other elements in Southeast Asia." Then, without saying which perspective he held, the president moved quickly to emphasize Indochina's current strategic importance, thus implying that the war's origins no longer mattered.

"If Indochina goes," Eisenhower warned his audience, "several things happen right away. The Malayan peninsula, with its valuable tin and tungsten, would become indefensible, and India would be outflanked. Indonesia, with all its riches, would likely be lost too. . . . So you see," he went on, "somewhere along the line, this must be blocked. It must be blocked now. That is what the French are doing." It followed that America's financial contribution to the war effort was money well spent; by assisting France, Americans were acting "to prevent the occurrence of something that would be of the most terrible significance for the United States of America—our security, our power and ability to get certain things we need from the riches of the Indonesian territory, and from Southeast Asia."[28]

It must be blocked now. That is what the French are doing. A more ringing endorsement of the war's importance would be hard to imagine. Reflecting on the speech over lunch with two British officials a few days later, Eisenhower said that Indochina was more crucial strategically than Korea. It was the neck in the bottle, and it was essential to keep the cork in. Unfortunately, getting this basic fact across to the American people and their representatives in Congress had not been easy. Ignorance was widespread: Many Americans thought Saigon was something to eat. The president assured his guests he had done his best with congressional leaders, but there was no telling if it was enough, and that's why he had devoted so much of the Seattle speech to the subject. Congress had to be convinced, he said, to support an "all-out" effort in Vietnam for a year or eighteen months. Without such congressional backing, American aid would end.[29]

By "all-out" effort, did Eisenhower mean potentially using U.S. ground forces? It's hard to be sure. He knew that lawmakers would be in no mood to send soldiers back to Asia immediately on the heels of the long and frustrating struggle in Korea, and he himself was not keen on such a prospect. In the short term, at least, the emphasis would have to be on other means. But something had to be done, and soon. Eisenhower doubted the Laniel government's commitment to the war, but he also feared it might be the last French government to fight at all. Therefore, the United States should move immediately to boost the level of American aid to Navarre's war effort. The president received support on this point from the Joint Chiefs of Staff, who said in August that the ultimate success of the Navarre Plan might depend on the allocation of additional U.S. aid. From Ambassador Dillon in Paris, meanwhile, came the warning that the "Indochina problem is rapidly reaching a crisis here," and that "to carry out the basic elements of the Navarre Plan, something like $200 million extra will be required." Dillon, a Francophile who owned vineyards in Bordeaux, urged that the funds be allocated, and that more be given later.[30]

Already Congress had approved the administration's request for $400 million for Indochina for fiscal year 1954, despite complaints among some in the Senate—notably freshman Republican Barry Goldwater of Arizona—that the money would merely support France's colonial oppression. Now the president moved to boost the amount. In September, with Congress out of session for the remainder of the year, he quietly approved an *additional* $385 million, to be taken out of the budgets of existing aid programs. He instructed aides to consult with select lawmakers prior to the announcement of the decision, confident he could get at least grudging support.

And so he did. Some of the congressional leaders consulted grumbled about the massive outlay, but none was prepared to block the administration on Indochina strategy. Unlike in previous years, when the war had elicited only sporadic interest on Capitol Hill, now, with an armistice in Korea and concerns on the rise regarding Communist expansion elsewhere in Asia, more and more House members and senators paid attention and issued pronouncements. And although some three hundred and fifty U.S. ships (or more than two each week) had already made the voyage to Vietnam over the previous three years, delivering all manner of war matériel to the French—trucks, tanks, automatic weapons, small arms and ammunition, artillery shells, engineering and hospital equipment, radios—the legislators were prepared to do more.

A select few Senate members, such as John F. Kennedy, the freshman Democrat from Massachusetts, offered biting critiques of the French for failing to grant "genuine independence" to Indochina, while others were more forgiving of the Paris government, saying effective independence was already in place. Almost no one, however, disputed the administration's interpretation of the stakes. Certainly not Senate majority leader William Knowland of California, who had railed against Truman for "losing" China and who would later so exasperate Eisenhower that the president claimed he confounded the age-old question "How stupid can you get?" In early September, Knowland stopped off in Vietnam during an extensive tour of Asia. Upon being briefed by French officials, he went before the microphones and thundered that Vietnam was now free and independent and that France's cause was also America's.[31]

IV

KNOWLAND'S VISIT, HOWEVER, WAS NOT THE MOST CONSEQUEN-tial by a U.S. senator to Vietnam that fall. That honor belonged to Mike Mansfield, a freshman Democrat from Montana who was destined to be the leading congressional voice on Vietnam matters in the years to come. Known as something of an Asia expert for having visited wartime China and postwar Japan and having taught college classes on the region's history, Mansfield in fact knew little about Indochina before the start of 1953. But already in February of that year, a mere seven weeks after being sworn in, he expressed his alarm over the situation. "Indo-China is at this time the most important area on the Continent of Asia," he wrote in a memo for his files, the gist of which he also conveyed to *The New York Times*. "Its loss would start a chain-reaction extending to the Persian Gulf and would give to the Soviets and the satellites the rubber, the tin and the oil which are in such short supply within the Soviet Union and which would mean so much to the conduct of a war." Admittedly, Indochina herself would probably supply only a small amount of the needed rubber, but her loss would open up the area in Southeast Asia that contained the riches the Kremlin badly needed. "In addition the loss of Indo-China would entail grave political consequences in the countries to the East, Malaya, Thailand, Burma, India, Pakistan, Iran and perhaps, beyond." Consequently, "I believe that military shipments should be stepped up considerably to that area."[32]

It could have been John Foster Dulles speaking. Though Moscow's involvement in Indochina was minimal—especially compared to Washington's—both the senator and the secretary of state were inclined in this early period to see the Soviet bear looming large and menacing behind the scenes, directing the struggle. Regarding the dire consequences of a defeat in Indochina, certainly, the two men were in full agreement, and in the months that followed, Mansfield held to that view. In early May, he attended a luncheon in Washington in honor of Ngo Dinh Diem, the Roman Catholic and ardently anti-Communist Vietnamese nationalist who was then living at the Maryknoll Seminary in Lakewood, New Jersey. In time, as we shall see, Mansfield would become Diem's great champion in Washington, indeed would become known as "Diem's godfather," but for the moment it is enough to note that the senator came away from the luncheon further convinced of Vietnam's importance—and of the need for a "Third Force" in between the French and the Viet Minh. The trouble in Vietnam, Diem told his attentive listeners, who also included John F. Kennedy, was the absence of a "rallying point between the Communists and the French." His mission, he said, was to create such a Third Force.[33]

Mansfield determined that he would have to experience Indochina for himself. He obtained authorization for a trip from the Foreign Relations Committee and logistical assistance from the State Department, which prepared an itinerary and coordinated with American diplomatic posts in Laos, Cambodia, and Vietnam. His arrival in Saigon on September 21 received little notice, which surprised no one who knew him, for he was by nature reticent and unassuming, the very antithesis of the charismatic and glad-handing politician. Neither witty nor silver-tongued, he was in many ways a prototypical gaunt and laconic westerner (though he was born in the east), who could be monosyllabic in public. To gain a more accurate assessment of the conditions, Mansfield had asked that 60 percent of his time be free from official inspections and briefings, that entertainment be kept to "an absolute minimum," and that no publicity accompany his various stops. Nevertheless, the range of opinions he heard was constricted, for he interacted almost solely with French officials and high-ranking French-appointed Vietnamese. Never did he come close to experiencing the war on the ground—he toured the Red River Delta by air—and he encountered few independent observers. An exception was Australian journalist Denis Warner, who told him the French strategy was gravely flawed and the war likely lost. Mansfield, Warner recalled, refused to accept the analysis, replying, "I'm sure you can't be right. I'm sure you can't be right."[34]

Navarre, on the other hand, sang a different melody, one much more to the senator's liking. He would implement the Navarre Plan, he assured Mansfield, and so would take the fight to the enemy. Mansfield returned home further convinced of the vital importance of the French effort and expressed confidence bordering on enthusiasm regarding Navarre's intentions for the fall campaign. "There are indications," he wrote in his report to Congress, "that the stalemate in Indochina may be coming to an end. The months ahead could witness the beginning of a series of significant military engagements." With increased American assistance as well as a buildup of the VNA, and with French devolution of sovereignty to the non-Communist governments, "only an outright invasion by the Chinese communists would be likely to rescue the Viet Minh from defeat." The report acknowledged the breadth of Ho Chi Minh's popular appeal and took note of the "current of nationalism [that] runs strong throughout Indochina," but its author was not willing to characterize Ho as a genuine nationalist. The Viet Minh leader's objective, Mansfield wrote, was merely to use a "form of misdirected nationalism" to gain the support of non-Communists.[35]

For Eisenhower and Dulles, the Mansfield Report was a godsend, providing just the kind of bipartisan legitimacy they wanted at a critical time in the war, when the U.S. aid effort was ramping up massively. He was a junior senator but a respected one, especially on Asian issues, and he was from the opposition party. His claim that the military outlook was good and getting better served to further strengthen the consensus on Capitol Hill that this was a battle that should be waged. The future of Southeast Asia, and ultimately Asia as a whole, and therefore the future security of the United States, depended on it. If someone as steady, sober-minded, and seemingly knowledgeable as Mansfield—a former professor of Asian history!—could voice this kind of unwavering support for the French cause, many lawmakers must have asked themselves, who am I to disagree?

V

THAT THE U.S. GOVERNMENT REMAINED STEADFAST WAS LOST ON none of the principal actors in Vietnam—not the French, not the Viet Minh, and not the non-Communist nationalist groups who picked this time to begin clamoring more loudly for major concessions from Paris. "We'll fight, but only for independence" was the new refrain among these groups. The Mayer government's unilateral devaluation of the piaster back in May still rankled many of them, including Bao Dai and his prime minister Nguyen Van Tam, and Joseph Laniel's July 3 promise to "perfect" (*parfaire*) the independence of the Associated States seemed like so much empty rhetoric. Paris, it was clear, still called the shots. At official ceremonies, French representatives still sat in the front row, relegating the Vietnamese to the back; on Saigon streets, French officials still rubbed in their presence by tearing around with screaming motorcycle escorts.

To many observers, Nguyen Van Tam seemed a pawn in French hands. A former lawyer and schoolteacher with a gray-streaked crew cut and a preference for white sharkskin suits, the fifty-eight-year-old had been born into a family of small merchants and had been educated in France. Seemingly indefatigable, he rose early and often worked past midnight and in his spare time wrote poetry. His hatred of the Viet Minh ran deep—he had had a hand in putting down Communist insurrections prior to and during World War II, and two of his sons were killed by Giap's forces in 1946. Another son now served as VNA chief of staff. Glancing at a map, Tam told an American journalist: "The most important thing is winning the village populations over to the cause. Our nationalist fervor has got to match the Viet Minh's, and once we take over from the French, Ho Chi Minh could well be forced into making a deal on our terms."[36] To underlings, however, Tam always stressed the need to be patient and to not press the French too hard, too fast.

In October, Bao Dai, in an effort to increase pressure on the French, convened a three-day "National Congress," and invited representatives (all chosen by Bao Dai) of all the significant religious and political factions outside the Viet Minh. This included the Hoa Hao, Cao Dai, and Binh Xuyen politico-religious sects and their affiliated parties. Going considerably further than Bao Dai wanted (thereby showing his weakness, even within anti–Viet Minh circles), the congress declared that all treaties with France be approved by a national assembly, to be elected by universal suffrage, and it passed a resolution refusing to join the French Union. Independence should be complete, proponents said, with no Vietnamese membership in any French-dominated commonwealth.

The delegates held their breath. They needed backing in high places, they knew, one place in particular. "Rightly or wrongly," one delegate recalled, "we had invested substantial hopes in the American connection. And these hopes had been encouraged, not officially but through a series of informal contacts with the USIA, the CIA, and embassy personnel."[37] But when they sought U.S. backing for the resolution, its sponsors found none. On the contrary, after the vote Ambassador Donald Heath summoned several key delegates, including Bao Dai's cousin Prince Buu Loc, to his residence and castigated them for adopting a measure that could only hurt the fight against Ho Chi Minh. The United States supported Vietnam and favored independence, he said, but it was also allied to France. The resolution went too far and must be softened. Bao Dai, summoned to Paris from his perch on the Riviera to explain the congress's action, agreed. The following day a new, milder version was passed, this one stating that Vietnam would not be part of the French Union "in its present form."[38]

Heath did not come away impressed, stressing in his report to Washington the delegates' "emotional, irresponsible nationalism": "It was apparent that [the] majority of the delegates had honestly no idea of [the] import of [the] language in [the] resolution they had just passed." And in another cable: "It is a matter of extraordinary difficulty to convey [the] degree of naiveté and childlike belief that no matter what defamatory language they use, the Vietnamese will still be safeguarded from [the] lethal Communist enemy of France and [the] United States."[39]

In Paris, the reaction to the congress was even more caustic, as newspapers and politicians of various stripes demanded to know what France was fighting for in Indochina. Ho Chi Minh and his Communists were evidently not the only foes. "Let them stew in their own juice," President Vincent Auriol thundered. "We'll withdraw the expeditionary force." Prime Minister Joseph Laniel said France had "no reason to prolong her sacrifices if the very people for whom they are being made disdain those sacrifices and betray them," a remark widely seen to be advocating early negotiations with Ho. Meanwhile, Paul Reynaud and Édouard Daladier, together with former colonial governor of Indochina Albert Sarraut, called for a full-fledged reevaluation of policy, while in the National Assembly the clamor for pulling up stakes and getting out of Indochina grew louder than ever before. Just how to manage the withdrawal remained a source of friction: The right sought to settle the conflict through a great-power initiative (perhaps including China) covering the whole of Southeast Asia, while the left insisted on the need for direct talks with the Viet Minh.

"What aim has this war still got?" asked Alain Savary, a young Socialist widely acclaimed for his intellectual brilliance. "It's no longer even a question of defending the principle of the French Union. To fight against Communism? France is alone. . . . Peace will not wait, it must be actively sought. You can talk to Moscow, Peking, London, and Washington, but this will not help you deal with the real issue. The only thing that will lead to an armistice is negotiation with Ho Chi Minh."[40]

Intellectuals too increasingly clamored for an end to the war. Many had rallied around the cause of Henri Martin, a Communist activist who served in the French Navy in Indochina and witnessed the violent clash in Haiphong in November 1946. Martin returned to France determined to agitate against the war. In July 1949 he began distributing political tracts to new recruits at the Toulon naval dockyard, urging them to oppose the conflict. Arrested in 1950 and tried on charges of demoralizing the army, Martin was convicted and sentenced to five years in prison. But his case continued to attract attention and supporters, not least Jean-Paul Sartre, who went to press in late 1953 with *L'Affaire Henri Martin*. By the time the book appeared, Martin had been discreetly released at the order of President Auriol.

Portentously, a perceptible anti-Americanism crept into the discourse, as commentators noted that, with the end of the fighting in Korea, France was the only Western nation shedding blood on a major scale to fight Communism. Why, critics asked, did Washington reserve for itself a course of action—negotiations, leading to a political solution—it denied to its allies? And why, some asked (especially on the right), did these self-righteous Americans feel free to lecture France on how to treat dependent peoples, given their discrimination against Negroes within America's own borders? The signing of the new U.S. aid agreement in Paris elicited little applause but numerous complaints about the division of labor in Vietnam. "One of the parties brings dollars, while the other makes a gift of its blood and its sons," Daladier acidly remarked, to wide acclaim.[41]

The Eisenhower administration brushed off the criticism, but it looked again for ways to keep its allies in Indochina focused on the task of winning the struggle. To the Paris government, it insisted that seven years of war had not been in vain, that her cause was both just and essential, and that negotiations should be avoided until France and the West could dictate the terms. To the non-Communist nationalist groups, it preached the message that the continued presence of the French Expeditionary Corps was essential to victory. (Subtext: The VNA by itself would get crushed in no time.) Said Heath in a speech on October 24: "There is only France who can make this military contribution at this vital moment which the destinies of the free world have now reached. . . . I have not the slightest doubt of the final victory of the Vietnamese National Army in unity with the noble military effort being made by the expeditionary corps of the French Union."[42]

VI

SO EAGER WAS THE WHITE HOUSE TO GET THESE POINTS ACROSS that it dispatched a special messenger to Indochina to articulate them. At midday on October 31, Vice President Richard Nixon, accompanied by his wife, Pat, a few staffers and Secret Service agents, and a handful of reporters, landed in Saigon. The group had spent the previous day in Cambodia, where Nixon had met King Norodom Sihanouk and Prime Minister Penn Nouth. The arrival in Saigon was preceded by a sudden squall that, sweeping across the tarmac in front of the taxiing plane, soaked both the honor guard and the reception committee. Nixon, his enthusiasm undamped, emerged and delivered a short impromptu statement, whereupon he was whisked away to meetings with Nguyen Van Tam and Henri Navarre.[43] That evening Ambassador Heath hosted a dinner for the visitors at the Majestic Hotel, and in the days that followed Nixon traveled to Dalat to meet with Bao Dai, to Laos for a session with Prince Souvanna Phouma, and to Hanoi, where High Commissioner Maurice Dejean presided over a formal dinner—complete with "starched linen napkins, sparkling crystal goblets, and silver candelabra"—and where Nixon visited a French garrison in the company of Navarre and the commander of French forces in Tonkin, General René Cogny. Outfitted with battle fatigues and a helmet, Nixon rode in a convoy of American-

VICE PRESIDENT RICHARD NIXON TRIES TO CHAT UP A SOLDIER IN THE VIETNAMESE NATIONAL ARMY AT A BASE NEAR DONG GIAO, NORTHEAST OF HANOI, IN EARLY NOVEMBER 1953.

earlier in the spring but offering a speeded-up timetable: There would be immediate small operations and raids followed by a large-scale offensive in September. Rear-area units in static defensive positions would be consolidated into *groupes mobiles,* and the VNA would be trained and equipped at an accelerated pace and given expanded responsibilities in the field. Reinforcements would be sought from France, including officers who would be used as cadres to build up the VNA. As in the Letourneau Plan, a final offensive in 1955 would destroy the enemy's *masse de maneuvre* and force him to sue for peace.[8]

French sources do not support this contention that the "Navarre Plan" was entirely American in conception and structure; they see the French commander as shaping the basic contours on his own. But there is no doubt that U.S. pressure for a more vigorous application of military power lay behind the scheme. That's clear from the documentary record, and Navarre himself would later lament the degree to which Washington's influence dictated French policy.[9] Whatever his exact role in the planning, Navarre pronounced himself pleased with the particulars, and O'Daniel returned triumphantly to Washington, confident he had a road map for victory in Vietnam. He claimed to detect an "increased aggressiveness in attitude" on the part of the French High Command and a greater openness to American ideas and recommendations. Navarre, he enthused, possessed "a new aggressive psychology to the war" and seemed determined "to see this war through to success at an early date."[10]

Others were doubtful, believing that O'Daniel's close personal rapport with Navarre caused him to exaggerate by a considerable margin the French commander's commitment to offensive action. The raw numbers remained a problem: Even though Navarre had a basic numerical superiority in terms of men under arms, for offensive operations he could muster the equivalent of only about three combat divisions as against the enemy's six, due to the French commitment to provide all major cities and hundreds of villages and posts with an increasingly flimsy measure of security.[11] These U.S. skeptics also found little to cheer in French counterinsurgency efforts, whether through the oil-spot method (occupying a central point in a given area and pushing outward from it) or the opposing "gridding" (*quadrillage*) approach, whereby one divided a territory supplied jeeps to a hot spot north of Hanoi, where he watched an artillery barrage.[44]

The hectic schedule left some in the entourage exhausted, but Nixon reveled in the fast pace, seemingly gaining in energy with each passing day. In speech after speech, he made the same basic points: that the defeat of Communism in Indochina was essential to the safety of the free world; that it was only in union with France that Vietnam could—and would—achieve her aims; and that no negotiated solution should be sought. "It is easy," he said in Dalat, "in the name of nationalism and independence to call for the immediate withdrawal of the French Republic. At first glance this meets with popular favor, but those who call for such a step must also know that, if it were taken, it would mean not independence or liberty but complete domination by a foreign power." In Hanoi, he declared himself convinced that all differences between France and the State of Vietnam could easily be solved, and added: "We must admit that in no circumstances can we negotiate a peace which would deliver into slavery the peoples whose will is to remain free, and we must know that by a close union of our efforts, this struggle will end in victory. . . . The tide of aggression has reached its peak and has finally begun to recede. The foundation for decisive victory has been laid."[45]

And with that, Nixon and his party were off from Hanoi, bound for home. No one could know then that nineteen years later, as president of the United States, Nixon would send B-52s to hit the city during the Christmas period in a massive and highly controversial air offensive. But what was amply evident even now, exactly a year after the Eisenhower-Nixon team's election victory, was the administration's determination to win in Vietnam, to keep the French fighting, and to rein in the Saigon nationalist groups. Any notion of cultivating a Third Force, one in between the Communists and the French, seemed to have vanished. Said an obviously impressed British diplomat to his superiors in London: "By this constant reiteration that the one immediate goal was the defeat of the enemy and that this must be done in union with France, Mr. Nixon has, I am sure, done something to bring the Vietnamese back to reality after pipe dreams of the National Congress."[46]

Nixon's confident pronouncements masked deep private chagrin. The Navarre Plan was sound and could succeed by 1955 as planned, he told the

National Security Council a few weeks later, but the administration should not count on it. The Communists had a sense of history, they had determination and skill, and they believed time was on their side. Bao Dai and the non-Communist groups were weak entities, while in the French High Command there was legitimate fear that Paris would seek premature negotiations. "There is a definite need to stiffen the French at home," Nixon said, because Washington's recent aid increase, though essential, would do little good if Navarre did not have full support from the metropole. For the French commander Nixon offered mostly praise, but he lamented Navarre's failure to utilize the VNA effectively and his reluctance to accept American advice regarding how the native army should be trained.[47] Even here, though, the vice president was sympathetic to the French dilemma. He told a group of State Department officers:

> Deep down I sense that Navarre, and Cogny, the Field Commander, and the other field commanders I talked to on the scene at the present time have very little faith in the ability of the Vietnamese to fight separately in independent units which don't have French noncoms. That may be a cover for the fact that the French naturally have a reluctance to build up a strong independent Vietnamese army because they know that once that is done and once the Vietnamese are able to handle the problem themselves, that despite all the fine talk about the independence within the French Union—when that time comes, the Vietnamese will kick out the French.
>
> My own opinion, of course, as I have expressed it publicly, and I believe it very strongly, is as far as the Vietnamese and the Cambodian and Laotians are concerned, and weak as they are and weak as they will be, even with their national armies, that their only hope to remain independent is to have their independence within the French Union, which the French are now willing to give, but which, unfortunately, they have not been able to sell to the Vietnamese, Cambodians, and Laotians.[48]

There was candor here, but also a seeming unwillingness to face the obvious paradoxes. If the Communists had the motivation and the "sense of history" on their side, and the good guys didn't, what did that say about the cause? And how could the French be induced to step up the war effort in order to hold Vietnam and at the same time commit to true independence for the Vietnamese? What would be the point of expanding their efforts to retain their colonial possession if they then had to give it up?

On negotiations, the vice president again spoke frankly, while again ignoring the contradictions. Diplomacy should be firmly resisted, he asserted, for it would inevitably lead to Communist domination of Indochina. The French "cannot get out," and "we cannot have them get out because if we do the Communists—the Viet Minh are the only ones capable of governing, the only ones capable of controlling the country"—would take over. "So what we end up with here is a hard choice. It is a real risk and a real gamble, but what we end up with here, with all that is at stake, it seems to me we have to continue our military aid and, in that connection, I think the military are going to be as flexible as they can be, and, if there is any doubt, they will put in the additional material equipment that is necessary."[49]

Hence Nixon's determination, while in Vietnam, to strike only upbeat notes, to urge Navarre on, and to trumpet the robust health of the French Union. The stakes were huge, and victory must come. Now was no time to give up. And indeed, though Nixon's optimistic pronouncements did little to lift spirits in metropolitan France, where the charcoal autumn sky matched the prevailing mood, they had a noticeable effect on *colons* and high French officials in Saigon and Hanoi. Navarre and Dejean had more of a bounce in their step after hearing him extol them for the job they were doing and simultaneously admonish the Vietnamese to keep their nationalist ambitions in check. The new U.S. aid package, Nixon had promised them, would soon make itself felt on the ground. How soon was soon? Nobody knew for sure, but Navarre and the high command took satisfaction from the fact that the campaigning season was by now well under way and Giap had yet to launch a major attack anywhere. In past years, he would have moved sooner than this. French intelligence speculated that he felt insufficiently strong to attack in the delta, and that he would concentrate his attention on the highland region of northwestern Tonkin.

Navarre was determined to meet the threat. Rather than concede the highlands and husband his resources for the defense of the deltas and of

Annam in the center, he moved to take on the enemy here, in the remote and menacing northwest. As part of that effort, he ordered the reoccupation of a post near the Laotian border. This seemingly innocuous action would trigger a series of moves and countermoves in several world capitals and ultimately bring the war to its climax. The post bore the unlikely name of "Big Frontier Administrative Center," or, in Vietnamese, Dien Bien Phu.

PART FOUR

THE CAULDRON, 1953–1954

CHAPTER 16

ARENA OF THE GODS

THE VILLAGE WAS SET A THIRD OF THE WAY DOWN A HEART-SHAPED basin measuring eleven miles in length and seven miles across at its widest point. It was surrounded by mountains, some round and gentle, others sharp limestone masses rising in irregular tiers to pointed peaks. A small river, the Nam Youm, ran past the village, through the plain from north to south. Although flat, the basin contained small features that sprouted up here and there, and there were numerous tiny hamlets and isolated dwellings scattered about. The inhabitants, perhaps ten thousand total, were mostly ethnic Tai who grew rice and mangoes and oranges on the fertile plain and marketed the opium brought down from the mountains by Hmong tribes, but there were also other tribal groups and Vietnamese. The Tai called the place Muong Thanh. To the Vietnamese, and to the French, it was known as Dien Bien Phu.

A strategic position it certainly was. The Laotian border lay just over the mountains, ten miles to the west, and the basin was one of the few hollows in the vast and largely impassable highland region, with its dense vegetation and forbidding terrain. The village was also at the junction of three routes. One went north, to China by way of Lai Chau, another was to the northeast to Tuan Giao, and the third ran southward to Laos via Muong Khoua. Whoever controlled the basin, legend taught, controlled the region and the entry to Laos and the upper Mekong—which was one reason the Tai referred to the bowl of land and its rim of hills as the Arena of the Gods.

Occupied in turn by the Chinese, the Siamese, the Hmong, and the Tai, Dien Bien Phu in 1889 was taken by French explorer-diplomat Auguste Pavie, who stuck around long enough to give his name to the horse path, the Pavie Piste, that ran north to Lai Chau. A French column subsequently camped in the village during operations against the Tai tribes, and in time it became an administrative post manned by a small group of local troops under French command. A lowly—and, one can guess, lonely—French colonial administrator took up residence as well, charged with the task of controlling the size of opium shipments, which in French Indochina was a state monopoly. In 1939, a small airstrip was built to allow supplies to be flown in from Hanoi (about a hundred and seventy miles away by air) for the garrison at Lai Chau, and during World War II the French used this strip for clandestine landings of agents of Force 136, an anti-Japanese resistance unit. On two occasions, French pilots used Dien Bien Phu to evacuate American fliers shot down over Japanese-controlled parts of Tonkin. When the Japanese launched their *coup de force* in March 1945, Dien Bien Phu became, for almost two months, the headquarters of French anti-Japanese resistance activity. Small planes from General Claire L. Chennault's U.S. Fourteenth Air Force used the airstrip to bring supplies to the French and to evacuate wounded, and two obsolete French Potez 25 fighter aircraft used it as a base of operations against the advancing Japanese.[1]

After the war, the post reverted to French control, but from an early point Viet Minh units operated in the area. In late November 1952, with the Viet Minh 316th Division and 146th Regiment closing in, General Salan ordered Dien Bien Phu to be evacuated. Almost immediately he made plans to retake it. His top-secret directive number 40, issued on January 10, 1953, read in part: "The reoccupation of Dien Bien Phu must constitute in the forthcoming period the first step for the regaining control of the Tai country and for the elimination of the Viet-Minh from the area west of the Black River."[2] Though Salan lacked the means to undertake this operation before he relinquished command to Henri Navarre, the idea took hold in the French High Command that Dien Bien Phu was key to the defense of northern Laos and especially the royal capital of Luang Prabang. The most likely invasion route, strategists reasoned, would be from Tuan Giao, where the Viet Minh had a modest forward

THE CAULDRON, 1953–1954 | 383

base, through Dien Bien Phu, and then over the border and down the Nam Ou valley to Luang Prabang.

In addition, Dien Bien Phu could be further vindication—following the example of Na San in 1952—of the theory of the *base aéro-terrestre* ("air-ground base," or, in American military parlance, "airhead"), by which a small number of air-supplied "hedgehogs" would be planted in the path of the advancing enemy and held for only limited periods by mobile units from the general reserve. For Salan, certainly, Na San was the shining symbol of French ability to withstand a massive Viet Minh assault on a prepared defensive position, and he made an early convert of Navarre. If Giap could again be goaded into a major battle as at Na San, and could again be forced to sacrifice thousands of men in vain, in a region of supposed Viet Minh domination, it would enhance France's position in the negotiations to come. It would also respond to American pressure for more aggressive military action.

The establishment of a strongpoint in northwestern Tonkin was advantageous for a third reason: It would provide crucial assistance to the Tai and Hmong tribal partisans who had operated with success against Viet Minh forces for some years. Navarre held a romantic attachment to this tribal "resistance," likening it to the activities of the French Resistance against the Germans in occupied France, and he argued that strengthening the tribes militarily could free up regular troops for mobile operations. Herein lay also a fourth consideration: The tribes were a source of opium, which was important to the French to finance their special operations section and which, when it fell into enemy hands, was used to fund Viet Minh special operations and arms purchases. Retaking Dien Bien Phu would ensure that the opium crop remained in effective French control.[3]

Beyond all this, perhaps there was yet another, final reason to make a stand here, less important to Navarre, who was after all still new to Indochina, than to his subordinate officers, many of whom had deep experience in the region. They felt a sense of attachment to this part of the world—to the sheer beauty of the landscape, to the tribal minorities whose leaders they had befriended, to the captivating young women with the swaying gaits who put leis of flowers around their necks. The peoples of these mountains and valleys were in peril and moreover had little love for the Viet Minh; France had a solemn duty to protect them.

Later on, after everything went wrong, French commanders would attack one another over the strategic purpose of reoccupying Dien Bien Phu.[4] The myth would take hold that top officials were from the start divided on whether the operation should be undertaken at all. In reality, the French command initially acted at Dien Bien Phu with a large degree of unity and with faith that the enterprise could succeed. On July 24, 1953, top civilian and military leaders—among them Navarre—meeting in Paris reached consensus on the importance of defending northern Laos if at all possible.[5] That desire grew still stronger in October, when Laos signed a mutual defense treaty with France that cemented Laotian ties to the French Union and Giap's forces thrust into eastern Laos. The Paris government hoped to sign similar treaties with Cambodia and Vietnam; the prospect of doing so would be much diminished if Laos was left to her fate.[6]

Nor is it easy to credit the postwar claim by Navarre's principal subordinate and commander of the Tonkin theater, Major General René Cogny, that his initial (grudging) support for the plan to retake Dien Bien Phu was based on his belief that it would be a lightly held "anchor point" used primarily to support mobile operations by local tribal forces. Cogny's primary concern was always the Red River Delta and making sure that he had maximum resources there, but the archival record shows quite clearly that he endorsed the *base aéro-terrestre* concept. His personal dislike for Navarre, which was real and which would in time turn to a deep and abiding hatred, should not obscure the fact that initially the two men largely agreed. For Cogny no less than for Navarre, the concept had the virtues of being versatile and of having both a defensive and offensive purpose: It was a "hedgehog" that would thwart a major attack, and it was an "anchor point" that would support mobile operations in the enemy's rear.

There were, to be sure, other potential sites for such bases in the highlands region. Na San was an obvious contender, but its location was not ideal, as the Viet Minh were now capable of easily outflanking it; in August, Navarre indeed ordered the evacuation of the Na San garrison for redeployment elsewhere. Lai Chau, the Tai tribal capital, also received consideration, but its location was problematic. Situated a mere thirty miles from the Chinese border, it was far from the main route into Laos, and its stunningly dramatic topography made it difficult to supply by air. And relatively easy air supply would be of central importance to the sort of operation gestating in Navarre's mind. Better placed than either Na San or Lai Chau, he and his commanders concluded, was Dien Bien Phu, especially as it had a reasonably good airstrip already in place. Although the site was ringed by mountains, the French—who considered themselves the master artillerists of the world—deemed these to be beyond artillery range, even if occupied by enemy forces. Machiavelli's famous admonition to always control the high ground did not apply. Giap would have no choice but to bring whatever artillery he had into the valley itself, where it would be pounded to bits by French counterbattery guns and aviation.

In Paris, however, nerves were on edge. The civilian leadership was in no mood to launch a major military operation. On November 15, Marc Jacquet, minister for the Associated States, embarked for Saigon. He told Navarre, cryptically: "The fall of Luang Prabang would make impossible the prosecution of the war." What did he mean? Let Laos fall in order to stop this war, which was costing France so much and which should be terminated? Or, to the contrary, keep Laos? Navarre chose the second interpretation. "After all," he said, "Dien Bien Phu will not cost me anything more than Na San cost Salan."[7]

Then, on November 18, Rear Admiral Georges Cabanier arrived in Saigon, sent by Paris to inform Navarre that he should try nothing extravagant and that, in any case, there was no longer any money in the treasury for the war. Possibly, Cabanier was even to tell Navarre to halt military operations and leave everything to the politicians, who would seek a cease-fire and negotiations. But Navarre was in Hanoi. He kept Cabanier waiting, fearing the admiral's message. For by then he had given the order: Dien Bien Phu would be retaken. Already two weeks before, Navarre had instructed Cogny to begin planning for the operation, to be code-named Castor. Cogny had obliged, over the objections of his staff. Colonel Jean Nicot, commander of the transport arm of the French Air Force, registered his opposition on November 11; he could not, he said, guarantee a steady flow of supplies to Dien Bien Phu. Navarre was unmoved. On the seventeenth, he met all of his major subordinate commanders, who one by one registered their concerns regarding Operation Castor. Cogny was among them. Navarre listened politely, then asked, "Is it possible?" Everyone murmured that it was. Very well, then, the commander in chief replied, the operation would take place in three days, weather permitting.[8]

At 8:15 A.M. on Friday, November 20, 1953, about sixty Dakotas took to the air one after the other from a Hanoi airfield, their noses painted blue, yellow, or red. Flanked by B-26 Invaders, they formed a column seven miles long. A little more than two hours later, at about 10:35, the first of them appeared from behind the crests above the basin. Twenty-two hundred "paras" (paratroopers), the cream of the French Expeditionary Corps, proceeded to drop into the valley north and south of the village. The operation, commanded by gruff, one-eyed Brigadier General Jean Gilles (he carried his glass eye in his jacket pocket when he jumped), was carried off with the loss of 15 dead and 53 wounded. The Viet Minh lost 90 men before giving way and allowing the French to dig in.[9]

THE FIRST LANDED "PARAS" KEEP A CLOSE EYE ON THE DESCENT OF THEIR COMRADES, AS OPERATION CASTOR BEGINS, NOVEMBER 20, 1953.

II

THE NEWS OF THE FRENCH REOCCUPATION OF DIEN BIEN PHU CAUGHT Viet Minh commanders by surprise. When word reached Vo Nguyen Giap, he was just preparing to present the 1953-54 offensive campaign to his division commanders at a forest camp in the Dinh Hoa district of Thai Nguyen province. The plan had taken shape over several months and was the product of considerable high-level discussion, involving also Chinese advisers. At the Fourth Plenum of the Communist Party (formally, the Vietnamese Workers Party), held in January 1953, senior strategists had determined to strike where the enemy was weak, in order to force the French to disperse their troops to the greatest extent possible, as far away from the Red River Delta as they could be lured. That was a main motivation behind the Laos invasion in the spring, and it remained the operating assumption throughout the summer. Giap gave close consideration to mounting a major operation against the heart of French defenses in the Red River Delta, but both he and Ho Chi Minh worried that the all-important "balance of forces" in the delta still tilted against them.

The Chinese too argued for a more cautious strategy centered on the northwestern highlands. "We should first annihilate enemies in the Lai Chau area, liberating northern and central Laos, and then extend the battlefield gradually toward southern Laos and Cambodia, thus putting pressure on Saigon," the Chinese Communist Party Central Committee declared in a telegram in August. "By adopting this strategy, we will be able to limit the human and financial resources of the enemy and separate the enemy's troops, leaving the enemy in a disadvantageous position. . . . The realization of this strategic plan will surely contribute to the final defeat of the colonial rule of French imperialists in Vietnam, Laos, and Cambodia. Of course, we need to overcome a variety of difficulties and prepare for a prolonged war."[10]

The Chinese role in the decision to avoid a major clash in the delta should not be minimized, but neither should it be exaggerated. Responsibility was shared. Just as the Navarre Plan grew out of joint U.S.-French planning, so did the Chinese and Viet Minh consult each other over which course to take at this critical juncture. Certainly, Ho and Giap could not ignore Chinese recommendations. For one thing, Beijing's aid had increased markedly over the previous year. For most of 1952, the monthly average was 250 tons, but by December it had risen to 450 tons. (U.S. aid to France, by contrast, now exceeded 8,000 tons per month.) In January 1953, the amount reached 900 tons, much of it in the form of arms and ammunition and motor vehicles. And with the end of the fighting in Korea in the summer, PRC aid could flow still more freely. Chinese military advisers and technicians also came across the border in larger numbers, while Vietnamese were sent in the other direction to undertake wireless and antiaircraft training in southern China. (In theory, at least, the antiaircraft weapons, mostly Russian 37mm, were to come in with a trained team of twenty operators per gun.)[11]

In October, Ho, Giap, and the other top party leaders met in high secrecy, around a bamboo table in a bamboo house on the side of a heavily forested hill in Thai Nguyen province. So sensitive were they to potential leaks that the party note taker was denied entry. By now reasonably well-informed about the details of the Navarre Plan—they were, as always, assiduous readers of the French press, and their intelligence network reached close to the French High Command—they formally agreed to concentrate during the coming campaign season on the northwest, where, as they saw it, the enemy was weak but would feel compelled to make a stand. In the process, he would spread his forces thinner and become more vulnerable to guerrilla and other attacks in his rear.[12]

"When you close your hand you make a fist that can strike a powerful blow," Ho Chi Minh told the assembled, opening and closing his raised right hand as he spoke, and with a cigarette in his left. "But if you spread your hand out, it is easy to break your fingers, one by one. We must find a way to force the solid bloc of enemy mobile groups to spread out into a number of pieces so that we can gradually annihilate them, one at a time, thereby causing them to suffer complete defeat."[13]

Truong Chinh, the party's senior theoretician, concurred. "The Tonkin lowland is the place where enemy forces are hard, where their defenses are stiff," he argued.

In other battlefields the enemy's dispositions are relatively weak and exposed, but they cannot abandon these areas, and this is especially true for the mountain jungle region. If we launch an attack into the Northwest region we will certainly draw in enemy forces and force the enemy's strategic mobile force to disperse to defend against our attack. . . . The enemy may only be able to bring in supplies and reinforcements by air. If we can overcome the problems with logistics and supplies, our forces will have many advantages fighting up there and we will be capable of attaining and maintaining military superiority throughout the entire campaign, or at least in a certain sector of the campaign area. In that way we may be able to win a great victory.[14]

Behind these confident assertions was a genuine concern that comes through even in the official accounts of the meeting. Despite seven years of immense sacrifice, of constant hardship and deprivation, the goal of "complete victory" (*toan thang*) remained far, far away. The sagging support for the war in metropolitan France was encouraging, but militarily the French held pretty good cards, especially in view of their strong positions in the Red River Delta and in Cochin China. With Washington's recent decision to massively increase U.S. aid to the French cause, a continuing stalemate on the battlefield was not out of the question.[15] Then too there was the buildup of the Vietnamese National Army. The conferees heaped disdain on this French attempt at "using war to nourish war, using Vietnamese to fight Vietnamese," as one delegate put it, but it's clear that they worried about the implications of an expanded VNA, one that, if still inferior in all respects to their own People's Army of Vietnam (PAVN), might show greater commitment and fighting ability than previously, and greater popular support. Victory would still come in the end, the delegates assured themselves and one another, but the task was far from finished.

Ho Chi Minh, hinting at possible morale problems among troops in the coming operation, concluded the meeting by noting that some soldiers, after the previous campaign in the highlands, had put their hands together and bowed toward the mountains and the jungles in a gesture of thanks and respect. These troops would have no desire to return to the area, Ho said, and they would have to be convinced of the importance of the mission. They would also need adequate supplies, including warm clothing: "Have we completed the sewing of this new style of padded jacket that I am wearing?" he asked. "When will we issue them to the troops? I want you men to go back and check on this. Warm jackets must be issued to each of our troops before they move out for this campaign."[16]

The decision made to concentrate on the northwest, Giap in the midautumn resisted Navarre's attempts to goad him into a major engagement in and around the delta. On October 14, Navarre personally supervised the launching of Operation Mouette (Seagull), directed at the important enemy supply center of Phu Nho Quan, just south of the delta. Six *groupes mobiles,* backed by tank and amphibious battalions as well as two French Navy marine units, broke through the limestone hills of Ninh Binh in a pincer movement designed to encircle the PAVN 320th Infantry Division. Regiments 48 and 64 stood fast and even counterattacked the vastly stronger French Union forces, in order to allow vital supplies and matériel to be removed from Phu Nho Quan. With that task completed, the Viet Minh troops withdrew again into the countryside, and the French entered a deserted town. All along the line, they had run into stiffer resistance than expected but without engaging the bulk of the enemy force. The 320th, considered less well equipped and trained than the 308th and the 312th, had been mauled, but it was far from decimated. Yet again the Viet Minh had shown their maddening ability (in French eyes) to slip away from serious trouble.[17]

Giap also ordered his ten-thousand-man 316th Division to leave its staging area near Thanh Hoa and move up the Song River toward Lai Chau.[18] That force was still en route when word of the Castor airlift operation reached the Thai Nguyen meeting. Clearly taken aback by Navarre's move, Giap told his assembled commanders: "This is an operation that works to our advantage." But he also expressed uncertainty about Navarre's intentions. According to a Vietnamese account of the meeting, Giap peppered subordinates with questions: Was this a temporary incursion? Did Navarre order it because he had learned of the movement of the 316th toward Lai Chau? Were the parachutists dropped into Dien Bien Phu to support Lai Chau, or would Navarre now abandon Lai Chau and move those troops to Dien Bien Phu? If the Viet Minh reacted strongly, would Navarre reinforce the airhead into a powerful entrenched camp like Na San, or withdraw? And how precisely were the French units deployed in the valley?

"We immediately telephoned our reconnaissance element preparing to go to Lai Chau," one of the subordinates recalled, "and told them to leave immediately for Dien Bien Phu, to work with local units in the area, reconnoiter the enemy situation, and send daily reports back to the intelligence department." At the same time, this officer continued, the Viet Minh command directed its technical reconnaissance (radio intercept) forces to continually monitor French activity not merely at Dien Bien Phu but also at Lai Chau and in northern Laos.[19]

These activities soon yielded valuable information, as did the loose lips of French commanders. It was a constant problem during the war, this habit of senior officers to speak too freely about plans and operations. The French and foreign press, taking good notes on what they heard, dutifully reported that an entrenched camp similar to Na San would be established at Dien Bien Phu and would provide support for a major Tai partisan movement. General Cogny rashly confided to a reporter that "if he could, he would have transported Na San *en bloc* to Dien Bien Phu." More damaging still, a series of reports referred to the 316th Division's progress toward Lai Chau, knowledge that could only have come from radio intercepts. The Viet Minh immediately changed their code for operational traffic, thus frustrating French intelligence operatives in the Service de documentation extérieure et de contre-espionnage (SDECE) for the better part of a week.[20]

Sensing the seriousness of the French commitment, Giap directed three other divisions, the 308th Iron, the 312th, and the 351st Heavy (artillery and engineering), to prepare to move toward Dien Bien Phu. French intelligence intercepted these orders, and its chief estimated that the 316th, already en route, would reach the general area by about December 6; the other three divisions, he anticipated, would arrive between December 24 and 28. Meanwhile Gilles's paras were encountering problems as they pushed battalion-strength patrols north and south of the camp. The terrain was rough, with heavy tropical growth, steep hillsides, and potentially treacherous stretches of open ground. The jungle guarded its secrets, and in its shadows lurked tigers and—the paras suspected—enemy troops. Sure enough, by November 25, the 148th Regiment as well as advance elements of the 316th Division had been spotted by aircraft on the approaches to the surrounding hills. Not good news, especially to the French officers and tribal guerrillas of the so-called GCMA (Groupement de commandos mixtes aéroportés), a highly secretive commando unit that was to use Dien Bien Phu as a base from which to launch operations in the area. Such action would be well-nigh impossible if the Viet Minh controlled the approaches to the village.

On December 3 Navarre, who knew of the advancing enemy divisions, issued a fateful order to Cogny, in the form of "Personal and Secret Instructions for the Conduct of Operation No. 949." Following some opening formalities, he came to the point: He had decided to accept battle in the northwest. Dien Bien Phu would be the center of operations and must be held at all costs. Lai Chau was to be evacuated as soon as the threat to it became too great to resist, and ground communications with Lai Chau to the north and Muong Khoua to the south were to be maintained as long as possible. Navarre envisioned a battle involving a movement phase of several weeks while the Viet Minh marched up to the base, followed by a week or ten days for their reconnaissance, and culminating in a few days of battle, resulting in the enemy's total defeat.[21]

It was a momentous decision, no less so for going against a core tenet of the Navarre Plan: the need to avoid a major engagement in the current campaign season. The French commander's calculation, which he knew would be tested soon enough, was that Giap's logistical problems so far from home would be too severe to overcome. He would not be able to maintain a large body of troops in the area due to the harshness of the terrain and the presence of the French Air Force. The Deuxième Bureau had made clear to Navarre that the PAVN was a real army with trucks and cannons, but how could it transport them as far as Dien Bien Phu? Answer: It couldn't. Its inherent inferiority in transport means ensured that, try as Giap might, he would not be able to match the weight of French weaponry and hence would be crushed when battle came.

A colossal miscalculation in hindsight, it was less so at the time. Giap himself feared that the task before him was too great. Following his defeats against de Lattre in the delta in 1951, the self-taught strategist had vowed never again to underestimate his foe or to fight on the foe's chosen ground. He had relearned the lesson at great cost at Na San in late 1952. Now again he confronted the choice of whether to accept a set-piece battle against the heart of the Expeditionary Corps. This would be no hit-and-run ambush but a major assault on a fortified French camp, using mobile trench warfare. It would be, to an extent, a repeat of the assaults at Vinh Yen and the Day River in 1951, which had ended disastrously for Giap's forces. True, those forces were now better trained and equipped, but so were the Expeditionary Corps.[22] Most vexing of all, how to bring his army to the battlefield? The troops would have to cover some three hundred miles on foot, and supply lines from China would be still longer, up to five hundred miles. The road system, rudimentary where it existed at all, would somehow have to carry every piece of equipment, every bullet, for thousands of soldiers over that distance. Even then the task was not complete, for these vulnerable supply lines would have to be kept open, in forbidding terrain, over a period of weeks, perhaps months.

Nor was it just a matter of transporting weapons and ammunition. A two-week supply of rice would mean a load of thirty to forty extra pounds per soldier. When added to his other gear, this exceeded the optimum load for a soldier moving by foot in the rugged landscape of the northwest. Porters were thus essential, but a porter too needed to eat. If he started with sixty pounds of rice, at the end of two weeks he would have only enough left to feed himself on the return journey to his starting point. By day fourteen, therefore, he could turn over only enough rice—two pounds—to feed a soldier for a single day. For Giap, there was no way around it: His units, operating at least part of the time without access to motorized resupply, would face immense challenges in a major operation in this area. If Navarre chose to garrison a division or so at Dien Bien Phu, virtually the entire Viet Minh *corps de bataille* would be required to launch an effective attack.[23]

Yet it could be done. As he studied his maps, many of them crude and approximate, and analyzed a stream of reports from Viet Minh intelligence sources, Giap came gradually to the conviction that he should accept battle at Dien Bien Phu. He would spring a trap against the trapper. His Chinese military advisers agreed; they saw an opportunity for the Viet Minh to score a major military victory in advance of possible negotiations in 1954.[24] Just how large a role the Chinese played in shaping Giap's thinking is unclear (he alludes to them only vaguely in his memoirs), but certainly there are Chinese fingerprints on the battle plan that Giap endorsed and that was presented to the party Politburo on December 6. The plan's fundamental premise was that the fortified French camp would be a formidable defensive complex, but that it suffered from a grave weakness, namely its isolation. The French garrison would have to be supplied largely by air, completely so if the People's Army could surround it. That would be the aim: to encircle the encampment with a ring of steel, and then close in.[25]

The battle envisioned in the plan would be the largest set-piece engagement of the war and would require the deployment of nine Viet Minh infantry regiments and all available artillery, engineer, and antiaircraft units, for a total of some 35,000 men. Adding in the campaign headquarters (1,850 men) plus 4,000 new recruits (to be sent to the front in separate contingents), plus 1,720 troops who would protect the supply lines, the total number of troops to be utilized was 42,570. The plan also called for a civilian porter force of 14,500 men and women, not including porters used in the rear area. Three hundred tons of ammunition would have to reach the front, along with 4,200 tons of rice, 100 tons of dried vegetables, 100 tons of meat, and 12 tons of sugar. As the essential first task, the plan called for a huge logistical effort to allow motorized transport through the mountainous terrain—hundreds of trucks must be able to travel hundreds of miles and reach close to the battle zone. Once under way, the battle could be expected to last forty-five days.[26]

That day the Politburo decided to launch the Dien Bien Phu campaign and to approve the military committee's battle plan. Giap would command, backed up in his general staff by his Chinese advisers Mei Jiasheng and Wei Guoqing and his Vietnamese commanders, notably Chief of Staff Hoang Van Thai. Ho Chi Minh, turning to Giap, issued the send-off: "You are the general commanding the troops on the outer frontier. . . . I give you complete authority to make all decisions. If victory is certain, then you are to attack. If victory is not certain, then you must resolutely refrain from attacking."[27]

III

EVEN AS THE TWO COMMANDERS IN CHIEF LAID PLANS FOR A MAJOR
and perhaps climactic military showdown in northwestern Tonkin, activity on the political front stepped up as well—in various world capitals. In the four months since the Korean armistice, the Chinese and Soviet leaderships had shown their determination to avoid if at all possible another war against the United States. Both came out of the summer of 1953 professing a desire to solve international disputes by diplomatic means— a preference reinforced on the Soviet side by the popular uprising in East Germany in June. On August 3, the Soviet newspaper *Red Star* carried an editorial arguing that the truce in Korea should help end the war in Indochina. The same month Chinese premier Zhou Enlai declared that a final conference on Korea's future should also address "other issues" in Asia. In late September, the Kremlin proposed a five-power foreign ministers' meeting to address international tensions. China, included as one of the five, endorsed this initiative in early October. Some weeks after that, before a group of Indian diplomats, Zhou spoke in sympathetic terms about the concept of great-power "peaceful coexistence."[28]

Georgy Malenkov, who had emerged as the leading figure in Moscow after Stalin's death the previous March, sought improved relations with the West in part to rein in a burgeoning defense budget and free up funds for needed economic projects. For Zhou and Mao, the Korean truce likewise offered a chance to devote more of China's resources to domestic concerns. They were contemplating the launching of the first five-year plan, as well as shifting governmental resources to the "liberation" of Nationalist-controlled Taiwan.[29] After four years of sharp confrontation with the United States and the West, they sought a break. Korea had been a huge drain on the country's finances, forcing Beijing to borrow $2 billion from Moscow to cover war costs. But Korea also left a more positive legacy, and this too inclined Chinese leaders toward endorsing a political solution in Indochina. The Korean negotiations had enhanced China's stature as a world power, for Beijing had succeeded in forcing Washington into a compromise—the Truman and Eisenhower administrations had been compelled to sit at the bargaining table with a government they did not formally recognize. It was an intoxicating feeling for a group of leaders still seeking international and domestic legitimacy, and it made them willing to play—or at least not averse to playing—the great-power negotiating game again.

Accordingly, in the fall of 1953, Moscow and Beijing made clear to DRV leaders that the door to a negotiated solution should be kept open. Ho Chi Minh and his associates were initially skeptical. Earlier in the summer, Ho had warned his colleagues that neither France nor the United States would ever accept major concessions at the bargaining table unless they were defeated on the field of battle.[30] Ultimately, however, a rough consensus emerged that there was little to lose and potentially a lot to gain from indicating a willingness to negotiate—while easing up not at all on the military side of the struggle. No less eager than the Chinese and Soviets to avert direct U.S. military intervention, senior DRV officials also were conscious of the fatigue and war-weariness among their people, both soldiers and civilians, and the consequent need to offer them more than the prospect of perpetual war. As a party report of the period concluded, the "struggle to restore peace in Vietnam" had become "the wish of the people." In late 1953, the Politburo took tentative but important steps to position itself on what another internal party study referred to as a "new front," that is, the diplomatic one.[31]

Thus on November 23, at the opening session of the World Peace Council meeting in Vienna, the DRV delegate announced that a Korea-type diplomatic settlement in Vietnam "is completely necessary and also possible." The Vietnamese people, he went on, "stand for an end to the Viet-Nam war and peaceful settlement of the Viet-Nam question by means of peaceful negotiations."[32]

Then, three days later, the Swedish newspaper *Expressen* published Ho Chi Minh's answers to questions posed by the paper's Paris correspondent, Svante Löfgren, who had heard Premier Joseph Laniel on the floor of the National Assembly express openness to peace proposals emanating from "Ho Chi Minh and his team." The resourceful Löfgren decided to test the proposition. He wrote to the Viet Minh leader and, to his surprise, got a response. Should France express a sincere willingness to "negotiate an armistice in Viet Nam and to solve the Viet Nam problem by peaceful means," Ho wrote, "the people and Government of the Democratic Republic of Viet Nam are ready to meet this desire." Presumably the negotiations would be bilateral, involving the DRV and France, but Ho said he would also be open to having a third-party mediator. Significantly, Löfgren had cabled his questions through Beijing, and the Chinese in all likelihood conferred with Moscow on the benefits that could come from the interview. Two days before *Expressen* printed Ho's answers, the Kremlin accepted a long-standing Western proposal for talks on the German question involving the United States, Britain, France, and the Soviet Union; by implication, the discussions would be expanded to include Indochina. A few days after the article appeared, Beijing used an editorial in *People's Daily* to indicate its explicit approval of Ho's offer.[33]

Following the *Expressen* interview, Ho explained his policy to the DRV National Assembly, which was meeting for the first time since 1946. Framing the matter entirely in terms of stopping America's aggressive designs, and echoing fully the line out of Moscow and Beijing, he noted that just as Indochina influenced world events, so the world affected the situation in Vietnam. Washington was sabotaging "the convening of political conferences," rearming Japan while keeping China out of the United Nations, and building up West Germany to prevent a reunification of that country. "Our camp is becoming stronger and stronger, more united and single-minded within the front of democracy and peace headed by the Soviet Union. Our present goal is to relax international tensions and to solve all the disputes in the world by means of negotiation."[34]

The word must have gone over well, or well enough, for two weeks later, on December 19, the Politburo discussed and approved a resolution concerning DRV policy toward "negotiations and talks." "A new front had been opened," a party account said of the thinking at this meeting. "Our Party believed that a diplomatic front that was initiated at the correct time and that was closely coordinated with our military operations on the battlefield would be an intelligent strategy to use to gradually, step by step, attain the fundamental goals of our nation." Not quite acknowledged in the account but plainly a subtext in the Politburo deliberations that day was that eight years of war and sacrifice had taken their toll, requiring a new approach.[35] That same day Ho delivered a radio address to the Vietnamese people, commemorating the seventh anniversary of the "Nationwide Resistance War." The veteran revolutionary vowed to continue the struggle to final victory but said again that his government stood ready to negotiate a cease-fire and a resolution of the war. But was France willing to bargain in good faith?[36]

More than willing, many in Paris would have replied. Ho Chi Minh's *Expressen* interview, reprinted in *Le Monde* on December 1, caused a sensation. Was this the opening to meaningful dialogue leading to an end to the disaster, an end to seven years of bloody and stalemated warfare? Yes, much of left-wing opinion answered. Earlier in November, the Socialists had forced a major debate in the Assembly, on the proposition that since France could no longer claim to be fighting to preserve the French Union (in light of the Bao Dai Congress in October) or to defeat the Asian Communist crusade (in light of the Korean armistice), the only thing to do was to end the war through direct bilateral talks with Ho Chi Minh. Ho might not be a genuine nationalist, Socialist deputy Alain Savary allowed, and his Viet Minh might not be all that popular, but neither was it correct to call Ho "Peking's puppet." He was no more China's puppet than Mao Zedong was the Soviet Union's puppet. Nor, Savary added, were French soldiers "American mercenaries." Édouard Daladier, meanwhile, complained of France's "deplorable complacency," if not "servility," toward the United States, while Jean Pronteau warned, with notable foresight, that Vietnam could be a thirty-year war.[37]

The Assembly ultimately rejected (by a vote of 330 to 250) a Socialist motion for immediate negotiations with the Viet Minh. Opponents prevailed by arguing that an affirmative vote would undermine morale among French troops and Bao Dai's ministers, and embolden the enemy. Laniel and Bidault breathed a sigh of relief, only to be rocked by Ho's offer in *Expressen*. Hitherto the two men had been able to maintain, as Laniel did on November 12, that their expressed support for negotiations—"*une solution honorable . . . une solution diplomatique du conflit*"—had elicited no response from the other side. That argument no longer worked, though Laniel could still insist that Ho's proposal was a nonstarter in that it failed to take the Associated States into account.[38]

Laniel and Bidault did their best to beat down expectations. On November 30, the premier assured the U.S. chargé d'affaires in Paris that

Ho Chi Minh's statement would not change French policy, and that bilateral Franco–Viet Minh talks were impossible. The same day Bidault told *Le Monde* that the statement was a mere "propaganda gesture."[39] When Defense Minister René Pleven, excited upon reading the *Expressen* transcript, floated the idea of having Alain Savary (whose liberal positions on colonial questions had gained respect among nationalists in North Africa and Asia) make contact with Viet Minh leaders in the Tonkin jungle, Bidault vetoed it.[40] All too aware of the worrying trends on the ground in Vietnam, and resigned to the need for a political solution, Laniel and Bidault still hoped to enter talks on a multilateral basis, and to do so from a stronger bargaining position, which meant giving Navarre more time to turn the tide. As before, they felt pressure from Washington to remain steadfast in opposition to early talks, and they also kept one eye on the non-Communist nationalists in Saigon. The VNA commander, General Nguyen Van Hinh, rejected Ho's overture as a "political maneuver," while Ngo Dinh Nhu, brother of Diem, blasted Laniel for even contemplating negotiations with Ho Chi Minh. Prime Minister Nguyen Van Tam, Hinh's father, was more circumspect, allowing that Ho's opening, while hardly satisfactory, warranted a response, including some kind of counteroffer. Tam told a reporter: "Neither Vietnamese opinion nor, I am sure of it, French opinion would understand if we did not do everything possible to stop this bloody war."[41]

IV

BUFFETED BY THESE COUNTERVAILING CLAIMS AND CHARGES, LANIEL and Bidault escaped the poisonous atmosphere in Paris for a three-power summit meeting in Bermuda with the leaders of Great Britain and the United States. Originally scheduled for June 1953, the conference was postponed when Winston Churchill that month suffered a serious stroke. This was perhaps an omen, for barely had the planes touched down in Bermuda, starting with Churchill's on December 2, when several conferees began suffering from the tropical flu. Churchill, frail-looking and hard of hearing (he tried all manner of hearing aid contraptions during the sessions), was in a sour mood from the start, and it seemed contagious. The French were incensed that "The Marseillaise" was not played on their arrival, while both "God Save the Queen" and "The Star-Spangled Banner" were played. The excuse given—that Laniel was not really a head of state—did not mollify them. Nor were they pleased by the way the British and American delegations focused most of their attention on each other, figuratively and literally turning their backs on the French. According to one American observer, British officials were "constantly conferring in quite audible stage whispers and only half smothered giggling and laughter while [the] French were speaking."[42]

Churchill's choice of reading en route to the conference, it may be said, was not the most auspicious preparation: C. S. Forester's *Death to the French*.

Laniel was spared the humiliation, having taken to his room with a 104-degree fever soon after arrival. Bidault had to carry the load, and the strain showed. Always inclined to drink when under pressure, he consumed a great deal of wine during the meals and fell asleep during one evening social event. He complained about his predicament, reportedly telling John Foster Dulles at a recess of one meeting: "I am in a very difficult position. Not only is my Prime Minister sick, but he is also a damn fool." Evelyn Shuckburgh, private secretary to British foreign secretary Anthony Eden, summarized in his magnificently readable diary what he saw: "Everybody very angry, appeals, sentiment, Bidault looks like a dying man, Laniel is actually dying upstairs. . . . Outburst by Eisenhower and Winston, former left the conference table in a rage, came back, having changed for dinner, sat another four hours."[43]

Strangely enough, in view of what was to come, the smoothest relationship at this fractious summit was that between Eden and Dulles. The two lounged together on the beach, the extremely fair-skinned Dulles donning a pair of gaudy shorts, and Eden—still recovering from a difficult operation six months earlier—soaking up the sun. They worked hard to construct a joint communiqué on the fifth and final day, even invading the hotel room of poor, bedridden Laniel to get the task done.[44]

Much of the discussion at the conference concerned nuclear weapons, with the Europeans expressing unified horror at the Americans' threat to use the bomb against Chinese targets if the Communists violated the Korean truce.[45] On European security, the Americans and British pressed the beleaguered Bidault to ensure swift French approval of the EDC.

LEADERS OF THE "BIG THREE" MEET IN BERMUDA IN DECEMBER 1953. FROM LEFT TO RIGHT: GEORGES BIDAULT, WINSTON CHURCHILL, JOHN FOSTER DULLES, ANTHONY EDEN, DWIGHT EISENHOWER, AND JOSEPH LANIEL, WHO WOULD SHORTLY TAKE TO HIS ROOM WITH A HIGH FEVER.

Should France fail to do so, Dulles warned, the United States would be forced to undertake an "agonizing reappraisal" of American policy toward European defense. Regarding superpower relations, Eisenhower generated nervous smiles from the Europeans with his graphic description of the new, post-Stalin Soviet Union. Russia, he declared, was "a woman of the streets, and whether her dress was new, or just the old one patched, it was certainly the same whore underneath." America intended to drive her off her present "beat" into the back streets.[46]

Indochina received less focused attention at Bermuda, in part because of French claims on the first day that the military trends were favorable, with the Viet Minh on the defensive. But the discussion of the war was revealing nonetheless. The negotiations question was plainly on French minds. Before his fever felled him, Laniel told Eisenhower that while many in Paris wanted immediate talks, he was determined first to estab-

lish a position of strength. Bidault, for his part, said he personally wanted
to stay the course but that French popular will was faltering, especially in
light of the cease-fire in Korea. Although Ho Chi Minh's recent proposal
was unacceptable, implying as it did bilateral talks, a five-power conference (including China) might represent a solution provided the Associated States were included.

In response, Eisenhower praised French efforts in Indochina but
called a five-power conference "a bad word for the United States." Still
framing the conflict in military terms, the president assured Bidault that
additional U.S. military aid was on the way, which to the Frenchman was
not exactly the point. Churchill, visibly exhausted, thanked France for
all she was doing for empire and freedom, including in Indochina, and
said he regretted that Britain had given up India. He urged the French
to consider longer terms of military service (which would permit troops
to "breed their own kind") and vaguely suggested that the British counterinsurgency experience in Malaya might have lessons for the French in
Indochina.[47]

And then it was over, this first meeting involving the three Western
leaders. No one doubted it would also be the last (as indeed it was). For
all their differences, however, for all the indecorous behavior and bad
chemistry, on Indochina the delegations seemed to agree: The final communiqué saluted "the valiant forces of France and of the three Associated States" and recognized "the vital importance of their contribution to
the defense of the free world."[48] But this boilerplate language evaded the
central issue: namely, when and under what format to enter negotiations.
Bilateral Franco–Viet Minh talks were ruled out, and Bidault's tentative
suggestion of a five-power conference, a "bad word" in the American lexi-
con, failed to find support where it counted. The war, Eisenhower had
made clear, should go on. General Navarre should be given more time.

CHAPTER 17

"WE HAVE THE IMPRESSION THEY ARE GOING TO ATTACK TONIGHT"

HENRI NAVARRE NEEDED NO ENCOURAGEMENT FROM THE POLI-
ticians. On his own, he had made the decisions first to occupy and then
to seek battle at Dien Bien Phu. He still believed, at the moment the
leaders' airplanes departed the Bermuda idyll half a world away in early
December 1953, that the remote Tonkin valley could be the scene for a
spectacular victory, like Na San a year earlier but bigger and more devastating. It would be Na San to the power of ten. But already there were
ominous signs of trouble, visible if not to the French commander then to
some of those around him. Battalion-size sorties outside the valley continued to run into difficulties. Major Jean Souquet's First Colonial Parachute Battalion, for example, came under fierce attack three miles to the
northeast on December 4. Eventually the battalion extricated itself, but
at the cost of fourteen dead and twenty-six wounded. Documents found
on Viet Minh corpses (who were clad in the quilted jackets Ho Chi Minh
had called for) indicated they were not regional troops, as hoped, but
regulars from Regiment 176 of the 316th Division.[1]

Major General René Cogny, aware of the division's rapid advance,
now ordered the full evacuation of Lai Chau. Most regulars were evacuated by air, but some 2,100 soldiers, most of them Tai auxiliaries, were
ordered to leave on foot, bound for Dien Bien Phu, fifty-five miles to the
south. They left in relays between December 5 and 11. Despite supporting air strikes, the poorly trained and lightly armed Tai soon ran into
trouble, suffering one ambush after another. Survivors, forced off the
tracks, tried desperately to elude rapacious pursuit or chose to give their

lives in heroic last stands. Final losses are impossible to determine, but one source has a mere 185 survivors reaching Dien Bien Phu by December 22. Not all the rest were killed, certainly—sizable numbers were able to melt into the jungle and thereby escape their pursuers—but the losses were staggering. Of the larger groups, only Lieutenant Wieme's three companies were able to straggle into Dien Bien Phu more or less intact by taking a circuitous route far to the east.[2]

The evacuation of Lai Chau was a major blow for the French-Vietnamese antiguerrilla forces operating in the Tai country. It also allowed the Viet Minh to extend their all-weather road from Kunming to the frontier near Phong Tho, down through Lai Chau, and toward Tuan Giao. Even the most skilled army press officer could not cover the fact that the loss of Lai Chau was, in these ways, a significant military defeat. Psychologically too it hurt, for the town was the capital of the Tai tribes and a symbol of French support and strength in the region. Now it was gone. On December 12, regiments of the 316th Division entered the abandoned town.[3]

The division's pace had been relentless, even for an army that had long since proved its ability to traverse wide stretches of difficult country at speed. Troops covered twenty miles by day, usually just off the roads, or up to thirty by night, since under darkness they did not have to worry about concealment from the air. Each man carried his weapon, a week's supply of rice (usually replenished at depots along the way), a water bottle, a shovel, a mosquito net, and a little salt in a bamboo tube. He marched from dawn to dusk, or vice versa, with a ten-minute rest every hour. The nighttime marches were blissfully cool but physically much more grueling. Upon arrival, groups of soldiers dug a foxhole in which to take shelter and sleep, spreading a piece of nylon on the bottom. Then they washed their feet with salt water. Some men had footwear, while some made do with sandals cut out of tires. Fatigue was constant, and food was sometimes limited to greens and bamboo shoots picked in the jungle.[4] Vietnamese accounts give few hints of the morale problems alluded to by Ho Chi Minh back in September, but surely they existed, among some units at least. The pace was too rapid, the conditions too punishing, the terrain too treacherous, for it to have been otherwise. But neither can it be doubted that the 316th showed extraordinary resilience and cohesiveness, moving so far so fast, nor that its positioning posed a serious danger to the garrison at the south end of the Pavie Piste.

The man given the task of meeting that threat was Colonel Christian Marie Ferdinand de la Croix de Castries, age fifty-one, a tall, debonair, aristocratic cavalryman who became commander at Dien Bien Phu early in the Lai Chau evacuation. De Castries, however, didn't convey much concern. It was his nature to assume a nonchalant air when confronted with major challenges, and conversely to be overly serious about less important matters. Descended from a long line of high military officers—one marshal, one admiral, and eight generals, one of whom had served with Lafayette in America—de Castries was dashing and courageous, a notorious womanizer, a dilettante with a file full of youthful peccadilloes. If there was a fashionable high-society event in interwar Paris, chances were de Castries was in attendance, each time with a different woman on his arm. A superb horseman, he had won two world riding titles in the 1930s—he was the only person to hold both the high- and broad-jump records. Taken prisoner by the Germans in the Battle of France, he escaped in 1941 and, as a major in the liberation army, led troops in the Italian, French, and German campaigns. In 1946 de Castries went to Indochina, and he returned for a second tour in 1951, sustaining injuries at Vinh Yen. Navarre had known him for years and had been his regimental commander during the victorious dash into Germany in 1944–45; the two cavalrymen got on well. Cogny gave his assent to the appointment, but mostly because he thought de Castries supercilious and vain and wanted him away from his own headquarters in Hanoi.[5]

De Castries arrived at Dien Bien Phu on December 8, sporting a glittering shooting stick, a scarlet foulard, and the red *calot,* or peaked overseas cap, of his old cavalry regiment. No shrinking violet he. Jean Gilles, relieved to be leaving, showed him around the camp and introduced him to the officers, some of whom were quick to point out that commando operations outside the valley were already encountering severe problems. The enemy was in close, they told him; they were hemmed in. For de Castries, whose dislike for static, defensive warfare was well-known, who indeed had been selected for the job in part because he, possessing the cavalryman's gambler mentality, would activate Navarre's plan for offensive operations, it should have been a sobering message. But he struck an upbeat tone in those early days, even as news filtered in of the terrible fate suffered by the Tai partisans struggling southward from Lai Chau. Probably the officers were exaggerating the difficulties of the mobile operations, he thought. And besides, the enemy would not have heavy weapons at his disposal. Even if by some miracle he got some of them in place on the hillside, the French artillery would soon annihilate them.[6]

And so, de Castries got to work supervising the construction of strong-points in the valley. Eventually there would be nine of them, all given female names—reputedly those of former de Castries mistresses (though also representing letters of the alphabet). Most of the garrison was packed in defensive positions around the airstrip—Dominique, Huguette, Claudine, and Eliane—while to the west stood the smaller Françoise. On two small hills to the north and northeast, a mile and a half away, there were Gabrielle and Béatrice, each holding a battalion. Beyond Huguette to the northwest, a series of loosely connected points manned by Tai auxiliaries was christened Anne-Marie, while three miles to the south, all by herself, stood Isabelle. Two battalions were given the tasks of supporting the central position with artillery fire and of defending a secondary airstrip. Much effort went into protecting the defensive positions with bunkers, trenches, and barbed-wire entanglements and into the construction of an underground central headquarters and hospital. There would be water filtration plants (amoebic dysentery was endemic), generating stations, maintenance repair shops for tanks, ammunition dumps, and general stores.

The problem was acquiring sufficient building material for this work—some thirty thousand tons, according to the estimate of Major André Sudrat, the engineering commander. Realizing quickly that having even a fraction of that tonnage flown in would be impossible (especially given that food and ammunition would have priority), Sudrat asked for what he considered the bare essentials: three thousand tons of barbed wire. If he expected the resources of the valley to provide a significant substitute for the missing shipments, he was soon disappointed. There was no cement, no sand, no stone, no brick, and curiously enough, almost no wood. The basin was almost completely devoid of trees, while the wooded slopes were trackless. Venturing farther out for timber was a fool's errand, for there lurked Viet Minh scouts and skirmishers. The

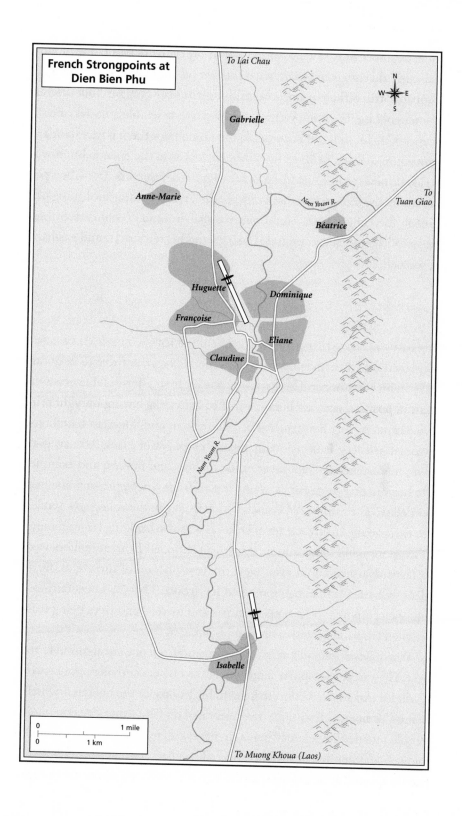

French Strongpoints at
Dien Bien Phu

To Lai Chau

N
W   E
S

Gabrielle

Anne-Marie

Nam Youm R.

To
Tuan Giao

Béatrice

Huguette

Dominique

Françoise

Eliane

Claudine

Nam Youm R.

Isabelle

0   1 mile
0   1 km

To Muong Khoua (Laos)

chief engineer thus saw no option but to order the demolishing of local peasants' dwellings to obtain what little wood could be had—thereby, of course, earning their enmity. With the shrubbery going to fuel the garrison's cooking fires, the valley soon began to resemble a barren moonscape. This in itself did not trouble the French; for them it was standard procedure to open fields of fire and deny cover to the enemy. But it was welcome news to the Viet Minh, whose forward observers, from their positions on the hills, could distinctly see the French coming and going like ants in the valley basin, could observe their routines, could learn their ways. With binoculars, even de Castries and his red scarf could easily be discerned.[7]

II

NO DOUBT THE BINOCULARS WERE OUT WHEN A SPECIAL VISITOR deplaned on Christmas Eve. It was General Navarre, there to celebrate mass with his troops. The garrison was by then a formidable entity, at least in terms of size, each day over the past weeks having brought reinforcements by air: Foreign Legion, Moroccan, and Algerian battalions; colonial artillery batteries with sizable numbers of black African gunners; intelligence and engineer units; doctors and nurses; and even, for the Legion, prostitutes of two *bordels mobiles de campagne*—mobile field bordellos. The number of French Union troops in the valley now totaled 10,910, and the steady stream of Dakotas was also bringing large amounts of weaponry and ammunition. American-supplied Bearcat fighters were in place. Navarre could even view the first platoon of three U.S.-made M-24 "Chaffee" tanks being readied for action. They had been airlifted into the camp in two sections—chassis and turret—and were being reassembled laboriously with a block-and-tackle rig.[8]

Word of the general's arrival soon spread from one strongpoint to the next. He was not a popular man among the officers and men, but he won credit for making this effort to be with his troops for the holiday—which, in the Continental tradition, was celebrated on Christmas Eve. He might be cold and distant, clumsy in his shyness, a mere armchair general, they told one another, but at least he's here. The visit raised spirits among the battalions and around the spindly, vaguely sinister-looking Christmas

GENERAL NAVARRE, LEFT, AT
DIEN BIEN PHU ON CHRISTMAS
EVE 1953. IN THE DRIVER'S SEAT
IS COLONEL DE CASTRIES,
COMMANDER OF THE GARRISON.

tree decorated with whatever colored bits of paper and cotton a group of soldiers and nurses had managed to find. By nightfall the strains of "Stille Nacht, heilige Nacht," sung by German legionnaires, could be heard rising into the darkness, accompanied by faint mortar shots in the distance. At the officers' mess of the Legion, meanwhile, there was more singing, and much coarse conversation, as the champagne flowed.[9]

It was, in part, an attempt at escape. You had to force yourself to celebrate the festivities as if the mountains shrouded in darkness and fog were not alive with enemy troops bent on your annihilation. You had to forget that you were surrounded on all sides. "There was a strange atmosphere in the camp," recalled Howard Simpson, the perspicacious USIA correspondent, who was in the camp one or two days earlier. "The officers remained cocky and determined, but the men, particularly the North Africans, Tai, and some of the Vietnamese, seemed to have been affected by the boredom, the lack of movement, and the threat of what was 'out there.' A troubled silence fell over the dark valley after sundown. Nervous gunners occasionally loosed a stream of seemingly slow-moving tracers into the night, jeeps with hooded headlights bumped over the rough roads, and the odiferous open latrines glowed with the phosphorescence of seething maggots."[10]

Navarre picked up on this underlying unease, indeed felt it himself. He was sullen and withdrawn on the visit—even by his usual standards. He made no uplifting speech, no effort to put heart into his men. "The military conditions for victory have been brought together," he assured both de Castries in an early closed-door meeting and a group of officers later on. But his words lacked conviction, for he also expressed worry about the large number of Viet Minh supply trucks reported en route to the area. "We can't cut the trails," he told the officers, many of whom disagreed.[11] Following mass that evening, Navarre presided over a holiday supper at de Castries's quarters but left quickly when Lieutenant Colonel Jules Gaucher of the Ninth Groupe Mobile, a burly, no-nonsense veteran who had been in Indochina since 1940 and who during the evening had consumed his share of drink, described in unsparing detail the difficulties of conducting operations even a few miles from the camp. The next day, after the fog lifted, Navarre departed as quickly as he had come.

Why, in light of his gloomy realism, did he not call the whole thing off, order an evacuation? The hour was late, to be sure—the PAVN 308th and 316th Divisions were already establishing defensive positions to prevent a withdrawal. But Giap did not yet have artillery in place and would not for several weeks. There was still time. An order to evacuate would have been personally embarrassing and would have brought forth charges of weakness, of snatching defeat from the jaws of victory, of quitting just when decisive victory was at hand. But it would have generated support as well, including among politicos in Paris who had given him a free hand to act as he wished. History offered many examples of commanders who, when faced with an untenable situation, chose to retreat and were praised for their wisdom, despite fervent initial opposition to the action.

As a U.S. undersecretary of state would say years later, in arguing vainly against making Vietnam a large-scale American war: "No great captain has ever been blamed for a successful tactical withdrawal."[12]

The idea crossed Navarre's mind, at least fleetingly. Four days after his Christmas visit to Dien Bien Phu, as reports confirmed the impossibility of maintaining an overland link to the entrenched camp, he ordered René Cogny to prepare top-secret plans for possible evacuation. The two plans—Operation Ariane, providing for the rescue of the withdrawing garrison, and Operation Xenophon, involving a fighting retreat to the south—were to be kept secret from the camp's commanders and were not to be implemented until the very last moment. But hadn't that moment arrived? No, the commander in chief determined, not yet. (Or he believed, in his heart of hearts, it had come and gone.) Cogny too, who took several weeks to prepare the evacuation plans, called such thinking premature. Success could still come, the two men said; the valley could still be the setting for a spectacular victory, a bigger, better Na San, one that could allow the civilians in Paris to, as they liked to say, negotiate with honor.

Those Paris leaders understood that it might all come down to this, to a battle royal in the remote highlands of northwestern Tonkin. Other observers grasped it as well, including officials in Washington, London, Moscow, and Beijing. Said a cable from the British embassy in Saigon on New Year's Eve: "All out attack on Dien Bien Phu now appears likely."[13]

Navarre's nemesis too sensed that a line had been crossed. As the year turned, and as the Viet Minh forward observers reported back to headquarters that the buildup at the camp was continuing apace, Vo Nguyen Giap announced that he was ready: He would move his command post from Thai Nguyen, three hundred miles away, to the immediate vicinity of Dien Bien Phu. He had to be right there on the scene, he told aides, for the task ahead was huge. Lest there be any uncertainty on that score, a letter from Ho Chi Minh had reminded him: "This campaign is a very important one, not only militarily but also politically, not only for domestic reasons but for international ones as well. So all of our people, all of our armed forces, and the entire Party must entirely unite to get the job done."[14]

III

THE ATTACK WAS PLANNED FOR THE LATE AFTERNOON OF JANUARY 25, 1954. At five o'clock, the troops would plunge straight into the heart of the French camp. The 308th Division, having massed in the west of the basin, would push as far as the central command post of Colonel de Castries, who on that side was unlikely to be fully garrisoned. The 312th would come from the northeast to cut down, blow by blow, Gabrielle (Doc Lap) and Anne-Marie (Ban Keo) and seize control of the airstrip. Moving out from the center to the periphery, the camp would be cut into pieces and swiftly crushed.

This operational plan had taken shape over several weeks and was the product of consultation between Vo Nguyen Giap and his Chinese advisers. Giap had left for the Tonkin highlands on January 5. In a departure from previous practice, he traveled much of the way by jeep, with the exception of one night and one day spent on foot crossing over the difficult Pha Din Pass, located between Thuan Chau and Tuan Giao. All along this route, most of it on the new axis of Provincial Route 13, Giap received regular updates on the situation at the front and kept in close communication with Wei Guoqing, the top Chinese representative. The two men shared one principal fear: that the French army would withdraw, as it had at Na San a few months earlier and at Hoa Binh early in 1952. Their concern rose one night as news came in of fires burning near the French camp. Had General Navarre ordered stocks to be destroyed before an evacuation? No, subsequent reports came back; the French were staying put. The fires had been lit to clear away brush on the outskirts of the camp.[15]

The details of the discussions between Vo Nguyen Giap and Wei Guoqing in these early weeks of 1954 have been lost to history, but one can guess there were tensions. In recently published memoirs, Giap says he had early doubts about the strategy of "swift attack, swift victory" (*danh nhanh, thang nhanh*), a clear reference to Chinese wave tactics as used in Korea. Better, perhaps, would be to proceed more slowly, through a method of "steady attack, steady advance," over a period of several weeks. Pham Ngoc Mau, the Viet Minh head of artillery, described the choice as between eating an orange by using a knife to cut it into pieces, or taking one's time and peeling the fruit by hand. Wei Guoqing argued for using the knife, and Giap relented, but he secretly asked his closest Vietnamese aides to keep him continually abreast of the pace of French reinforcements. If the January 25 attack failed, he feared, it would inflict huge damage on the People's Army and hand the French a major military and political victory.[16] He had not forgotten Ho Chi Minh's admonition: Unless you are certain of victory, don't proceed.

The journey to the new headquarters took about a week. An advance party selected for the command post a grotto near a waterfall in the Muong Phong hills, about nine miles north of Dien Bien Phu. Surrounded by jungle cover, the cave was under fifteen feet of solid rock, and giant boulders concealed the entrance. About forty-eight hours after arriving, Giap convened a meeting involving all his top commanders, including Hoang Van Thai, his chief of staff, and Le Liem, the political commissar. Almost certainly Wei Guoqing and other Chinese advisers were present too, although few Vietnamese texts mention them, even as they do note the presence of a Romanian artist painter and two journalists, one Italian and one Chinese.[17]

Who was Wei Guoqing, this phantom general whose presence in Vietnamese histories of this period is usually so ill defined? He came from Guangxi, not far from the Vietnamese frontier near Lang Son. A member of the Zhuang national minority, which traced its bloodlines to the Tai stock that one finds at Dien Bien Phu, he had joined the Chinese Communist Party in 1931 and taken part in the Long March. After distinguishing himself in the civil war of 1948, he had become after 1949 the leading figure in his native province and from 1950 directed the Chinese Military Assistance Group (CMAG), charged with overseeing Beijing's assistance to the Viet Minh. Apart from a year away on sick leave, he had subsequently been a close adviser to Giap and was often present at headquarters.[18]

The meeting on January 14 affirmed the plan to unleash a furious attack on the French fortress eleven days thence. The objective would be twofold: to annihilate an important part of the enemy's force, and to liberate the northwestern sector and create the conditions for a territorial extension of the base of the Pathet Lao. Some weeks earlier Giap had sent seven battalions from his 304th and 325th Divisions slicing into central Laos, linking up with the Pathet Lao and threatening to cut Laos in half at her narrowest point. The offensive took the French by surprise (the Deuxième Bureau temporarily lost sight of the units), and though it ran out of steam, it showed Giap what could be accomplished once Dien Bien Phu had been taken. Just how much the conferees on January 14 revisited the attack-fast versus nibble-away-slowly options is not clear, but we know they came out of the meeting still committed to the former. The French garrison was deemed likely to be still vulnerable on January 25, while the People's Army had neither the resources nor the experience to engage itself in a lengthy operation.

IV

THERE FOLLOWED TEN DAYS OF RELENTLESS PREPARATION, AS ferocious as any in the history of warfare. The general mobilization of labor initiated a month earlier now took on a breathtaking pace. For on this day, January 14, nothing was yet ready. The artillery was not in place on the crests above Dien Bien Phu, and the trails to get it there had not been made ready nor even fully marked out. Farther away, huge tasks remained to get materials to the highlands, from the Chinese border at Mu Nam Quam over Provincial Route 13 to the Red River and thence via Provincial Route 41 to the area of Dien Bien Phu—a total distance of almost five hundred miles. All along this route, engineering crews and soldiers, assisted by porters, worked day and night to clear and widen and repair the roads and to keep convoys moving. The route was divided into eight sections, their endpoints marked by major obstacles such as ravines or waterways where checkpoints were set up. The Russian-made Molotova two-and-a-half-ton trucks, now numbering about six hundred, as well as a smaller number of American Dodge trucks captured by the Chinese in Korea or the Viet Minh in Vietnam, traveled only one section each; at the checkpoints, their contents were taken off by porters and reloaded on the vehicles assigned to the next stretch.[19]

French aircraft were a constant menace, and the casualties among the porters, though never published or perhaps tallied, were undoubtedly high. (A particular menace: the new American antipersonnel bombs that spread lethal showers of small steel splinters.) But the work continued, as thousands of porters stood ready to fill in the craters or build bypasses; French crews reported with dismay that the cuts they succeeded in making in roads were often repaired within hours. To complicate the pilots' task, elaborate efforts were made to camouflage the route wherever possible. Log bridges were constructed just under the surface of a stream to hide them, and treetops were pulled together with ropes and cables to screen the roads. Vehicles were covered with leafy branches, and tire tracks were rubbed out as soon as the trucks had passed. A primitive but effective air-warning system was fashioned, whereby spotters in treetops clanged alarm triangles or blew whistles to warn of approaching planes (none of which were jets and thus could be heard well in advance of arrival). Pilots would report seeing long lines of truck headlights suddenly go dark, long before they reached the target.[20]

When bomb damage or natural obstacles proved too great to overcome quickly, porters were called in to carry loads themselves, often over considerable distances. They would don makeshift shoulder pads and bamboo carrying rigs, and frequently they would team up. Photographs exist of four-man teams using shoulder poles to carry the barrels and the breechblocks of 75mm Japanese mountain guns up steep wooded hillsides.

Bicycles, for years a favored mode of transport for the Viet Minh, were again called into service. Most were French-made, manufactured at Saint-Étienne or in the Peugeot factories. A specially equipped bicycle—with wooden struts to strengthen the frame and bamboo poles to extend the handlebars and the brake levers—could take more than an elephant could carry. "We mobilized all available supply bicycles," Vo Nguyen Giap would recall, "reaching a total of 20,000."

> Every supply bicycle was initially capable of transporting 100 kilograms, and this was later increased to 200 or even 300 kilograms. One civilian coolie laborer from Phu Tho named Ma Van Thang was able to transport a total of 352 kilograms on his bicycle. The carrying capacity of transport bicycles was more than ten times greater than that of porters carrying loads on "ganh" [bamboo or wooden] poles, and the amount of rice consumed by the people transporting the supplies was reduced by a similar amount. The superiority of the transport bicycles also lay in the fact that they could operate along roads and trails that trucks could not use. This method of transportation greatly surprised the enemy's army and completely upset his original calculations.[21]

But the most dramatic feats were accomplished at the end, after the trucks had snaked their way to the endpoint, at Na Nham on Route 41. From here, in order to avoid detection by the French, the artillery pieces had somehow to be dragged to their emplacements, on a trail that ten days before the attack date had still to be blazed. Unloaded from the

A PARADE OF SPECIALLY MODIFIED BICYCLES (MANY OF THEM
FRENCH-MADE PEUGEOTS), LOADED WITH FOOD AND MUNITIONS,
ON A ROAD TO DIEN BIEN PHU IN JANUARY 1954.

trucks, the cannons were to be transported through a chain of mountains
without going through a valley, in order to cut through the foothills of
the 1,100-meter-high Pu Pha Song mountain; then they were to descend
again in the direction of the Pavie Piste, which linked Dien Bien Phu to
Lai Chau, which they would cross near Ban To; then they were to scale
another new height in order to position the battery at Ban Nghiu, from
where they would fire on the French garrison at point-blank range.

It took seven days and nights of nonstop labor to get the heavy guns
in place, with the use of block and tackle, drag ropes, and braking chocks
to keep them from careening back down the slopes. The half-ton 75mm
mountain guns were not the problem; they could be broken down into
eleven loads that, while heavy and cumbersome, were manageable. The
105mm howitzers, however, represented an almost absurd challenge on
inclines that reached as steep as sixty degrees. Commander Tran Do
of the 312th Division was among the infantry pressed into this "silent

battle" of "cannon-pulling" of the 105s. "Every evening when the white fog . . . began to descend over the plains, columns of human beings set out on the road," he later wrote. "The [six-mile] track was so narrow that if a slight deviation of the wheels took place the artillery piece would have fallen into the deep ravine. The newly-opened track was soon an ankle-deep bog. With our own sweat and muscles, we replaced the trucks to haul artillery pieces into position."

Fatigue and lack of supplies were a constant concern, Tran continued. Meals consisted only of rice, often undercooked, as the kitchens had to be smokeless by day and sparkless by night. And yet the work went on: "To climb a slope, hundreds of men crept before the gun, tugging on long ropes, pulling the piece up inch by inch. On the crest, the winch was creaking, helping to prevent the piece from slipping." Then it got worse: "It was much harder descending a slope. The sight was just the reverse: Hundreds of men held onto long ropes behind the piece, their bodies leaning backwards, and the windlass released the ropes inch by inch." In this way, whole nights were spent toiling by torchlight to gain five hundred or a thousand meters.[22]

Always there was pressure to do more, to go faster. When a staffer informed Pham Ngoc Mau, an artillery commander, that the 105mm cannon could be moved at a speed of approximately 150 meters per hour, he received a blistering reply. "Speed my ass! You can't simply say like everyone else that we can't do a fucking two hundred meters per hour!" The relentless pace inevitably led to accidents and other mishaps, and to questioning. At one point, during a particularly grueling uphill stretch, a cannon began tilting, one wheel sinking into the side of the trail. For a time, it seemed the whole apparatus might thunder down into the ravine, taking the soldier-porters with it. The men moaned. "We're dying for nothing," they complained. "What good is it to have trucks if we're using our own arms as motors?"[23] Though such moments of despair appear to have been relatively rare, meetings were organized to boost the morale of the troops and to seek ways to make the labor less excruciating and dangerous. One such improvement: the installation of a device under the beam of the cannons to allow them to slide on the ground without having to be lifted, which both eased the burden on the men and reduced the risk of accidents.[24]

V

THE FRENCH COMMAND KNEW OF THE IMPENDING ATTACK. ON JANUARY 20, intelligence operators intercepted and decoded Viet Minh messages indicating that the assault would commence on the evening of the twenty-fifth, by the light of the moon in its second quarter. Shouts of joy rang out among operational officers in Hanoi and Saigon; at long last, the enemy would emerge and receive the drubbing that was his due. As the news spread among the officers and men at the garrison, again there were smiles and expressions of delight. False bravado? To some extent, maybe, especially among senior officers privy to information about the depth and breadth of Viet Minh preparations. But most everyone was eager to get on with the show. Time and again the soldiers had been told an attack seemed imminent, yet nothing had happened; the succession of false alarms was frustrating and nerve-racking. Ennui was a frequent companion in the remote valley, as the men dreamed of home, of wives and girlfriends, of cold beers at the neighborhood café, of warm baths and favorite meals. The dark rotgut that was issued to them in the form of *vinogel*—a canned, jellylike wine concentrate to which water must be added—only made them pine harder for real drink; the women in the camp bordellos provided gratification but not love.

The constant flow of aircraft bringing men and supplies was a source of comfort, however, adding to the conviction that the battle, when it came, would surely go France's way. Every fifteen minutes they landed (weather permitting), day after day after day, U.S.-supplied C-47 Dakotas and C-119s. In due course, this rate of delivery would be seen as far too limited—one postwar estimate said it would have taken twelve thousand flights, or five months of essentially nonstop deliveries, to make the valley into a fully defensible field position—but for the moment, it seemed fully adequate to most. By mid-January, twelve battalions were in place, charged with defending the strongpoints. In the north, Gabrielle had the Fifth Battalion of the Seventh Algerian Regiment and a Legion mortar company; Béatrice had the Third Battalion of the Thirteenth Legion Demi-Brigade; and Anne-Marie had the Third Tai Battalion and a Legion mortar company. There were similar-size concentrations in the center at Huguette, Dominique, Françoise, and Eliane, while in the area of de Castries's command post, Claudine had the Eighth Colonial Parachute Battalion, two tank platoons, artillery, a Legion heavy-mortar company, and security, intelligence, and medical units. At Isabelle in the south was installed the Third Battalion of the Third Legion Infantry Regiment, the Second Battalion of the First Algerian Rifle Regiment, one tank platoon, artillery, and a Tai partisan company.

January also witnessed a steady flow of visitors to the entrenched camp. Most pronounced themselves pleased with the buildup, with the positioning of the strongpoints, with the presence of twenty-eight guns and sixteen heavy mortars ready to open fire on Viet Minh positions. When someone expressed skepticism that it would be enough, de Castries did his level best to change the person's mind.[25] Cogny and Navarre, for their part, were more cautious than their camp commander as the anticipated Viet Minh attack date approached. The intelligence reports were sobering. As early as December 27, the French Air Force had picked up evidence of the passage of heavy Viet Minh equipment toward Dien Bien Phu. Already then intelligence analysts estimated that Giap would deploy 49,000 men, including 33,000 combatants, figures that would turn out to be within 10 percent of reality. On January 9, aerial photographs showed that 105mm howitzers had left Viet Minh rear-base areas in the direction of the highlands.[26]

Navarre hedged his bets. He found ominous the news that de Castries's chief of staff had been killed by a sniper within the perimeter on December 28. On the last day of the year, Navarre confessed to U.S. ambassador Donald Heath that Dien Bien Phu might be overrun despite his best efforts. The Viet Minh, he told the American, now might have the means to move 105mm cannons up on the heights overlooking the approach to the valley. The following day Navarre informed Paris that, "faced with the arrival of new possibilities which very serious intelligence has been announcing for two weeks . . . I can no longer—if these materials truly exist in such numbers and above all if the adversary succeeds in putting them to use—guarantee success with any certainty."[27]

That was the key question: Would Giap be able to put his major weaponry to effective use? Navarre and Cogny in January still clung to the belief that he couldn't. If he followed the conventional practice of firing his guns from behind the crests, the trajectory would be wrong and he'd be too far away to do serious damage; if he fired them from the forward slope, he would be easily identified and destroyed. The garrison's artillery commander, the one-armed Colonel Charles Piroth, encouraged them in this belief, insisting that he could handle easily whatever Giap threw his way. Cogny, increasingly fearful that the outlying strongpoints—especially Béatrice and Gabrielle on the north end—would be swiftly overrun in the battle and be almost impossible to retake, hoped he was right. Artillery would be decisive, he knew, one way or the other.

That Cogny and Navarre actively disliked each other didn't help French planning. They had never been close, but recently the mutual animosity had become obvious to all, not least to their respective staffs in Hanoi and Saigon. They were, in almost every way, opposites. Whereas Navarre was short and trim, taciturn and socially awkward, and ill at ease around journalists, Cogny was a giant of a man at six foot four and 210 pounds, an extrovert who had a flair for public relations and was a born leader of men. Now forty-nine, he had doctoral degrees in law and political science and had survived the tortures of the Buchenwald concentration camp, emerging at the liberation severely malnourished—he was down to 120 pounds—and with a limp. (He walked with a cane the rest of his life.) Under de Lattre, he had commanded a division in Tonkin, earning raves from his men for wading through waist-deep paddies with them and fording streams to see what was happening on the other side. He had remained in Indochina after the great man's death. Far more thin-skinned than Navarre, easily wounded by even the slightest criticism, he also had a well-earned reputation for arguing orders, even in front of privates. For all that, Navarre had nevertheless appointed him in May 1953 to command of the key northern region.[28]

Historians have sometimes made too much of the Cogny-Navarre clash—Cogny, as we have seen, was not hostile to Operation Castor, whatever his postwar claims—but by the middle of January 1954 their feud threatened to become a major distraction. Cogny openly fumed at "the air-conditioned general" moving pins on his wall map in his palatial Saigon office while the real fighters dealt with real problems in the north. The security situation in the Red River Delta was growing more serious each day, he warned Paris, with the Viet Minh maintaining guerrilla activity at a very high pitch and with more and more of its six thousand villages falling out of government hands. (At most, a third of them could now be considered friendly.) The vital rail link between Hanoi and Haiphong was being cut virtually daily, often through the use of new remote-controlled mines, as was the Hanoi-Phu Ly–Nam Dinh road. Cogny's faith in the Vietnamese National Army (VNA), meanwhile, never high, plummeted in the early weeks of the year, as a result of several alleged acts of treachery—including instances of soldiers allowing Viet Minh commandos to enter French-held compounds under the cover of darkness and massacre the men (often legionnaires) who were holding them. In Hanoi, January witnessed an uptick in brazen grenade attacks on French Union soldiers, notably on the streets around the Citadel.[29] Cogny expressed confidence that he could counteract these Viet Minh tactics, but only if he had adequate troops at his disposal.

He was especially incensed by Navarre's decision to proceed with Operation Atlante, an ambitious strike into Viet Minh–held territory in south-central Vietnam that got under way on January 20. Following an amphibious landing at Tuy Hoa, in which U.S.-supplied Grumman Hellcat fighters tore into the coastline with napalm, more than thirty infantry battalions with supporting artillery and armor swept through a large Viet Minh zone with the objective of securing the coastal area of central Vietnam from Nha Trang to Hue, and secondarily to give the new light battalions of the VNA a chance to show their mettle in battle. Cogny questioned the importance of the objective and said the operation was drawing aircraft and troops from his larder. He felt vindicated when Atlante in the early going failed to yield the hoped-for results. The Viet Minh proved elusive as always, fading into the hills, and in one counterattack they wiped out an entire *groupe mobile* made up of French troops who had fought with the U.S. Second Division in Korea.[30]

VI

AT DIEN BIEN PHU ON JANUARY 25, EVERYONE IN THE ENTRENCHED camp waited with nervous anxiety. And waited. By nightfall, no attack had come. A Dakota circled above the basin, like some silver metallic hawk, ready to drop flares at the first sight of advancing enemy troops, but none emerged. By sunrise the next morning, all was still quiet. At 1:50 that afternoon, Navarre and Cogny arrived at the camp, along with two other dignitaries: Marc Jacquet, the minister for the Associated States, and Maurice Dejean, the high commissioner for France in Indochina. De Castries, his red scarf blowing in the breeze, was there to meet the plane, as was Piroth, his empty sleeve tucked into his belt. Immediately the group headed to de Castries's command post, the only dugout protected by steel plates. While Paule Bourgeade, de Castries's beautiful young secretary (whose lipstick-stained cigarette butts were prized possessions among the paras), prepared coffee, the group grappled with the question: Why had Giap held his fire the night before?

No obvious answer presented itself. Perhaps, someone offered, he will attack this evening. The moon will still be out, and perhaps he just needed an additional day for final preparations. This seemed as good a theory as any, and the discussion moved on to the state of the garrison's defenses. De Castries, unflappable as always, calmly announced himself ready for the undertaking. Jacquet took Piroth aside and said, "Colonel, I know there are hundreds of guns lying idle at Hanoi. You ought to take advantage of a minister's presence [that is, Jacquet himself] to get a few sent you on the side." Piroth declined the suggestion with the air of a military man having to endure a civilian offering battlefield advice. "Look at my plan of fire, M. Minister. I've got more guns than I need."

Someone asked if he was sure. "If I have thirty minutes warning," Piroth replied, "my counterbattery will be effective." The follow-up hung in the air, unasked: What if he didn't have thirty minutes warning?[31]

As the afternoon drew to a close, Navarre turned to Jacquet: "We have the impression they are going to attack tonight. I would prefer not to expose a minister to any risks." Soon thereafter the official Dakotas lifted off and disappeared in the clouds. There would be no attack that night either, or the next night, or the night after that.[32]

What happened? Why did the Battle of Dien Bien Phu not begin on that moonlit evening in late January 1954? For years, historians aware of the initial plan assumed that the Chinese got cold feet and prevailed on

Giap to issue a cancellation. It now appears, however, that the decision was Giap's and that he made it in the face of opposition, or at best grudging acquiescence, from the Chinese.

There were actually two postponements. The first was issued on January 24. That day a Viet Minh soldier from the 312th Division fell into French hands; under interrogation, he revealed what the French already knew, that the attack would commence the following day at five o'clock. Viet Minh radio monitoring of the French picked up on this leak, and Giap ordered that the attack be pushed back twenty-four hours, to five P.M. on January 26.[33]

Those twenty-four hours would prove critical. Giap was under pressure from his Chinese advisers, from some of his senior commanders, and from his frontline troops to attack with full force, and to do it quickly. These advocates insisted that everything was ready and that a further postponement would create dissension in the ranks and among the tens of thousands of porters who had given their absolute all to prepare the ground. But Giap was worried. He was not sure all the elements were in place for a successful attack. On the night of the twenty-fifth he was anxious, returning again and again to the question, could his troops prevail? Several things troubled him, starting with the size of the battlefield. Dien Bien Phu was three times larger than Na San, and Viet Minh units were not trained to operate on such a large expanse, against a formidable foe possessing tanks, heavy artillery, and airpower. His own force was huge, at more than five divisions, but were the units capable of the necessary discipline and control? Could his artillery, not used to working on such a major scale, execute coordinated calibration from protected but suboptimal sites? It worried Giap that one artillery regiment commander had recently disclosed that he did not know how to operate his cannon. Finally, there was the question of time. Up to now, battles had seldom lasted longer than twenty hours. Most began at twilight and ended in the early morning. Would the troops be able to handle a drawn-out battle, involving much fighting during daylight hours?[34]

More basically, Giap sensed that the situation had changed. Tactics approved in December no longer made as much sense in January, for the French were now much stronger. They had doubled in overall strength, and their fortifications were much improved, with barbed wire and artillery. Meanwhile the People's Army did not yet have all its artillery in place. An attack now, Giap concluded, would be "an adventure."

"I couldn't close my eyes," Giap recalled of that night, spent in his one-room hillside hut with its small cot and bamboo table overlaid with maps of the valley. "I had a terrible headache. Thuy, a medic, wrapped a mugwort compress around my forehead."

The next morning Giap summoned Wei Guoqing, who was surprised to see the compress. "The battle is about to begin," the Chinese adviser remarked; how did Giap think it would likely unfold? "That's the issue I'd like to discuss," came the reply. "From observing the situation, I believe the enemy has moved from a temporary to a solid defense. For that reason, I think we must not follow our agreed plan. If we fight, we lose."

"How should we solve this?" Wei Guoqing responded.

"My thought is immediately this afternoon to order a delay in the offensive, withdraw our soldiers to their training positions, and prepare again under the directive, 'Steady Attack, Steady Advance.'"[35]

Wei Guoqing, depending on which source one consults, either supported the delay or grumbled that Giap lacked "Bolshevik spirit." Perhaps he did both. Regardless, that afternoon a contentious meeting at the Viet Minh commander's post—during which several subordinate Viet Minh commanders pressed for going ahead with the attack that evening—ended with a postponement of the operation and a switch to the "steady" directive.[36] Several more weeks would be taken to get everything into place, to study the French defenses more thoroughly, and to make sure not a single ingredient for victory had been left out. Nothing would be left to chance. The orange would be peeled by hand, slowly.[37]

"In taking this correct decision," Giap later wrote, echoing Ho Chi Minh's words to him in December 1953, "we strictly followed [the] fundamental principle of the conduct of a revolutionary war; strike to win, strike only when success is certain; if it is not, then don't strike."[38]

What if he had chosen differently? What if he had bowed to the pressure and launched the attack? It's a tantalizing counterfactual question. No one can know the answer with any degree of certainty, of course, but it seems impossible in hindsight to argue against the veteran commander's reasoning. The fact is that Giap's forces were not yet prepared for the immense task at hand; an attack on January 25 or 26 could easily have ended in disaster. From this perspective, neither Navarre's original conception regarding Operation Castor nor de Castries's and Piroth's confidence before Jacquet and Dejean on the twenty-fifth seems so absurd. The People's Army came much closer to military failure at Dien Bien Phu than is generally believed.

CHAPTER 18

"VIETNAM IS A PART OF THE WORLD"

B EYOND THE VARIOUS MILITARY CONSIDERATIONS, ONE OTHER
factor may have contributed to Vo Nguyen Giap's decision to call off
the January 25 attack. The Berlin conference of foreign ministers was
scheduled to open at this very time, and Indochina would certainly come
up for consideration. An unsuccessful attack upon the French garrison
could have an enormous impact on the tenor of that discussion, and on
any decisions reached by the four powers (France, Britain, the United
States, and the Soviet Union) regarding Indochina's future. At this stage
of the game, General Giap and Ho Chi Minh knew, all military plans had
to be considered in light of their international diplomatic ramifications,
and vice versa. As Ho had put it in his report to the DRV National Assembly a month earlier, in December 1953, Vietnam had become "a part
of the world."[1]

Ho Chi Minh remained suspicious of great-power negotiations concerning Indochina, as did his top lieutenants. The timing was not yet
right. If there were to be talks, Ho wanted them to be bilateral discussions
between the DRV and France. Even these should be entered carefully,
and there should be no letup in military pressure. But Viet Minh officials
also understood that they might be powerless to stop the convening of a
five-power conference of the type Moscow proposed and to which Paris
and Beijing seemed receptive. If the other leading powers, and especially
the United States, agreed to such a meeting, it would be held, whatever
the Vietnamese might have to say about it.

And on this point, available DRV internal sources are clear: At the start of 1954, it was American policy more than French policy that was of chief concern to Ho Chi Minh and the Politburo. The United States was now the principal enemy, not France.[2] Should President Dwight Eisenhower choose to further increase his involvement in the French cause, perhaps by sending ground troops to the war theater, or by ordering air strikes on Viet Minh positions, it would have enormous implications for the balance of military forces. Conversely, should the American president alter his hostile attitude toward diplomacy and come out in favor of a negotiated settlement, that too would change the dynamics in a fundamental way.

Yet again the question loomed, for Viet Minh leaders and for their counterparts in Paris, Beijing, Moscow, and London: *What will the Americans do?*

No easy answer presented itself as the opening of the Berlin meeting drew near or in the early days after it commenced. On the one hand, Washington continued to maintain, publicly and privately, that the essentials for victory were in place and that a better French execution of existing strategy was the only thing required. The Navarre Plan had not yet delivered much, it was true, but neither had it failed, and significant operational results were not expected for several more months. On January 16, Eisenhower approved NSC-177 (later NSC-5405), a policy paper that affirmed Indochina's critical importance to American security and adhered to an essentially optimistic assessment of the overall military situation. "With continued U.S. economic and material assistance," the paper stated, "the Franco-Vietnamese forces are not in danger of being militarily defeated by the Viet Minh."[3]

On the other hand, senior officials gave close and unprecedented consideration to what to do if the battlefield situation deteriorated, or if the French suddenly called it quits. Sending U.S. ground forces seemed out of the question, at least in the president's mind; he told an NSC meeting on January 8 that he could not imagine putting American troops anywhere in Southeast Asia, except perhaps in Malaya, in his mind a crucial link in America's defensive perimeter. Vietnam would swallow U.S. divisions whole, he said. But Eisenhower in the same meeting showed markedly more interest in other forms of intervention. When Treasury Secretary George Humphrey expressed opposition to the suggestion by

Admiral Arthur Radford, the chairman of the Joint Chiefs of Staff, for the use of U.S. air strikes to assist the French at Dien Bien Phu, Eisenhower interjected that it might be necessary to "put a finger in the dike" to protect vital interests in the region. To NSC adviser Robert Cutler's suggestion that it could be a French finger, Eisenhower and Radford chorused in unison that France had been the problem all these years. It might take American airpower, both men agreed. With no consensus in the group, and no danger of imminent French collapse, the NSC left the question of air strikes open and agreed in the meantime to meet a request from Paris for additional B-26 bombers, needed, the French claimed, to counter an improvement in the enemy's antiaircraft capability.[4]

Eisenhower also created a high-level, ad hoc working group representing the State and Defense departments, the CIA, and the NSC staff to undertake an analysis of the Southeast Asian situation and produce an action plan for the region. The group's charge included consideration of committing U.S. ground forces or airpower to Indochina, and it was instructed to proceed from the assumption that a defeat in Indochina would be a major blow to American national security. As a third step, the president ordered the creation of a smaller, top-secret Special Committee on Indochina, chaired by Undersecretary of State Walter Bedell Smith, whose task was to "come up with a plan in specific terms, covering who does what and which and to whom" in Indochina and the surrounding region.[5]

Late in the month the Smith committee recommended, and Eisenhower approved, the dispatch of two hundred uniformed U.S. Air Force mechanics to Indochina to service American-supplied aircraft, including the new B-26s, on the understanding that "they would be used at bases where they would be secure from capture and would not be exposed to combat." The president also agreed to send U.S. civilian pilots hired by the CIA, using planes from the agency's proprietary airline, the Civilian Air Transport (CAT), to assist the French with air transport. Within a few weeks, a squadron of C-119 transports based in Formosa, painted gray and manned by two dozen CAT pilots, began flying supplies into Dien Bien Phu. Their contribution would be crucial, for these "Flying Boxcars" had a six-ton capacity, as compared to the two-and-a-half-ton capacity of the French-piloted Dakotas. The supply of Dien Bien Phu would have been impossible without them.[6]

"Don't think I like to send them there," Eisenhower said in front of Press Secretary James Hagerty, with reference to the technicians. "But we can't get anywhere in Asia by just sitting here in Washington doing nothing. My God, we must not lose Asia. We've got to look this thing in the face."[7]

Secretary of State John Foster Dulles did not involve himself directly in these decisions, having meanwhile departed for Berlin. European security issues were at the top of the agenda for the meeting, but Dulles knew that the Soviets intended also to table a formal proposal for a five-power conference—that is, including Mao Zedong's People's Republic of China—to deal with Asian issues, among them Indochina. He was determined to resist. In its first year, the Eisenhower administration had steadfastly rejected negotiations on Indochina, and it remained committed to that position. With equal vehemence, the White House had refused to countenance any action that might be construed as even tacit recognition of the PRC's legitimacy, let alone as signifying its membership in the great-power club; neither Dulles nor the president had any intention of changing that posture now. As Ike had put it in Bermuda, a five-power conference was a "bad word for the United States."

In phrasing it that way, Eisenhower may have been suggesting he was hemmed in by partisan politics. If so, he himself was partly to blame. His own Republican Party, as we have seen, had made China the partisan shibboleth of American politics with its attacks four years earlier on Truman and Acheson for allegedly "losing" the country to Mao and his Communists. "Red China," it was thenceforth branded, to distinguish it from the Republic of China in Taiwan, and it generated in American political discourse—notably in the 1952 election campaign, with Eisenhower's tacit consent—an intensity almost religious in nature. U.S. officials, Britain's foreign secretary Anthony Eden lamented in late November 1953, "find it difficult to pursue a realistic policy towards China." The following day Eden returned to the theme in a personal communication to Winston Churchill: "In the existing state of American opinion, the US administration would find it politically impossible to sit down with a high level meeting of the big Five."[8]

Or as Selwyn Lloyd, minister of state in the British Foreign Office, put it: "There is now in the United States an emotional feeling about Communist China and to a lesser extent Russia which borders on hysteria."[9]

It was the great difference between the United States and her main transatlantic partner, Britain: the degree to which fear of the Communist world conspiracy permeated political and popular discourse. Eden and Churchill and other British Conservatives were mystified by the seeming support in Middle America for extreme Red-baiters such as Senator Joseph McCarthy, who applied constant pressure on the White House to live up to their rigid standards of anti-Communist purity. No less than their Labour counterparts, these Tories shook their heads at the brutal antics of Scott McLeod, a McCarthy acolyte appointed by Dulles who (as head of the Bureau of Security and Personnel) was conducting an anti-Communist witch hunt in the State Department that, by the time it finished, ruined the careers of scores if not hundreds of officers and other staff. Among them were a number of China specialists.[10]

But it was not merely McCarthy and his ilk. For years, British analysts had marveled at the deep American aversion—across party lines—to negotiating with adversaries; at the ruling out of compromise and the demand for "unconditional surrender" ("the simple American ideal," as one Briton put it); and at the unwillingness to recognize China or admit her into the United Nations.[11] For years, they had noted the periodic anti-British broadsides in Congress and in the American press—especially the Hearst and Scripps-Howard papers—because of London's willingness to engage with Beijing and Moscow. "Appeasers," the British were called, guilty of disloyalty, of cowardice, of cozying up to robbers and murderers. In late 1953, the frustrations seemed to build—in large part, the British speculated, because of American irritation at the failure to achieve outright victory in Korea. Selwyn Lloyd queried veteran U.S. diplomat W. Averell Harriman about it over dinner one evening in New York City. The American was sympathetic. He condemned the prevailing temper and the Eisenhower administration's habit of always taking publicly rigid diplomatic stances, and he pleaded for Britons to be tolerant from "the wisdom borne of your maturity."[12]

Harriman needn't have worried. London policy makers were not prepared to be anything other than forbearing. They reminded one another that at the end of the day, as one put it, "we and [the Americans] are basically on the same side." And "anyhow, lecturing a patient in a state of hysteria will never do the slightest good." Britain simply had to accept that domestic political considerations shaped U.S. foreign policy in crucial ways. Although obsessive hostility toward China "may not reflect an actual majority of opinion throughout the United States, the disturbing factor which emerges is that the United States Administration appear to be convinced that opinion in the Middle West (i.e. isolationist and xenophobic) must at all cost, at any rate for the present, be 'appeased'; and that we can, with some certainty, expect current United States foreign policy to take this into account as a major, and, perhaps often, as a paramount consideration."[13]

Yet despite this British determination to avoid raising hackles in Washington, Anglo-American differences over China policy, and over the fundamental notion of negotiating with Communists, would play themselves out in the first half of 1954, with profoundly important implications for the Indochina War. For the first time since 1945–46, when she had facilitated France's return to Indochina, Britain would in these six months play a central role in the conflict, generating in the process much angst and anger in Washington—and more accusations of craven weakness in the face of the Communist peril. Time and again the Eisenhower administration would press London to agree to an internationalization of the military struggle in support of France; each time the British would resist, pointing instead to the need for a negotiated political solution. This despite the fact that British officials, who held to their own version of the domino theory, were hardly less keen than the Eisenhower team to see a French victory in the war.

II

ONE MAN WOULD DOMINATE THIS ACTIVE BRITISH DIPLOMACY ON Vietnam: Anthony Eden, foreign secretary and Churchill's heir apparent as prime minister. Nineteen-fifty-four would be a triumphant year for this talented, handsome, vain, intensely ambitious man, in large part because of Indochina. His annus mirabilis, one author called it, which is saying something, given that Eden had to that point enjoyed a spectacular political career. Born of landed gentry in County Durham in 1897, Eden survived the trenches of World War I, unlike two of his three brothers and a third of his Eton class. For his actions at the Somme in 1916 he won the Military Cross. In the interwar period, he moved steadily up the greasy pole of politics, becoming in 1935 the youngest foreign secretary ever. Few were surprised by this ascent: Here was a man, after all, who read Persian and Arabic literature in the original and presented an image of effortless suavity—"He had the talent for looking wonderful no matter what he wore," noted one keen observer of his sartorial elegance—bolstered by an unrivaled knowledge of international affairs and diplomatic history. Only much later would many come to realize that the easy charm and unruffled competence were to some extent a facade, that Eden was, in the words of his authorized biographer, "an exceptionally tense, lonely, and shy man."[14]

Eden resigned in 1938 in protest of Neville Chamberlain's policy of appeasement, but he returned to the office during World War II. In 1951, he came back yet again, and the chattering classes predicted he would soon be prime minister. Eden believed it, for Churchill privately told him he'd hand over power in a year. One year became two, and now it was going on three. The waiting was intensely frustrating, not least because Churchill, his zest diminished, chose to focus most of his energy on Eden's own area of responsibility, defense and foreign policy. It didn't help Eden's mood that his own health had been bad for much of 1953, the result of chronic overwork and a botched cholecystectomy in London in April that required several follow-up procedures, one of which almost killed him.

He felt better at Bermuda in December 1953, sunbathing on the beach with Dulles, and as the new year dawned, he was determined to assert himself on the world stage. It would be a momentous year, he sensed, for world politics and for his personal political ambitions; he was right on both counts. Eden's diplomacy in 1954 would confirm the judgment of many—not least Eden himself—that he was a negotiator of the first rank, capable always of thinking two or three steps ahead, of finding openings, of sensing his adversary's vulnerabilities and closing in for the kill. It would confirm the sense of seasoned Eden watchers that he was a man of overweening self-esteem and confidence in his own judgment, one re-

sult of which was to make him reluctant to delegate. And it would confirm that, his recent health problems notwithstanding, he was as prone
to overwork as ever, to long days and short nights that drove him and his
staff to the edge of exhaustion.

Eden gave a hint of the trouble to come with Washington in a cabinet
memorandum late in 1953. He reminded his colleagues of Britain's pragmatic approach to relations with Beijing, and of the decision early on to
extend diplomatic recognition to Mao's government and accept China as
a legitimate member of the great-power club. British policy, he said, was
a combination of containment and compromise, not—as in the case of the
Americans—containment and confrontation. Aggressive Chinese expansion would be resisted, but more generally London's policy rested upon
"acceptance of the facts of the situation, the avoidance of provocation,
gradual progress towards more normal trading and diplomatic relations,
and the need to keep a toe in the door in case divergences between China
and Russia develop and can be exploited." Maintaining good relations
with Beijing would also help London secure its interests in Malaya and
Hong Kong.[15]

Eden therefore came to Berlin fully prepared to agree to a future
great-power meeting that would include China. He knew Dulles would
balk. For the U.S. leadership, Eden warned Churchill, there could be no
question of admitting "the bloody Chinese aggressor into the councils
of peaceful nations." Though he and Dulles had gotten on quite well at
Bermuda in December, Eden had left that meeting troubled by what he
sensed was a growing gulf in Anglo-American relations. The U.S. approach to the matters under discussion at Bermuda had been crude, he
thought, and Eisenhower in particular had been frightening with his casual talk of using nuclear bombs in the Far East and his reference to post-
Stalin Russia as the "same old whore" in a new dress.[16]

On Indochina specifically, Eden's memoirs claim that he arrived in
Berlin convinced of the need for a negotiated solution.[17] That may be
clearer than the truth, for the contemporaneous documentation suggests
he remained, in January 1954, desirous of gaining a turnaround of the
military situation before any settlement. No fan of revolutionary nationalism in the developing world, he would have liked to see Ho Chi Minh's
cause decisively defeated. But Eden was a realist; such an outcome was

unlikely to happen, he knew. From an early point in the conference he expressed a willingness to bring the great powers together to discuss the matter, and he got the cabinet to endorse his view that it would be unwise to oppose a proposal to include China in such a meeting.

Eden's French counterpart, Foreign Minister Georges Bidault, was equivocal. Personally his instinct was to stand firm and to insist that Beijing first give a token of its goodwill, since "it has persisted in contributing to the equipment and training of the Viet Minh troops."[18] He still clung to the belief that French commander Henri Navarre's Operation Atlante, then just under way, could dramatically alter the military picture below the eighteenth parallel in France's favor, and that Dien Bien Phu could deal a crushing blow to Giap's ambitions. The Americans would support him in this hard-line position, he believed.[19] But Bidault also knew that Paris officialdom would expect him to make progress toward ending *la sale guerre*. In the view of most members of Joseph Laniel's center-right coalition, a five-power conference including China seemed likely to hasten this development and therefore should be embraced. French public opinion, meanwhile, was losing faith in the war effort seemingly on a daily basis. A poll carried out during the Berlin meeting found that only 7 percent of respondents favored fighting to keep Indochina. Bidault didn't doubt that there would be uproar, should the government refuse to follow every possible lead for an armistice, including an international conference with China.[20]

Even Charles de Gaulle, whose intransigence in 1945–46 had done so much to start the bloodshed, had given up on military victory in Indochina, Bidault knew. In recent weeks, the general had told numerous associates and reporters that France should disengage from the struggle. "We have no really direct interest in Indochina," de Gaulle informed an American journalist in mid-January. "That is a reality. What is taking place there now is merely a prestige war. Not even the prestige of France is involved anymore. Indochina is of international interest more and more and of French interest less and less. . . . We will regret [leaving] greatly, but we must go."[21]

It all pointed to the prospect of considerable Western disunity when the delegations arrived on January 25 for the start of the conference, held in the interallied building on the Potsdamerstrasse in the American sector of Berlin. No doubt relishing the prospect, Soviet foreign minister Vyacheslav Molotov immediately proposed a meeting including China to discuss "measures for reducing international tension." Dulles objected, insisting several times in the early days that the United States would not take part in a five-power conference, for to do so would mean conversing about world problems with unrepentant aggressors. Molotov refused to be put off, stressing the important role that China, "a great power," could play in lessening world tension. The Russian suggested the meeting could be held in May or June and implied that the agenda could be confined to Korea and Indochina.

There matters might have rested had it not been for Eden, who now cast himself in the role of the honest broker. He received strong support from Churchill, who was keen to meet the Soviets halfway in furtherance of his personal "peace offensive."[22] With progress on the other agenda items—the German question and the matter of a peace treaty for Austria, still left unresolved from World War II—extremely unlikely, both men were eager to gain something, anything, from the weeks and weeks of speechifying in Berlin; an agreement for a five-power meeting seemed the best bet. That such a deal would come despite American objections didn't deter Eden and may have added to his motivation. Dulles's obstreperous refusal to admit China to international society annoyed him, for one thing. More broadly, he resented Britain's standing as the junior partner in the "special relationship," and he felt the (largely unspoken) resentment of one whose adult life had seen the gradual replacement of his nation by the United States as the preeminent force in world affairs. Though intellectually Eden knew that his country was a cash-strapped, declining power, he sought ways to assert her strength and independence, which, among other things, could strengthen the government's as well as his own personal standing with voters at home. Here was such an opportunity.[23]

Eden accordingly embarked on a great personal mission to win an agreement for a five-power meeting, to be convened in May or June at a locale to be determined. He had noticed a chink in the Americans' armor: At a preconference strategy session on January 23, Dulles had allowed that he might be willing to meet with the Chinese concerning one matter, namely Korea, about which many unsettled issues remained. Dulles had

ANTHONY EDEN AND
GEORGES BIDAULT LEAVING
JOHN FOSTER DULLES'S
RESIDENCE DURING THE
BERLIN CONFERENCE,
FEBRUARY 1954.

suggested that Molotov would never accept such a limited agenda, and he was right; the Soviet diplomat initially refused to consider anything other than an "international" agenda. Little by little, however, over a period of almost three weeks, Eden got the two men to come around. Bidault, at once insistent on negotiations and tempted by his dream of making China cease aiding the Viet Minh as the price of her participation, signed on as well and won approval for his preferred venue: Geneva. On February 18, the Berlin conference agreed that "the problem of restoring peace in Indochina will also be discussed at the Conference [on the Korean question], to which representatives of the United States, France, the United Kingdom, the Union of Soviet Socialist Republics, and the Chinese People's Republic and other interested states will be invited."[24]

III

THE FOREIGN SECRETARY HAD ACHIEVED THE SEEMINGLY IMPOS-sible. How had he done it? By persistence and shrewdness—and fortuitous timing. "Eden was quick, he was skillful," an American delegate at the conference later acknowledged admiringly. "His rather languid manner concealed a lively, imaginative, perceptive mind. . . . He had an almost inbred, instinctive effort, in any conflict, in any collision, great or small, to find a compromise solution."[25]

Molotov and Bidault proved the easiest to convince, the former because he got the essentials of what he wanted—a meeting to which his restive Chinese allies were formally invited, and where more than just Korea would be discussed—and the latter because he ultimately saw no choice. The government in which he served would fall if it emerged that he had passed up a great-power conference on Indochina. Dulles was the tough one to crack, immovable in the early sessions and behind closed doors. It wasn't one thing that caused the secretary to change, but several interrelated considerations. He came, first, to see what Bidault and Eden saw: that opposition to Molotov's proposal would bring down the only French government willing to attempt the continued defense of Indochina. Of equal concern, the fall of Laniel would almost certainly kill any chance of gaining French ratification of the European Defense Community, for Laniel's cabinet was more positively inclined toward the scheme than any successor government was likely to be.

A letter home to Eisenhower in the second week hinted at Dulles's agonizing shift: "Last night I urged Bidault to pass over any suggestion of Indochina negotiation, saying that even to initiate discussion put us on slippery ground, and might lead to further decline in morale in Indochina and France. However, he feels that the bottom will fall out of the French home situation unless he does something here to indicate a desire to end [the] Indochina war. I shall do everything here to minimize possible risks, but dare not push Bidault beyond [the] point which he thinks will break his position in France, as he [is] our main reliance for both EDC and Indochina."[26]

Upon his return to Washington, the secretary of state told the National Security Council: "If Bidault had not gone back to Paris with something to show on Indochina, the Laniel government would have fallen at once and would have been replaced by a government which would not only have a mandate to end the war in Indochina on any terms, but also to oppose French ratification of EDC." To Senator Hubert H. Humphrey in executive session, he was blunt: Either the conference proposal would be accepted, or "our influence would have been zero in France, both in relation to Indochina and in relation to the EDC."[27]

"One cannot help wondering," a startled British observer remarked a few days later, "whether even Mr. Dulles did not come to the conclusion in Berlin that future prospects in Indochina were not very rosy and that therefore no opportunity of exploring the possibilities of a negotiated way out should be neglected."[28] This was going too far. Dulles had not changed his mind regarding the stakes in Vietnam, and he was nowhere near seeking a "negotiated way out." His horror at the thought of dealing with Communist regimes remained. He hoped France could hang on militarily until the monsoon rains came, then regroup and be in a stronger position come fall.

Still, there's no doubt Dulles in Berlin showed a degree of flexibility that few in the international community thought he possessed. He was not quite the rigid ideologue of legend. Or at least his rigidity could coexist, paradoxically, with a certain dexterity in everyday conduct. Not even his irritation at Eden for putting him on the spot (he talked badly about the foreign secretary with Bidault, not knowing that the Frenchman was meanwhile saying acid things about him to Eden) dissuaded him.[29] Nor did the certainty that he would take a beating at home.[30] To cover the administration with GOP hard-liners, Dulles secured inclusion in the communiqué of a caveat that the holding of the Geneva meeting should not "be deemed to imply diplomatic recognition in any case where it has not already been accorded." At his demand, it also made no mention of "five powers," no reference to hosts and guests, and it welcomed "other interested states" to attend.

Would that phraseology be enough to satisfy right-wing critics? Upon his return to Washington, Dulles went on the offensive, insisting before the Senate Foreign Relations Committee on February 24 that he had had no option at Berlin but to agree to include Indochina in the upcoming conference, lest the Laniel government fall. But he also guaranteed the lawmakers that the United States "will not go into that conference with any obligation to stay there and will not be bound by anybody's vote other than its own, and we will be in a position to exert a considerable degree of power because of the extent to which the French are dependent, certainly to carry on the struggle, upon our military aid." That evening, in a nationwide television broadcast titled "Report on Berlin," he spoke of the "vital importance" of the struggle waged by French Union forces in Indochina and assured viewers that the wording of the communiqué in no way signified a change in America's China policy.[31]

IV

DULLES UNDERSTOOD, MORE CLEARLY IT SEEMS THAN EITHER BIDAULT or Eden did, that the decision to convene a Geneva conference on Indochina started the clock ticking at Dien Bien Phu. More than they, he worried that the announcement would cause the enemy to intensify his efforts in the valley and elsewhere in order to show the Geneva delegates a flurry of victories, thereby taking the conflict to its climax. The prospect of a peace conference, Dulles warned Bidault on the final day in Germany, increased the Communist desire for a "knock out this season."[32] His concern was justified, though it remains hard to assess the counterfactual question of how things would have gone in the absence of a Berlin deal. Certainly the evidentiary record shows plenty of warning signs for the French prior to the February 18 announcement and plenty of French official optimism afterward. But it also shows that DRV leaders did in fact make battlefield decisions in late February and in March with Geneva firmly in mind. Just as Dulles anticipated, Ho Chi Minh and his colleagues wanted to be in the best possible military position when the diplomats descended on the Swiss lakeside city.

Initially, at least, the Berlin communiqué had little discernible impact on the ground. When French defense minister René Pleven, in the midst of a tour of Indochina, flew into Dien Bien Phu on February 19, he found a garrison brimming with optimism. Everyone, from Colonel de Castries to the lowliest gunner, told him they looked forward to the Viet Minh assault, fearing only, they said, that Giap might abandon the attempt, just as he had done on January 25. This bullish bravado impressed Pleven and his entourage, which included General Paul Ely, the chairman of the Chiefs of Staff Committee, but the sight of the surrounding heights, dominated by enemy troops, filled them with apprehension.[33]

Pleven got a similarly upbeat message on his next stop, in Luang Prabang, which was under direct threat from a renewed Laotian offensive that Giap had launched soon after canceling the Dien Bien Phu attack. With Viet Minh forward elements only thirty miles away, French officers assured Pleven they were ready, and the Royal Laotian government indicated it would remain rather than evacuate, suggesting it believed the defenses were sufficiently robust. Then, on February 24, while Pleven was still in the city, the Viet Minh forces suddenly halted, withdrawing soon afterward in the direction of Dien Bien Phu. Some immediately connected the move (rightly, we now know) to the Berlin announcement and Giap's desire to score a smashing victory prior to the Geneva gathering.

In his reports to Laniel and to the National Defense Committee, Pleven duly noted these expressions of optimism, but his conclusions were sober. He had set out to determine if time was on the side of France or the Viet Minh, and everything he saw indicated the latter. He considered it doubtful that General Giap would be able to inflict a decisive defeat on the Expeditionary Corps so long as China did not intervene directly and the Viet Minh lacked airpower. In southern Vietnam and in the Red River Delta, the French still held strong cards. All the same, he continued, the balance of forces was not shifting in France's direction, and Navarre would likely have little to show for his efforts in the present campaign season except increasingly heavy casualties. Notably, Operation Atlante was in February running into all kinds of difficulty. Beijing's aid to the DRV was growing each day and would present more and more problems. The VNA, meanwhile, showed emerging promise but would not become truly effective until its men felt they had something to fight and die for, something other than merely French interests. As for the Bao Dai government, it inspired little support among ordinary Vietnamese.[34]

On Dien Bien Phu, Pleven was even more blunt. Whereas the garrison might look forward with eagerness to the showdown, he said, "Personally, I do not look forward to it."[35]

It all pointed to one inescapable conclusion, as far as the defense minister was concerned: France must use every effort at Geneva to gain an acceptable settlement to the war. Prior to the conference, she should press for military advantage and should work hard to prepare the VNA to be able to take over from the Expeditionary Corps—remote though the latter prospect might be.[36] She should also reject bilateral Franco–Viet Minh talks, since such negotiations would be seen as betraying Bao Dai and his supporters. But Geneva, as an international meeting where the

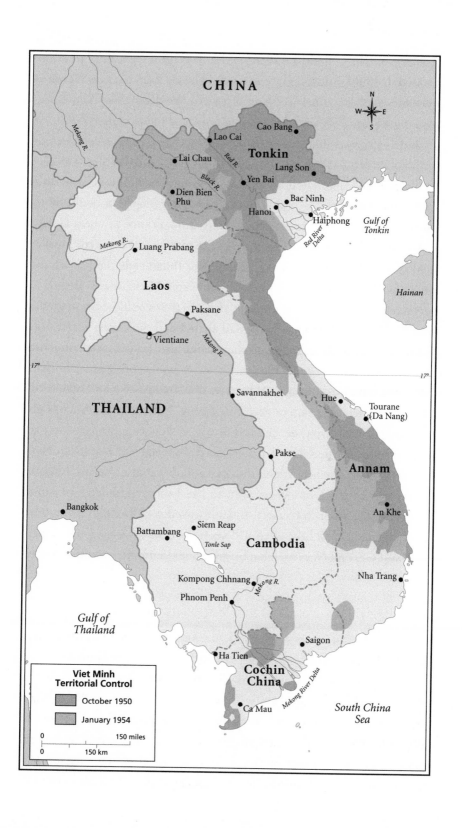

CHINA

N
W   E
S

Mekong R.

Lai Chau

Lao Cai

Cao Bang

Red R.

Tonkin

Lang Son

Black R.

Yen Bai

Dien Bien
Phu

Bac Ninh

Hanoi

Haiphong

Red River Delta

*Gulf of
Tonkin*

Mekong R.

Luang Prabang

Laos

Hainan

Paksane

Vientiane

Mekong R.

17°   17°

THAILAND

Savannakhet

Hue

Tourane
(Da Nang)

Pakse

Annam

Bangkok

An Khe

Battambang

Siem Reap

Tonle Sap

Cambodia

Kompong Chhnang

Mekong R.

Nha Trang

Phnom Penh

Saigon

*Gulf of
Thailand*

Ha Tien

Cochin
China

Mekong River Delta

Ca Mau

*South China
Sea*

**Viet Minh
Territorial Control**

October 1950

January 1954

0   150 miles

0   150 km

Associated States could be represented, was an opportunity that must be seized. The resulting agreement would be far from perfect, Pleven acknowledged, but neither would it necessarily be disastrous. Above all, it would get France off a road that could only lead to her ruin.

Bidault agreed that direct talks with Ho Chi Minh were out of the question, at least at present, but he was less enchanted with other parts of Pleven's message. He told aides that the military outlook was rosier now than at the start of the year and that Dien Bien Phu could be the setting for a glorious victory that would allow France to enter Geneva in a position of strength. The fortress, he and Laniel insisted, must be held at all costs.[37] Once at the conference, Bidault planned to use the threat of American intervention to extract from Moscow and Beijing an agreement to cease backing the Viet Minh. If they could be persuaded to abandon Ho Chi Minh, as Stalin had abandoned the Greek leader Markos in 1947, Bidault reasoned, France could secure a compromise settlement on favorable terms. Or at least it seems he reasoned as such—with Bidault, it's hard to be sure, so torn was he, in author Jean Lacouture's words, "between his rancor and his dreams."[38] Neither the Soviets nor the Chinese had given the slightest hint that they were prepared to play his game, so one may wonder what he really believed. But he stuck to his determined posture. When India's leader Jawaharlal Nehru, hitherto largely silent on the Indochina war, in late February issued a proposal for a cease-fire prior to Geneva, Bidault waved it off (with Washington's encouragement).[39] There were still several weeks left before the conference, and General Navarre must be given maximum time to do damage.

V

IN LIGHT OF WHAT WAS TO COME, IT SEEMS PREPOSTEROUS, THIS idea that France could appreciably strengthen her military position—and therefore her diplomatic position—before Geneva. Yet Bidault was far from alone in believing it. As we have seen, at Dien Bien Phu de Castries struck a tone of serene certitude in these weeks, seemingly out of conviction. Giap, he reasoned, had wisely avoided battle on January 25, knowing his forces could not prevail, and since then the garrison had only become stronger. Sure, Giap had shelled different points in the valley on a regular basis since late January, but these were desultory bombardments, in the late afternoon or early evening, that seldom did real damage; to de Castries, they merely confirmed that the Viet Minh were outmatched. Piroth, the artillery commander, puzzled over his failure to locate the enemy's guns but nevertheless exuded confidence, even refusing to dig his own guns in to provide shelter for their crews. Who could hit them, after all? Much better to have open emplacements, so as to be able to fire at all angles of the compass. Piroth would go no further than to place his guns in pits with sandbag walls to protect against mortar shells.

Lieutenant Colonel Jules Gaucher, commander of both the central sector of the camp and of the Thirteenth Demi-Brigade at Béatrice, wrote to his wife in February 22: "For now, the Viets leave us almost in peace. This is a decisive period. . . . One has to ask oneself if the Viets are really going to attack us. We have created such a defensive system that it would be a big mouthful to swallow, and that gives pause to the gentlemen opposite, who have already countermanded the order to attack [on January 25]. But I still believe that for the sake of prestige they'll have to come, though we are already causing them heavy loss with our artillery and aircraft." In another letter, this one dated March 5, the colonel expressed no fear at the prospect of battle: "Things are still calm, but they tell us that a brawl is coming soon. Is it true? It's true they must wish to do something spectacular before Geneva. But I believe that if they do, they'll break their teeth."[40]

Visitors to the camp—and there was a constant stream of them in February and early March, as there had been in January; typically they arrived from Hanoi in the morning and departed in the late afternoon—often got caught up in the fervor. The bustling activity, with thousands of men digging and building, hauling and stacking, against the constant droning of C-47s landing and taking off, was reassuring even to the most seasoned military tourist. U.S. General John "Iron Mike" O'Daniel, for example, though troubled by the positioning of some of the strongpoints and the seeming weakness of the bunkers, declared that the base could "withstand any kind of attack the Viet Minh are capable of launching" and summarized the military situation as one where "the French are in no danger of suffering a major military reverse. On the contrary they are gaining strength and confidence in their ability to fight the war to a successful conclusion."[41] In Saigon, Navarre told Ambassador Heath privately and journalists publicly that he'd be disappointed if no battle developed at Dien Bien Phu, for it was there he saw a golden opportunity to inflict a major defeat on the enemy. The camp, he told Heath on February 21, was "a veritable jungle Verdun" that would cause huge Viet Minh losses and would not fall. The Communists had not achieved their major objectives in the current campaign season, he reminded reporters four days later, having failed to take Dien Bien Phu and having seen their offensive against Luang Prabang blocked.[42]

Most of the scribes were skeptical. Robert Guillain of *Le Monde,* who had just published a series of probing articles on Dien Bien Phu, after traveling by rail through Thailand and Laos to reach Hanoi, reportedly said to some colleagues after Navarre left the room: "Ours is a wonderful profession. The Commander in Chief has just explained everything to us dogmatically, and I, a humble journalist, would stake my life on it that he is either making a terrible mistake or lying to us. I would be ready to swear that the situation he has described has nothing in common with reality. What the Commander in Chief lacks, like his entourage, is our fresh, unbiased view of events."[43]

Graham Greene came for a visit too. Once again wintering in Saigon, he was on assignment to write a piece on Indochina for *The Sunday Times.* He flew into Dien Bien Phu early on a Tuesday morning and stayed twenty-four hours. A guide gave him a tour of the camp, whereupon de Castries hosted him for lunch at the senior officers' mess. The commander, Greene recalled, "had the nervy histrionic features of an old-time actor," and the novelist observed with fascination de Castries's reaction when artillery commander Piroth and another officer mentioned the Na San evacuation of the previous year. "Be silent," de Castries thundered, hitting the table with his fist. "I will not have Na San mentioned in this mess. Na San was a defensive post. This is an offensive one." Puzzled, Greene asked his guide after lunch what de Castries had meant by "offensive post." The officer scoffed at the notion. What we need for an offensive base, he told the Briton, is not a fleet of tanks but a thousand mules.[44]

For Guillain, Greene, and other outside analysts, it was not merely that Dien Bien Phu was much more vulnerable than official optimism allowed, or that the security situation in the Red River Delta remained dire (even though Giap had withdrawn four divisions from that area), or that Operation Atlante to the south was going less well than advertised, or that formerly pacified areas of Cochin China were increasingly under threat.[45] These military matters, while important, were not ultimately going to decide the war. The real nub of the problem was political. France, though she had already granted more independence to Bao Dai than Ho Chi Minh in 1945–46 ever asked for, had not convinced the mass of Vietnamese that she would make good on her promise of full sovereignty. Partly for that reason, and partly because of its own dithering and infighting and corruption, the Bao Dai government enjoyed little popular support. In a December shakeup, Bao Dai had inserted his cousin Buu Loc as prime minister in place of the Francophile Nguyen Van Tam, but it had made little difference, perhaps because Bao Dai himself seemed more and more removed from the struggle. When he wasn't ensconced at his villa on the Côte d'Azur, he looked as if he should be. "How do you think it feels getting oneself killed in the jungle," complained a young graduate of the École militaire inter-armes in Dalat, "for that man who comes up here to swear us in wearing a Riviera suit, a polka-dot tie, and inch-thick crepe soles?"[46]

On March 8 began yet another round of negotiations, this one in Paris, between the French government and Bao Dai's representatives. Back and forth they went on what constituted full independence, on what sort of association the two countries ought to have. A French observer spelled out his side's interpretation of the Vietnamese position: "Having promised independence to the Associated States, we would have to leave Indo-China even if we won a total victory. So what are we fighting for, and for whom?" To which the Vietnamese replied: And what are *we* currently fighting for but to preserve your inequitable system?[47]

The questions still hung in the air a few days later when the anticipated yet still shocking news came in: Dien Bien Phu was under attack.

VI

IT BEGAN LATE IN THE AFTERNOON OF MARCH 13, A SATURDAY. A distant thunder sounded from the hills. Then, within seconds, the ear-splitting noise of high explosives shook the earth in the camp, as 105mm and 75mm howitzers and 120mm mortars rained down from above.[48] Strongpoint Béatrice, which for some days had been completely surrounded by enemy approach works, was the initial target, in part because of its crucial location and in part because it was manned by a first-rate unit, the Third Battalion of the Thirteenth Legion Demi-Brigade. "Bunker after bunker, trench after trench, collapsed, burying men and weapons," one surviving legionnaire at Béatrice said of that first artillery barrage. At 5:10, two Viet Minh regiments from the 312th Division leaped from their approach trenches barely two hundred yards from Béatrice. Savage fighting ensued. At 6:15, Major Paul Pégot, the legionnaire commander, called for artillery fire on areas just in front of his final line of resistance. At 6:30, a Viet Minh artillery round hit the Béatrice command post, killing Pégot and his entire staff. Soon thereafter another shell tore open the chest and ripped the arms off Lieutenant Colonel Gaucher. He died within minutes. (The previous day he had written his wife of the impending attack: "Finally the long wait will be over and hopefully it will end in a positive way.")[49]

Their two leaders gone, the men at Béatrice fought desperately to survive, but it was hopeless. At 10:30, the radio of the Tenth Company fell silent. At 11:00, the Eleventh Company radioed in that the enemy was just outside the command bunker. Shortly after midnight, the last radio went dead. Béatrice had fallen, with the French losing 550 men out of 750. Viet Minh dead totaled 600, with another 1,200 wounded.

The French initially fared better at Gabrielle. That first night the 312th Division made two separate attempts to take the strongpoint; both were repelled. Anne-Marie likewise held fast in the face of three separate assaults, though at heavy cost. At daybreak on the fourteenth, an impromptu truce was agreed to, allowing both sides to collect their dead and wounded. The entire garrison was stunned by the previous night's events. Gaucher was dead, Béatrice in enemy hands. The supposedly invincible Thirteenth Demi-Brigade, which had fought Rommel's Afrika Korps to a standstill at Bir Hakeim, had seen one of its battalions overrun—in a few hours. To make matters worse, the attack had not even been a surprise—radio intercepts had picked up both the date and the hour of the attack. Just as the French had always anticipated, the battle had begun when it was still light enough for Viet Minh artillery to find its targets, but too late for Bearcat fighters based at Dien Bien Phu to intervene effectively. For many days, moreover, enemy movements had made clear that Béatrice and Gabrielle would be the initial targets. (See map on p. 526.)

What de Castries and his subordinates did not know, however, was the full extent of enemy preparations. Since that crushing disappointment seven weeks earlier, when their commander in chief had canceled the attack mere hours before it was set to start, Viet Minh soldiers and porters had been hard at work, day after bruising day. General Giap ordered that artillery positions be better prepared, that more ammunition and supplies be on hand, and that overwhelming supremacy in men and firepower be established; only then would the operation commence. Huge effort was expended installing 75mm and 105mm guns in casements sunk into the forward slope of the hills surrounding the basin. It was riskier than the conventional deployment on the reverse slope, but it promised a bigger payoff: The gunners would be able to fire "down the tube" at the French targets. Many guns were placed singly in deep and narrow casements, thus preserving the integrity of the rock as protection from aerial attack and artillery fire. If done right, only the cannon's mouth protruded when engaged. To draw enemy fire and air attacks, dummy guns were built and positioned. All the while, artillery officers and their Chinese advisers carefully mapped the French defenses and determined the coordinates of specific targets. Periodic shelling of the garrison in February and early March allowed gunners to fine-tune their targeting.[50]

Simultaneously, Giap ordered the digging of a vast trench system around the camp. The shovel now became the prime weapon, as hundreds of men toiled day and night to dig trenches and tunnels, often under fire and often advancing only five or six yards in a day. By early March, French listening posts were reporting the disconcerting sound of thumps and scrapes by shovels close to the camp's perimeter. By March 12, the workers could be seen in broad daylight, brazenly digging under the protection of lookouts. By then, the trenches had snaked their way toward the fortress, in one observer's words, "like the tentacles of some determined, earthbound devilfish."[51]

Anxious to reduce the enemy's air capabilities at the source, Giap ordered daring commando raids on French airfields in the Red River Delta. In early February, a handful of Viet Minh soldiers crawled through the drainage pipes undetected and entered the Do Son air base south of Haiphong, where they proceeded under the cover of darkness to destroy five Dakotas and one hundred thousand liters of fuel. On February 20, after some American air force technicians had arrived at the base (part of the two-hundred-man contingent authorized by Eisenhower in late January), it was discovered that infiltrators had contaminated the fuel stocks by pouring water in the tanks. On March 4, commandos entered Gia Lam air base and placed gasoline satchels wired with explosives under ten Dakotas, destroying all of them. Despite elaborate defenses at Gia Lam, all but one of the infiltrators got away. Three days after that, Viet Minh units destroyed four B-26 bombers and six Morane spotter planes at Cat Bi airfield, home to another contingent of uniformed U.S. mechanics. On March 10, Viet Minh guns shelled the Dien Bien Phu airstrip for the first time, and on the twelfth, the eve of the attack, a handful of commandos slipped past the garrison's defenses to destroy some of the steel grilling of the airstrip—and, while they were at it, to confirm specific target locations for the Viet Minh artillery.[52]

Giap's attack plan involved three phases. In the first phase, the outlying posts of Béatrice, Gabrielle, and Anne-Marie would be overrun. Viet Minh forces would then close in on the main positions crowded around the airstrip and the camp's headquarters. The final phase would involve an attack on whatever remained, including the other outlying strongpoint, Isabelle in the south. To undertake the operation, Giap had at his disposal the PAVN 308th and the 312th Divisions, both complete, as well as two regiments of the 316th, one regiment of the 304th, plus the 351st Heavy Division. The 308th was in the hills to the east and the 312th to the north. The 316th, recently returned from its incursion into Laos, waited in the background for the time being, while the 304th occupied the heights to the east of Isabelle.[53]

Nothing was left to chance. "We had observed everything and made a minute study of the terrain several nights before the attack, using models too," a Viet Minh officer later told a French interviewer. "Every evening, we came up and took the opportunity to cut barbed wire and remove mines. Our jumping-off point was moved up to only two hundred yards from the peaks of Béatrice, and to our surprise your artillery didn't know where we were. Finally, some Tai deserters had given us a lot of information."[54]

In Giap's mind, a great deal would hinge on the outcome of the initial attack on March 13. Victory on Béatrice would galvanize his men and prepare them to handle the inevitable setbacks later on, while conversely French morale would likely plummet if a strongpoint were lost right at the start. Ceaselessly Giap and his lieutenants hammered home the message to their men that they could win, that they would win; only an early victory, he knew, would really convince them. He had taken to heart the veteran warrior's maxim: "Always win the first fight."[55]

VII

COLONEL DE CASTRIES, EVIDENTLY HIMSELF A BELIEVER IN THE maxim, was despondent on the morning after Béatrice succumbed, his mood matching the heavy gray clouds overhead. Already there were murmurings about his performance the previous night, about his tentative messages to the strongpoints, his decision to remain holed up in his command post the entire time, his failure to launch a vigorous counterattack. Now he had to fashion a plan, and fast, for the onslaught would resume within hours. One key strongpoint was gone, and hundreds of men with it. The airstrip had been rendered more or less unusable, pitted with holes and bristling with pieces of broken grids like the teeth of a saw. Chief gunner Piroth, meanwhile, had used up six thousand rounds of 105mm howitzer shells, or about a quarter of his total stock, in trying to answer Giap's furious and deadly artillery barrage.

Piroth's demeanor was worrying. Hitherto the picture of steadfastness, of breezy self-assurance regarding what his guns could accomplish, the forty-seven-year-old had become a morose automaton overnight. He seemed to be in trance, several officers later recalled, unable to comprehend what was happening. De Castries was concerned enough that he asked the chaplain to keep an eye on him. Later in the day, Colonel Pierre Langlais, Gaucher's successor as commander of the central sector, happened by Piroth and saw the vacant stare.

"Is everything all right?" Langlais asked.

"We're done for," the artillery chief murmured. "I've told de Castries he must put a stop to it all. We're heading for a massacre, and it's my fault."[56]

That night the Viet Minh resumed the attack. Heavy fighting continued throughout the night on Gabrielle, defended by the Fifth Battalion of the Seventh Algerian Regiment and a heavy mortar company of the Legion. The Viet Minh gained several footholds, but the tenacious Algerians just managed to hang on to part of the position. Early on March 15, the French launched a counterattack, using a new parachute battalion (the Fifth Vietnamese) that had been air-dropped in on the fourteenth, to restore the situation on Gabrielle. But the action, though supported by seven Chaffee tanks, was undermanned and poorly planned and had to be abandoned in the face of major losses. Gabrielle too was gone, with the loss for the Algerian battalion of 540 dead, 220 captured, and 114 escaped. The Viet Minh counted 1,000 dead. Heavy shelling by Viet Minh guns had made a shambles of French earthworks, not only in the northern sector but in the center too. As in the worst days of Verdun in 1916, enemy shells ground the whole top layer of soil into fine sand and caused bunkers and trenches to implode.[57] French defensive fire, meanwhile, though more effective than on the first night, still had not proven equal to the task.

Colonel Piroth fell into extreme despair. "I'm completely dishonored," he muttered to a fellow officer. "I have guaranteed de Castries that the enemy artillery couldn't touch us—but now we're going to lose the battle."[58] Perhaps too he remembered his dismissive assertion to Marc Jacquet on January 26: "I have more guns than I need." Sometime that morning of March 15, Piroth slipped away to his dugout. Being one-armed, he could not charge his pistol. He lay down on his cot, pulled the pin from a grenade with his teeth, and clutched it to his chest. De Castries initially tried to keep the circumstances of the death secret, reporting to Hanoi that Piroth was killed by enemy action. But news of the suicide leaked out and soon spread from one unit to the next.[59]

The morgue to which Piroth's body was taken had long since filled to capacity. Scores of corpses lay jumbled together, on stretchers or on bare ground. In the surgery, Drs. Grauwin and Gindrey, stripped to the waist,

TWO MEMBERS OF THE SIXTH COLONIAL PARACHUTE
BATTALION RUN FOR COVER AT STRONGPOINT ISABELLE
ON MARCH 16, THREE DAYS INTO THE BATTLE.

had been operating almost nonstop for two nights and days. Within hours on the night of March 13–14, the hospital, located near the camp's headquarters complex, had been crammed with wounded, many of them needing urgent attention to major trauma. French, legionnaires, Algerians, Africans, and Vietnamese; officers and men—all waited their turn in the cramped space, amid the stench of vomit and blood and voided bowels and bladders. The surgeons fought to save limbs and avoid the onset of gangrene, but for some it was already too late: That first night Grauwin and Gindrey carried out fourteen amputations. At one point, Grauwin complained that the battalion aid posts were sending him all their wounded rather than trying to treat them—until he learned that they too were overflowing. Some ambulance drivers had even risked the dangerous journey all the way up from Isabelle.[60]

March 15 was a low point for the men of the garrison, for—astonishing though it may seem in hindsight—their spirits in the days thereafter began to lift, or at least stopped sinking. There was a sense that they had weathered the worst of the storm. Even after Anne-Marie fell on the seventeenth (the Tai battalion serving as the backbone of its defense having deserted), many French officers saw no reason why victory could not come in the end. Giap might have gained effective control of the northern sector, but he had suffered enormous losses in doing so, with as many as 2,500 dead in the mass frontal assaults of the first days. Surely he could not keep that up. His success against the northern strongpoints, moreover, would be harder to replicate against the heart of the garrison's defenses in the center.

And indeed, Giap had his own problems, the high number of battlefield dead being only one. His ammunition was running low, as was medicine for the wounded. His units had only one full-fledged surgeon, Dr. Ton That Tung, who with his team of six assistants had responsibility for some fifty thousand men. Head injuries due to lack of steel helmets were a particular problem, and the situation was not made easier by the swarms of yellow flies that laid eggs in the wounds. The infirmary was infested with ticks, and there was an acute shortage of beds. The feeder roads built through the jungle in December and January, deteriorating under the French aerial attacks and the rains, were kept open, but passage was often excruciatingly slow, with high casualties among sappers, truck drivers, and laborers. Especially deadly were the latest American-supplied antipersonnel bombs. As the first phase of Giap's three-phase battle plan drew to a close on March 17, his political officers accordingly took up the task of maintaining troop morale. Harangues and patriotic speeches hammered on the twin points: No lives had been given in vain, and victory must be achieved at any cost. Declared Giap in his special message to the troops: "His [enemy] morale is affected, his difficulties are numerous, but don't underestimate him. If we underestimate him, we'll lose the battle."[61]

In Hanoi and Saigon, meanwhile, Cogny's and Navarre's staffs were left reeling by the previous days' developments, as were High Commissioner Maurice Dejean and his aides. They now began to whisper the impermissible: that all might be lost. The comparative lull in fighting that began at Dien Bien Phu on March 17 was welcome news, as was the profession of optimism on the part of some commanders in the camp, but overall the situation looked extremely grim. Only the rapid intensification of air support to the garrison, together with a breakthrough in Operation Atlante, Navarre concluded, could avert out-and-out disaster.[62] The airstrip had been rendered more or less unusable, so now the imperative was parachuting supplies and men, and somehow evacuating wounded. In addition, it would be essential to attack the enemy's rear, harassing his supply lines, cutting his communications, neutralizing his artillery batteries, and drawing a ring of death around the garrison using napalm. Dejean immediately approached the U.S. embassy in Saigon for the top-priority dispatch of more B-26 bombers, Bearcat fighters, and C-47 transports. He also asked for American authorization to use the borrowed C-119s—with French crews—for the "massive use of napalm."[63]

The requests were under consideration in Washington when a high-profile French visitor arrived for consultations with senior U.S. officials. It was chief of staff of the armed forces Paul Ely, France's highest active officer, who only a few weeks earlier had accompanied René Pleven on his tour of Indochina. Important though that trip had been, this one would be even more so.[64] For it would set in motion the most intensive period of Franco-American and Anglo-American deliberations on Indochina since the outbreak of war seven-plus years earlier. For more than a month the discussions would last, and they would reveal deep fissures in relations among the three Western allies as they debated the most pressing question of all: Should the United States, either alone or in concert with Britain and other allies, intervene directly in the war?

CHAPTER 19

AMERICA WANTS IN

LITTLE DID ANYONE IN WASHINGTON KNOW THAT WHEN GENERAL Paul Ely's plane touched down at National Airport on Saturday morning, March 20, 1954, after a fourteen-hour transatlantic flight, it marked the start of the most intensive period of American policy making on Indochina, a period that would last more than a month and would take the nation to the brink of war. Allied military leaders were always descending on the American capital, and if this wasn't quite a routine visit—Ely was his country's chief active military officer, and his forces faced a serious predicament in Vietnam—neither was his arrival greeted with a great deal of anticipation in a city where preponderant attention was focused on the Army-McCarthy hearings about to begin. News of the Viet Minh attack on Dien Bien Phu had filtered in and was a source of concern, but hopes remained high that the French could withstand the attack and that, regardless, the battle in remote Tonkin would not be decisive. When the NSC convened on March 18, President Eisenhower did not exhibit any particular urgency about Dien Bien Phu, even after CIA director Allen Dulles reported the agency's assessment that the fortress had only a fifty-fifty chance of holding out. The soldier-president noted that France had air supremacy and napalm, as well as heavily fortified positions, which meant that the Viet Minh's two-to-one numerical superiority mattered little. Director Dulles did not disagree and said the pessimistic French reports from Saigon might be a ploy to exaggerate the extent of their ultimate victory.[1]

If anyone did see Ely's visit as a potential watershed moment, it was Admiral Arthur C. Radford, the chairman of the Joint Chiefs of Staff—that is, Ely's American counterpart. An Asia-firster in the mold of MacArthur who had an abiding faith in the efficacy of airpower, Radford saw Dien Bien Phu as both an impending disaster and an opportunity: as the potential setting of France's symbolic defeat in the war, and as a chance for the United States to strike a blow against the real menace in the region, the People's Republic of China. The admiral would be a principal player on Indochina in the weeks to come, as the lead advocate of direct U.S. intervention in Vietnam, with airpower and if necessary with ground troops. On March 19, the day before Ely's arrival, he met with General Jean Valluy, the former commander in chief in Indochina who now was chief of the French military mission and French member of the NATO standing group in Washington. Valluy had just returned from Paris, and he told Radford that Ely would bring a sobering message: Paris authorities had concluded that victory could not be achieved in 1954 or 1955 and that France could carry on the fight into 1956 only if the United States contributed military forces to the campaign.[2]

On Saturday morning, as snow flurries dusted the city, Radford went to the White House for a ninety-minute off-the-record meeting on Indochina with Eisenhower and the Dulles brothers. Though no notes were taken, Radford must have relayed Valluy's comments. From there, the admiral went to meet Ely's plane, and that evening he hosted a small stag dinner at his home in the Frenchman's honor, attended also by Allen Dulles and Vice President Nixon and a few others. A graduate of Saint-Cyr and a veteran of both world wars, the gaunt, leathery Ely knew Washington well: Before becoming chief of staff, he had been the French member of NATO's standing group on military strategy, which convened in the U.S. capital. On this night, the subject of direct American involvement in the war apparently did not arise, but Ely acknowledged that Dien Bien Phu might fall, leading to a further deterioration of French morale. The garrison's fate was actually not crucial in military terms, he said, for France still held the advantage in the two major deltas in Vietnam, but psychologically a great deal hinged on the outcome in the basin.

In meetings with U.S. officials over the following days, Ely asked for twenty-five additional B-26 bombers and American volunteers to fly them, as well as eight hundred parachutes required for the continued support by air of the forces at Dien Bien Phu. Eisenhower approved the requests and did his best to buck up French morale. While posing for photographers after an Oval Office meeting on the morning of March 22, the president was heard to remark to Ely that things sometimes had looked bleak for the Allies during World War II, "but we won in the end and we will win again." Radford chimed in: "The French are going to win. It is a fight that is going to be finished with our help."[3]

It was a congenial start to Ely's visit, and he no doubt expected more of the same when he arrived at Foggy Bottom the next day for a session with Secretary of State John Foster Dulles. Not only was Dulles widely perceived in the mid-1950s as the prime architect of American foreign policy; he had also made clear his fervent desire to prevent a Viet Minh victory in Indochina. But the secretary was notably cautious on this day, refusing to be drawn into a discussion of what Washington would do if China sent aircraft into the war. Before any such decision could be reached, he told Ely, several factors would have to be examined, and it

PRESIDENT EISENHOWER RECEIVES GENERAL ELY (MIDDLE) AND
ADMIRAL RADFORD IN THE OVAL OFFICE, MARCH 22, 1954.

was premature for him even to venture an opinion. U.S. prestige would be involved with any move to intervene, and thus extreme care had to be taken. Certainly the United States would insist on playing a larger role in war planning and training of the VNA than was currently the case, and she would expect a greater French commitment to granting full independence to the Associated States.[4]

Dulles maintained his careful line in a meeting with Eisenhower on the morning of March 24 and in a subsequent telephone conversation with Radford. The United States should not intervene, he told both men, unless Paris provided concrete assurances that the two governments could work well together. Any commitments would have far-reaching implications, and the administration should not move without good answers to crucial questions, concerning not only Indochina but France's status as a key player in the West. Significantly, the president and the JCS chairman seemed prepared to move farther, faster. Eisenhower agreed with Dulles that political preconditions had to be met prior to a major U.S. intervention in Vietnam, but he added that he would "not wholly exclude the possibility of a single strike, if it were almost certain to produce decisive results."[5]

Radford, for his part, engaged in hours of private talks with Ely and even persuaded the general to remain in Washington an extra day so they could properly examine the various exigencies. The results of this final meeting, which took place on March 26, remain unclear, but they would be the subject of intense controversy in the months and years to come. The agreed record of the session said they discussed potential responses to a Chinese aerial intervention in the war, but the conversation ranged also to the specific military assistance Washington might provide to the beleaguered garrison at Dien Bien Phu. Both men knew of a plan— code-named Vulture (Vautour)—conceived by U.S. and French officers in Saigon, involving massive nighttime attacks on Viet Minh positions surrounding the basin by U.S. carrier-based aircraft as well as B-29s from Clark Air Base in the Philippines. Some 350 planes could be over the valley with two days notice, the American said. Ely later claimed that Radford strongly supported this plan and intimated that he could overcome Dulles's reservations and gain the president's approval. Radford admitted only that he had told Ely that American planes could be over the valley within two days of a formal request. He never made any promises, he insisted, and emphasized that higher authorities would have to make the final decision.[6]

Probably at least some miscommunication occurred. The two chose not to use an interpreter for this final session and were barely conversant in each other's language. The Frenchman may also have heard what he wanted to hear, reading more into the JCS chairman's assertions than he should have, and confusing American capability with American intent. Yet in all likelihood, as one judicious historian of the episode has concluded, "Ely received the impression that Radford intended."[7] The admiral personally favored using airpower at Dien Bien Phu and more broadly sought expanded U.S. involvement in the war; he had even at times advocated the use of atomic weapons against China. Aware that Ely had been disappointed in Dulles's words, Radford may well have wanted to buck him up, to prevent any further diminution in the French military's will to continue. And besides, Radford might well have told himself, wasn't it official U.S. policy, as articulated in NSC-5405 and in countless other documents, to prevent a Viet Minh victory? Hadn't President Eisenhower himself, back in January, fully shared Radford's position that American airpower might have to be used? What was Vulture but an affirmation of those twin views?[8]

Just the day before, on March 25, in an NSC meeting that focused heavily on the war, Eisenhower had provided additional grist for Radford's mill. To Secretary of Defense Charles Wilson's suggestion that one might "forget about Indochina for a while and concentrate on the effort to get the remaining free nations of Southeast Asia in some kind of condition to resist Communist aggression against themselves," Eisenhower was unequivocal. "The collapse of Indochina," he shot back, "would produce a chain reaction which would result in the fall of all Southeast Asia to the Communists." A Viet Minh victory would be a disaster, and it was necessary to contemplate new measures to prevent it. Accordingly, the president went on, "this might be the moment to explore with the Congress what support could be anticipated in the event that it seemed desirable to intervene in Indochina." Congress, he declared, was the key: Lawmakers "would have to be in on any move by the United States to intervene in Indochina. It was simply academic to think otherwise."[9]

Radford was in the room when Ike uttered those words, and he grasped the implications. The president of the United States had just said that the fall of Indochina would be a calamitous development and that he was contemplating expanded U.S. involvement to keep this from occurring. Congress would have to be on board prior to any intervention, Eisenhower had made clear, but the JCS chairman could be forgiven for thinking that such backing would be forthcoming, no matter how distasteful many lawmakers might find the prospect of another Asian war so soon after Korea. Few of them, he could sensibly conclude, would ultimately be prepared to stand in the president's way. Little wonder if Radford made certain assurances about American steadfastness to Ely the following day.

Had Radford known of John Foster Dulles's comments at dinner on March 25, he would have been further emboldened. The secretary of state, who had also witnessed Eisenhower's outburst before the NSC earlier that day and seemed to have shifted his stance somewhat in response, told Australia's ambassador in Washington, Percy Spender, a close personal friend, that Vietnam was too important to leave to the French. The Laniel government did not appreciate the stakes in the struggle and seemed inclined to go into Geneva in a vacillating frame of mind. Some way simply had to be found to make the French hold on militarily until the start of the monsoon season brought its annual respite.[10]

II

IN THE FINAL DAYS OF MARCH, AS THE BATTLE RAGED ON IN DIEN Bien Phu, the administration thus began to prepare congressional and public opinion for the possibility of direct American intervention in Indochina. As *The New York Times* reported on March 28, a public education offensive was under way, led by Dulles, to explain to the public "what is at stake in Indochina."[11] According to Richard Rovere in *The New Yorker*, Dulles had undertaken "one of the boldest campaigns of political suasion ever undertaken by an American statesman," in which congressmen, journalists, and television personalities of all stripes were being "rounded up in droves and escorted to lectures and briefings" on the crucial importance of achieving victory in Vietnam. Should Indochina be "lost," the color charts showed that Communist influence would radiate outward in a semicircle from Indochina to Thailand, Burma, and Malaya, and far to the south to Indonesia. The briefing officers also listed the raw materials that would fall into Soviet and Chinese hands and be denied forever to the West, and they warned darkly that an American failure here likely would cause anti-Communist resistance to falter throughout Asia, from India to Japan. The secretary of state, Rovere wrote, was represented in the briefings as believing that "we should not flinch at doing anything that is needed to prevent a Communist victory," including, if necessary, committing American ground forces.[12]

Operation Vulture per se was thus not the issue in this public education effort: A large-scale one-off air attack to save the Dien Bien Phu fortress was but one possible form of intervention and not perhaps the preferred option. (Even advocates wondered if the hour had not passed for such an operation.) The aim, rather, was to test the waters more generally, to gauge the likely response on Capitol Hill and beyond to the use in Vietnam of American military force, in whatever scenario and to whatever extent.

Explicit congressional authorization would be required. Eisenhower had made that clear. He had only slim majorities in both houses, after all (48–47–1 in the Senate, 221–213–1 in the House), and he could scarcely depend on Republicans to remain unified. In the upper house, especially, the debate over Joseph McCarthy's sensational charge that the army had covered up alleged foreign espionage activities had badly split the GOP caucus. More generally, Republicans lacked a consensus on foreign policy and on how far to go to check Communist expansion in Asia. The right wing of the party was unreliable; Majority Leader William Knowland of California, for example, expressed equal distaste for sitting down at the bargaining table with Communists (Geneva, he declared, could be a "Far Eastern Munich") and for sending U.S. forces to rescue the French. The Democrats, meanwhile, who had by and large supported administration foreign policy through 1953, were in a restive mood as winter turned to spring. Remembering well the GOP's attacks on Truman for his unilateral decision to send American troops to Korea in 1950, some now said they were not eager to rally to the aid of a Republican president contemplating a similar move.

A centerpiece of the administration's public education campaign was John Foster Dulles's "United Action Speech" (as it came to be known), delivered before the Overseas Press Club in New York City on March 29. The secretary, following his usual custom, drafted it himself, with input from aides as well as congressional figures—lest they "say they were not advised." Eisenhower too went over it carefully. It was important to get both tone and content right. To encourage a favorable reception to the speech, the president also called in Republican legislators, including Knowland and House Speaker Joseph Martin, and conveyed his own concern over the worsening situation in Vietnam. Vice President Nixon, who attended, recorded in his diary that Ike referred to the situation at Dien Bien Phu as desperate, so much so that he would consider the use of a diversionary tactic such as a landing by Chiang Kai-shek's Nationalist forces on China's Hainan Island or a naval blockade of the Chinese mainland. "I am bringing this up at this time," the president said, "because at any time within the space of forty-eight hours, it might be necessary to move into the battle of Dien Bien Phu in order to keep it from going against us, and in that case I will be calling in the Democrats as well as the Republican leaders to inform them of the actions we're taking."[13]

Did the president mean what he said here, or was he merely using strong language—America might have to "move into battle" at any time; he would *inform* lawmakers rather than *consult* with them—to assess the lawmakers' reaction and to make Dulles's speech that evening seem safely moderate by comparison? It's hard to know. Certainly, his convening of the meeting on minimal notice and his choice of words showed how engaged he had become by late March on the Indochina issue. And it is telling that, in reading over the draft of Dulles's speech, Eisenhower toughened the language in several places.[14]

That evening a sense of anticipation filled the room as Dulles stepped up to the lectern a little after nine o'clock, stiff and somber as always. Word had spread that he would deliver more than the ordinary after-dinner foreign policy overview. He didn't disappoint, though the precise meaning of his words would be intensely parsed in newsrooms and chancelleries the world over in the days to come. A guideline for action more than an actual statement of policy, the speech stressed the importance of Indochina to American interests and raised the prospect of military action to "save" it. Even a partial Viet Minh victory would be disastrous, Dulles declared: "If the Communist forces won uncontested control over Indochina or any substantial part thereof, they would surely resume the same pattern of aggression against other free peoples in the area."

The propagandists of Red China and Russia make it apparent that their purpose is to dominate all of Southeast Asia. Southeast Asia is the so-called "rice bowl" which helps to feed the densely populated region that extends from India to Japan. It is rich in many raw materials, such as tin, oil, rubber, and iron ore. It offers industrial Japan potentially important markets and sources of raw materials. The area has great strategic value. Southeast Asia is astride the most direct and best developed sea and air route between the Pacific and South Asia. It has major naval and air bases. Communist control of Southeast Asia would carry a grave threat to the Philippines, Australia, and New Zealand, with whom we have treaties of mutual assistance. The entire Western Pacific area, including the so-called "offshore island chain," would be strategically threatened.

But it was even worse than that. The Viet Minh victories, Dulles continued, had come about because of active Chinese Communist assistance. Mao's lieutenants were training Ho Chi Minh's forces, were supplying them with arms, even directing them in the field. Should the United States and her allies fail to thwart this Chinese expansionism, Beijing leaders would conclude that as long as they refrained from open invasion they had freedom to do as they wished. Of this idea they had to be disabused. Should Beijing choose to "send its own army into Indo-China, the grave consequences might not be confined to Indo-China."[15]

How, then, to thwart these Communist designs? Dulles called for a coalition of nations composed of the United States, Great Britain, France, Australia, Thailand, the Philippines, and the Associated States that would pledge collectively to defend Indochina and the rest of Southeast Asia against aggression. This was United Action, and its ambitions were, it seemed, enormous: to deny *any* Viet Minh takeover in Indochina— whether as a result of a total battlefield victory or a compromise agreement made at the bargaining table. Either Ho Chi Minh would have to surrender, Dulles and Eisenhower (for the president had approved every word) appeared to be saying, or the United States would have to join the war against him.

Of course, they didn't say that. Not quite. The speech was carefully crafted—it went through twenty-one drafts—to sound menacing while remaining vague on specifics; as one Dulles deputy recalled, it did not actually commit "anyone to anything."[16] Dulles and Eisenhower hoped the strong words would have a deterrent effect on the Chinese and would boost French morale, that the speech would torpedo the upcoming Geneva negotiations and induce Britain to pledge support to a multilateral intervention should one be required. With respect to the domestic front, the speech was a means to test the waters, to see how the public would respond to the prospect of U.S. involvement in the fighting. As Dulles and Eisenhower surely understood, in describing the danger in such grandiose terms, in terms they seldom used in private meetings, they risked hemming themselves in. It might be very difficult to change course after you've all but declared that the loss of Indochina could lead to mass starvation all over Asia, that the Viet Minh were puppets of a Soviet-Chinese allied leadership bent on world domination. But they said it anyway. It's hard to avoid the conclusion that the two men had made up their minds: All of Indochina would have to be held, with direct American intervention if necessary.

III

THAT WAS CERTAINLY THE CONCLUSION DRAWN BY MANY WHO HEARD the speech or read the transcript. "The Eisenhower administration has decided that Indo-China will not be allowed to fall into Red hands— whatever the cost," declared *The Wall Street Journal* the next day. Echoed *U.S. News & World Report*: "Blunt notice is given to Communists that [the] U.S. does not intend to let Indochina be gobbled up, even if it means big war." *The New Republic,* commenting on Eisenhower's approval of the text, likewise said the address could have only one possible meaning: "The administration has decided to do whatever is necessary to win in Southeast Asia—if necessary it will commit US ground forces." And in *The New York Times,* the lede of James Reston's front-page news analysis read, "The Eisenhower Administration has taken a fundamental policy decision to block the communist conquest of Southeast Asia—even if it has to take 'united action' with France and other countries to do so." How did Reston know this? Because "the highest authority" told him so.[17]

Of course, Southeast Asia was not the same as Indochina, so the *Times* and *The New Republic* may have been hedging their bets slightly on what the immediate implications were for the fighting in Vietnam. But that distinction was lost on many observers, as was the distinction between intervening with airpower at Dien Bien Phu (which Dulles in particular doubted would do much good) and elsewhere in Indochina. On Capitol Hill, the predominant reaction to the speech—especially among Democrats—was surprise and uncertainty. Was the administration trying to lead the nation into war? And what was "United Action" precisely? "I followed Secretary Dulles's speech very carefully," remarked Democratic senator John Stennis of Mississippi, "and I have not been able to decide exactly what he means by 'united action.'" Senator Arthur Watkins, a Republican from Utah, warned the White House not to follow Truman's example "and take action without consulting the Congress."[18]

Misgivings came also from a more unexpected quarter in the aftermath of the speech: the Joint Chiefs of Staff. On March 31, Admiral Radford convened a meeting of the group to ascertain his colleagues' views about recommending the commitment of U.S. naval air and air force units for the defense of Dien Bien Phu—and, by extension, their views of the Indochina struggle more broadly. If he expected full support for such a recommendation, he was soon disappointed. None of the other service chiefs was keen on the idea. General Matthew Ridgway, chief of staff of the army, said any benefits to be accrued from intervention to support the garrison would be outweighed by the costs. The use of airpower at Dien Bien Phu would not decisively affect the military picture in Vietnam, Ridgway said, but would greatly increase the risk of general war. Nor did the army chief like the way Radford had introduced the matter. "Unless the question emanated from proper authority," he continued, "any such recommendation—for or against—was clearly outside the proper scope of the authority of the JCS." To advocate a specific policy would be to "involve the JCS inevitably in politics."[19]

Underlying Ridgway's opposition, and that of his subordinates in army intelligence, was a deeply skeptical view of what the use of airpower could accomplish in Vietnam. Dismissed as a parochial argument by some, as reflecting a desire to rationalize an institutional army viewpoint, it was in fact a reasoned position. To Ridgway, recent history showed clearly that airpower alone could not effectively interdict lines of communication if the adversary had the resources and the motivation to keep supplies moving, as the Viet Minh clearly had. The Italian campaign in World War II had demonstrated this, as had Korea. In Indochina, moreover, the obstacles were greater, for unlike in Italy and Korea the approaches to the front were not constricted by a peninsula. The Viet Minh had shown time and again the relative ease with which they could overcome French aerial interdiction efforts, and there was little reason to believe aircraft operating from American carriers would have markedly more success. The imminent start of the rainy season, with its heavy cloud cover and low ceiling, would further reduce effectiveness.[20]

The White House took note of the alarms raised in Congress and among the service chiefs. During a press conference on March 31, Eisenhower, after affirming his "complete agreement" with Dulles on Indochina policy, said he "could conceive of no greater disadvantage to America" than to send U.S. forces "in great numbers around the world, meeting each little situation as it arises."[21] That phraseology, of course, signified little about what he might do or not do in Indochina, but some interpreted it as an attempt to soothe congressional concerns. The next morning the president told the NSC he was troubled by the division of opinion within the JCS regarding Radford's air strike plan but then said the intervention question was not for the Joint Chiefs but for "statesmen" to answer. And the decision would have to be made soon. But not by the full NSC—Eisenhower announced he would not delegate the decision to the NSC but would pursue it after the meeting with a smaller group in the Oval Office.

No records of this second meeting have been found, but it must have been a dramatic session. Two days earlier, on March 30, General Vo Nguyen Giap had launched the second phase of his attack plan on Dien Bien Phu, and the reports coming into the White House were ominous: The garrison had suffered withering blows in two nights of savage fighting, much of it at strongpoints Eliane and Dominique. Radford's prediction of an imminent Viet Minh conquest seemed to be coming true. The transcribed summaries of Dulles's telephone conversations from later in the day indicate that a sense of urgency pervaded the second gathering, and that those in attendance agreed on the need for a meeting with the bipartisan congressional leadership. The tenor of these telephone conversations, following on the heels of the NSC and Oval Office meetings, implied the very real possibility of implementing the Vulture plan or some variant. Eisenhower, shortly after the second session, told two newspaper chieftains over lunch that he might have to send squadrons from two aircraft carriers to bomb the Reds at Dien Bien Phu—then added, "Of course, if we did, we'd have to deny it forever."[22]

The next morning, Friday, April 2, Eisenhower met with Dulles, Radford, NSC head Cutler, and Secretary of Defense Wilson in the Oval Office. The issue on the table: how to nudge Congress to approve military action? Dulles presented a draft congressional resolution on Indochina that he hoped to show lawmakers at what now shaped up to be a key session the following day. The operative paragraph read:

> That the president of the United States be and he hereby is authorized, in the event he determines that such action is required to protect and defend the safety and security of the United States, to employ Naval and Air Forces of the United States to assist the forces of which are resisting aggression in Southeast Asia, to prevent the extension and expansion of that aggression, and to protect and defend the safety and security of the United States.

The nonmention of army ground forces in this passage is perhaps telling, or perhaps not. Naval forces can after all include marines, and, depending on the interpretation of the subsequent phrases, army ground troops could be used to prevent further Communist aggression, and/or to defend American security.[23]

Dulles dominated much of the discussion that morning. Over the previous days he had become increasingly persuaded of the Dien Bien Phu battle's enormous symbolic importance—far greater than the strategic value of the actual territory in contest—and of the very real possibility that its fall could trigger an immediate French withdrawal from Indochina. Such a withdrawal would be disastrous, and thus a way must be found to stiffen French spines. Dulles still doubted that a one-off air intervention could save the garrison, however, and said he saw the congressional resolution as a tool by which to deter Beijing and realize United Action with allied governments. Radford, chastened by the lack of support he had received from the other Joint Chiefs, sung an unexpected tune: The outcome at Dien Bien Phu, he now opined, would be determined within hours and therefore U.S. intervention was not advisable at present. Ike listened intently. He liked the draft, he said, but—ever the savvy pol—he instructed Dulles to gauge congressional leaders' thinking on the subject before presenting them with the text. It should be made to appear that the resolution was their idea, Ike advised, and not one "drafted by ourselves."[24]

IV

THE MEETING BEGAN AT NINE-THIRTY IN THE MORNING. IT WAS April 3, a Saturday. As tourists began arriving on the Mall to catch the explosion of cherry blossoms, a few blocks away in Foggy Bottom, fourteen somber-faced men filed into a conference room at the State Department. In the months and years to come, this meeting would take on mythical status, in part due to the reporting of *Washington Post* correspondent Chalmers M. Roberts, and in part due to the statements at the meeting by Senate minority leader Lyndon Johnson, who as president of the United States eleven years later would take his country into large-scale war in Vietnam. Roberts filed two articles, the first on the front page of the *Post* in the late spring, the second some weeks later in *The Reporter*, a weekly. So detailed were they, and so apparently accurate, that they touched off an FBI investigation of Roberts's sources.[25]

The second article bore the title "The Day We Didn't Go to War," a standard bit of journalistic hyperbole that nevertheless contained more than a grain of truth. This was a pivotal moment, as the participants well understood. Joining Johnson from Congress were fellow Senate Democrats Richard Russell of Georgia and Earle Clements of Kentucky; Republican senators Eugene Millikan of Colorado and Knowland of California; House Speaker Joseph Martin, a Republican from Massachusetts;

and House Democratic leaders John W. McCormack of Massachusetts and J. Percy Priest of Tennessee. With Eisenhower away at Camp David, Dulles presided and was joined on his side by Admiral Radford, Deputy Secretary of Defense Roger Kyes, Undersecretary of State Walter Bedell Smith, Navy Secretary Robert B. Anderson, and Assistant Secretary of State and future U.S. senator from Kentucky Thruston B. Morton.[26]

The atmosphere was electric from the start. Dulles, who may have had the draft resolution already in his possession that day, opened by saying that the meeting had been called at the president's request, with an eye toward organizing a response to the crisis in Southeast Asia. Then he cut to the chase: What the administration sought was a joint resolution by Congress authorizing the president to use air and naval power in Indochina. The mere passage of such a resolution might make its actual use unnecessary, he went on, but that only made its consideration more vital. The president believed it essential for Congress and the White House to be on the same page with respect to the war.

Radford then gave the legislators a comprehensive rundown of the military situation, painting a grim picture of the conditions at Dien Bien Phu. The fortress was in desperate straits, he declared, and might succumb at any time. Dulles voiced full agreement with Radford's assessment and said defeat at Dien Bien Phu could have calamitous political implications, setting off a French move to withdraw entirely and leading to the Communist conquest of all of Indochina. America's defensive line in Asia would in turn be gravely endangered. If Indochina was allowed to fall, "it was only a question of time until all of Southeast Asia falls along with Indonesia." To prevent such a catastrophe, the secretary urged Congress to give the president solid backing "so that he could use air and seapower in the area if he felt it necessary in the interest of national security."

Knowland immediately offered his support but quickly fell silent as probing questions poured forth from several of his colleagues. Clements asked Radford if the notion of using air strikes to try to save the French at Dien Bien Phu had the approval of the rest of the Joint Chiefs of Staff.

"No," the admiral replied.

"How many of the three agree with you?"

"None."

"How do you account for that?"

"I have spent more time in the Far East than any of them and I understand the situation better."

The full-court press continued: What about allied involvement? "We want no more Koreas with the United States furnishing 90 percent of the manpower," Lyndon Johnson said plainly, repeating a complaint made some weeks before by William Knowland. Dulles and Radford replied that the action they were contemplating would be on a much more limited scale than the effort in Korea, since French and Vietnamese troops would do all the fighting on the ground. The legislators were not mollified. They doubted France's willingness and capability to maintain her share of the responsibility and expressed a concern that Johnson would have thrown back at him a decade later: Once the flag was committed, it would be impossible to limit U.S. involvement to air and sea power. Ground troops would inevitably follow. By acclamation, the eight lawmakers voted their response to the secretary's plea: Before they would ask the rest of Congress to back any commitment of American military power to Indochina, they must be assured that it would be part of a multilateral effort. Could Dulles offer that assurance?

The secretary hedged. He realized he was caught in a catch-22. He could not secure foreign commitments to join a coalition without proof that his own government was fully on board. But the legislators were now telling him that a precondition for congressional backing was gaining allied support in advance. He tried to satisfy them by saying he had begun consultations with Britain and the Philippines and would soon talk to the French, and he added he felt confident that Australia, New Zealand, Thailand, and the Philippines were unofficially on board, willing to contribute troops to a defense coalition. All well and good, the legislators said, according to personal notes taken by Russell, but it was London that mattered. What about the likelihood of a British commitment? Dulles admitted he was "unenthusiastic."[27]

And with that, the meeting broke up, a little more than two hours in. A consensus had been reached that if sufficient foreign commitments were obtained, a congressional resolution could be passed authorizing the president to deploy American armed forces in the area. Dulles phoned the president that afternoon and tried to put the best face on what had occurred. "On the whole it went pretty well—although it raised some serious problems." Congress would be quite prepared to go along on "some vigorous action" but only if "we were not doing it alone" and only "if the people of the area are involved too." Eisenhower agreed. "You can't go in and win unless the people want you," he told Dulles. "The French could win in six months if the people were with them."[28]

Dulles got to work immediately on securing allied support for United Action. He arranged for the Australian and New Zealand ambassadors to come to his home the next afternoon, April 4, and began preparations for a campaign to get London to join the coalition. He also met with Henri Bonnet, the French ambassador to Washington, telling him that a negotiated peace would equal surrender and that partition of Vietnam—an idea slowly gaining currency in London and elsewhere, in which the Viet Minh would have control of the northern portion—was synonymous with defeat. French prestige in North Africa and elsewhere was at stake, he warned Bonnet; therefore Paris simply had to stay in the fight. Would Congress sanction U.S. military intervention? Bonnet asked. Only if such action was part of a coalition of powers, including Britain, and only if France remained an active participant, the American replied. Bonnet pressed the point: What if London refused? "The difficulties would be greatly increased," Dulles acknowledged, "if the British would not agree," but it might still be possible to proceed. Bonnet was reassured; the secretary had implied that British involvement was not essential, a position that seemed, Bonnet said, to accord with Dulles's March 29 speech in New York.[29]

In fact, though, British participation *was* essential, at least under present circumstances, as Dulles made clear when Ambassadors Percy Spender of Australia and Sir Leslie Munro of New Zealand arrived at his home the following afternoon. Hardly had the visitors taken their seats in the library before he and Radford and Walter Bedell Smith lit into them on the vital importance of avoiding a French defeat, lest all of Southeast Asia fall and Japan seek accommodation with Communist China. A new military force was needed, Dulles said, and it had to include Great Britain, or Congress would not give its approval. Yet Winston Churchill's government seemed altogether too inclined to seek the "least bad" exit from Indochina, perhaps by way of partition.

At this point, Dulles rose and walked over to a bookcase. He pulled out the first volume of Churchill's monumental history of the Second World War. Opening it to a certain page, he pedantically read aloud the Briton's account of the 1931–32 episode when Henry L. Stimson, then the U.S. secretary of state, had tried in vain to enlist British assistance in a joint effort to check Japanese expansionism. Churchill in the book excused London's behavior on the grounds that Great Britain had no reason to expect corresponding American involvement in Europe, where the truly vital problems lay. That was a reasonable argument at the time, the solemn secretary told his guests as he closed the book and returned it to the shelf, but no longer. Today the United States was fully involved and had "definitely proved" her deep concern with European developments.[30]

Spender and Munro listened attentively but kept their counsel. They were not unsympathetic to the American's claims, and they promised to pass on to their governments his specific request of naval support, probably in the form of a carrier from each. But they could do no more. Dulles plainly hoped that by taking Canberra and Wellington into his confidence he could meaningfully alter London's policy, but this was a long shot at best, given the intimate nature of Commonwealth diplomacy and the residual subservience of the junior partners to British supremacy on global military strategy. Upon leaving the Dulles residence, the two ambassadors informed not only their home governments of the contents of the discussion, but also the British embassy in Washington.[31]

Eisenhower, meanwhile, had returned from Camp David. At 8:20 that same Sunday evening, April 4, he held an off-the-record meeting with five foreign policy advisers in the upstairs study at the White House: Dulles, Smith, Radford, Kyes, and State Department counselor Douglas MacArthur II. According to his assistant Sherman Adams, the president agreed "to send American forces to Indo-China under certain strict conditions": that (1) the intervention take the form of a united action including Great Britain and other concerned states, that (2) France agree to maintain her own commitments in the area, and that (3) the Paris government pledge to grant full independence to the Associated States, so as to avoid any hint of colonialism. Though Adams didn't say it, there can be no doubt the conferees that evening saw the first two conditions as of more immediate importance than the third and moreover felt securing the first could be essential to gaining the second.[32]

How to interpret Eisenhower's decision to seek support from Congress on the issue of intervention? Scholars have lauded his inclusion of the legislative branch at a key juncture in the policy making; they often also praise his refusal to take the unilateralist path trod by so many of his successors in the White House. But historians have disagreed in their assessments of his underlying motivations. Some assert that he deliberately used the April 3 meeting to isolate hawks within the administration such as Radford and Vice President Nixon, whose desire for direct military intervention he did not share. According to this interpretation, Eisenhower had no intention of permitting the use of American military force in Indochina in the spring of 1954, and he cleverly used congressional doubts as a means to avoid action while simultaneously protecting his political flank from the inevitable fallout following French defeat.[33] Others depict a president who was himself a hawk, who believed the apocalyptic rhetoric about Indochina's transcendent importance, and who was serious about intervention, but who was determined to have Congress—and therefore allied governments—on board. With the long and frustrating Korean experience fresh in everyone's minds, it was inconceivable to him to put Americans in harm's way in Asia again without the explicit backing of Capitol Hill.[34]

The evidence makes it hard to come down firmly on one side or the other, but the best argument is the second one, or a variant thereof: that Eisenhower actively contemplated taking the United States directly into the war and sought a blank check from Congress to free his hands and strengthen his bargaining position vis-à-vis allies, or at least that he wanted to keep open the option of military involvement. A president scheming to use congressional nervousness as a pretext to avoid deeper involvement would not have tried to remove such constraints on his future decision-making authority; Eisenhower did.[35] A president determined to stay out of the war would also have spoken more elliptically about the nature of the threat in Indochina, and would have instructed top aides to do likewise. He would not have worked so hard to bring the British around. Taken as a whole, Eisenhower's statements and actions from the time of General Ely's arrival on March 20 until April 4—and, as we shall see, in the days thereafter—suggest a man who was fully prepared to intervene with force under certain circumstances and who sought to maintain his freedom of maneuver for whatever contingencies might arise.

V

WHEN MACARTHUR LEFT THE WHITE HOUSE THAT EVENING OF April 4, he decided to go back to Foggy Bottom and check his mail for any late messages. At 10:15 P.M. he read a top-secret cable from the Paris embassy. It was a stunner: The Laniel government had decided formally to request American intervention at Dien Bien Phu, in the form of Operation Vulture. Two days earlier, on April 2, Colonel Raymond Brohon, a midlevel French officer, had arrived in Hanoi, charged with determining General Navarre's views on Vulture and, more broadly, whether the general thought American air strikes could save Dien Bien Phu. U.S. Admiral Radford, Brohon noted, had told Paul Ely he supported such action. If Navarre signaled his approval, Paris leaders had decided on March 29, the French government would put the request forward to Washington.[36]

Navarre was initially skeptical—he questioned Vulture's military utility and feared it could bring Chinese retaliation—but by April 3 he had warmed to the plan. Overnight the situation at Dien Bien Phu had grown still more ominous. Portions of Eliane and Dominique in the north-central part of the camp had fallen to the enemy, and the wounded could no longer be evacuated—the last flight out had left on March 26. The garrison was now totally dependent on air-drops that, on account of Viet Minh antiaircraft fire and the steady compression of the perimeter, were increasingly landing in enemy territory. On April 4, after Brohon had returned to France, Navarre radioed Paris his approval: "The intervention of which Colonel Brohon has told me can have a decisive impact, especially if it is made before the Viet Minh [major] assault."[37] Defense Minister Pleven, who that afternoon had been accosted by hostile Indochina veterans at the Ceremony of the Flame at the Arc de Triomphe, immediately called a meeting of a newly formed "war committee"—composed of the service chiefs and some key cabinet members—for late that evening. In short order, they voted to ask for American air strikes. Even those members fearful of "international complications" arising from U.S.

intervention went along, as did those who doubted that even large-scale aerial bombardment could save the day. A desperate situation called for desperate action. But all also agreed that the intervention must be immediate and massive.[38]

Time was short. The meeting adjourned quickly so that U.S. ambassador Douglas Dillon could be brought to Hôtel Matignon (the French prime minister's official residence) for consultation. But could he be summoned this late—it was after eleven P.M.—on a Sunday night? He could. Dillon arrived close to midnight to find Foreign Minister Bidault waiting. Prime Minister Laniel soon arrived and got right down to business: On behalf of the French government, he hereby requested that the United States intervene immediately with heavy bombers capable of delivering two-ton-or-heavier bombs, in order to save the entrenched camp at Dien Bien Phu. No other option existed. Given the heavy Chinese involvement on the side of the Viet Minh, including material aid, technical advisers, and communications system, it seemed entirely appropriate, Laniel added, for the American government to initiate the actions General Ely and Admiral Radford had discussed in Washington. Dillon was noncommittal. He said that in his personal view, Congress would have to be consulted before any action could commence, but he promised to submit the request to his government right away.[39]

Dillon's cable arrived at the State Department at 9:43 P.M. local time. MacArthur read it half an hour later. By 10:30, he had passed on the details to Dulles, Radford, and Smith. Dulles did not act immediately, in part because he was busy preparing a telegram from Eisenhower to Winston Churchill that amounted to, in one historian's words, "a request for war."[40] Eisenhower in his correspondence was usually not given to oratorical flourish, but this time he and the secretary laid it on thick, rather in the way the Briton himself might do. After paying tribute to the "gallant fight" being put up by the French at Dien Bien Phu, Eisenhower warned that, whatever the final outcome there, greater efforts by the Western powers would be required to save Indochina from Communism. Simply to urge the French to redouble their efforts was no solution, not when the stakes were this high: The loss of Indochina could lead to a disastrous shift in the power ratio "throughout Asia and the Pacific" and severely undermine the global strategic position of both the United

States and Britain. Even Berlin did not matter as much in grand strategic terms. Following a defeat in Vietnam, Southeast Asia could swiftly fall, and Australia and New Zealand would be threatened. Japan would be deprived of non-Communist markets and sources of food and would almost certainly have to make an accommodation with the Communist world. "This has led us," the president continued, "to the hard conclusion that the situation in Southeast Asia requires us urgently to take serious and far-reaching decisions."

Specifically, Eisenhower wrote, there should be a coalition of nations committed to stopping Communist expansion in the area and "willing to join the fight if necessary. I do not envisage the need of any appreciable ground forces on your or our part. If the members of the alliance are sufficiently resolute it should be able to make clear to the Chinese Communists that the continuation of their material support to the Viet Minh will inevitably lead to the growing power of the forces arrayed against them."

Eisenhower concluded by offering to send Dulles to London "at the earliest date convenient to you" and by invoking a previous moment of similar peril: "If I may refer again to history, we failed to halt Hirohito, Mussolini, and Hitler by not acting in unity and in time. That marked the beginning of many years of stark tragedy and desperate peril. May it not be that our nations have learned something from that lesson?"[41]

One must ask again: Would a president determined to avoid military intervention in Vietnam send this kind of letter—cajoling, flattering, bribing, bullying—to his old wartime partner, drawing direct parallels between their titanic struggle against the Axis powers and the present threat? Hardly. Would he reference the all-important question concerning fighting troops under United Action by saying he did not envisage the need for "*appreciable* ground forces" on Britain's or America's part? Not likely. Historian Kevin Ruane is surely right that Eisenhower's missive ("a model of psychological profiling with barbs aimed at all the prime minister's weak points") constitutes powerful proof that he was utterly serious about intervention under the right conditions.[42]

The letter, sent by cable through the American embassy in London, went out six minutes before midnight. Due to problems in transmission, it did not reach Churchill until six P.M. the following day, April 5. The day after that came the reply:

"My dear friend,

"I have received your most important message of April 4. We are giving it earnest cabinet consideration. Winston."[43]

VI

HOW TO RESPOND TO THE FRENCH REQUEST FOR IMMEDIATE AERIal intervention at Dien Bien Phu consumed White House attention early on April 5. First thing that morning Dulles telephoned the president and told him of Laniel's conversation with Dillon and of his petition for air strikes. Eisenhower expressed irritation at Radford's seeming indiscretion in the talks with Ely—the admiral had implied more than he should have—and said there could be no talk of early intervention absent explicit congressional support. Certainly the administration should take "a look to see if anything else can be done," he went on, but "we cannot engage in active war." Dulles concurred. He dispatched a cable to Paris informing Dillon that the United States would not intervene "except on [a] coalition basis with active British Commonwealth participation." Congress, he added, would likewise have to be on board.[44]

Bidault, informed of the rejection later in the day, took it hard. The time for coalitions had passed, he told Dillon, for the fate of Indochina would be determined in the next ten days at Dien Bien Phu. As the American got up to leave, Bidault vowed that French troops would not quit even if they must fight alone. May God grant them success, he said.[45]

Or perhaps God plus some additional American aircraft. The following day, April 6, Bidault summoned Dillon back to the Quai d'Orsay and made a new request, this one for ten to twenty B-29 bombers, complete with maintenance personnel and bombs, to be put at the immediate disposal of France. As the runways in Indochina were probably too short to handle the B-29s, the French government hoped the aircraft could be based at U.S. facilities in the Philippines. It amounted to a Plan B, similar to Operation Vulture except involving no American airmen. The Frenchman expressed hope that prompt intervention by these B-29s over the following few days could break up the Viet Minh reinforcement columns moving toward Dien Bien Phu and thereby save the day.[46]

Dillon, sympathetic as usual to the Laniel government's perspective on Vietnam, recommended to Dulles that the administration grant the request. Failure to do so, he warned, would allow Paris to lay significant blame for the fall of Dien Bien Phu on the United States and would "strengthen the already powerful group in [the] French Government who wish for peace at any price in Indochina." Senior policy makers feared he might be right, but they rejected Plan B as well when the NSC met on Tuesday afternoon, April 6. The French had little experience with B-29s, Admiral Radford noted, and could not put them into effective use in time to make a difference at Dien Bien Phu. Even the B-26s already given to them had not been used efficiently. Eisenhower concurred. The group decided instead to give the French other aircraft, including Corsairs and light navy bombers, plus technicians and maintenance crews, subject to approval by Congress.

Congress in fact was the elephant in the room that afternoon, figuring into every part of the discussion. The Smith committee formed by Eisenhower back in January had submitted a report the day before rejecting negotiations and calling for "military victory" in Indochina using U.S. ground forces if necessary, but the NSC refused to go that far. Eisenhower, after declaring that the war was still eminently winnable and that even the fall of Dien Bien Phu would not necessarily be a defeat "since the French would have inflicted such heavy losses on the enemy," said "with great emphasis" that a fundamental reality had to be faced: Unilateral American intervention was impossible. "Even if we tried such a course, we would have to take it to the Congress and fight for it like dogs, with very little hope of success." John Foster Dulles agreed. The April 3 meeting with legislative leaders had shown, he said, that it would be impossible to get congressional support for unilateral action. Intervention would have to be multilateral and would have to include Great Britain. Accordingly, Dulles continued, he had with the president's approval begun to work on allied governments and in particular to convince Britain of two salient facts: that her own position in Malaya would be gravely endangered if Indochina was lost, and that her "two children" Australia and New Zealand would likewise be imperiled.

As Eisenhower and Dulles no doubt knew, a prearranged colloquy on Indochina was at that very moment under way in the U.S. Senate, a few blocks away. Massachusetts Democrat John F. Kennedy, fifteen months into his first term in office and exhibiting the same contradictory impulses on Vietnam that he would later show as president, framed the discussion with an address blasting the administration for its lack of candor about the war. The time had come, he proclaimed, "for the American people to be told the truth about Indochina." While he favored the concept of United Action, Kennedy feared where such a policy would lead the nation: "To pour money, matériel, and men into the jungles of Indochina without at least a remote prospect of victory would be dangerously futile and destructive." For that matter, he wondered, would the United States ever be able to make much difference in that part of the world? "No amount of American military assistance can conquer an enemy which is everywhere and at the same time nowhere, 'an enemy of the people' which has the sympathy and covert support of the people." No satisfactory outcome was possible, Kennedy concluded, unless France accorded the Associated States full and complete independence; without it, adequate indigenous support would remain forever elusive.

The Massachusetts senator's support for United Action was seconded by many colleagues of both parties, as was his belief that gaining greater indigenous support was a prerequisite for success. Few, however, articulated his skepticism regarding what U.S. power could accomplish on the ground, and even Kennedy indicated a willingness to vote for a multilateral military intervention if it came to that. Turning the discussion to the practical implications of United Action, Mike Mansfield, Democrat from Montana, asked JFK what he thought John Foster Dulles had in mind when he announced the concept before the Overseas Press Club in New York nine days prior.

"There is every indication," Kennedy answered, "that what he meant was that the United States will take the ultimate step."

"And that is what?" Mansfield asked.

"It is war."[47]

Back at the other end of Pennsylvania Avenue, the NSC meeting, having taken up much of the afternoon, ended with an agreement to seek a regional grouping for the defense of Southeast Asia against Communist aggression. The conversation had been muddled at points, with no clear sense of what policy to pursue, or even of Dien Bien Phu's and Indochina's ultimate importance to the West, but by the end the principals were in basic accord. When a plainly skeptical George Humphrey, secretary of the treasury, asked whether the Dullesian notion of United Action might not eventually lead to "a policy of policing all the governments of the world," Eisenhower responded firmly. Indochina, he lectured Humphrey, was the first in a row of dominoes. If she fell, her neighbors would soon topple as well. Where would the process end? "George," he said, "you exaggerate the case. Nevertheless in certain areas at least we cannot afford to let Moscow gain another bit of territory. Dien Bien Phu itself may be just such a critical point."[48]

The president evidently liked the domino metaphor, for he used it again the next day in what would become the most famous press conference of his presidency—and arguably of the entire Cold War. Asked to comment on Indochina's strategic importance, he warned that the possible consequences to the free world of defeat in Indochina were incalculable because of the "falling domino principle." If Indochina fell, the rest of Southeast Asia would "go over very quickly," he declared, a disintegration that would have "the most profound influences." Though the underlying imagery was not new to 1954 or even to the Eisenhower administration—recall Acheson's "rotten apple" metaphor from 1947—it had not been articulated this way in public before; the metaphor quickly captured the popular imagination and came to define an era in American foreign policy. Lest any of the reporters doubt his determination, the president also said that America could afford no more losses to Communism; that Geneva would likely not bring an acceptable peace settlement; and that independence for the Associated States was not a condition for U.S. intervention. He did not tell them that simultaneously a carrier strike force, already present in the South China Sea, was moved to within one hundred miles of Hainan Island and had commenced air reconnaissance of Chinese air bases and other military installations.[49]

That afternoon John Foster Dulles received a phone call from Republican senator Alexander Wiley of Wisconsin, chairman of the Foreign Relations Committee. Everyone was talking about Indochina, Wiley said, and he wondered how he should comment. Dulles said every effort was being made to create a solid front of nations pledged to denying the area to the Communists. Everything would hinge on the British, who remained noncommittal, and on the French, whose government was close to collapsing and "who have been drawing on us like an unlimited bank account." The time might be near, Dulles judged, for a showdown.[50]

And indeed, a showdown was coming. On April 10, Dulles embarked on a climactic trip to Europe, a final, all-out effort to make United Action a reality. "One of the most concentrated periods of diplomatic arm-twisting in the nation's history," a leading scholar has called it, and so it was.[51] For the stakes were huge, and time was running out.

The first stop: London.

CHAPTER 20

DULLES VERSUS EDEN

Y APRIL 1954, JOHN FOSTER DULLES HAD LOGGED SOME HUNDRED thousand miles in his capacity as secretary of state, visiting most of the non-Communist capitals of Europe and Asia and even making it to Africa and South America. More than two hundred miles per day he averaged. He was America's great traveling salesman, transforming U.S. diplomacy by his use of the airplane, by his willingness to dash off overseas on short notice, by his penchant for the quick in-and-out visit lasting mere hours. Constantly he was on the go, to-ing and fro-ing around the globe, returning home just long enough to huddle with Eisenhower and speak to a congressional committee or two before grabbing his homburg and flying off again to some distant locale. Or so it seemed to the exhausted newsmen who covered him, one of whom is said to have quipped, "Don't just do something, Foster; stand there."[1]

But he couldn't just stand there, not this time. If Indochina was to be saved from the Communists, the threat and perhaps the actuality of direct American military intervention would be necessary. Of that Dulles was certain. Congress had made starkly clear that it would not approve such action except as part of a multilateral intervention including Great Britain, yet the Churchill government had so far proved maddeningly resistant to United Action. The French too had to be brought around; even as they clamored for immediate American air strikes to save the battered Dien Bien Phu garrison, they stubbornly resisted talk of internationalizing the war, and they seemed alarmingly close to giving up the fight altogether. The future of Indochina, of Southeast Asia, and therefore of

America's and the West's position in the Far East, Dulles believed, could well depend on the outcome of the talks set to begin over dinner in London on April 11 and continuing there and in Paris over the next three days.

Dulles had great confidence in his abilities as a negotiator and statesman, but he was under no illusion that his task in Europe would be easy. The American embassies in the two capitals had provided extensive reports of local governmental and popular attitudes in the weeks prior, and he had also met with the respective ambassadors to Washington, Britain's Roger Makins and France's Henri Bonnet. From them he knew that although all three Western governments desired a French victory in the war, they differed on how best to try to achieve it, on what could be accomplished by military means, and on what could be expected from the negotiations scheduled to begin in Geneva at the end of the month. Yet the enormity of Dulles's task in creating even the semblance of unity on these issues became evident only after he arrived and the discussions began. Only then was the depth of the Anglo-American schism on Indochina brought fully into the open; only then was the full extent of the mutual suspicions between Paris and Washington made clear.

In London, frustrations with the Eisenhower policy had grown steadily in the weeks since the Berlin conference, and not only on account of Indochina. The Bravo hydrogen bomb test at Bikini atoll in the Marshall Islands on March 1 generated enormous concern in British official and popular thinking and fed already-existing fears of a new and perhaps uncontrollable nuclear arms race. The fate of the crew of the unfortunately named Japanese fishing trawler *Lucky Dragon,* which though outside the supposed danger zone of the Bravo test still felt the effects of the fallout—twenty-three seamen suffered radiation sickness, and one died—increased worldwide fear. Prime Minister Winston Churchill, remembering the chillingly casual way in which Eisenhower at Bermuda in December 1953 had referred to the bomb as just another weapon, expressed his horror at the power of the new H-bomb. He wrote to Eisenhower in mid-March and—as he had at Bermuda—pointed out the vulnerability of the densely populated British Isles, and London in particular.[2] The revelation that the Bravo test, at fifteen megatons, was three times greater than expert predictions added to the fear that, as one

British official wrote in his diary, the process was out of control: "Very great excitement everywhere about it, as if people began to see the end of the world."[3]

There ensued a raucous H-bomb debate in the House of Commons, which Churchill barely survived. Privately disdainful of "the bloody invention," in the chamber he gamely defended the Americans' right to test the bomb, even welcoming the new weapon's deterrent value, but his performance was wooden and halting and read entirely from a text. There were constant Labour interruptions as he spoke, while his own side sat glum and silent behind him. Even some Tories hinted that the old man should resign. Critics both in Parliament and in the press depicted a prime minister fawningly servile to Eisenhower, and a British government far too ignorant of America's nuclear program—and her foreign policy generally. Inevitably, Indochina came into the picture, as Labourites said they would seek to quash any thought of joining a U.S.-led intervention to defeat Ho Chi Minh. Such an intervention, they said, could lead swiftly to a dangerous and uncontrollable escalation of the conflict, drawing in China and the Soviet Union and culminating in World War III.[4]

Such fears resonated also at the highest levels of government. At a meeting of the full cabinet on April 7, Churchill read aloud Eisenhower's letter of April 4, whereupon Anthony Eden summarized a paper setting out his own views. The American proposal contained a fatal flaw, Eden said, for it wrongly assumed that the threat of retaliation against China "would cause her to withdraw her support from the Viet Minh." Such a threat would hardly be potent enough to make Beijing buckle, at least initially, and therefore the West would be faced with a terrible choice: either "to withdraw ignominiously or else embark on a warlike action against China." Nor would such military action be likely to achieve success. "Neither blockade nor the bombing of China's internal or external communications, which the United States Government appear to have in mind, were considered by our Chiefs of Staff to be militarily effective when these were discussed in connection with Korea," Eden maintained. "They would, however, give China every excuse for invoking the Sino-Soviet Treaty and might thus lead to a world war." The time to contemplate a warning to Beijing, he concluded, was later, after an agreement at Geneva, when Mao Zedong could be cautioned against breaching the accord.[5]

The cabinet endorsed Eden's position and then considered the nature of possible action inside Indochina. Eisenhower's letter to the prime minister had acknowledged that some American and British ground troops might need to be deployed; no one in the room doubted that land forces would indeed have to follow air and naval action. And would aerial action against China include the use of nuclear weapons? This was a question that must be put to Dulles during his visit.

Eden's reluctance to threaten China also had another source: He did not believe that Beijing's aid to the Viet Minh was decisive. A rough assessment by the Joint Intelligence Board showed that the scale of U.S. assistance to the French was "immeasurably greater" than the Chinese aid to the DRV. "Exactly," wrote Eden in the margin of the report. Even if one somehow persuaded the Chinese to withdraw their support, he and other British believed, the Viet Minh would still present a formidable threat for a very long time to come, because the keys to victory were not in China but in Vietnam and the rest of Indochina. Given the continuing weakness of the Bao Dai regime and the Vietnamese National Army, and the inability or unwillingness of the French to send major ground reinforcements, and given the need for France to play her full part in the defense of Western Europe, British policy makers concluded the best that could be hoped for was a negotiated settlement at Geneva leading to the partition of Vietnam.[6]

Such a solution was anathema to the Eisenhower administration, London officials knew—Concede territory to Communists? At the negotiating table? In an election year?—but they saw no reasonable alternative. Still, they worried that Eisenhower, so determined in his letter to Churchill, would be impossible to stop. Evelyn Shuckburgh, Eden's generally pro-American private secretary, wrote in his diary on April 8 of the period since the arrival of the letter: "two terrible days . . . the Eisenhower plan for the Far East worrying everybody."[7]

II

ON SUNDAY EVENING, APRIL 11, DULLES HOSTED EDEN FOR DINNER at the American embassy. Once the dishes were cleared and the cigars smoked, they got down to what one Foreign Office representative called "a singularly unfortunate series of discussions."[8] Dulles began with a falsehood, asserting that the Joint Chiefs of Staff had recommended, two weeks earlier, the use of air and naval power in Indochina, and that consequently carriers had been deployed from Manila. (In fact, as we have seen, only Admiral Radford among the Joint Chiefs supported such action.) The administration had decided, however, that there were two prerequisites to military action: the granting by France of complete independence to the Associated States, and the declaration by a coalition of countries of their readiness for united action. Should those two preconditions be met, the secretary continued, there was every reason to believe that Congress would authorize the president to use air and naval forces in Indochina, and perhaps even ground troops. Making no mention of an explicit warning to Beijing—he sensed Eden would never go along—Dulles asked for British consent to a public declaration of common purpose.[9]

Eden resisted. His government could not enter such an agreement before the Geneva Conference, he said, and he indicated skepticism that any allied intervention could be confined to the air and sea. Ground forces would inevitably soon follow. The prospects for holding Indochina were in any event dim, though consideration could certainly be given to drawing a line elsewhere in the region. The two men then sparred over the makeup of the still-hypothetical coalition. Eden stressed that Asian representation would have to be broadened beyond the Americans' suggestion of Thailand and the Philippines—both, he told aides, were too pro-U.S. to be representative of Asian opinion—and specifically mentioned India and Burma. Dulles, intensely suspicious of India's neutralist inclinations and her conciliatory attitude toward Communist China, immediately objected and said Washington would have to counter by offering membership to Formosa (Taiwan) and South Korea, maybe even Japan. Then what? he asked. There would be endless bickering among the members while the Communists gobbled up more territory.[10]

Throughout the evening Dulles made little effort to hide his feeling that Eden himself was largely to blame for the impasse. While the foreign secretary spoke, one observer recalled, Dulles doodled, "looking up occasionally out of the corner of his eye to give Eden a rather quizzical or skeptical look."[11]

The next morning, April 12, it was the subordinates' turn, but they too failed to find common ground on the key issues. There followed a second Eden-Dulles session that again yielded no real breakthrough. Dulles tried invoking history, comparing the present situation to the Japanese invasion of Manchuria in 1931 and Hitler's occupation of the Rhineland, two occasions when the West had failed to act and paid a dear price; Eden rejected the analogy. Dulles tried scare tactics, asserting that U.S. willingness to assume additional responsibilities in Southeast Asia "would diminish if agreement could not be reached now to make this stand"; the Briton was unmoved. And he tried pleading, invoking the shortage of French air mechanics in Indochina to ask for some British personnel so that Congress would in turn approve an increased American presence; again, Eden refused to be engaged.[12]

Dulles hit hard that day, but to many in the Foreign Office, he was the voice of moderation next to that of his rabidly anti-Communist assistant secretary of state for Far Eastern affairs Walter Robertson, a high-bred and bellicose Virginian. Robertson still seethed over America's failure to prevent Chiang Kai-shek's defeat in the Chinese civil war, and he referred to Chinese premier Zhou Enlai as a "charming gentleman who would cut his grandmother's throat if he saw advantage in it." In an afternoon encounter with Shuckburgh, Robertson vowed that neither he nor Dulles had any intention of sipping whiskey with the Chinese at Geneva. "You do not take a drink, when the court rises, with the criminal at the bar." But this is not a court, Shuckburgh protested—you are meeting them at a diplomatic conference. "No, we are not, we are bringing them before the bar of world opinion." Shuckburgh could not let that one pass. "I beg your pardon, but you are not bringing them, they are coming."

In his diary, Shuckburgh recorded the rest of the exchange: "I asked this Robertson whether Dulles had entirely given up any idea of trying to play the Chinese off against the Russians at Geneva. He scorned such a thought, said it was no use, never would be, what good had it done you (British) to recognize China, they just spurn you. A wholly inelastic and opinionated man."[13]

The final communiqué, agreed upon on the morning of April 13, was vacuous and open to varying interpretations. "We are ready to take part with the other countries principally concerned," read the key sentence, "in an examination of the possibility of establishing a collective defense." Just when this "examination" might commence, and with which participants, was left unclear, though Dulles claimed in a cable to Eisenhower that Eden had agreed to make Ambassador Makins available for pre-Geneva planning sessions. The cable was upbeat in tone—Dulles closed with a quip that the *London Daily Worker* had called him the most unwelcome visitor to England since 1066—but it could not hide the fact that the secretary had failed to achieve his main objective. United Action was hardly closer to becoming reality. Though Eden was hammered in Parliament that afternoon for even agreeing to a communiqué, the percipient Shuckburgh got closer to the truth in his assessment. "The actual agreement is so favorable to us," he wrote in his diary, "and so far from what Dulles's speeches before he came here led everyone to suppose he would demand, that the extremists [in the Commons] were quite discomfited, and the opposition cloven in half. A.E. enjoyed this very much."[14]

III

DULLES HOPED FOR BETTER RESULTS IN PARIS, A CITY HE KNEW well from his days as a student at the Sorbonne. He had always been fond of the French capital, of the lovely boulevards, the graceful architecture, the palpable respect for tradition and history so comparatively lacking in American cities. But his opinion of the French government and the men who led it, never particularly high, had reached a nadir. In London, he had mused with Eden about France's decline and her "inevitably ceasing to be a Great Power," and he had urged that the Anglo-American partners give this problem "careful thought." (Eden, a Francophile since his youth, had withheld comment but had himself told colleagues in the Foreign Office a few days earlier that "the French become daily more helpless and contemptible.")[15] Now he was back in the City of Light, hoping yet again to buck up Joseph Laniel and Georges Bidault, both on Indochina and the European Defense Community, and to persuade them not to set their hopes on Geneva.

The talks were rather less extensive than those in London, and the visit shorter, reflecting the lower importance attached by the administration to the Paris portion of the trip—for United Action and the prospect of potential multilateral military intervention in Indochina, it was the British who mattered most. Dulles tried in vain to get his hosts to grant full sovereignty to the Associated States (Bidault's response: What would be the point of continuing the struggle if Indochina was no longer tied to France?) and said Britain had agreed to send her ambassador in Washington to participate in an informal Indochina working group that would meet prior to Geneva. In order to get congressional support for an increased American share in the struggle, the secretary of state went on, it was imperative to get the other countries to see that events in Indochina threatened them all. Absent such allied consensus, lawmakers and the general public would almost certainly reject U.S. intervention.

Bidault, convinced that United Action was primarily an effort by the Americans to torpedo the prospects for a diplomatic solution, had no quarrel with Dulles's emphasis on securing congressional and popular support, but he countered that he had his own public opinion to consider. The imperatives of French domestic politics required that his government seize every opportunity for a negotiated settlement to the war, he insisted, and for this reason the anticipated early start-date of the working group's deliberations was problematic. Under no circumstances could French policy makers leave themselves open to the charge that they hoped for failure at Geneva, or that they sought a major new expansion of the fighting prior to the conference. Public opinion would not stand for it. Thus there could be no internationalization of the conflict involving a coalition of countries until after the Geneva Conference had clearly failed.[16]

Bidault was right: His political maneuverability was sharply limited. The French left continued to argue that the war was wicked, refused to acknowledge that its prosecution could serve the country's interests, and agitated for a negotiated settlement on the best terms that could be obtained. The attitude of the right—that is, of officialdom and the political parties supporting the Laniel government—was more complex, though it too proceeded from the conviction that the war was distasteful and deeply debilitating. Concern for French credibility and prestige internationally, and the lingering hope of rescuing something from the massive French investment in the struggle, prevented leaders and other opinion makers on the right from embracing a policy of abandonment, while at the same time making them suspicious and resentful of Washington's efforts to deepen U.S. involvement. Might it still be possible, the government and its supporters wondered, to thread the needle at Geneva: to bring an end to the war on terms that could be profitable to French material interests in Indochina and could be made to look honorable?

In London, meanwhile, Eden was starting to feel uneasy about the way the Dulles talks had gone. He feared that the White House might twist the capacious language of the communiqué to serve the cause of military intervention, and he worried about how the talks would be perceived at the Colombo conference of former Asian colonies scheduled to meet in a few days. Britain must not alienate her commonwealth partners before that meeting by seeming to back the wrong side in what most everyone at Colombo would interpret as a colonial war. More than that, in Eden's view it was vital to have as many Asian states as possible associated with any new security arrangements. India loomed especially large in this regard, and Eden knew that Nehru already thought him too cozy with the Eisenhower administration. Accordingly, the foreign secretary asked underlings for a draft telegram instructing Makins in Washington to reiterate Eden's views to the U.S. government in unambiguous terms. The key sentence in the final version, sent on April 15 and bearing signs of Eden's own input—he had a proclivity for the double negative—read: "I am not convinced that no concession could be made to Communists in Indochina without inevitably leading to Communist domination of the whole of South East Asia, particularly if we have the proposed security system."[17]

Makins delivered the message as instructed, but to no avail: On April 16, Dulles, now back in Washington, told the ambassador that the administration would call a meeting of the prospective members of the new security organization, namely Australia, Britain, France, New Zealand, the Philippines, Thailand, and the Associated States, to occur on April 20 in Washington. Eden was outraged at the news, and it did not help his mood that Makins concluded the cable by stating, "I presume that I can agree to such a proposal." The cable arrived on April 17, Easter Saturday, when the Foreign Office was largely deserted; with no one around to look over his shoulder, the workaholic Eden that day and the next sent Makins six telegrams, all of which he penned himself. "I cannot possibly accept this," he declared. No agreement of this kind had been reached in

London, and convening such a meeting now, before Geneva, would raise all sorts of suspicions in people's minds, and rightly so, particularly if it occurred in Washington. "If this enterprise is to have [a] fair chance of success, it must appear as a spontaneous effort by those countries and not as a response to an American crack of [the] whip."[18]

"I am not aware that Dulles has any cause for complaint," he snapped in another cable, his anger still rising. "Americans may think the time past when they need to consider the feelings or difficulties of their Allies. It is the conviction that this tendency becomes more pronounced every week that is creating mounting difficulties for anyone in this country who wants to maintain close Anglo-American relations. We at least have to constantly bear in mind all our Commonwealth partners, even if the United States does not like some of them; and I must ask you to keep close watch on this aspect of our affairs and not to hesitate to press it upon the United States."[19]

This last outburst came after Makins requested copies of the British texts concerning the London talks, to compare with the American versions. The ambassador had informed Dulles of Eden's instruction that he not attend the April 20 session, whereupon Dulles had calmly quoted to him from the American records, which indicated full agreement between him and Eden that there would indeed be consultations in Washington prior to Geneva. Makins's description of Dulles as sad rather than angry probably only fueled Eden's irritation, and he was in any event predisposed to question the ambassador's interpretation of events, finding him to be too often overly sympathetic to the Americans' point of view. The differing British and American accounts—the former indicates no agreement on pre-Geneva working group talks—make it impossible to determine who was right, though Eden's overheated reply may indicate he knew he had been outmaneuvered and had, perhaps without fully realizing the implications, given his counterpart the tacit approval he sought. Makins and Denis Allen, certainly, subsequently said they thought the Americans were in the right in their interpretation of what had occurred in London.[20]

Dulles's cool demeanor with Makins masked deep resentment. In prohibiting his ambassador from attending the ambassadors' meeting, "Eden has reversed himself and gone back on our agreement," Dulles

THE CAULDRON, 1953–1954 | 491

told his sister Eleanor in the front hall of his Washington home, after hanging up with the ambassador. "He was visibly disturbed" as he said this, Eleanor recalled.[21] British nonparticipation would render the working group notion all but meaningless, the secretary knew, and indeed the agenda of the April 20 session was altered to comprise only routine briefings on the forthcoming Geneva Conference. Dulles suspected that a desire to appease India lay behind Eden's about-face, but this was only partly true. The Briton did think it important at least to get New Delhi's acquiescence to any new Asian security pact, but he made little effort to understand Indian attitudes or policy. Knowing Nehru to be a vain man like himself, he thought flattery would be enough to keep the Indian on board in support of British policy, while privately he dismissed him as "blind beyond the end of his nose" and a "miserable little Indian Kerensky."[22]

It was in any event a key moment, this "Easter reversal" by Eden. James Cable, then a junior member of the Foreign Office, captured its importance in his unsparing evaluation of the foreign secretary's actions that weekend. "The replies he fired off were the petulant reaction of a cornered rabbit," Cable wrote of the six telegrams sent on April 16 and 17. "It was a deplorable performance and it lastingly impaired relations between Eden and Dulles, but it did check the dangerous drift towards a futile war. Although the United States would subsequently return to the charge again and again, Eden's Easter outburst may reasonably be regarded as the turning point of the April crisis. Henceforth Eden had a personal position to defend."[23]

IV

THE SKIRMISH WITH EDEN WAS NOT THE ONLY THING OCCUPYING Dulles's mind that Easter weekend. He also had to contend with the controversy kicked up by Vice President Nixon on Good Friday, April 16. Speaking before the American Society of Newspaper Editors, Nixon, whose hawkishness on the war had lessened not at all since his trip to Indochina six months earlier, and who had been encouraged by organizers to express himself openly on the understanding that he would be identified in press accounts only as a "high administration official," described the stakes in Indochina in alarmist terms. France seemed to lack "the will to win," he told the editors, even though the loss of Dien Bien Phu would be an enormous blow. Should the fortress fall, the Paris government would seek at Geneva to "settle in Indochina at any cost." Such an outcome would be disastrous for America's interests. A French withdrawal would cause Indochina to become Communist-dominated "within a month," and the U.S. position in Asia would be gravely imperiled. An editor asked the obvious follow-up: Should American troops be sent to Indochina in the event of such a French withdrawal? "The United States as a leader of the free world cannot afford further retreat in Asia," Nixon began.

Then came the kicker: "It is hoped the United States will not have to send troops there, but if this government cannot avoid it, the administration must face up to the situation and dispatch forces. Therefore, the United States must go to Geneva and take a positive stand for united action by the free world. Otherwise it will have to take on the problem alone and try to sell it to others. . . . This country is the only nation politically strong enough at home to take a position that will save Asia."[24]

The statement captured headlines all over the world the following day. Many papers attributed it, as per the agreement, to a "high administration official," but *France-Soir* identified the speaker as Nixon, as did (in more elliptical language) *The Times* of London. Soon several American papers followed suit, and Nixon felt compelled to fess up. He insisted, however, that the comments were merely his personal opinion, expressed impromptu in response to a hypothetical question. Many were skeptical, then and later. For one thing, the speech was perfectly timed, coming just as Dulles was bending every effort to win allied backing for United Action. For another, why had Nixon answered this supposedly out-of-the-blue question at such length, and by reading—many of those present could see—from a prepared text? There seemed nothing impromptu about it.

To *The Wall Street Journal* and *The Washington Post*, it was perfectly obvious that Nixon's answer had been cleared in advance. Yes, agreed Arthur Krock of *The New York Times,* this was an administration-sanctioned trial balloon, floated to gauge the public's attitude concerning the dispatch of ground forces to Vietnam.[25] Nixon immediately denied these claims, and no evidence has surfaced to show he coordinated his comments with either Eisenhower or Dulles ahead of time. But the vice president also insisted, both then and in later interviews and in his memoirs, that everything he said that day was consistent with U.S. policy, as articulated in Dulles's New York City speech on March 29 and elsewhere.[26] The administration had long declared Indochina to be a vital theater of the Cold War, and all he had done before the editors was affirm that position. This is a wholly plausible claim. The difference, of course, is that whereas the secretary of state's remarks on March 29 were a study in artful obfuscation, open to wide interpretation, these by Nixon were anything but ambiguous.[27]

If Dulles and Eisenhower were displeased with Nixon's choice of words, they didn't show it. Dulles teased Nixon on the phone about getting his name in the paper and assured him that the president was not disturbed by what he had said. Eisenhower, in a subsequent phone conversation, told Nixon not to worry, he probably would have said the same thing himself. Publicly the president refused to comment on the matter, leading journalists to speculate he approved of the remarks. Nixon, *The Wall Street Journal* declared, had "expressed a carefully considered administration view."[28]

Whether intended as such or not, the statement did serve as a useful trial balloon for American planners, though which direction it drifted was not clear. Many editors who heard the speech in person were favorably impressed, it seems, or at least bought the underlying message. "More than a generation ago Lenin set down the dictum that the conquest of the world for communism lay, first, in the conquest of Asia," pontificated *The New York Times*. The dictum had been followed, the paper continued, and much of Asia had since 1945 been lost to the West. The process could not be allowed to continue, for on the outcome at Dien Bien Phu hinged "survival in a free world, for us as well as for the Indochinese. This is the reason that the Vice-President and our Administration take the case seriously and the reason we must do likewise." *The Wall Street Journal* announced it would support a decision to send troops and declared: "The premise of this decision, which Mr. Nixon stated with a candor and persuasiveness that does him great credit, is that Indo-China is vital to the security of the United States. Therefore, should it unhappily come to the ultimate choice, the United States must do what must be done." And America must do it despite the fact—the paper added prophetically—that the "road through Indo-China will be a long one for the United States."[29]

Nixon, like most ambitious politicians an assiduous reader of his own press coverage, welcomed these and other expressions of editorial support.[30] He was taken aback, however, by the negative response in Congress, where many legislators feared that the *Journal*'s assessment was all too correct: The war, once entered, would last a long time. Hadn't they made clear to the White House, moreover, that intervention would have to be multilateral? Why, then, was the vice president implying that the United States might act regardless of allied backing? Democrats voiced these concerns the loudest, but even Republicans acknowledged that the administration still had a job to do to build popular support. In a Gallup poll after Nixon's speech, 68 percent of those surveyed opposed sending U.S. ground forces to Indochina.[31]

Whether this mixed response to the speech had any appreciable effect on administration policy that April is hard to say. Probably it didn't, except perhaps to remind top officials that unilateral intervention involving U.S. ground forces would not be an easy sell at home. Top policy makers were as committed after the speech to implementing United Action as they had been before and as leery of any kind of compromise settlement with the Communists at Geneva. Eisenhower and Dulles were exasperated by the London government's attitude on both of these matters but had not given up on changing Britain's policy or, if that failed, finding a way to proceed militarily without her. Both men were furious with France for seeking large-scale American aid while insisting on retaining full authority over war policy, and for refusing to grant full independence to the Associated States; but they still saw no option but to keep the French in the fight until the rainy season brought relief, and to stiffen the Laniel-Bidault team's backbone in preparation for Geneva. On April 24, more than a week after Nixon's speech, presidential press secretary James Hagerty would write in his diary that the option of using American airpower "to support French troops at Dien Bien Phu" remained alive.[32]

Walter Robertson, the assistant secretary of state for Far Eastern affairs and a figure largely lost to history, gave a sense of the administration's determination in a dinner conversation with an American journalist in Paris on April 22. Robertson was a hawk with a tendency toward hyperbole, but even so his comments are revealing. "We must recognize," he told C. L. Sulzberger of *The New York Times*, "that it is impossible for us to lose Southeast Asia—which would follow the loss of Indochina." America's "whole civilization would be affected," and therefore intervention was the only answer. "What is the difference," Robertson asked, "whether the Communists start a war of aggression or we lose our civilization because we have failed to take a sufficiently powerful stand?" To Sulzberger this was a reiteration of Eisenhower's domino theory as expressed two weeks earlier, and a recipe for "preventive war," but the journalist noted that Robertson also said a war—any kind of war—would mean the end of "'our civilization'—even in budgetary terms, quite apart from the destructive power of new weapons. [Robertson] remarked that the national debt was then $275 billion and 'another war would bankrupt the country.'" Still, the United States must go in, and with as much force as necessary. "This is a time," Robertson warned, "to tighten our belts, a time for unpopular decisions and higher taxes—not for a soft, easy, luxurious life."

Robertson added that the Vietnamese hated the French and that Washington was stuck with France's puppet emperor, "the horrid little Bao Dai." He muttered dejectedly: "If only Ho Chi Minh were on our side we could do something about the situation. But unfortunately he is the enemy."[33]

V

ROBERTSON AND SULZBERGER WERE DINING IN PARIS BECAUSE JOHN Foster Dulles and top aides had returned to the French capital—less than a week after leaving—for more talks, this time in tripartite form involving also the British. Officially the meeting was to be devoted to NATO affairs, but Indochina dominated from start to finish. No one present doubted the importance of the moment: This was the last chance to develop a unified Western position in advance of the Geneva Conference, set to begin a few days thence.

Bidault made the first move, in a session with Dulles on the morning of April 22, before the British delegation had even arrived. In recent days had come more grim news from Dien Bien Phu, and General Navarre once again pressed for immediate and massive U.S. air support, à la Operation Vulture, despite deep private doubts that any such intervention would come in time to save the garrison. (On April 21, he wired Paris: "From now on, it is as much for the United States that we are fighting as for ourselves.") General Valluy sounded out U.S. officials in Washington on April 18 but got a noncommittal response—it would be up to Eisenhower, he was told, and the president had not yet made up his mind. Dejected Paris policy makers considered negotiating a truce to allow the evacuation of the wounded, but the view prevailed that such a truce would give the Viet Minh too great a propaganda advantage heading into Geneva. What alternative remained? Perhaps only one, Bidault concluded: The government might have to accept United Action and its odious political elements, if that was the price to be paid for relieving Dien Bien Phu.[34]

But Bidault still could not bring himself to accept the Americans' prescription, not fully. Dulles would have to bend a little too. At that first session on April 22, the Frenchman, looking exhausted and depressed and joined on his side only by General Ely, painted a dark picture of the situation at Dien Bien Phu; in the past few days, it had become, he said, virtually hopeless. Disagreements and recriminations between the top generals—a clear reference to the now-unbridgeable chasm between Navarre and René Cogny—made things even worse. Nor was any kind of breakout from the camp possible, since the wounded could not be moved and the able-bodied troops would not leave them behind. Only one thing now had any chance of saving the situation, Navarre and Ely continued, namely a massive air intervention, of the kind only America could undertake, involving two to three hundred carrier-based aircraft. Britain could be forgotten, since her participation would be minuscule anyway. Alongside such immediate action at Dien Bien Phu—here came Bidault's concession—an internationalization of the struggle of the type Washington wanted would be possible, even though the French government had been opposed to it up to now.[35]

Dulles liked what he heard. At last Paris had moved toward acceptance of United Action. Much as he may have wanted to strike a deal right then and there, however, the secretary knew he could not. A collective defense system would have to be in place *before* any intervention; Congress had made that clear. Or at least Great Britain would have to be directly and explicitly on board. And there was one more thing, he told Bidault: France would have to give the Associated States an "independent" role in the new system, meaning they would be able to negotiate themselves to receive American aid. Bidault shook his head. If Dien Bien Phu fell, France would have no need for a coalition, he replied, and indeed would not want one, for in such an eventuality the French people would see a coalition as doing nothing but prolonging French bloodshed in Southeast Asia. According to Dulles's account, the Frenchman concluded the meeting with an ominous warning: If the fortress fell, France would want to pull out completely from Southeast Asia and assume no continuing commitments, "and the rest of us would have to get along without France in this area."[36]

It was an inauspicious start to the proceedings. Bidault, according to several sources, left the meeting enraged by the Americans' stubborn fixation on United Action when he could think only of Dien Bien Phu, while Dulles for his part told the British delegation over lunch that the French were on the verge of quitting Vietnam altogether.[37] When the tripartite talks got under way that afternoon, Bidault's mood had not improved. He was garrulous, ironical, and obscure, and more than a few of the twenty-odd people in the room, aware of his weakness for drink, thought he was inebriated. A British observer suspected exhaustion more than alcohol, but the effect was the same: Nobody really understood what the Frenchman was saying. "[He] said he was casting himself to the wolves, into the waves, under the train, but we could not quite make out which wolves, waves, train." Bidault also read out a "declaration of French intentions" that indicated a French commitment to defending the Associated States at all costs, but later in the meeting he seemed to dismiss it as merely "*une tendance,*" which he did not plan to publish.[38]

Turning to Dulles, the foreign minister noted the presence of American ships in the Gulf of Tonkin and Dulles's repeated public statements that America would not tolerate the expansion of Communism. If Washington wished, it could now reconcile those twin realities by assisting France at Dien Bien Phu. "He merely looked glum," Bidault later remembered, "and did not even promise to repeat my request to Washington."[39]

AS TOP NATO LEADERS MEET IN PARIS TO DISCUSS THE NEXT COURSE OF
ACTION IN INDOCHINA, FRENCH PARATROOPS FILE INTO THE NOSE OF A
U.S. AIR FORCE GLOBEMASTER AT ORLY AIRPORT IN THE CITY'S OUTSKIRTS
ON APRIL 23, 1954, BOUND FOR DIEN BIEN PHU.

But Dulles did offer a response, the nature of which has been shrouded
in controversy for half a century. According to Bidault, the American
took him aside during an intermission and asked him whether atomic
bombs could be effective at Dien Bien Phu. If so, Dulles allegedly went
on, his government could provide two such bombs to France. Bidault
said he turned down the request, on the grounds that the bombs would
destroy the garrison as well as the Viet Minh, while dropping them farther away, on supply lines, would risk war with China. When informed a
few months later of Bidault's claim, Dulles said he could not recall making such an offer and insisted there must have been a misunderstanding. Given Bidault's visible exhaustion on the day in question and his
muddled speech-making, and given the lack of any British or American
confirmation of the claim, it is reasonable to suppose Dulles might have
been right. On the other hand, Bidault's version is supported by senior
French official Jean Chauvel in his memoirs, and by General Ely in his
diary, which was kept on a daily basis. Ely wrote that he was of two minds

about "the offer of two atom bombs. The psychological impact would be tremendous, but the [military] effectiveness was uncertain, and it carries the risk of generalized warfare."[40]

Moreover, Bidault's contention that Washington might offer atom bombs to his government had an inherent plausibility. At several points that spring, U.S. strategists had considered the possible use of the bomb, and according to one interpretation, Operation Vulture had always, from its inception, had an atomic dimension. In early April, a study group in the Pentagon examined the possibility of using atomic weapons at Dien Bien Phu and concluded that three tactical A-bombs, properly employed, would be sufficient to obliterate the Viet Minh effort there.[41] Admiral Radford used this finding to suggest the use of the A-bomb to the NSC on April 7. And on April 29, mere days after this supposed Bidault-Dulles encounter, the use of "new weapons" in Indochina was raised for discussion in a meeting of the NSC Planning Board. Some participants in that meeting argued that using atomic power in Vietnam could deter China from retaliating in response to expanded conventional attacks, while failure to employ it would lead Mao and his government to conclude that the United States lacked the will to take advantage of its technological might. National Security Adviser Robert Cutler raised the matter with Eisenhower and Nixon the next morning, and they replied that atomic weapons would likely not be effective at Dien Bien Phu. But they agreed, according to the meeting note taker, that "we might *consider* saying to the French that we had never yet given them any 'new weapons' and if they wanted some *now* for possible use, we might give them a few."[42]

Dulles himself, at this very Paris meeting, formally raised the matter of atomic weapons and their possible use, though without explicit reference to Indochina. In a speech to the NATO Council on the evening of April 23, he declared that Soviet advantages in manpower were too great—in military, political, or economic terms—for the West to overcome. Therefore, nuclear weapons must be considered part of NATO's "conventional" arsenal. The secretary went on to assert that it must be "our agreed policy," in the case of either general or *local* war, to use atomic weapons "whenever or wherever it would be of advantage to do so, taking account of all relevant factors."[43] Dulles sought here to speak to the furor in Europe resulting from the recent H-bomb tests, and he may also have been wanting to keep Moscow and Beijing guessing as to what the West might resort to in Indochina; but his language is a further indication that the use of the bomb in the jungles of Tonkin in the spring of 1954 was, from the administration's perspective, decidedly within the realm of possibility.

Much of the discussion on April 23 was taken up by NATO business, but Indochina remained on everyone's minds. A night's sleep had done Bidault good—he was sharper in the morning session, and he looked better. But the arrival of a letter from General Navarre sent him into despair again, and in the afternoon he took Dulles aside, letter in hand. Dien Bien Phu would fall very soon, he told the American. De Castries's combat-worthy force was down by two-thirds, to a mere three thousand men; no more reserves remained. Air-dropped supplies continued to land behind Viet Minh lines. After the garrison's fall, General Giap would move his forces to the Red River Delta and launch an offensive against Hanoi—before the rainy season got fully under way. In such a situation, Bidault continued, Paris would have no choice but to seek a full cease-fire by the quickest possible means. Only one thing could forestall this calamitous sequence of events: immediate and massive air support for the besieged garrison by American B-29s. Would the United States, he asked, reconsider her rejection of Operation Vulture?

Dulles listened intently and said he would have an answer by the following day, after conferring with Eisenhower and with Admiral Radford, who was en route from Washington. This reply gave Bidault hope, even as time was running out at Dien Bien Phu (Giap had commenced his third phase), and other French officials that day also thought Operation Vulture might still happen. General Ely, for example, considered making an appeal to the Viet Minh for a cease-fire in order to collect the wounded from Dien Bien Phu. He added in his diary: "After refusal, get U.S. intervention."[44]

Dulles now in fact was inclined to accept the French version of events, at least to a degree. Still dubious that air strikes at Dien Bien Phu would be militarily effective, much less that they would save the garrison, he nevertheless saw them as the only ready means to bolster France's will to resist. His conviction on this point deepened over dinner as Defense Minister René Pleven disabused him of the hope that any cease-fire would be limited to Dien Bien Phu. It would apply to the whole of Indochina, Pleven insisted. The West's bargaining power at Geneva would be effectively nil, and the Communists would secure a resounding victory. Dulles knew what he must do: He must gain British support for United Action—the sine qua non of congressional assent to military intervention—and he must do it fast. Eden, bracing himself for what lay ahead, cabled Churchill that Dulles seemed to want air strikes, then went to bed, he recalled later, "a deeply troubled man." His private secretary, Evelyn Shuckburgh, took a sleeping pill but still managed only four hours.[45]

VI

SATURDAY, APRIL 24, DAWNED SUNNY AND WARM, A GLORIOUS PARIS spring day. Overnight Dulles had cabled the president, who was spending the weekend in Augusta, Georgia, informing him of the Bidault request for intervention at Dien Bien Phu. "The situation here is tragic," Dulles wrote. "France is almost visibly collapsing under our eyes." Dien Bien Phu had achieved symbolic importance all out of proportion to its military significance, and if the fortress fell, most likely "the government will be taken over by defeatists."[46]

The message alarmed Eisenhower, and he gave serious thought to returning to Washington to monitor the crisis. He opted to stay put for now, but the matter consumed his attention on the Saturday. That morning he called acting secretary of state (in Dulles's absence) Walter Bedell Smith, who told him the situation was evolving so rapidly—in both Paris and Vietnam—that making considered appraisals was almost impossible. The president nevertheless offered a couple: The French were contemptible for constantly seeking U.S. aid while insisting on Washington remaining a junior partner; and Eden and the British were foolish for failing to see that it was preferable to fight the Communists in Indochina, where hundreds of thousands of French Union troops were engaged, rather than in some other country lacking such a force. Admiral Radford should be urged, Eisenhower continued, to stop in London on his return from Paris and ask the British military chiefs baldly why they'd rather fight "after they've lost 200,000 French."[47] A subsequent presidential cable to Dulles lauded the secretary for his efforts thus far and suggested he hand Premier Laniel a message from Eisenhower urging France to commit to staying in the fight, "regardless of the possibility of the physical over-running of the gallant outpost" of Dien Bien Phu.[48]

The message could hardly be clearer: In the president's mind that final weekend in April 1954, military intervention in Indochina was a very live possibility.

Eisenhower's cable arrived in Paris in midafternoon, local time, by which point the climactic Dulles-Eden encounter was about to begin. The setting was Ambassador Dillon's residence on Avenue d'Iéna. The British suspected what was coming, and any doubt was removed by what they saw on arrival: There to greet them in the garden were not only Dulles and his wife and the ambassador and his, but a phalanx of senior U.S. army and navy officers, including Radford. Dulles immediately guided the guests into the study and, after acknowledging that Dien Bien Phu might now be beyond saving, made the case for joint Anglo-American intervention in Indochina. Only such a commitment would keep the French in the war, Dulles declared, and thus would be highly beneficial even if it failed in its immediate objective of preventing the fall of the fortress in remote Tonkin. Radford, who seemed to the Britons present to be yearning for war, said that the impending fall of Dien Bien Phu would leave no option but for the United States and Great Britain to more or less take over the fighting, pushing the French into the background and hoping by these actions to so inspire the Vietnamese that they would rally against the Viet Minh—and also prevent a massacre of French troops by disaffected VNA units. If Her Majesty's government would participate nominally in an air bombardment (Radford suggested the contribution of RAF squadrons in Malaya and Hong Kong), the administration was prepared to seek congressional support for American intervention, Dulles said. But it would never happen absent allied (read: British) involvement.

Once again Dulles had presented the British with a choice: Would it be joint action or appeasement?[49] Eden refused to be drawn but restated his doubts that air strikes would do any good and his fear that the kind of intervention proposed could result in a dangerous Cold War conflagration. More and more skeptical of the domino theory, Eden doubted that defeat in Indochina would cause neighboring countries to fall one by one. Intervention would also be "hell at home," he remarked, sure to inflame

British public opinion. The Americans offered no sympathy. Dulles, the foreign secretary later remarked, seemed in a "fearfully excited state" during the exchange, and did not demur when Radford and the "even more vehement and emotional" Walter Robertson spoke of bombing China to teach her a lesson once and for all.[50]

When Bidault joined the discussion at four-thirty P.M., the Americans continued the offensive. What would be the position of the French government, Dulles demanded to know, if Dien Bien Phu fell? Would it continue the war? Bidault equivocated. He and Laniel would want to pursue the struggle, he said, but would have to contend with a highly problematic military and psychological reaction. Dulles persisted: Would Paris, as René Pleven had asserted the night before, declare before Geneva a full cease-fire covering all of Indochina? No, the Frenchman replied, there would be no such declaration, and he would enter the negotiations with considerable freedom of maneuver. Thus reassured, Dulles produced a draft letter, addressed to Bidault, stating that while U.S. intervention at Dien Bien Phu was now impossible, Washington was nevertheless ready to move "armed forces" into Indochina, provided France and other allies so desired, for the purpose of defending Southeast Asia. The letter was handed to Eden, who skimmed it and passed it on to Bidault. Several minutes ticked by as he read it and considered his options. He was still primarily interested in Dien Bien Phu, and he remained leery of internationalization, but perhaps this was a way to salvage something out of the wreckage. He cleared his throat and said yes, he would be prepared to receive the letter formally.[51]

Suddenly events stood at a new watershed: United Action was back with a bang, and the war seemed about to be internationalized. Eden quickly interjected that his government did not feel bound by the Dulles-Eden communiqué of April 14 to intervene in the Indochina War. He could promise no more, he said, than to return to London at once to consult with his cabinet colleagues. But the foreign secretary understood that the crucial moment had arrived; as he noted in a cable to the Foreign Office just before heading to the airport: "It is now quite clear that we shall have to take a decision of first-class importance, namely whether to tell the Americans that we are prepared to go along with their plan or not." Just prior to departure, he received a call from Maurice Schumann, the French secretary of state for foreign affairs, advising him that both Laniel and Bidault hoped he would gain approval from his colleagues to proceed "on the lines desired by Mr. Dulles."[52]

The dilemma was acute, as Shuckburgh observed in his diary that evening: "If we refuse to cooperate with the US plan, we strain the Alliance. If we do as Dulles asks, we certainly provoke the bitterest hostility of India and probably all other Asiatic states and destroy the Commonwealth. Also, a war for Indo-China would be about as difficult a thing to put across the British public as you could find."[53]

Eden and his team landed at 10:20 P.M., got into two waiting cars, and drove straight to Churchill's country estate, Chequers, arriving shortly before midnight. There to greet them was the prime minister, wearing a silken two-piece suit covered by a dressing gown. Drinks were distributed, whereupon Eden laid out the essentials of the situation. Churchill heard him out, then ruminated on "our glorious Empire, our wonderful Indian Empire, we have cast it away"—the implication being, thought Shuckburgh, why should Britain fight for a decrepit French colonial effort after that? Then a cold supper, during which general agreement was reached that Britain should reject the American request. In London the following morning, the cabinet, in a rare Sunday meeting to which the chiefs of staff were also summoned, needed little persuasion to confirm the rejection. The chiefs of staff said the proposed action would be ineffective and added that even a total collapse in Indochina would not decisively affect the British position in Malaya. The domino theory did not hold.[54]

VII

BUT THE WEEKEND DRAMA WAS NOT OVER. THAT SAME MORNING in Washington Walter Bedell Smith, having learned that the French cabinet had in fact *declined* late on Saturday night to accept Dulles's letter and instead wanted simply an air bombardment at Dien Bien Phu, made a new offer to the French ambassador: If Paris could persuade the British to join even nominally a coalition dedicated to preventing Communist expansion in Southeast Asia, and if the Laniel government would agree to grant America strategic command in Indochina, then the administration could seek a congressional resolution that would allow a carrier-based strike force to go into action at Dien Bien Phu in three days' time, or by April 27. The action might come too late to save the fortress, but it could stiffen French resistance elsewhere in Indochina.

Eden learned of this new American proposal in the early afternoon during a hastily arranged meeting with René Massigli, the French ambassador. Immediately the ministers and the chiefs of staff were told to return for a second session, which convened at four o'clock. Eden made no attempt to hide his fury. This was a naked attempt by Washington to make Britain responsible for any failure to prevent Communist expansion in the region, he told the group, and he resented "this indirect approach [by the Americans] to the United Kingdom Government through the French." It spoke volumes that Smith had spoken only to the French ambassador in Washington and not to the British. The plan for a strike at Dien Bien Phu would be unsuccessful and was likely a red herring, Eden continued; the real objective would turn out to be China. The cabinet had no authority from Parliament to support such action, and it might be condemned by the United Nations. A dangerous escalation might follow, leading ultimately to a "third world war."

Churchill agreed. He told the group he disliked being asked to "assist in misleading Congress" into authorizing a military operation that would not salvage the situation for France and that could take the world to the brink of a major war. The request must be rejected. No voice rose up in opposition, and the meeting reaffirmed the consensus of the earlier meeting. Eden flew to Geneva, touching down briefly at Orly airport in Paris to inform Bidault of the government's decision. The Frenchman, never confident he would get a positive reply, took the news stoically.[55]

Not so Admiral Radford, who made the case for intervention personally to Churchill at Chequers on April 26. He held nothing back. Defeat at Dien Bien Phu, and failure by the United States and Great Britain to take appropriate action to try to prevent it, would be a huge victory for Communism and a turning point in history. The French government would fall, the EDC would fail to win ratification, and NATO itself might be destroyed. Southeast Asia would be lost, Japan would turn toward Communism, and Australia and New Zealand would be in danger. Nationalists in North Africa would rise up against the French, which would spread unrest and disquiet into the rest of Africa and the Middle East. In short, the effects would be global and calamitous. But it was not too late. Radford said he had been present at a meeting with congressional leaders at which the legislators made clear that they would approve action to save Indochina—*if* Great Britain was willing to cooperate. There was no time to waste, however, for each day that passed meant a proportionate gain for the Communist powers at the West's expense. Now was the hour to make a stand against China, and the prime minister need not fear that the Russians, who were fearful of war, would join in the struggle and openly aid the Chinese.

Churchill did not deny that the fall of Dien Bien Phu could be a momentous turning point in history. He was reminded, he said, of the situation at Warsaw in 1919, when the Russians, sweeping westward, were stopped by Pilsudski with the advice and help of General Weygand and Lord d'Abernon. The tide was halted and indeed turned back. The question was if the same thing could be done this time. Churchill thought not, and said it was in any event premature to take action prior to Geneva. Diplomacy, what he called "conversations at the centre," must now assume primary importance. Such negotiations might or might not prove successful, but they would be understood by the British people far better than taking up arms in far-off Southeast Asia. A great part of his life and strength, the prime minister concluded, had been directed toward strengthening the bond between English-speaking peoples and in particular between Great Britain and America. But the two allies could not now allow themselves to commit to a policy that might lead to their destruction and that was almost certain to be militarily ineffective. "The loss of the fortress must be faced," Churchill said bluntly, and France had insufficient forces to hold down all the rest of Indochina. The sensible policy was for France to withdraw to areas she could realistically hold, and for London and Washington to await the outcome at Geneva before taking further measures.[56]

One of Churchill's assertions in particular stuck in Radford's craw. The prime minister said he doubted Britain would be willing to help save Indochina for France when she had not been willing to save India for herself. It was almost incomprehensible, Radford confided to Richard Nixon three days later, that the same Churchill who had understood the seriousness of the Communist menace so fully back in 1947 and 1948 could make such a foolish statement, could equate the two crises in terms of their importance.[57]

Radford thanked the prime minister for his time and said he would report the full content of their conversation to Eisenhower upon returning to Washington the next day. In the absence of close Anglo-American cooperation, he added obliquely, both the United States and the United Kingdom would drift to disaster.[58]

It did not help Radford's cause that British officials judged him a rather dim bulb, lacking in subtlety and always seeming, as one said, to be "raring for a scrap" with Beijing. It irritated them that he would come to England to pressure them into joining what Eden contemptuously referred to as "Radford's war against China."[59] The Foreign Office surmised that Radford's unvarnished stridency was not fully representative of the administration's position, which was true enough but missed a crucial point: It had been Eisenhower's idea to have the admiral dash across the Channel after Paris to try to talk some sense into the selfish and pusillanimous British.

When a dejected Radford boarded his plane for the return flight across the Atlantic, it brought to an end a remarkable fortnight in American diplomacy. On two occasions—starting in this same city on April 11—John Foster Dulles had come to Europe to make the case for an internationalization of the Indochina War. Both times he had shown a willingness to mislead his allied counterparts regarding the state of congressional and military opinion in the United States and the necessary conditions for American military intervention. Yet both times he had failed to find support where it mattered most, in London. Anthony Eden had refused to play along. He and his colleagues saw the stakes and the possibilities in Indochina differently than their American cousins, and they were much more fearful of the dangers of escalation. The poor chemistry between the two men, evident for months, had evolved into obvious and open dislike. Nor was the feud likely to end anytime soon: Both were now in Switzerland for the start of the Geneva Conference. There would be no avoiding each other there, no avoiding the need to strategize about the crucial negotiations to come.

In Washington, Dwight Eisenhower, sounding very much the hawk, fumed about London's obstructionism and "morbid obsession" with World War III. The British, he complained in his diary on April 27, were showing "woeful unawareness" of the risks "we run in that region." And the French were no better. "The French have used weasel words in promising independence and through this one reason as much as anything else, have suffered reverses that have really been inexcusable," the president told childhood friend Swede Hazlett the same day. Even as he railed against his allies, however, Ike continued to frame the issue in military terms. To Hazlett, he said he wanted to see the Communists "take a good smacking in Indo-China," while to Republican legislative leaders, he warned of the dangers of not coming to France's aid. "Where in the hell can you let the Communists chip away any more? We just can't stand it."[60]

Therein lay the rub, as Eisenhower knew. Having determined that Indochina must be held, and having stated publicly that failure to hold it could have disastrous consequences for American and Western security, his administration felt pressure to act forcefully to prevent such a calamity from occurring. Its credibility was on the line, both internationally and at home—or so the president and his aides feared. The public information campaign launched a month earlier had achieved considerable gains domestically—Congress and the press largely bought the administration's claims regarding Indochina's vital importance, and its domino theorizing—but that very success also had the effect of reducing the president's maneuverability. Fail now to prevent a Viet Minh victory, and a lot of powerful voices in American society would attack the White House for standing by as the Communists gained a crucial piece of territory.

Yet the prospect of unilateral intervention involving U.S. ground troops carried its own political risks, Eisenhower understood, with memories of an unpopular war in Korea still fresh in people's minds and with Republicans facing midterm elections in the fall. Sure, people would initially rally around the flag and around the president, as they always did in times of international crisis. But Vietnam was too remote from Middle America, and the core issues too murky, for the support to last long. It would be a "little war," and under the administration's massive retaliation policy, such interventions were to be avoided—nations that persisted in hostile action were to be warned, given a chance to be peaceful, then hit with the full force of American striking power if they failed to relent.

A-bombs and H-bombs would take the place of GIs as the counter to aggression.

And there were other grounds too, Eisenhower knew, to question the wisdom of going in alone. The number of troops required, for one thing, would likely be large, given the size of the area involved. Viet Minh forces in Indochina in late April 1954, as superimposed on a map of the United States, were spread from Vermont down to Savannah, Georgia. Fighting had been raging, in this analogy, around a fort near Rochester, New York, while nightly attacks were common in New England, in the Carolinas, and with thrusts made into western Pennsylvania.[61] Nor was it clear where the U.S. troops would come from. Of the twenty-two current combat divisions (nineteen army and three marine), five were tied down in Europe, unavailable to be withdrawn for limited war elsewhere. Nine were committed in Korea, or were standing by in Japan to prevent a resumption of fighting in Korea. That left eight divisions at home in the United States, in training or standing by in case of a "big war," a number that Pentagon planners insisted was close to the minimum force required at home for basic security. Finally, in geostrategic terms, would the United States be perceived as a colonialist aggressor in the eyes of the world if she went in unilaterally? Would America's prestige (and Eisenhower's own personal historical legacy) be irrevocably tied to achieving victory in such a war? Yes and yes, the president feared.

And so, he determined, the focus would have to remain on collective action, both diplomatically at Geneva and militarily in Vietnam. London would have to be coaxed into coming on board, or some means be found to get around what Radford, on his return to Washington, despairingly called Britain's "veto power" over U.S. policy.[62] Perhaps it would be possible to cobble together a coalition without her. But it wouldn't happen quickly, not quickly enough to affect the situation at Dien Bien Phu. For all the disagreement and ill will between the Churchill and Eisenhower governments, on this point they were now in full accord: The garrison was in all likelihood doomed. No allied intervention would be sufficient. Only a miracle could save it.

CHAPTER 21

VALLEY OF TEARS

TUESDAY, APRIL 27, 1954, DAWNED GRAY AND DAMP AT DIEN BIEN
Phu. So thick were the clouds during the night's storms that hardly any
planes got through, and twenty Dakotas, laden with supplies to be air-
dropped over the camp, turned around and flew back to their base in
the delta. Only fifty volunteers were dropped in as reinforcements for
the garrison. The following night the Dakotas again were forced to turn
back, though some eighty legionnaires succeeded in parachuting in over
strongpoint Isabelle.

The abortive missions were a common occurrence now, for the monsoon season had begun. Some five months it would last, during which
sixty inches of rain could be expected to fall in the Tai highlands. Life in
the garrison, arduous enough before, now became almost unimaginably
grim, particularly in the lowland sector in the west of the camp and at
Isabelle to the south, as the ground turned to mud and as the perimeter
continued to shrink in the face of shellfire, mortars, and sniping. Movement was largely confined to the crumbling labyrinth of trenches, where
the liquid mud could be knee-deep and where the men, unwilling to risk
making a dash for the latrine trench, relieved themselves on the spot. It
was Passchendaele 1917 all over again. Food was in short supply, and exhaustion from lack of sleep a constant concern. Most of the paratroopers
and legionnaires had now been in action for at least forty-five days—the
point after which, studies of World War II soldiers show, fatigue no longer causes merely dangerous carelessness but physical and emotional
breakdown.[1] Support aircraft, meanwhile, were often denied sight of the

ground, if not by turbulent masses of cumulonimbus clouds, then by the *crachin,* the dry fog characteristic of the Tonkin highlands at all times of the year.

The rains worsened the already-miserable conditions for the wounded in the camp and for the medical staff, headed by the estimable Major Grauwin. The team of doctors and its one fully trained nurse—Geneviève de Galard-Terraube, age twenty-nine, who along with a few prostitutes was the only woman left in the camp and whom the Paris press heralded as the "Angel of Dien Bien Phu"—had worked indefatigably for weeks on end and had succeeded in creating a makeshift but reasonably well-functioning surgery. But now the system suffered a breakdown. On April 17, the hospital reported its first confirmed case of gangrene, and in the days thereafter, monsoon rains began seeping in everywhere. Space limitations became still more acute, and the Moroccan sappers of the 31st Engineering Battalion were set to work, night after night, to dig new tunnels into the ground in order to make room for the wounded, some eight hundred of whom were awaiting evacuation. Grauwin meanwhile faced an enemy of a different sort, as maggots invaded the infirmary and laid their eggs under bloody bandages and plaster casts. "At night," Grauwin later recalled, "it was a shocking sight to watch those repugnant little white worms moving over the hands, the faces, and in the ears of the sleeping wounded." He tried to reassure the panic-stricken men that the maggots, by eating dead and infected tissue, were hastening the healing process.[2]

Through it all they carried on, these dwindling battalions, and, remarkable though it seems, kept their discipline largely intact. April to this point had seen 701 men killed, 1,948 wounded, 375 unaccounted for, and 47 deserters.[3] Yet volunteer replacements continued to come forward and, despite the weather problems, to descend into the camp. Their numbers were never large enough to make up for the casualties—which ran between fifty and a hundred per day in late April—but they were a welcome sight nonetheless. Even more extraordinary, many of the troops maintained the belief, well into the first week of May, that victory would come in the end, that the enemy would be broken and have to withdraw. These men reacted with incredulity whenever a newly arrived comrade would speak of the pessimism that reigned in Hanoi. How could this be? The enemy was suffering no less than they were, after all, indeed had it much worse, judging by the far greater number of casualties he was incurring. His trenches must be filling up as quickly as theirs. As long as the key strongpoints held, the men told one another as they peered out of the bunkers at the darkened mountains surrounding them, their eyes red with exhaustion, it would all work out in the end. The politicians in Geneva would make a deal, or a relief column would arrive from Laos. Or, best of all, the rumors were true and the Americans would send in their B-29s and annihilate the Viet Minh positions and supply lines.

The senior officers had a more sober view of the prospects, but even they entertained the hope that one or more of these deliverances would come to pass. Late each afternoon they would gather, in a dugout by the central command post, with de Castries's principal subordinates Colonel Langlais and Lieutenant Colonel Bigeard summing up the situation. (All three men had won promotion on April 16, with de Castries now brigadier general.) Some days earlier Langlais had estimated effective combat strength of the garrison to be 2,400 men, down from 11,000 men available at the start of the battle plus four battalions parachuted in after it began. Someone asked how this could be: There had not been 12,000 dead or wounded. Langlais replied that he counted only soldiers, not shadows. Many hundreds of men had stopped fighting and indeed at night went to pillage the air-dropped supplies. Should there be a punitive expedition against these slackers, the so-called Rats of Nam Youm? No, Langlais had determined. There were already so many dead, so many wounded, what good would it accomplish? The matter could be pursued later, if anyone made it out.[4]

Outside the valley, meanwhile, French morale was low and going lower. In Saigon and Hanoi, Generals Navarre and Cogny, their mutual animosity stronger than ever, understood what the commanders in the fortress did not yet (happily for them) fully grasp: that there were hardly any additional resources available to commit to the battle.[5] Only one strong airborne battalion, the First Colonial, remained in reserve, and the nonairborne mobile troops were already too committed to ongoing ground operations in the Red River Delta and the Central Highlands to create diversions that would draw Giap's units away from Dien Bien Phu. Was there no way, then, to change the strategic climate in France's favor? The prospect of massive American aerial intervention a fading

LOUDSPEAKERS URGE FRENCH UNION FORCES AT DIEN BIEN PHU TO GIVE
UP DURING THE CLIMACTIC FINAL DAYS OF THE BATTLE: "SURRENDER.
YOU WILL BE TREATED WELL. SHOW FLAGS AND COME OUT IN GOOD
ORDER. THOSE WITH RIFLES, POINT THE BARREL TOWARD THE GROUND."

hope, there remained but one possibility. In order to create a threat to the
rear of Viet Minh positions around Dien Bien Phu, Navarre and Cogny
considered an approach from Laos. Code-named Operation Condor,
the plan appeared promising on paper yet faced two major problems.
First, transporting and supplying the eight battalions called for in the
plan would mean reducing by as much as a third the number of aircraft
available to Dien Bien Phu—this at a time when the garrison needed all
the supplies and reinforcements it could possibly get. Second, the plan
depended on the use of Laotian troops, who were largely untested in
battle and who—it was widely assumed—were too "soft" and too "peace-
loving" to be a match for the battle-hardened and resourceful Viet Minh.

Nevertheless, a limited version of Condor was launched, though neither its commanders nor Navarre nor Cogny entertained much hope it would arrive in Tonkin in time to do much good.[6]

II

ON THIS DAY, THOUGH, APRIL 27, THE COMMAND AT DIEN BIEN PHU had more pressing concerns than whether help might arrive from the west. Foremost among these was the deepening supply problem. It wasn't merely that some planes were forced to turn back on account of the weather; it was that some pilots had stopped flying, fed up with having to dip lower and lower through the flak to compensate for the shrunken drop zones. On the night of April 23–24, one of the mostly American-piloted C-119 "Flying Boxcars" had been hit by two 37mm shells from a Soviet antiaircraft gun. The pilot made it back to base, but the next day the American pilots, who were being paid roughly $2,000 a month for the job, announced they would no longer make the run to Dien Bien Phu; the risks were simply too great, and the French fighter pilots whose job was flak suppression were not doing a good enough job. It took two days for General Cogny to win General Navarre's approval to have French pilots fly the Boxcars, and it remained to be seen if these men would be up to the task.

Meanwhile, the enemy drew ever closer. Two weeks earlier Vo Nguyen Giap had abandoned mass assaults in favor of *grignotage,* or "nibbling away" of the French positions, in a replay of the trench warfare tactics of the Ypres salient in World War I. Hundreds of sappers were deployed to push assault trenches ever closer to the fortifications, a practice, Giap told associates, that would allow the Viet Minh "completely to intercept reinforcements and supplies." Lead elements would dig a deep hole at the bottom of the trench and pass the dirt to the rear, where it would be immediately put in sandbags, while other workers brought forward logs and wooden beams to provide the diggers with overhead cover. It was a simple, beautifully efficient system. On most nights the defend-ers of Eliane could hear the clinking of picks and shovels almost under their feet, sometimes with their naked ears and sometimes using crude geophones made of a combination of wine canteens and medical stethoscopes. This too was reminiscent of Passchendaele forty years earlier, when German troops heard miners from Wales digging beneath them on Messines Ridge, in preparation for blasting them out.[7]

Why did Giap shift tactics? With the French seemingly on the ropes in the second week of April, why did he not seek a swift and conclusive victory, a *coup de grâce*? Mostly because neither he nor his subordinate commanders could accept the casualty rates the French had been inflicting on them in the first month of the fighting. They needed a respite. Of the total number of dead and wounded that the Viet Minh suffered during the battle for Dien Bien Phu, close to half had been suffered already by April 5. Roughly four thousand of these were fatalities. Many of the losses occurred during intense fighting on strongpoints Dominique, Eliane, and Huguette, but French aerial attacks also could have devastating effect. C-47 transports were equipped with depth-charge racks to allow napalm drums to be unloaded swiftly. These were fused to explode twenty yards above the ground. Larger C-119s swept low, then pulled up abruptly while napalm cans slid out. The actual damage done by these attacks was often marginal, especially when poor weather and antiaircraft fire made accurate targeting impossible, but the mere anticipation that such a weapon could fall from the sky was acutely unnerving to defenders.

By mid-April, various reports indicated growing despondency among Viet Minh troops. Fiery speeches by political commissars about sacrifice, duty, and the need to stamp out Franco-American imperialism were duly given, but these worked best on new recruits anticipating quick success; they rang hollow to weary veterans of the frontal attacks who had witnessed comrades being slaughtered all around them and who themselves might have sustained wounds. French radio intelligence picked up agitated dispatches from lower-unit commanders reporting that some units were refusing orders, and a Viet Minh deserter told the French on April 20 that new recruits were despondent about the difficulties of the struggle. The commissars had to press all the harder, especially at recovery stations where soldiers were convalescing, insisting that the fight must go on as long as necessary, regardless of losses.[8]

Many of the new recruits had walked to Dien Bien Phu, often in groups of about a hundred, usually for long distances through difficult terrain, only to find conditions worse after they arrived. Though the

People's Army had the luxury of rotating units between the trenches and rest areas in the surrounding jungle, this brought only limited relief. Even in the rear areas, men generally slept only on bamboo mats or banana leaves on plastic mats. Few had mosquito nets, and malaria was endemic. Quinine to treat the illness was in short supply, so much so that soldiers would have to pass around a cup of water containing one dissolved tablet, take a sip, and send it on. When the rains started for real about April 25, the conditions deteriorated, and not only for those in the trenches. Sickness increased, and the situation for the wounded, deplorable to begin with, deteriorated further. Gangrene cases proliferated. Ton That Tung remained the only real surgeon on his side, and along with his six assistants he waged a hopeless struggle to treat the wounded, lacking modern drugs and instruments and sometimes forced to operate while standing knee-deep in water. As before, head injuries were a particular problem, and Tung taught the assistants his method of removing foreign bodies by suction and then closing the skull. With no electrocoagulators at their disposal, the team resorted to touching the blood vessels with white-hot platinum wire.[9]

Referring to this very day, April 27, Ton That Tung would later hint at the extreme hardships he and his staff faced:

0:45 A.M. Somebody rings me up for the next operations. While waiting for the arrival of the wounded, I sit alone in front of the operating room, a straw hut lit by the vacillating light of a kerosene lamp. The song of crickets is drowned in the gurgle of the brooks. Our artillery thunders at regular intervals as though to mark time. The sudden change in the weather makes me feel bad. I recall president Ho's advice: "You must overcome all difficulties." So many difficulties have cropped up. Dien Bien Phu, an idea, a place for testing people's endurance.[10]

A Viet Minh nurse, Nguyen Thi Ngoc Toan, later commented on the brutal conditions:

It was raining very hard and there was a lot of standing water, so there were places cut to allow water to run off, because the bunkers for the wounded had to be kept dry. So the wounded had platforms to lie on. But you had to go out to check the wounded, especially the ones with head wounds, wounds to the skull and brain, and if we discovered that they had died we had to carry out the policy for handling the dead. We had to bind their hands and feet, so that the mortuary people could handle them properly. And when we found someone who had died, we had to follow the procedures to pro-tect and guard them. This was because we also had civilian coolies moving by, and maybe the coolies needed a shirt or a pair of pants, so they would strip clothing from the dead. The guy I replaced had put them outside and had not guarded them properly, and that is why he was disciplined. So I was very frightened of this job. The work was tense and nerve-wracking, and you had all these kinds of things to worry about.[11]

The Politburo of the Vietnamese Workers Party (VWP) was con-cerned enough about flagging morale to discuss the matter in a meet-ing on April 19. Agreement was reached on the need to work harder to buck up soldiers' confidence and to press on for final victory in the battle as soon as possible. Political commissars at Dien Bien Phu vowed to do better, acknowledging "erroneous tendencies" that affected the fulfill-ment of vital tasks. On April 27, they launched a "campaign for moral mobilization and 'rectification' of Rightist tendencies." Giap's statement that day urged marksmen and machine gunners to kill the enemy one by one—"for each bullet fired, an enemy killed"—and promised decorations for the most successful.[12]

In his memoirs of the battle, Giap wrote with candor of this period in late April:

The principal trait of that phase of the battle had been the violent character of the combat. . . . [T]he battle having lasted a very long time, more troops—who had to fight without interruption—became fatigued, worn and subject to great nervous tension. . . . It was pre-cisely at these moments when rightist tendencies appeared among our cadres and soldiers—in the fear of suffering many casualties, [in giving way to] fatigue, in subjectivity, in overestimation of the enemy. . . . These rightist tendencies remained serious, and partly limited the scope of our victories.[13]

"Rightist tendencies" was political shorthand for lack of commitment, doubt, and combat fatigue. Officers, both junior and senior, were themselves not immune to these maladies as they contemplated the prospect of continued fighting and still more casualties among their men. One of them, a twenty-five-year-old company chief of peasant stock and bearing the initials N.T., years later recalled his feeling upon seeing his entire unit decimated. "You are going to die," he had told himself in the midst of the action, "there is nothing more to think about." Though shot in the head, he survived, and he soon rose in rank over the dead bodies of his immediate superiors. Ordered by commanders to launch an offensive against one of the strongpoints, he asked to postpone the attack for a few days because of the exhaustion of his men, who had spent nearly a week digging trenches. "Our men are already overly tired," he said. "We will certainly win the battle if the attack occurs only one day later." His plea was rejected. Only three of his seventy-one men survived the engagement. N.T. vowed quietly to himself that he would never again comply with that kind of order, and in later years he would gain the reputation among superiors as being "unruly" for his determination to minimize casualties among his troops.[14]

Senior commanders also had to contend with the possibility that a French force would arrive from Laos to relieve the garrison (they had become aware of Condor), and—more seriously—the possibility that the United States would intervene with massive airpower. Such a bombardment, they knew, would catch tens of thousands of Viet Minh infantrymen in the open and would surely also destroy the army's forward supply depots at Tuan Giao. Even if none of this happened, even if everything went according to plan, victory at Dien Bien Phu might turn out to be a defeat if Navarre used this time—when much of the Viet Minh troop strength was concentrated here, in the remote northwest—to organize his defenses in the vital Red River Delta. The uncomfortable fact for Giap was that whereas Dien Bien Phu absorbed perhaps 5 percent of the French battle force in Indochina, it tied down as much as 50 percent of Viet Minh forces and the vast bulk of the military aid from China.

These were arguments for launching the third phase of the battle as soon as possible, and Giap took comfort from the fact that his logistical preparations for the final phase were now almost complete. Before dawn that morning, April 27, scores of Viet Minh trucks, their drivers taking advantage of the miserable weather and low cloud cover, had arrived near the battle zone, laden with ammunition. Similar-size deliveries had occurred in the days before that, some containing also 75mm recoilless guns and fuel.[15]

But timing was key. The Geneva Conference was under way, and within a week or two, it would turn its attention to Indochina. If Giap's forces could score an all-out victory at Dien Bien Phu prior to then, it would be a giant boost to Viet Minh negotiators. By the same token, to fail before the eyes of the world by launching the assault prematurely would have potentially disastrous consequences at Geneva. Giap knew he had to choose his moment carefully.

III

JUST HOW THE DRV LEADERSHIP FELT ABOUT GENEVA, AND ABOUT negotiations more broadly, is not easy to discern from the record, but it's clear that top officials retained their earlier skepticism and uncertainty. They were poised, after all, to score a smashing victory at Dien Bien Phu, an outcome certain to undermine drastically the French public's willingness to continue the war. In the Red River Delta, their forces now effectively controlled the central portion of the Hanoi-Haiphong road, while in the country as a whole perhaps 80 percent of the population lived in Viet Minh–held areas. Why risk negotiations in such a situation? In particular, why risk multilateral talks of the type Viet Minh diplomats had never taken part in before?

But in Ho Chi Minh's mind there were also compelling reasons to give diplomacy a serious try, while remaining vigilant as always in pressing the military advantage. For one thing, the morale problem at Dien Bien Phu hinted at an important and growing problem for a revolutionary war now in its eighth year: The Vietnamese people, including those in liberated areas, were tired, were longing for a respite from the fighting, were showing signs of losing their fervor for the cause. They wanted an end to the severe economic dislocation necessitated by the demands of war, and they wanted better living standards. The balance of forces, however, still suggested the struggle could go on for a very long time. For vulnerable though the French were in large parts of Indochina, they retained the edge in firepower and had full command of the air. In Saigon and much of the Mekong Delta in the south, their position was strong and would likely remain so for a long time to come. There remained, moreover, the threat of American military intervention, a threat likely to increase as time went by and an outcome to be avoided if at all possible: Defeating France and her Vietnamese collaborators was difficult enough without also adding the mighty United States into the mix. "Our main enemy," wrote party theoretician Truong Chinh of the internal deliberations that spring, was not France but "the U.S. empire." As the French "grew weaker by the day," the Americans "intervened more actively in Indochina by the day."[16]

Keeping the United States out of Vietnam meant cultivating support for the DRV internationally, and that too argued for being open to diplomacy. Alienating world opinion by forswearing the chance for peace would be unwise. "We have always followed the situation in the world" and "coordinated with the wishes for peace of the people of the world," one official said. A negotiated agreement would therefore be a "victory" as it met "the pressing needs of the world's peace lovers." In the view of deputy prime minister and foreign minister Pham Van Dong, the DRV needed "the sympathy and the support of all peoples" to contain its enemies and protect its sovereignty."[17]

Party officials were less keen to talk about yet another possible consequence of a prolongation of the fighting, namely that the struggle would become increasingly fratricidal over time. Already now, Vietnamese were killing other Vietnamese in larger numbers. Viet Minh strategists remained confident they had the vast majority of people on their side, and they were as contemptuous as always of what party documents habitually referred to as the "puppet army" created by the French, but in quiet moments they expressed concern about the changing nature of the war. The revolutionary cause they championed was based on the principles of national unity and derived its legitimacy from its status as the only real representative of the populace. In the spring of 1954, the revolution was not yet seriously threatened, but how would things look in six months or a year, or in two years?

Above all, Ho Chi Minh knew, negotiations for an end to the war would have to be attempted in Geneva because his patrons in Moscow and Beijing said so. Repeatedly since the end of the Berlin conference in February, the Communist giants had made clear their desire for a political solution in Indochina and had even made their continued material and rhetorical backing of the war effort contingent on the DRV declaring a willingness to seek peace. The Soviet Union still sought improved relations with the West and also hoped to induce France to agree to a tacit quid pro quo—Moscow's help in facilitating a settlement in Indochina in exchange for Paris saying *non merci* to the proposed European Defense Community. China, for her part, viewed the Geneva meeting as an opportunity to solidify her membership in the great-power club and to forestall an American military intervention near her southern borders. Both Communist powers perceived as well a chance to drive a wedge between the Western powers. Said premier and foreign minister Zhou Enlai on February 27, during a meeting with his associates in the Foreign Ministry: "While France seems interested in reaching a peaceful solution to the Indochina issue, the United States is not. Therefore, it seems that France is reluctant to let the United States put its nose into Vietnam."[18]

But how to reach such a "peaceful solution"? The Kremlin came down early on the side of partition, a Korea-type solution that would temporarily divide Vietnam in half. Such a solution would respect France's continuing strength in Cochin China while also acknowledging the Viet Minh's effective control of large areas of Tonkin and Annam. It would serve China's security needs as well, by forestalling an American intervention and by giving her a friendly "buffer" state on her southern frontier. And it would stop the war, if not forever, at least for a time. Already in late January 1954, Moscow instructed its ambassador in Paris to float the partition idea with French leaders. "There would be a provisional armistice line drawn at the 16th parallel," a U.S intelligence assessment said of this Soviet overture, and "the French would evacuate Hanoi and the Tonkin Delta."[19] The French reacted with caution but did not rule out the idea, and the Soviets were further encouraged when the British government in subsequent weeks began making supportive noises about partition.

The Chinese too were attracted to the idea. Beijing's ambassador in Moscow, Zhang Wentien, told Foreign Minister Vyacheslav Molotov on March 6 that a division along the sixteenth parallel would be "very advantageous" for Ho Chi Minh and as such "should be accepted if it is put forward officially." A few days later Zhou Enlai told Ho via telegram that conditions were ripe for a greater emphasis on the diplomatic struggle, and that, no matter what the likely outcome of the Geneva Conference, "we should actively participate in it." Partition should be seriously considered, Zhou went on, because "if a ceasefire is to be achieved, it is better that a relatively fixed demarcation line be established so that [the Viet Minh] can control an area that is linked together." As for where the line ought to be, the Chinese statesman singled out the sixteenth parallel as "one of our options."[20]

The VWP Politburo met three times in March to discuss negotiating strategy for Geneva, more specifically the notion of partition. Details from the meetings are sketchy, but we can guess that the sessions were stormy. Earlier in the month, the DRV ambassador in Beijing, Hoan Van Hoang, had shown little enthusiasm for partition when his Soviet counterpart brought up the matter. How can you find a demarcation line, Hoang asked, when there are no front lines? Over time, though, as the early assault on Dien Bien Phu failed to yield a decisive victory, the thinking in the Politburo swung in favor of partition, or at least against outright opposition. Members agreed to consider the possibility, so long as the division was temporary. The demarcation line would reflect the balance of military forces and would be as far south as possible. A party statement avoided mention of partition but extolled Geneva as "a victory for the forces of democracy" that, "together with big victories in the military field," would make "our people in the occupied areas happy, and the puppets confused and concerned."[21] VWP instructions concerning the May Day celebrations stressed the need to encourage the people to write petitions to the government to express their "support of the Geneva Conference with a view toward finding ways for peacefully solving the Korean problem and putting an end to the war in Indochina."[22]

Still, it must have been with mixed feelings that Ho Chi Minh in late March arrived in Beijing, accompanied by Pham Van Dong, the DRV's deputy prime minister and foreign minister, for a pre-Geneva strategy session. His powerful allies were telling him to take half a loaf rather than the whole thing, even though his forces were winning on the battlefield. This was hardly what he wanted to hear, even if he had his own reasons for exploring a compromise diplomatic settlement. He and his comrades had not fought for seven-plus years to gain only partial control of the country. Now he had to listen as Mao and Zhou urged him to score a victory at Dien Bien Phu and thereby achieve results at Geneva, but they also cautioned him to have "realistic expectations" regarding how much could be achieved in the negotiations—shorthand, in all probability, for the estimation that the DRV would not come away from the conference with control over all of Vietnam. The Vietnamese, according to Chinese sources, agreed on both points.[23]

From there the Vietnamese went on to Moscow, accompanied by Zhou Enlai, for meetings with top Kremlin leaders including Nikita Khrushchev and Foreign Minister Vyacheslav Molotov. Khrushchev, emerging as the main man in the post-Stalin leadership struggle, shared Stalin's general lack of interest in Indochina; like Stalin he saw struggle there mostly in terms of what it meant for European issues, and he hoped at Geneva to undermine the EDC, with its plan for German rearmament. Khrushchev cautioned his visitors against expecting great results from the conference but pledged—cryptically—that the Soviet Union would support the DRV's interests. When Zhou Enlai returned to the Soviet capital later in April, Molotov insisted on the need to have a realistic Soviet-Chinese-Vietnamese strategy at Geneva, since the Western powers would surely stand up for their interests. But even though the Americans would no doubt try to sabotage the conference, Molotov continued, savvy negotiating by the Communist allies could bring forth a political settlement on favorable terms. Zhou Enlai agreed.[24]

Much would depend, though, on the outcome at Dien Bien Phu. As April drew to a close and the various delegations arrived in Geneva, the Communist allies were in full accord that General Giap needed to score a knockout blow against the French garrison, and to do so before the Indochina discussions began in earnest—or at least before they reached their critical stage. Mao Zedong, always a keen student of military tactics and

strategy, had insisted already on April 3 that the fortress "should be conquered resolutely" and that once conditions were ready, the Viet Minh
should start a general attack as swiftly as possible.[25] Giap had waited,
determined to have every piece in place before initiating the final phase
of the battle. He could delay no longer.

IV

THE ASSAULT BEGAN ON MAY 1, AT THE USUAL TIME: LATE AFTER-
noon. All day long evidence had accumulated in General de Castries's
command bunker that something was afoot, and by early afternoon the
deadly smell of all-out assault hung in the air. Probing attacks down the
trench lines were being made in greater strength, and radio intercepts
detected the presence of Viet Minh battalions in concentration. The
previous three nights had seen more downpours, and on April 29 some
parts of the garrison reported three feet of standing water in the trenches.
Their boots and clothing perpetually soaked, the men were also hungry, for everyone was now on half rations. April 30 brought a modicum
of good news, in the form of an agreement by the American crews from
CAT to resume their C-119 flights, in exchange for a promise from the
French Air Force to do a better job of suppressing enemy flak (a promise
it failed to keep). Supply drops increased dramatically that day and on
May 1, and when the assault began, there was again three days of food
available, along with desperately needed ammunition.

Just before five o'clock in the afternoon, the artillery barrage commenced. More than one hundred Viet Minh field guns opened up over
the whole area of the camp. Bunkers and soggy trenches collapsed under
the bombardment, many of their occupants buried alive. After three
hours, the firing slackened, whereupon the entire 312th and 316th Divisions stormed up the eastern hill positions of Eliane and Dominique and
the 308th targeted Huguette. Dominique 3, defended by a motley mix of
Algerians and Tai, fell quickly, and by 2 A.M. Eliane 1 had succumbed as
well. In nine hours of fighting, the garrison had lost 331 killed or missing.
Was this the beginning of the end? Senior French commanders feared
it was. Colonel Langlais wired Hanoi soon after the assault began: "No
more reserves left. Fatigue and wear and tear on the units terrible. Sup-

plies and ammunition insufficient. Quite difficult to resist one more such push by Communists, at least without bringing in one brand-new battalion of excellent quality."[26]

General de Castries followed with his own message, sent to General Cogny shortly before midnight: "In any case extremely heavy losses require as of tomorrow night a solid new battalion. Urgent reply requested."[27]

Cogny obliged, sending in part of his last remaining airborne force, the First Colonial Parachute Battalion, the next night. More ammunition and supplies were dropped as well, but as on previous nights a high proportion of the tonnage—in this case roughly a third—landed in Viet Minh hands, or in sections of the camp too dangerous to enter for fear of snipers, with the result that the packages were left unretrieved. The new troops were a welcome sight, but they could not make up the heavy losses suffered by the other battalions. Intense fighting continued, with the Viet Minh suffering colossal losses but pressing forward relentlessly. Slowly the French perimeter was bent inward and compressed, as the mortar shells rained down on the French positions. On the night of May 4, de Castries and his staff had to listen helplessly as Huguette 4, defended by eighty legionnaires and Moroccan riflemen against an entire Viet Minh regiment plus four additional battalions (roughly three thousand men), fell after a desperate hours-long stand. At 3:55 A.M. a terse radio message from one of the last surviving officers announced that only a few men remained on their feet. His listeners then heard his death cry, uttered as he was shot by Viet Minh troops who had fought their way into his trench.[28]

After sunrise that morning, de Castries cabled Cogny the news of the enemy advance in the face of enormous losses and asked for the immediate dispatch of the remainder of the First Colonial Parachute Battalion. The concluding passage stands out for its unsparing assessment of the situation at that moment, fifty-three days into the battle:

> The provisions of all kinds are at their lowest; for fifteen days they have been reduced little by little. We don't have enough ammunition to stop enemy attacks or for harassing fire that must continue without pause; it appears that no effort is being made to remedy this situation. I am told of the risks to the aircrews, but every man

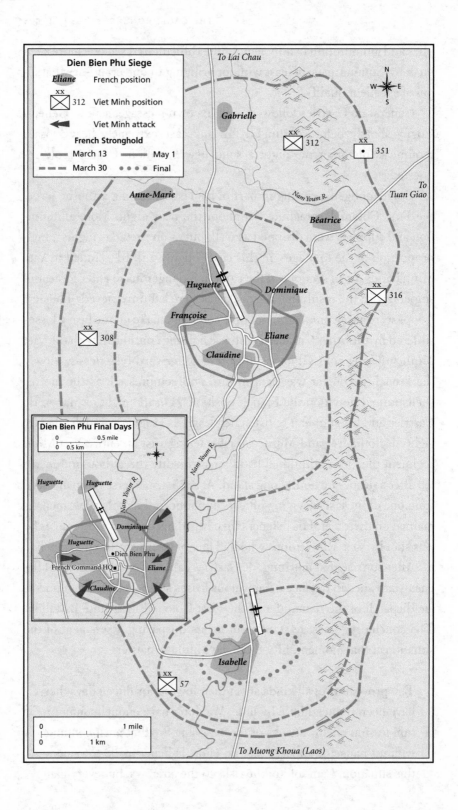

Dien Bien Phu Siege

Eliane   French position

XX
312   Viet Minh position

◀   Viet Minh attack

French Stronghold
- – – March 13   —— May 1
- – – March 30   •••• Final

To Lai Chau

N
W—E
S

Gabrielle

XX
312

XX
• 351

Anne-Marie

Nam Youm R.

To
Tuan Giao

Béatrice

Huguette

Dominique

XX
316

Françoise

Eliane

XX
308

Claudine

Nam Youm R.

Dien Bien Phu Final Days

0   0.5 mile
0   0.5 km

N
W—E
S

Huguette

Huguette

Nam Youm R.

Dominique

Huguette

• Dien Bien Phu

French Command HQ ■

Eliane

Claudine

Isabelle

XX
57

0   1 mile
0   1 km

To Muong Khoua (Laos)

here runs infinitely greater risks—there cannot be a double standard. The night drops must begin at 8 P.M. instead of 11 P.M. The morning hours are lost because of the fog, and due to the planning of night drops with long intervals between aircraft the results are ridiculous. I absolutely need provisions in massive quantities.

The very small state of the center of resistance, and the fact that the elements holding the perimeter can't leave their shelters without coming under fire from snipers and recoilless rifles, means that more and more of the cases dropped are no longer retrievable. The lack of vehicles and coolies oblige me to use extremely exhausted units for recovery tasks; the result is detestable. It also causes losses. I cannot even count on retrieving half of what is dropped, although the quantities sent to me represent only a very small portion of what I have requested. This situation cannot go on.

I insist, once more, on the broad authority that I have requested in the matter of citations. I have nothing to sustain the morale of my men who are being asked for superhuman efforts. I no longer dare to go see them with empty hands.—end—[29]

De Castries did not hold out much hope that the plea would do any good. Hitherto Hanoi had not been able to provide remotely enough supplies; why should that change now? Headquarters was indeed now giving him authorization to consider a possible breakout attempt from the valley, a sure sign in de Castries's mind that Hanoi was fast losing faith that the situation could be salvaged. The plan bore the unfortunate code name Albatross and called for the able-bodied survivors to break through enemy lines to the southeast at nightfall, under cover of artillery fire, air support, and small arms fire from the walking wounded, who would be left behind, along with more seriously wounded and the hospital staff. The breakout group would make for the Laotian frontier and would rendezvous with the Condor column about ten days thence, somewhere near Muong Nha. Navarre welcomed Albatross as an alternative to leaving the garrison to die, but Cogny was unenthusiastic. The escapees were sure to be routed, he argued, if not at the initial breakout, then soon thereafter; they were too exhausted, and the enemy too entrenched, for it to be otherwise. The Viet Minh would make propaganda hay of the rout, and the French press would not look kindly on such a nonheroic action. But Cogny agreed it should be left to General de Castries to decide whether to attempt the breakout once on-the-spot resistance had become hopeless.[30]

Strangely enough for a commander whose position was more precarious with each passing hour, whose men were fighting for their very lives, de Castries had ample time to consider Albatross during the daylight hours of May 5. With all the reserves committed, and with ammunition levels low, there was simply not much left to plan or direct other than an attempted breakout. Still, he hardly relished the opportunity. Told by Cogny that under no circumstances should he surrender, he now faced the delicate task of preparing for a potential breakout without shattering the morale of his troops. He summoned his senior subordinates to his command post and briefed them on the plan. No one expressed enthusiasm, but all agreed it might have to be implemented depending on what transpired in the coming days.

Not yet, though. The situation was bad but not yet desperate enough to initiate an escape plan that even its few proponents considered risky in the extreme. The enemy continued to suffer vastly greater casualties and surely had his own supply problems; if the fortress could hold out a few more days, Giap might have to call a halt and withdraw, at least temporarily. The mood brightened further on the morning of May 6, with the largest supply drop in almost three weeks, a total of almost 196 tons. Ninety-one volunteers also parachuted in during the early hours, many of them Vietnamese. (These paras would be the last reinforcements to reach Dien Bien Phu.) Meanwhile a weak Viet Minh probe against Eliane 3 was easily repelled, and a more serious attack on two Huguette positions was also beaten back.[31]

Soon the fog lifted to reveal that most rare of sights in these weeks: clear blue skies. Seemingly on cue, the air above the valley filled with aircraft, bringing further hope to de Castries's desperately weary men. With French Air Force and Navy bombers and fighters concentrating on flak suppression, some transport pilots volunteered to come in lower to achieve better success releasing their loads over the drop zone. Art Wilson, a CAT pilot carrying ammunition for Isabelle, took a hit from a 37mm flak shell in his tail and lost elevator control but completed his run and made it safely back to base at Cat Ni.

Next into the circuit was another CAT pilot, Captain James B. Mc-Govern. A giant bear of a man—his nickname was "Earthquake Mc-Goon," after a hulking hillbilly in the comic strip *Li'l Abner,* and his pilot seat had to be specially designed to accommodate his massive frame—McGovern was a legend among Indochina pilots, just as he had been a legend among Chennault's Flying Tigers in China in World War II. With a booming voice and an insatiable appetite for food and drink, the native of Elizabeth, New Jersey, was a fixture at bars from Taipei to Saigon, and he did not hesitate when offered the chance to fly the Dien Bien Phu run. This was his forty-fifth mission to the remote valley, and he had with him copilot Wallace Buford of Ogden, Utah, as well as two French crewmen. As McGovern eased the C-119 in for the final run over the drop zone, he was hit in the port engine; he feathered it quickly, only to have a second 37mm shell tear into one of the plane's tail booms. With six tons of ammunition aboard, the aircraft was a gigantic bomb, and the two pilots fought desperately to regain control. They made it out of the valley to the southeast, the plane yawing badly, but it was hopeless. "Looks like this is it, son," McGovern coolly radioed another pilot, seconds before the plane plummeted to earth behind the Laotian border, cartwheeled, and exploded in a huge black cloud.[32]

The following day a telegram from the American consulate in Hanoi informed Washington that, according to French officials, "a C-119 was shot down yesterday by ack ack fire south of Dien Bien Phu. Entire crew, composed of two CAT American pilots (names unknown) and two French crew members, reported lost."[33] Since March 13, thirty-seven CAT pilots had made nearly seven hundred air-drops over the basin, the importance of which to the garrison's survival would be next to impossible to exaggerate. McGovern and Buford would be the only ones to lose their lives.[34]

V

ABOUT THE TIME MCGOVERN'S PLANE ENTERED THE DROP ZONE on that fateful final run, the French command in the camp below received a shocking message from Hanoi. Cryptographers had picked up news of the date and time of the final Viet Minh assault: It was to be launched shortly after sundown that very day, May 6. For General de Castries and his subordinates, this was a bombshell of a different kind. They would not be prepared, they knew. True, more ammunition had come in overnight, but many of the parachuted packets would not be retrievable until after dark, by which point it might be too late. The enemy trench works had drawn ever closer, and the garrison was acutely undermanned. But it would be vital to persevere for the next few days, especially with a column en route from Laos and with the Geneva Conference about to commence discussion of Indochina. "We must hang on," Colonel Langlais told a gathering of officers at ten A.M. "We must force a draw. On the other side they're just as exhausted as we are."[35] If the defenders could withstand the assault and in the process inflict heavy losses on Giap's forces, he might choose to halt the proceedings for a period of weeks, or might be compelled to do so by a cease-fire agreement at Geneva. If, on the other hand, the Viet Minh commander succeeded in overwhelming the last strongpoints, he might be perceived far and wide as the victor in Indochina. These broader considerations were hardly the central concern of the officers in the bunker that morning, but they grasped that the stakes were huge—that on the defense of their tiny patch of territory in the coming days could hinge the entire war.

What a task they faced! Giap's attacking force consisted of four infantry divisions, plus thirty artillery battalions and some one hundred guns. In response, the defenders could offer very little except the courage and fortitude borne of desperation. In this respect it was to their advantage that their perimeter had shrunk: It now consisted mostly of portions of Huguette, Claudine, and Eliane, perhaps one thousand yards square, plus the isolated Isabelle three miles to the south. To cover the approach to the hospital, which that morning held more than sixteen hundred wounded, an improved strongpoint christened Juno had been created between Claudine and Eliane. Total troop strength stood at roughly 4,000, though in terms of infantry in the central sector it was closer to 2,000. There were Foreign Legion and Vietnamese parachutists, Moroccan Rifles, Tai from various dissolved units, French paratroop battalions (half of them Vietnamese), Arab and African gunners, and, down on Isabelle, still some Algerians. The greatest concentration of men, some 750 parachutists, was deployed at the point of maximum import and danger, the top of Eliane.[36]

At four P.M., the Viet Minh artillery bombardment began. Its purpose was mostly to cover the assembly of assault infantry in forward positions, and it featured the unleashing of a wholly new weapon in the 351st Heavy Division's arsenal: the "Stalin Organs." Modeled on the twelve-tubed Katyusha rocket launchers that the Red Army had used with devastating effect against the Wehrmacht in World War II, these projectors announced their presence with the terrifying screeching noise of their rockets, which one legionnaire likened to the sound of a passing train. The explosions that followed were louder and often more destructive than those of shells of larger caliber, for the explosive made up a greater proportion of the rocket's weight. Several of the rockets scored direct hits, destroying munitions stores, pulverizing sodden earthworks, and doing serious damage to the medical supplies depot. That night the garrison's senior medical officer cabled Hanoi: "Situation of the wounded extremely precarious due to flooding and collapse of several dugouts. . . . Urgent need of all medical supplies; my stocks are destroyed."[37]

For two hours, the pounding by the Stalin Organs continued, whereupon the Viet Minh switched to their more accurate conventional artillery, unleashing a barrage on the whole of the entrenched camp. The heavy rain simultaneously resumed, flooding the trenches. Shortly before seven o'clock the soldiers came forward in massed groups at every point on the perimeter, the bodies of those killed bearing down the barbed wire and forming a bridge for those behind to cross upon. All the outposts were under attack, and by ten P.M. the Elianes were in deep peril and Claudine 5 had been overrun. Hard-pressed and undermanned though they were, however, the desperate defenders counterattacked and for a time even succeeded in driving the Viet Minh back. At ten-thirty a ragtag band of legionnaires from three companies counterattacked Claudine 5 and reclaimed it from the enemy regiment, three thousand strong, to which it had just succumbed. Bigeard and Langlais desperately shuffled their remaining manpower to meet the various dangers, but they knew the arithmetic of the battle ran inexorably against them. Dakotas in the air above carried a company from the First Colonial Battalion but could not make the drop; even had they done so, it would not have made an appreciable difference.

Sometime before eleven (accounts differ on the exact time), a massive explosion shook the earth under Eliane 2. In a tactic reminiscent of the Union at Petersburg in 1864 and the British at the Hawthorn Redoubt in 1916, the Viet Minh had driven a mine shaft under Eliane 2 and loaded it with three thousand pounds of TNT. Veterans recalled a muffled rumbling under their feet, followed after a pause by a giant geyser of earth and stones thrown into the air. The garrison suffered massive casualties, but the key French blockhouse did not fall, and the Viet Minh foolishly paused before advancing. This delay gave the defenders under Captain Jean Pouget precious time to man the lip of the crater and open a murderous fire on the approaching infantry. Three hours later, with Pouget's men still holding out, he asked for reinforcements. He could hold Eliane 2, he told HQ over the wireless, with just one additional company. None was available, replied the major on the other end. "Not another man, not another shell, my friend. You're a para. You're there to get yourself killed."[38]

Pouget did not die. After acknowledging the major's message, he announced his intention to sign off and to disable the radio. A Viet Minh operator who had been eavesdropping broke in and told him not to wreck the set just yet—a song was coming on. Through the static Pouget could hear the strains of "Chant des Partisans," a wartime anthem of the French Resistance. "The swine," he grumbled, grasping the irony. He put three bullets through the radio and went out to join his men. A few minutes before five o'clock, he and his last handful of soldiers were surrounded and captured.[39]

The end was near. On May 7, the sun went up for the last time on the fortified French camp. Eliane 4 and 10 were still holding out at daybreak, but by midmorning both were gone. With the enemy now a mere three hundred yards from his command post, General de Castries's only hope was to hold the west bank of the river until nightfall and then attempt the Albatross breakout. Via radio, he updated Cogny on the situation, then asked for, and received, authority to launch the breakout at his own judgment. A transcript of their conversation survives, and it is among the more poignant such documents to come down to us from any war. De Castries, despite the unrelieved gloom of his situation, is imperturbable, stoic, haughty—qualities that at the beginning of the siege seemed wrong to many but now are what give his senior officers the strength to carry on. Cogny, by contrast, from the safety of his perch in Hanoi, is the one stammering banalities. De Castries says he will stay behind with the wounded and the noncombatants and will send the breakout group southward toward Isabelle, whose troops he will order to break out at the same time. Cogny agrees.

The Viet Minh commanders, meanwhile, were surprised by the rush of events. They had anticipated ordering a lull for consolidation before storming the remaining French positions on the west bank of the river. By early afternoon, however, with reports coming in that the garrison was close to collapse and that a breakout attempt might occur, General Giap (or, some accounts say, his deputy chief of staff General Thanh, due to Giap's temporary absence) ordered the immediate initiation of a general offensive and the closing off of any attempted French escape to the south. Units of the 312th Division crossed the river to the west bank, and the 308th Division advanced from the west to meet them. By four P.M. Eliane 3 had been taken, and there was hand-to-hand combat around Eliane 11 and 12. The French reported "massive V.M. infiltration over the entire western front of the central position."[40]

The last radio contact with Hanoi occurred shortly before five o'clock. Some hours earlier de Castries and his principal subordinates had concluded the game was up, and that a breakout would only result in a massacre. The commanders of the units chosen to participate had sent word that their men were too weary to attempt a fighting breakout, much less a jungle journey of any length. Cogny now insisted that there be no capitulation:

"*Mon vieux,* of course you have to finish the whole thing now. But what you have done until now surely is magnificent. Don't spoil it by hoisting the white flag. You are going to be submerged [by the enemy], but no surrender, no white flag."

"All right, *mon général,* I only wanted to preserve the wounded," de Castries replied, his voice calm and collected.

"Yes, I know. Well, do the best you can, leaving it to your [static: subordinate units?] to act for themselves. What you have done is too magnificent to do such a thing. You understand, *mon vieux.*"

There was a silence. Then de Castries bade his farewell: "*Bien, mon général.*"

"Well, good-bye, *mon vieux*," said Cogny. "I'll see you soon."[41]

Less than an hour later, a squad of Viet Minh soldiers, specially detailed from among the thousands who were now pressing into the center of the camp, entered de Castries's post, where they found him impeccably attired in clean uniform and wearing his red spahi cap. They took him prisoner while another soldier hoisted the red flag of the Viet Minh on the roof above.

The work was not done, though. In the south, Isabelle remained unsubdued. Its commander, Colonel André Lalande, a tough veteran of Narvik, El Alamein, and the Vosges, had been given permission to try a breakout on his own and had decided to go for broke. Into the evening hours, he remained uncertain about which route to take, but at nine o'clock, a two-battalion mixed force of legionnaires, Algerians, Tai, Vietnamese, and Frenchmen crawled through the barbed wire and headed south along the banks of the Nam Youm, desperately groping for a way through the encircling Viet Minh lines. They didn't find it. Instead they found waiting enemy units; firefights soon broke out to their front, flank, and rear. By midnight, it was all over. "*Fini*, repeat, *fini*," the post radioed Hanoi. Lalande and his principal lieutenants were captured. Only about seventy men, most of them Tai, got away and made it through the hundred miles of hostile terrain to safety in Laos.

The Battle of Dien Bien Phu was over. The Viet Minh had won. Vo Nguyen Giap had overturned history, had accomplished the unprecedented, had beaten the West at its own game. For the first time in the annals of colonial warfare, Asian troops had defeated a European army in fixed battle.

VI

THE NEWS OF GENERAL DE CASTRIES'S CAPTURE AND THE HOISTING of the red flag above his command bunker reached Paris—seven hours behind Dien Bien Phu—at about noon on May 7. It was a lovely spring day in the capital, with the chestnut trees in the Bois de Boulogne and along the quays in flower. The National Assembly chamber was packed at 4:45 P.M. when Prime Minister Joseph Laniel, the big and stolid textile millionaire who had governed France for ten shaky months, rose to announce the garrison's fall. Unbeknownst to him, half a world away Isabelle was going under at that very moment.

"The Government has been informed," he declared, his voice choked with emotion and barely audible, "that the central position of Dien Bien Phu has fallen after twenty hours of uninterrupted violent combat." Following a stunned silence, punctuated by gasps of disbelief, all but the Communist Party legislators and a few of their allies rose to their feet. A woman legislator could be heard sobbing as Laniel continued:

> Strongpoint Isabelle is still holding. The enemy has wanted to obtain the fall of Dien Bien Phu prior to the opening of the conference on Indochina. He believes that he could strike a decisive blow against the morale of France. He has responded to our goodwill, to France's will for peace, by sacrificing thousands of [his] soldiers to crush under their number the heroes who, for fifty-five days, have excited the admiration of the world. . . .
>
> France must remind her allies that for seven years now the Army of the French Union has unceasingly protected a particularly crucial region of Asia and has alone defended the interests of all. All of France shares the anguish of the families of the fighters of Dien Bien Phu. Their heroism has reached such heights that universal conscience should dictate to the enemy—in favor of the wounded and of those whose courage entitles them to the honors of war—such decisions as will contribute more than anything to establish a climate favorable to peace.[42]

The archbishop of Paris ordered a solemn mass to honor the dead and the prisoners at Dien Bien Phu, and the Paris Opera postponed a much-anticipated series of performances by the Moscow Opera Ballet (its first visit since the end of World War II). Television canceled its evening schedule, and the radio stations replaced entertainment shows with French classical music such as the Berlioz *Requiem*. Many cinemas, theaters, and restaurants closed for two days as a mark of respect. Édouard Herriot, the former premier who at age eighty-one had experienced many of his country's modern misfortunes, observed, "A veil of mourning has fallen over France."[43]

It was as though a switch had gone off: The war that for seven-plus years had received only intermittent and fleeting attention from the French public suddenly was on everyone's mind. The defeat coincided with two of France's greatest holidays—the ninth anniversary of V-E Day and the feast day of Joan of Arc—but there would be little rejoicing this year. When Laniel's car rolled past the Tomb of the Unknown Soldier at the Arc de Triomphe, passersby shouted and cursed. "Send him to Dien Bien Phu," cried some. "Shoot him!" others yelled. At the same spot, Defense Minister René Pleven drew shouts of "Resign! Resign!" Asked *Le Franc-Tireur*: "Who placed de Castries and his men in this trap? Who is officially or unofficially responsible? Who? What party? What minister? What general?" Others cast blame on the United States for declaring France's struggle in Indochina vital to the West's security yet failing to intervene in the hour of need. Still others called on Frenchmen and -women to look inward. "The fighters at Dienbienphu died because we lied to ourselves," *Le Figaro* declared. "What these sacrifices demand is an examination of our conscience."[44]

Robert Guillain of *Le Monde* was savage in his judgment. "We'll show the people, the people of France above all," he cabled the newspaper from Hanoi. "They have to be shown what their neglect, their incredible indifference, their illusions, their dirty politics have led to. And how best may we show them? By dying, so that honor at least may be saved. Our dead of Dien Bien Phu died, I claim, protesting, appealing against today's France in the name of another France for which they had respect. The only victory that remains is the victory of our honor."[45]

A foreign observer, American correspondent Benjamin Bradlee of *Newsweek,* was not impressed by the appraisals. "France is stunned and intensely, patriotically proud of Dienbienphu's defenders," he wrote from Paris. "But there is no inclination to unite in patriotism—no desire to avenge defeat. France offers the shameful spectacle of a country almost unanimously looking for someone to blame."[46]

Henri Navarre, interestingly, fared quite well in the early rounds of this blame game, despite being the principal architect of the disaster. It was Paris that had ordered him to defend Laos the previous summer, most analysts declared, and then inexcusably failed to give him adequate means to carry out his task. If the general took comfort from this metropolitan reaction, he failed to show it, for his mind was now focused on how to retrieve the military situation. As he looked at his chessboard, he saw hope: By concentrating his defenses on the Red River Delta and adopting a static posture in the rest of Indochina, he could maintain the situation until Paris sent out substantial reinforcement for the fall 1954 campaign season. Parts of the delta might have to be sacrificed in order to mass available forces in the crucial area around the Hanoi-Haiphong corridor, but there was no immediate danger of wholesale collapse. In the southern half of the country, meanwhile, including the Mekong Delta, the picture remained reasonably good, Navarre believed; Giap certainly did not have the necessary resources to mount a major challenge there anytime soon, especially after losing thousands of his best troops at Dien Bien Phu. His survivors were exhausted and would need a period of rest and recuperation, and the monsoon season, which still had months to run, would limit his ability to move men and matériel.

This was a classic glass-half-full reading of things. Navarre knew it was possible to argue a very different case, at least with respect to Tonkin: to see a glass with hardly any drops at all. As recently as two years earlier, in the spring of 1952, the Viet Minh had had only about 15,000 men in the Red River Delta; by March 1953, the figure was 50,000, and now it was close to 100,000. Eight million Vietnamese resided in this triangle-shaped, Connecticut-size plain, the vast majority of them hostile to the colonial overlord. Though theoretically held by the French, the delta was also the Viet Minh's main base of operations, supplying 80 percent of the People's Army's food and 70 percent of its recruits. Whereas the previous autumn it was possible still to say that the delta was French by day, Viet Minh by night, now it was mostly Viet Minh at all hours. The French held only Hanoi and Haiphong and a handful of the larger towns. Connecting roads were insecure—even by day. As for the vital sixty-mile rail and road link between Hanoi and Haiphong, it was more vulnerable with each passing week. No French traffic moved before noon; even then the convoys would have to speed up, some seven miles out of Hanoi, to run the Viet Minh gauntlet. Often they would be cut down as the mortars and bazookas opened up. With Giap now free to shift the bulk of his forces to the delta, would France be forced to give up Tonkin altogether and shift her efforts to maintaining control of Cochin China and southern

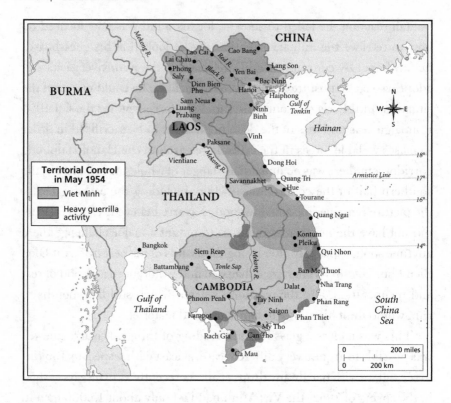

Annam? Publicly Navarre denied that this was so and that all was lost in the north; privately he understood that the outlook was bleak and getting bleaker.

VII

AS THE FRENCH COMMANDER SUSPECTED, GENERAL GIAP OPTED, even before the smoke had cleared at Dien Bien Phu, to shift the bulk of his fighting force there to the delta. By the last week of May, advance elements of the four divisions that had overrun the fortress reached Moc Chau, seventy-five miles west of Hanoi. He was not yet prepared to launch an all-out assault on French positions in the delta—his troops needed a period of rest and recuperation, and the Geneva negotiations must be given a chance to play themselves out—but he wanted to be fully prepared when the day and hour came. French intelligence analysts were probably correct in estimating that his Dien Bien Phu divisions would be ready to attack the delta by June 15–20.

Giap's more immediate concern was the disposition of hundreds of enemy wounded at Dien Bien Phu, and thousands of enemy prisoners. With the fighting over, it was possible, for the first time since the battle began, for him to determine the real strength of the garrison. The total was astonishingly large: When the shooting stopped on May 7, more than ten thousand French Union service personnel of all nationalities, including the lightly wounded, emerged into the open.[47] The discrepancy between that figure and the number of fighting troops at General de Castries's disposal in the final weeks can be explained in part by the sizable number of noncombatant personnel at headquarters and elsewhere. But by far the largest addition to the sum was supplied by the Rats of Nam Youm, the slackers who early on had decided to sit out the battle in abandoned dugouts and trenches along the banks of the river. Their number, at the end, approached four thousand.

In short order, the prisoners were put on the road, the better to keep them under control and to prevent any French rescue attempt. Some were destined for camps along the lower Song River in Thanh Hoa province, 300 miles to the southeast by road; the majority was marched in a northeasterly direction, to Bac Kan province in the Viet Bac, upward of 450 miles away. The seriously wounded remained behind, along with some medical staff and engineers. The Viet Minh, lacking the medical or transport facilities to care adequately for the gravely ill either on the spot or their own rear areas, agreed, with a curiously old-fashioned conventionality that they on occasion exhibited, that about nine hundred of the wounded should be evacuated by air from the basin to French hospitals. Some wounded started out on the march but were returned to the valley when it became clear that they were not remotely up to the ordeal of walking even a few hours through the jungle. Also sent back: a group of mostly North African POWs, needed for reconstructed scenes of "the fall of Dien Bien Phu" staged for the film cameras.[48]

The ordeal of the marchers, who numbered some nine thousand, has been told before.[49] A harrowing story it is. As a group, they were in poor physical condition even before they set out from the valley floor, and now they would be compelled to cover some twelve miles per day for forty days over difficult terrain and during the rainy season. The daily ration of 800 grams of rice, supplemented by the occasional banana or handful of peanuts, provided insufficient nourishment, and the prisoners soon shed whatever body fat they had been able to retain during the siege. Their immune systems thus compromised, many proved unable to fight off infection and disease, and malaria, beriberi, and dysentery were endemic. Nor, in their weakened condition, could prisoners long help carry bamboo litters bearing ailing comrades; soon the seriously ill were simply left to suffer and die, all alone, with the jungle and its rats and ants closing in around them. The few doctors among the marchers were kept separated with the other officers and forbidden from giving even minimal care to the French wounded, forcing desperate men to resort to desperate actions—such as the soldier who cut off his own gangrenous arm with a pocket knife.

Few of the grievously wounded survived more than a day or two, and even many of the technically fit succumbed before the end of the march. Those in their thirties and forties often held up better than those in their twenties. Senegalese and North Africans and Vietnamese had higher rates of survival than did French and Legion POWs, despite the fact that the Vietnamese—"traitors" for having fought on the side of the enemy—were singled out for tougher treatment. The predominantly central European background of the legionnaires, with their fair skin and hair, no doubt made them particularly ill equipped to deal with the harsh weather, and both they and the French troops also appear to have been more susceptible to disease than were the other groups. The individualistic, may-the-Devil-take-the-hindmost attitude of many in the Legion may also have made a difference, as they were sometimes unwilling to come to the aid of weaker comrades.[50]

These personal tragedies may rightly be laid at the feet of the Viet Minh. Instances of outright wanton brutality or sadism on the part of the guards were by all accounts very few; severe beatings generally were administered only to escapees who were recaptured—and then often only if these were Vietnamese or recidivist escapees. Surviving prisoners also recalled occasional acts of kindness by their captors, who themselves often had to get by on very meager rations. Overall, though, the Viet Minh guards and political officers (*can bo*) showed scant concern for the survival of the captives and for abiding by the Geneva Conventions, even as more and more of the POWs succumbed to the brutal conditions.

In response, it could be said that the marchers had it coming to them, in view of the suffering the French had inflicted on Vietnamese over these past decades; this does not negate the point that the Viet Minh, from start to finish, showed callous disregard for the prisoners, only a minority of whom were French nationals. The *can bo* concerned themselves mostly with waging psychological warfare through evening lectures and self-criticism sessions in which the captives were told they were "war criminals" who must confess the error of their ways. The *can bo* also sought to turn prisoners against one another by appealing to racial differences and expounding on the evils of imperialism. Why, the North Africans were asked, did you come to fight in Vietnam when your own countries are still under colonial control?[51]

Those who survived to reach the camps (the first of which had been set up in late 1950, following the Viet Minh victory on the RC4) found conditions hardly better there. The relentless psychological conditioning continued, some of it now carried out by former French Union prisoners who had turned—"crossovers," they were called—and been trained by the Viet Minh and Chinese in the use of Communist propaganda techniques. Malaria remained endemic, and the death rate from waterborne intestinal diseases—only the officers' camp was provided with pots to boil water—skyrocketed. (Camp 70, for example, counted 70 deaths out of 120 in July–August 1954, many from amoebic dysentery.) Physical labor was compulsory, and those too ill or too weak to work received no rations.[52]

There is no way to know with accuracy how many prisoners died in the months following their march out of the valley, but certainly the period of captivity killed far more of the garrison than had the entire battle. One careful estimate, by a representative on the International Control Commission in March 1955, had the number of prisoners from the Dien Bien Phu garrison handed back by the Viet Minh at the time of the POW exchange (which began on August 18, 1954) at 3,900, or some 43 percent of those who began the trek. Not all the remainder died, certainly— some managed to disappear in the jungle, and as many as a thousand legionnaires may have been directly repatriated to Communist countries of origin. Nevertheless, the picture that emerges is extremely grim. Add in the roughly 3,500 dead or missing in action from the battle itself, and

FRENCH UNION POWS ARRIVE IN HANOI AFTER
THEIR RELEASE, AUGUST 25, 1954.

one is left with the following dark interpretation: Of the approximately 15,000 men who served in French uniform in the valley of the Nam Youm, fewer than half ever went home, wounded or unwounded. Historian Martin Windrow puts the death ratio at 60 percent, a statistic, he rightly notes, that rivals the very worst battles of the twentieth century.[53]

The Viet Minh, of course, paid a heavy human price for their victory at Dien Bien Phu. Various casualty figures have been put forth over the years, including by a Franco-Vietnamese team that in 1955 began an aborted project to recover bodies for an ossuary; consensus remains elusive, but a safe estimate is that the Viet Minh suffered on the order of 10,000 deaths, from start to finish, and at least 15,000 wounded. According to internal sources uncovered by historian Christopher Goscha, Giap's troops experienced an astonishing killed-in-action rate of 32 percent during the first-wave attack in March—that is to say, three out of ten Vietnamese men who went over the top in the initial assault did not return. In the subsequent waves the death rate dropped, but it never went below 20 percent. Among the wounded, these documents show, almost a quarter (23.7 percent) suffered injuries to the head or neck. Many, it goes without saying, would never recover, even if they lived.[54]

VIII

IT REMAINS TO BE ASKED IF IT COULD HAVE TURNED OUT DIFFER-ently. Might the battle of Dien Bien Phu, if the French command had conducted it another way, have yielded a different result? Could it have ended in a victory for French Union forces instead of a defeat, thereby perhaps changing the whole complexion of the war?

In strategic terms, Navarre's original decision to make a stand at Dien Bien Phu had more to recommend it than conventional historical wisdom has suggested. He was not wrong to want to create an initiative outside the delta, or to see the valley as the best available place to bar Giap's path to Luang Prabang, the royal capital of Laos, which France was committed to defending. Nor was it necessarily unreasonable to see in Operation Castor an opportunity to repeat the success of Na San the previous year, but on a greater scale: that is, Navarre believed he could create at Dien Bien Phu a focus of action that would draw into play, on terms favorable to him, the bulk of the enemy's mobile force. And it made sense to try to deny the enemy the lucrative opium harvest of the area. The counterargument would be that Navarre would have been better off sacrificing northern Laos in order to husband his resources in the more vital Red River Delta and force Giap to attack him there, and that he should have anticipated much more readily than he did the logistical problems that ensued and that ultimately would be the garrison's undoing. Fair points both. Then again, had General Giap followed the original plan and launched the attack on January 25—which, as we have seen, he came very close to doing—his troops might have suffered a colossal defeat. Navarre's conception would have been fully vindicated. Castor would have gone down in history as a military masterstroke, its architect a strategist of the first order. Many of the same military experts—not least, it should be said, American ones—who after May 7 savaged Navarre's decision to establish a garrison that could be supplied and reinforced only by air had earlier lauded his choice and predicted it would result in a smashing victory.

Of course, Giap did not attack on that final Monday in January. He waited seven more weeks, until twilight on March 13. By then, it had long since become clear to Navarre, to Cogny, and to de Castries that their hopes of operating beyond the valley, indeed beyond the range of their own artillery, were in vain. By then, they grasped that the Viet Minh had defied the forecasts and assembled an enormous stock of ordnance as well as superiority in numbers. A battle of position and attrition now seemed more or less inevitable, and the question is whether the French commanders could have done more in tactical terms to prepare for the encounter. The answer must be yes, even if some things were beyond their power to remedy—notably the inability of the French Air Force, stretched to the limit and lacking sufficient aircraft and crews, to provide adequate air cover. They might have, for one thing, used that limited airpower more effectively. They committed the common error of overestimating the strategic capabilities of airpower, dropping huge tonnages of bombs on Routes 41 and 13 to interdict Viet Minh supplies and having little to show for it. The Viet Minh proved too adept at getting the materials through. French planners would have been better off concentrating their bombing effort on the basin itself.[55]

Inside the valley, the layout of the position left much to be desired. The network of defensive strongpoints was poorly conceived, with Isabelle too far away to really support the central position with artillery fire, and Gabrielle and Béatrice too weakly defended to play their assigned roles in defending the airstrip. At no time did Cogny order de Castries to test whether his reserve forces could reach these strongpoints at night and under fire. Probably none of them, and certainly not Isabelle, should have been occupied, for although they forced the Viet Minh to begin the assault farther from the airstrip, the battalions that ostensibly defended them would have been better used to launch counterattacks from the central position. Such counterattacks often showed good results when Bigeard and Langlais launched them and indeed were a major reason the garrison held out as long as it did. The U.S.-supplied Chaffee tanks proved crucial in these raids, and it seems undeniable that de Castries should have demanded, and received, another dozen tanks—or as many as could have been flown in and reassembled. But de Castries seems never to have grasped the importance of the counterattacks, both to retake hill positions once they had been lost and to get at the Viet Minh's antiaircraft artillery, much of which was close to the airstrip and an ideal target for sallies from the main position. Though a courageous and intelligent commander, he was miscast for this role, being inadequately attuned to the particulars of trench warfare—and Dien Bien Phu was, in Bernard Fall's words, "in many ways a piece of Argonne Forest or Verdun transported into a tropical setting."[56]

Even matters so basic as strengthening the gun pits and reinforcing the roofs of the essential service installations, including that of the hospital, would have made a big difference. Most of the bunkers were too weak to stand up to the Viet Minh artillery fire, or for that matter to the monsoons; nor was any effort made to camouflage them. The meager resources of the valley didn't help in this regard—even wood, it will be recalled, was not readily available—but certainly de Castries and his engineering commander should have done much more than they did to prepare the position for the assault they knew was coming. As it was, the flimsy fortifications made the garrison much more vulnerable than it should have been.

Finally, mention must be made of the personal schism between Henri Navarre and René Cogny, which grew deeper and wider as the spring progressed (and which, after the war, led the latter to file suit—unsuccessfully—against the former). By the end, the two men felt a profound and abiding mutual disdain and were barely speaking, a situation hardly conducive to nimble and imaginative decision making. Nor was Navarre willing to relieve Cogny of his command in favor of someone with whom he could work. Instead, in a stunning failure of leadership, he allowed the feud to fester, week after crucial week.

How the battle would have run had some or all of these problems on the French side been rectified is of course impossible to know, but it's not fanciful to imagine a different outcome. Giap scored a tremendous victory and showed tactical brilliance in his use of antiaircraft and artillery and his employment of World War I siege tactics and techniques. The sequence in which he attacked the three northern strongpoints—first Béatrice, then Gabrielle, then Anne-Marie, which the demoralized Tai abandoned without a fight after seeing at close hand the fall of the two stronger outposts—has been justly praised by military historians, and did much to shape the outcome of the battle. Nevertheless the French could have held Dien Bien Phu, if not indefinitely, then certainly through the rainy season and into the autumn. Even with the shortcomings and the mistakes on the French side, Giap was compelled to use the whole range of his resources, and his forces were severely bloodied by the end. He had his hands full throughout, even though the enemy had 3,000 to 4,000 "internal deserters" who decided to sit out the battle. (What if all these Rats of Nam Youm, or even half of them, had chosen instead to fight?) Had the fortress held out even just a few more days, Giap might have been compelled to order another pause—which in turn would have allowed the Condor column to arrive from Laos to bolster French defenses.

To argue for this counterfactual is not to say that, as a result, the French could have won the war. For even if French Union forces had held the valley and brought about the destruction of Giap's main force divisions, and even if that result had seriously undermined the morale of Viet Minh troops elsewhere in Indochina, the overall balance of strength would still have tilted against France. The extent of the *pourrissement* (deterioration) in the countryside rendered the reestablishment of French control an unlikely prospect at best, not merely in Tonkin but in large swaths of Annam and Cochin China as well. The VNA remained a weak military instrument, while on the home front in France, morale was sinking ever further, as more and more Frenchmen and -women concluded that the war no longer had any valid objective and as the French Army continued losing officers at a frightful clip—an average of six hundred killed per year, the equivalent of a whole graduating class from the military academy at Saint-Cyr.

None of which diminished the momentousness of the occasion when the small and intense French foreign minister, who had been at the center of Indochina policy for eight years, who was as closely associated with this war as anyone on his side, arose slowly from his seat in the Palais des Nations in Geneva on the afternoon of May 8, walked to the lectern, and acknowledged before the delegates and the world the fall of Dien Bien Phu.

PART FIVE

PEACE OF A KIND, 1954

CHAPTER 22

WITH FRIENDS LIKE THESE

W HEN GEORGES BIDAULT STRODE TO THE PODIUM AT THE PALAIS des Nations that Saturday afternoon, May 8, 1954, the Geneva Conference was already approaching the end of its second week. The formal Indochina discussions would begin only now, with Bidault's speech, but the behind-the-scenes jockeying on the war had been intense from the start, from the arrival of the first delegations on April 24–25. The Chinese, some two hundred strong and clad in blue high-neck suits, created a stir among the journalists who assembled at Cointrin airfield to greet prime minister and foreign minister Zhou Enlai's plane on the twenty-fourth. This was, everyone knew, a kind of international coming-out for the Beijing government, and a horde of photographers clicked away furiously as the courtly and handsome Zhou, with his high forehead, wide mouth, and piercing black eyes, descended the stairway, flashed a smile, and made quickly for his waiting car.[1]

Neither Vyacheslav Molotov that evening, nor Anthony Eden the following day, nor even Bidault a day after that, caused anything like this commotion, and there was no journalistic frenzy when a somber John Foster Dulles emerged from his plane late on April 25 and read a statement he had drafted a few minutes earlier while en route. A "durable peace" in Indochina ought to be achievable, he said, but it was not up to the Western powers to bring it about. "We hope to find that the aggressors come here in a mood to purge themselves of their aggression."[2]

Zhou Enlai, having declined to share a headquarters with the Russians, chose for his residence the splendid and ornate Le Grand Mont-Fleuri, a twenty-six-room mansion five miles from Geneva in the picturesque lake-side village of Versoix. Bidault, Molotov, and Eden found similar abodes, though in the case of Eden, only after several bad nights in the Hotel Beau Rivage. He railed at aides about the traffic noise outside his window and the lousy food service and said he could not bear the presence in the same hotel of Chinese support staff, whom he suspected of eaves-dropping. A frantic search for new accommodations followed, and on April 29, Eden and his wife, Clarissa, along with a few top aides, de-camped for Le Reposoir, a superb villa north of the city decorated with fine furniture and artwork. Only the Americans, more than a hundred strong, opted to stay together as a unit, in the ultramodern, cheerless Hotel du Rhône, a selection meant to show, some thought, that Dulles was merely passing through and that his delegation would be ready to leave at any time.[3]

And the Vietnamese? They were not yet there. They didn't need to be, for the first item on the agenda was Korea, and moreover the ques-tion of who among the Vietnamese would attend had yet to be settled. The Paris government struggled to round up representatives from the Associated States, whose leaders, especially Bao Dai and his minis-ters, were suspicious of the whole endeavor and fearful of the probable outcome. These Vietnamese also objected to any DRV participation in the conference, and they initially received the backing of Bidault, less because he shared their views than because he hoped to have no Viet-namese participation at all. Mistrustful of the Viet Minh, the Frenchman also understood that Bao Dai's cabinet, along with the U.S. government, represented the greatest obstacles to a negotiated settlement in Geneva; as such, it would be best to deny both Vietnamese entities a voice in the proceedings. Bidault's conviction on this score hardened on May 3, when Bao Dai declared that his government would attend only if France guar-anteed it would not partition Vietnam. But Molotov and Zhou Enlai re-jected out of hand any attempt to deny a seat to the Viet Minh, and even Dulles, though he shared the emperor's opposition to partition, told Bi-dault that Viet Minh participation was inevitable.

Bidault said he agreed, then changed his mind. Later he changed it again, and then yet again. It was his pattern, in these early days in Geneva, to go back and forth on the core issues, to temporize, as he waited anxiously for news from Dien Bien Phu and as the Laniel government, accused of insufficient ardor for a diplomatic solution, worked feverishly to survive a vote of confidence in the National Assembly. Ultimately Bidault agreed to the Viet Minh's presence at the conference, and he secured the Bao Dai government's participation by committing himself, in a letter to the emperor on May 6, to oppose partition. But his general indecision on all matters irritated the other chief delegates, including Dulles, who complained to Eden that the French seemed incapable of making up their minds on any subject.

Eden concurred. Privately, though, he fumed at the American's failure to acknowledge the obvious: that U.S. policy was in significant measure responsible for Bidault's lack of resoluteness. The Eisenhower administration, after all, like Shakespeare's whining schoolboy, was "creeping like snail unwillingly" to Geneva and had made no secret of its dim assessment of the prospects for an acceptable deal. Even now, Eden suspected, they were whispering dangerous ideas in Bidault's ear—that he should hold firm, that the Communists, being Communists, would never abide by any agreement, that there was still the prospect of a U.S.-led military intervention in support of the Expeditionary Corps should the talks fail. Such notions, the Briton knew, appealed to Bidault, for although he grasped that he had no option but to seek a diplomatic settlement—French public opinion demanded it—he still clung to the possibility that he could salvage something from the Indochina mess he had done so much to create. At the start of May he still hoped that the threat, and if necessary the reality, of American intervention might change the dynamics on the ground, saving if not Dien Bien Phu then at least the French position in the Red River Delta.

It was true: The Eisenhower administration was hardly in a position to complain about Bidault's temporizing, given its own confused and uncertain posture as the conference got under way. Dulles, stern and unsmiling even in the most salubrious of circumstances, was in a sour mood from the get-go, as he contemplated having to appear on the same stage as the Chinese Communists. He was also dismayed at his government's failure to secure a declaration of joint intention among the Western powers and annoyed with the British for, as he saw it, pressuring Paris to accept a cease-fire. He cabled Washington on April 29: "UK attitude is one of increasing weakness. Britain seem to feel that we are disposed to accept present risks of a Chinese war and this, coupled also with their fear that we would start using atomic weapons, has badly frightened them."[4]

Eisenhower too was frustrated on that second to last day of April, as he prepared to convene a crucial meeting of the National Security Council. In recent days, he had complained to friends about the French failure to heed his advice to internationalize the war, and he fully shared his secretary of state's irritation at Britain's fecklessness. The question was what to do. "The president was extremely serious and seemed to be greatly concerned about what was the right course to take," Vice President Nixon wrote in his diary that evening of the NSC session, which began at ten A.M. and lasted three hours. Following reports on the military situation and the early jostling in Geneva, Nixon, Admiral Radford, and Harold Stassen, director of the State Department's Foreign Operations Administration, urged the president to consider American military intervention. Stassen wanted American ground forces to replace French troops in Cochin China, while Nixon and Radford favored air strikes at Dien Bien Phu and perhaps elsewhere.

Eisenhower was skeptical. It was all "well and good," he commented in response to Stassen, to say that American GIs should take over from French soldiers. "But if the French indeed collapsed and the United States moved in, we would in the eyes of many Asiatic peoples merely replace French colonialism with American colonialism." That wouldn't do: Any intervention would have to be multilateral and would have to follow from a request by the Associated States. As for air strikes, Ike said he might be amenable to such action but only if it could be shown that it would stiffen the French resolve to remain in the war. Stassen, undaunted, warned darkly that people around the world would question America's courage if she failed to act, if necessary unilaterally. The president shook his head. Going in alone would signify an attempt to police the entire world and risked bringing world condemnation, he said. Allies were essential; without them, the leader was just an adventurer like Genghis Khan. And the cause of the free world would never succeed if precious resources were squandered in local engagements.

Nixon sensed an impasse and tried a new tack: Might it not still be possible, he asked the group, to put together a coalition without the British, who, after all, had been "as much a liability as an asset" in Asia? They had failed to stand up to Japan prior to World War II, and they were failing now again. Walter Bedell Smith, the acting secretary of state, liked this suggestion and noted that it would meet the president's condition for intervention and thereby allow air strikes against Viet Minh positions at Dien Bien Phu. Even if the fortress should fall, such action might, as the president had suggested, induce France to carry on in the war. Eisenhower said he had been thinking along precisely these lines but wondered whether it would be possible to cobble together a coalition without Britain. It worried him that the Menzies government in Australia, for example, seemed unwilling to act independently of London. Nixon was not so sure: His sources in Canberra indicated that Menzies, who was in an election campaign and had to be careful in his public statements, might in the end follow America's lead.

The meeting drew to a close. No one was quite sure what had been decided, though Nixon in his diary recorded a general consensus that a "united action pact," excluding if necessary Britain, would be pursued, and that American airpower might be used to keep France in the fight. Ground troops were another matter, with Eisenhower near the end of the session emphasizing they should not be part of the equation. The American public was frightened of that prospect, he said, and would register opposition to it.[5]

As so often on Vietnam (not least when Nixon himself was president), this was the audience the White House thought the most about: the American public. Not the Western allies, not the Soviets or the Chinese, not the Vietnamese. Having worked successfully since late March to build up congressional, journalistic, and popular support for United Action, the administration was now in the awkward position of having to explain why no such coalition agreement had been reached. *The Washington Post* spoke of a "major defeat for American diplomacy," and there was bewilderment on Capitol Hill; Republicans in particular felt themselves pulled in two opposing directions. On the one hand, their reading of the public mood indicated little support for another land war in Asia.

On the other, they had argued louder than anyone against striking any diplomatic bargains with Communists anywhere. No such deal would be worth the paper it was written on, for Communists were wicked and could never be trusted.

Perceptive observers saw the problem. "The American position at Geneva is an impossible one," columnist Walter Lippmann informed his readers that same day, April 29, "so long as the leading Republican senators have no terms of peace except unconditional surrender of the enemy and no terms for entering the war except as a collective action in which nobody is now willing to engage." Echoed *Newsweek*: "Top officials, at this point, are unwilling to make war and unable to join in negotiated peace."[6]

That 1954 was an election year made Republicans all the more jittery. They had gained victory two years earlier in part by blasting Democrats for "losing China" and by assuring voters that "unnecessary wars" like Truman's in Korea (as Robert Taft had put it) would not happen on their watch. More than Democrats, they—and not merely McCarthy and his crowd—had urged Americans to believe the United States to be so powerful that setbacks in foreign policy could be explained only by criminal stupidity or treason. How to proceed in those circumstances? The GOP could enter the fall campaign with American boys once again fighting "another Korea," an inconclusive war on the periphery of the Communist empire; or, conversely, the party could find itself having to explain to voters how another piece of territory had been allowed to slip behind the bamboo curtain for want of effective American support.

II

UNDERSTANDING THIS REPUBLICAN DILEMMA—WOULD IT BE TAGGED as the war party or the appeasement party?—is essential to understanding the curious scene that was the Geneva Conference in May and June. The Swiss, veterans at hosting big gatherings of this kind, stood ready to help arrange lavish banquets of the kind made famous by the Congress of Vienna, but instead found they had very little to do. The Russians too were disappointed, having shipped vast stocks of caviar in the expectation of feasts that never took place. The Viet Minh delegation, hastily appareled in ill-fitting Western suits, was kept largely isolated by its security officers so as to minimize the chances of infection by the capitalist bug—there were evening sing-alongs and language classes, late-afternoon group strolls among the blooming chestnut trees and lilacs, and supervised games, but certainly no solo ventures around Geneva, with its well-stocked shops and brightly lit cafés and stylish nightclubs.[7]

As for the Americans in Geneva, social contacts with Communists were anathema. If anyone had other ideas, Dulles's instructions to the team quashed them. To counter any hint that Washington's participation in the conference implied any softening in the U.S. refusal to recognize Mao Zedong's government, the secretary of state forbade any contact—verbal or physical—with the Chinese. This of course meant that no American could sit at the same table as the Chinese, a problem in terms of the seating arrangement in the working sessions. The matter was resolved by the provision of separate small tables for each delegation, laid out in a U formation, a scheme hardly conducive to diplomatic intercourse.

Dulles practiced what he preached. He kept social interactions to a minimum and repaired early each day to his accommodations in suite 545–546 in the Hotel du Rhône. When on one occasion he unavoidably found himself in close proximity to Zhou Enlai, the Chinese extended his hand in greeting. Dulles turned away.[8]

Subordinates were not always so good about avoiding contact. Chester L. Cooper, a young CIA officer who would later write one of the best early histories of U.S. involvement in Vietnam (and whose first task at Geneva was to determine whether Ho Chi Minh, who had not been heard from in the West in several months, was still alive and, if so, still held the leadership of the DRV; yes and yes, Cooper soon determined), at one point spotted a familiar face among the Chinese group, a former classmate from MIT. Several days later, by sheer coincidence, the two men found themselves alone in an elevator. They hugged, exchanged a few brief sentences, and laughed, then hastily recovered their composure as the elevator doors opened. They did not speak again.[9]

This American game of pretending the Chinese did not exist was observed with bemusement by Anthony Eden, who enjoyed a firmer domestic base than did Dulles, and by Georges Bidault, who did not. The

Frenchman had his own suspicions about Beijing's intentions, and he rejected urgings to meet one-on-one with Zhou Enlai, but his animus did not extend to refusing handshakes. Eden, meanwhile, worried that the Americans sought intentionally to kill the prospect of a negotiated deal. His dislike of their approach, and of Dulles personally, threatened to get the better of him, as an alarmed Evelyn Shuckburgh, opinionated as always, noted in his diary already on the second day in Geneva: "A.E. is so anti-American today that it is hard to get him to look for positive ways of bringing Dulles to a more patient frame of mind."[10]

Dulles's impatience had to do with the continuing failure to generate Western unity in advance of the start of the Indochina portion of the conference, and with what he characterized as the "imprecision" of Eden's strategy. He was in a surly mood when he called on the Briton before lunch on April 30. That morning Dulles had delivered a hard-hitting speech, whereupon Zhou Enlai had delivered a tough one himself, accusing Washington of imperialist intervention in Indochina. Eden had not come to Dulles's defense. Shuckburgh's diary again:

> [Dulles] said nobody was supporting the US; nobody had said a word to defend them against Zhou Enlai's attacks; the alliance was nearly at an end; Asia lost; France finished, etc. "We have seen the best of our times . . . and the bond cracked between father and child" (Lear?) . . . He wants someone to make a speech, like his, attacking communism. I think one of us had better do it. A.E. says, "They would think in London I was mad". . . . One major worry is the almost pathological rage and gloom of Foster Dulles, which we really must do something to allay. (Not easy; A.E. is fed up with Dulles, refuses to make concessions to his feelings, and almost resents seeing him.)[11]

The following evening they tried again, this time over dinner. It went badly. After the spouses left the room, Dulles and three aides, including Undersecretary of State Walter Bedell Smith, who had arrived from Washington earlier in the day, and the hard-line assistant secretary of state Walter Robertson, launched into a long disquisition on Anglo-American relations. The ties, formerly so strong, were in complete disarray, Dulles remarked. Eden, with only one colleague on his side (Lord Reading, the minister of state at the Foreign Office), felt ganged-up upon. The Americans said Great Britain had let them down, but they no longer sought any material assistance in Indochina from her—not a single airplane, or soldier, or pound. They knew Britain was fully stretched (an assertion Eden found contemptuous). Rather, all they wanted now was "moral support." Eden asked what kind of action would require this moral support. That had not yet been determined, came the reply, but later in the discussion Dulles alluded to the possibility of maintaining a bridgehead, or foothold, for two years until Vietnamese troops had sufficient training to defend their country. To Eden and Reading's ears, this sounded unmistakably like a plan to take over military operations from the French, and it alarmed them. When Reading remarked that the bridgehead notion "meant that things would remain on the boil for several years to come," Dulles retorted: "That would be a very good thing."[12]

Little wonder that Eden believed, as he put it to Her Majesty's ambassador in Washington some days later, that whereas his concept of a Southeast Asian defense organization was designed to guarantee a diplomatic settlement, the Eisenhower administration seemed to be contemplating a concept that would help them reconquer Indochina—an idea quite unacceptable to the London government.[13]

Winston Churchill, for his part, when informed of Dulles's demeanor and agenda in Geneva, said he had had his fill of the American, finding him a "dull, unimaginative, uncomprehending man; so clumsy I hope he will disappear."[14]

Churchill got his wish: Dulles did disappear—from Geneva. From the start, he had said he would remain in Switzerland only for a short period, and on May 3, a week after arriving, he made good on the vow and left for Washington. His departure proved a godsend, for at that moment, subordinates on both the American and the British sides feared the Eden-Dulles rift was beyond repair and might scuttle the whole enterprise. It helped as well that his replacement as head of the U.S. delegation was Walter Bedell Smith, the only one among the American foursome at the May 1 dinner whom Reading and Eden thought showed any comprehension of the complexities involved. A veteran bureaucratic infighter, Smith had been Eisenhower's chief of staff during World War II and later

served as ambassador to Moscow and director of the CIA. Since inauguration, he had served as Dulles's number two, and it's interesting to speculate what might have happened had Eisenhower selected him for the top
job. With his abrupt speaking style and quick temper, and his ramrod-
straight soldierly bearing, he did not at first glance resemble anyone's idea
of the flexible and accommodating diplomat. In the April deliberations
in Washington, moreover, he had been notably hawkish on Indochina.

But there was another side to the man, as French diplomat Jean
Chauvel's portrait suggested: "Rather a small, thin man whose face, all
bumps and furrows, made him look as if he had chewed some bitter pill.
He did in fact have stomach trouble and was thus prone to attacks of indi-
gestion and to brief but violent fits of temper . . . an intelligent man, who
appreciated what was concrete, understood politics, and did not deal in
false coin."[15]

Lord Reading saw Dulles's departure as "pure gain." "He was beginning to act as a powerful irritant upon Anthony and others and seemed
to devote himself to telling us where to get off, though never how we
got on. Bedell is, of course, quite a different proposition and the relations between him and Anthony are increasingly 'frank and friendly.'"
Reading also appreciated that Smith seemed to have tighter rein on
subordinates—by which he no doubt meant Robertson, a loathsome figure to the British delegation.[16]

For Eden, the improvement was instantaneous. "I went to see Foster
off," he wrote in his diary on May 3. "It was meant as a gesture but I don't
think it did much good. Americans are sore, mainly I suspect because
they know they have made a mess of this conference. . . . Bedell came
to dinner. We arranged the ground at length & I gave him proposals for
talks to supplement any Indo-China agreement. I think that we made
progress." It pleased Eden to hear Smith urge him "not to pay too much
attention to some of the stupid things being said in the USA," and in
the first days of May he used words such as "sympathetic" and "reasonable and receptive" to describe the American. Perhaps too Eden had an
inkling of the fact that Smith disliked his own boss Dulles, considering
him a pompous blowhard. On May 5, Eden made a concession to Smith
for five-power military staff talks on Southeast Asian regional security—a
concession he might not have made to Dulles.[17]

III

BY THE TIME THE INDOCHINA PART OF THE CONFERENCE COM-
menced on May 8, therefore, the prospects for Western unity in the negotiations had begun to tick upward. But there was a long way to go. Even
now, as Bidault prepared to initiate the proceedings, the three delegations were not in full agreement on what the talks should accomplish:
Eden had a commitment to a negotiated settlement of the war that neither
Bidault nor Smith fully shared. The Frenchman in previous days had
continued to vacillate, and not even the news of Dien Bien Phu's fall on
May 7 had lessened his determination to drive a hard bargain. Smith,
for his part, acting substantially on instructions from Washington, said
his government wanted nothing to do with a deal that would subvert the
governments of the Associated States or sell out the interests of the West,
a line echoed by Bao Dai's foreign minister Nguyen Quoc Dinh. On the
other side, Zhou Enlai went through the first week saying little and revealing less, and the Viet Minh delegation, led by Pham Van Dong, was
likewise inscrutable after its arrival on May 4. Only Molotov seemed to
share Eden's desire to move expeditiously to start the talks, and it was
their joint efforts on May 5-7—prodding their respective allies, assuring
them that no harm would come from conversing—that brought things to
this point.

No one envied Bidault his task that afternoon. The little man had not
only to open the conference but also to acknowledge the fall of Dien Bien
Phu, and in the presence of the world's press as well as Pham Van Dong
and his Communist allies. Looking gray with fatigue, his voice quiet at
the start, Bidault paid tribute to the defenders of the fortress and recalled
the civilizing role of France in Indochina. If that didn't cause Pham Van
Dong's blood pressure to rise, Bidault's description of the war—"this
conflict that was imposed on us"—and his insistence that France fought
only for defensive purposes, surely did. Bidault then proposed "that the
Conference should start by adopting the principle of a general cessation
of hostilities in Indochina supported by essential guarantees of security. . . . These guarantees are intended to preserve the security of the
troops of both sides and to protect the civil population against any abu-

sive exploitation of the truce." There ought also to be a release of prisoners and the disarming of irregulars, he went on, and any final settlement should be guaranteed by the member nations of the Geneva Conference.[18]

It was now the Viet Minh's turn, but Pham Van Dong was not yet prepared to show his hand. Perhaps he was too stunned—the French foreign minister had come close to demanding the Viet Minh's surrender, twenty-four hours after the fall of Dien Bien Phu. A thin man with hollow cheeks, Pham Van Dong had helped lead, it will be recalled, the Vietnamese delegation in negotiations with the French during the abortive Fontainebleau conference in 1946. Thereafter he had continued to rise in the party, becoming DRV deputy prime minister in 1949 and in 1951 taking a seat on the Politburo. A tenacious negotiator whose bargaining style shifted easily into caustic truculence, he was no one's idea of the affable interlocutor.

When Pham Van Dong took the podium on May 10, he pointed out that Bidault had offered no political proposals but only military ones, based on an "outdated colonialist outlook," and moreover that he had utterly failed to take account of the actual military situation on the ground. Following a vehement, sarcastic denunciation of American "imperialists" and their intervention in Indochina, Pham Van Dong put forward the DRV's core points, on which he had reached agreement in the days prior with Molotov and Zhou Enlai.[19] In particular, he called for the independence and sovereignty of the three Indochinese states, elections to create a unified government in each of them, the withdrawal of foreign troops and advisers, and the inclusion in the Geneva talks of the Viet Minh–backed Pathet Lao and Khmer Issarak "resistance" governments. Also, persons who collaborated with the opposite side in the war would be free from repression, and there would be an exchange of prisoners. Implementation of these provisions would be preceded by a cease-fire, followed by readjustment of occupied territory to separate the two sides and a ban on the importation of new troops, weapons, and munitions into Indochina. As a sop to the French, Pham Van Dong pledged the DRV's willingness to consider membership in the French Union based on free will and said his government recognized France's considerable cultural and economic interests in Vietnam, Cambodia, and Laos.[20]

The sides were thus far apart, but the gap was not as wide as one might have expected. That Pham Van Dong would offer any kind of compensation at all to the enemy seems surprising in retrospect, in light of the crushing victory three days earlier at Dien Bien Phu. More tellingly, his proposal clearly envisioned partition, followed by national elections, as the best way to end the war. The three Communist countries, as we have seen, had reached basic agreement on the desirability of partition already weeks earlier, and on May 1 a senior Soviet official in Geneva had repeated his government's support for such a solution.[21] With the stunning development in the Tonkin highlands, however, one might have expected Pham Van Dong now to put forth a maximalist demand: immediate French withdrawal and the formation of a national government led by the Viet Minh. From his perspective, after all, a cessation of hostilities would appear counterproductive, now that General Giap plainly had the Expeditionary Corps in so much trouble. Pham Van Dong's failure to stake out such a position resulted in part from Chinese and Soviet pressure in recent months to maintain a flexible negotiating posture. But it also suggests that the DRV leadership continued to have its own reasons for wanting a settlement, continued to see the overall balance of forces as uncomfortably close, continued to worry about morale problems among its own troops and its own supporters. The vehement denunciation of U.S. policy pointed yet again to another concern: that a prolongation of the fighting would bring the powerful Americans into the war.

Colonel Michel de Brébisson, one of the French negotiators at Geneva, saw ample evidence that the Viet Minh wanted an end to the war. "The eight years of war they have waged with increasing intensity have led their troops to a certain degree of tension in the precarious economic situation in which they live," he wrote at the time. "The population they control is weary of the burden of this war. Dien Bien Phu was a victory that exerted a high price. They may be able to take over the Tonkin delta, but this will exact a higher price and will give rise to fresh depredations. Finally, and above all, the danger of internationalization [of the war] is not excluded." DRV leaders themselves, it will be recalled from the previous chapter, in candid moments described their predicament in strikingly similar terms.[22]

None of which is to suggest that the Viet Minh leadership was desperate for an early agreement at Geneva, or that it had overcome its earlier skepticism regarding the prospects for multilateral diplomacy. On May 11, the Vietnamese Workers Party issued a set of instructions, warning against "peace illusions" among the Vietnamese people and cautioning them that Geneva would not bring an end to the struggle for independence and national unity. Simultaneously, Vo Nguyen Giap continued to make preparations for a large-scale assault on the Red River Delta. And in its deliberations with the Chinese and Soviets at Geneva, the Viet Minh delegation affirmed the need to drive a hard bargain.[23]

That the Viet Minh proposal implied support for partition was lost on neither Bao Dai's State of Vietnam, which on May 12 categorically rejected "partition, direct or indirect, definitive or provisional, in fact or in law, of the national territory," nor on the Eisenhower administration, which followed suit the next day.[24] Though Anthony Eden reported hopefully to the Foreign Office that some members of the U.S. government now recognized that partition represented a viable option, contemporaneous American sources give a different picture. Twice on May 14—once to the cabinet and once to his brother, CIA director Allen Dulles—John Foster Dulles said he did not think it possible to "draw a line," given both the present balance of forces and the geography of Indochina. Nor, he anticipated, would partition end the Viet Minh insurgency in the south. The Joint Chiefs of Staff, long of the opinion that Tonkin was the key to the defense of Southeast Asia, warned additionally that partition would provide Ho Chi Minh with contiguous territory within which he could reorganize his forces. And Walter Bedell Smith, in a meeting with Bidault and Eden on May 15, said such a solution would mean the loss of Tonkin forever and thus should be avoided.[25]

Yes, Bidault concurred, and this was impossible: France could not agree to surrender Haiphong and Hanoi. Physical separation of the combatants was necessary, but it should be in the form of enclaves controlled by each side throughout the country (the so-called leopard skin approach), not partition into two separate regroupment zones.[26] The Laniel government expected to retain control—for France or for Bao Dai's government—in the south, but it also hoped to keep a foothold in the Red River Delta. Dien Bien Phu did not change this calculation, at least not in Bidault's mind or that of cabinet colleagues such as Maurice Schumann and René Pleven. Drawn up by General Navarre's staff in Saigon at the urging of Paris, the leopard skin plan gave the Viet Minh the Ca Mau peninsula in the far south, three enclaves around Saigon, a huge slice of Annam in the center, and most of Tonkin; the French Union, however, got all of the urban areas in the country, including Hanoi and Haiphong, and the Viet Minh were also to withdraw all forces from Cambodia and Laos. The plan would protect French political and economic interests in Indochina and also allow the French High Command to resume combat operations if necessary.[27]

But there were murmurings of dissent from some French military planners, who questioned the leopard skin plan's strategic value. "Nothing would be more dangerous than an armistice which will involve, from one end of the territory to the other, the two sides' cohabitation," remarked the French military attaché in Bangkok, after a meeting in which Chinese officials made clear to him their support for partition. Anthony Eden, for his part, was shocked to see how much Navarre's scheme gave up to the Viet Minh, while the British chiefs of staff charged that the plan "abandons Vietnam" by leaving enemy "footholds all over the country."[28]

To compound the problem for Bidault, the fall of Dien Bien Phu had strengthened the forces of peace in France. The Laniel government was living on borrowed time. On the eve of the garrison's fall, Laniel won a vote of confidence on his government's Indochina policy by a vote of 311 to 262. A mere six days later, on May 13, this margin had been reduced to two votes: 289 to 287. The government had public opinion against it, while in the press, more and more commentators spoke out in favor of partition, if that would secure an agreement. In *Le Monde*, for example, the respected Robert Guillain saw numerous formulas for the division of Vietnam into two regroupment zones, any one of which provided the means to "internationalize the peace."[29]

IV

BIDAULT, HOWEVER, PINNED HIS HOPES ON SECRET TALKS THAT might do the opposite, namely, internationalize the war—less because he sought such an escalation than because he hoped to use the prospect of it to force concessions from the Communist powers. From mid-May, bilateral Franco-American negotiations considered the scenarios under which joint military action could occur. French and American archival sources differ on the origin of the endeavor, but what is clear is that Dulles, on May 11, cabled conditions for U.S. intervention to Ambassador Douglas Dillon in Paris, who waited until after Laniel survived his vote of confidence to deliver them on May 14. The request must have the backing of the National Assembly, Dulles asserted, and must be addressed to other countries as well. The French troop level in Indochina must be maintained, and agreement must be reached on the training of Vietnamese troops and the nature of the command structure for joint intervention. Finally, the secretary of state maintained, the French government was expected to grant full independence to the Associated States and to give them the right to secede from the French Union.[30]

Eden, having secured provisional agreement from the other delegations to move the conference into restricted session—where, he believed, the real negotiating could commence—knew nothing of these Franco-American contacts until he learned about them in the Swiss newspapers on Saturday morning, May 15. The articles said that discussions would shortly begin in Paris, where Dulles would meet Laniel. Eden was flabbergasted. He confronted Bidault and Smith the next day; the former was evasive, but the American confirmed the reports were correct. Distressed at Washington's inability to keep a secret, Smith, in strict confidence, showed Eden some of the top-secret telegrams setting out the details of the intrigue. Eden thanked him for this gesture but said Britain could not possibly proceed with the five-power staff conversations he had agreed to on May 5. He reconsidered this refusal two days later, after Bidault assured him France would not request intervention unless and until the Geneva Conference had failed to bring about a settlement, but his suspicions remained. Paris and Washington seemed as uninterested as ever in giving negotiations a serious try, and the belligerence the Americans had shown during the disastrous encounter over dinner on May 1—with their talk of holding a bridgehead in Vietnam for two years while the VNA was being properly trained—evidently had not dissipated.[31]

A skeptic could ask whether the Franco-American plan was really meant to succeed. Could any French government, given the mood in the National Assembly, ever meet the American preconditions? And why was the scheme leaked to the press? Was this not simply a means by which the White House could show toughness to hawks at home and to Communists in Geneva while setting the bar so high, there was little chance of intervention actually occurring?

The evidence suggests there was more to it than that. Eisenhower did seek to keep the bar high and to bring Congress in on any decision for intervention, but he and Dulles, in the last half of May, worked hard to do what Vice President Nixon had advocated on April 29: create an allied coalition without the British. Thus, on May 19 at the White House, Dulles reminded Eisenhower that America's proposed military intervention "did not make UK active participation a necessary condition." The president concurred but noted the importance therefore of Australia, New Zealand, the Philippines, Thailand, and, of course, the Associated States. The next day Dulles met with Australia's ambassador to Washington, Percy Spender, and New Zealand's minister for external affairs, Clifton Webb, who was stopping off in Washington on his way home from Geneva. Congressional criticism of Britain as a U.S. ally was growing, Dulles told them, and "the United States is prepared to persevere with an organization which does not include the United Kingdom." Could the administration count on Canberra and Wellington to join this coalition, if necessary without Britain's participation? The two men were noncommittal, just as Spender and New Zealand's Leslie Munro had been noncommittal when Dulles, six weeks earlier, had urged them to use their influence on the stubborn British. They promised merely to consult with their respective governments.[32]

"With friends like these . . . ," Dulles might well have muttered. He was fed up. Fed up with dithering allies who always wanted more time, more consultation, more negotiation, who failed to see the need for swift and resolute action. He articulated his frustration in a letter to Dean Rusk, former assistant secretary of state and current head of the Rockefeller Foundation, who as secretary of state himself a decade later would face his own frustrations regarding allies' views of Vietnam. "I do not think that any adequate thought has been given to the implications of our so-called 'alliances,'" Dulles wrote. "How much should it in fact tie our hands with respect to many areas as to which there is no agreement?" The letter implied that the two men had already discussed the matter the previous week, and Dulles said there might be an important meeting on the subject a few weeks thence, in mid-June, for which he would value Rusk's input.[33]

That was in the future: In the here and now, Dulles had to work within the existing system, which meant continuing the quest for collective action. The president had indicated he would not order unilateral intervention, certainly not without the backing of a Congress that showed scant enthusiasm for going in alone. Dulles therefore continued the Franco-American negotiations over intervention, continued to apply pressure on Australia and New Zealand, continued to warn the British and French against agreeing to partition. The latter task became more difficult on May 25, for in restricted session on that day, Pham Van Dong explicitly endorsed the concept—or as explicitly as was possible without uttering the word. Each side would have complete administrative and economic control over its territory, he said in his characteristically staccato French, and would withdraw its military forces from the other zone. A similar arrangement would be implemented in Laos and Cambodia, with one zone for the royal governments of the Associated States and one for the Viet Minh–supported Pathet Lao and Khmer Issarak. Pham Van Dong stressed that his proposal did not represent a violation of the national unity of each country; the division in each case would be temporary and would lead to elections for reunification.

Pham Van Dong knew the general concept he was outlining would find favor in the British delegation and among many in the press corps. More important, he knew partition had growing support in the French camp. Georges Bidault, anxious to assuage the fears of the South Vietnamese government, remained hostile, but several officials—Claude Cheysson and Raymond Offroy, both of them Indochina specialists, as well as Jean Chauvel and Colonel de Brébisson—were convinced of the wisdom of attempting some kind of division of Vietnam, one that would give each side one of the deltas. A week earlier de Brébisson had commenced a series of face-to-face sessions with the Viet Minh's Colonel Ha Van Lau, the first such Franco–Viet Minh meeting of the conference. Their initial charge was to discuss the evacuation of the wounded from Dien Bien Phu (it will be recalled that several hundred had been too ill to march to Viet Minh prison camps and had been left behind) as well as a possible exchange of prisoners, but in the days thereafter, they also considered other issues of contention, including the mechanics of a cease-fire and how to achieve the regroupment of the two sides. In the weeks to come, these two colonels, who had fought on opposite sides since the outbreak of the struggle—de Brébisson had been among the first French troops to disembark in Saigon, in November 1945, and Ha, a former clerk in the French colonial administration, had been political commissar in the 320th Division—would contribute as much as anyone to the final work of the conference.[34]

Slowly, almost imperceptibly, Smith seemed to be coming around to the need for some kind of division of the country. At a press conference on May 27, he admitted that one could not ignore Ho Chi Minh's well-disciplined and formidable fighting force, which controlled a significant proportion of the territory. This Viet Minh position of strength on the battlefield could not be wished out of existence. What the Eisenhower administration sought, Smith continued, was some means of reconciling this reality with American principles, leading to a "termination of hostilities on an honorable basis."[35] (See map on p. 538.)

That was the rub, of course: What constituted "honorable"? With voices in Congress and the American press branding partition a sellout—*U.S. News & World Report* compared "Winston Churchill's proposal" to Chamberlain allowing partition of Czechoslovakia at Munich, while *Time* said British leaders "look alarmingly like appeasers"—Smith's superiors in Washington still sought to preserve flexibility and to avoid committing the United States fully to any particular plan concerning the political aspects of the cease-fire.[36] Better no agreement at all, the White House believed, than one that would reward "Communist aggression."

In restricted session on May 29, Eden and Smith squabbled over the Briton's proposal that the French and Viet Minh military commands should meet to discuss "the cessation of hostilities, beginning with the question of regrouping areas in Vietnam." The American warned that his government would reserve the right to judge whether the recommendations coming out of these bilateral discussions prejudiced the U.S. position with respect to the independence of Vietnam, Cambodia, and Laos. This was a holding action, and it annoyed Eden, though not as much as what Smith did next: He declared his desire—no doubt with American domestic opinion firmly in mind—to make his reservation public. Eden countered by saying he would not release his own proposal to the press, so that Smith would not feel compelled to announce his reservation. "For some reason or other this apparently annoyed the Americans," he wrote in his diary, an understatement of the first order. Smith was outraged by what he called, in a cable to Dulles, Eden's "exhibition of impatience and pique." Despite the foreign secretary's plea, both his proposal and the unenthusiastic American reception to it were leaked to the press.[37]

Eden would have blanched had he seen what else Smith said to Dulles that day: "I want you to know that I believe it will be a sad day for Britain and America when Eden becomes Prime Minister. I am convinced, after long association, that he is without moral or intellectual honesty, and his vanity and petulance are not counterbalanced, as in the case of Churchill, by genuine wisdom and great strength of character."[38]

That evening Eden got more alarming news. At 7:36 a cable arrived at the Foreign Office from Sir Gladwyn Jebb, Britain's ambassador in Paris, who asked that it be sent on to Geneva immediately. It contained a bombshell: According to Maurice Schumann, the French undersecretary of state for foreign affairs, the Franco-American negotiations regarding possible U.S. intervention in Indochina had that day achieved a breakthrough, with the result that "agreement has now practically been reached with the Americans on all points." The French government didn't actually want this intervention, Schumann told Jebb; what it wanted was the "deterrent effect" that an agreed-upon plan, involving both American airpower and ground forces, would have on the Viet Minh negotiators and their Soviet and Chinese backers. This last assertion did little to mollify Eden. Convinced, as he wrote Churchill the following day, that the Americans "want to intervene," he determined he would reiterate in the strongest terms Britain's unwillingness to support any plan for military action while the Geneva talks had even one breath of life in them. Schumann might claim that France did not want an escalation of the war, but "their wavering between pusillanimity and intransigence may well bring it about."[39]

When Eden confronted Bidault about the matter, the Frenchman confirmed the veracity of Schumann's claim. If the Geneva negotiations failed to yield an acceptable peace, Eisenhower would go to Congress and request authorization for intervention. Airpower would be used, and probably also three marine divisions. The administration had even dropped its requirement that France give the Associated States the right to secede from the French Union. Eden heard Bidault out, then restated his government's refusal to commit to military action, whereupon Bidault said he himself saw the plan mainly as a political weapon designed to strengthen the French diplomatic hand.[40]

Was this true also of the Americans? Did they too see this roll of distant thunder primarily as a means to induce the Communists in Geneva to lower their demands? Was the show of strength more show than strength? Or was Eden right in insisting to Churchill that Washington wanted to intervene? The evidence is not conclusive, but almost certainly it was some of both. To imagine that the Eisenhower administration viewed this Franco-American arrangement purely as an elaborate ruse is difficult, to say the least; surely the president and his aides knew that if no settlement emerged from the negotiations (as they expected and half-hoped would be the case), they would face enormous pressure to implement the plan. Loath for ideological as well as pragmatic partisan reasons to be associated with a "Far Eastern Munich," and fearful of the geopolitical as well as domestic political consequences of allowing a Viet Minh military victory, the administration continued to plan for possible military intervention, continued to lean on Australia and New Zealand to join in the endeavor even if Britain would not. On June 2, Bedell Smith, acting on instructions from Washington, told a press conference that the United States could not associate herself "with any formula which partitions or dismembers Vietnam."[41]

V

THEN SOMETHING CHANGED—OR MORE PRECISELY, TWO THINGS. First, word arrived in Washington that neither Australia nor New Zealand was willing in the foreseeable future to participate in military action in Indochina. Canberra, the more influential of the two ANZUS partners, had in fact quietly been coming to this position over a period of weeks. Eager, on the one hand, to remain on good terms with the United States and to keep the Americans committed to underwriting the defense of Southeast Asia, the government was reluctant, on the other, to come out in open opposition to British policy. What tipped the balance was the state of the war on the ground. With Giap's victory at Dien Bien Phu and the increasing pressure on the delta, Australian military officials saw little hope for French Union forces in Tonkin, and even in Annam and Cochin China the prospects were bleak. An American-led multilateral intervention would undoubtedly help the situation, but not enough to turn things around, at least in the short or medium term, and consequently the best means of blocking further Communist expansion was through an early cessation of hostilities. The Menzies government agreed; on May 23, Richard Casey, the minister for external affairs, concluded in a secret cable that the optimum solution would be an armistice "with some political solution (even entailing partition)."[42]

It's telling that U.S. ambassador Amos J. Peaslee, when informed of this Australian position, remarked that its endorsement of a political over a military solution did not accord with his understanding of American policy. And it's telling that Casey, in formally presenting his argument to the Australian cabinet on Friday, June 4, asserted that Washington sought to prolong the war through multilateral armed intervention. He won cabinet approval for a policy of seeking a diplomatic settlement and for his claim that, notwithstanding Canberra's interest in keeping America engaged in the defense of Southeast Asia, "Australia's destiny was not so completely wrapped up with the United States as to support them in action which Australia regarded as wrong." Certainly, few in Canberra thought of America's warlike breast-beating on Indochina as a mere ruse designed to scare the Communist delegations into making major concessions.[43]

This is why Australia's decision to support a political settlement has historical importance: Not long after word of it reached the White House, the Eisenhower administration began to sing a different tune. At the end of May, Peaslee gave Washington hints of what was to come, and Ambassador Spender officially informed the State Department on June 4. The following evening Dulles indicated the administration was inclined to seek a negotiated solution to the war. "France would have to accept whatever terms they would get if they were to obtain a cease-fire," Spender reported him as saying. Dulles also hinted the United States "would not engage in unilateral intervention . . . without the support of

Australia and New Zealand." (Wellington had in the meantime also said it would not commit to United Action.) To Roger Makins, the British ambassador in Washington, the secretary of state was clear as could be: Any American military action in Vietnam would have to be as part of a coalition force.[44]

If the news from down under was one reason for this apparent change in American thinking, there was also a second: a growing appreciation of just how dire the situation was on the ground in Vietnam. That same weekend witnessed the start of the five-power military staff talks in Washington, which featured chiefs-of-staff-level discussions by representatives from the United States, Great Britain, France, Australia, and New Zealand. Some two weeks earlier a French military mission led by General Paul Ely, chief of the French general staff, and including also the former Indochina commander Raoul Salan, had visited Indochina. They returned with a sobering assessment of the war map. Major reinforcements were essential, they told the Committee on National Defense, and because of the sorry state of the Vietnamese National Army, these would have to come from France. This in turn would mean changing the law to allow conscripts to be sent. Even then it might be necessary to focus defenses on the truly vital parts of the Red River Delta—essentially the Hanoi-Haiphong corridor—and to sacrifice the rest.[45]

This same basic message was articulated by the chief French representative in the five-power talks, General Jean Valluy, the commander of the Expeditionary Corps at the start of the war in 1946 and now the head of the French Military Mission to the United States. Morale among French Union forces had plummeted, a despondent Valluy told Admiral Radford late on June 2, while the VNA had become a rabble, deserting right and left. The Viet Minh, on the other hand, enthused by their victory at Dien Bien Phu, were laying preparations to attack the delta in force, using as many as one hundred battalions. Could the delta be held? Valluy was skeptical and said so both to Radford and in the five-power talks that commenced the following day. He offered up some tough rhetoric on the importance of holding Tonkin and the desirability of United Action, but he knew that three of the other four delegations in Washington wanted nothing to do with multilateral intervention. As the talks progressed, Valluy hinted that French military opinion was now resigned to partition, whether through a negotiated agreement at Geneva or through a unilateral military withdrawal southward by French Union forces. Conceding that Ho Chi Minh would accept a cease-fire only if he won control over Hanoi, the Frenchman suggested seeking a division line as far north as possible, ideally at the eighteenth parallel.[46]

For Arthur Radford and like-minded members of the American military, such "defeatist" talk was contemptible. During the Washington talks, the admiral continued to press for United Action, continued to insist that the West faced a choice between military intervention and the rapid loss of all of Indochina and perhaps Southeast Asia too, continued to argue that Tonkin was the key to the whole region. He insisted that major troop reinforcements from France, combined with air and naval action by the United States, could hold Tonkin for the six or nine months American missions would need to train effective Vietnamese forces. But though Eisenhower and Dulles remained sympathetic to the admiral's assessment of the stakes—U.S. News & World Report said that week that the president saw much wisdom in Radford's plan—they had now to contend with the state of affairs on the ground in Vietnam, and the hardening views of the key allied governments. Moreover, they had to consider the opposition to Radford's analysis from within the U.S. military. Army chief of staff General Matthew Ridgway, who with his formal bearing, cold gray eyes, and steel-trap mind exuded seriousness and gravitas, had not abandoned his deep skepticism concerning the utility of airpower in Vietnam. He was certain, moreover, that U.S. ground forces would inevitably be part of the equation—and in large numbers. This would put huge strains on Pentagon planners, given America's existing troop commitments around the globe, and would constitute, Ridgway warned, a "dangerous strategic diversion . . . in a non-decisive theater."[47]

Anthony Eden sensed the change in American thinking. On June 5, he was the picture of gloom before the British cabinet, telling his colleagues that a deal was unlikely because Bidault was indecisive and because Washington was only interested in military intervention. But later that day word came in from Makins in Washington that the Americans had a new policy, which was not to intervene in Indochina unless the Chinese did so by arms and airplanes. Eden in his diary scoffed at the idea that Beijing might intervene in force—"why they should when they are winning already I cannot imagine"—but he interpreted the policy change, if indeed it was real, as a sign that the interventionists (he listed Radford, Dulles, and Admiral Robert B. Carney, the U.S. delegate to the five-power staff talks) had suffered a setback.[48]

Bidault too felt a new wind blowing, and it made him shiver. What would be the point of continuing the Franco-American talks, he asked Dulles through Ambassador Henri Bonnet, if intervention was no longer a live option? And what incentive would the Communists at Geneva then have to compromise? Dulles replied that the situation had changed: Whereas six weeks earlier American air and naval power and a "token land force" would have been enough, now four or five U.S. divisions would in all likelihood be required. The military outlook was dire, and morale both in France and among allies in Vietnam had plummeted. Nor had the French government met the preconditions for U.S. involvement. The testy exchange concluded with Bonnet charging that agreement had been reached between the two governments when Washington all of a sudden pulled back.[49]

VI

IF AMERICAN MILITARY INTERVENTION IN VIETNAM WAS AT LONG last off the table, the Eisenhower administration still could not bring itself to take the next step and support a negotiated settlement. Even as each of the other main players in Geneva gravitated toward partition as the preferred solution—Viet Minh and French negotiators made significant progress on the particulars in secret meetings on June 4, 5, and 10, even as Georges Bidault personally remained noncommittal—the administration was loath to sign on. (At least publicly; privately, Bedell Smith told Australia's Casey on June 13 that he personally accepted the idea of partition.)[50] In domestic political terms, it would be better for the conference to collapse than for it to agree to a compromise with Communists, especially of the Chinese variety.

Hence the equanimity with which U.S. officials greeted the splits that emerged in restricted sessions in mid-June. The disagreements concerned the authority and composition of an international supervisory commission that would monitor the peace, and the status of Cambodia and Laos.

Resolution seemed impossible, and many delegates, Eden among them, concluded that a breakup of the conference was imminent. Dulles was pleased, or at least not disturbed. "It is our view," he cabled Bedell Smith on June 14, "that final adjournment of Conference is in our best interest, provided this can be done without creating an impression in France at this critical moment that France has been deserted by US and UK and therefore has no choice but capitulation on Indochina to Communists at Geneva and possible accommodation with Soviets in Europe."[51]

But what if such capitulation and accommodation occurred, or what if the Communists used the failure of the conference as an excuse to try to conquer the whole of the Indochinese peninsula? Robert Bowie, the director of the State Department's Policy Planning Staff, articulated precisely that fear at a meeting of the NSC on June 15. Here was the United States, Bowie said, withdrawing from the Geneva Conference because she found the Communist proposals unacceptable, yet she was unwilling to do anything to bolster the French position. The likely result: The Viet Minh would charge down the peninsula and get more of Indochina than they were demanding at the conference. In the wake of such a development, Nehru and other "Asiatics" would swing to the Communist side. Far better, Bowie asserted, to defend "South Vietnam," if necessary with four U.S. divisions.[52]

Although U.S. diplomats in Saigon had made similar noises for several weeks, this was a revolutionary idea in the halls of power in Washington.[53] Bowie had not merely asserted that partition served American interests better than allowing the negotiations to fail; he had said the southern half of Vietnam was militarily defensible. The five-power staff talks had come to the same conclusion, with a consensus that a line from Thakhek (in Laos) to Dong Hoi—that is, about 17°50' north—could be defended. For the moment, Bowie found few takers for his argument, but his advocacy gained force among high officials in the days thereafter. Already by June 17, John Foster Dulles could be heard singing a new tune at another meeting of the NSC. Seconding Eisenhower's comment that the native populations of Southeast Asia viewed the war as a colonial enterprise, the secretary, according to the note taker, said "perhaps the time had come" to let the French get out of Indochina entirely and then try to "rebuild from the foundations." And later in the same meeting: "For the

United States or its allies to try to fight now in the Delta area was almost impossible, if for no other reason than that the French have no inclination to invite us in. They are desperately anxious to get themselves out of Indochina. . . . Probably best to let them quit."[54]

The "perhaps" and the "probably" were important. Although in hindsight Dulles's words constituted a watershed moment—the first clear sign of a monumental policy shift, from keeping the French fighting and resisting negotiations to moving France out of Indochina altogether and "rebuild[ing] from the foundations," without the taint of colonialism—at the time, in mid-June 1954, neither he nor President Eisenhower knew what they wanted. They still groped hesitantly for some means of reconciling the competing imperatives on Indochina: to keep the nation out of "another Korea" while avoiding any hint of "appeasement" of the Communists. Seeing danger whichever way they turned, especially in a congressional election year, the two men still saw advantages in letting the Geneva meeting collapse without an agreement. On June 12, Smith candidly told Eden that he had just received a "plain spoken" personal message from Eisenhower instructing him to do everything in his power to bring the proceedings to an end as quickly as possible. "We decided," the president himself would recall of this period in June, "that it was best for the United States to break off major participation in the Geneva Conference. The days of keeping the Western powers bound to inaction by creating divisions of policy among them in a dragged-out conference were coming to an end."[55]

In Paris, however, one man had a different idea. On June 18, six days after the Laniel government failed to win a vote of confidence (306 to 296), Pierre Mendès France, who had spoken out against this war longer and more fervently than any other leading politician, became France's new prime minister. In soliciting the National Assembly's support, the veteran Radical deputy didn't merely proclaim as his first objective a cease-fire in Indochina; he vowed that he would resign within thirty days of his investiture if an agreement had not been reached. His last act before resigning, he added, would be to introduce a bill for conscription to supplement the professional army in the field, which the Assembly would have to vote on the same day. Mendès France was sufficiently encouraged by the results of the de Brébisson-Ha secret discussions to make this pledge, but he knew it was a gamble. How would the delegations at Geneva respond? Would he be able to bring the Viet Minh, the Americans, the Chinese, the Soviets along? And what about Bao Dai's State of Vietnam, which that week had had her own change of leadership, one little noticed at the time but with enormous implications for the future? Buu Loc was out as prime minister, replaced by Ngo Dinh Diem. Would Diem, who immediately announced his opposition to any settlement involving partition, upset the Mendès France timetable?

So many questions, so much to work out. And the clock was now ticking.

CHAPTER 23

"WE MUST GO FAST"

I T WAS A GAMBLE, BUT A CONSIDERED ONE. PIERRE MENDÈS FRANCE had announced to the world that he would resign as French premier if he could not end his country's eight-year war in Indochina within one month (that is, by end of the day on July 20, 1954). Since agreeing on June 13 to be premier-designate, Mendès France, well-known for his colossal zest for work and immense powers of concentration, had immersed himself in the details of the military situation in Vietnam. The more he learned, the more he realized he had to move quickly to secure an agreement. There was still a war on. The picture in the Red River Delta was growing more and more bleak, senior military officers told him on June 14; desertions from the VNA were reaching epidemic proportions, and the Hanoi-Haiphong road was in constant danger of being cut, not for hours as was happening already, but permanently. Within weeks, Vo Nguyen Giap would be ready to launch a large-scale attack from various points on the delta's perimeter. Worse yet, the Viet Minh commander might not need to initiate such an all-out assault; so extensive was the *pourrissement* in the delta that the French position might quickly collapse anyway. "We must act quickly," the officers implored the premier-designate, "we must make them put their cards on the table as soon as possible."[1]

But it was not merely the dismal military situation that caused Mendès France to stake his political future on securing a rapid agreement at Geneva. For years, as we have seen, he had been a Cassandra in parliament, using his credentials as an economist to argue that France could not afford the war, could not afford to fight a major military campaign in Asia while seeking recovery at home. And without such an economic recovery, the country's broader foreign policy objectives, including in Europe and North Africa, would be unattainable.[2] Everything was connected to everything else. Admittedly, liquidating the Indochina enterprise short of success would not be easy—there would be denunciations from some commentators at home, and French prestige abroad would suffer a blow—but what alternative was there? "To govern is to choose," Mendès France had once declared (*gouverner, c'est choisir*), and he had been withering in his criticism of previous French governments for avoiding the tough decisions on Indochina. Now he would get the chance to follow his dictum.

And besides, all was not necessarily lost. Grim though the military prospects might be, diplomatically Mendès France saw reason to be hopeful. From Jean Chauvel's telegrams he knew that the bilateral Franco–Viet Minh negotiations in Geneva were making slow but steady progress, which seemed to indicate that the Viet Minh too sought an early end to the war. The other leading delegations, meanwhile—with the exception of the Americans, that is, who he knew suspected his left-wing credentials—were pleased by his selection, and the task now was to strike quickly, while he had the advantage of freshness and could count on broad support in the Assembly. By announcing this deadline, he hoped to create a psychological situation closely approximating a truce. After all, a major enemy offensive operation during the four-week window would bring international opprobrium, and since only the enemy was in a position to be able to launch such an operation in the near future, the cost to French maneuverability in the field would be minimal. In Korea, the negotiations had been allowed to drag on for months and months; he could not let that happen here.[3]

But there were risks as well in setting a deadline, huge risks, and Mendès France knew it. His own reputation would suffer a blow, possibly a fatal one, if he failed to deliver a deal by July 20. Furthermore, his country's adversaries might be tempted to slow down the negotiations with the aim of securing last-minute concessions as the clock ticked down. Tensions among the Western powers, palpable enough in recent weeks, could increase as the three governments worked to establish a common position before the deadline. Nevertheless, Mendès France took the plunge. At two A.M. on June 18, 1954, some hours after electrifying the delegates in the National Assembly with his Indochina wager, Pierre Mendès France became premier of France, by a vote of 419 to 47, with 143 abstentions. It was one of the strongest majorities in the history of the Fourth Republic. The left-wing press cheered the result, and "Mendèsiste" delight could be seen also in the more centrist papers such as *Le Monde, Franc-Tireur, Combat,* and *France Observateur.*

His rise to the highest political office in the land was at once extraordinary and entirely to be expected. A descendant of Marrano Jews who had fled the Portuguese Inquisition of 1684, Pierre Mendès France was born in Paris in 1907. From an early age, he assumed the wholly secular sense of identity long held by middle-class Jewish families of the Third and Fourth republics, who trusted that an assimilationist but condoning France would satisfy their sense of belonging. Ambitious and brilliant, he had served as the precocious undersecretary of finance in Léon Blum's second ministry in 1938 and as de Gaulle's minister of economic affairs in 1944–45. Yet Mendès France remained to an extent an outsider throughout the wartime and early postwar years, an emerging political star who drew his strength not from party maneuvering or parliamentary skill but from the force of his intellect and his moral fervor, from his willingness to face hard truths, make tough choices, and get things done. To his young supporters and staffers, he was "PMF," after FDR, and to the journalistic allies who founded the weekly magazine *L'Express* to promote his cause, the future had at long last arrived.[4]

Mendès France retained much of the Geneva delegation headed by Jean Chauvel, while the Ministry for the Associated States he entrusted to Guy La Chambre, a veteran Radical Party member and former minister for the air. The Foreign Ministry Mendès France kept for himself, because the chief initial task he had set for himself—making peace in Indochina—he viewed as essentially diplomatic.

Thus came to a sudden end the Bidault phase of the Geneva Conference, after seven and a half weeks—and the Bidault phase of the Indochina War, after seven and a half years. Almost continuously the former history teacher had been at the center of things, from before the real shooting started in 1946, but he would not be there for the denouement. At Geneva he had initially pursued the policy of the victor, calling for a

cease-fire based on the leopard skin formula (the irregular outline of territorial zones controlled by the opposing sides) and stubbornly refusing
to discuss the political future of Vietnam or even to meet with Pham Van
Dong. "I am not used to associating with assassins," Bidault haughtily
declared, adding: "What do I have to hear from him? I know that he has
only one idea: to kick us out the door."[5] As the weeks passed, however,
Bidault saw the need to shift ground somewhat, to appear more flexible.
He allowed the de Brébisson–Ha Van Lau talks to proceed, even as he
continued to rule out a personal encounter with Pham Van Dong. But to
the end he was ambivalent, temporizing, circumspect.[6] He never could
bring himself to link the military and political questions, or to abandon
hope for some kind of deus ex machina, inevitably involving U.S. military intervention. Even after many in his own delegation embraced partition as the only real solution, he remained resistant, proclaiming into
mid-June that only the leopard skin suited him.[7]

It could be argued—and was argued, by Bidault and his supporters,
and by some observers since—that this approach yielded real results for
France. By resisting partition and by laying preparations with Washington for possible military escalation, so the argument goes, Bidault
elicited concessions from the Communist side, concessions impossible
to imagine at the time of Dien Bien Phu's surrender six weeks earlier.
The alternative view is that Bidault's "diplomatic somnambulism" (to
use Raymond Aron's phrase), his evident revulsion at having to negotiate
with Pham Van Dong and his Soviet and Chinese allies, only delayed an
agreement.[8] Vyacheslav Molotov, upon returning to Moscow in late June,
complained to the Central Committee that the Frenchman's reluctance
to discuss an armistice line contributed to the sluggish progress of the
conference. China's Zhou Enlai agreed, as did Britain's Anthony Eden,
as indeed did key players in the French delegation. On June 19, with Bidault finally off the stage, Jean Chauvel told Eden that the French team
was now able to discuss seriously the partition of Vietnam.[9]

For Eden, it was as though the clouds had suddenly parted. Where
just days earlier he had despaired to colleagues that the conference
seemed likely to collapse without agreement (a result, he ruefully noted,
that would please the Americans), rendering all his hard work over the
previous months meaningless, he now saw reason to be hopeful, even op-

timistic. Bidault was gone, and the new man wanted a deal. Not only that, in recent days both Molotov and Zhou, seeking to exploit the changed situation in Paris, had made concessions. On June 15, Molotov had proposed a compromise on the composition of the supervisory commission to come out of the conference, suggesting that neutral India could be named chair. He also affirmed his willingness to tackle military issues first, so long as political matters were not neglected. Zhou, for his part, said cryptically on June 14 and explicitly on June 16 that the situations in Vietnam, Laos, and Cambodia were not wholly alike and should be treated separately. Laos and Cambodia could be considered neutral nations like India and Burma, he told Eden, and as such could be given the right to remain in the French Union provided they had no American or other foreign bases. On June 18, Zhou issued the proposal again in formal session and was followed by Pham Van Dong, who indicated the willingness of his government to remove its forces from Laos and Cambodia so long as no foreign military bases were established anywhere in Indochina.[10]

II

EDEN SAW ZHOU ENLAI AS THE REAL FORCE BEHIND THIS COMMU-nist diplomatic maneuver, and his judgment seems correct in hindsight. Molotov was content to let him play the key role. In the first several weeks of the conference, Zhou had mostly adhered to a firm line and showed scant signs of the refined charm that would enchant so many interlocutors in the years to come. Most of the time he had been the bitter challenger with the chip on his shoulder, quick to lash out, notably against Walter Robertson, the hard-line American assistant secretary of state who as head of the Far East desk helped shape the administration's China policy. His words dripping with sarcasm, Zhou would mock Robertson's pronouncements, reminding him and all within earshot of Washington's errors of judgment concerning Chiang Kai-shek and the survivability of the revolution.[11]

But not this time. This time when Robertson rose to tell the conference (in tones Eden in his diary said constituted a "violent attack") that the new Communist proposals were unacceptably imprecise, Zhou

Enlai held his fire and reiterated his offer.[12] Why his new conciliatory tone? Contemporary observers assumed that Mao Zedong was eager to keep the Geneva Conference from breaking up and to prevent the United States from establishing a military presence in Laos and Cambodia. With the odious Bidault gone and a longtime foe of the war taking power in Paris, and with the Eisenhower administration seemingly intent on letting the negotiations fail, now was the time, these analysts imagined Mao and Zhou thinking, to move aggressively to secure a deal.

Recently released Chinese archival documentation supports this interpretation. It shows that the Chinese, Soviet, and Viet Minh delegations met on June 15 in Geneva to evaluate the changed situation in Paris and to coordinate strategy. Zhou Enlai took a firm line, warning Pham Van Dong that the Viet Minh's refusal to acknowledge the presence of their troops in Cambodia and Laos threatened to kill the negotiations and squander a golden opportunity to secure a political agreement. Zhou accordingly proposed that the Communist side adopt a new line favoring withdrawal of all foreign troops from the two kingdoms, including the "volunteers" sent by the DRV, so that "our concessions on Cambodia and Laos will result in [the other camp's] concessions on the question of dividing the zones between the two sides in Vietnam." Molotov, having previously held several private discussions with Zhou, strongly backed the proposal. Pham Van Dong was noncommittal but ultimately seemed to imply assent.[13] "The Chinese delegation has presented a proposal that contains a number of concessions," he wrote in a cable to the DRV Central Committee, "such as acknowledging that there are dissimilarities between the Laotian and Cambodian problems and the Vietnam problem and that there are dissimilarities between [the] Laotian problem and the Cambodian problems as well, and the position that all foreign troops would be withdrawn from Laos and Cambodia (the proposal means that if our troops are present they too will have to be withdrawn)."[14]

It was a huge blow to the DRV's attempt to secure recognition for her "sister" governments in Laos (Pathet Lao) and Cambodia (Khmer Issarak). Pham Van Dong had arrived in Geneva seeking to replace the French colonial state of Indochine with a new, revolutionary Indochina, in which the three "resistance governments" would join together under the leadership of the DRV. The dream was now dying. Zhou Enlai, seeking to advance the negotiations and to show wary non-Communist governments in Asia—notably India, Burma, and Indonesia—that the Viet Minh would not try to export Communism beyond Vietnam's borders, had made clear that the situation in Laos and Cambodia was different from that in Vietnam and would be judged accordingly.[15] In a long telegram to the Chinese Communist Party (CCP) leadership, he underscored his determination to secure Viet Minh agreement on the need to show flexibility on the key outstanding issues. Without such flexibility, "the negotiation cannot go on, and this . . . will not serve our long-range interests." Zhou went on:

> If we take the initiative to make concessions in Cambodia and Laos, we will be able to ask for more gains in Vietnam as compensation to us. Our position in Vietnam being relatively strong in various aspects, we will not only be able to keep our gains there, but also will be capable of gradually consolidating and expanding our influence. . . . The emphasis of our strategy at this stage should be to encourage the [peace] initiatives of the French, to keep the French from listening to the Americans completely, to make sure the British support stopping the war, and to quickly reach an armistice agreement as long as the conditions seem reasonable.[16]

Vietnamese sources, meanwhile, suggest Zhou Enlai may also have had another motivation for the new line: a desire by the CCP to incorporate Laos and Cambodia into *China's* sphere of influence, if only to keep them from falling into Vietnam's. Better to give the two states neutral status than to allow Ho Chi Minh's government to dominate all of Indochina.[17]

On June 19, the day before the chief delegates were scheduled to leave Geneva to return home to consult with their governments, Zhou Enlai told Canadian diplomat and China expert Chester Ronning that a settlement was within reach if only France would commit herself to a political solution. China and her allies had made important concessions, Zhou said, and now the French should follow suit. The next morning he reiterated these points to Eden and also expressed his keen desire to meet the new French premier. Eden, stopping in Paris en route to London later in the day, happily passed the message on to Pierre Mendès France. He urged the Frenchman to meet with Zhou at the earliest opportunity. Mendès France, having received the same recommendation from Jean Chauvel, agreed.[18] But where should the meeting occur? The Chinese foreign minister would not go to Paris as long as his government was not recognized by France, while Mendès France feared he would be perceived as a supplicant if he went so soon to Geneva. Dijon was suggested, but the two sides settled instead on the Swiss city of Bern, on the pretext of thanking the Swiss Confederation president for providing a locale for the negotiations. The meeting was arranged for the following Wednesday, June 23, in the French embassy.[19]

An epic encounter it would be. Zhou Enlai, attired not in his usual blue high-collared tunic but in a gray business suit and tie, looked younger and more relaxed than he had in Geneva, and he made an immediate winning impression on Mendès France: *"L'homme était impressionnant."* Zhou opened sternly—China feared neither threat nor provocation and considered both to be illegitimate means of negotiation—but then followed a conciliatory line. He had lived in France and felt an attachment to the French people, he said, and moreover his view aligned with the French view, meaning military questions should take precedence over the resolution of political issues in Indochina. Achieving a cease-fire was the first priority. Much to the Frenchman's satisfaction and relief, Zhou then made clear that he accepted not only the view that Laos, Cambodia, and Vietnam should be evaluated separately but also, indirectly, the view that there existed "two governments in Vietnam." Following an armistice, he went on, there should be elections for reunification of that country under a single government.

Zhou declared that his government—like that of the Democratic Republic of Vietnam—intended to move swiftly toward recognition of Laos and Cambodia and to follow a policy of nonintervention toward both. He even hinted that Beijing would have no objection if one or both of the kingdoms chose to be attached to the French Union. What would not be acceptable, however, would be for the United States to misinterpret this Chinese and DRV policy as an excuse to turn the kingdoms into "bases of aggression." In order to facilitate national reunification, both Phnom Penh and Vientiane should grant recognition to the resistance movements—Khmer Issarak and Pathet Lao—for the sake of unity. The latter, being a significant presence in Laos, should be granted a zone of administrative control, but Viet Minh forces that penetrated Laotian territory might be withdrawn after an armistice.

Mendès France liked what he heard, and he could see by the expression on Jean Chauvel's face that the ambassador was pleased as well. The premier agreed that there should be no American bases in Cambodia or Laos, and he voiced support for elections in Vietnam. The vote could not happen immediately, though, and there was moreover the issue of what kind of temporary division to have in the meantime. Did the Chinese government support partition? Zhou Enlai initially evaded a direct answer but then said he favored a formula involving "large sectors." Mendès France agreed that a "horizontal cut" was possible, but not as far south as suggested by the Viet Minh at Geneva. Everything else, he continued, depended on a resolution of this issue of the regroupment zones. Zhou concurred and said "this [is] also Mr. Eden's opinion." With hard work, he speculated, the military negotiators in Geneva ought to be able to reach agreement "within three weeks," at which point the foreign ministers could return and be ready to sign the documents. Mendès France, finding this time limit (July 15) to be uncomfortably close to his own July 20 deadline for the settlement of *all* outstanding problems, replied that three weeks "should be regarded as a maximum."[20]

The meeting drew to a close. Both sides were pleased with the outcome and said they understood each other well, but neither doubted that tough slogging remained. Mendès France flew back to Paris, while his Chinese counterpart, having earlier held sessions with the leaders of the Cambodian and Laotian delegations (he promised them that Beijing would respect their sovereignty and independence), departed for a series of meetings in Asia, among them a two-day secret session with Ho Chi Minh.

The following day in Paris, June 24, Pierre Mendès France summoned his four principal Indochina advisers to his home for a strategy session: General Ely, who had returned for a short visit from Saigon; Alexandre Parodi, the general secretary of the Foreign Ministry; and La Chambre and Chauvel. Their task: to establish the French diplomatic strategy for the climactic (as they saw it) portion of the Geneva meeting.

Militarily, the picture looked grim—since Dien Bien Phu's fall six weeks earlier, the Viet Minh had solidified their control over much of Tonkin and had assembled and deployed the main bulk of their fighting force around the delta; French intelligence estimated they were now in a position to launch a major assault at any time (though the analysts thought Giap would probably bide his time, pending the outcome at Geneva). Viet Minh reconnaissance units were active along the northern face of the delta's perimeter, and there were signs also of increased infiltration along the southern face. The French, meanwhile, were evacuating isolated outposts and concentrating their forces around Hanoi and along the Hanoi-Haiphong axis, leaving the defense of other areas to VNA units of dubious reliability. Nam Dinh, the third largest city in the delta, would soon have to be abandoned, French planners recognized. To the south, apart from a coastal strip held by French Union units, central Vietnam was now mostly under Viet Minh domination. The important naval and air base of Tourane (Da Nang) was increasingly at risk, while in the area

VIETNAMESE CIVILIANS ARE COMPELLED INTO SERVICE TO MAKE FORTIFICATIONS AT PHU LY, SOUTH OF HANOI, ON JUNE 22, 1954.

between Qui Nhon and Nha Trang the Viet Minh had the initiative and were increasing their pressure.

Chauvel, long an advocate of partition and sensing the momentum coming his way, argued that this dire military picture called for accepting a line at Tourane, or roughly the sixteenth parallel, though the effort should be made to get it drawn higher, at the seventeenth. No one objected. On the subject of the election for reunification, the five men agreed on the need to avoid fixing a specific date, or at least setting it as far into the future as possible. La Chambre stressed that Bao Dai's State of Vietnam would need time to consolidate her position in the south. Yes, Chauvel replied, and it would be imperative to get American assistance for this task.

But would Washington even accept partition? Chauvel felt confident that Undersecretary of State Walter Bedell Smith had come around on the matter and saw no realistic alternative, but what about Eisenhower and Dulles? "The United States has a tendency to think in terms of an anticommunist crusade," Chauvel acknowledged, which was why the Eisenhower administration wanted to retain Haiphong as a base for future operations in Asia—presumably for a war to drive the Communists out of Indochina and perhaps out of China too. The British government, on the other hand, still desirous of normalizing relations with Beijing, would accept a DRV-dominated Vietnam if the Geneva powers could guarantee the country's neutrality. A crucial question in the coming weeks would be whether the Anglo-Saxons would adopt a single position, and which one it would be.

None of the men present in the premier's home that day believed they could retain Hanoi or Haiphong in any negotiated agreement. Possibly they could hang on to one or two of the Catholic bishoprics in the north, General Ely opined, or at least secure for them some kind of neutral status, but Chauvel foresaw a full French withdrawal from Tonkin, in three stages: to Hanoi, then to Haiphong, and finally out of northern Vietnam. Mendès France's suggestion that perhaps the United States would be satisfied if Haiphong was retained for a year or two was met with a collective shake of the head. Chauvel said he could think of no justification for keeping the port city. Better to focus on securing a line of division, with no Viet Minh enclaves below it. The others agreed.[21]

"We must go fast," Mendès France declared at this point, "not only because of the time limit we have set for ourselves, but also because the situation is quite favorable. Everybody is more or less undecided at present and is searching for the way. If France displays determination and indicates clearly what it regards as important, what it will not surrender at any cost, and what concessions it is prepared to make, it will reverse the present situation and regain the political initiative at the negotiations."[22]

That day, June 24, 1954, Pierre Mendès France did what Georges Bidault and Joseph Laniel had always refused to do: He formally agreed to seek the temporary division of Vietnam, as a means of bringing the long and bloody Indochina war to an end.[23]

III

THAT SO MUCH OF THE DISCUSSION AT THE FRENCH PREMIER'S home that fateful day should revolve around American policy and American intentions is revealing. No one present doubted that any partition agreement would require U.S. backing, tacit or formal, or that one had to go through the Americans to have any hope of gaining the backing of Bao Dai's State of Vietnam, whose pro-Washington leanings were increasingly evident. The Saigon government had not been a key player at the Geneva Conference, but from the start it had made clear its misgivings about the whole enterprise and its staunch opposition to any division of the country. Bao Dai, aware that the French had long since lost faith in him, more and more saw his fortunes as being tied to the United States. Facing pressure from various quarters to replace the ineffectual Buu Loc as prime minister in anticipation of the post-Geneva environment, Bao Dai selected a man who, in addition to being a staunch anti-Communist and committed nationalist, had lived in America and had several influential American backers: Ngo Dinh Diem.

A portly and ascetic bachelor and devout Catholic, Diem had impeccable nationalist and anti-Communist credentials. Already in 1933, he had been a minister in then-Emperor Bao Dai's government, but he had resigned within months in protest of France's unwillingness to give Vietnam greater autonomy. Later, at the end of World War II, Diem turned down Ho Chi Minh's offer to collaborate with the Viet Minh—he reportedly called Ho a war criminal to his face—and in 1947–48 he refused to back the "Bao Dai solution" unless the French granted Vietnam true independence. When Bao Dai subsequently asked Diem to form a government, he declined. In 1950 he opted for exile abroad. He visited Europe, stopping in Rome for an audience with the pope before moving on to two Maryknoll seminaries in New Jersey and New York. He meditated and did some writing, but occasionally he emerged from behind the cloistered walls to travel to New York City and Washington or to address academic audiences. At Cornell University in February 1953, for example, Diem castigated France for clinging stubbornly to a bankrupt colonial system and called for the United States to assume a direct role in training the Vietnamese National Army.

All the while, Diem showed a talent for connecting with people who could help his cause. Through Wesley Fishel, a university professor, he was introduced to New York's Francis Cardinal Spellman, who in turn brought him together with lawmakers in Washington. Two were fellow Catholics: Montana Democratic senator Mike Mansfield and Massachusetts Democratic representative-then-senator John F. Kennedy. Diem also met periodically with midlevel officials in the State Department and won the confidence of such individuals as Supreme Court justice William O. Douglas and Georgetown University administrator Edmund Walsh.[24]

No other Vietnamese politician possessed anything like this network of contacts in the United States, or engaged in this kind of lobbying, and some authors have concluded that U.S. officials must have forced Bao Dai's hand in June 1954 and pushed through their "protégé." This is going too far. For one thing, the evidence is strong that senior American policy makers in spring 1954 were at best dimly aware of Ngo Dinh Diem's existence and credentials. (As late as May 22, Dulles told the U.S. delegation at Geneva there was "no immediate substitute" for the current regime.)[25] For another, Diem had a power base also in Vietnam, and even before his departure in 1950, he had turned down an offer by Bao Dai to become prime minister. In May 1953, he left American soil and settled at a Benedictine monastery in Belgium, from which he lobbied on his own behalf in the important Vietnamese community in Paris. This effort yielded results, and by the spring of 1954, his anti-French posture put him on every short list of contenders to succeed Buu Loc.[26]

Yet the American connection mattered enormously in the end. Consider Bao Dai's own explanation for why he chose Diem as premier. "From my earlier experience with him, I knew that Diem had a difficult character," he wrote in his memoirs.

> I was also aware of his fanaticism and his messianic tendencies. But, in the present situation, there was no better choice. He was well known to the Americans, who appreciated his intransigence. In their eyes, he was the man best suited for the job, and Washington would not be sparing in its support of him. Because of [Diem's] past and because of the presence of his brother at the head of the "Movement for National Union," he would have the cooperation of the fiercest nationalists, those who had brought down [Nguyen Van] Tam and then Buu Loc. Finally, because of his intransigence and his fanaticism, he could be counted on to resist communism. Yes, he was truly the right man for the situation.[27]

Also suggestive is that Bao Dai, who did not attend the Geneva Conference personally, chose Diem's brother Ngo Dinh Luyen to be his representative in communications with the American delegation. Beginning in the third week of May, Luyen pressed U.S. officials in Geneva, including Walter Bedell Smith, for their views about a change of government in general and one headed by Ngo Dinh Diem in particular. Smith and his aides passed along to the State Department their impression that Bao Dai was "obviously trying to find out whether the U.S. is disposed to replace France in Indochina to an extent which would virtually free Bao Dai from the need for taking into account French views." They concluded that Bao Dai "might well play the Ngo Dinh Diem card if he could be sure we would support him; otherwise not." A few days later, after Nguyen again asked if Bao Dai could count on American backing if he adopted "an entirely new stand," Secretary of State John Foster Dulles cabled the U.S. delegation: "In view of role which U.S. may be called upon to play in Indochina, we have given much thought to Bao Dai's offer. . . . I believe this offer should be discreetly exploited."[28]

A smoking gun? Not quite. But it's one more piece of evidence that Bao Dai insisted upon—and received—American approval before proceeding with the Diem appointment. Did the appointment also depend on Vietnamese internal politics, on Diem's powerful backing among Vietnamese Catholics, and on the shrewd maneuverings by him and his aides (notably his brother Ngo Dinh Nhu) in the decisive weeks in May and early June? Unquestionably. The Eisenhower admistration did not *engineer* his appointment, as is often alleged. But its role was nonetheless vital.

Interestingly, many who interacted with Diem in this period seconded Bao Dai's description of him as a "difficult character" with "messianic tendencies"—and not merely French officials, who were predisposed to view him harshly for his unshakable nationalist convictions. Among leading lights in the Vietnamese community in Paris, he came across as obscurantist and long-winded and utterly humorless. To Douglas Dillon, the U.S. ambassador to France, Diem was a "Yogi-like mystic" who appeared "too unworldly and unsophisticated to be able to cope with the grave problems and unscrupulous people he will find in Saigon," while to Robert McClintock of the U.S. embassy in Saigon, who was on hand when Diem arrived to assume power in late June, he was a "messiah without a message." With notable foresight, McClintock saw in Diem "a curious blend of heroism mixed with a narrowness of view and egotism which will make him a difficult man to deal with."[29]

Yet these observers also identified more positive attributes in the man. His hostility to Communism was deep and profound, as was his hostility to the French—a terrific one-two punch. Even his detractors acknowledged his personal probity and courage. And there was the simple fact that the competition was weak. Each of the other candidates to succeed Buu Loc had his own shortcomings, some of them more crippling than Diem's. As for the incumbent and those who came before him, the less said the better. Said Dillon from Paris: The U.S. government should accept the "seemingly ridiculous prospect" that Diem could take on the job if "only because the standard set by his predecessors is so low."[30]

To no one's surprise, Diem was hostile on the issue of partition, even more so than Buu Loc had been. It would be a disaster, he insisted, a reward for international Communist aggression, a betrayal. In Washington, though, attitudes were more mixed. Smith, having returned from Geneva on June 20, argued in favor of accepting the inevitability of a division of Vietnam and the desirability of guaranteeing it, so as to discourage the DRV from trying to violate the agreement. But Pentagon planners reiterated the old view that the Red River Delta was vital to the defense of all of Southeast Asia. A north-south partition, at whatever line south of the delta, would therefore merely be a prelude to the loss of the entire region. This view had support within the Policy Planning Staff—upon learning of the results of the Zhou–Mendès France meeting in Bern, some of its members advocated "busting up" the Geneva Conference in order to "achieve a new climate" more amenable to the continuation of military resistance in Vietnam. At the very least, these analysts maintained, the administration should make unambiguously clear that it would accept no division below the line from Thakhek (in Laos) to Dong Hoi, just south of the eighteenth parallel, and that if necessary, it would send U.S. troops to protect that line.[31]

Saigon ambassador Donald Heath thought the sentiment in Washington ran almost wholly in this direction. "All the people below the Secretary and Under Secretary are unanimous that we should intervene with or without the French," he wrote Philip Bonsal, the director of the State Department's Office of Philippine and Southeast Asian Affairs, who was in Geneva. Bonsal answered that the view in Geneva was different. American delegates to the conference doubted that intervention could produce more advantageous results than those to be gained from a negotiated agreement.[32]

Eisenhower and Dulles in effect split the difference, with enormous long-term implications. Averse though they were to having any compromise agreement of any kind with Communist foes, they also were in no mood to rush in without allied support. The new French leader had made his intentions clear, as had the British. "Personally I think Mendès France, whom I do not know, has made up his mind to clear out on the best terms available," Churchill wrote Eisenhower on June 21. "If that is so, I think he is right." The prime minister added that "in no foreseeable circumstances, except possibly a local rescue, could British troops be used in Indochina, and if we were asked our opinion we should advise against US local intervention except for rescue."[33]

The only real answer, Eisenhower and Dulles determined, was to accept the likelihood that part of Vietnam would be lost at Geneva and to plan for the defense of the rest of Indochina and Southeast Asia. They had been contemplating this solution for several weeks, as we've seen, but only now did they take concrete steps to realize it. On June 24, Dulles told congressional leaders that any Geneva agreement would be "something we would have to gag about," but he expressed optimism that the United States could "salvage something" in Indochina "free of the taint of French colonialism." Specifically, Washington would assume responsibility for the defense of Cambodia, Laos, and southern Vietnam, with the first task the drawing of a line the Communists would not cross. Then, the secretary continued, the United States would "hold this area and fight subversion within with all the strength we have," using economic and military assistance to the non-Communist governments as well as an American-led regional defense grouping modeled in part on NATO.[34]

It was a monumental decision, as important as any made by an American administration on Indochina, from Franklin Roosevelt's to Gerald Ford's. Its true import would become clear only with time, but even on that day the weight of the secretary of state's words were hard to miss. The United States would thenceforth take responsibility for defending most of Indochina, he told the lawmakers, and without "the taint of French colonialism."

IV

THE AMERICAN POLICY SHIFT HELPED SMOOTH WHAT OTHERWISE might have been a fractious Anglo-U.S. "summit" meeting in Washington in the last week of June. Dulles acknowledged on June 26 that partition was less objectionable in Vietnam than early nationwide elections—neither he nor Dwight Eisenhower doubted that Ho Chi Minh would win such a vote, and win handily. Agreement was also reached on the establishment of an Anglo-American study group, to convene in Washington for the purpose of considering, among other things, the necessary steps to create a Southeast Asian security pact (tentatively called the Southeast Asia Treaty Organization, or SEATO).

The tangible results of the summit were a joint communiqué, issued by Churchill and Eisenhower on June 28, and a secret list of Seven Points, drawn up the following day by Dulles and Eden. The communiqué was put out partly at the request of Mendès France who, though he had decided to seek a political solution on the best terms he could get, wanted the appearance of allied unity in order to strengthen his bargaining position at Geneva. He asked that the communiqué include a statement that a "serious aggravation" could result if no acceptable settlement was reached at Geneva. He got his wish—the statement warned that if the conference failed, "the international situation will be seriously aggravated."[35] In the Seven Points, meanwhile, Dulles and Eden laid out the minimum terms their two governments would "respect."[36] Notably, an agreement would have to preserve the integrity of Cambodia and Laos and assure the removal of Viet Minh forces; preserve the southern half of Vietnam and, ideally, an enclave in the Red River Delta; include no provisions that would risk the loss of the retained area to Communist control; and include the possibility of ultimate reunification of Vietnam.

The French government saw much to like in both the communiqué and the Seven Points. The former showed the world that France's allies maintained a strong interest in Indochina and the Geneva Conference, while the latter amounted to an acceptance (privately, at least) by Washington of partition as a solution.[37] At the same time, Mendès France was puzzled by some of the ambiguities in the Seven Points. What did Dulles and Eden mean by "respect"? And wasn't it potentially contradictory to speak of the possibility of national reunification while also ruling out a Communist takeover? What if Ho Chi Minh won the national elections? To Mendès France and Chauvel it seemed clear that Washington was still hedging its bets, still unwilling to fully commit itself to the negotiations. And this was a problem: As Chauvel said, the ultimate success of the conference depended on the Soviets and Chinese applying pressure on the Viet Minh while the United States did the same to Bao Dai's State of Vietnam. He was not willing to wager money that either would happen.[38]

CHAPTER 24

"I HAVE SEEN DESTINY BEND TO THAT WILL"

W HILE THE THREE WESTERN POWERS WERE TRYING TO COORDI-
nate strategy, and while the negotiations continued among the second-
string officials at Geneva, a different kind of diplomacy was being carried
on elsewhere. Chinese premier Zhou Enlai, en route to Beijing, made
several stops to woo Asian leaders with talk of "peaceful coexistence."
In New Delhi he assured India's prime minister Jawaharlal Nehru of Beijing's nonaggressive intentions in Southeast Asia and its commitment to
a compromise settlement in Indochina. The two men agreed that Laos
and Cambodia should remain neutral so as to transform them into "a
bridge for peace," and they concurred on the need for Sino-Indian cooperation in forming a nonaligned movement of decolonized Afro-Asian
states. With Nehru and then with Burmese leader U Nu in Rangoon,
Zhou issued joint public statements pledging mutual support for peaceful coexistence and for the right of countries having different social systems to coexist without interference from outside. "Revolution cannot be
exported," the Sino-Burmese statement said; "at the same time, outside
interference with the common will expressed by the people of any nation
should not be permitted."[1]

The Delhi and Rangoon sessions were the easy ones. Zhou knew he
would face a much sterner test in his next encounter, with Ho Chi Minh
on July 3–5 in the southern Chinese city of Liuzhou. It worried Zhou
that the DRV delegates in Geneva, led by Ta Quang Buu, vice minister
of defense and a senior negotiator, had become more belligerent in recent
days. On June 26, Buu lashed out at the French for having a top-level

meeting with Zhou but not with them; two days later he called for a line of division in Vietnam very far to the south, near the thirteenth parallel, or some three hundred and fifty miles from the French proposal of the eighteenth parallel. French forces should be given only three months to evacuate the north following the armistice, he further demanded, and the Pathet Lao should be granted virtually sovereign rights over the eastern half of Laos. Zhou saw various reasons for this hardening of the Viet Minh's posture—Mendès France's seeming desire for peace at any price; the worsening French military position, as demonstrated by the High Command's evacuation of the entire southern part of the Red River Delta, in Operation Auvergne, launched in late June; and the temporary absence from Geneva of senior statesmen to surround and moderate the Viet Minh demands—but the task now was to get Ho to order a pulling back.[2]

For the most part he succeeded, as recently released Vietnamese and Chinese documents make clear, though there were testy moments. Much of the first day was devoted to consideration of the military situation and the balance of forces on the ground, with Vo Nguyen Giap sketching out the big picture. Dien Bien Phu had represented a colossal defeat for France, he began, but she was far from defeated. She retained a superiority in numbers—some 470,000 troops, roughly half of them Vietnamese, versus 310,000 on the Viet Minh side—as well as control of Vietnam's major cities (Hanoi, Saigon, Hue, Tourane [Da Nang]). A fundamental alteration of the balance of forces had thus yet to occur, Giap continued, despite Dien Bien Phu, at which point Wei Guoqing, the chief Chinese military adviser to the Viet Minh, spoke up to say he agreed.

"If the U.S. does not interfere," Zhou asked, "and assuming France will dispatch more troops, how long will it take for us to seize the whole of Indochina?" In the best-case scenario, Giap replied, full victory could be achieved in two to three years. Worst case? Three to five years.

That afternoon Zhou offered a lengthy exposition on the massive international reach of the Indochina conflict—much greater than the Korean War—and on the imperative of preventing an American intervention in the war. Given Washington's intense hostility to the Chinese Revolution, and given the ominous words in Vice President Richard Nixon's April 16 speech, one must assume the current administration would not stand idly by if the Viet Minh sought to win a complete victory. Consequently, "if we ask too much [at Geneva] and if peace is not achieved, it is certain that the U.S. will intervene, providing Cambodia, Laos and Bao Dai with weapons and ammunition, helping them train military personnel, and establishing military bases there."

Korea provided a sobering lesson: "The key to the Korea issue lay in U.S. intervention. It was completely beyond our expectation that the [American] reinforcement would arrive so quickly. . . . If there had not been U.S. intervention, the Korean People's Army would have been able to drive Syngman Rhee's [troops] into the ocean." Because of American intervention, "we only achieved a draw at the end of the war, and were unable to win a victory." The experience must not be repeated in Vietnam. "The central issue," Zhou told Ho, is "to prevent America's intervention" and "to achieve a peaceful settlement." Laos and Cambodia would have to be treated differently and allowed to pursue their own paths, provided they did not join a military alliance or permit foreign bases on their territory. The Mendès France government, having vowed to achieve a negotiated solution, must be supported, lest it fall and be replaced by one committed to continuing the war.[3]

Ho Chi Minh raised no major objections to any of this, but over the next two days disagreements emerged, mostly concerning what constituted an acceptable line of division between the two regroupment zones. Ho did not insist on the thirteenth parallel, as had Ta Quang Buu in Geneva, but he pressed hard for the sixteenth. Zhou answered: "We will endeavor to execute the will of President Ho but implore President Ho for general permission to permit flexibility." Zhou noted that Route 9, the only line of transport linking Laos to the sea, ran closer to the seventeenth parallel, and that therefore this might be a suitable boundary. Ho Chi Minh was unmoved, but it seems he did not entirely close the door to a slight adjustment to the demarcation line, above 16 degrees.[4]

The two men went their separate ways, Zhou making for Beijing and Ho returning to Vietnam. In short order the Central Committee of the Vietnamese Workers Party issued an internal instruction (known as the "Fifth July Document"), the contents of which reflected the agreements between Zhou and Ho at Liuzhou. But the full examination of Viet Minh options occurred a few days later at the party's Sixth Central Committee Plenum. A remarkable session it was, as Ho Chi Minh and General Secretary Truong Chinh took turns articulating the need for an early political settlement so as to prevent a military intervention by the United States, now the "main and direct enemy" of Vietnam.[5]

"In the new situation, we cannot follow the old program," Ho declared. "Before, our motto was, 'war of resistance until victory.' Now, in view of the new situation, we should uphold a new motto: 'peace, unification, independence, and democracy.'" A spirit of compromise would be required by both sides to make the negotiations succeed, and there could be no more talk of wiping out and annihilating all the French troops. A demarcation line allowing the temporary regroupment of both sides would be necessary.

The plenum endorsed Ho's analysis, passing a resolution supporting a compromise settlement to end the fighting. But Ho and Truong Chinh plainly worried that, following such an agreement at Geneva, there would be internal discontent and "leftist deviation" and in particular that analysts would fail to see the complexity of the situation and underestimate the power of the American and French adversaries. They accordingly reminded their colleagues that France would retain control of a large part of the country, and that people living in this area might be confused, alienated, and vulnerable to enemy manipulations. "We have to make it clear to our people," Ho said, that "in the interest of the whole country, for the sake of long-term interest, [they must] accept this, because it is a glorious thing and the whole country is grateful for that. We must not let people have pessimistic and negative thinking; instead, we must encourage the people to continue the struggle for the withdrawal of French troops and ensure our independence."[6]

Ho Chi Minh instructed the DRV delegation in Geneva to move ahead quickly to reach a settlement: "In view of France's positive attitude . . . we must use the formula of being positive, aggressive, and pushing [for] an agreement. We must not be passive, sitting back to wait."[7]

In Beijing, meanwhile, Zhou Enlai informed the Central Committee of the Chinese Communist Party on July 7 that Liuzhou had gone well and that all efforts should go toward securing a deal at Geneva. Mao Zedong agreed. "For the purpose of uniting with the majority and isolating the few (the United States)," he told the group, "we should make concessions when such concessions are necessary, and should adhere to our own stand when such adherence is possible."[8]

For the Chinese as well as the Viet Minh, clearly, one thing mattered most of all: keeping the United States out.[9]

II

THE FINAL PHASE OF THE GENEVA CONFERENCE BEGAN ON JULY 10, when Pierre Mendès France arrived to take charge of the French delegation. Soviet foreign minister Vyacheslav Molotov was already in place, having returned from Moscow on July 8, and Zhou Enlai and British foreign secretary Anthony Eden were soon due as well. This left the Americans, who to this point had resisted strong French and British pressure to have a top official—meaning either Secretary of State John Foster Dulles or Undersecretary of State Walter Bedell Smith—on hand for the climactic sessions. With only ten days to go until his self-imposed deadline, it infuriated Mendès France that Dulles might not come and might not send his top deputy. What message would that send about Western unity? Dulles coolly replied that no "united front in relation to Indochina" existed among the Western allies in any case, and he further maintained that an acceptable settlement would be more likely to result if the other side was kept guessing about Washington's ultimate intentions. To Ambassador Douglas Dillon in Paris, he said the administration would want no part of an agreement that might superficially resemble the Seven Points but would contain clauses allowing the Communist takeover of all of Indochina within mere months.[10]

He had another worry too. In the first week of July, the administration faced a drumbeat of domestic criticism for seemingly cooperating in what would amount to a Communist victory parade in Geneva—"another Munich," a "second Yalta." California Republican William Knowland's pronouncements on this theme on the floor of the Senate caused much consternation in the White House. "Immediate problem before us," Press Secretary James Hagerty wrote in his diary, "is Knowland's speech and the fear that many of us have that it indicates a growing fear in the country, fanned to life, of course by the isolationists, that it would be better to wash our hands of the whole mess and even get out of the United

Nations." Knowland urged that neither Dulles nor Smith should return to Geneva. Vice President Richard Nixon agreed, as did Senate minority leader Lyndon Baines Johnson, a Texas Democrat, who said "it would be better not to be represented at a high level at Geneva."[11]

President Dwight D. Eisenhower understood, as he had always understood, that Geneva had the potential to create all kinds of political problems at home. But he also grasped that staying away presented problems of its own. Hagerty, showing an impressive ability to argue both sides of an issue, spoke in favor of fighting for U.S. aims on the spot in Switzerland, with Dulles or Smith present, lest America look like "a little boy sulking in his tent." At a cabinet meeting on July 10, the president said he had not yet made up his mind on the matter, but indicated he leaned toward sending one of the two men. Dulles privately recommended against such a course, whereupon Eisenhower agreed to withhold a decision until the nature of the final agreement had been clarified. If it looked like an acceptable settlement was in the offing, Dulles or Smith would head for the airport.[12]

This was scarcely acceptable to the French government, or to Eden, who continued to apply the pressure for top-level American representation, not later but right away. Eisenhower compromised by dispatching Dulles to Paris to confer with the French and British leaders. He arrived on July 13 and, after dinner at Matignon, proceeded to tell Mendès France and Eden that Washington should remain in the background, as a kind of "wicked partner," so as to keep the Communists guessing.

"But do you know," replied Mendès France in English, "that the absence of an American minister in Geneva delights the delegations from the East? Do you know that the mere announcement of your arrival in Paris has sown confusion among them? Your presence in Geneva would strengthen the West's position."

Dulles turned to his real objection. "What you sign in Geneva will be bad," he grumbled. "We do not want, by our presence, to encourage a new Yalta."

"But we want your presence precisely so that the agreement will not be bad! So that it will conform to your Seven Points of June 29."[13]

Dulles had arrived in Paris deeply skeptical that the French in fact would adhere to the Seven Points, but he was impressed by the premier's assurances. The Viet Minh in recent days had softened their tone in Geneva, Mendès France pointed out; they were now offering (as per Ho Chi Minh's instruction) a partition line at the sixteenth parallel and gave indications they might budge further. They had also recognized the unity of Laos under the royal government but were holding out for a regroupment zone for the Pathet Lao. They would not accept any U.S. bases or military personnel in Laos, they could live with a French training mission, and they showed a willingness to compromise on the issues of Vietnam elections and the composition of the supervisory commission. France, the premier continued, would press hard for a division at the eighteenth parallel—anything south of the RC9 was unacceptable, he maintained—and would lay preparations for a continuation of the war if the negotiations failed.

Eden, witnessing the scene, marveled that "Mendès France fought his corner brilliantly" while the American "cut a sorry figure" who "kept quoting Yalta." This last assessment seems harsh, for Dulles showed a keen grasp of the implications of what he heard. After lunch on July 14, Mendès France promised to seek an agreement embodying the Seven Points in exchange for Dulles pledging to send Bedell Smith back to Geneva. Upon his return to Washington, the secretary told colleagues that the administration must avoid any "Yalta business" but also that it must support France. The United States, he now said, could not "withdraw inconspicuously" without generating talk of "too many stiff-necked Presbyterians, of sanctimoniousness, and of invoking lofty moral principles." He lauded Mendès France for his decisiveness and sincerity.[14]

With six days to go until the deadline, the French leader felt he had what he needed to land a deal. But the drama was not over. Important disagreements remained. The Paris government had kept Bao Dai's State of Vietnam largely ignorant of the details of the negotiations, and a big question now was whether the new prime minister, Ngo Dinh Diem, who had made no secret of his steadfast opposition to partition, and to the whole Geneva endeavor, could be persuaded to accept the agreement taking shape—or at least induced to refrain from raising a ruckus against it. On July 12, Donald Heath, the U.S. ambassador in Saigon, gingerly outlined the Seven Points for Diem and said Washington would "respect" a cease-fire that "preserves at least the southern half of Vietnam." Diem was unimpressed. He instructed his chief negotiator in Geneva, Foreign Minister Tran Van Do, to urge the French not to surrender Hanoi and Haiphong. Do did so in a session with Jean Chauvel the following day, but he struck a moderate tone, perhaps because he was a realist. He seemed prepared to accept a partition deal, Chauvel reported, and, added Mendès France, "did not appear to delude himself greatly regarding the scope of his [Diem's] demands." On the fifteenth, Do told Eden that although Diem wanted an enclave in the north, he himself considered the idea naïve in view of the military situation. In restricted session two days later, Do formally rejected the principle of partition—which "takes no account of the unanimous desire for national unity of the Vietnamese people"—but then assured Eden that this was merely for the record.[15]

An astute observer might say that Tran Van Do's objections, however halfhearted, were a warning of trouble to come. So they were, especially given Diem's hostile attitude toward the proceedings. The new premier used every chance in his first weeks in office to denounce the Geneva Conference and to trumpet his determination not to be bound by its results. No less than Ho Chi Minh, he sought a unified Vietnam. For the moment, though, French officials had reason to feel confident that the State of Vietnam would not expend great energy to try to prevent an agreement.

The last days before the deadline witnessed a dizzying array of bilateral encounters and ad hoc meetings, as well as discussions between military representatives of the opposing commands. Pierre Mendès France and Pham Van Dong occupied the starring roles, with Zhou, Eden, and Molotov also seizing the spotlight. India's foreign minister Krishna Menon was a Zelig-like figure in these final hours, seemingly always there in the background, ready to supply a supportive nod of the head or word of encouragement. Walter Bedell Smith, however, who arrived in Geneva on July 16, remained almost completely aloof from the discussions. His stated excuse was an attack of ulcers, but he also had instructions to avoid associating the United States with the sordid business at hand. "The American delegation was insulated and isolated from what was going on," recalled a member of his team, "except for what crumbs of information we could pick up from better-informed friends and colleagues in

PIERRE MENDÈS FRANCE AND ZHOU ENLAI IN GENEVA ON JULY 19, 1954,
JUST BEFORE THE FINAL BREAKTHROUGH IN THE NEGOTIATIONS.

other delegations. Smith himself was in close touch with developments, primarily through phone conversations with Eden. But the general was in an even more forbidding mood than usual during this period, and it was a courageous man who attempted to mix a solicitous call at Smith's bedside with a quest for information."[16]

Gradually, despite inevitable setbacks (as late as the morning of July 18, Eden could telegraph Churchill that the chances of reaching a deal were only fifty-fifty), the shape of an agreement began to emerge.[17] On July 18, Zhou Enlai broke the deadlock over the composition of the commission that would supervise the various cease-fire agreements; he proposed, and won approval for, India, Canada, and Poland. That day and the next there was progress as well on the specifics of the cease-fire agreements for Vietnam, Cambodia, and Laos.

Still, it was only on July 20, with the clock ticking down, that the main issues were resolved.[18] For days, the French and the Viet Minh had been deadlocked on whether the line of partition ought to be at the eighteenth or sixteenth parallel; now, with the encouragement of the Soviets and Chinese, attention focused on a line six miles north of the RC 9 (or roughly 17° N), which would keep Hue and Tourane (Da Nang) in non-Communist hands and give French Union forces—and the Vietnamese troops that would succeed them—a short defensible line as the northern boundary of South Vietnam (as it would thenceforth be called). General elections would be held within two years of the signing of the agreement—the exact date to be determined by representatives of the two Vietnamese governments—and there would be a regrouping of forces within 245 days in order to achieve partition. Vietnam, Laos, and Cambodia would be effectively neutralized—none could join alliances or host foreign military bases.

Throughout the day, Pham Van Dong and Mendès France jousted over these terms. By late afternoon, they were in accord that the demarcation line should be the seventeenth parallel and that the elections should be scheduled for no later than July 1956. The French premier had wanted the timetable for the voting to be left open, while Pham Van Dong relaxed his demand for six months, suggesting one year, possibly even eighteen months. Molotov, whose timely intervention had also helped secure the seventeenth parallel as the demarcation, said, "Shall we say two years?" Mendès France agreed; Pham Van Dong, with more hesitation, nodded as well. Anthony Eden could barely hide his satisfaction.

By 5:15 P.M., the news was out: Agreement had been reached! Preparations began for a signing ceremony in the Palais des Nations, so the armistice agreements and the concluding document could be initialed before midnight. Lost in the frenzy was the fact that not everything had been decided, and in particular that the agreements concerning Laos and Cambodia were still barely beyond draft stage. Sure enough, at eight o'clock came word that Sam Sary, head of the Cambodian delegation, objected to the terms and would refuse to sign the agreement. Enforced neutralization represented an intolerable restriction of his country's freedom of action, he announced, not because Phnom Penh wanted foreign troops, arms, or bases, but because it could not be denied the right to have them if it chose.[19] He did not budge when the Big Five, including even Bedell Smith, pleaded with him to come around. The hours passed. Midnight came and went. At two A.M., Molotov, impressed with the Khmer's determination, tried a new tack. Bases were impossible, the Russian affirmed, but "one might consider certain forms of common defense. Suppose it were said that Cambodia could call for external aid in case of a particular threat, a danger?" Fine, the others replied, too exhausted now to object, though Mendès France won approval for an amendment giving the same right also to Laos. Sam Sary pledged to sign the agreement the following day.[20]

Accounts differ as to when the three agreements (all dated, to save face for Mendès France, at midnight on July 20) were actually signed, but the American record is probably more or less correct: three-thirty A.M. on July 21 for Vietnam and Laos, eleven A.M. for Cambodia.[21]

In Hanoi, the French Army radio station interrupted its broadcast of the Tour de France bicycle race. A woman's breathless voice broke in: "*L'armistice vient d'être signé à Genève.*" Outside a florist shop in the city, a French lieutenant shook his head: "The armistice will only mean something to me the day I won't have to buy any more wreaths for my buddies. Today I'm ordering six." But as he spoke, the rumble of artillery began to taper off.[22]

Success had come at last—at least as defined by Mendès France. He had met his deadline, more or less. The final cease-fire agreement between France and the DRV provided for partition at the seventeenth parallel, and a demilitarized zone (DMZ) six miles wide (three miles on each side) along that parallel. French forces were to regroup south of that line, and Viet Minh forces to the north. The terms allowed for free movement of populations between the zones for three hundred days, prohibited either zone from joining a military alliance or receiving military reinforcement, and created a commission composed of India (chair), Canada, and Poland to monitor compliance. The cease-fire agreement explicitly recognized that the demarcation line was only "provisional," as did the Final Declaration, an unsigned document approved by oral statements at the final plenary session on the afternoon of July 21. "The

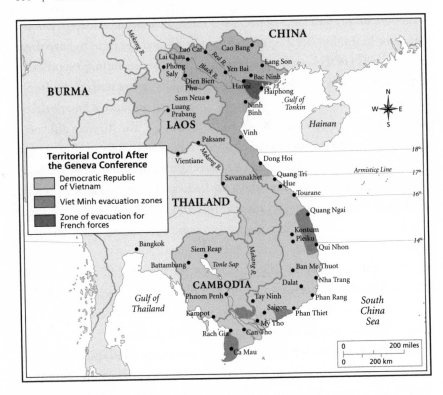

Territorial Control After the Geneva Conference
- Democratic Republic of Vietnam
- Viet Minh evacuation zones
- Zone of evacuation for French forces

military demarcation line is provisional and should not in any way be interpreted as constituting a political or territorial boundary," the Final Declaration stated. It also provided for "free general elections by secret ballot" throughout Vietnam, to be held in July 1956, with consultations between representatives of the two zones to begin a year before that, in July 1955.[23]

Neither the State of Vietnam nor the United States formally associated themselves with the outcome of the conference, but Smith did make a unilateral declaration in which Washington "took note" of the cease-fire agreements bringing the war to an end and declared that it would "refrain from the threat or the use of force to disturb them." Moreover, the United States would "view any renewal of aggression in violation of the aforesaid agreements with grave concern and as seriously threatening international peace and security." As for the election provisions, Smith continued, "we shall continue to seek to achieve unity through free elections, supervised by the United Nations to ensure that they are conducted fairly."[24]

In his weekly radio address to the French people, Mendès France laid out what had just occurred and what it meant for his country: "Believe me, on that night of the twentieth of July, within an hour of the end of our negotiations, when unforeseen difficulties arose to imperil our efforts, suddenly we felt a presence among us, commanding and imperious, a presence which dominated us, which forces us to conclude because no one could ignore or resist it."

He paused for a long second, then went on, slowly, his voice laden with emotion. "That force was yours. It was the profound feeling, among both our friends and our adversaries, that there could be no possible doubt about the determination of the French people to make peace or to take whatever measures were necessary to face the alternative. There could be no mistake about it that night. I have seen with my own eyes how overwhelming is the will of a great people, when it is clearly expressed and deeply felt. Yes, I have seen destiny bend to that will."[25]

Only later would the grim tallies for France be known. Between September 1945 and July 1954, Paris sent a total of 489,560 soldiers to the Indochinese peninsula: 233,467 French nationals, 72,833 legionnaires, 122,920 North Africans, and 60,340 Africans. In addition, hundreds of thousands of Indochinese troops served with the French forces or in associated armies. By the end of the Geneva Conference, approximately 110,000 troops from the French Union side had been killed in combat or were presumed dead.[26]

III

THE QUESTION LOOMS: WHY DIDN'T THE VIET MINH GET A BETTER deal? Or, to put it differently, why did the French prove to be better negotiators than fighters? Early in the proceedings, after all, Bidault had complained that he was playing with "a two of clubs and a three of diamonds," whereas the Viet Minh had several aces, kings, and queens. Dien Bien Phu fell just as the talks got under way, and in the weeks thereafter, the military outlook for French Union forces got steadily grimmer.[27] Hanoi was increasingly vulnerable and might be permanently cut off from Haiphong at any moment. Desertions from the VNA were exploding in number, on occasion reaching eight hundred per day, and civilian morale in French-held areas in Tonkin was plummeting. In Laos, the

Pathet Lao controlled more than a third of the territory. In supposedly secure southern Vietnam, the French were vulnerable to any incident because their forces were concentrated in the north, while in metropolitan France the public was fed up with the whole endeavor and seeking a swift exit. "Considering all this information," remarked a member of the French delegation at Geneva, "one is entitled to think that the division of the country at the 13th Parallel would have more accurately reflected the true state of affairs than the partition at the seventeenth parallel which we achieved."[28]

But it didn't happen that way. The old maxim that you can't win at the bargaining table what you're unable to achieve on the battlefield failed in this case to apply—as the Viet Minh would remember bitterly in the years to come.

Historians have generally explained this outcome at Geneva by pointing to the pressure placed on the Viet Minh delegation by its Soviet and Chinese allies.[29] There's no doubt this was of paramount importance. Neither Communist power wanted to see an escalation of the fighting; both were eager to avert a direct American military intervention and to keep Mendès France's government from falling on account of his failure to make his deadline.[30] Both also saw at Geneva an opportunity to demonstrate their commitments to "peaceful coexistence," regionally in Asia as well as beyond, and more broadly to make a positive impression on the international stage and thereby enhance their prestige. The Soviets, moreover, hoped to accommodate some of France's desires on Indochina as a means of reducing the French commitment to the Western alliance in general and to the EDC in particular, while the Chinese wanted to solidify their own influence in Indochina and to check Viet Minh expansionist ambitions.

Zhou Enlai in particular played a critical role in facilitating the ultimate agreement of July 20–21. Content in the conference's early weeks to maintain a fairly low profile, his more activist posture from mid-June onward proved decisive, as the courteous elegance and diplomatic savvy for which he would in time be heralded came to the fore. "The godfather of the partition solution," U.S. delegate Chester Cooper would call Zhou, and this seems fair. For although partition had been bandied about as a potential solution for many weeks prior to Geneva, it was the Chinese premier's subtle but forceful advocacy, coming at a time when many predicted the imminent dissolution of the conference, that made all the difference. As Cooper put it, "once [Zhou] advanced the idea, it achieved enough momentum that by early July, it was not a question of *whether* there would be a partition, but *where* the dividing line in Vietnam would be."[31]

Of course, behind Zhou Enlai there loomed always the imposing figure of Mao Zedong. Zhou always deferred to Mao in matters of significance—usually in a fawningly servile way—and there is no doubt that Zhou acted, in these climactic days in Geneva, at the behest of his leader.[32] In this sense it is Mao Zedong who could be considered the *true* godfather of partition. Whatever one's position on the matter, the broader point stands: The Chinese contribution to the final settlement of the Indochina War was crucial.

That DRV officials chafed under the pressure from their powerful allies is undeniable. "He has double-crossed us," Pham Van Dong is alleged to have muttered to an aide after one of the final haggling sessions, in reference to Zhou, a remark that has the ring of truth.[33] But the argument should not be taken too far. The Viet Minh, as we have seen, had their own reasons for wanting a negotiated settlement in mid-1954, their own concerns about the balance of forces on the ground, their own fears of American intervention. Even before Geneva, internal documents show, they thought in terms of the area around the sixteenth parallel as a possible line of division, and they reiterated this suggestion in the early, secret Franco–Viet Minh negotiations in Geneva. The demand for the thirteenth parallel came later, after the investiture of Mendès France and his promise to end the war in a month or resign; most likely it was an attempt to drive a hard bargain in an altered environment rather than a firm negotiating position. And if the sixteenth parallel was the real Viet Minh objective all along, the common assertion in the literature that the acceptance of the seventeenth parallel was a surrender forced on the DRV by her allies seems excessive. A concession, yes, but not a surrender.[34]

Surrender is a term better applied to the Viet Minh's acceptance of another Sino-Soviet proposal: namely, to delay the elections for reunification well beyond the six months demanded by Pham Van Dong. Confident that the Viet Minh would win any nationwide election, the DRV foreign minister and his colleague Ta Quang Buu clung to this demand up until the final few days. Western officials understood only too well that Ho Chi Minh would win in such a vote, which was why they wanted as long a delay as possible, or—even better—no fixed date at all. "I have never talked or corresponded with a person knowledgeable in Indochinese affairs," Dwight Eisenhower later famously remarked, "who did not agree that had elections been held as of the time of the fighting, possibly 80 percent of the population would have voted for the Communist Ho Chi Minh as their leader rather than Chief of State Bao Dai."[35]

Neither Zhou nor Molotov seemed willing to force the issue. Zhou did not object when Mendès France, at their pivotal meeting in Berne on June 23, said elections could not be held in Vietnam until the people had been given sufficient time to cool off and calm down. The Chinese premier said the final political settlement should be reached via direct negotiations between the two governments in Vietnam, and he gave no sense that these negotiations needed to happen right away. He even assured Mendès France that Paris could play a useful role in the talks and that he saw no reason why the eventually united State of Vietnam could not remain within the French Union.[36] Molotov, for his part, was initially a bit more helpful to the DRV's cause, pressing as late as July 16 for elections to take place in June 1955. That very day, however, he backed off and said any time in 1955 would be acceptable. The Western representatives refused, and with time running out on July 20, he made his suggestion of July 1956.

The Western negotiators made their own concessions, but fewer than each of them had initially thought would be necessary to secure an agreement. Anthony Eden had arrived in Geneva deeply desirous of gaining a deal, and he never gave up even when prospects were at their lowest—at times, it seemed his will alone kept the conference going. Arguably he did as much as anyone to facilitate a successful outcome, and his performance from start to finish drew tributes from all sides—except perhaps from the American duo of Dulles and Smith. Australia's foreign affairs minister R. G. Casey wrote in his diary of Eden's "almost inhuman good humour and patience." Echoed France's Jean Chauvel: "Towards his foreign partners he had the best conference table manners I have ever seen."[37]

But it was more than that. Eden's advocacy—fully supported by Winston Churchill in London—greatly complicated the Americans' not-so-secret hopes of seeing the conference break up without agreement. He disrupted the Eisenhower administration's preferred narrative—that negotiations with Communists had yet again been a fruitless endeavor, proving once more that talk should be resolutely avoided unless they involved the terms of said Communists' surrender—just as he had confounded it for several months, going back to the Berlin conference in January–February. This was no ordinary ally speaking, after all; this was Great Britain, America's most important partner in world affairs, the one whose opinion mattered most. The personal feud between Eden and Dulles was real and deep and important, as we have seen, but it should not obscure the fact that the two countries disagreed fundamentally about how to proceed in Indochina, and that Britain's stance limited Washington's options.

"I was continually producing proposals," Eden recalled, "because if I did not we stuck fast. On the other hand, we were constantly being criticized for doing so, particularly in the American press. . . . I had been compelled to adopt the role of intermediary between the Western powers and the Communists. My activities in this respect were open to every kind of misrepresentation. I was concerned about their effect on Anglo-American relations."[38] This account omits important elements in Eden's calculations—a Geneva agreement would strengthen his political standing at home, as he waited impatiently for Churchill to vacate 10 Downing Street, and also elevate Britain's standing in East-West matters generally—but overall it seems right: The foreign secretary did serve a vital intermediary role, especially in the early phases of the conference.

He was less vital after that because by then Pierre Mendès France was on the scene. The premier took an enormous risk that he could end the war within a month of taking office, and he won. He made clear his determination both to achieve a settlement and to gain concessions for France, and he succeeded. The right-wing *Le Figaro,* not normally a supporter, on July 21 paid tribute to his efforts, while making a nod also to Laniel and Bidault, who went before:

> We are in mourning. Half our positions in the Far East are lost, and the rest are severely shaken. The free world, which must concede

a new territory to Communist expansion in Asia, is also in mourning. But once things have gone this far, a failure by Mendès France in Geneva would have made the immediate future look dark and stormy indeed.

Let us be thankful to him for his success. Soon, French blood will no longer flow in a hopeless battle.

M. Mendès France has worked hard and well for his nation in Geneva. It would be unjust to permit him to bear alone the burden of surrenders that had already been written into the record before he came to power. It would be equally wrong to forget—and we can be sure he would not think of doing so himself—that his predecessors in Geneva undertook the task, started the talks, and laid out solutions.[39]

At a press conference in Washington that same day, President Eisenhower expressed satisfaction that an agreement had been reached to stop the bloodshed in Indochina. But he emphasized that the United States was not a party to the accords or bound by them, for the agreement contained elements that the administration could not support. The task now, he continued, would be to pursue the formation of a collective defense organization to prevent further direct or indirect aggression in Southeast Asia.[40] Privately, Eisenhower knew what every other informed observer knew: that the terms of the agreement at Geneva were far better, from France's perspective and the West's perspective, than would have been expected on the day the proceedings opened. He felt a measure of vindication. America's tough words, starting with Dulles's speech in September 1953 that warned of major retaliation if China intervened directly in the war, had had their effect. The threat of direct U.S. military involvement caused nervousness in Beijing and Moscow and helped persuade the Viet Minh to accept concessions in the final agreement—the sources make that clear.

Which is not to say the administration should get great credit for conscious policy planning. Quite the contrary, senior policy makers were usually uncertain and hesitant as they tried to maneuver around an imposing set of obstacles: a grim battlefield situation in Vietnam and a poor bargaining position in Geneva; powerful—and contradictory—

congressional pressure to prevent any territorial loss to the Communists and, at the same time, to avoid "another Korea"; the troubles and the fall of a Laniel government in which Washington had vested so much hope, with respect not merely to Indochina but also to the European Defense Community. Nevertheless, at the end of the day Eisenhower and Dulles had a deal they could live with. They had two years before the elections, two years in which to build up the South Vietnamese government, free of the taint of French colonialism. Canada, a loyal ally, had a seat on the International Control Commission and could be counted on to "block things."[41] All in all, hardly a catastrophe.

For others, including two of the principal craftsmen of the agreement, the time to look ahead had not yet come; it was enough now to reflect on what had been and what had been achieved. "The agreements," said Anthony Eden in the wee hours of July 21, "are the best that our hands could devise." Jean Chauvel was more somber: "There is no good end to a bad business."[42]

PART SIX

SEIZING THE TORCH, 1954–1959

CHAPTER 25

"WE HAVE NO OTHER CHOICE
BUT TO WIN HERE"

THEY ARRIVED AT DAYBREAK IN HANOI'S OUTER NEIGHBORHOODS, the green-uniformed troops of the People's Army, in Molotova trucks, in jeeps, on bicycles, and on foot. In the lead were infantry of the 308th Division, many of them veterans of Dien Bien Phu, carrying their mortars and machine guns as well as bouquets of gladiolas. Word spread quickly among the city's residents, who rushed out on the sidewalks to cheer the procession. "Long live President Ho!" they chanted. "Long live the People's Army!" "Free Vietnam!" Already the gold-starred red flags of the Democratic Republic of Vietnam fluttered from almost every window, and banners had been hung proclaiming *"Doc lap!"* (independence). It was the eve of the formal Viet Minh takeover of the city, under the terms of the Geneva Accords. It was Saturday, October 9, 1954.

Later in the day, a very different scene played itself out. Near the Citadel at the city's heart, a lone French bugler sounded taps as the tricolor was lowered for the last time. A steady rain fell. A small contingent of battle-weary officers and men watched passively as a silently weeping colonel accepted the furled flag. In eight years of war, the French Expeditionary Corps had won more engagements than it had lost, had killed far more enemy soldiers than it had lost, yet victory had not come. "We shall never come back," a French colonel murmured, his head bowed. "My heart is heavy when I think of the great heritage we are abandoning."[1]

The French withdrawal occurred sector by sector, almost street by street, the engines of the armored cars growling in low gear. The last three streets were those converging on the road leading to the Paul Doumer Bridge that spanned the rain-swollen Red River. At long last, in the early evening, the last car made its way up the slope of the bridge. The three French officers who had been directing traffic glanced around, looked at one another, then walked slowly up the slope. The Vietnamese onlookers, sensing the moment, surged forward to the edge of the bridge. After a few minutes, the three men were gone from view. In that instant, Hanoi, the apple of French colonialism's eye since a detachment under Lieutenant Francis Garnier marched into town in 1873 and claimed it for France, passed fully into Viet Minh control.

The following day General Vo Nguyen Giap, after a victorious parade by his troops through the heart of the city, said under clear blue skies: "After eight years of resistance and eighty years of struggle for the liberation of the nation, our beloved capital is now completely free."[2]

One man was conspicuously absent during the celebration: Ho Chi Minh, who would slip into Hanoi unannounced two days later in the back of a captured French three-quarter-ton truck, shake hands with members of the International Control Commission, then disappear behind closed doors with a few aides. He would not be seen in public until

VICTORIOUS VIET MINH TROOPS PARADE THROUGH HANOI,
OCTOBER 10, 1954. THE TOP BANNER READS: "VIETNAM: PEACE,
UNITY, INDEPENDENCE, LONG LIVE DEMOCRACY"

the arrival of Indian prime minister Jawaharlal Nehru on October 17.[3] In a newspaper editorial on October 18, Ho explained that he did not wish to waste his compatriots' time with a public gala ceremony. "Our mutual love," he said, "does not depend on appearance." But the satisfaction Ho felt in these first days was immense. It was thirty-five years since he had made his appeal in vain to the great powers at the Versailles Peace Conference, and nine years since that glorious day in September 1945 when he declared Vietnamese independence before the cheering throngs in Ba Dinh Square. At the start of 1946 he and his lieutenants fled Hanoi for the Viet Bac, just as the fighting began. Now they were back, having prevailed over a great Western power on the field of battle. Never before had a colonial people achieved such a feat.

It was dizzying, on some level, hard to fully digest even now, five months after the smashing victory at Dien Bien Phu. The sight of the departing French signified the breaking of a bond, and for many educated revolutionaries, Ho Chi Minh among them, the moment was not without its bittersweet element. "I felt a sudden twinge of sadness, in the midst of the cheering and singing," recalled Luu Doan Huynh, a veteran of both the French and American wars, half a century later. "We were never happy slaves under the *colons,* and yet when I went into the jungle in 1946 I carried with me a book of French poetry! I believed in the eternal truths: *liberté, égalité, et fraternité.* And now it was over. Separation had occurred."[4]

II

FOR HO CHI MINH, THERE WERE OTHER, MORE IMPORTANT REA-sons to temper the celebrations that mid-October day. To begin with, the price of victory over France had been enormous, in both blood and treasure. From 1946 to 1954, the Viet Minh suffered some 200,000 soldiers killed, and an estimated 125,000 civilians also perished, the majority of them in Tonkin.[5] Much of the DRV zone, moreover, lay in ruins. Roads and railways had been cut, bridges blown up, buildings destroyed. Rice production in the Red River Delta had declined precipitously. By the end, in Geneva, Ho had been almost as desperate for a cease-fire as his counterpart in Paris, Pierre Mendès France. Now he and his colleagues were faced with the task of rebuilding their war-torn economy, and of carrying out a revolutionary transformation of the DRV. In many areas, it meant starting essentially from scratch, for the departing French had dismantled post offices and hospitals and stripped factories of tools and machinery, even lightbulbs in some cases.

Most of all, for Ho Chi Minh, there was no getting around the fact that his victory, however unprecedented and stunning, was incomplete and perhaps temporary. The vision that had always driven him on, that of a "great union" of all Vietnamese, had flickered into view for a fleeting moment in 1945–46, then had been lost in the subsequent war. Now, despite vanquishing the French military, the dream remained unrealized, as the country was divided into two zones and as the ethnic and social and political contradictions within Vietnamese society threatened to become more sharply defined—already the two entities were becoming known around the world as North and South Vietnam. In Saigon, Ho knew, Bao Dai's regime under Prime Minister Ngo Dinh Diem was working to expand and strengthen its authority. If Diem could have broad American backing in that effort, as seemed highly likely, then the temporary partition at the seventeenth parallel might not be so temporary at all. Even the Soviet Union and China, Ho feared, would be unlikely to work hard to end the split by insisting that the elections for reunification scheduled for 1956 take place; they had bigger fish to fry in global politics, he knew, and especially China might prefer to have a weak and—in every sense of the word—divided Vietnam over a strong and united one.

Ho Chi Minh accordingly determined that he would have to tread carefully, the better to win broad support from the outside world and thereby better the chances of the elections taking place. Even as he secretly left behind Viet Minh cadres in the south to agitate for the 1956 elections and to undermine Diem's government, he determined he would project the image of that now-familiar figure: Ho the conciliator.[6] The new government, he told a group of party officials on October 16, represented the will of the people and would subject itself to popular criticism. The same day he urged foreigners to remain in Hanoi and to continue their jobs, emphasizing that he envisioned a very slow transition to socialism. In choosing his residence, he rejected the Governor-General's

Palace near Hoan Khiem Lake, for the reason that it was too ostentatious, and selected instead a small gardener's house on the palace grounds. During Nehru's visit, Ho assured his guest that the Hanoi government would maintain correct and cordial relations with Laos and Cambodia and would seek diplomatic contact with countries on both sides of the East-West divide. On October 18, he offered the same assurances to his old acquaintance and negotiating partner Jean Sainteny, who had been sent by Pierre Mendès France as a special envoy to represent French interests in North Vietnam. Ho told Sainteny that he hoped France would retain a cultural and economic presence in the DRV and insisted he was not a pawn of hard-liners in his government.[7]

Sainteny responded in kind. Even before the meeting, he warned Paris that Viet Minh leaders would never give up the struggle for a reunited Vietnam under Hanoi's control, and that any attempt to create a permanent division of the country would ultimately provoke renewed war and ruin all attempts to facilitate improved French-Vietnamese relations. Following his encounter with Ho, Sainteny dwelled on this theme while also stressing the Viet Minh leader's forthcoming attitude. Ho Chi Minh, he stressed, sought to resume the dialogue where it had been interrupted at Fontainebleau in 1946 and evinced no bitterness about the life-and-death struggle that had just concluded. "Democratic Vietnam asserts that it is ready to talk, to negotiate, to keep a very acceptable position open for us, in other words to respect the Geneva agreements and to 'play the game,'" Sainteny said. He stressed that the DRV would be no puppet of the Soviet Union or China: It would be a Communist state, certainly, but it wanted to follow an independent line. France's policy should be aimed at supporting this independent policy.[8]

Mendès France accepted all of this, but he had to take into account other considerations. His success in putting an end to the fighting had not liberated him from Indochinese matters. In particular, his desire to create a basis for amicable relations with Hanoi came up against the promise he had made to Saigon, at the conclusion of the Geneva Conference, that France would have diplomatic relations only with South Vietnam—it was the price for getting the Diem government to stop subverting the negotiations. Thus even while French opinions of Diem's performance and the VNA's capacity grew steadily dimmer through the late summer and into the fall, Mendès France determined there could be no fundamental change in French policy. Senior aides agreed.[9]

The result: Sainteny was not accorded full ambassadorial status, and the French government steadfastly refused to receive a DRV counterpart to Sainteny's delegation. His authority severely constrained, Sainteny focused much of his effort in the cultural realm. He achieved some successes. The prestigious Lycée Albert Sarraut and the University of Hanoi reopened their doors with French administrators and instructors, the latter even employing a French chancellor who also retained the deanship of the Hanoi Medical School. With Sainteny's urging, Ho's government also kept the French personnel of the renowned École français d'Extrême-Orient and of the Pasteur Institute of Hanoi, and it set aside the equivalent of $15,000 a month in convertible Bank of Indochina piasters to pay these employees.[10]

Mendès France might have been able to circumvent the commitment to the Saigon government—on the grounds that fulfilling the provisions of the accords ultimately meant maintaining productive relations with

HO CHI MINH MEETS WITH JEAN SAINTENY IN HANOI ON
DECEMBER 16, 1954. ON HO'S RIGHT IS PHAM VAN DONG.

Hanoi—had it not been for the pressure put on him by the United States, and had it not been for the increased need he felt, in the autumn of 1954, to maintain strong Franco-American ties. This latter task became more difficult on August 30, when the French Assembly, by a vote of 319 to 264, killed once and for all French participation in the European Defense Community. The action was greeted with consternation in Washington and reduced further France's eroding leverage with the Eisenhower administration.

Moreover, the EDC vote occurred just as Paris faced mounting nationalist pressures in North Africa—in Tunisia, Morocco, and especially Algeria. In the minds of Mendès France and top officials at the Quai d'Orsay, France would need American backing (or at least acquiescence) to maintain her ascendancy in the Maghreb. Add in that France remained dependent on U.S. aid to support her army in Vietnam, and that domestic public opinion was clamoring ever louder for an end to the Indochina commitment—"What are we still doing there?" was the common refrain—and the prime minister saw ample reason to fall into line with American policy. He instructed Sainteny to avoid close association with the Hanoi leadership, and he abandoned plans to boost French commercial contacts with the DRV and the People's Republic of China. When Guy La Chambre, the minister for the Associated States, recommended new overtures to Ho Chi Minh, Mendès France's reply was unambiguous: "In Southeast Asia it is the Americans who are the leaders of the coalition."[11]

III

AND AMERICA'S INTENTIONS WERE ALREADY CLEAR. AS WE HAVE seen, the Eisenhower administration refused to identify itself with the Geneva Accords, and it resolved, even before the agreement was reached, to take responsibility for "saving" southern Vietnam without "the taint of French colonialism" and making it a "bastion of the free world." After the conference, the administration moved energetically to implement this vision, trying now to do alone what it had previously sought to do in association with France: Create and sustain an anti-Communist government in Vietnam. This government, freed from the encumbrance of the old colonial presence and possessing genuine nationalist legitimacy, could, U.S. officials believed, compete effectively with Ho Chi Minh's North Vietnam—provided it received proper guidance and support from the United States.

In a press conference on July 24, Secretary of State John Foster Dulles laid down the fundamental American objective. "The important thing from now on," he declared, "is not to mourn the past but to seize the future opportunity to prevent the loss of northern Vietnam from leading to the extension of Communism throughout Southeast Asia and the Southwest Pacific." A principal endeavor, Dulles continued, would be to secure a regional defense grouping similar to NATO, whose members could draw a clear boundary, across which no further Communist expansion would be tolerated: "Transgression of this line by the Communists would be treated as active aggression calling for reaction of the parties to the Southeast Asia Pact."[12] Embodied in the Manila Pact of September 8 (ratified by the U.S. Congress in February 1955), the loosely structured alliance, popularly known as the Southeast Asia Treaty Organization (SEATO), included the United States, Britain, France, Australia, and New Zealand, together with the only three Asian countries Washington could convince to join: the Philippines, Thailand, and Pakistan.

This was a poor imitation of the robust "United Action" concept that Eisenhower and Dulles had sketched out back in the spring. Key nations in the region—India, Indonesia, Burma—refused to sign up, and because of restrictions in the Geneva settlement, South Vietnam, Laos, and Cambodia were barred from formally participating. Pakistan joined the pact less because of a desire to contain Communist aggression in Southeast Asia than because she saw SEATO as a means to gain leverage against rival India. The Philippines, meanwhile, had virtually no history of involvement in or cooperation with mainland Southeast Asian countries. Nor did the member nations pledge to do very much—they bound themselves only to "meet common danger" in accordance with their own "constitutional processes" and to "consult" with one another. British foreign secretary Anthony Eden, a principal architect of the Geneva deal, showed how much importance he attached to the endeavor when he opted to skip the Manila meeting altogether. He sent a subordinate instead.

For all that, Dulles nevertheless took satisfaction in the pact. He had what he wanted, which was an alliance that made few hard-and-fast commitments on its members (including the United States) but that might well deter Communist expansion in the region. He also secured inclusion of a separate protocol that specifically designated Laos, Cambodia, and southern Vietnam as areas that, if threatened, could "endanger" the "peace and security" of SEATO signatories. This protocol was crucial in Dulles's eyes, for it provided a legal basis for intervention in Indochina of the type that had been missing in the spring debate concerning United Action, and it was a pointer that Washington would not stand idly by if South Vietnam looked likely to go Communist. In this way, SEATO endowed the seventeenth parallel with a political character that the Geneva Accords had prohibited, and it laid the basis for a separate statehood for the southern area. As Dulles candidly told the Senate Foreign Relations Committee, "In fact the military regrouping [zones] will be apt to gradually become a live de facto political division."[13]

With SEATO thus providing the foundation for establishing a U.S.-protected state in southern Vietnam, the administration set about making that state a viable entity. In the National Security Council's words, the United States should "make every possible effort, not openly inconsistent with the U.S. position as to the armistice agreements . . . to maintain a friendly non-Communist South Vietnam and to prevent a Communist victory through all-Vietnam elections."[14] The new venture retained the same name as its French-sponsored predecessor—the State of Vietnam—and Bao Dai stayed on as chief of state. But in American eyes the similarities ended there. In particular, U.S. planners sought to fulfill quickly and unambiguously a provision in the Geneva deal that they had sought for years: the formal abolition of French rule. These officials did not doubt that France would continue to exert significant cultural and economic influence in Vietnam, but they were confident that Western efforts against Ho Chi Minh's revolution from now on could be undertaken without the taint of colonialism. Now, at last, a genuine Third Force—neither French-backed nor Communist—could develop and sustain genuine support among the Vietnamese people.

The man to lead that force was, of course, Ngo Dinh Diem, who arrived in Saigon on June 25, 1954, and took formal power on July 7. Diem considered the subsequent Geneva agreement to be a disgrace and saw the division of the country as a personal betrayal. But he also realized swiftly that he had no option but to accept it; such was the immensity of his task below the seventeenth parallel. He encountered a city wracked by political intrigue, and his government lacked broad authority and strength.[15]

Nor did Diem help matters with his early performance. His absence of some four years from Vietnam and of more than two decades from ministerial service had left him out of touch with his compatriots and unable to seize and galvanize a heavy and cumbersome administrative mechanism. His early contacts with the International Control Commission (ICC) were tentative and stilted, in contrast to Ho Chi Minh's forthcoming and assured approach. Diem evinced little charisma or practical managerial talent, and his senior subordinates for the most part lacked administrative experience. Unlike Ho, he showed not a grain of humor. Press reaction to his arrival in office was muted and unenthusiastic. With his younger brother and closest adviser Ngo Dinh Nhu—a charismatic, intelligent, scheming, witty, and strikingly handsome figure, who had an ego to match—he strove to establish a highly centralized government unrestrained by dissent, in which Bao Dai's oversight powers would be vitiated and French influence eliminated, and in which all non-Communist parties would be subordinated into a single government-sponsored party, the Nhu-led Can Lao Nhan Vi (Personalist Party).[16]

The CIA's Saigon station, which had worked hard in previous weeks to smooth the way for Diem's assumption of power, voiced early doubt that he could offer serious competition for Ho Chi Minh. In August, Paul Harwood, the station's covert action chief, noted that Diem's unwillingness to delegate authority beyond a tight inner circle was creating a government by coterie, one disinclined to pursue political compromise. Such an approach was not, Harwood dryly remarked, "a political asset which will attract mass support."[17]

It didn't help in this regard that Diem entered a State of Vietnam that was deeply splintered, in which armed religious sects dominated in the Mekong Delta and the Binh Xuyen crime syndicate controlled much of Saigon.[18] These groups lacked any sense of cohesion and common purpose. Neither the French nor the Vietnamese who had supported Bao

Dai's previous regimes were eager to come forward and back the new government, especially as there were complex administrative and military arrangements still to be worked out with France, whose army continued to wield power in the south and was slated to remain there for two more years to protect French citizens and property. Diem made no secret of his desire to neutralize France's influence in South Vietnam, and the *colons* in Saigon wholly reciprocated the animosity. All the while, the politically ambitious chief of staff of the Vietnamese National Army, Nguyen Van Hinh, a French citizen who was married to a French woman, seemed to be laying plans to launch a coup. Diem removed him from his command and ordered him out of Vietnam, but Hinh flouted the directive by charging around Saigon on his motorcycle, waving the expulsion notice.

Yet Diem was sanguine about his ability to surmount these challenges. Neither the sects nor the Binh Xuyen nor the French presented serious problems for his government, he assured U.S. senator Mike Mansfield when the latter came calling at Diem's private lodgings on September 2. As for Hinh, he appeared to be "coming around." Mansfield was sympathetic but skeptical, having heard from Ambassador Donald Heath that Diem was "utterly honest but tended to operate in a cloister," and from other Americans on the scene that the Saigon leader was self-centered and intellectually obdurate. But Heath also stressed that "if Diem goes, there is no replacement for him in sight."[19]

Mansfield agreed. He returned to Washington convinced that Diem, whatever his flaws, must be backed, or America's grand design in Indochina would founder. Diem's program "represents genuine nationalism," the senator told the Senate Foreign Relations Committee in mid-October; only Diem offered any hope of creating a government worthy of American backing. With no viable alternatives available, Mansfield maintained, the U.S. course was clear: "In the event that the Diem government falls . . . I believe that the United States should consider an immediate suspension of all aid to Vietnam." Diem, sensing an opportunity, had one hundred thousand copies of the senator's report printed and distributed.[20]

And no wonder: Mansfield was a figure of rising influence on Vietnam matters, whose recommendation was widely interpreted as representing American policy. He was the Congress's resident Indochina expert, after all—he had taught Asian history before coming to Washington and had visited Vietnam twice, albeit for a total of only twelve days—and was known to get along well with Dulles, having accompanied the secretary of state to Manila for the SEATO meeting. Now he would assume what his biographer Don Oberdorfer calls "an extraordinary role" on Indochina. In Manila, he had emphasized to Dulles that Diem might be "the last chance" for a leader who could prevent a Communist takeover of southern Vietnam. When Guy La Chambre subsequently told Dulles that Diem was "totally ineffective" in securing broad-based popular support and should be replaced, the secretary of state replied that he "did not believe any useful purpose would be served in getting rid of Diem since no better substitute had been advanced." Dulles capped his claim by asserting that "Senator Mansfield had recently been in Indochina" and quoting Mansfield's perspective that Diem was the "last chance."[21]

"From that day on," Oberdorfer writes, "the Montana senator was the State Department's principal interlocutor on support for Diem in the mid-1950s, and the most important backer in Congress of the Saigon leader."[22] From the perspective of a Republican White House still feeling vulnerable to partisan charges that it had "allowed" half of Vietnam to be given away at Geneva, it was a huge plus to have a respected Democrat in its corner, and Dulles and his aides wasted few chances in the fall of 1954 to cite Mansfield's views on Diem to back up their own. After Mansfield in a September 24 cable extolled Diem's commitment to achieving "genuine national independence and internal amelioration" and said all other potential leaders were too closely identified with the French colonials, Dulles quoted from it at length in a top-level meeting the next day, adding that "the senator's views would carry a lot of weight in the Foreign Relations Committee, especially with the Democrats." Later the same day Undersecretary of State Walter Bedell Smith also referred to the cable in a meeting with La Chambre. Mansfield's championing of Diem and of the U.S. commitment to South Vietnam, Smith stressed, would have "great influence in Congress, particularly with Democrats." The Frenchman, hemmed in by his government's need to maintain smooth relations with Washington, reluctantly agreed to a secret commitment to support Diem and to urge all anti-Communist forces in South Vietnam to do likewise.[23]

In domestic terms, Mansfield's advocacy came at a critical time, for even now there were doubters. A National Intelligence Estimate in August, echoing the assessment of the CIA's Saigon station, cautioned that even with robust backing by the United States, the chances of establishing a strong government with broad popular support were "poor." The Joint Chiefs of Staff, when asked to create a program for training the South Vietnamese military, said it would be "hopeless" to build an army without a "reasonably strong, stable civil government in control." Secretary of Defense Charles E. Wilson recommended that the United States get out of Indochina "as completely and as soon as possible." With the French experience firmly in mind, Wilson warned that he could "see nothing but grief in store for us if we remained in that area."[24]

A cartoon by Daniel Fitzpatrick in the *St. Louis Post-Dispatch*, meanwhile, showed Uncle Sam gazing into a dark swamp labeled "French Mistakes in Indochina." The caption asked, "How would another mistake help?"[25]

Prophetic sentiments, all of them, but they did not carry the day where it counted: in the White House. Eisenhower and Dulles had their own doubts about the prospects in Vietnam, and in particular about the Diem government's long-term viability, but they did not waver in their determination. To do nothing would risk the loss of all of Indochina, and that remained anathema to them, for geopolitical as well as domestic political reasons. Accordingly, the administration moved energetically to reorganize and retrain the Vietnamese National Army, eventually winning the acquiescence of the Joint Chiefs in doing so. Still skeptical about the advisability of undertaking a training program "from a military point of view," the JCS agreed in mid-October to go along "if it is considered that political considerations are overriding." Never mind that this Joint Chiefs position was, strictly speaking, illogical: In their minds, it was precisely the political weaknesses of the current Saigon government that made the creation of an effective South Vietnamese army an impossible task. Perhaps the Chiefs were referring to U.S. domestic politics, in which case their position made more sense; or—most likely of all—they were being savvy bureaucrats, putting on record their objections to the training program and thereby giving responsibility to civilian officials while simultaneously allowing the effort to move forward.[26]

On October 22, 1954, the State Department instructed the Military Assistance Advisory Group (MAAG) immediately to formulate and initiate with the Vietnamese government a "program for training that number of Vietnamese armed forces necessary to carry out internal security missions." The following day in Saigon, Ambassador Heath delivered a letter (drafted several weeks before) from Eisenhower to Diem offering expanded American assistance to the Saigon government for the purpose of "developing and maintaining a strong, viable state, capable of resisting attempted subversion or aggression through military means." The United States had of course already been providing assistance, but much of it was through the French; this time, Eisenhower stressed, the aid would be given "directly to your government." The letter did caution Diem that U.S. assistance would be conditioned on the Saigon government's readiness "to give assurances as to the standards of performance it would be able to maintain," and on its commitment to "undertaking needed reforms."[27] In its public announcement of the new policy, however, the administration played down any such concerns. The core concern of the president's letter, officials said, was to emphasize America's support and "to strengthen the hand of the Premier and give his regime ammunition to use against his political enemies."[28] Thus began, it could be said, the formal U.S. commitment to South Vietnam.

Half a world away in Paris, John Foster Dulles pressed Pierre Mendès France to do more to support the Diem government. It was October 23, mere hours after Diem received Eisenhower's letter. Time was running out in Vietnam, Dulles warned, and he reminded the Frenchman that Mansfield's report carried great weight in Washington. Mendès France, "aghast" when informed by Dulles that if Diem fell, the United States might disengage from Vietnam entirely, could only grit his teeth and repeat La Chambre's assurances from a few weeks before: The French government, though it doubted that Diem could succeed, would stand behind him.[29]

IV

ALL OF WHICH UNDERSCORES JUST HOW POOR WERE THE PROSpects for the Geneva Accords from the very start. Only one of the major players at the conference, it turned out, namely Ho Chi Minh's DRV, had indicated an intention to adhere to the provisions for reunification spelled out in the settlement, and the most powerful player of them all, the United States, was adopting a policy that flew in the face of those provisions. No other major player was willing to push the matter. The new leader of the Soviet Union, Nikita Khrushchev, did not want a fracas over elections in Vietnam to interfere with his policy of improved relations with the West. Chinese officials, preoccupied with the tense confrontation with the U.S. Seventh Fleet in the Taiwan Straits over the Quemoy and Matsu islands, also stayed largely silent, content to issue tepid protests. France, consumed after early November 1954 by the outbreak of war in Algeria, remained unwilling to seriously contest U.S. aims (as Mendès France again made clear when he visited Washington that month). Great Britain, cosponsor with the Soviet Union of the Geneva Conference, initially worked to ensure the implementation of the accords but backed off when Washington made its position clear. Anthony Eden griped that his government was being "treated like Australia" by the White House, but he was not willing to risk a serious falling-out with his powerful ally on account of Indochina.[30]

Nevertheless, a fragile peace settled across Vietnam in the second half of 1954. Some 132,000 French Union troops (roughly half of them Vietnamese auxiliaries) withdrew to the south, while a slightly smaller number of Viet Minh soldiers, administrative cadres, and their families moved north. Both Vietnamese governments claimed to rule the entire country, but neither wanted to press the issue, not yet anyway. Both understood that they had urgent tasks to complete, not the least of which was to consolidate authority within their own zone.

For Ho and the DRV, the economic problems at year's end were overwhelming. Most factories in the north were shuttered, and many of the owners had left the country. In Hanoi, foreign journalists reported that scores of restaurants and shops had gone out of business, while in the port city of Haiphong only one of thirty French-owned factories remained open. Fuel for motor vehicles was in short supply, and the railroads were idle. Even more pressing, rice production continued to decline, and floods in December along the central coast raised the specter of major famine. The price of the commodity in the markets skyrocketed. And whereas Tonkin had traditionally been able to rely on the more fertile Cochin China for much of its food, now the Saigon government blocked economic exchange between the two zones. In 1955, only emergency rice imports from Burma, financed by the Soviet Union, prevented a recurrence of the disastrous famine of 1945. Nor did it help the economic recovery that many urban professionals and shopkeepers and Catholics—fearing what Communism would bring—fled to the south.

At first, the government moved cautiously as it grappled with these problems. To reassure well-to-do farmers and the urban bourgeoisie, it initially vowed to respect private property and religious freedom. To Sainteny and members of the ICC, it continued to pledge support for the Geneva Accords and a desire to maintain harmonious relations with neighboring countries. But much as in China, where an initial policy of moderation in 1949–50 was followed by much harsher measures, officials in short order adopted more radical approaches.

The centerpiece was an ambitious land reform program first implemented in liberated areas of the north in late 1953 and now expanded to cover the whole of North Vietnam. The aim was to alleviate food shortages (the 1945 famine was still fresh in the mind) and break the power of the large landowners—to bring about, as the regime put it, equality for the greatest number among the rural masses—and over the long term it achieved considerable results in this regard. But the cost was immense. Instead of offering incentives to the people to spur production, doctrinaire officials categorized people in five groups, from "landlord" to "farm worker," then sent platoons of cadres to arraign the landlords and other "feudal elements" in what were called "agricultural reform tribunals." In reality, however, the distinction between social categories was not always clear, and many families of modest means saw their land seized. Small landholders were classified as large ones. Panic set in. Fearful of arbitrary indictment, peasants trumped up charges against their neighbors, while others accused their rivals of imaginary crimes. Anyone suspected of having worked for the French was subject to execution as a "traitor." Others were condemned merely for showing insufficient zeal and ardor for the Viet Minh.[31]

"My father was an active militant with the Party during the war," one Viet Minh cadre from the village of Son Duong, in Phu Tho province, recalled. "Our house was frequently used for meetings of Party leaders and my father was named treasurer because he was rich. . . . I was not at home when the land reform was begun, but I learned that they seized everything we had except for the water buffalo shed, which was given back to us because someone mentioned that my younger brother and I were in the armed forces. . . . To survive, the family sold buffalo dung as fertilizer, but the money was confiscated because 'the fertilizer belonged to the people.' "[32]

Executions became commonplace, though the scale of the killing is still unclear—estimates have run as high as 50,000 victims, but more credible assessments put the figure between 3,000 and 15,000.[33] Thousands more were interned in forced labor camps. Most of the victims were innocent, at least of the stated charges. Ho Chi Minh, it seems, knew about the arbitrary persecution and violence but did little to prevent it. When Mrs. Nguyen Thi Nam, an important landlord and Viet Minh sympathizer, was condemned to death by a people's tribunal and executed, Ho expressed frustration but did little more. "The French say that one should never hit a woman, even with a flower," he reportedly declared, "and you, you allowed her to be shot!" Later, on February 8, 1955, Ho used the occasion of a conference on the land reform to condemn the use of torture and humiliation: "Some cadres are using the same methods to crush the masses as the imperialists, capitalists, and feudalists did. These methods are barbaric. . . . *It is absolutely forbidden to use physical punishment.*"[34]

Some did not get the message, or did and ignored it. The brutal actions continued. In August 1956, Ho Chi Minh issued a public acknowledgment that "errors have been committed," and he promised that "those who have been wrongly classified as landlords and rich peasants will be correctly reclassified." Other officials dutifully echoed his admission, disclosing that even loyal Viet Minh veterans had been wrongly tried and executed. Truong Chinh, general secretary of the party and a key proponent of the program, was relieved of his post, as were other senior officials, including the minister of agriculture. The tribunals were ended. These measures helped reduce the tensions but not fully—late in the year in coastal Nghe An province, where Ho was born and raised, farmers in one district openly rioted, requiring the dispatch of government troops to restore order. In Hanoi, meanwhile, intellectuals chafed under what they saw as authoritarian state cultural policies.[35]

None of this unrest, however, really posed a fundamental test of the regime's authority. Ho Chi Minh's stature remained unchallenged; more than ever he was, for a great many of his compatriots, the embodiment of Vietnamese nationalism. Under him operated a bureaucracy that was capable, disciplined, and ruthless—techniques such as imprisonment, execution, press censorship, and indoctrination programs were standard—as well as a potent military seasoned by the long war against France. Furthermore the food situation slowly improved, and the land reform program, for all its horrors, distributed land to more than half of all families in the north. Meanwhile the mass exodus of middle-class professionals and entrepreneurs and Catholics, though a drain on talent and though embarrassing from a public relations angle, removed a major source of potential opposition to DRV authority.

V

IN THE SOUTH, THE SITUATION WAS EVEN MORE VOLATILE. DIEM'S government, with a cabinet made up of inexperienced appointees, faced an array of difficulties and had done little to solidify its position as 1954 drew to a close. The religious sects and the Binh Xuyen continued to apply pressure, and Franco-U.S. friction remained pronounced, notwithstanding Paris leaders' assurances that they would follow America's lead in Vietnam.[36] Rumors flew of French-sponsored schemes to overthrow the government. But Diem, aware that the French lacked leverage and that he enjoyed staunch American backing, remained seemingly unruffled. And indeed, whenever a challenge to Diem's rule by dissident Vietnamese arose during these weeks, American officials warned that his overthrow would result in a withdrawal of U.S. assistance, leaving the south ripe for a DRV takeover. The plotters duly backed off.

Washington's effort to bolster Diem's authority included initiatives aimed equally at building popular support for him and undermining his adversaries, northern as well as southern. Conventional and unconventional means would be used. "The Central Intelligence Agency was given the mission of helping Diem develop a government that would be sufficiently strong and viable to compete with and, if necessary, stand up to the Communist regime of Ho Chi Minh in the North," Chester Cooper, then a CIA official, remembered later.[37]

Taking charge of this effort was Colonel Edward G. Lansdale, a soft-spoken but charismatic forty-eight-year-old air force colonel attached to the CIA. A former advertising man who had been raised in Los Angeles and had worked under "Wild Bill" Donovan in the wartime Office of Strategic Services (OSS), Lansdale had a reputation in Washington as a master of psychological warfare and counterinsurgency. He had played a significant role in suppressing the left-wing Huk insurgency in the Philippines in the early 1950s and in building support for Philippine president Ramón Magsaysay. (Lansdale, one account goes so far as to say, "virtually invented" Magsaysay.)[38] Now he was asked to perform the same feat in South Vietnam. "Do what you did in the Philippines," Secretary of State John Foster Dulles instructed him. CIA director Allen Dulles repeated his brother's orders and added a personal message: "God bless you."[39]

Lansdale set up shop in Saigon in June 1954, before Ngo Dinh Diem's arrival and even before the outcome in Geneva was known. In short order, he created what became in effect a parallel (and autonomous) unit to the regular CIA station, a covert intelligence operation called the Saigon Military Mission, made up of a dozen soldiers and analysts who specialized in black ops and who had two other things in common: a devotion to Lansdale and a willingness to live dangerously. To sow dissension in North Vietnam, the team undertook sabotage efforts across the seventeenth parallel—destroying printing presses, contaminating fuel supplies, counterfeiting Viet Minh documents to frighten peasants, even recruiting soothsayers to conjure up fake forecasts of catastrophe under Communism. The CIA team also formed secret squads of anti-Communist Vietnamese who infiltrated the north in order to stash weapons and ammunition for use in possible future uprisings, and more generally to gather information and foment unrest. The squads accomplished little. Most of their members were rounded up and tried; some switched sides and claimed allegiance to Ho Chi Minh's government.

All the while, Lansdale worked to ingratiate himself with Ngo Dinh Diem. He succeeded so well that Diem, normally distrustful of anyone outside his immediate family, quickly invited him to move in to the presidential palace. Lansdale declined the offer, on the grounds that he remained officially an air force colonel, but he was a fixture in Diem's office in the difficult early months, often being summoned for late-night meetings in which Diem showed his predilection for delivering lengthy monologues. Whereas other visitors invariably found this prolixity excruciating, Lansdale didn't mind it—true, the Saigon leader might talk until dawn, he conceded, but only because his interests were so broad, ranging beyond politics to education, economics, and agriculture. However late the hour, Lansdale always arrived at the palace gate in full uniform.[40]

Very often the conversation turned to domestic adversaries and how to deal with them. The quiet colonel soon proved his worth in this regard. When word came in October that Nguyen Van Hinh was stepping up plans for a coup, Lansdale hustled the general's top lieutenants off to Manila and kept them entertained there until the danger passed. In November, at Lansdale's urging, Washington pressured Bao Dai into ordering General Hinh's departure—almost two months after Diem had ousted him.

EDWARD LANSDALE AND NGO DINH DIEM IN AN UNDATED PHOTO,
TAKEN AT THE PRESIDENTIAL PALACE IN SAIGON.

"I had only to lift my telephone, and the coup d'état would have been over," Hinh said soon after. "Nothing could have opposed the army. But the Americans let me know that if that happened, dollar help would have been cut off. That would not matter to the military; if necessary, we soldiers could go barefoot and eat rice. But the country cannot survive without American help. We would only have played into the Viets' hands with a revolt."[41]

Lansdale also helped facilitate the mass movement of refugees from north to south—though almost certainly his role has been exaggerated in some accounts. Beginning in a serious way in the summer of 1954, waves of refugees, most of them Catholic, went to the south under the provisions of the Geneva Accords permitting civilian regroupment. (Article 14d: "Any civilians residing in a district controlled by one party who wish to go and live in the zone assigned to the other party shall be permitted and helped to do so.") As hundreds of thousands of refugees descended upon Haiphong in August and awaited evacuation, the French Air Force and Navy, realizing they were unprepared for the onslaught, asked Washington for assistance. The Pentagon ordered the U.S. Navy to mobilize a task force to assist in the evacuation, and in short order, ships were steaming from Subic Bay in the Philippines, bound for Haiphong.

All told, French and U.S. ships would make some five hundred trips in three hundred days, ferrying almost nine hundred thousand people southward, in perhaps the largest civilian evacuation—and largest sea migration—in history to that point. Entire northern Catholic communities abandoned most of their worldly possessions and set off en masse, their priests in the lead, in what the U.S. Navy dubbed Operation Passage to Freedom. The result was a major reordering of the religious balance of Vietnam. Before the exodus, most Vietnamese Catholics lived north of the seventeenth parallel; afterward the majority lived south of it. By 1956, the diocese of Saigon had more Catholics than Paris or Rome. By then, more than a million of Vietnam's Catholics lived in the south, 55 percent of them refugees from the north.[42]

The United States and the State of Vietnam reaped significant propaganda benefits from the mass exodus to the south in 1954–55. It seemed a perfect example of refugees "voting with their feet," a damning indictment of the Viet Minh regime, and it was especially notable for the fact that comparatively few people went in the other direction, from south to north. The evacuation received wide play in the American press, with readers learning that the travelers, once they completed the journey, were given "welcome kits" of soap, towel, and toothpaste, and tins of milk labeled "From the people of America to the people of Viet Nam—a gift." Left out of the accounts was that the exodus was not altogether spontaneous. Though many Catholics needed no incentive to leave the north, Lansdale and his CIA team initiated a campaign to convince the skeptics. In Catholic areas in the north, they broadcast the messages that "Christ has gone to the south" and "The Virgin Mary has departed the north" in order to be with Diem, a devout Catholic. They promised "five acres and a water buffalo" to every relocated refugee. In another gambit, Lansdale arranged for leaflets to be dropped over the same areas showing a map of North Vietnam with a series of concentric circles emanating from Hanoi. The none-too-subtle suggestion: that Hanoi was a likely target for a U.S. atomic bomb.[43]

Even some Americans on the scene questioned the claims. "At one point I recall arguing with Lansdale over a propaganda story about village children whose eardrums had been ruptured by the insertion of chopsticks during a Viet Minh torture session," Howard Simpson of the U.S. Information Service, who was in Saigon as a kind of unofficial press adviser to Diem in the period, later wrote. "There was something about the account that didn't ring true. I had seen and heard enough of torture by both sides during my time in the field. Chopsticks had never featured as a preferred instrument. . . . Lansdale only flashed his all-knowing smile and changed the subject. The chopstick story soon spread through Haiphong and was picked up by the Saigon press and some Western correspondents. The veteran psywarrior obviously knew his business."[44]

VI

NOVEMBER 1954 WITNESSED A CHANGING OF THE GUARD IN SAIgon, one with unexpected results. U.S. ambassador Heath packed his bags, to be replaced by special presidential envoy General J. Lawton "Lightning Joe" Collins. The unflappable Heath had worked quite effectively with the French for three years, keeping them in the fight and reasonably content. That very success made him a figure of suspicion among some in the State Department and the Pentagon, who thought him too pro-Paris, too tolerant of French intrigues against Diem—and too ambivalent in his own assessment of the premier's leadership. That Heath during his tenure had also been adept at reassuring nationalists in Saigon that Washington supported their desire for a free and independent Vietnam was small comfort to these critics. French foot-dragging "must be ruthlessly overcome," Admiral Felix Stump, commander of the Pacific Fleet, declared in calling for Eisenhower to appoint a single individual with overall authority to oversee the entire U.S. effort in Vietnam.[45] Dulles liked the suggestion, as did Eisenhower. They tapped Collins, a former chief of staff of the army during the Korean War; as one of Eisenhower's corps commanders in Europe in World War II, he had earned a reputation for decisive leadership and toughness. In early November, Collins, who it will be recalled had visited Vietnam in 1951, found himself in Saigon as the president's special representative with wide authority and the rank of ambassador.[46]

His arrival initially heightened French nervousness. General Paul Ely, the French high commissioner, believed Washington was replacing Heath because "because his realism caused him to oppose the State Department in defending positions which were very close to ours." Ely, who had worked with Collins when both men were assigned to the NATO Standing Group and who liked him personally, predicted that Collins's mission would generate a very unfavorable reaction in Paris, where "it would be taken as meaning that the U.S. was going to take over in Indochina." He did not come to the airport to greet the American. Sure enough, in his first press conference Collins proclaimed that he was in South Vietnam "to give every possible aid to the government of Ngo Dinh Diem and to his government only."[47]

Before long, however, Lightning Joe showed a different side of his personality: his capacity for independent thought. With Ely he hammered out a joint Franco-American command to train the Vietnamese National Army, and though the early operation of this Training Relations Instruction Mission (TRIM) was far from smooth, it did function, thanks in good part to the effective Collins-Ely partnership. Ely made no secret of his low opinion of Diem, informing Collins that the premier was "a losing game." Collins, in short order, decided the Frenchman had a point. "Diem is a small, shy, diffident man with almost no personal magnetism," he noted in a cable to Dulles a few days after arrival. "I am by no means certain he has [the] inherent capacity to manage [the] country during this critical period." A few weeks after that, Collins went further. "Diem still represents our chief problem," he reported to Washington, and his assessment of Diem's shortcomings "has worsened rather than improved." The "time may be approaching rapidly" when thought should be given to "possible alternatives." How soon? Collins set January 1 as the deadline; if Diem had not shown an ability to govern effectively by then, a replacement should be sought.[48]

It was hardly the message Washington expected or wanted. The day after this top-secret cable arrived, Dulles sent three subordinates, including the zealously anti-Communist assistant secretary for the Far East, Walter Robertson, to Mike Mansfield's office, copy in hand, to solicit his reaction. The senator responded as expected: He backed Diem fully and warned against giving up on him "for some unknown and untried combination." Collins's proposal for a short deadline was foolish, Mansfield added, for no leader could be expected to show significant results in so brief a period of time. His statements were passed on to Dulles for use within the administration and with the press, and were also sent to Collins in Saigon. Later in December, when Collins once again complained about Diem and even gingerly suggested that the United States consider cutting her losses and withdrawing from Vietnam, Robertson again hustled to Mansfield's office for a reply. Mansfield repeated his defense of Diem, and Robertson made sure Dulles got the word.[49]

Collins also got pushback from Lansdale, who pressed his argument that Diem should be supported and that South Vietnam was too important to abandon. "I feel we have too much to lose to consider losing or withdrawing," he told Collins on January 3. "We have no other choice but to win here or face an increasingly grim future, a heritage which none of us wants to pass along to our offspring."[50]

Collins wavered. In January, the tenor of his telegrams changed, as the Saigon government showed signs of life. Land reform legislation was drafted, and a provisional assembly was organized to write a constitution. Diem even gave signs—faint and tentative, but signs nonetheless—

that he understood the need for social and political reform and would act accordingly. Collins told Washington he now saw hope for Diem, saw signs of progress in the government's performance, and he affirmed in stark terms the importance of the U.S. commitment to South Vietnam. Mistrust of French intentions now crept into his analysis, as he warned Dulles that France sought a new government that would be submissive to her, most likely with Bao Dai as its leader. Keeping the French in line would thus be essential. "If Diem has firm support and guidance and active French cooperation, or at least acquiescence, his government has a reasonable prospect of success," the ambassador concluded in late January. "I cannot guarantee that Vietnam will remain free, even with our aid. But I know that without our aid Vietnam will surely be lost to Communism."[51]

It further pleased Collins that Diem's regime enjoyed economic independence from the French Union's franc zone as of January 1, and that South Vietnam now became the direct beneficiary of U.S. economic aid. The United States channeled much of that money through her Commercial Import Program (CIP), which was modeled on the Marshall Plan. Washington gave dollars to the Saigon government, which then sold them to South Vietnamese importers. These businessmen purchased the dollars with piasters at one-half the official exchange rate; they then used these cut-rate dollars to buy American goods. South Vietnamese officials also collected tariffs on these U.S.-subsidized imports. It was a brilliant scheme, at least on paper. Not the least of its benefits was that the government could use the piasters it collected from the selling of the dollars to pay the cost of the army, police, and civil service.[52]

It all put Secretary of State Dulles in a buoyant mood when he made his first visit to South Vietnam in February. Dulles assured Diem privately that the Eisenhower administration had "a great stake" in him, and he announced at a press conference, "Today I do not know of any responsible quarter which has any doubts about backing Diem as the head of this government." Never mind the continuous French efforts to have Diem replaced, and never mind Collins's previously articulated skepticism. The assembled journalists got the unambiguous message that the Diem experiment was a success, and Collins, standing by the secretary as he spoke, gave no indication that he disagreed.[53]

VII

DIEM SAVORED THE MOMENT, BUT NOT FOR LONG. HIS TROUBLES with the sects were about to worsen. The Cao Dai and the Hoa Hao had both raised armed forces several years before, when the French were anxiously seeking any local military assistance they could get against the Viet Minh. The French had supplied weapons and money in exchange for a commitment by both sects to defend their respective areas. In the vacuum of power following the Geneva Accords, however, Cao Dai and Hoa Hao leaders had seized the opportunity to expand their control, levying taxes and raising troops in their sectors.[54] When the French in February 1955 stopped their payments, sect leaders demanded that their armies be integrated intact into the VNA and stationed in their home territories, and moreover that the government continue the French subsidies. Diem refused. With Lansdale's help, he instead used American funds to cajole factions of the sect forces to his side—as much as $3 million in one case. The total amounts distributed may have reached $12 million or more, but Lansdale denied that the payments constituted bribery. The money, he remarked, was merely "back pay." Thus the Cao Dai's Trinh Minh Thé, whom American analysts had viewed as a potential Third Force leader since he defected with his men from the French Union army in 1951, purportedly received payment after Lansdale convinced him to reintegrate his army with Diem's military, the idea being that Thé would share the money with his men.[55]

But the biggest obstacle to Diem's consolidation of power in the south came from the Binh Xuyen gang—forty thousand strong, well armed, and swollen with profits from gambling, extortion, and prostitution. Diem's attempts to control security forces and police in Saigon had met with blatant opposition from Binh Xuyen leader Bay Vien, a Bao Dai protégé, and the premier moved to step up the pressure. In mid-January, he refused to renew the gambling license of Bay Vien's Grande Monde casino in Cholon, whereupon Bay Vien announced he would join with the religious sects in a "united front" against Diem's "dictatorial" regime. Green-bereted Binh Xuyen troops set up arbitrary checkpoints and road barriers in the Saigon-Cholon area and installed sandbag and barbed-wire defenses around their headquarters on the rue Catinat, within rifle range of Diem's palace. In late March, the sects issued an ultimatum demanding that Diem reconstitute his government to include a cabinet of "National Union," and they gave him five days to comply.[56]

A showdown loomed. Many informed observers thought the odds were against Diem, especially since the French were providing intelligence and other tacit support to the Binh Xuyen. U.S. officials were split, not only on the question of whether Diem's tough approach was wise, but on how to deal with the French: One group saw the French as spoilers and wanted them out of Vietnam as soon as possible; the other thought they could still play a stabilizing role. Lansdale was in the former camp, while Collins, whose assessment of the Saigon leader had again turned gloomy, was in the latter.

On March 28, Diem, having refused to respond to the sects' ultimatum, issued one of his own. The Binh Xuyen forces were to vacate promptly the installations they had occupied in and around Saigon. The following night open warfare erupted briefly between government forces and Binh Xuyen police and commandos. French armored units appeared quickly and blocked the streets, and the gunfire ceased. Charges and countercharges flew regarding who fired the first shots, and a French officer on Ely's staff mediated an uneasy truce. Diem's view of the French role grew still dimmer, as he suspected them of having incited the Binh Xuyen to violence.

Diem's hold on power was weakening seemingly by the day. French banking and commercial interests still dominated much of the economy in the south and thus were a force to be reckoned with. Their leaders in Saigon urged the Paris government to act now to install a new leader who would be more malleable and more pro-French. General Ely noted in his diary that whereas previously he had been prepared to retain Diem as a part of a coalition government (for the sake of Franco-American cooperation), that day was gone; now it would be necessary to convince the Americans to abandon Diem in favor of Bao Dai.[57] Bao Dai weighed in from his château on the Côte d'Azur, directing Diem to join him in France for "consultations." Diem ignored the order. Collins, for his part, informed Washington on March 31 that the government's days were numbered and that active consideration should be given to alternative leaders. He suggested Bao Dai or one of two senior Vietnamese political figures, Foreign Minister Tran Van Do or former defense minister Phan Huy Quat. Dulles phoned Eisenhower, read him part of Collins's cable, and suggested they should once again seek Mansfield's input. The president initially demurred, then changed his mind and agreed such consultation would be helpful. The next day Mansfield insisted that all available alternatives were worse than Diem, and that if Diem left, the likely result would be a civil war that would benefit no one but Ho Chi Minh.[58]

This analysis accorded with Dulles's own, and his instructions to Saigon counseled Collins to tread carefully. Congress would be unlikely to fund a successor regime perceived as bearing a "French imprint," he noted, and the administration needed Democratic support on a range of legislative issues—notably the proposed interstate highway system—and on the crisis in the Taiwan Straits. Implicit in the secretary's message was the worry that Diem's replacement by someone championed by the French would represent an embarrassing diplomatic defeat for the United States and victory for France.[59]

Collins did as instructed, but privately he continued to argue for a change in leadership. He noted Diem's deepening political isolation and his stubborn unwillingness to broaden his advisory system to include people outside his immediate family. As April progressed, the chaos in Saigon became pronounced, a fact duly reported by journalists on the scene, some of whom also picked up on Collins's pessimism. "The chances of saving South Vietnam from chaos and communism are slim," C. L. Sulzberger wrote in *The New York Times* on April 18. "Brooding civil war threatens to tear the country apart. And the government of Ngo Dinh Diem has proven inept, inefficient, and unpopular. Almost from the start the French wished to get rid of the little Premier. Now they appear to have sold the idea to General Collins, our special ambassador." The influential columnist Joseph Alsop, also reporting from Saigon, wrote Diem off as "virtually impotent."[60]

Subtly at first, and then dramatically, the White House modified its position. Dulles's missives to Saigon became open-ended regarding what should occur, even as he reminded Collins that regime change would be problematic in U.S. domestic political terms. Then, in late April, with Collins back in Washington for consultations, Eisenhower and Dulles went further, in effect conceding the ambassador's point, made during lunch with the president on April 22, that "the net of it is . . . this fellow is impossible." They took the plunge. At 6:10 and 6:11 P.M. on April 27, 1955, top-secret cables went out from the State Department to the embassies in Saigon and Paris initiating a process designed to remove Diem and replace him with a leader selected by Generals Collins and Ely (while every effort was to be made to make the new government appear to be chosen by the Vietnamese). Diem was to be told that "as a result of his inability to create a broadly based coalition government, and because of Vietnamese resistance to him," the United States and France "are no longer in a position to prevent his removal from office."[61]

Then, near midnight the same day, came word from Saigon: Fighting had erupted in the streets of the city between the Binh Xuyen and the VNA. Almost certainly Diem had been tipped off about the ouster orders, perhaps by Lansdale, who was by his side almost continuously throughout the crisis. With nothing to lose and much to gain, he then in all likelihood initiated the battle.[62] Diem always denied being the instigator, and it's not outside the realm of possibility that the Binh Xuyen fired first; conclusive evidence remains elusive. Whatever the case, the violence worked immediately to Diem's advantage: At 11:56 P.M., Dulles canceled the earlier directives calling for Diem's removal, less than six hours after they had been issued. In the days thereafter, fierce gunfights continued, leaving five hundred dead and two thousand wounded, and government troops gradually got the upper hand. Leading sect figures surrendered. Trinh Minh Thé was killed by a shot to the back of the head while he watched his troops engaging Binh Xuyen forces, the identity and allegiance of his assassin forever a mystery. Soon the crime syndicate was routed, and Bay Vien, the vice kingpin of Saigon-Cholon, fled to a cushy retirement in Paris. The religious sects retreated slowly into the Mekong Delta background, never again to threaten Diem's rule.

No less portentous for the future, Diem's actions in the "Battle of Saigon" made him a heroic figure to many in the U.S. Congress and press. In the Senate, California Republican William Knowland offered a lengthy paean to Diem's fortitude and courage, and Minnesota Democrat Hubert Humphrey proclaimed that "Premier Diem is an honest, wholesome, and honorable man. He is the kind of man we ought to be supporting, rather than conspirators, gangsters, and hoodlums . . . who are diabolical, sinister, and corrupt." Mansfield chimed in too, extolling Diem as the leader of a "decent and honest government." Members of the House Foreign Affairs Committee registered their opposition to the administration's withdrawing support from Diem. Democratic congressman Thomas Dodd of Connecticut demanded that Collins be fired in favor of "someone who measures up to the needs of the hour."[63]

Publisher Henry Luce, in his weekly editorial in *Life*, could barely restrain himself: "Every son, daughter or even distant admirer of the American Revolution should be overjoyed and learn to shout, if not pronounce, 'Hurrah for Ngo Dinh Diem!'" Diem's decision to confront the "Binh Xuyen gangsters," Luce went on, "immensely simplifies the task of U.S. diplomacy in Saigon. That task is, or should be, simply to back Diem to the hilt." *U.S. News & World Report* made the same argument in more restrained language, as did *The New York Times*. The latter added a prediction: "If Premier Ngo Dinh Diem should be overthrown by the combination of gangsters, cultists, and French colonials who have been gunning for him, the communists will have won a significant victory."[64]

A watershed moment had come. By the start of May 1955, Ngo Dinh Diem had obtained what he had long sought, namely full power in Saigon and firm American backing for his government. Just days earlier he had appeared politically finished; now he was more entrenched than ever. That the underlying problems with his government had not gone away was either forgotten or pushed aside by his U.S. backers, who were focused on the here and now at the expense of longer-term strategic considerations. Lightning Joe Collins had raised profound questions about the Diem experiment's viability; these were now filed away and were not to be articulated by a high-level official again for a very long time.

On May 6, the U.S. government, relieved of the pain of reorienting the policy, reaffirmed its commitment to the regime: "The United States has great sympathy for a nationalist cause that is free and effective. For this reason we have been and are continuing to support the legal government of Ngo Dinh Diem."[65]

By this expression of support Eisenhower narrowed the options on Vietnam—for himself and for his successors. Diem's government had not lived up to the "standards of performance" on which the administration conditioned U.S. aid, but now the president backed him anyway, increasing America's stake by supplanting the French, in the face of repeated objections from Eisenhower's "personal representative" on the scene. The White House found it far preferable to stand firm, chiefly because it feared the implications of letting Diem fall. His demise would deliver a blow to American credibility on the world stage, while at home it would embolden the administration's critics and cause furor among Diem's growing band of influential supporters. As so often in U.S. policy making on Vietnam, staying the course proved the easiest bet in the short term.

But Eisenhower might have chosen differently. He might have accepted Collins's argument that using Diem to build a strong, capable democratic alternative to Ho Chi Minh's DRV was in all likelihood illusory; at a minimum, it required using America's leverage to force far-reaching changes in how Diem governed, or more ambitiously, it involved working with the French to bring in a new leader, one more likely to win broad-based popular support. Or he might have been bolder and pursued a "Titoist" solution for Vietnam. Ho's primary concern, in this line of reasoning, was to gain and maintain Vietnam's independence from France, just as it was Marshal Tito's to gain Yugoslavia's independence from the Soviet Union. If the United States could aid Tito, as she had been doing for several years, why should she have to vanquish Ho? Why indeed. Paul Kattenburg, a discerning State Department intelligence analyst who was in Saigon at the time and who would later pen a penetrating account of America's Vietnam adventure, remarked to a colleague, in the winter of 1954–55, that the most profitable U.S. course would be to offer Hanoi $500 million in grant aid for the reconstruction of war damage. Ho could not refuse such an offer, Kattenburg maintained, since it would afford a means for him to maintain independence from Soviet and Chinese domination. The sum of money was considerable, but it was lower than what Washington seemed to be committing itself to spending on behalf of Ngo Dinh Diem.[66]

For France, the outcome of the Battle of Saigon was a bitter blow, a stunning demonstration of her waning influence in South Vietnam. For many colonists and a goodly number of French officers, the revolt of the sects had been a last-ditch chance to maintain some authority on the ground. That hope was now gone, replaced by resentment and rancor.

Franco-American antagonism in Saigon grew markedly in May, poisoning even the professional relationships between journalists from the two countries. "Some French officers I had known and worked with passed me on the rue Catinat without a sign of recognition," the USIA's Howard Simpson later wrote. "If the murderous looks of the old French *colons* on the Continental's terrace had been knife blades, I would have died a hundred times over."[67]

At the highest levels, the tension level was a notch or two lower but still palpable. In a dramatic confrontation in Paris in the second week of May, Prime Minister Edgar Faure (who had succeeded Pierre Mendès France in February) argued forcefully that Diem was "not only incapable but mad" and that France could "no longer take risks with him." If Washington persisted in its support, France would have to disengage from Vietnam. Dulles was unmoved. The United States would henceforth frame her policies independently, he said, and would not feel bound to consult with Paris before acting. Diem might represent a "gamble," but he should nevertheless get unreserved support. Having thus established the bottom line—and made clear the power relationship—the secretary appealed for France to stay in Vietnam and support Diem until the Vietnamese could decide their own fate through elections. Faure nodded sullenly. He knew he had no real cards to play.

He knew, that is to say, what every other serious observer now knew, including not least Ho Chi Minh and his colleagues in Hanoi: The French were Out in South Vietnam, and the Americans were In.

CHAPTER 26

MIRACLE MAN

THE IMPORT OF THE MOMENT WAS NOT LOST ON LEADERS IN HANOI. They understood only too well that with his victory over the sects in early May 1955, Ngo Dinh Diem had achieved his long-sought objective: the consolidation of power in Saigon as well as staunch American backing for his government. French military and political influence in South Vietnam, meanwhile, had suffered a blow from which it would almost certainly never recover.

For Ho Chi Minh and his colleagues in the north, it was a stinging setback. Once again they had miscalculated, wrongly assuming that France would maintain a strong presence in the south through the elections for reunification scheduled for July 1956—elections that virtually all informed observers thought Ho would win—and thereby keep the United States from becoming more heavily entrenched. "It was with you, the French, that we signed the Geneva agreements, and it is up to you to see that they are respected," Pham Van Dong, soon to be named DRV premier, had told a visiting French official on New Year's Day 1955.[1] On the first day of the year, it was still possible for Pham Van Dong to believe that France would follow through in that way; now, four months later, the hope seemed forever dashed. As they had done in 1946, during the negotiations that preceded the outbreak of major fighting, DRV leaders had overestimated the power of what they liked to call "democratic elements" in Paris to tilt French policy in Hanoi's direction, or at least to ensure compliance among all concerned with the elections provision of the accords. In reality, few in French officialdom were so committed. With events in North Africa increasingly clamoring for attention, Indochina receded from view, and moreover there was the ever-present need to maintain smooth relations with Washington. Try though local French commanders might to assist the sects in their battle with Diem, they never had the full backing of authorities in the metropole.

And so, seemingly overnight, French political and military influence in South Vietnam withered. On May 20, 1955, French forces withdrew from the Saigon area and assembled in a coastal enclave. From there, their numbers steadily dwindled, until on April 28, 1956, the last French soldier departed Vietnam—signifying the symbolic end, some said, of France's century in the Far East. Earlier in the month, on April 10, there occurred the last parade of French troops in Saigon. Foreign legionnaires in sparkling white kepis, paratroopers in camouflage uniforms and dark red berets, and bearded Moroccans with tan turbans marched by, their flags rippling in the breeze. In the crowd were Vietnamese who wore medals they had won in the service of France. Some could be seen wiping

FRENCH TROOPS ON PARADE FOR THE LAST TIME
IN SAIGON, APRIL 10, 1956.

away tears as the troops disappeared out of view, bound for their waiting ships.[2]

That month Paris also shut down the Ministry for the Associated States and moved its functions to the Foreign Ministry. And to fully sever the old colonial connection, France withdrew her high commissioner from Vietnam (to be replaced by an ambassador, who was not appointed for more than a year).[3]

Gone now was the authority of the only great power that was both bound by the Geneva Accords and—up until that moment—capable of action in the south, in view of the politico-military means still at her disposal there. DRV leaders, well aware of Diem's hostile view of the accords, grasped immediately that the odds that the 1956 elections would take place had just gotten much longer. And indeed, barely had the shooting stopped in the streets of Saigon when Diem launched a propaganda campaign to condemn the Geneva Accords in general and the elections provision in particular. He refused to enter into preparatory consultations with Hanoi on the matter of the elections (according to paragraph 7 of the Final Declaration, these consultations were to begin by July 20, 1955), on the grounds that the State of (South) Vietnam was neither a signatory at Geneva nor a party to the Final Declaration, and moreover that only a duly elected representative body for the south could authorize the Saigon government to take a position on the subject.

For good measure, Diem and his American supporters claimed that the accords had declared "fundamental freedoms and democratic institutions" as prerequisites for any election (rather than as anticipated consequences, as article 14A actually specified). Since—according to the time-honored American line—no one could ever vote for a Communist regime of his own free will (Communism being wholly divorced from the mainstream of normal human beliefs), these conditions must not yet exist in Vietnam. Ergo, it would be impossible for a legitimate election to take place, even if supervised by the International Control Commission, as Geneva provided.

The claims were dubious at best. "When France signed the Geneva Agreement," one exasperated British official remarked, "it signed also on behalf of the southern part of Vietnam. The Geneva Agreement also clearly stipulates that the signatories of the agreement and their successors in their functions shall be responsible for ensuring the observance and enforcement of the terms and provisions thereof."[4] The United States, this and other British analysts maintained, had openly declared that she would not disturb the implementation of the accords and could not therefore now legitimately support Diem in his refusal to even enter consultations with Hanoi. French officials argued likewise, as did those from the ICC member nations India, Canada, and Poland. As for the "freedom and democracy" claim, the critics were derisive. "Unfortunately," another British observer acidly remarked, "there seems little doubt that the freer the elections in Vietnam—at present, at least—the greater will be the Viet Minh majority."[5]

American officials heard these counterarguments and were sensitive to them. Though determined to keep the 1956 elections from actually taking place—Ho Chi Minh, they acknowledged in private moments, would in all likelihood win handsomely—they couldn't be seen as actively working toward that end. For appearances' sake, Diem should go through the motions of consulting with the North Vietnamese on the plans and conduct of the elections. If he didn't, how could he legitimately claim that they would not be fair? "The over-all United States position in the world would be harmed by U.S. identification with a policy which appeared to be directed towards of avoidance of elections," the National Security Council concluded, and "world opinion, and for that matter domestic U.S. opinion, would have difficulty in understanding why the U.S. should oppose in Vietnam the democratic procedures which the U.S. had advocated in Korea, Austria, and Germany."[6]

But U.S. planners were not willing to act on the basis of this analysis and pressure Diem to participate in the preparatory consultations. The bottom-line American objective had not changed: to maintain a separate, non-Communist bastion in southern Vietnam. More than ever, Washington policy makers saw Diem as the vehicle for executing that policy. Doubts about him remained in some circles, to be sure, but in mid-1955 virtually no one in official Washington was prepared to use American leverage to try to move him from his intransigence. The leverage was indeed fast disappearing, for by backing Diem through the darkest days of the sect crisis and not enforcing the conditions set down by President Eisenhower the previous fall, the administration had in effect locked itself into a defense of the south. No longer could it blame the situation in Vietnam on French colonialism and wash its hands of the entire mess. A dynamic took hold that would persist right through the end of the Diem years: As U.S. involvement steadily grew, so did the stakes for policy makers who faced the unpalatable choice of either abandoning the commitment or acquiescing to the Saigon leader's actions or lack thereof. In a dependent relationship, these men learned, the protégé can often control the benefactor by threatening to collapse.[7]

II

TO COMPOUND HANOI'S SENSE OF ISOLATION, NO OTHER PARTICI-pant at Geneva was prepared to work hard to compel Diem to accept the elections provision of the accords. Britain and France valued relations with the United States far too much to defy her over Indochina, and neither the Soviet Union nor China would force the issue. The Soviets, as co-chairs (with Britain) of the Geneva Conference, could have threatened to bring the players back to Geneva, thereby allowing Hanoi to make its case before world opinion. But the Moscow leadership under Nikita Khrushchev did not wish to jeopardize a recent calming in East-West relations for what Soviet leaders had always considered a minor sideshow in the Cold War; as a result, the Kremlin was content to pass the buck to France, arguing that Paris was primarily responsible for ensuring that the political provisions of Geneva were implemented. The Chinese government too refused to risk broader policy objectives elsewhere in the world—including a resolution of the conflict over Taiwan—for the sake of rigidly backing the North Vietnamese position.[8]

Once again the DRV was getting the diplomatic cold shoulder from her closest international allies. In the summer of 1955, when Ho Chi Minh, in the company of General Secretary Truong Chinh and other senior officials, visited first Beijing and then Moscow, he received polite expressions of diplomatic support as well as pledges of increased financial aid ($200 million from China and $100 million from the USSR), but no assurances that either Communist giant would bring its pressure to bear on the Western powers regarding national elections for Vietnam. The Soviets even questioned Ho's Marxist-Leninist bona fides, as they had done for three decades. Foreign Minister Vyacheslav Molotov did agree to approach the British about reconvening the Geneva Conference, but the effort was halfhearted at best—when London refused, Molotov quickly dropped the matter.[9]

What to do? The apparent failure of the Geneva program forced the DRV to recalibrate. Any shred of hope that reunification with the south would happen quickly or easily had been dashed. At the Central Committee's Eighth Plenum in August, a subdued Ho remarked on the curious fact that while the world situation had become appreciably calmer in recent months, the situation in Southeast Asia was, if anything, more tense, due especially to America's growing commitment to thwarting revolution in the region. Yet if the diplomatic route to reunification was looking more and more impassable, the military option appeared chancy at best. For the foreseeable future, the Diem regime, with its U.S. backing, would in all likelihood be too strong to overtake by force, and moreover the DRV still faced huge tasks in the area of reconstruction and the creation of a socialist society. As well, North Vietnam's public insistence on the fulfillment of the Geneva Accords precluded too open a breach of it by herself.[10]

Accordingly, Ho's government vowed again to unify the country by peaceful means through general elections. At the same time, a new concern permeated the deliberations in Hanoi: What if Diem actually succeeded in building up popular support in the south? Then the hope for early reunification, already dimming, might be gone forever. To win support among southerners and create the impression that they were sacrificing some of their objectives in order to achieve a national agreement, Hanoi leaders in September announced the creation of the Fatherland Front. While emphasizing the essential unity of Vietnam, this program said that reunification would happen slowly and would not involve (at least immediately) the communization of the southern half. Moderation was the watchword. The front's purpose, Ho Chi Minh announced at the founding congress, was "to unite with all patriots whatever their political tendencies, religions, etc.," who rejected the nefarious U.S.-Diem plot to divide the country in perpetuity.[11]

The program was a hard sell. The emphasis on moderation rang hollow alongside the recent mass exodus of refugees to South Vietnam and with the proliferation of reports concerning the DRV's brutal land reform campaign. Diem's propaganda machine publicized and embellished these reports far and wide in the south, to considerable effect. The Saigon premier also launched a campaign of repression, under the slogan "Denounce the Communists," which summoned the population into mass meetings to denounce Viet Minh members and sympathizers; the South Vietnamese army and police arrested thousands of suspected subversives and sent them to detention camps. The regime escalated the effort in January 1956 by issuing Ordinance No. 6, which gave officials almost unlimited powers in combating political opponents. Henceforth, the edict read, anyone considered a danger "to the defense of the state and public order" was to be thrown in jail or placed under house arrest until "order and security" had been achieved—however deep into the future that might be. Hundreds of executions occurred, some of them by beheading or disembowelment. The harsh methods were not without effect. Gradually, through 1956 and 1957, clandestine Viet Minh organizations in the south were decimated.[12]

To solidify his hold on power, Diem also moved cleverly to remove any lingering threat posed by Bao Dai by calling a referendum to decide whether to maintain the monarchy or to establish a republic with himself as president. To ensure the right outcome, the government prohibited campaigning for the emperor, stuffed ballot boxes, intimidated voters, and showered urban and rural areas with anti–Bao Dai propaganda. On voting day, October 23, 1955, Diem claimed he won 98.2 percent of the ballots, having spurned Pentagon suggestions that he aim for a more credible 60 to 70 percent. (His 605,025 votes in Saigon were one-third more than the city's registered voters.)[13]

Even friendly observers expressed dismay at these electoral tactics. "The one-sided 'election campaign' and the methods employed to assure an almost unanimous vote for Diem were quite outrageous," one ardent supporter of South Vietnam later wrote. "The use of these methods to secure the victory of a good cause boded ill for the future of a regime whose leader liked to advertise his acts as morally inspired." State Department officials privately agreed but publicly claimed to see in the election the further "evolution of orderly and effective processes in an area of Southeast Asia which has been and continues to be threatened by Communist efforts to impose totalitarian control."[14]

Flush with victory, Diem proclaimed the birth of the Republic of Vietnam (RVN), with himself as her first president. He stood supreme. Six months after facing near-certain demise, he was now in uncontested control of South Vietnam, having defeated the sects, having virtually eliminated political and military French influence, and having deposed Bao Dai. Soon thereafter Diem abolished elected village councils and replaced them with appointed administrators, many of them Catholics who had moved down from the north and who were unknown to the villagers. With no trace of irony, Diem again renounced the nationwide elections prescribed in the Geneva Accords, because they could not be "absolutely free."

It's no surprise that many later analysts, in judging these and other actions and statements by Diem in the course of 1955, depicted him as a power-hungry and hypocritical autocrat, a reactionary mandarin, a pliant U.S. puppet, and nothing more. But this is insufficient. As recent scholarship has demonstrated, Diem was a modernizer of sorts, a man who had his own vision for Vietnam's future and who sought to strike a balance between progress and Vietnam's cultural traditions. "We are not going to go back to a sterile copy of the mandarin past," Diem told journalist Marguerite Higgins. "We are going to adapt the best of our heritage to the modern situation."[15] Along with his brother and chief adviser Ngo Dinh Nhu, he embraced the ideology of personalism, which was rooted in the efforts of humanist Roman Catholic intellectuals in interwar France to find a third way to economic development, between liberal democracy and Communism. A key figure was philosopher Emmanuel Mounier, who expounded his ideas in books and in the journal *Esprit*. For Nhu, an intellectual and a graduate of France's L'École des chartes, personalism's emphasis on the value of community, rather than individualism, while at the same time avoiding the dehumanizing collectivism of socialism, held tremendous appeal and could complement the traditional concern of Vietnamese culture with social relationships.[16]

At least theoretically. In hindsight, it seems clear, personalism for Diem and Nhu was more than a cover for crass personal interests or a rationalization of policies pursued for other reasons; it was a motivating factor in its own right, even if not quite the driving force that some sympathetic historians have suggested. In late 1955, however, it remained to be seen whether the brothers were truly committed to working hard to realize the personalist vision, and, if so, whether the ideology could work in the real world of practical politics. In particular, how would they square the ideology's emphasis on Vietnamese autonomy and Vietnamese solutions with the RVN's real and continuing dependence on American aid? Hypersensitive to questions concerning his nationalist legitimacy, especially in light of the DRV's battlefield successes against the French, Diem from the start was obsessed with the specter of collaboration. Dependence on the United States could, he feared, taint his credentials as a nationalist, thus playing into the hands of his enemies. But what option did he have? U.S. material and political support was, and would continue to be for some time to come, vital to his political survival.

III

AMERICAN PLANNERS WERE NOT UNAWARE OF DIEM'S NEOCOLOnial conundrum, and the more sagacious among them understood that it could cause problems for the U.S.–South Vietnamese relationship down the line. But they took comfort from the fact that, during his first eighteen months in office, Diem worked reasonably amicably with his American advisers. Edward Lansdale, especially, was seemingly always there, just off center stage, prodding Diem, urging him on, counseling restraint when the need arose. Lansdale even designed the ballots for the Diem–Bao Dai referendum, cleverly placing Diem's name against a red background (the Asian color of happiness) and Bao Dai's in green (the color of a cuckold). On a range of political and military issues confronting the regime in the course of 1955, Lansdale offered his counsel, which Diem always accepted even if he did not always choose the recommended course. "South Vietnam, it can truly be said, was the creation of Edward Lansdale," author Neil Sheehan would say, an exaggeration that nevertheless gets at the American's fundamental importance.[17]

Nor did Lansdale matter only in terms of his counsel to Diem. He also sent admiring dispatches to Washington concerning the South Vietnamese leader and his prospects. Whatever appearances to the contrary, Lansdale insisted, Diem could defeat his multiple enemies; no other candidate for the leadership offered the same hope. The message hit home with policy makers, as the USIA's Howard Simpson recalled: "[Lansdale's] cables were vibrant accounts of what he had witnessed during the Saigon fighting. The events and conversations he reported backing Diem's actions had an impressive 'I was there' quality, and these trumped the more staid diplomatic correspondence between government officials."[18]

The claim for influence should not be overstated. President Eisenhower and Secretary of State John Foster Dulles had already decided, before Lansdale was on the scene, to create and sustain a non-Communist bastion in southern Vietnam; to the extent that they had doubts in the early months, these concerned Diem and whether to keep him, not whether to maintain the American commitment. Key players such as Mike Mansfield were likewise predisposed to welcome Lansdale's bullish missives, as were other members of the emerging "Vietnam Lobby"—a group loosely coordinated by Diem's New York publicist, Harold Oram, and counting among its members Supreme Court justice William O. Douglas and Senators Mansfield and John F. Kennedy.[19] Donald Heath, the diminutive career diplomat who served as U.S. ambassador in Saigon until November 1954, was himself an important adviser to the new government, his car often parked outside the palace. Other Americans were likewise providing assistance, in ways large and small, notably Professor Wesley Fishel, who headed a Michigan State University Group that advised Diem on issues relating to public administration and policing.

But that in a way is the point: Lansdale matters in historical terms because he gave momentum and conceptual clarity to a policy that was already emerging. He described the stakes and the tasks in Vietnam in ways that resonated with Americans, insisting, as he constantly did, on the need to be *for* something, not merely *against* Communism. "Democracy" and "freedom" were his watchwords, not "empire" or "intervention," and he stressed that Americans were in Vietnam not to be colonizers like the French but to build a nation. Their motives were wholly altruistic. Through development aid and technical know-how, the United States would help the Vietnamese and other newly independent nations transition from the "traditional" world to the modern one without falling prey to the false attractions of Communism. For despite differences in culture or history, all societies traveled toward the same universal end point, one already reached by the United States, the "first new nation." Consequently, Lansdale and other modernization devotees argued, nation building would serve American interests while also creating a safer, more peaceful world.[20]

Today we know that the results did not often match the claims. Combining reformist zeal with the easy resort to military force, nation-building efforts sometimes created authoritarian, dictatorial regimes rather than liberal states—including in Vietnam. In practice, American modernizers tended to be distrustful of populist politics and inclined to favor elite-led societies; often they turned to modernization as a means of counterinsurgency and social control. But the message resonated powerfully in its day, and Edward Lansdale was a particularly skillful exponent of it. "Ed was low-key but he could always convince people," one colleague remembered. "God! The way Ed explained the situation in Vietnam. If we gave up, all of Asia would go down the drain. It was just remarkable. . . . Of course he was an advertising man, a salesman, very soft-spoken, very quiet, very smooth."[21]

Moreover, Lansdale's views were more complicated—and contradictory—than some later critics allowed. His certainty that the American way was right for all concerned did not prevent him from extolling the need for U.S. officials to show empathy for local values and practices. "Let's cut the American self-delusion," he declared, with reference to CIA colleagues concerned only with espionage and State Department officers who belittled the Vietnamese. Though tone deaf to foreign languages, Lansdale took genuine interest in foreign cultures and enjoyed spending extended time with villagers in the Philippines and Vietnam, charming some of them by taking out his harmonica and gamely trying to learn the local songs and always taking care to be gracious and polite. In this way, Southeast Asia became for Lansdale, in historian Jonathan Nashel's apt formulation, "simultaneously exotic and proto-American."[22]

IV

A COURTEOUS AND SOFT-SPOKEN AMERICAN COMES TO SOUTHERN Vietnam completely convinced of the moral virtue of his anti-Communist ends and gives scant concern to the means he employs to realize those ends. It all sounds uncannily like another figure who made his appearance just as Ngo Dinh Diem's Republic of Vietnam came into being at the end of 1955: Alden Pyle, the title character in Graham Greene's *The Quiet American,* which was published in Britain in December and came out in the United States the following March. In the novel, set in Cochin China in 1952, Pyle—the quiet American of the title—is a new arrival in Saigon who works for the CIA and is intent on encouraging an indigenous Third Force that is neither Communist nor colonialist. He befriends British journalist Thomas Fowler, who introduces him to his young Vietnamese mistress Phuong. A tempestuous love triangle develops. When Fowler learns that Pyle has supplied a Third Force general with matériel used in a bombing in a Saigon square, he betrays the American to the Viet Minh, who murder him and dump his body in a canal.

As we have seen in an earlier chapter, Lansdale was almost certainly *not* the model for Pyle—Greene began writing the novel long before he knew of Lansdale—and there are notable differences between them. Lansdale was considerably older than Pyle, for one thing, and lacked his schoolboy innocence. He also did not possess the bookishness and inexperience that Pyle exhibits in the novel; nor was he quite as earnest as Pyle. Yet the similarities are nonetheless striking, and it's easy to see why Greene—much to his frustration—never could quite dispel the notion among literary critics and journalists that he had patterned Pyle after Lansdale.

The novel won lavish praise from British critics. "The best [Greene] novel for many years, certainly since *The Power and the Glory,*" declared Donat O'Donnell, the pen name of Conor Cruise O'Brien, in the *New Statesman.* Evelyn Waugh, writing in *The Sunday Times,* found the work "masterly, original, and vigorous," while Nancy Spain (*Daily Express*) thought it "as near a masterpiece as anything I have ever read in the last twenty years." In the view of *The Times Literary Supplement,* "it is quite impossible to close the discussion simply by closing the book," in view of the issues at stake. "A particular excellence of *The Quiet American* lies in the way in which [Greene] builds up the situation finally to explode in the moral problem which for him lies at the heart of the matter. . . . The effect is powerful and long-lasting, and it is by this effect that the whole book must be judged." And in *The Manchester Guardian,* Norman Shrapnel pronounced the novel "superb, the sort of prize for devotion to duty that comes to a reviewer once in several years. . . . Attack the book at its weakest points and nothing essential fails."[23]

Many American reviewers felt differently. Not all of them: Contrary to later myth, the novel received broadly favorable notice in various U.S. publications, with critics lauding Greene for his skillful pacing, his evocative sense of place, and his taut, clean style. The *Chicago Sun-Times* called it "the best novel about the war in Indo-China," while *The New York Times* said it was "written with Greene's great technical skill and imagination." Even some of these reviewers, however, as well as those who were wholly negative in their evaluations, faulted the author for what *Newsweek* called "This Man's Caricature of the American Abroad." Why did Greene invent such a shallow, cardboard figure as Pyle, one who was never allowed to win any of his debates with Fowler, the cynical and well-traveled British narrator? The only explanation was that the author had allowed his palpable anti-Americanism (resulting, some of the reviewers speculated, in part from his being temporarily denied a visa to enter the United States in 1952) to drive his story. A. J. Liebling, in a caustic and supercilious review in *The New Yorker,* took particular umbrage at the direct connection between Pyle and the killing of innocents and concluded that Greene—who, Liebling delighted in pointing out, could not manage to get American idiomatic English right—merely resented America's assumption of world leadership. "There is a difference," Liebling charged, "between calling your over-successful offshoot a silly ass and accusing him of murder."[24]

Greene plainly touched a nerve among these reviewers, testy about his portrayal of their national character. What they missed was the complexity of both Fowler and Pyle (though not, it must be said, of Phuong, the Vietnamese woman they both covet, who is the real cardboard figure in the book, a physically beautiful and demure airhead who spends her time reading gossip about the British royals). Fowler is jaded and sardonic and content to caricature all things American through one-dimensional analysis, but the novel also shows a dark element in his own character. He feels threatened by Pyle's vitality and courage and chooses to betray him, perhaps out of sexual jealousy, and he shows scant concern for the ordinary people of Vietnam and what will happen to them. Even after he sets up Pyle to be killed by the Viet Minh, moreover, he admits sneaking admiration for the young American's willingness to commit to a cause: "All the time that his innocence had angered me, some judge within myself had summed up in his favor, had compared his idealism, his half-baked ideas founded on the works of York Harding, with my cynicism." After all, Fowler is reminded, "Sooner or later . . . one has to take sides. If one is to remain human."[25]

In the famous nocturnal watchtower scene, the Briton tells Pyle that the peasants in the field care only about securing enough rice, to which Pyle replies that they want to think for themselves. "Thought's a luxury," Fowler answers. "Do you think the peasant sits and thinks of God and Democracy when he gets inside his mud hut at night?" Having apparently conceded this point, Pyle asserts that peasants do not make up the whole of the Vietnamese population. What about the educated? Would they be happy under the Communists? "Oh no," says Fowler, "we've brought them up in our ideas."[26]

Generations of college students have debated who gets the better of this exchange. For British journalist Richard West, an admirer of the novel who freely admits to seeing Vietnam "through Greene-tinted spectacles," the answer is clear: It is the American who wins. "In this debate, I find myself wholeheartedly on the side of Pyle," West writes in a sympathetic essay published shortly after Greene's passing in 1991. "It is wrong and arrogant to suppose that because a man lives in a mud hut, he cannot think about God or indeed democracy." In the late 1960s, West had made a film about the inhabitants in a small village in the Mekong Delta, and though no "expert on their thinking," he found them to be interested in the outside world and avid listeners to the BBC. In the French period, West rightly notes, the countryside was often the center of discontent and militancy, and he argues that Pyle was right to predict that peasants would resent Communist rule, "partly perhaps because they want to think for themselves."[27] Fowler, in other words, is not immune to the kind of shallow analysis he so often ascribes to Pyle and to Americans generally. He seems blind to the possibility that situations could arise in which Pyle's idealistic innocence might prove much more humanly useful than his own weary realism.

Of course, behind the innocence there lurks another, more sinister element, a self-righteous and brutal efficiency that Pyle shows no hesitation in deploying. Utterly confident in the theories he picked up in some books while a student at Harvard, he is prepared to do whatever it takes to support them. If some Vietnamese civilians are killed in the process of establishing the Third Force, it is a necessary price to pay. It is this darker element in Pyle's can-do naïveté that Greene stresses in the novel; over time it is what would give *The Quiet American* its prescience, its seemingly perpetual contemporary resonance. This quality in the U.S. advisory effort in South Vietnam was not clearly evident initially, though, and thus most American reviewers felt free to be dismissive of the characterizations and to recognize nothing of themselves in Alden Pyle.[28]

It follows that Americans did not pay much attention to Greene's contemporaneous account, published in *The New Republic* not long after the U.S. release of the novel, of his most recent visit to Vietnam. "The South," he wrote, "instead of confronting the totalitarian North with the evidences of freedom, has slipped into an inefficient dictatorship; newspapers suppressed, strict censorship, men exiled by administrative order and not by judgment of the courts." And in a second article in the following issue: Diem "represents at least an idea of patriotism . . . but he is separated from the people by cardinals and police cars with wailing sirens and foreign advisers droning of global strategy, when he should be walking in the rice fields unprotected, learning the hard way how to be loved and obeyed—the two cannot be separated. . . . The name I would write under his portrait is Patriot Ruined by the West."[29]

V

WHAT AMERICANS SAW INSTEAD, IN THE SPRING OF 1956, WAS A Saigon regime that had gone a long way toward consolidating its authority in South Vietnam. The advance of Communism, which had seemed so ominous just two years before, appeared to have been halted. Washington's post-Geneva policy of fashioning a pro-Western bulwark in Indochina showed abundant signs of succeeding—and at relatively low cost. True, some Americans acknowledged, Diem's government was thoroughly authoritarian, but how could it be otherwise, in view of the myriad challenges he faced to his rule? Reform would certainly be necessary, but it could come in time. For as U.S. ambassador G. Frederick Reinhardt would later remark, Diem was securing his leadership, not "running a Jeffersonian democracy." Reinhardt's boss felt the same way. "I must say," the ambassador noted, "that Mr. Dulles made my life a lot easier by taking a pretty philosophic view of the question, saying that a truly representative government was certainly our objective in the long run, but one shouldn't be unrealistic in thinking it was something to be achieved in a matter of weeks or days."[30]

Few leaders in Congress and the press questioned this logic at the time. Many among them who followed the Vietnam struggle belonged to an advocacy group called the American Friends of Vietnam (AFV), which was really the Vietnam Lobby in more organized form and which offered full-throated support for America's mission in Vietnam—and by extension for Diem's rule. As the group's founding document in 1955 succinctly put it: "A free Vietnam means a greater guarantee of freedom in the world." In short order the group gained a large and distinguished membership, including Democratic senators John F. Kennedy, Mike Mansfield, and Hubert H. Humphrey, Republican senators Karl Mundt and William Knowland, academics such as Arthur M. Schlesinger, Jr., Wesley Fishel, and Samuel Eliot Morison, and even American Socialist Party leader Norman Thomas. Still more impressive was its roster of media barons: Whitelaw Reid, editor of the *New York Herald Tribune*; Walter Annenberg, publisher of *The Philadelphia Inquirer*; Malcolm Muir, publisher of *Newsweek*; William Randolph Hearst, Jr., of the *New York Journal-American*; and, at the top of the heap, Henry Luce of the Time Inc. empire. Through these and other friendly publications, the AFV produced a barrage of pro-Diem propaganda in the period, while drastically limiting the number of articles even remotely critical of the Saigon government.[31]

Time, with its huge midcentury circulation, led the way, as usual. In historian Robert Herzstein's words, by this point the magazine "no longer covered Diem; it celebrated him." In issue after issue, Americans learned that the South Vietnamese premier had brought "peace and stability" to his country and deserved Americans' unqualified support. Schoolchildren across the United States, who would be of draft age in five or ten years, took weekly *Time* quizzes; securing a good grade meant knowing that Diem was a great patriot and ally of the West. Every so often the magazine acknowledged quietly that the Ngo family echoed "authoritarian overtones," but it would go no further; even then, it trumpeted the regime's achievements.[32]

The overall effect of this onslaught was considerable, if not in the upper reaches of the executive branch—the administration was after all already deeply committed to South Vietnam—then in Congress and in the broader American populace. Thanks in part to the AFV's efforts, a narrative took hold among opinion makers that Diem was the right man to lead Saigon, and that the outlook in the struggle for Vietnam was rosy thanks to his courage and strength and thanks to America's unstinting support. The White House, sensing the opportunity, aided the AFV by meeting with its officers and sending speakers to the group's conferences. When the organization's chairman, retired general William J. Donovan, sent a letter to Eisenhower in February 1956 urging the administration to oppose all-Vietnam elections scheduled for that summer, the president replied promptly that he was in full agreement. Later that spring, through Eisenhower's urging, Donovan's successor as AFV chief, retired general John W. O'Daniel, appeared before the House subcommittee on Far Eastern affairs. O'Daniel lavished praise on Diem and said South Vietnam would thrive with continued U.S. backing. The legislators accepted his account without question and offered their own encomiums to Diem and also to the efforts of O'Daniel and his organization.

On June 1, 1956, the AFV held its first major conference on Vietnam, titled "America's Stake in Vietnam," at the Willard Hotel in Washington. The administration dispatched Assistant Secretary of State Walter Robertson to assure the delegates of "the determination of this Government that there shall be no weakening in our support for Free Vietnam." But the keynoter that day was Senator Kennedy, a late addition to the program when Mike Mansfield proved unavailable. JFK had changed on Vietnam, at least in public. Gone was the JFK who as a young congressman in 1951 had visited Indochina and asked such searching questions about the ability of the West to have its way in that part of the world. Kennedy had begun to qualify that position already in 1954, when he backed the concept of United Action to save the French position at Dien Bien

Phu. Now the alteration was still more pronounced. JFK praised Diem's leadership in extravagant terms, then declared that "Vietnam represents the cornerstone of the Free World in Southeast Asia, the keystone in the arch, the finger in the dike," and a "test of American responsibility and determination." The United States, he continued, had been present at South Vietnam's birth and had given assistance to her life: "This is our offspring. We cannot abandon it." Neither the United States nor "Free Vietnam is ever going to be a party to an election obviously stacked and subverted in advance."[33]

Was this the possible presidential aspirant talking, positioning himself for a White House run by proclaiming his anti-Communist bona fides before an audience composed partly of influential publishers and journalists? Perhaps. Democrats, Kennedy knew, had been hammered for allegedly "losing China" half a dozen years before; it made sense to cover that flank by talking tough. Still, it's significant in historical terms that JFK would feel the need to speak in such unambiguous terms in a public setting. His speech was greeted by enthusiastic applause. Few remembered the dissenting remark by distinguished University of Chicago professor Hans J. Morgenthau the same evening: "I shall defend the legal validity of that [Geneva] agreement to the last drop of my blood."[34]

In the audience for Kennedy's speech was another speaker at the conference, a young doctor who in the months to come would do more to shape American popular views of the Vietnam struggle at mid-decade than any other person. Largely forgotten today, his was for a time a household name in America—in January 1961, at the time of his premature death of cancer at thirty-four, a Gallup poll ranked him third among the world's "most esteemed men," right behind Dwight Eisenhower and the pope. His name was Thomas A. Dooley.

Born into privilege in St. Louis, Dooley was an indifferent student at Catholic schools who barely made it through his medical studies. Upon graduation, he took the only job he could get, signing on with the Navy Medical Corps. In 1954, now twenty-six and assigned to the USS *Montague,* he spent significant time ashore in the refugee camps in Haiphong monitoring the health condition of refugees seeking to relocate from North Vietnam to the south in Operation Passage to Freedom. Fluent in French and possessing boundless energy, Dooley worked tirelessly to combat contagious diseases before the exiles boarded navy vessels, earning accolades from superiors, a Legion of Merit, and a personal decoration from Ngo Dinh Diem.[35]

The experience also instilled in Dooley a fierce and unrelenting anti-Communism. When William Lederer, a reporter for *Reader's Digest* and future co-author of the Cold War classic *The Ugly American,* visited Haiphong in early 1955 looking for human interest stories on the refugee crisis, he met Dooley, who described his work in gripping terms. Lederer said it had the makings of a "helluva book" and offered to help create it. Dooley jumped at the chance. The result was *Deliver Us from Evil,* which first ran in abridged form in *Reader's Digest*—at that time the most popular magazine in the world, with a circulation of twenty million—then came out in hardback to enthusiastic reviews. With its gruesome tales of Viet Minh atrocities, and its trumpeting of Dooley's own and America's good deeds in the crisis, the book became a runaway best seller in 1956; sales exploded at about the time of the AFV conference in June (when Dooley was booted out of the service for his "extraordinarily active" homosexuality—quietly, for the navy did not wish to have a spectacle on its hands, having already decorated Dooley and endorsed his book).

Movie-star handsome and a gifted orator, Dooley also embarked on a nationwide lecture tour, giving eighty-six talks in seventy-four cities. At least three-fourths of the talks were broadcast. Audience mem-

TOM DOOLEY AND KIRK DOUGLAS, THE ACTOR WHO WOULD PLAY HIM IN THE FILM VERSION OF DOOLEY'S BOOK, *DELIVER US FROM EVIL,* CONVERSE IN A RESTAURANT IN APRIL 1956.

bers reported being spellbound as he wove his tale; many broke down in tears as Dooley piled image upon wrenching image. "What do you do for children who have had chopsticks driven into their ears [by the Viet Minh]?" he would ask. "Or for old women whose collarbones have been shattered by rifle butts? Or for kids whose ears have been torn off with pincers? How do you treat a priest who has had nails driven into his skull to make a travesty of the Crown of Thorns?" In Dooley's telling, the refugees were hapless victims, unable to think or act for themselves, utterly dependent on the heroic efforts of American doctors and sailors, while the Viet Minh were irredeemably evil, so devoid of conscience that Dooley referred to them simply as that "ghoulish thing."[36]

Diem recognized what he had. He cabled a message to Dooley in the midst of the speaking tour to thank him for "the wonderful service you have rendered Vietnam. . . . [Y]ou have eloquently told the story . . . of hundreds of thousands of my countrymen seeking to assure the enjoyment of their God-given rights." Other letters of praise came from President Eisenhower, Eleanor Roosevelt, Chief Justice Earl Warren, and Cardinal Spellman.[37]

In due course, *Deliver Us from Evil* would be revealed for what it was: a wholly unsubstantiated account of the Passage to Freedom, studded with misleading claims and outright falsehoods. A group of U.S. officials who served in the Hanoi-Haiphong area during Dooley's time there reported already in 1956 that his account was "not the truth" and that his accounts of Communist misdeeds were "nonfactual and exaggerated." Their report, however, was kept secret. Lederer himself acknowledged in 1991 that the atrocities Dooley described "never took place." Even more damning, one of the corpsmen who had served under Dooley's command in Haiphong said years later that he never witnessed any of the barbaric spectacles detailed in the book.[38]

At the time, however, in the mid-1950s, many Americans were ready to believe. To them, Dooley's appalling account only confirmed what so many others in the culture were already saying: that Communists, in evangelist Billy Graham's words, were "inspired, directed, and motivated by the devil himself, who has declared war on Almighty God." That Dooley knew little about Vietnam or geopolitics—in his book and lectures, he got even elementary facts wrong—did not matter much, for his legions of adoring fans knew even less. By the millions, they bought what he was selling, literally and figuratively. Others would plead Ngo Dinh Diem's cause in the mid- and late 1950s, but no one touched so many Americans, in such an emotional way, as the doctor from St. Louis.

VI

JULY 1956 CAME AND WENT. ACCORDING TO THE FINAL DECLARA-tion at Geneva, the elections for the reunification of Vietnam, to be super-vised by the ICC, were to be held in this month, but no voting took place, and July ended without incident in Vietnam and without much interna-tional comment. American planners breathed a sigh of relief; they had successfully bypassed an election they were certain their guy would lose. In the months thereafter, as U.S. aid dollars, technical know-how, and products poured into South Vietnam, some Washington officials spoke hopefully about a "Diem miracle," about the RVN being a "showcase" for America's foreign aid program. Saigon store shelves were well stocked with consumer goods, and food supplies were abundant. More than a thousand Americans were now in South Vietnam, assisting Diem in vir-tually all areas of civil and military administration, and the U.S. mission in Saigon was the largest in the world. American economic and security assistance totaled about $300 million per year starting in 1956—a man-ageable sum for taxpayers, even if it made Diem's small state the fifth-largest recipient of American foreign aid.

The vast bulk of American assistance to South Vietnam was mili-tary. This accorded with Diem's own preferences, and with John Foster Dulles's view, expressed already in the summer of 1954, that a strong and effective South Vietnamese army would be an essential prerequisite to achieving political stability. (The Pentagon, it will be recalled, had said the opposite in 1954: that evidence of political reform ought to be a condition for expanded military aid.) From 1956 to 1960, 78 percent of American assistance to South Vietnam went into Diem's military budget, a figure that excluded security items such as police training and direct equipment transfers. Conversely, only 2 percent of American funds went into programs such as health, housing, and community development.[39]

Under Lieutenant General Samuel T. Williams, the Military Assistance and Advisory Group (MAAG) undertook a crash program to build the new South Vietnamese Army (formally the Army of the Republic of Vietnam, or ARVN) into an effective fighting force. A native of Texas and a veteran of both world wars as well as Korea, Williams was a tough, no-nonsense commander with a leathery face and a stiff mustache, who bore the nickname "Hangin' Sam" for imposing the death penalty on a rapist in his regiment in Korea. The name also suited his character, that of a strong disciplinarian prone to issuing fierce tongue-lashings toward underlings.

Williams arrived in Saigon in 1955 wholly ignorant of the social, political, and cultural complexities of Vietnam and not in any big rush to learn. He was, however, a keen student of guerrilla warfare, having paid close attention to irregular operations in Korea. To be successful, he reasoned, the guerrilla must win the backing of a significant portion of the civilian population as well as access to supplies from friendly powers. Armed with this support, small and well-led guerrilla units could successfully tie down much larger conventional forces arrayed against them. They could achieve and retain the allegiance of the population by emphasizing the purity of their motives: to defeat colonialism, to stamp out corruption, to end governmental repression, to implement reforms. To defeat these guerrillas, Williams continued, superior military power would not be enough; rather, government officials needed a combined approach, involving political, psychological, economic, and administrative as well as military elements. In a succinct summation of what would later be called the "counterinsurgency" doctrine, Williams declared: "The major political and psychological mission is to win the active and willing support of the people." Absent that, and absent a concomitant effort to cut the guerrillas off from supplies provided by the sponsoring power, no lasting victory could be achieved.[40]

There was wisdom and prescience in this line of analysis, yet Williams was curiously unwilling to act on his own prescription. He dismissed as "communist propaganda" all reports of corruption and nepotism in the ARVN, even when presented with strong evidence that some officers embezzled official funds, ran prostitution rings, trafficked in drugs, and extorted the very peasants whose support Williams supposedly considered it so vital to win.[41] He also decided—on the basis of his Korean experience—that the guerrilla threat in South Vietnam was not so dire after all. The real danger, rather, was a massive conventional invasion across the seventeenth parallel. The DRV would use guerrillas, to be sure, but only to draw defenders away from border areas. Once the defenders fell into the trap of vacating the border, the hammer blow would follow. "Communist guerrilla strategy is simple," Williams said to Diem.

> By using a small amount of arms and equipment and a few good military leaders, they force [their opponents] to utilize relatively large military forces in a campaign that is costly in money and men. In Korea in 1950, the South Koreans were using three divisions to fight less than 7,000 guerrillas in the Southeast. When the North Koreans attacked, the South Korean Army suffered from this diversion as their army was not strategically or tactically deployed to meet the North Korean attack.[42]

Building from this analysis, Williams rejected the need for comprehensive political reform that might facilitate popular support for the government and instead urged Diem to build his conventional forces. Diem needed little convincing. He and Williams formed a strong bond, and the two men would have regular sessions that lasted several hours. Typically, Diem held forth. "Sometimes the general was able to get in some important points," an American aide recalled, "but most of the time it was a case of General Williams making small talk while the president just plain rambled." The two would sit with an interpreter at a small table, upon which a tea service and a tray of Vietnamese cigarettes were laid out. Diem would pick up one cigarette after another—the interpreter would light them—take a puff or two, and then move to another brand. The hard-pressed translator would attempt to take notes, translate, and keep his lighter at the ready.[43]

Williams set to work. Limited by the Geneva Accords to a total of 342 U.S. military personnel, he used various subterfuges to get the number up to 692. Utilizing these men he then reorganized and trained the ARVN, while Washington supplied approximately $85 million per year in uniforms, weapons, trucks, tanks, and helicopters. The United States also paid the salaries of ARVN officers and enlisted men, underwrote the costs of training programs, and bankrolled the construction of military facilities.

Gradually, a new, leaner South Vietnamese military took shape, its numbers totaling 150,000 troops organized into mobile divisions. Problems, however, remained. The army suffered from an acute shortage of officers, and many of those in senior positions were of marginal quality, in part because of Diem's habit of choosing loyal rather than competent people for key posts. Trained specialists such as engineers and artillerymen were also lacking, and there were persistent concerns about the level of logistical support for troops in the field. "In the event of organized full-scale guerrilla and subversive activity by 'planted' Viet Minh elements, control of relatively large undeveloped areas of Free Vietnam would likely pass to the Viet Minh," the Joint Chiefs of Staff concluded in a sober assessment in 1956. If faced with a conventional attack across the seventeenth parallel, meanwhile, the ARVN could likely hold out a mere sixty days, the Chiefs said.[44]

For that matter, would Diem's forces show sufficient fighting spirit to really engage the enemy at all? Low morale, a chronic problem for the Vietnamese National Army units operating under the French, remained a worry even now, two years after the cessation of hostilities. Few U.S. advisers were proficient in French, and almost none of them had even a basic command of Vietnamese. Nor were there nearly enough South Vietnamese interpreters and translators. The linguistic barriers were immense, especially as there were no expressions in Vietnamese for most American military terms and phrases. Misunderstandings were common, and mutual frustrations festered. Even more alarming to American analysts, many Vietnamese troops questioned why the United States— another big, white Western power—seemed so eager to help them and direct them. "Probably the greatest single problem encountered by the MAAG," one of its officers wrote at the time, "is the continual task of assuring the Vietnamese that the United States is not a colonial power—an assurance that must be renewed on an individual basis by each new adviser."[45]

With time, of course, these complications could be worked out, and the South Vietnamese Army could be a professional and dedicated and well-trained force built on U.S. lines, capable of countering any threat to

Diem's rule. Or so MAAG officials told themselves. To Washington, they generally painted an optimistic picture, noting that the military training mission was proceeding apace and that the possibility of renewed fighting on a significant scale was remote. For Eisenhower and Dulles, however, it was welcome news, especially as other foreign policy issues rose to the fore. In the fall of 1956, the Middle East exploded in the Suez Crisis and the second Arab-Israeli war, resulting in major tensions between Washington and its British and French allies. Simultaneously, Nikita Khrushchev, who the previous year had cemented his control over the post-Stalin Kremlin leadership, sent Red Army units to crack down ruthlessly on anti-Soviet rebels in Hungary. Eisenhower opted for a policy of restraint in Hungary, but the twin crises, together with the prospect of rising tensions in Africa, made him more than willing to pay the price for continued calm in Vietnam.

Ngo Dinh Diem, meanwhile, prepared to embark on a triumphant visit to the United States. Four years had passed since his previous American stay. Back then he had been a mostly anonymous exile, speaking before modest-size audiences on college campuses and cultivating relationships with public figures who he anticipated could help him attain power at some point in the future. This time, Diem knew, the reception would be of a different type altogether; this time he would be hailed as the conquering hero, America's loyal ally, who as the fearless and clear-sighted leader of Free Vietnam had stood valiantly to stem the Red tide. Little did he or anyone else know that this would be his final trip to America, or that the visit would mark the high point of South Vietnam's long and complex relationship with the United States.

CHAPTER 27

THINGS FALL APART

THE TRIP ALMOST DIDN'T HAPPEN. ON FEBRUARY 22, 1957, AS NGO Dinh Diem prepared to give a speech at the fairgrounds in Ban Me Thuot in the Central Highlands, a shot rang out. Do Van Cung, South Vietnam's minister of agrarian reform, went down, clutching a bleeding side and left arm. "They have shot me," he gasped. Diem, unflappable as always in the face of physical danger, calmly bent down to check on his colleague, even though he surely understood that the bullet was intended for him, and even though he had no way of knowing that the assassin's automatic pistol had jammed (hurriedly fitting the magazine, he had neglected to push it home fully) and that there would be no more shots. Diem then raised himself and gazed over the assembled crowd, a newspaper account said, "with his sharp and heavy look in an attitude of the most striking impassability." A few minutes later, after the assailant had been dragged away by police, Diem began his prepared remarks. "Dear compatriots . . . "[1]

The attempted murder was a sign of things to come, an omen, but few remembered it when Diem's plane touched down at Washington National Airport on May 8. The mood was expectant among the assembled dignitaries and journalists. The White House had pulled out all the stops for this state visit, even putting President Eisenhower's personal plane, the *Columbine III,* at Diem's disposal. Reporters were urged to give the stay maximum coverage, and officials set a schedule for the coming days that many a world leader would envy. In addition to a state dinner, there would be a speech to a joint session of Congress, an address to the National Press Club, private meetings with Eisenhower, Secretary of State John Foster

Dulles, and Vice President Richard Nixon, as well as a ticker-tape parade on Broadway in New York City. Diem would also take his turn as host, at a formal dinner for Eisenhower at the South Vietnamese embassy.

Most telling of all, perhaps, Eisenhower endured the heat and sweltering humidity of this summerlike day in Washington to be on hand at the airport to greet Diem personally, a gesture he had made only once before to a visiting head of state. "You have exemplified in your part of the world patriotism of the highest order," Eisenhower said to Diem at a makeshift news conference after escorting him along the polished ranks of the honor guard. Diem, perspiring in a heavy double-breasted dark suit, waved away the compliment. It was the courage of his people, he told Eisenhower, and "your own faith in my country" that "accomplished the miracle of Vietnam." The two men posed for photographs, then rode off in the backseat of an open limousine, entering Washington by the Lincoln Memorial. Crowds edged the curbs, getting deeper as the motorcade neared the White House. Several military bands played martial airs, and a bagpipe group in kilts skirled, as the two presidents passed.

EISENHOWER AND DIEM PREPARE TO DEPART WASHINGTON NATIONAL
AIRPORT SHORTLY AFTER DIEM'S ARRIVAL, MAY 8, 1957.

Reporter Russell Baker of *The New York Times* succinctly summarized official Washington's hopes for the visit: "The prime purpose of the present trip is to demonstrate to President Diem the depth of the Administration's liking for him and what he has done."[2]

Journalists did their best to help out, competing to outdo one another in praising the Miracle Man for his enlightened leadership and his rock-ribbed steadfastness. The American Friends of Vietnam had urged them on, declaring in a telegram, sent to more than a hundred publishers and editors, that Diem ought to be accorded "the warmest welcome" with "positive editorial comment."[3] Diem, gushed *The New York Times,* was "an Asian liberator, a man of tenacity of purpose, a stubborn man . . . bent on succeeding, a man whose life—all of it—is devoted to his country and his God." For the *St. Petersburg Times,* he was the quintessence of "the nationalist leader, struggling to stand against both the Red tide and reaction." Under the headline "Welcome to a Champion," *The (Washington) Evening Star* praised Diem as a "valiant and effective fighter," while to *The Boston Globe* he was "Vietnam's Man of Steel." *The Washington Post* acknowledged that America's "massive aid" had had something to do with South Vietnam's success; a huge part of the answer, though, lay "in the determination and the resources of character of this remarkable man." Not to be outdone, *The Saturday Evening Post* pronounced Diem "the mandarin in a sharkskin suit who's upsetting the Reds' timetable."[4]

Even skeptics, who had never imagined the South Vietnamese leader would last in power this long, struck a new chord. "I had always thought of him," one witty scribe remarked, "as Per Diem—good only for a day."[5]

American ethnocentrism permeated much of the reporting, with emphasis given to Diem's can-do optimism, his love of freedom, his Western attire, and most of all, his faith. Diem, the administration's press release pointedly noted, was "a deeply religious man." Would the point have been underscored had Diem practiced the Buddhism of the vast majority of Vietnamese, so alien to American sensibilities at midcentury? Hardly. But he was the good Catholic Christian, a fact that had not mattered much to U.S. planners at the time of his appointment by Bao Dai in 1954 but was worth a lot now, at his American coming-out party.

Diem proved himself shrewd at playing to the mood in the U.S. capital, mixing in equal doses of humility, gratitude, and determination in his public utterances. His speech to Congress, delivered in heavily accented English, was enthusiastically received, as lawmakers repeatedly interrupted him with applause. Time and again he thanked the United States for her outpouring of "moral and material aid," without which South Vietnam could never have "overcome the chaos brought about by the war and the Geneva Accords. . . . I could not repeat too often how much the Vietnamese people are grateful for American aid." Then a warning: If the aid programs were curtailed or eliminated, the Communists could sweep right in.

Behind closed doors, Diem asked for stepped-up assistance, and although U.S. officials refused to be drawn in—Congress, they informed him, sought to reduce foreign aid spending, not expand it—they assured their guest that America's core commitment to his government could not be firmer. During his after-dinner toast on the second evening, Eisenhower lauded Diem's ability to withstand whatever the Communists threw at him, attributing it to the Saigon leader's understanding of "how much moral values and the concept of human dignity could count for in the minds of men." Through Diem's inspired leadership, South Vietnam had become an international symbol of what a small nation could do to resist outside aggression. Eisenhower concluded by raising a glass to President Diem, the Vietnamese people, and "the great and lasting friendship between our two countries."[6]

Then it was on to New York for two event-packed days. Diem was stunned and delighted by the parade from lower Broadway to City Hall, for which a crowd estimated at 250,000 lined up to cheer him, throwing bunting and confetti and streamers at the motorcade.[7] Mayor Robert Wagner presented him with the city's Medal of Honor and predicted that history would judge him one of the great leaders of the century. That evening, May 13, the AFV and the International Rescue Committee (IRC) put on a banquet in Diem's honor at the Ambassador Hotel. Henry Luce presided, and Francis Cardinal Spellman gave an invocation. Guests included John D. Rockefeller, Eleanor Roosevelt, Senators John F. Kennedy and Mike Mansfield, and William Randolph Hearst, Jr. "The word *friends* should be my theme for tonight," an emotional Diem declared to the gathering after dinner had been served. "Looking at the newspapers since I have arrived in your country, one would think that everybody in

America is now a friend of Vietnam."[8] As if to demonstrate the point, IRC chairman Leo Cherne then read the guests a telegram from President Eisenhower praising Diem for showing "the highest qualities of heroism and statesmanship."[9]

From there Diem flew to Michigan, then Tennessee, then Los Angeles, and finally Honolulu. Everywhere the accolades continued to rain down. When he boarded the plane for home on May 19, only one verdict was possible: The U.S. visit had been a smashing triumph, a diplomatic tour de force. The red carpet had been rolled out, literally and figuratively, and in those early hours in the capital Eisenhower had set the tone by extolling Diem's leadership and declaring him "an example for people everywhere who hate tyranny and love freedom." The adulatory press had steered clear of criticism of Diem's authoritarian rule, while to the world he had demonstrated in a way he never had before that he had the full support of the most powerful nation on the earth.

Nor was it just the international community that took away this message; Middle America did too. This is what makes these eleven days in May 1957 so important historically. As a result of Diem's stay and the fawning coverage it received, America's commitment to Vietnam had been personalized in way it never was before—this in a culture in which, as the saying goes, all politics is personal. A Cold War political commitment made by a comparative handful of elites had become a U.S. *public* commitment, thereby reinforcing it, deepening it, in a way only dimly visible at the time. The visit crystallized the self-congratulatory perception in the popular mind of Ngo Dinh Diem as the lionhearted fighter, the devout Christian in suit and tie, the Miracle Man of Asia, fighting off the rapacious Communists with America's selfless help. Ticker-tape parades and speeches to joint sessions of Congress have a way of doing that, as do images of a U.S. president standing patiently on the tarmac in the humid noonday sun, waiting for his guest's plane to touch down.

II

IT IS IRONIC, IN LIGHT OF THE EUPHORIA AND BULLISH CONFIDENCE surrounding Diem's visit, that it was precisely at this time that another narrative took hold concerning South Vietnam, one much more somber.

Some who adhered to this point of view still detected reasons for long-term optimism; others saw only darkness the deeper they peered into the tunnel. Diem's repressive system of governance elicited particular concern. "South Vietnam today is a quasi-police state characterized by arbitrary arrests and imprisonment, strict censorship of the press, and the absence of an effective opposition," an analyst wrote in *Foreign Affairs* in January 1957. "All the techniques of political and psychological warfare, as well as pacification campaigns involving extensive military operations, have been brought to bear against the underground." Though the repression was in theory aimed at Communists, in practice it targeted anyone, of whatever political stripe, who dared challenge the government.[10]

Even *Life* magazine, otherwise staunchly pro-Diem, felt moved to assert, in an issue that hit the newsstands on the eve of the Saigon leader's arrival in Washington: "Miraculous though their recovery and progress have been, Diem and Vietnam still have plenty of problems. . . . For all its electoral and constitutional show, South Vietnam appears in many ways to be as much of a police state as its Viet Minh rival to the north, and Diem may easily be mistaken for another dictator."[11]

More and more, the regime resembled a narrow royal oligarchy, in which real power resided with Diem and his brothers—Ngo Dinh Can, based in Hue and the virtual warlord of Central Vietnam; Ngo Dinh Thuc, the Catholic archbishop of Hue and primate of Vietnam; and, especially, Ngo Dinh Nhu, the president's main political adviser who together with his wife, the lacquered and bejeweled Madame Nhu, became increasingly influential in the Presidential Palace. The family's main instrument of rule was its own covert political apparatus, the Can Lao party, whose members, many of them Catholics, held principal posts in the government bureaucracy, as well as in the officer corps and police.

The new American ambassador in Saigon, Elbridge Durbrow, a pudgy career foreign service officer, had barely arrived before he expressed concerns about this centralization of power and Diem's seeming determination to quash all forms of political opposition. A mere week before Diem's departure for the United States, Durbrow warned the State Department that the Saigon leader had "become more intolerant of dissenting opinions" and that he continued to "rely heavily on a small circle of advisers including members of his family." Diem might be the undisputed leader in the south, Durbrow continued, but he lacked broad popular support, having alienated a great many people with his rigidity and his easy resort to repression. No doubt Durbrow's grim assessment grew partly from conversations he had with CIA officers in Saigon, who continued to despair at the Saigon leader's poor leadership qualities and the lack of competent, motivated people available to staff his government.[12]

Even some members of the AFV experienced buyer's remorse that spring. Norman Thomas, the American Socialist leader, resigned his membership in the organization, remarking in a letter to Mike Mansfield that the United States needed to show positive support for democracy "against fascist as well as communist forms of oppression." More notably, Joseph Buttinger, co-founder of the AFV, began to express unease about the large number of political prisoners in Saigon jails, most of them non-Communist nationalists. It bothered Buttinger not merely that Diem ignored repeated entreaties to release the prisoners but that he lied to the U.S. press on this matter during his American tour.[13]

Buttinger was not yet prepared to give up on his project, however, and the AFV as a group continued in the succeeding months to champion Diem and the U.S. commitment to him at every turn. Compared to the chaos in many ex-colonial areas of Asia and Africa, organization leaders pointed out, South Vietnam was the very picture of stability. Moreover, nation-building efforts were succeeding, and the Commercial Import Program (CIP) continued to hold inflation in check by making available sizable quantities of consumer goods. The AFV also drew attention to the fact that fifteen hundred American specialists advised Saigon officials on everything from farming techniques to traffic control, and that one particular outfit, the Michigan State University Group under Wesley Fishel—himself an AFV member—brought a cadre of academics who instructed South Vietnamese on education, law enforcement, and personnel management.[14] Most important of all, spokesmen said, U.S. and South Vietnamese officials appeared to be working well together, including on important projects such as land reform and rural resettlement.

The AFV also poured its energies into promoting Hollywood's adaptation of *The Quiet American,* which changed the story to make Pyle the completely good American and Fowler a Communist dupe who betrays Pyle solely out of sexual jealousy. In the novel, Pyle works for the Economic Mission, while in the film his employer is the more noble-sounding "Friends for Free Asia." No longer is he the upper-class New England boy from Harvard but an aw-shucks Texan who went to Princeton. And whereas in Greene's version the Pyle-backed Third Force leader Trinh Minh Thé is responsible for the bombing in the square, in the movie the blame is pinned on the Communists.

The film, skillfully directed by Joseph L. Mankiewicz and shot on location in Saigon, in other respects tracks closely to the plot and the dialogue of the novel, but this was small comfort to Graham Greene, who expressed mocking disdain upon learning of the alteration. "If such changes as your Correspondent describes have been made in the film," he wrote in a letter to the editor of the London *Times,* "they will make only the more obvious the discrepancy between what the State Department would like the world to believe and what in fact happened in Vietnam. In that case, I can imagine some happy evenings of laughter not only in Paris but in the cinemas of Saigon." In his memoir *Ways of Escape,* Greene referred to "the later treachery of Joseph Mankiewicz." Elsewhere he wrote that "the book was based on a closer knowledge of the Indo-China war than the American [filmmaker] possessed and I am vain enough to believe that the book will survive a few years longer than Mr. Mankiewicz's incoherent picture."[15]

Contrast this with the view of Edward Lansdale, who was a consultant on the film and who, in a letter to Ngo Dinh Diem, praised its alterations from Greene's "novel of despair. . . . I now feel that you will be very pleased with the reactions of those who see it." In October 1957, Lansdale invited representatives of "virtually all [U.S. government] departments, agencies, and services concerned with psychological, political, and security affairs" to attend a pre-screening of the film in Washington; "they all," he wrote the chairman of the AFV, "seemed to enjoy it as much as I did."[16]

On January 22, 1958, the AFV sponsored the "world premiere" of the film at Washington's Playhouse Theater, a screening attended by, among others, Senator Mansfield, Supreme Court justice William O. Douglas, and General J. Lawton Collins. "History has somewhat negated the story of the book by Graham Greene, and the motion picture, in our opinion, sets the record straight by placing the turbulent event period of 1954 [*sic*] into a more accurate historical perspective," the group's press release declared.

> The motion picture gives appropriate weight to the constructive role played by the United States in assisting the Vietnamese in their quest for national independence. Mr. Greene's book, written before it became clear that Free Vietnam would survive, denies the possibility of a third alternative between communism and colonialism. The record since Dienbienphu is demonstrably clear—that third force, Vietnam ruled by the Vietnamese, has become a reality. Consequently, in attempting to set the historical record in order, this motion picture has a most important function.[17]

III

THE AFV'S JUDGMENT WAS PREMATURE. APPEARANCES DECEIVED. The well-stocked store shelves in Saigon and the shiny new motor scooters on its streets hid the degree to which the U.S. aid program, necessary though it was, was failing to promote a robust South Vietnamese economy that could in time stand on its own. In fiscal year 1957, American aid supported the entire cost of the Vietnamese armed forces, almost 80 percent of all other government expenditures, and nearly 90 percent of all imports.[18] The assistance created a semblance of middle-class prosperity while fostering a dependent relationship; a well-heeled minority of Vietnamese benefited, while the majority saw little or no gain. With the market saturated with consumer goods of all kinds, merchandise accumulated on the docks, left to rot by importers who hadn't the money to pay for it. A study by U.S. political scientists found that South Vietnam "is becoming a permanent mendicant," dependent on outside support, and asserted that "American aid had built a castle on sand."[19]

In the countryside, where 75 to 80 percent of South Vietnamese lived, Diem failed to cultivate broad popular backing. Many local officials presided over what historian Philip E. Catton calls "a virtual reign of terror." They employed bribery and extortion to enrich themselves and did not make fine distinctions in determining who constituted a genuine threat to the community's safety and well-being. "If people attempted to resist the authorities," Catton writes, "local officials often clamped down even harder, thus encouraging a vicious action-reaction cycle between the government and the rural populace."[20]

On land reform, Diem resisted the advice of American experts such as Wolf Ladejinsky, a Ukrainian-born economist who had planned successful agrarian redistribution programs in Japan and Taiwan and who encouraged the Saigon leader to think boldly. Diem allowed landowners to keep up to one hundred hectares of rice land—an enormous amount in regions where the land was so fertile—and another fifteen for burial grounds and ancestor worship. This was more than ten times that allowed in Japan and Taiwan, and it meant that little acreage was available for redistribution. Savvy landowners got around even these restrictions by transferring title to some of their land to family members. In other cases, local officials lacked the will to force compliance, or the efforts became ensnared in red tape. To compound the problem, Diem's policy required peasants to pay for land they had been given free by the Viet Minh in the war against the French, thus fueling the resentment.[21]

It was Diem's single greatest liability as a leader, this proclivity to alienate groups whose backing he needed. He had created a relatively stable South Vietnam, but in order to do so he had resorted to draconian measures—measures that, while temporarily hindering the ambitions of local Communist activists, ultimately facilitated their objectives by fomenting hatred of the government. The arbitrary and often capricious nature of many arrests by the police angered many in the urban elite, who then found avenues for expression closed off by the regime's brutal actions. Newspapers whose editorial line or whose reporting displeased the Ngos were suppressed with regularity, and the Nhu-led Vietnam Bureau of Investigation went after subversives with a ruthlessness that would have made FBI director J. Edgar Hoover wince. Many intellectuals bemoaned the pervasive and growing influence of the covert Can Lao party, the reach of which extended into virtually every facet of South Vietnamese political life. Can Lao members, most of them Catholic, held the key positions in the administration, the armed services, the National

Assembly, the judiciary, the police, and the trade unions, from which they exercised influence clandestinely, often by way of political and economic blackmail.

Conditions were ripe for a backlash, and it occurred. The second half of 1957 witnessed a marked increase in antiregime activity by hard-pressed Communist cadres and other victims of regime repression. On July 17, for example, armed men gunned down seventeen patrons in a bar in Chau Doc. On September 14, the district chief of My Tho and his family were stopped on a highway in broad daylight and assassinated in cold blood. On October 10, a bomb thrown into a café in Saigon wounded thirteen people, including two plainclothes police officers. And on October 22, thirteen U.S. servicemen were injured in three separate attacks directed at American installations in Saigon.[22]

A new insurgency had begun, provoked by Diem's suffocating repression, though few non-Vietnamese perceived the change at the time.[23] One who did was Bernard Fall, who since the French defeat in 1954 had further cemented his position as America's leading expert on the Indochina conflict. As 1957 began, Fall felt restless at home in the United States. He longed to be back in the Vietnam that captivated and charmed him, the Vietnam that his wife, Dorothy, called his mistress and that he referred to as a "bad love affair." Although Dorothy was pregnant with their first child that spring, Fall sought and secured an invitation from the South Vietnamese embassy in Washington to spend three months in country examining developments since partition in 1954.[24]

He arrived in June 1957. "I keep looking over the roadsides in the usual wide and wary sweeps of wartimes," he wrote in an early letter to Dorothy, "but there's nothing more dangerous in sight than a buffalo emerging suddenly from the underbrush. The [French] watchtowers, now showing the wear and tear of the war years and of neighboring scavengers eager to use their bricks for building materials, are unmanned. The country's at peace at last . . . but for how long?"

The question assumed more urgency as Fall's visit wore on. He compared the U.S. presence favorably to that of the French ("they want to go home p.d.q.," he wrote of the Americans; "no colonialists they"), but as he traveled the countryside and interrogated people from all walks of life, he grew despondent. His alarm increased when he compared notes with François Sully, a fellow veteran of the French Resistance in World War II who reported for *Time* and would later write for *Newsweek* before being expelled by Diem for writing negatively of the regime. Though government officials assured Fall that South Vietnam was stable and the security situation under control, his findings indicated the opposite. It struck him, notably, that the obituaries in the South Vietnamese press showed an abnormally high death rate among village chiefs (crucial figures in Vietnam, as the link between the government and 90 percent of the population). Digging further, he determined that 452 village officials had died within a year, or more than one per day. He then made two maps, one showing where they had perished and another indicating the location of guerrilla activity in the same time period. The result indicated a clear link. Saigon, Fall observed, was ringed by villages whose leaders had been assassinated and replaced by Communists.

For Fall, the finding was highly significant. The killings were not random; they conformed to a pattern. The victims were village chiefs who had been landlords and were not much loved by the villagers. The insurgents got the double benefit of being Robin Hoods to the local population and putting other village notables on notice that they could be next. When Saigon appointed a new acting village chief, chances were he too would soon be found with a machete in his back or a bullet in his head. How would number three on the list respond? Simple, Fall surmised: Unless he wanted to die a martyr's death, he'd quietly declare his fidelity to the revolution. And just like that, another village would have gone Communist. The change would be invisible to the outsider; everyday life would go on as before. ARVN units coming through the village would be greeted courteously, but the insurgents who came through later would get the intelligence and the rice and the use of the U.S.-supplied radio set. The ARVN hadn't been outfought per se, but it had been "outadministered," which in the end would matter even more.[25]

Fall sought out the minister of the interior and said to him, "Your Excellency, you are in trouble in Vietnam. Do you know that?"

"Yes, I know that," the minister answered.

"Did you tell President Diem?"

"Nobody can tell President Diem we are in trouble. He believes we are doing fine."

"Do the Americans know?"

The minister shook his head. He did not think so.[26]

In fact, though, some Americans did know. Ambassador Durbrow, in a 1957 year-end report produced not long after Fall left Vietnam, declared that the Diem "miracle" was increasingly a mirage. The South Vietnamese president's autocratic style and suspicious nature, combined with his lack of vision and his seeming unconcern with broadening his base of support, augured poorly for the future. So did his seeming inability to delegate authority, or to differentiate the vital from the trivial. In Durbrow's analysis, the regime's concentration on security at the expense of the economic and social needs of the mass of southerners was fraught with risk, and its easy resort to repression and intimidation to suppress opposition played into Communist hands by alienating key groups in society. He concluded by hinting at America's lack of leverage: It was regrettable, he wrote, that the United States had not found more ways to make her influence more effective.[27]

Durbrow's cautionary notes were sounded also by the CIA and by the military attachés from the three branches of the armed services. But they were resolutely rejected by General Samuel Williams, head of the Military Assistance Advisory Group (MAAG). Williams thought Durbrow far too critical of the Saigon regime, and he disliked him personally. The ambassador, he told an aide, was "better suited to be senior salesman in a good ladies shoe store than to be representing the U.S. in an Asian country."[28] Officially Durbrow outranked Williams, but the general did not like it and sought whenever possible to make decisions on his own. Frequently their meetings degenerated into shouting matches. Williams sharply rejected Durbrow's claim that Diem was headed for trouble. The people supported the Saigon leader, Williams insisted, and he was adamant that the guerrilla threat could be contained without undue difficulty.

It was a welcome message in Washington in early 1958, where President Eisenhower had more pressing foreign policy concerns—notably tensions over the status of Berlin and the fallout from the Soviets' successful launch, in October 1957, of their unmanned Sputnik satellite. In November 1957, moreover, Mao Zedong had paid a seemingly successful visit to Moscow, boasting to students that "the East wind prevails over the West wind."[29] South Vietnam's problems loomed small in comparison. In May 1958, on the anniversary of Diem's visit to Washington, Eisenhower sent the Saigon leader a warm personal note, extolling him as "the foremost advocate of our interests in the area" and praising the Republic of Vietnam as an example to free nations everywhere.[30]

Even as the president wrote these words, however, there were fresh signs of the deterioration, from the northern provinces of Quang Nam and Thua Thien to the Ca Mau peninsula in the extreme south. In Tay Ninh province, in the heart of the rubber plantation region near the Cambodian border, revolutionary leaders began to integrate their local military forces into combined units to defend against sweeps by government troops. In August, soon after the U.S. embassy reported that "in many remote areas the central government has no effective control," guerrilla units attacked and briefly captured the province capital in Tay Ninh.[31]

Nor did it help Diem's popularity that his government remained so dependent on American power, a fact that led to increased anti-U.S. animus as well. "For many Vietnamese peasants," a Pentagon chronicler would write of this period, "the war of Resistance against French–Bao Dai rule never ended; France was merely replaced by the U.S., and Bao Dai's mantle was transferred to Ngo Dinh Diem." Consequently, when resistance to Diem increased in the late 1950s, the "opprobrium catchword *'My-Diem'* (American-Diem) thus recaptured the nationalist mystique of the First Indochina War." Or as Robert Scigliano would write of the period, "So deeply has the *My-Diem* relationship been established in the minds of the peasants that Vietnamese government officials have been addressed, with all respect, as *'My-Diem'* by peasants doing business with them."[32]

IV

THE GROWING DISCONTENT IN THE COUNTRYSIDE IN SOUTH VIETnam, and the corresponding rise in insurgent attacks, pointed to the need for party leaders in Hanoi to make a decision: Should they move away from their policy of pursuing reunification through peaceful means? That they were wrestling with this choice at such a late date is exceptionally important in historical terms—far from imposing the insurgency on the south, as successive U.S. administrations and some scholars would later assert, the DRV leadership went through a wrenching series of deliberations about whether to support it; some Politburo members argued for the need to focus exclusively on building a socialist state in the north. Moreover, they wondered, could an insurgency against the Saigon regime even succeed, given Diem's success in thwarting all challenges to his rule?

Contributing to Hanoi's caution was the restraining influence of its principal allies, China and the Soviet Union. The Chinese had no objection to a low-level insurgency in South Vietnam—after all, such a conflict could increase Hanoi's dependence on Beijing while avoiding the risk of major U.S. involvement—but they continued to warn against the resumption of large-scale war as had existed up to 1954. Conditions were not yet ripe for such an escalation of the struggle, Mao Zedong warned Ho Chi Minh when the latter came calling at Mao's summer retreat at Beidaihe in the summer of 1958, and might not be for a very long time—a decade, perhaps, or even a century. The Soviet leadership, meanwhile, were even more adamant that revolutionary fires in the south must not be stoked, not now and perhaps not ever. So eager was the Kremlin to avoid renewed international tensions over Vietnam that it even floated the idea of admitting both Vietnams into the United Nations, a move that left DRV authorities sputtering with impotent rage. (The Western powers, fearful of the implications for Germany, quietly rejected the suggestion.)[33]

But the North Vietnamese could not ignore the increasingly desperate appeals of their southern comrades. Slowly they moved toward a more aggressive policy.[34] A central figure in the shift was Le Duan, a former political prisoner of the French who had been a top Viet Minh leader in the south before being named acting secretary-general of the party in Hanoi. The son of a carpenter in Quang Tri province, Le Duan was small in build and plainspoken in manner, and he lacked the educational pedigree and elite family credentials of many party leaders, some of whom mocked his coarse accent and his early job as a railway attendant. But he possessed a formidable intellect, and he did not want for self-confidence. Beginning in mid-1956, when he penned a short report titled "The Path to Revolution in the South," he nudged his comrades to do more to support the revolution below the seventeenth parallel, even as they continued to give primary emphasis to building socialism in the north.[35]

In late 1958, Le Duan conducted a secret inspection tour of the south. Upon his return, the Politburo gathered in special session to assess the situation and decide on future actions. Conditions in the south, Le Duan warned, were dire. The Diem government's brutal crackdown had left the revolution drastically weakened. People were suffering terribly. At the same time, the broad popular hostility to the Saigon government represented a golden opportunity that should be grasped to hasten the reunification of the country. If Hanoi did not take charge of the effort, southerners would proceed on their own, and the DRV would become irrelevant. Henceforth Le Duan concluded, liberation of the south must have equal priority with consolidation of the north.

Le Duan's argument won the day, but not before intense debates during the Central Committee's Fifteenth Plenum in January 1959. Ho Chi Minh, who at almost seventy no longer involved himself in the DRV's day-to-day decision making, urged continued restraint. A return to armed violence on a broad scale could create a pretext for American intervention, Ho stressed, and therefore the southern revolutionaries should remain content with small victories. The plenum's final resolution reflected Ho's cautionary words, even as it approved Le Duan's call for a return to revolutionary war to press for victory in the south. The measure hedged, in other words, on the relative degree of political and military pressure to be applied:

> The fundamental path of development for the revolution in South Vietnam is that of violent struggle. Based on the concrete conditions and existing requirements of revolution, then, the road of violent struggle is: to use the strength of the masses, with political strength as the main factor, in combination with military strength to a greater or lesser degree depending on the situation, in order to overthrow the ruling power of the imperialist and feudalist forces and build the revolutionary power of the people.[36]

Diem's policies, the resolution underscored, were responsible for the decisive shift in strategy: "Because the enemy is determined to drown the revolution in blood, and because of the . . . revolutionary mood in the South, it will be necessary to a certain extent to adopt methods of self-defense and armed propaganda activities to assist the political struggle." And then, another vow of restraint: "But in the process of using self-defense and armed propaganda units, it is necessary to grasp thoroughly the principle of emphasizing political strength."[37]

In the wake of this crucial decision—which has been called Hanoi's opening shot in the Second Indochina War—North Vietnamese planners took a number of steps to expand their involvement in the south. In March 1959, they ordered southern leaders to begin construction of a revolutionary command area in the Central Highlands, a strategically vital area populated mostly by minority peoples. Some weeks later two units, Groups 559 and 759 (so named because of the date of their formation—May and July 1959), were formed to enhance the DRV's ability to infiltrate matériel and men into the south through Laos and by sea. The land trails, which had been hacked out of the jungle during the war against the French, would become known to the world as the Ho Chi Minh Trail. In short order, the first organized shipment of cadres and supplies began to move, initially by bicycle or on foot, later—after the trails were expanded—by truck. Most of the personnel in these early trips were "regroupees," former Viet Minh supporters from the south who had gone to the north for training and indoctrination after the Geneva Conference. Their task now was to return home to provide the insurgency with a solid nucleus of experienced and loyal cadres.[38]

Tran Van Tra, at that time a junior official in Hanoi, offers his own explanation for the dispatch of the first regroupees. Late one summer evening in 1959, Tra was relaxing at home, catching the nighttime breeze after a sweltering hot day. He tried to tune in some light music on his radio when his dial came across a BBC report of a platoon-size engagement on the Plain of Reeds in the northern Mekong Delta. Tra was stunned: Could real fighting already be taking place? On the spot, he determined that the insurgent forces must receive military instruction if they were going to stand a chance of prevailing, and that this meant sending a training group to the south. Tra presented his idea to Le Duan, suggesting a force of one hundred regrouped southerners. Le Duan liked the idea but said a force that size would have to be approved by the Politburo. "Can you make do with fewer?" he asked. "Maybe fifty," Tra replied. Le Duan thought for a moment. The figure might still be too high. "If it is only a small number I could approve it and take personal responsibility," he offered, "and then report it to the Politburo. OK, let's settle for twenty-five."[39]

The trek southward was often excruciatingly taxing. "The further south we got," one cadre recalled, "the worse our situation became. Finally we were down to a few kilos of rice which we decided to save for the last extremity. For two months we ate what we could find in the jungle—leaves, roots, animals, jungle birds." Arrangements were made to create "way stations" along the route, which were to be stocked with rice, vegetables, and water. They often ran short. "So each individual learned to save his own food and water," another regroupee later said. "The farther along we got, the worse the hunger we faced. As food grew scarcer, comradeship broke down. People became more and more intent on saving their own lives."[40]

Yet the infiltration continued, and the pace gradually quickened. Simultaneously, Hanoi moved to give organizational structure to the new politico-military struggle, a process culminating in the founding in late 1960 of the National Front for the Liberation of South Vietnam or, for short, the National Liberation Front (NLF). Modeled on the Viet Minh, the NLF would seek to be a broad-based organization led by Communists but designed to rally all those disaffected by Diem by promising sweeping reforms and the establishment of genuine independence.[41] Militarily, the scattered forces in the south were brought together into a new People's Liberation Armed Forces (PLAF). Like the Viet Minh armed forces in the French war, the PLAF was given a hierarchical structure, with local self-defense units operating at the village level, guerrilla forces under regional command, and regulars directed from southern headquarters. Overall direction would be provided by a Central Office for South Vietnam (COSVN), which in turn would report to the Central Committee in Hanoi. The political apparatus, meanwhile, would closely resemble that of the Diem government, with officers at hamlet, village, district, and provincial levels, and numerous organizations designed to draw as many people as possible into the cause.[42]

V

IN THE MINDS OF SOUTHERN INSURGENT COMMANDERS, HANOI'S move to step up its involvement in the south came not a moment too soon. For simultaneously, the Diem government had opted to escalate its efforts to crush the revolutionary movement through a new draconian directive known as 10/59. Passed in May 1959, Decree 10/59 restored the French guillotine to Vietnam and gave the regime vast new repressive powers by widening the scope of political crimes to include virtually all forms of political opposition. Within three days of a charge, a special roving court could sentence to death "whoever commits or attempts to commit . . . crimes with the aim of sabotage, or of infringing upon the security of the State," as well as "whoever belongs to an organization designed to help or to perpetuate [these] crimes." There would be no right of appeal. The number of arrests skyrocketed as local officials, aided by the roving tribunals, arbitrarily consigned opponents of all kinds to life in prison or death—or used the threat of conviction as a lever by which to extract bribes from a frightened populace.[43]

The 10/59 law was effective as a tactic of intimidation, but like so many of Diem's policies it also boomeranged, dealing a heavy blow against whatever progress the regime had made in legitimating its claim to rule. In many parts of South Vietnam, the decree gave fuel to the insurgency. "Thanks to the 10/59 decree," said a poor peasant in My Tho province who had been largely unconnected to the revolution before then, "new life was blown into the political movement, and a patriotic appeal was made to overthrow the government of Mr. Diem because this government was killing people like that, so it led to another war and renewed fighting."[44]

In other areas too, government attempts to thwart the Communist challenge faltered. In 1959, Diem undertook to relocate lowland-dwelling peasants in fortified "agrovilles" where they could be kept isolated from what Saigon officials now derisively called the "Viet Cong" (Vietnamese Communists). In theory, these fortified concentrations were designed to be self-sustaining and to provide a range of social services for their inhabitants. In practice, the promised amenities seldom materialized. Even worse, the measure required peasants to leave their old homes, with their family tombs and gardens and groves, for a barren plot of land in an unfamiliar place. Government financial assistance was minimal—about five dollars plus a small loan to help pay for the acre and a half of land that each farmer received. Though only a fraction of the half million peasants initially targeted for the program ultimately participated, the agrovilles became for many peasants an enduring symbol of their hatred for the South Vietnamese regime. Or as the *Pentagon Papers* chronicler would later put it, the relocations "catalyzed the most widespread and dangerous anti-GVN sentiment."[45]

Many in the countryside had no love for either side in the conflict and sought only to steer clear of trouble. This did not mean, though, that villagers were necessarily politically equidistant from the government and the revolutionaries. As political scientist David Elliott writes of My Tho province in this period, "a probable majority of the villagers were seething with indignation against the GVN and its local officials," even if they were afraid to show their anger in a rapidly evolving situation. "At the time," Elliott quotes a peasant as saying, "the people were outwardly deferential to the government, but inwardly they didn't respect it. Their outward deference was based on fear of imprisonment and death. They were really scared, but they still protected the cadres."[46]

In Ben Tre province in the southern Mekong Delta, a Viet Minh stronghold during the French war, Diem's campaign to stamp out all Communist influence had by one measure been phenomenally successful: In the period 1954–59, some 90 percent of cadres in Ben Tre were killed or thrown in jail. But the revolutionary forces in the province did not completely disappear, and in 1959, led by Nguyen Thi Dinh, a widow whose husband had died in the notorious French island prison in Paolo Condore in 1938, they gained rapidly in popular support.[47] Madame Dinh organized protests and instructed women on how to confront government troops. She taught them the signals for when to disperse and when to stand their ground in the village square. She pleaded for weapons and, when told none were available, proceeded anyway with plans to stage an uprising in the province. Launched in January 1960, this carefully coordinated series of insurrections achieved considerable success, as insurgents seized isolated posts and captured local leaders. Some of the officials were executed; others were set free after being warned. Cadres also infiltrated the agroville at Thanh Thoi and destroyed it with the assistance of villagers who had been relocated there. In several districts, land held by "reactionary landlords" was seized and redistributed to poor peasants. Diem responded with a show of force, and ARVN forces succeeded in regaining control, but at considerable expense and loss of life.[48]

"The forces encircling the posts had been ordered to burn down any posts they captured," Madame Dinh later said of the assaults on a government-held village. "The people immediately tore up the flags, and burned the plaques bearing their house numbers and family registers. On the roads, the villagers cut down trees to erect barriers and block the movement of the enemy. . . . All the posts were surrounded by the people who made appeals to the soldiers through bullhorns. . . . It was a night of terrifying thunder and lightning striking the enemy on their heads. Attacked by surprise, they were scared out of their wits and stayed put in the posts."[49]

Some American observers insouciantly dismissed the growing unrest as inconsequential, as of no real importance when set against the larger picture of South Vietnamese stability and growth. In early 1959, for example, the newly retired director of the U.S. aid program in Saigon gave a glowing report of the progress achieved since 1954 and pronounced the current situation "good." On July 7, the fifth anniversary of Diem's ascension to power, *The New York Times* gushed: "A five-year miracle, not a 'plan,' has been carried out. Vietnam is free and becoming stronger in defense of its freedom and of ours. There is reason, today, to salute President Ngo Dinh Diem."[50]

At MAAG headquarters too, senior officers continued to insist that the picture was bright. Like their French predecessors in 1953, who stubbornly insisted that their forces "controlled" the Red River Delta inside the perimeter of the De Lattre Line, U.S. commanders used the absence of direct challenge against main ARVN forces in many areas of the south as proof that those forces were "in control." Like the French before them, these American generals were not, as Bernard Fall would put it, "technically or psychologically geared to evaluate the far subtler challenges presented by revolutionary war."[51] When the ARVN stepped up sweep operations in the second half of 1959, inflicting heavy losses in lives and property to the peasants, thus increasing their resentment of the regime, it did so with full U.S. endorsement and support.

VI

SOME AMERICAN ANALYSTS, HOWEVER, DID PERCEIVE THE NATURE of the threats. Almost to a person, they didn't like the trend lines. Wolf Ladejinsky, who still believed in the South Vietnamese experiment and in the importance of maintaining a robust American assistance program, was despondent after senior Saigon officials told him that Diem was relying far too much on military methods to defeat the Viet Cong. When these men tried to persuade Diem of the importance of winning the active support of the peasantry, he offered that same reply he always gave to such pleas: that military security must come first.

Ambassador Durbrow, after listening to Ladejinsky recap the conversation, voiced his own fear that the Communists would exploit the growing disaffection in the rural areas to intensify opposition to the government. But the problems went beyond the countryside. To Durbrow it was increasingly apparent that Diem was losing the confidence of urban intellectuals as well as administrative and business leaders. Even those who owed their positions to the regime and professed personal loyalty to Diem chafed at the restrictions on press freedom as well as the administrative inefficiency and widespread nepotism and corruption.

But Durbrow saw little point in arguing for a change in U.S. policy. The Operations Coordinating Board (OCB), created by Eisenhower early in his tenure to bring together national security views across a range of agencies and therefore a good barometer of midlevel official attitudes, announced gravely in early 1959 that the Communists had begun a "carefully planned campaign of violence" against Diem using tactics employed with success against the French. The OCB further reported increased dissatisfaction, within the South Vietnamese military and government, with Diem's repressive leadership and the stifling power of his family. What could the United States do? Precious little, the OCB concluded. Washington's influence remained "greatly limited" due to Diem's "extreme sensitivity."[52]

The characterization was apt. As the decade drew a close, American leverage with Diem, not high to begin with, had declined further. Try as U.S. officials might to get him to broaden his government, to show more sensitivity to the needs of his people, to show greater tolerance for the expression of political opposition, they got nowhere. Instead Diem, his utter confidence in his own political instincts wholly unimpaired, turned increasingly inward, relying almost exclusively on an ever-shrinking circle of confidants headed by his brother Ngo Dinh Nhu. More than ever, personal loyalty, rather than ability and efficiency, became the criterion for promotion and reward. More than ever, Catholics were favored. And more than ever, Diem and Nhu regarded the formal apparatus of Western-style democracy—such as giving greater authority to the National Assembly and allowing it to be a forum for substantive debate—as a dangerous distraction that would do little but give voice to dangerous political opponents among the urban elite.[53]

The Americans did not understand this danger, the brothers allowed, but then Americans were naïve and softhearted, lacking maturity in world affairs and a deep grasp of Vietnamese realities. Nhu in particular argued this line. Disdainful, like many French-educated Vietnamese intellectuals, of the brash Anglo-Saxons, he contemptuously told an ARVN officer that the French might have been the colonial masters, but at least they understood Vietnam, whereas the United States "helps us with a lot of money but doesn't know anything about Vietnamese affairs."[54]

It bothered the brothers no end that they had been pinned with the *My-Diem* "puppet" tag. They hated relying so heavily on U.S. assistance, hated what this dependence did to their nationalist credentials and their freedom of maneuver. But though they would try at all times to maintain maximum autonomy, they knew there could be no question of severing the tie. "If you bring in the American dog," Diem told a reporter, "you must accept American fleas."[55]

CIA officers and embassy personnel in Saigon were well aware of this creeping anti-Americanism infesting the House of the Ngos, and it frustrated them. Behind closed doors, they returned the favor with a few choice words of their own, especially for the vain and arrogant Nhu, who demanded continued U.S. aid on a massive scale even as he gave Washington the proverbial one-finger salute. But they could do no more than quietly grumble. They knew what Diem knew: that the United States, determined to maintain a non-Communist bastion in southern Vietnam and seeing no plausible leadership alternative anywhere on the scene, needed Diem at least as much as he needed the United States. In the perpetual contest of wills, between stopping the American assistance or enacting comprehensive reforms, Diem won easily, just as he always had (apart from a moment's wavering at the height of the sect crisis in 1955).

And so, America's Vietnam planners chose once again to travel that familiar and easy and well-trod course: the course of least immediate resistance. They had opted to forge ahead and hope for the best, rather than face the unpleasant task of initiating a fundamental change in policy. This had been the pattern under Harry Truman, and it had continued through Dwight Eisenhower's two terms. Never blind to the obstacles standing in their way, U.S. decision makers through the decade of the 1950s stayed firm in their commitment to thwart Ho Chi Minh's revolutionary ambitions. Even if the odds for success were long, it was always safer, easier—in domestic political as well as geopolitical terms—to soldier on, to muddle through, especially given that for America the superpower colossus, the Saigon commitment remained small, in both material and manpower terms. Diem, for all his deficiencies, had beaten the odds before; perhaps he could do so again.

Eisenhower has been praised by some historians for his prudence in keeping the United States out of the Indochina quagmire. But this analysis largely conflates his overall restraint in foreign policy—including in the broader Cold War—with his more aggressive approach to crises in the Third World, including in Vietnam. In 1954, he and Dulles were prepared to intervene directly to save the French position in the Indochina War, and came close to doing so; in the years thereafter, they gambled that they could build a new state in southern Vietnam with a mercurial and unproven leader. As the Saigon government skidded and careened down treacherous roads in the late 1950s, Eisenhower, his attention mostly on other foreign policy concerns and his trusted Dulles no longer by his side as of early 1959, ordered no reevaluation, even though an insurgency was under way in South Vietnam and even though Diem continued business as usual, rejecting all calls to enact far-reaching reforms and insisting on framing the problem as primarily military in nature.

698 | EMBERS OF WAR

As the Viet Cong attacks increased in frequency and intensity, Eisenhower indeed deepened U.S. military involvement in a way that had extremely important implications for the future. In mid-1959, the White House authorized American advisers to accompany South Vietnamese Army battalions on operational missions to offer combat guidance. Though the advisers were still forbidden to enter "actual combat," the change was highly significant—hitherto they had been confined to corps and division headquarters, training commands, and logistic agencies and had been obligated to remain behind whenever their units were on patrol. Now they would be in the field, in harm's way, their "advising" duties greatly expanded.

And still the challenges only mounted. Already in April 1959, before infiltration from the North had even begun, the CIA could report that the Viet Cong had achieved de facto control over much of Ca Mau in the far south. By the end of the year, sizable areas of South Vietnam—including some very close to Saigon—were under Communist control. "If you drew a paint brush across the South," an intelligence agent told Senator Mansfield at the time, "every hair of the brush would touch [an insurgent]."[56] The Viet Cong campaign of assassination, targeting village leaders and other notables, picked up pace in 1960, yielding more than two hundred monthly killings in February, March, and April, and a total for the year of more than sixteen hundred. The Central Highlands, hitherto firmly in government hands, was more and more up for grabs. That November, Diem barely quashed a coup attempt by disaffected ARVN generals upset by his cronyism and his management of the war effort.

The Joint Chiefs of Staff, in belated acknowledgment that the principal and most immediate security threat came not from the North Vietnamese military but from the southern insurgency, now outlined a plan to fight an antiguerrilla, or counterinsurgency, war in the south. Finalized in late 1960, the strategy operated from several core assumptions, none of them new: that Diem's government at present offered "the best hope" for defeating the Viet Cong; that Diem in fact could cope with the Communist threat provided that "necessary corrective measures were taken"; and that the United States had a vital stake in helping to eradicate the insurgency. The plan provided for an increase in the size of the South Vietnamese Army and the Civil Guard, to be financed mostly by Washington. In return for this assistance, the Saigon regime would implement a series of measures designed to achieve and maintain economic and political stability and thereby win the hearts and minds of the general population. Intelligence and counterintelligence operations would be better coordinated, and more resources would be devoted to psychological warfare and civic action programs. Overall, the scheme, which had White House support, gave continued priority to the military dimensions of the problem, much to the collective satisfaction of MAAG and the Ngo family.[57]

VII

THERE OCCURRED IN THAT FATEFUL YEAR OF 1959 ONE OTHER EVENT that, with the knowledge of what was to come, perhaps looms largest of all.

In the early evening of July 8, eight American advisers stationed at a camp serving the South Vietnamese Seventh Infantry Division near Bien Hoa, twenty miles north of Saigon, gathered for dinner in the usual fashion. Earlier that afternoon, Master Sergeant Chester Ovnand, forty-four, had finished a letter to his wife in Copperas Cove, Texas, and dropped it in the mess hall mailbox. Ovnand had just about completed his tour of duty and was looking forward to returning home. Major Dale Buis of Imperial Beach, California, age thirty-eight, had arrived in Bien Hoa just two days before and during the afternoon had shown his new colleagues pictures of his three young sons. Tall and strong, Buis had played high school football and was known around the camp as a good-humored prankster.

The quarters were situated about a hundred yards from a river, in a grassy meadow ringed by a simple two-strand barbed-wire fence. On duty in front of the building were two South Vietnamese Army guards, who faced a road on the side away from the river. As the dishes were cleared, two of the officers drifted away to play tennis, while the others settled in to watch a movie, *The Tattered Dress* starring Jeanne Crain. At previous film screenings, the guards had been known to leave their posts to view the film through the windows of the gray stucco dining hall, a fact no doubt duly noted by the two Vietnamese women from the nearby town who usually attended but were not present this time (and who were later alleged to be Viet Cong agents).

At some point after the opening credits rolled, six Viet Cong guerrillas crept up from the river and slipped through the fence undetected. Two edged to the front of the building to cover the guards, two positioned a French-made submachine gun in the mess hall's rear window, and two placed their gun muzzles against the pantry screen. When Ovnand snapped on the lights to change reels, the guerrillas opened fire. Ovnand and Buis were hit and died within minutes, the former after crawling up a flight of stairs. Captain Howard Boston of Blairsburg, Iowa, was seriously wounded but survived. One of the guards was killed, as were a Vietnamese cook and his eight-year-old son. The others in the room might have met the same fate, had not Major Jack Hellet of Baton Rouge, Louisiana, leaped across the room to turn out the lights—and had not one of the guerrillas mishandled a homemade bomb (two milk cans filled with explosive and welded together) and blown himself up. Within minutes, Vietnamese troops arrived, but the remaining attackers had gotten away.[58]

Ovnand's wife, Mildred, was sipping coffee and watching NBC's *Today* show in her small brick Texas home when she got the first inkling of her husband's death. The show's correspondent announced that two U.S. servicemen had been killed outside Saigon. Soon thereafter the phone rang. "I heard a man say, 'I'm with the AP in Dallas,'" she recalled years later. "When did you first hear about your husband?"[59]

In Imperial Beach, eight-year-old Kurt Buis was darting about the house with his brothers, six and four, when the word arrived. "I only knew something awful had happened," he said later. "A doctor came and gave my mother a sedative." Then an aunt arrived and took the boys for a drive to give them the news.[60]

Ovnand and Buis were not the first Americans to die by hostile fire in Vietnam. Peter Dewey of the Office of Strategic Services had been killed by the Viet Minh in September 1945, it will be recalled, and pilots James McGovern and Wallace Buford were shot down after delivering supplies to the besieged French post at Dien Bien Phu in May 1954. But Ovnand and Buis were the first to be killed in the Second Indochina War—or, in the official American euphemism for an undeclared war, the Vietnam

Era. Theirs are the first two names on the Vietnam Veterans Memorial in Washington, at the apex, on Panel 1E, Row 1, directly below the large engraved "1959."[61]

U.S. military officers and intelligence analysts in Saigon suspected immediately that the Bien Hoa attack exemplified an important transition in the conflict, from the serious yet irregular and piecemeal actions by the Viet Cong during the previous two years to a program of sustained and carefully coordinated terrorism and military action that would gain in intensity and size in the months and years to come. And so indeed it would be. A new chapter in the struggle for Vietnam had begun.[62]

But in the United States, the event passed by largely unremarked, a seemingly minor incident in a faraway land. *Time* published a short three-paragraph account written by a newly arrived young reporter, Stanley Karnow, and there were brief mentions also in a few newspapers and on the *Today* show. That was all. The White House stayed silent, and few on Capitol Hill took notice.[63]

No one knew then, in the summer of 1959, that Bien Hoa would in a few years become a gigantic American base, complete with a seedy strip of brothels and bars. And no one knew then that Chester Ovnand and Dale Buis were merely the first of more than 58,000 Americans whose names would be etched on that stark and moving monument in the nation's capital, its black granite walls gradually sunken within a gentle slope, within sight of the Lincoln Memorial.

DIFFERENT DREAMS, SAME FOOTSTEPS

O N JANUARY 20, 1961, JOHN F. KENNEDY TOOK THE OATH OF OFFICE as the thirty-fifth president of the United States. He was forty-three, the youngest man ever elected to the job. During the campaign, Kennedy had criticized Eisenhower's foreign policy as unimaginative and stuck in the past, and once in office he surrounded himself with mostly young advisers of intellectual verve and sparkling résumés, who proclaimed they had fresh ideas for invigorating the nation. On Vietnam, however, as on most policy issues, continuity was the watchword in the early months. The Kennedy team, no doubt mindful of the fact that they had come in with the slimmest electoral majority of the twentieth century, undertook no wide-ranging discussion of the involvement they had inherited in Southeast Asia, no comprehensive review of options, no major analysis of the struggle's importance to American national security. A White House aide of the time, when asked years later how the U.S. interest in Vietnam was defined in 1961, answered that "it was simply a given, assumed and unquestioned." The given was that Ho Chi Minh could not be allowed to prevail in Vietnam, that the Saigon government must survive, that failure to thwart the Communists here would only make the task harder next time.[1]

The continuity was to be expected, of course. It's the way of Washington, not least in the area of diplomacy and statecraft. A new administration comes to power, with so much to learn, so much to do, so many powerful constituencies to accommodate. Invariably, staying the course looks prudent and sensible, especially on second-tier policy issues that are not at the forefront of popular consciousness. At least for now. Later, when things have settled down a bit and everyone's had a chance to read and digest the briefing papers, there will be ample time to reconsider options.

But Kennedy, more than most national political figures of the time, might have gone against the grain and ordered a full-scale review of Vietnam policy. For a decade, he had taken a special interest in the struggle there, and he was more informed about the issues on the ground than virtually any senior Democrat in Washington. More interesting, Kennedy had long shown a capacity for nuanced and independent thought on international affairs, not least on the Indochina conflict. Already in the autumn of 1951, during his visit to Vietnam, he had seen through the French expressions of optimism and bravado and voiced trenchant doubts about the ability of Paris—or, by extension, any outside force—to overcome Ho Chi Minh's nationalist cause. To act "apart from and in defiance of innately nationalistic aims spells foredoomed failure," JFK told a Boston audience a few days after returning home that fall, adding that a free election would in all likelihood go in favor of Ho and the Communists.[2]

Later in the decade, Kennedy moved closer to Cold War orthodoxy, as we have seen. He now spoke less and less of "nationalistic aims" and the French analogy and more of falling dominoes and the urgent need to thwart Communist aggression. But the skepticism did not go away; it was always there, just under the surface. Sometimes he expressed it openly, as in 1957, when he went well beyond official U.S. policy in supporting Algeria in her war of independence against France. "The most powerful single force in the world today," JFK declared in a Senate speech on the North African crisis that summer, "is neither communism nor capitalism, neither the H-bomb nor the guided missile—it is man's eternal desire to be free and independent." Washington must respond effectively to this hunger, he went on, which meant urging Paris to pursue negotiations leading to Algerian independence.[3] Both before and after becoming president, Kennedy showed an appreciation for the vicissitudes of history and—increasingly, as time wore on—for the limits of American power. From time to time, he expressed doubts about the ability of the West to use military means to solve Asian problems that were at root political in nature; on several occasions, and notably in the fall of 1961, he resisted aides' calls for committing U.S. ground forces to Vietnam. He also deflected the departing Eisenhower's urgings that he intervene militarily in

Laos ("the key to the entire area of Southeast Asia," Ike insisted), where the anti-Communist position had eroded significantly over the previous two years and where the DRV-supported Pathet Lao now seemed on the cusp of victory. And always the French experience gnawed at him, as when he confided to an aide, early in his presidency, "If [Vietnam] were ever converted into a white man's war, we would lose it as the French had lost a decade earlier."[4]

A commitment had been made, however, and Kennedy maintained it, as Richard Nixon, his Republican opponent in 1960, surely would have done had he won the election. Publicly, JFK and his aides voiced full-throated support for the Saigon regime and gave every indication that achieving victory in Vietnam was crucial to American interests. More than that, over the first year, as the Saigon government's problems steadily deepened and the insurgency grew stronger, and while the president resisted options for even faster escalation, they dramatically increased the U.S. military commitment. Already in May 1961, Kennedy reported to Congress that four thousand local officials had been killed in South Vietnam in the previous year alone. In 1962, vast quantities of the best American weapons, jet fighters, helicopters, and armored personnel carriers arrived, along with thousands of additional military advisers. That year a full field command bearing the acronym MACV (Military Assistance Command Vietnam) superseded MAAG (Military Assistance Advisory Group) with a three-star general, Paul D. Harkins, in command.

A secret U.S. war was under way. Ostensibly, Americans were serving purely as advisers and never engaging the Viet Cong except in self-defense; in reality, their involvement extended further—in the air as well as on the ground. "I'd heard stories that U.S. pilots were actually dropping bombs," Associated Press bureau chief Malcolm Browne, who arrived in the fall of 1961, later recalled, so "I went out to Bien Hoa, the biggest military airfield in South Vietnam, to have a look. I was barred from entering but I watched from outside the perimeter fence and saw two-seat T-28s taking off with full racks of bombs. When they returned, I could see that their racks were empty and there were smoke stains behind the guns. As often as not, a Vietnamese was sitting in the back and the actual pilot was blond and blue-eyed and obviously not from Vietnam. By reporting that, I was threatened with expulsion. The official American line was that the U.S. role in Vietnam was subordinate to that of our Vietnamese ally."[5]

The truth was plain to see. Homer Bigart, the venerable military correspondent of *The New York Times,* minced no words in a front-page article in February 1962. "The United States is involved in a war in Vietnam," the piece began. "American troops will stay until victory." Bigart noted the "passionate and inflexible" U.S. support for South Vietnamese president Ngo Dinh Diem and speculated that the United States "seems inextricably committed to a long, inconclusive war." He quoted Attorney General Robert F. Kennedy, who on a visit to Saigon that month vowed that America would stand by Diem "until we win."[6]

Never mind that a principal stated rationale for the containment policy in Asia, namely the need to check a worldwide Communist expansionist conspiracy directed from Moscow, demonstrably no longer pertained, if it ever had. For years, evidence had accumulated of a Sino-Soviet split; by 1960, Soviet economic and military assistance to China had ceased, Soviet technicians had been withdrawn, the ideological war of words between Moscow and Beijing had become intense, and international Communism had become fragmented. U.S. intelligence analysts were well aware of these developments, yet at the highest levels, officials made few adjustments. In January 1962, the Joint Chiefs of Staff warned Secretary of Defense Robert McNamara of the strategic advantages that could accrue to the "Sino-Soviet bloc" if the United States did not deepen her involvement in Indochina.[7]

By mid-1962, American military advisers in Vietnam numbered 8,000, by the end of the year over 11,000, and by the time of Kennedy's assassination in Dallas in November 1963, almost 16,000. Just three weeks before the Dallas tragedy, Ngo Dinh Diem had himself been murdered along with his brother Nhu, after a U.S.-sanctioned coup d'état by dissident generals. The coup followed months of widespread anti-government agitation in urban as well as rural areas. Notably, Buddhist monks protesting the Roman Catholic Diem's religious persecution poured gasoline over their robes and ignited themselves in the streets of Saigon. Intellectuals stepped up their long-standing complaints about government corruption and Diem's penchant for concentrating power in the hands of family members, and they condemned his policy of jailing critics to silence them. Kennedy and his aides vacillated before determining that Diem and the influential Nhu should go.

In 1964, under President Lyndon B. Johnson, the number of military advisers grew to 23,000, and Congress voted to authorize the president to use military force as he saw fit in Southeast Asia. The vote came after U.S. destroyers, operating in the Gulf of Tonkin, off the coast of North Vietnam, twice within three days reported coming under attack from North Vietnamese patrol boats. Many senior Democrats—including the entire Senate leadership on foreign policy—expressed misgivings about a deepening American involvement in the war, but they were not about to defy their president in an election year and with U.S. troops in harm's way. Despite a lack of evidence that the second attack had occurred, Johnson ordered retaliatory air strikes against selected North Vietnamese patrol boat bases and an oil depot.[8]

The aid and advisers helped, but not enough to achieve American purposes. Political turmoil was endemic in Saigon, no less after Diem's ouster than before. The string of governments that followed his fall continued to suffer from infighting and lack of broad popular support. Militarily too, the Viet Cong scored steady gains, despite the inferiority of their weaponry and training. A pattern repeated itself. The Viet Cong, like their Viet Minh forerunners, liked to operate at night and in the bush; the Army of the Republic of Vietnam (ARVN), with its formidable U.S.-supplied firepower, was afraid of the darkness and the jungle, just as the French Union forces had been. At twilight, the enemy took over. Virtually no ARVN officers had fought on the side of the Viet Minh in the earlier struggle; most, indeed, had served under the French. A clear majority were from privileged backgrounds, well-to-do, urban, disdainful of the peasantry that still made up the vast bulk of the Vietnamese populace.

Journalist Theodore White offered a sobering assessment in a letter to his friend John F. Kennedy, describing a scene eerily reminiscent of that which pertained during JFK's visit a decade earlier: "The situation gets steadily worse almost week by week. . . . Guerrillas now control almost all the Southern delta—so much that I could find no American who would drive me outside Saigon in his car even by day without military convoy. . . . What perplexes the hell out of me is that the Commies, on their side, seem able to find people willing to die for their cause."[9]

For true believers on the American side, the problems were all surmountable, and there could be no thought of turning back. Edward Lansdale, whose role in U.S. policy making on Vietnam had dwindled in the second half of the 1950s, reemerged early in the Kennedy years to argue for a robust prosecution of the war *and* for the need to be sensitive to local Vietnamese needs and mores. His faith in the precepts of counterinsurgency was undiminished and uncomplicated, never mind that previous attempts at such warfare—including by the French, in this very place—had yielded meager results. "Just remember this," he told a group of U.S. military officers in 1962, with perfect matter-of-fact simplicity. "Communist guerrillas hide among the people. If you win the people over to your side, the Communist guerrillas have no place to hide, and you can find them. Then, as military men, fix them . . . finish them!"[10]

For Lansdale and others of like mind, the French experience was largely irrelevant to America's concerns. France, after all, had been fighting a colonial war; the United States would be fighting one of popular opposition to Communism. She would represent the Third Force, neither Communist nor colonialist. Furthermore, the French had lacked military strength and sophistication, shackled as they were by their humiliating defeat in 1940 and their dependence on African colonial units and the German-dominated Foreign Legion, devious and narrow of vision. The United States, on the other hand, was honest and selfless and massively powerful, not least in political terms. Untainted by colonialism, possessor of the mightiest arsenal the world had ever seen, she was the champion of freedom, the engine in the global drive to stamp out rapacious Communist expansion. On the human side, the French experience with the cupidity and the fence-sitting *attentisme* of their Vietnamese collaborators would not repeat itself, Lansdale willed himself to believe (the evidence from the late 1950s might have given him pause), because this time the Vietnamese truly had something to fight for.

And besides, hadn't the British shown in Malaya that Communist insurgencies could be defeated? The so-called Emergency, which had been proclaimed in 1948 and was declared finished in 1960, when the British defeated the Communist Malayan National Liberation Army (MNLA), seemed to offer lessons that could be applied to the revolutionary situation in Vietnam. Or so it appeared—when pressed, Lansdale had to concede the particular advantages the British enjoyed in Malaya, beginning with the fact that the guerrillas were almost all ethnic Chinese, isolated from the bulk of the population; few Malays joined the movement. They also faced chronic and debilitating food shortages and, unlike the Viet Minh and now the Viet Cong, they did not have the benefit of neighboring sanctuaries or powerful outside patrons. Finally, the MNLA always had to cope with a colossal inferiority in numbers—perhaps as high as 35 to 1 (300,000 men under arms versus 8,000 guerrillas), as compared to a ratio of no better than 1.5 to 1 during the Franco–Viet Minh War.[11]

Other observers, seeing the parallels between the French war and this new American one, and sensing the dangers of innocence in a difficult and complex society such as Vietnam, found themselves thinking more and more of that fictional Lansdale, Alden Pyle. "We used to sit in the small French cafés [in Saigon] and talk about Greene's book," journalist David Halberstam—whose captivating, sprawling *The Best and the Brightest* remains an essential source on America's war—later recalled of himself and other reporters covering the early 1960s buildup. "It seemed at that time . . . the best novel about Vietnam. There was little disagreement about his fine sense of the tropics, his knowledge of the war, his intuition of the Vietnamese toughness and resilience, particularly of the peasant and the enemy." Only one element, Halberstam went on, raised reservations: "It was only his portrait of the sinister innocence of the American that caused some doubt, that made us a little uneasy." The public affairs officer at the U.S. embassy, Halberstam added, was particularly bitter about Greene's novel: "He called it an evil book, made worse, he said, because it was so effective, so slick."[12]

The "innocence" notion should not be exaggerated. By the early months of 1963, if not before, a bleak realism permeated much U.S. official analysis about the war's prospects, at least behind closed doors. In the intelligence community, pessimism was now the order of the day, and apprehension was also growing in Congress, even on the part of former Diem stalwarts such as Senate majority leader Mike Mansfield. Kennedy too grew increasingly wary, hinting to aides in the final months of his life that he wanted to withdraw from Vietnam following his reelection in 1964.[13] Johnson, for his part, in 1964 began to question the long-term prospects in the struggle, even with major American escalation, and to wonder about the war's ultimate importance to U.S. national security. In September, for example, he said of the hapless Saigon leaders: "I mean, if they can't protect themselves, if you have a government that can't protect itself from kids in the streets, what the hell can you do about an invading army?" A few months after that, LBJ dejectedly noted that "a man can fight if he can see daylight down the road somewhere. But there ain't no daylight in Vietnam, there's not a bit."[14]

But like his predecessor, Johnson was careful to articulate these sentiments only privately and even then only to a select few. In public, he and his top advisers—all of them holdovers from Kennedy—stuck close to the received wisdom, insisting that the outcome in Southeast Asia was critically important to American interests and that they were committed to defending their Saigon ally against aggression "imposed from the outside." Whatever problems might be hampering the war effort would be overcome in due course. And whatever the price of victory, the cost of defeat would be far greater. The sentiments, sometimes the very rhetoric, echoed that of their Paris counterparts a decade before. And by using such unambiguous language in public, U.S. leaders found—again like the French before them—that backing away could be extremely difficult. Hawks, they knew, stood ready to remind them of their stark words should they so much as hint at a change in course. By their categorical public pronouncements, that is to say, as well as by their escalatory actions, both American presidents painted themselves into a corner.

It mattered here that Kennedy's and Johnson's freedom of maneuver was already constrained by the choices of their predecessors—by Truman's tacit acknowledgment in 1945–46 that France had a right to return to Indochina; by his administration's decision in 1950 to actively aid the French war effort; and by the Eisenhower team's move in 1954 to intervene directly in southern Vietnam, displacing France as the major external power. LBJ had the added burden of Kennedy's expansion of U.S. involvement in 1961–63. For more than a dozen years, the United States had committed herself to preserving a non-Communist toehold in Vietnam, and both men feared that to alter course now, even under the cover of a fig-leaf negotiated settlement, could be harmful in terms of "credibility"—their country's, their party's, their own. They weren't willing to risk it. If this stance speaks poorly for their political courage, it also had political logic behind it. Then again, so did the skeptics' reply: that the credibility would suffer much more if America got sucked into a bloody and drawn-out slugfest—as seemed all too possible—in a conflict of peripheral strategic import in forbidding terrain seven thousand miles from the coast of California.

The skeptics had been there all along, since before the shooting started. During World War II, Franklin Roosevelt was their champion, and it's not fanciful to believe that had he lived beyond 1945, FDR would have tried to keep France from forcibly reclaiming control of Indochina, and might well have succeeded, thereby changing the flow of history. But Roosevelt died, and soon thereafter patterns of thought were laid down that would drive U.S. policy for the next twenty years. American leaders in this era always had real choices about which way to go in the anti–Ho Chi Minh struggle, choices evident not only in retrospect but also at the time, yet the policy always moved in the direction of deeper U.S. involvement. Successive administrations could have shifted course, but they never did. Hence the danger in focusing exclusively on contingency: It can blind us to the continuities that permeate the entire American experience in Vietnam. And hence the vital importance, if we are to understand the U.S. war, of reckoning seriously with the earlier era.[15]

Ultimately, Kennedy and Johnson found what their predecessors in the White House as well as a long line of leaders in the French Fourth Republic had found: that in Vietnam, the path of least immediate resistance, especially in domestic political terms, was to stand firm, to maintain the commitment, and to press on, in the hope that somehow things would turn out fine (or at least be bequeathed to a successor). As Democrats, JFK and LBJ felt the need to contend with the ghosts of McCarthy and the charge that they were "soft on Communism." Truman too, as we have seen, acted partly with this concern in mind, as indeed did Eisenhower—his monumentally important decisions of 1953–54 cannot be understood apart from the charged domestic political atmosphere in which they were made. But the perceived power of this political imperative was even greater in the early 1960s, as the two presidents, feeling the vulnerability that all Democrats felt in the period, sought to avoid a repeat of the "Who lost China?" debate, this time over Vietnam. This concern was seldom discussed in the major magazine and newspaper articles that examined decision making on Vietnam, and it is hardly mentioned in the vast documentary record. It was so self-evident that it hardly, or rarely, needed to be voiced.[16]

In North Vietnam as well, policy makers affirmed their determination to achieve victory in the conflict, through escalation if necessary. Already in December 1963, in the aftermath of the Diem coup, Hanoi leaders decided to step up the fighting in the south, in the hopes that further deterioration would either cause the Americans to give up the fight and go home or leave them insufficient time to embark on a major escalation of their own. Ho Chi Minh, whose role in the party hierarchy had shifted in recent years away from day-to-day policy maker to that of elder statesman, urged his colleagues to seize on the "disorder" in South Vietnam and expand military as well as political pressure on the Saigon regime. Even if the United States should step up her role tenfold, Ho asserted, "we shall still be victorious."[17]

Yet having made this decision, North Vietnamese officials moved warily. General Vo Nguyen Giap, mastermind of the bruising victory over France and a figure of immense prestige in the leadership, warned his colleagues that the United States represented a military test of monumental proportions; he urged caution until the People's Army of Vietnam had been properly trained and equipped with modern weapons. Not everyone in the Politburo embraced this message, but they also had to contend with the counsels of restraint emanating from Moscow and, to a lesser extent, Beijing. Neither Communist patron was keen to see an Americanized war in Vietnam, one that could confront them with difficult choices and potentially bring them into direct contact with the U.S. Seventh Fleet. Their own bilateral relationship deeply fractious, each sought to keep the other from gaining too much influence in Hanoi. The Soviet Union in particular pressured North Vietnam to go slowly and to avoid provoking Washington. The North Vietnamese obliged, even as they used the final weeks of 1964 to step up the infiltration of men and matériel into the south. Said Premier Pham Van Dong, during a meeting with Mao Zedong in October 1964: "If the United States dares to start a [larger] war, we will fight it, and we will win it. But it would be better if it did not come to that."[18]

But come to that it did. In early December, after Johnson won a landslide election victory to become president in his own right (his refrain in the campaign: He sought no wider war and would not send American boys to fight a war that Asian boys should fight for themselves), he and his aides agreed on a two-phase escalation of the fighting. The first involved "armed reconnaissance strikes" against the Ho Chi Minh Trail infiltration routes in Laos, as well as retaliatory air strikes against North Vietnam in the event of a major Viet Cong attack. The second phase anticipated "graduated military pressure" against the north, in the form of aerial bombing, and almost certainly the dispatch of U.S. ground troops to the south. Phase one would begin as soon as possible; phase two would come later, after thirty days or more.

In February 1965, following Viet Cong attacks on American installations in South Vietnam that killed thirty-two Americans, Johnson ordered Operation Rolling Thunder, a bombing program planned the previous fall that continued, more or less uninterrupted, until October 1968. Then, on March 8, the first U.S. combat battalions came ashore near Da Nang. The North Vietnamese met the challenge. They hid in shelters and rebuilt roads and bridges with a tenaciousness that frustrated and awed American officials. They also increased infiltration into the south. Ho Chi Minh, convinced that Washington had committed too much prestige to Vietnam to back down, predicted to associates that Lyndon Johnson would come in with guns blazing but that it would not be enough. Like the French, the Americans would taste defeat in the end.[19]

Perhaps, for Ho, it had to come to this. He had always seen the United States as a principal player in Vietnam's drama, after all, ever since that June day in 1919 when he donned his rented morning coat and tried in vain to gain an audience with Woodrow Wilson at Versailles. Later, in the dizzying summer of 1945, Ho had again pleaded for U.S. backing, to no avail, a pattern that would repeat itself in 1946 and 1947, after the serious fighting began. Ultimately, his Democratic Republic of Vietnam had triumphed over France, but the price of victory had been immense, as Washington massively bolstered the enemy's war-making machine, enhancing its destructive capacity exponentially (as did the Chinese aid for the DRV, though to a lesser degree). Then at the moment of glorious success in 1954, the Americans, determined to maintain a non-Communist bastion in southern Vietnam, helped deny the Viet Minh the full fruits of victory as they set about creating and building up the Republic of [South] Vietnam.

"It will be a war between an elephant and a tiger," Ho had said back in 1946, of the war then about to commence. "If the tiger ever stands still the elephant will crush him with his mighty tusks. But the tiger does not stand still. He lurks in the jungle by day and emerges only at night. He will leap upon the back of the elephant, tearing huge chunks from his hide, and then he will leap back into the dark jungle. And slowly the elephant will bleed to death."[20]

This time the elephant would be even bigger. But the outcome, Ho vowed, would be the same.

In Paris, leaders reacted to these developments with shudders of recognition and a sense of déjà vu. They knew this script by heart. On March 18, 1965, President Charles de Gaulle, whose unwavering determination to reclaim Indochina for France at the end of World War II had done so much to start the bloodshed, and who had been summoned back to power in 1958 as his country struggled to defeat another insurgency, this one in Algeria, told his cabinet that major war was now inevitable. The Americans had failed to learn from France's example, he said, and the fighting "will last a long, long, long time." The following month de Gaulle offered a more precise estimate: Unless the Johnson administration moved to halt the war immediately, the struggle would go on for ten years and would completely dishonor the United States. When U.S. ambassador Charles Bohlen called on de Gaulle in early May, he found the French leader in a philosophical mood, accepting the wholesale escalation of the fighting with "oriental fatalism."[21]

Another Frenchman, long since transplanted to the United States, felt a gripping sense of foreboding as 1965 progressed. Bernard Fall, over the previous decade, had become America's most respected expert on the First Indochina War (as it was now called), the author of numerous books and articles notable for their informed and dispassionate analysis. (Many a U.S. officer got his first real appreciation of the complexity of the Vietnam struggle by reading Fall's *Street Without Joy: Indochina at War 1946–1954*, published in 1961.) Fall was less categorical than de Gaulle about America's prospects in Vietnam, and he rejected as "facile" (a favorite adjective) the casual way some critics of U.S. involvement invoked the French analogy. The United States in 1965, after all, was immensely more powerful than her Western ally had ever been, especially in the air. "Before Dien Bien Phu," Fall wrote late that year, "the French Air Force had for *all* of Indochina (i.e., Cambodia, Laos, and North and South Vietnam) a total of 112 fighters and 68 bombers. On Sept. 24, 1965, the United States flew 167 bombers against North Vietnamese targets alone, dropping 235 tons of bombs and *simultaneously* flew 317 bomber sorties 'in country' [South Vietnam], dropping 270 tons of bombs."[22]

Even as he made this comparison, however, Fall doubted it would make a decisive difference in the end. The unleashing of massive American firepower might make the war "militarily unlosable" in the short term, he wrote elsewhere that autumn, but at immense cost: the destruction of Vietnam. He quoted Tacitus: "They have made a desert, and called it peace." Even then Ho's Communists would not be vanquished, for in this conflict military prowess meant only so much—the war had to be won politically if it was to be won at all. This was the pivotal point about the French analogy, Fall maintained; this was the lesson that must be learned. But few in Washington seemed prepared to do so. Few seemed prepared to acknowledge the salient facts about counterinsurgency warfare that the French had learned the hard way: that results can be measured only over a period of many years; that success requires an effective host government that in the end can carry the burden on its own; and that notwithstanding counterinsurgency theory's emphasis on nonmilitary measures, massive and brutal firepower will invariably be used, resulting in the widespread killing of civilians and increasing local resentments. Decades later, in a new century, Americans were still struggling to come to grips with these realities.[23]

One wonders what Bernard Fall would have made of these later military interventions and the debates surrounding them: In 1967, he was killed while accompanying a U.S. Marine battalion in an operation near Hue. Certainly, this astonishingly prolific writer, had he lived, would have produced more important books and articles on the struggle for Vietnam, works that would have reached a wide audience and added enormously to Americans' collective knowledge. Not least, I'm guessing, Fall would have reminded us early and often that any serious effort at understanding America's Vietnam debacle must range beyond the period of heavy U.S. involvement, to the era that came before. For as Fall once said, Americans were "dreaming different dreams than the French but walking in the same footsteps."[24]

By the end of 1965, 180,000 U.S. troops were on the ground in South Vietnam. More were on the way.

ACKNOWLEDGMENTS

THIS BOOK HAS MY NAME ON THE COVER, BUT IT'S VERY MUCH A collective enterprise. I am deeply grateful to the authors whose books and articles I read and reread over the past decade, and on whose shoulders I stand. The same goes for archivists at repositories in several countries, who patiently showed me how to navigate their collections and responded with alacrity when I emailed or phoned with this or that follow-up query. I'm also forever indebted to three dear friends who read the entire manuscript and set me right about facts or interpretations, who pushed me when I needed pushing, and who provided succor at just the right time: Chris Goscha, Jim Hershberg, and Ken Mouré. I can't thank them enough. Other colleagues provided incisive critiques of individual chapters: Chen Jian, Will Hitchcock, Jack Langguth, Mark Lawrence, Tim Naftali, Andrew Preston, and John Thompson.

Many friends have been generous in sharing documents, and in notifying me of collections I needed to consult. Here I thank, in particular, Chen Jian, Chris Goscha, Matthew Jones, Merle Pribbenow, Priscilla Roberts, and Kevin Ruane. Merle Pribbenow also made a tremendous contribution by making available to me his translations of Vietnamese military documents, and by providing new translations seemingly instantaneously. During one memorable two-week stretch, it seemed that every time I opened my email there was a new document from Merle, pertaining to this or that military campaign we had been discussing.

George Herring and Ben Weber were delightful travel companions on a memorable visit to Dien Bien Phu, and I thank them for indulging my desire to traverse the area around Colonel de Castries's battlefield headquarters and the nearby strongpoints. Nor will I soon forget George's keen interest and superb input as he and I discussed my then-embryonic book project by the pool at the Metropole Hotel in Hanoi, or our harrowing trip to Phat Diem, in which our driver seemed determined to set a new land speed record between the two points and thought nothing of using both sides of the road to make it happen.

I owe a great debt to my many wonderful students at the University of California, Santa Barbara, and Cornell University, and in particular to a remarkable group of research assistants at the two institutions: George Fujii, Justin Granstein, Michael Mazza, and Kim Quinney. Samuel Hodges, at the time a Brown University junior, provided excellent help during a return visit to his hometown of Santa Barbara.

For their willingness to help in various ways, large and small, I thank Joanna Ain, Richard Aldrich, Arthur Bergeron, James Blight, Robert Brigham, Jessica Chapman, Jessy Chiorino, Campbell Craig, Craig Daigle, Philippe Devillers, William Duiker, Daniel Ellsberg, Dorothy Fall, Susan Ferber, Dominique Franche, Warren Frazier, Marc Gilbert, Pierre Grosser, Robert Hanyok, Tsuyoshi Hasegawa, Pembroke Herbert, Will Hitchcock, Pierre Journoud, Audrey Kahin, Walter LaFeber, Janet Lang, John Lee, William Loomis, Erez Manela, Zachary Matusheski, Glenn May, Anne Mensior, Edwin Moïse, Lien-Hang Nguyen, Andrew Preston, Priscilla Roberts, Kevin Ruane, Jennifer See, Jack Talbott, Keith Taylor, Martin Thomas, Stein Tønnesson, Trinh Quang Thanh, Thuy Tranviet, Hannah Stamler, Kathryn Statler, Vu Tuong, James Waite, Geoffrey Warner, Kenneth Weisbrode, Odd Arne Westad, George Wickes, Mark Wilson, Emoretta Yang, John Young, and the late Luu Doan Huynh and Jon Persoff. For expert work on the maps I thank Don Larson and his team at Mapping Specialists.

At a critical early point in the project, Mark Lawrence and I teamed up to organize an international conference on the Franco–Viet Minh War and to gather the papers from that meeting into an edited volume. Mark's role in the success of both endeavors was enormous, and I'm grateful as well to Betty Sue Flowers, then director of the Lyndon Baines Johnson

Library and Museum, for agreeing to host the conference and for enthusiastically backing what we were trying to do.

Much of this book was written during a marvelous sabbatical year in England. I thank the Leverhulme Trust for providing a generous fellowship, the University of Nottingham for giving me a perfect institutional home, and Matthew Jones for his key role in shepherding the Leverhulme nomination through. I'm also grateful to Tony Badger of Clare College, Cambridge, for securing a second affiliation for me that year, as a Mellon senior fellow at Cambridge.

At Random House I thank my editor, David Ebershoff, for his steadfast support and superb editing, and Clare Swanson and Loren Noveck for their excellent labors. Special thanks to Jason Epstein, who had the idea for a book on the early years in Vietnam and encouraged me to give close attention to the Second World War, and to Scott Moyers, my original editor, who has been a keen and unstinting supporter throughout. My literary agent, John Hawkins, did not live to see this work published, but I am eternally grateful to him for betting on me early and for providing sound counsel throughout.

I'm fortunate to be surrounded by wonderful colleagues at Cornell: in the History Department, the Southeast Asia Program, and at the Mario Einaudi Center for International Studies. Three Einaudi Center colleagues deserve to be singled out for their skillful and energetic support in the latter stages of this project: Nishi Dhupa, Elizabeth Edmondson, and Heike Michelsen. At Cornell I also received very helpful feedback from the History Department's Comparative History Colloquium and from the brown-bag seminar of the Judith Reppy Institute for Peace and Conflict Studies. Elsewhere, I benefited from trying out my ideas before learned audiences at the University of Cambridge, Harvard University, the University of Nottingham, and the l'Institut d'études internationales de Montréal.

My final and most important acknowledgments are to my family. My beloved parents have provided boundless support and encouragement for longer than I can remember and in more ways than I can convey. I'm also grateful to my sister and brother, who somehow knew when to ask how the book was going and when not to. As for my wife, Danyel, I am lost for words. All I will say is that she contributed to this book much more than she might modestly accept. Always patient, always wise, at just the right moments she summoned up, as if by magic, calm where before there was only storm. I dedicate this book to her and to our two children, Emma and Joseph, who grew up with this book and tolerated the disruptions created by it with their usual good cheer. All three fueled my efforts more than they can ever know.

NOTES

PREFACE

1 Near the end of the trip, Kennedy would be rushed to an Okinawa hospital with a temperature of 106. The doctors initially doubted he would live, and he received his last rites.

2 1951 travel journal, Box 11, Book 3, October–November 1951, pp.116ff, John F. Kennedy Personal Papers, John F. Kennedy Library (hereafter JFKL). See also Geoffrey Perret, *Jack: A Life Like No Other* (New York: Random House, 2001), 170.

3 1951 trips, Mid and Far East, travel diary, Box 24, Robert F. Kennedy Pre-administration Personal Files, JFKL; Robert Mann, *A Grand Delusion: America's Descent into Vietnam* (New York: Basic, 2001), 83.

4 Seymour Topping, *On the Front Lines of the Cold War: An American Correspondent's Journal from the Chinese Civil War to the Cuban Missile Crisis and Vietnam* (Baton Rouge: Louisiana State University Press, 2010), 151–55; *The Pentagon Papers: The Defense Department History of Decisionmaking on Vietnam*, Senator Gravel edition (Boston: Beacon Press, 1971), 1:68.

5 JFK travel journal, 1951, JFKL.

6 Robert Dallek, *An Unfinished Life: John F. Kennedy, 1917–1963* (Boston: Little, Brown, 2003), 166–67; *Pentagon Papers* (Gravel), 1:72.

7 Arthur M. Schlesinger, Jr., *Robert Kennedy and His Times* (Boston: Houghton Mifflin, 1978), 1:96.

8 Important works that cover parts of this story, and that are cited in the pages that follow, include those by Mark Bradley, Pierre Brocheux, Laurent Cesari, Jessica Chapman, Chen Jian, Chester Cooper, Philippe Devillers, William Duiker, David Elliott, Duong Van Mai Elliott, Bernard Fall, Lloyd Gardner, Christopher Goscha, Ellen Hammer, George Herring, Stanley Karnow, Jean Lacouture, A. J. Langguth, Mark Lawrence, David Marr, Edward Miller, Jonathan Nashel, John Prados, Pierre Rocolle, Alain Ruscio, Neil Sheehan, Martin Shipway, Ronald Spector, Kathryn Statler, Martin Thomas, Stein Tønnesson, Frédéric Turpin, Martin Windrow, and Marilyn Young. Also essential are the following reference works: Christopher E. Goscha, *Historical Dictionary of the Indochina War: International and Multidisciplinary Perspectives* (Honolulu: University of Hawaii Press/Nordic In-

stitute of Asian Studies, 2011); Alain Ruscio, *La guerre "française" d'Indochine (1945-1954), Les sources de la connaissance: Bibliographie, filmographie, documents divers* (Paris: Les Indes savantes, 2002); Michel Bodin, *Dictionnaire de la guerre d'Indochine, 1945-1954* (Paris: Economica, 2004); Jean-Pierre Rioux, *Dictionnaire de la France coloniale* (Paris: Flammarion, 2007); and Edwin Moïse's excellent online bibliography of the Vietnam Wars, which can be found at www .clemson.edu/caah/history/facultypages/ EdMoise/bibliography.html. A fine atlas of the struggle is Hugues Tertrais, *Atlas des guerres d'Indochine, 1940-1990: De l'Indochine française à l'ouverture internationale* (Paris: Autrement, 2004). Special recognition needs to be extended to the quartet of Devillers, Fall, Goscha, and Lawrence, whose influence on this study has been especially great.

9   Although a great many Vietnamese archival sources remain inaccessible to scholars, it's possible to learn a lot about Vietnamese—Communist as well as non-Communist—decisions in this period from official histories and memoirs, and from French, American, and British archival collections. Nevertheless, this book is not a full history of the DRV in this period, much less of all of Vietnam. Important recent studies that are more Vietnam-centric include Christopher E. Goscha, *Vietnam: Un état né de la guerre, 1945-54* (Paris: Armand Colin, 2011); François Guillemot, *Dai Viêt, indépendance et révolution au Viêt-Nam. L'échec de la troisième voie, 1938-1955* (Paris: Les Indes savantes, 2011); David Marr, *Vietnam 1945-1950: War, State, Revolution* (Berkeley: University of California Press, forthcoming); Pierre Brocheux and Daniel Hémery, *Indochina: An Ambiguous Colonization, 1858-1954*, trans. Ly Lan Dill-Klein et al. (Berkeley: University of California Press, 2009); David W. P. Elliott, *The Vietnamese War: Revolution and Social Change in the Mekong Delta, 1930-1975* (Armonk, N.Y.: M.E. Sharpe, 2007); Shawn McHale, "Understanding the Fanatic Mind? The Viet Minh and Race Hatred in the First Indochina War (1945-1954)," *Journal of Vietnamese Studies* 4 (Fall 2009); Jessica M. Chapman, "Debating the Will of Heaven: South Vietnamese Politics and Nationalism in International Perspective, 1953-56," Ph.D. dissertation, University of California–Santa Barbara, 2006; and Edward Miller, "Grand Designs: Vision, Power, and Nation Building in America's Alliance with Ngô Dình Diêm, 1954-1960," Ph.D. dissertation, Harvard University, 2004. A useful older work is Greg Lockhart, *Nation in Arms: The Origins of the People's Army of Vietnam* (Wellington, N.Z.: Allen & Unwin, 1989). A major outlet for new research is the *Journal of Vietnamese Studies*.

10 Historians remain divided on what to call the conflict, referring to it variously as the French Indochina War, the First Indochina War, the First Vietnam War, the Franco–Viet Minh War, the Anti-French War, the First War of National Resistance, or simply the Indochina War. Here I most often use the French Indochina War and the Franco–Viet Minh War, recognizing that both have their limitations.

11 Works that explore this intersection include Mark Atwood Lawrence, *Assuming the Burden: Europe and the American Commitment to War in Vietnam* (Berkeley: University of California Press, 2005); Mark Atwood Lawrence and Fredrik Logevall, eds., *The First Vietnam War: Colonial Conflict and Cold War Crisis* (Cambridge, Mass.: Harvard University Press, 2007); Christopher E. Goscha and Christian F. Ostermann, eds., *Connecting Histories: Decolonization and the Cold War in Southeast Asia, 1945-1962* (Washington, D.C.: Woodrow Wilson Center Press, 2009); Tuong Vu and Wasana Wongsurawat, eds., *Dynamics of the Cold War in Asia: Ideology, Identity, and Culture* (New York: Palgrave Macmillan, 2009); Hans Antlöv and Stein Tønnesson, *Imperial Policy and South East Asian Nationalism* (Surrey,

U.K.: Curzon, 1995); and Marc Frey, Ronald W. Pruessen, and Tai Yong Tan, eds., *The Transformation of Southeast Asia: International Perspectives on Decolonization* (Armonk, N.Y.: M.E. Sharpe, 2003).

12 Though my emphasis in this volume is on high politics and military affairs, I am in full accord with David Elliott's argument that we also need local histories of the Vietnam struggle, which can capture what macrohistories cannot. See David W. P. Elliott, "The Future of the Past: Some Questions about the Vietnam War for the Next Generation of Historians," unpublished paper in the author's possession. See also Elliott, *Vietnamese War.*

13 See, e.g., A.J. Stockwell, "Southeast Asia in War and Peace: The End of European Empires," in Nicholas Tarling, ed., *The Cambridge History of Southeast Asia,* volume 4 (Cambridge, U.K.: Cambridge University Press, 1992), 1–32.

14 Paul Mus, *Destin de l'empire français: De l'Indochine à l'Afrique* (Paris: Éditions du Seuil, 1954), Part 1.

15 Neil Sheehan, introduction to Jules Roy, *The Battle of Dienbienphu,* trans. Robert Baldick (New York: Harper & Row, 1965; reprint New York: Carroll & Graf, 1984), xiv.

16 Westmoreland quoted in David F. Schmitz, *The Tet Offensive: Politics, War, and Public Opinion* (Lanham, Md.: Rowman & Littlefield, 2005), 69.

17 On this point as applied to Kennedy and Johnson in 1961–65, see Fredrik Logevall, *Choosing War: The Lost Chance for Peace and the Escalation of War in Vietnam* (Berkeley: University of California Press, 1999).

18 Daniel Ellsberg, *Papers on the War* (New York: Simon & Schuster, 1972), 42–135.

19 "Problem" comment quoted in Thomas A. Bass, *The Spy Who Loved Us: The Vietnam War and Pham Xuan An's Dangerous Game* (New York: Public Affairs, 2009), 71. "Embers" quote is in David Halberstam, keynote address, conference on "Vietnam and the Presidency," JFKL, March 10, 2006, available at www.jfklibrary.org/Events-and-Awards/Forums.aspx?f=2006 (last accessed Feb. 25, 2012).

20 Quoted in Marilyn B. Young, *The Vietnam Wars, 1945–1990* (New York: HarperCollins, 1991), 46.

21 On the American war as a colonial struggle, see, e.g., Michael Adas, "A Colonial War in a Postcolonial Era: The United States' Occupation of Vietnam," in Andreas W. Daum, Lloyd C. Gardner, and Wilfried Mausbach, eds., *America, the Vietnam War, and the World: Comparative and International Perspectives* (New York: Cambridge University Press, 2003), 27–42.

22 Former *New York Times* Saigon correspondent A. J. Langguth, in his fine history of the American war, refers to Ho Chi Minh's "lifelong admiration for Americans." *Our Vietnam: The War, 1954–1975* (New York: Simon & Schuster, 2000), 55.

PROLOGUE: *A Vietnamese in Paris*

1 The petition was cited in full in the socialist newspaper *L'Humanité* on June 18, 1919. See also Sophie Quinn-Judge, *Ho Chi Minh: The Missing Years 1919–1941* (Berkeley: University of California Press, 2003), 11–28; Pierre Brocheux, *Ho Chi Minh: A Biography* (New York: Cambridge University Press, 2007), 11–14; and William J. Duiker, *Ho Chi Minh: A Life* (New York: Hyperion, 2000), 54–63.

2 Ho did get a short, formal reply from an aide to Wilson's representative Colonel House, dated June 19, 1919. See David A. Andelman, *Shattered Peace: Versailles 1919 and the Price We Pay Today* (Hoboken, N.J.: Wiley, 2008), 124–25.

3 See the excellent analysis in Erez Manela, *The Wilsonian Moment: Self-*

Determination and the International Origins of Anticolonial Nationalism (New York: Oxford University Press, 2007).

4 Quinn-Judge, *Missing Years,* 20.

5 For the material covered in this chapter, helpful sources include Daniel Hémery, *Ho Chi Minh, de l'Indochine au Vietnam* (Paris: Gallimard, 1990); Duiker, *Ho Chi Minh*; Brocheux, *Ho Chi Minh*; E. V. Kobelev, *Ho Chi Minh* (Hanoi: Gioi, 1999); Quinn-Judge, *Missing Years*; Paul Mus, *Ho Chi Minh, le Vietnam et l'Asie* (Paris: Éditions du Seuil, 1971); Huynh Kim Khanh, *Vietnamese Communism, 1925–1945* (Ithaca, N.Y.: Cornell University Press, 1982); David G. Marr, *Vietnamese Anticolonialism, 1885–1925* (Berkeley: University of California Press, 1971); Thu Trang-Gaspard, *Ho Chi Minh à Paris* (Paris: Éditions L'Harmattan, 1992); and Alain Ruscio, ed., *Ho Chi Minh: Textes, 1914–1969* (Paris: Éditions L'Harmattan, 1990).

6 Ho's official birth date is 1890, but his sister, when questioned by French officials in 1920, gave the year as 1892 or 1893. See Quinn-Judge, *Missing Years,* 260n25.

7 For the making of French Indochina, see Pierre Brocheux and Daniel Hémery, *Indochina: An Ambiguous Colonization, 1858–1954,* trans. Ly Lan Dill-Klein et al. (Berkeley: University of California Press, 2009). A broader study that places the French Empire in this period in context is Jane Burbank and Frederick Cooper, *Empires in World History: Power and the Politics of Difference* (Princeton, N.J.: Princeton University Press, 2010), chaps. 10–11. Also useful is Frederick Quinn, *The French Overseas Empire* (New York: Praeger, 2001).

8 Both quotes are from Brocheux and Hémery, *Indochina,* 14.

9 Alice L. Conklin, *A Mission to Civilize: The Republican Idea of Empire in France and West Africa, 1895–1930* (Stanford, Calif.: Stanford University Press, 1997); and J. P. Daughton, *An Empire Divided: Religion, Republicanism, and the Making of French Colonialism, 1880–1914* (New York: Oxford University Press, 2006).

10 Brocheux and Hémery, *Indochina,* 15–33.

11 On the emergence of this opposition to French rule, see Marr, *Vietnamese Anticolonialism*; and William J. Duiker, *The Rise of Nationalism in Vietnam, 1900–1941* (Ithaca, N.Y.: Cornell University Press, 1976). On colonial prisons, see the rich and penetrating study by Peter Zinoman, *The Colonial Bastille: A History of Imprisonment in Vietnam, 1862–1940* (Berkeley: University of California Press, 2001).

12 See note 6 above.

13 Stanley Karnow, *Vietnam: A History* (New York: Viking, 1983), 131.

14 Daniel Hémery, "Jeunesse d'un colonise, genèse d'un exil: Ho Chi Minh jusqu'en 1911," *Approches Asie,* no. 11 (1992), 82–157.

15 A British official who had met him said Ho spoke excellent idiomatic English. Saigon to Foreign Office (hereafter FO), April 10, 1946, FO 959/7, The National Archives of the United Kingdom, Kew, London (hereafter TNA).

16 Brocheux, *Ho Chi Minh,* 10; Luu Doan Huynh, interview with the author, Hanoi, January 2003.

17 The date of his return to France has long been in dispute, with some authors maintaining it was late 1917 and others pointing to the spring of 1919, i.e., mere weeks before he presented the petition at the Paris Peace Conference. The French police, notably, concluded it was the latter. See Quinn-Judge, *Missing Years,* 20. Interestingly, Quinn-Judge also suggests he may have made another trip to the United States in the interval, i.e., in 1917–18, working for a wealthy family in Brooklyn.

18 Quoted in Andelman, *Shattered Peace,* 128.

19 See Ho Chi Minh, "The Path Which Led Me to Leninism," in *Ho Chi Minh on*

Revolution: Selected Writings, 1920–66, ed. Bernard B. Fall (New York: Praeger, 1967), 34.

20 Ibid., 24.

21 Manela, *Wilsonian Moment,* 6–7.

22 Karnow, *Vietnam,* 132; Brocheux, *Ho Chi Minh,* 19.

23 Quoted in Stanley Karnow, *Paris in the Fifties* (New York: Three Rivers Press, 1997), 216. See also Brocheux, *Ho Chi Minh,* 20–21.

24 Quoted in Brocheux, *Ho Chi Minh,* 22. Sternel was a pseudonym the activist used in his writings. I have not been able to identify his real name.

25 Quoted in William J. Duiker, *Sacred War: Nationalism and Revolution in a Divided Vietnam* (New York: McGraw-Hill, 1995), 27.

26 Duiker, *Ho Chi Minh,* chap. 4.

27 On the developments in these years, see, e.g., Brocheux and Hémery, *Indochina,* chap. 5; Huynh Kim Khanh, *Vietnamese Communism;* Duiker, *The Rise of Nationalism in Vietnam;* Hue-Tam Ho Tai, *Radicalism and the Origins of the Vietnamese Revolution* (Cambridge, Mass.: Harvard University Press, 1992); David G. Marr, *Vietnamese Anticolonialism.*

28 Zinoman, *Colonial Bastille,* chap. 9.

29 A fine study articulating this argument is Martin Thomas, *The French Empire Between the Wars: Imperialism, Politics, and Society* (Manchester, U.K.: Manchester University Press, 2005). See here also Burbank and Cooper, *Empires,* 388.

30 Duiker, *Ho Chi Minh,* 242.

CHAPTER 1: *"The Empire Is with Us!"*

1 On the fall of France, two important and engaging studies are Ernest R. May, *Strange Victory: Hitler's Conquest of France* (New York: Hill & Wang, 2000); and Julian Jackson, *The Fall of France: The Nazi Invasion of 1940* (New York: Oxford University Press, 2003).

2 Quoted in Jean Lacouture, *De Gaulle: The Rebel, 1890–1944* (New York: W.W. Norton, 1990), 224.

3 Charles de Gaulle, *Mémoires de Guerre: L'Appel, 1940–1942* (Paris: Plon, 1954), 78–80; David Schoenbrun, *As France Goes* (New York: Atheneum, 1968), 47–48, 214–15. See also Jean-Louis Crémieux-Brilhac, *La France libre: De l'appel du 18 juin à la Libération* (Paris: Gallimard, 1996).

4 Julian Jackson, *France: The Dark Years, 1940–1944* (Oxford, U.K.: Oxford University Press, 2001), 389.

5 Despite de Gaulle's conviction on this point, he was not an instinctive imperialist. Unlike many ambitious military officers, during the interwar period he sought as much as possible to avoid assignments to the colonies, and he viewed France as fundamentally a Continental power whose prime focus must be on the German frontier to the east. In the short term, however, de Gaulle understood his cause was intimately linked to France's overseas possessions. See Julian Jackson, *Charles De Gaulle* (London: Haus, 2003), 80–81.

6 Martin Thomas, *The French Empire Between the Wars: Imperialism, Politics and Society* (Manchester, U.K.: Manchester University Press, 2007).

7 Charles de Gaulle, *The Complete War Memoirs of Charles de Gaulle,* trans. Jonathan Griffin and Richard Howard (New York: Carroll & Graf, 1998), 160.

8 The armistice divided France into an occupied zone and an unoccupied zone. Occupied France included Paris and the entire Channel and Atlantic Seaboard. The

south of the country, below a heavily guarded demarcation line, made up the unoccupied (Vichy) zone. The French Navy was to be deactivated. In November 1942,
the German Occupation would be extended to cover the whole of France.

9 On Vichy and the empire, see Jacques Cantier and Eric Jennings, eds., *L'Empire
   colonial sous Vichy* (Paris: Odile Jacob, 2004).
10 François Kersaudy, *Churchill and de Gaulle* (New York: Atheneum, 1982), 85.
11 Andrew Shennan, *De Gaulle* (London: Longman, 1993), 54; Jackson, *Dark Years*,
   392.
12 Winston S. Churchill, *The Second World War*, 6 vols. (London: Cassell, 1948–53),
   3:682.
13 Martin Thomas, *The French Empire at War, 1940–1945* (Manchester, U.K.: Manchester University Press, 2007), 38. The French Army lost approximately 100,000
   killed, roughly equal to the rate of casualties at Verdun in 1916. In addition, the
   Germans took some 1.6 million POWs.
14 Bui Diem with David Chanoff, *In the Jaws of History* (Boston: Houghton Mifflin,
   1987), 15. See also David G. Marr, *Vietnam 1945: The Quest for Power* (Berkeley:
   University of California Press, 1995), 79–80; and Thomas A. Bass, *The Spy Who
   Loved Us: The Vietnam War and Pham Xuan An's Dangerous Game* (New York:
   Public Affairs, 2009), 31.
15 Henri Lerner, *Catroux* (Paris: Albin Michel, 1991), 52–54. For Catroux's version of
   events during these months, see his book, *Deux actes du drame indochinois* (Paris:
   Plon, 1959).
16 On Japanese decision making in this period, see Minami Yoshisawa, "The Nishi-
   hara Mission in Hanoi, July 1940," in Saya S. Shiraishi and Motoo Furuta, eds.,
   Indochina in the 1940s and 1950s (Ithaca, N.Y.: Cornell Southeast Asia Program,
   1992), 9–54; Hata Ikuhiko, "The Army's Move into Northern Indochina," in
   James W. Morley, ed., *The Fateful Choice: Japan's Advance into Southeast Asia,
   1939–1941* (New York: Columbia University Press, 1980), 155–63; and Sachiko
   Murakami, "Japan's Thrust into French Indochina, 1940–1945," Ph.D. disserta-
   tion, New York University, 1981. Grew is quoted in H. W. Brands, *Traitor to His
   Class: The Privileged Life and Radical Presidency of Franklin Delano Roosevelt*
   (New York: Doubleday, 2008), 570.
17 Jean Decoux, *À la barre de l'Indochine* (Paris: Plon, 1949), 41–46; FO to Consul
   General (Saigon), June 29, 1940, FO 371/24328, TNA.
18 Memcon Saint-Quentin and Welles, June 20, 1940, in Department of State,
   Foreign Relations of the United States (hereafter *FRUS*), *1940, The Far East*
   (Washington, D.C.: Government Printing Office), IV:29. See also Hornbeck memorandum, June 20, 1940, *FRUS, 1940, Far East*, IV:29; *New York Times* (hereafter
   NYT), August 2, 1945; John E. Dreifort, *Myopic Grandeur: The Ambivalence of
   French Foreign Policy toward the Far East, 1919–1945* (Kent, Oh.: Kent State University Press, 1991), 196; and Catroux, *Deux actes du drame indochinois*, 54–55.
19 Catroux quoted in Dreifort, *Myopic Grandeur*, 197–98. See also Catroux, *Deux
   actes du drame indochinois*, 62–66.
20 Joseph Buttinger, *Vietnam: A Dragon Embattled*, vol. 1: *From Colonialism to the
   Vietminh* (New York: Praeger, 1967), 235; and Archimedes L.A. Patti, *Why Viet
   Nam? Prelude to America's Albatross* (Berkeley: University of California Press,
   1982), 32. Yosuke Matsuoka is quoted in William Morley, *Fateful Choice*, 302.
21 Thomas, *French Empire at War*, 48–49; Arthur J. Dommen, *The Indochinese Experience of the French and the Americans* (Bloomington: Indiana University Press,
   2001), 48.

22 Jean Chauvel, *Commentaire* (Paris: Fayard, 1971), 238–39; Dreifort, *Myopic Grandeur*, 203–4.

23 Francois Charles-Roux, *Cinq mois tragiques aux affaires étrangères (21 mai–1 novembre 1940)* (Paris: Plon, 1949), 255; and Paul Baudouin, *The Private Diaries of Paul Baudouin* (London: Eyre and Spottiswoode, 1948), 198–99, 223–24.

24 Mark Philip Bradley, *Imagining Vietnam and America: The Making of Postcolonial Vietnam, 1919–1950* (Chapel Hill: University of North Carolina Press, 2000), 45. On U.S. thinking in the interwar period, see also, in a broader context, Anne L. Foster, *Projections of Power: The United States and Europe in Colonial Southeast Asia, 1919–1941* (Durham, N.C.: Duke University Press, 2010).

25 Dreifort, *Myopic Grandeur*, 208–13; Georges Gautier, *9 mars 1945, Hanoi au soleil de sang: La fin de l'Indochine française* (Paris: SPL, 1978), 43–45.

26 Hata, "Army's Move," 194–98; Marr, *Vietnam 1945*, 19.

27 David G. Marr, *Vietnamese Tradition on Trial: 1920 to 1945* (Berkeley: University of California Press, 1984), 400; *Histoire de la révolution d'août* (Hanoi: Foreign Languages Press, 1977), 19–22.

28 Pierre Brocheux, *Ho Chi Minh: A Biography* (New York: Cambridge University Press, 2007), 70–73; William J. Duiker, *Ho Chi Minh: A Life* (New York: Hyperion, 2000), 250–57; and Jean Lacouture, *Ho Chi Minh: A Political Biography* (New York: Random House, 1968), 74–78.

29 Huynh Kim Khanh, *Vietnamese Communism, 1925–1945* (Ithaca, N.Y.: Cornell University Press, 1982), 259–63.

30 Ho Chi Minh, "Letter from Abroad" (1941), in Ho Chi Minh, *Selected Works* (Hanoi, 1960), 2:153.

31 Brocheux, *Ho Chi Minh*, 74.

32 Ibid., 75. On this point, see also Daniel Hémery, "Ho Chi Minh: Vie singulière et nationalisation des esprits," in Christopher E. Goscha and Benoît de Tréglodé, eds., *Le Viêt Nam depuis 1945: États, contestations et constructions du passé* (Paris: Les Indes savantes, 2004), 135–48.

33 An excellent source on Decoux's policies is Eric Jennings, *Vichy in the Tropics: Pétain's National Revolution in Madagascar, Guadeloupe, and Indochina, 1940–1944* (Stanford, Calif.: Stanford University Press, 2004), 130–98. See also Ellen J. Hammer, *The Struggle for Indochina, 1940–1955* (Stanford, Calif.: Stanford University Press, 1955), 31; Marr, *Vietnam 1945*, 74; and Patti, *Why Viet Nam?*, 33.

34 Marr, *Vietnam 1945*, 78; Jennings, *Vichy in the Tropics*, 188–94.

35 Decoux, *À la barre de l'Indochine*, 444.

36 Jennings, *Vichy in the Tropics*, 145. On the persecution of Gaullists in Indochina as compared to the rest of the empire, see the recollections of Philippe Devillers, who spent part of the war in Indochina: Devillers, *Histoire du Viêt-Nam de 1940 à 1952* (Paris: Éditions du Seuil, 1952), 86. Historian Martin Thomas concludes that Decoux's government was "the most actively repressive within the Vichy empire." Thomas, *French Empire at War*, 196.

37 Colonel Jacomey to Tonkin Command, May 19, 1941, 1K401/C1, *Service historique de l'armée de terre, Vincennes*; Richard J. Aldrich, *The Key to the South: Britain, the United States, and Thailand During the Approach of the Pacific War, 1929–1942* (Oxford, U.K.: Oxford University Press, 1993), 288–93; Thomas, *French Empire at War*, 196–97.

38 F. C. Jones, *Japan's New Order in East Asia, 1937–1945* (Oxford: Oxford University Press, 1954), 260–63; Stein Tønnesson, *The Vietnamese Revolution of 1945:*

Roosevelt, Ho Chi Minh and de Gaulle in a World at War (London: Sage, 1991), 38; Dreifort, *Myopic Grandeur*, 216.

39 In September 1940 a joint team of army and navy cryptographers had broken the Japanese diplomatic code, allowing them to read what Tokyo was telling its diplomats around the world. The operation was known as MAGIC and the cryptographers as the "magicians."

40 David M. Kennedy, *Freedom from Fear: The American People in Depression and War, 1929-1945* (New York: Oxford University Press, 1999), 509-11; Jean Edward Smith, *FDR* (New York: Random House, 2007), 513-18.

41 Quoted in Jonathan Fenby, *Alliance: The Inside Story of How Roosevelt, Stalin and Churchill Won One War and Began Another* (San Francisco: MacAdam Cage, 2007), 79-80.

CHAPTER 2: *The Anti-Imperialist*

1 William D. Hassett, *Off the Record with F.D.R.: 1942-1945* (New Brunswick, N.J.: Rutgers University Press, 1958), 166. See also Robert Daniel Murphy, *Diplomat Among Warriors* (New York: Pyramid, 1965); and Raoul Aglion, *Roosevelt and De Gaulle: Allies in Conflict* (New York: Free Press, 1988). For Hull's views, see Cordell Hull, *The Memoirs of Cordell Hull* (New York: Macmillan, 1948), 2:961-62.

2 Kenneth S. Davis, *FDR: The War President, 1940-1943* (New York: Random House, 2000), 379.

3 Mario Rossi, *Roosevelt and the French* (Westport, Conn.: Praeger, 1993), 67-68.

4 David B. Woolner, "Storm in the Atlantic: The St. Pierre and Miquelon Affair of 1941," M.A. thesis, McGill University, 1990; Conrad Black, *Franklin Delano Roosevelt: Champion of Freedom* (New York: Public Affairs, 2005), 706-10; and Martin Thomas, *The French Empire at War, 1940-1945* (Manchester, U.K.: Manchester University Press, 2007), 133-39.

5 See Georges Catroux, *Dans la bataille de la Méditerranée* (Paris: Plon, 1949), 278-79.

6 Elliott Roosevelt, *As He Saw It* (New York: Duell, Sloan, & Pearce, 1946), 115; Samuel I. Rosenman, ed., *The Public Papers and Addresses of Franklin D. Roosevelt* (New York: Macmillan, 1938-50), 10:69.

7 Willard Range, *Franklin D. Roosevelt's World Order* (Athens: University of Georgia Press, 1959), 102-4; Foster Rhea Dulles and Gerald Ridinger, "The Anti-Colonial Policies of Franklin D. Roosevelt," *Political Science Quarterly* (March 1955): 1-18.

8 Paul Orders, " 'Adjusting to a New Period in World History': Franklin Roosevelt and European Colonialism," in David Ryan and Victor Pungong, eds., *The United States and Decolonization: Power and Freedom* (New York: St. Martin's, 2000); Dulles and Ridinger, "The Anti-Colonial Policies of Franklin D. Roosevelt."

9 Range, *Franklin D. Roosevelt's World Order*; Warren F. Kimball, *The Juggler: Franklin Roosevelt as Wartime Statesman* (Princeton, N.J.: Princeton University Press, 1991), 109.

10 Walter Lippmann, *U.S. War Aims* (Boston: Little, Brown, 1944), 50-51.

11 Kimball, *Juggler*, 130.

12 Roosevelt, *As He Saw It*, 37; Davis, *FDR: War President*, 269-73; and Martin Gilbert, *Finest Hour: Winston Churchill, 1939-1941* (London: Heinemann, 1983), 1163. On the differing Anglo-American conceptions of empire in this period, see

also Niall Ferguson, *Empire: The Rise and Demise of the British World Order and the Lessons for Global Power* (New York: Basic, 2003): 291–94.

13 Kimball, *Juggler*, 133. A fine study of the charter and the broader context in which it was articulated is Elizabeth Borgwardt, *A New Deal for the World: America's Vision for Human Rights* (Cambridge, Mass.: Harvard University Press, 2006), 14–86.

14 Winston Churchill, *The Second World War*, vol. 4: *The Hinge of Fate* (Boston: Houghton Mifflin, 1950), 209.

15 Foreign Ministry Report, "L'Amerique et les colonies," March 12, 1945, Y-International, file 655, Ministère des affaires étrangères, Paris (hereafter MAE). An excellent summary of the report is in Mark Atwood Lawrence, *Assuming the Burden: Europe and the American Commitment to War in Vietnam* (Berkeley: University of California Press, 2005), 24–25. See also Jasmine Aimaq, *For Europe or Empire? French Colonial Ambitions and the European Army Plan* (Lund, Sweden: Lund University Press, 1996), 101.

16 Jean Lacouture, *De Gaulle: The Rebel, 1890–1944* (New York: W.W. Norton, 1990), 1:394–402; Warren F. Kimball, *Forged in War: Roosevelt, Churchill, and the Second World War* (New York: William Morrow, 1998), 173–74.

17 Memo–Hopkins, Eden visit, March 27, 1943, Box 138, Harry Hopkins Papers, FDR Library.

18 Minutes of Subcommittee on Political Problems, April 10, 1943, quoted in Lloyd C. Gardner, *Approaching Vietnam: From World War II Through Dienbienphu* (New York: W.W. Norton, 1989), 25. See also John B. Judis, *The Folly of Empire* (New York: Oxford University Press, 2006), 124–25.

19 Edward M. Bennett, "Mandates and Trusteeships," in Alexander DeConde, Richard Dean Burns, and Fredrik Logevall, eds., *Encyclopedia of American Foreign Policy* (New York: Scribner, 2002), 2:381–86.

20 Kimball, *Juggler*, 131.

21 Robert Dallek, *Franklin D. Roosevelt and American Foreign Policy, 1932–1945* (New York: Oxford University Press, 1979), 428–29; Gardner, *Approaching Vietnam*, 22–23.

22 Gaddis Smith, *American Diplomacy During the Second World War*, 2nd ed. (New York: McGraw-Hill, 1985), 93.

23 *FRUS, The Conferences at Cairo and Tehran, 1943*, 448–50, 484–86.

24 *FRUS, Cairo and Tehran*, 509–68 passim; Kimball, *Juggler*, 143. See also William Roger Louis, *Imperialism at Bay: The United States and the Decolonization of the British Empire, 1941–1945* (Oxford: Oxford University Press, 1977), 283–86; Akira Iriye, *Power and Culture: The Japanese-American War, 1941–1945* (Cambridge, Mass.: Harvard University Press, 1981), 158–63; Gary Hess, *The United States' Emergence as a Southeast Asian Power, 1940–1950* (New York: Columbia University Press, 1987), 81–82.

25 Hess, *United States' Emergence*, 89–90. FDR quoted in Washington to FO, January 19, 1944, FO 371/41723, TNA.

26 Cadogan minute, on minute by Strang, January 12, 1944, FO 371/1878, TNA. See also Eden to PM, December 23, 1943, CAB 121/741, TNA.

27 See Anthony Eden's memo, dated February 16, 1944, and accompanying annex, in CAB 121/741, TNA. See also Kimball, *Forged in War*, 302–3.

28 Quoted in Ted Morgan, *Valley of Death: The Tragedy at Dien Bien Phu That Led America into the Vietnam War* (New York: Random House, 2010), 25. See also

David Stafford, *Roosevelt and Churchill: Men of Secrets* (Woodstock, N.Y.: Overlook, 2000), 256.

29 *Life* quoted in Walter LaFeber, "Roosevelt, Churchill, and Indochina: 1942–1945," *American Historical Review* 80 (December 1975), 1288.

30 Harriman to Hopkins, September 10, 1944, Harriman file, Box 96, Hopkins Papers, FDR Library.

31 The arguments of these "conservatives" in official Washington are ably explored in Lawrence, *Assuming the Burden,* 52–58.

32 Charles de Gaulle, *The War Memoirs,* vol. 3: *Salvation, 1944–1946* (London: Weidenfeld & Nicolson, 1950), 187.

33 Lawrence, *Assuming the Burden,* 31–32.

34 Jonathan Fenby, *Alliance: The Inside Story of How Roosevelt, Stalin and Churchill Won One War and Began Another* (San Francisco: MacAdam Cage, 2007), 287–88; Aglion, *Roosevelt and De Gaulle,* 177–78.

35 Aglion, *Roosevelt and De Gaulle,* 180–81; Lacouture, *De Gaulle,* 1:537–45.

36 *NYT,* July 11, 1945.

37 Muggeridge quoted in Alistair Horne, *La Belle France: A Short History* (New York: Alfred A. Knopf, 2005), 375.

38 See aide-memoir, August 25, 1944, FO 371/41719, TNA. On Franco-British scheming re this matter, see also Massigli to Foreign Ministry, October 2, 1944, Asie/Indochine, file 45, MAE.

39 Mark Lawrence, "Forging the 'Great Combination': Britain and the Indochina Problem, 1945–1950," in Mark Atwood Lawrence and Fredrik Logevall, eds., *The First Vietnam War: Colonial Conflict and Cold War Crisis* (Cambridge, Mass.: Harvard University Press, 2007), 105–29.

40 Stettinius memo, January 4, 1945, Record Group 59, Box 6177, National Archives and Records Administration (hereafter NARA); LaFeber, "Roosevelt, Churchill, and Indochina," 1291; Christopher G. Thorne, *Allies of a Kind: The United States, Britain, and the War Against Japan* (London: Hamish Hamilton, 1978), 94.

41 Washington to FO, January 9, 1945, FO 371/46304, TNA.

42 Rosenman, ed., *Papers and Addresses of Roosevelt,* 13:562–63. See also Thorne, *Allies of a Kind,* 628.

43 See, for example, George C. Herring, *America's Longest War: The United States and Vietnam, 1950–1975,* 4th ed. (New York: McGraw-Hill, 2002), 10.

44 Quoted in Rossi, *Roosevelt and French,* 144.

45 J. G. Ward minute, February 17, 1945, FO 371/46304, TNA. See also Gardner, *Approaching Vietnam,* 50–52.

46 Jim Bishop, *FDR's Last Year: April 1944–April 1945* (New York: William Morrow, 1974), 491–92; Stein Tønnesson, "Franklin Roosevelt, Trusteeship, and Indochina," in Lawrence and Logevall, eds., *First Vietnam War,* 66. Tønnesson in this essay presents a powerful case that FDR did not give up his opposition to a French return in the final months of his life. See also Tønnesson's larger work, *The Vietnamese Revolution of 1945: Roosevelt, Ho Chi Minh and de Gaulle in a World at War* (London: Sage, 1991).

47 De Gaulle quoted in H. W. Brands, *Traitor to His Class: The Privileged Life and Radical Presidency of Franklin Delano Roosevelt* (New York: Doubleday, 2008), 814.

48 Kimball, *Juggler,* 154.

49 See, e.g., British official documentation for fall 1945, much of which states forthrightly that FDR went to his grave seeking to prevent a French return to Indochina,

and which implicitly therefore sees historical importance in the FDR-Truman transition.

CHAPTER 3: *Crossroads*

1 Jean Decoux, *À la barre de l'Indochine* (Paris: Plon, 1949), 328.
2 David G. Marr, *Vietnam 1945: The Quest for Power* (Berkeley: University of California Press, 1995), 13, 55–56; Stein Tønnesson, *The Vietnamese Revolution of 1945: Roosevelt, Ho Chi Minh and de Gaulle in a World at War* (London: Sage, 1991), 221; Decoux, *À la barre de l'Indochine*, 328.
3 Summary of MAGIC intercepts, SRS 306, January 20, 1945, MAGIC Far East Summaries, Box 4, Record Group 457, NARA; Stein Tønnesson, "Franklin Roosevelt, Trusteeship, and Indochina," in Mark Atwood Lawrence and Fredrik Logevall, eds., *The First Vietnam War: Colonial Conflict and Cold War Crisis* (Cambridge, Mass.: Harvard University Press, 2007), 65–66; G. Sabbatier, *Le Destin de l'Indochine* (Paris: Plon, 1952), 138–39.
4 John E. Dreifort, *Myopic Grandeur: The Ambivalence of French Foreign Policy toward the Far East, 1919–1945* (Kent, Oh.: Kent State University Press, 1991), 239.
5 Bernard B. Fall, *Last Reflections on a War: Bernard B. Fall's Last Comments on Vietnam* (New York: Doubleday, 1967), 130; Marr, *Vietnam 1945,* 59; Duong Van Mai Elliott, *The Sacred Willow: Four Generations in the Life of a Vietnamese Family* (New York: Oxford University Press, 2000), 110.
6 Tønnesson, *Vietnamese Revolution of 1945,* 242–43.
7 Douglas Porch, *The French Foreign Legion: A Complete History of the Legendary Fighting Force* (New York: HarperCollins, 1991), 512; Marr, *Vietnam 1945,* 59.
8 Sabbatier, *Le Destin*; Tønnesson, *Vietnamese Revolution of 1945,* 239; Marr, *Vietnam 1945,* 326–27.
9 Ellen J. Hammer, *The Struggle for Indochina, 1940–1955* (Stanford, Calif.: Stanford University Press, 1955), 41; Elliott, *Sacred Willow,* 110.
10 John T. McAlister, Jr., *Viet Nam: The Origins of Revolution* (New York: Alfred A. Knopf, 1969), 114–15; Tønnesson, *Vietnamese Revolution of 1945,* 244.
11 Martin Shipway, *The Road to War: France and Vietnam, 1944–1947* (Providence, R.I.: Berghahn, 1996), 68; Robert Gildea, *France Since 1945* (New York: Oxford University Press, 1996), 17; Mark Mazower, *Dark Continent: Europe's Twentieth Century* (New York: Alfred A. Knopf, 1998), 209–10.
12 Christopher G. Thorne, *Allies of a Kind: The United States, Britain, and the War Against Japan* (London: Hamish Hamilton, 1978), 621; Dreifort, *Myopic Grandeur,* 241; Marr, *Vietnam 1945,* 327; Hammer, *Struggle for Indochina,* 43.
13 Joseph Buttinger, *Vietnam: A Dragon Embattled,* vol. 1: *From Colonialism to the Vietminh* (New York: Praeger, 1967), 302; D. Bruce Marshall, *The French Colonial Myth and Constitution-Making in the Fourth Republic* (New Haven, Conn.: Yale University Press, 1973), 193.
14 Frédéric Turpin, "Le RPF et la guerre d'Indochine (1947–1954)," in *De Gaulle et le Rassemblement du Peuple Français (1947–1955)* (Paris: Armand Colin, 1998), 530–31; Marshall, *French Colonial Myth,* 195.
15 Quoted in Tony Judt, *Postwar: A History of Europe Since 1945* (New York: Penguin, 2005), 100.
16 Shipway, *Road to War,* chap. 2; Hammer, *Struggle for Indochina,* 44.
17 The declaration is excerpted in Philippe Devillers, *Paris-Saigon-Hanoi: Les archives de la guerre, 1944–1947* (Paris: Gallimard/Julliard, 1988), 53–54.

18 Marr, *Vietnam 1945*, 329.

19 Martin Thomas, *The French Empire at War, 1940–1945* (Manchester, U.K.: Manchester University Press, 2007), 213; Hammer, *Struggle for Indochina*, 43–44; Philippe Devillers, *Histoire du Viêt-Nam de 1940 à 1952* (Paris: Éditions du Seuil, 1952), 144.

20 Shipway, *Road to War*, 60; Frederick Quinn, *French Overseas Empire* (New York: Praeger, 2000), 233.

21 Tønnesson, *Vietnamese Revolution of 1945*, 315; Shipway, *Road to War*, 126; Buttinger, *Dragon Embattled*, 303.

22 David G. Marr, *Vietnamese Tradition on Trial: 1920 to 1945* (Berkeley: University of California Press, 1984), 415–16; David W. P. Elliott, *The Vietnamese War: Revolution and Social Change in the Mekong Delta, 1930–1975* (Armonk, N.Y.: M.E. Sharpe, 2007), 33; Buttinger, *Dragon Embattled*, 294.

23 See the analysis in Pierre Brocheux, *Ho Chi Minh: A Biography* (New York: Cambridge University Press, 2007), 83–85.

24 William J. Duiker, "Ho Chi Minh and the Strategy of People's War," in Lawrence and Logevall, eds., *First Vietnam War*, 158–59. Ho quoted in Brocheaux, *Ho Chi Minh*, 83.

25 Devillers, *Histoire du Viêt-Nam*, 111.

26 Ho quoted in Hoang Van Hoan, *A Drop in the Ocean: Hoang Van Hoan's Revolutionary Reminiscences* (Beijing: Foreign Languages Press, 1988), 187–88.

27 Elliott, *Sacred Willow*, 112–13; Marr, *Vietnamese Tradition*, 416; William J. Duiker, *Ho Chi Minh: A Life* (New York: Hyperion, 2000), 296.

28 Marr, *Vietnamese Tradition*, 408; William J. Duiker, *Sacred War: Nationalism and Revolution in a Divided Vietnam* (New York: McGraw-Hill, 1995), 45.

29 Marr, *Vietnam 1945*, 96; Elliott, *Sacred Willow*, 107.

30 Motoo Furuta, "A Survey of Village Conditions During the 1945 Famine in Vietnam," in Paul H. Kratoska, ed., *Food Supplies and the Japanese Occupation in South-East Asia* (Houndsmills, U.K.: Macmillan, 1998), 236–37; Nguyen Thi Anh, "Japanese Food Policies and the 1945 Great Famine in Indochina," in Kratoska, *Food Supplies*, 211–21; Elliott, *Sacred Willow*, 107–8; and Marr, *Vietnam 1945*, 101. See also Robert Templer, *Shadows and Wind: A View of Modern Vietnam* (Boston: Little, Brown, 1998), 48ff.

31 Ngo Vinh Long, *Before the Revolution: The Vietnamese Peasants under the French* (New York: Columbia University Press, 1991), 133.

32 Marr, *Vietnam 1945*, 104.

33 Nguyen Thi Anh, "Japanese Food Policies," 221; Elliott, *Sacred Willow*, 113; William J. Duiker, *The Communist Road to Power in Vietnam* (Boulder, Colo.: Westview, 1996), 90; Templer, *Shadows and Wind*, 50.

34 The three were Laurence Gordon, Harry Bernard, and Frank Tan. On the GBT and its activities, see Dixee R. Bartholomew-Feis, *The OSS and Ho Chi Minh: Unexpected Allies in the War Against Japan* (Lawrence: University Press of Kansas, 2006), 63–94.

35 Marr, *Vietnamese Tradition*, 407; William J. Duiker, *U.S. Containment Policy and the Conflict in Indochina* (Stanford, Calif.: Stanford University Press, 1994), 28.

36 Lloyd C. Gardner, *Approaching Vietnam: From World War II through Dienbienphu* (New York: W.W. Norton, 1989), 62; Elliott, *Sacred Willow*, 113.

37 Fenn unpublished memoir, quoted in Bartholomew-Feis, *OSS and Ho Chi Minh*, 154–55.

38 Charles Fenn, *Ho Chi Minh: A Biographical Introduction* (New York: Charles Scribner's Sons, 1973), 132.

39 Bartholomew-Feis, *OSS and Ho Chi Minh*, 156–57; Fenn, *Ho Chi Minh*, 75–77.

40 Fenn, *Ho Chi Minh*, 76–78; Bartholomew-Feis, *OSS and Ho Chi Minh*, 156–57.

41 Tran Trong Trung oral history, Hanoi, June 12, 2007 (I thank Merle Pribbenow for making this oral history available to me); Gary Hess, *The United States' Emergence as a Southeast Asian Power, 1940–1950* (New York: Columbia University Press, 1987), 170; and Duiker, *Ho Chi Minh*, 293–94.

42 See the fine account in Bartholomew-Feis, *OSS and Ho Chi Minh*, 193–205. See René J. Défourneaux, *The Winking Fox: Twenty-two Years in Military Intelligence* (Indianapolis: ICA, 2000), 134–96; and Lisle Rose, *Roots of Tragedy: The United States and the Struggle for Asia, 1945–1953* (Westport, Conn.: Greenwood, 1976), 53–54.

43 This is a theme in Bartholomew-Feis, *OSS and Ho Chi Minh*. And see also the recollections of Henry Prunier, a member of the mission, in Christian G. Appy, *Patriots: The Vietnam War Remembered from All Sides* (New York: Viking, 2003), 38–41.

44 René J. Défourneaux, "A Secret Encounter with Ho Chi Minh," *Look*, August 9, 1966, 32–33; Bartholomew-Feis, *OSS and Ho Chi Minh*, 205–15; Tran Trong Trung oral history, Hanoi, June 12, 2007. I thank interviewer Merle Pribbenow for making this oral history available to me.

45 Quoted in Robert Shaplen, *The Lost Revolution: The U.S. in Vietnam, 1946–1966* (New York: Harper & Row, 1966), 35.

46 Ronald H. Spector, *In the Ruins of Empire: The Japanese Surrender and the Battle for Postwar Asia* (New York: Random House, 2007), 96–101; T. O. Smith, *Britain and the Origins of the Vietnam War: U.K. Policy in Indo-China, 1943–1950* (New York: Palgrave Macmillan, 2007), 21–33.

47 An indispensable account is Mark Atwood Lawrence, *Assuming the Burden: Europe and the American Commitment to War in Vietnam* (Berkeley: University of California Press, 2005), 68–74. And see *Causes, Origins, and Lessons of the Vietnam War:* Hearings before the Committee on Foreign Relations, U.S. Senate, 92nd Cong., 2nd sess., June 9–11, 1972 (Washington, D.C.: Government Printing Office, 1973), 167, 175–76.

48 Ronald H. Spector, *Advice and Support: The Early Years of the U.S. Army in Vietnam, 1941–1960* (Washington, D.C.: Center for Military History, 1985), 45.

49 Spector, *Advice and Support*, 45; Hess, *United States' Emergence*, 152–53; Thorne, *Allies of a Kind*, 95.

50 Dreifort, *Myopic Grandeur*, 248–49.

51 Ibid., 249–50.

52 *NYT*, September 16, 1945; Charles de Gaulle, *The Complete War Memoirs of Charles de Gaulle*, trans. Jonathan Griffin and Richard Howard (New York: Carroll & Graf, 1998), 926.

CHAPTER 4: *"All Men Are Created Equal"*

1 William S. Logan, *Hanoi: Biography of a City* (Seattle: University of Washington Press, 2000), 77.

2 Ibid., 95–96.

3 Mark Sidel, *Old Hanoi* (New York: Oxford University Press, 1999), 27.

4 William J. Duiker, *Ho Chi Minh: A Life* (New York: Hyperion, 2000), 316; David

G. Marr, *Vietnam 1945: The Quest for Power* (Berkeley: University of California Press, 1995), 489.

5   William J. Duiker, *Sacred War: Nationalism and Revolution in a Divided Vietnam* (New York: McGraw-Hill, 1995), 48; see also Bui Diem with David Chanoff, *In the Jaws of History* (Boston: Houghton Mifflin, 1987), 33–36.

6   This is a main theme in Marr, *Vietnam 1945*.

7   Joseph Buttinger, *Vietnam: A Dragon Embattled*, vol. 1: *From Colonialism to the Vietminh* (New York: Praeger, 1967), 210; Duiker, *Sacred War*, 48; Stanley Karnow, *Vietnam: A History*, 2nd ed. (New York: Penguin, 1997), 162.

8   Xuan Phuong and Danièle Mazingarbe, *Ao Dai: My War, My Country, My Vietnam* (Great Neck, N.Y.: EMQUAD, 2004), 53–54.

9   Gilbert Pilleul, ed., *De Gaulle et l'Indochine, 1940–1946* (Paris: Plon, 1982), 193.

10   François Guillemot, "Viêt Nam 1945–1946: L'élimination de l'opposition nationaliste et anticolonialiste dans la Nord: Au coeur de la fracture vietnamienne," in Christopher E. Goscha and Benoît de Tréglodé, eds., *Le Viêt Nam depuis 1945: États, contestations et constructions du passé* (Paris: Les Indes savantes, 2004), 1–9; Duiker, *Ho Chi Minh*, 316–17.

11   Marr, *Vietnam 1945*, 529–31.

12   Ibid., 532.

13   Bernard B. Fall, ed., *Ho Chi Minh on Revolution: Selected Writings, 1920–1966* (New York: Praeger, 1967), 53–56.

14   Marr, *Vietnam 1945*, 536.

15   *Vietnam: A Television History*, episode 1: "Roots of a War," PBS, transcript.

16   Duiker, *Ho Chi Minh*, 330; Marr, *Vietnam 1945*, 365.

17   Marr, *Vietnam 1945*, 368.

18   Bui Diem, *In the Jaws of History*, 38.

19   Archimedes L. A. Patti, *Why Viet Nam? Prelude to America's Albatross* (Berkeley: University of California Press, 1981), 198; Duiker, *Ho Chi Minh*, 318; Françoise Martin, *Heures tragiques au Tonkin* (Paris: Éditions Berger, 1948), 152; Jean Sainteny, *Histoire d'une paix manquée, Indochine 1945–1947* (Paris: Amiot-Dumont, 1953), 71–77.

20   Michael Maclear, *The Ten Thousand Day War* (New York: Avon, 1982), 12; Patti, *Why Viet Nam?*, 223–24. For the recollection of another American who was in the city then, see René J. Défourneaux, *The Winking Fox: Twenty-two Years in Military Intelligence* (Indianapolis: ICA, 2000), 197–202.

21   Marr, *Vietnam 1945*, 500.

22   Patti to Indiv, September 2, 1945, Record Group 226, Box 199, NARA; Mark Philip Bradley, *Imagining Vietnam and America: The Making of Postcolonial Vietnam, 1919–1950* (Chapel Hill: University of North Carolina Press, 2000), 134–35; Ronald H. Spector, *Advice and Support: The Early Years of the U.S. Army in Vietnam, 1941–1960* (Washington, D.C.: Center for Military History, 1985), 57.

23   September 19, 1945, FO 371/49088, TNA.

24   August 16, 1945, FO 371/49088, TNA. See also Antony Beevor, *Paris: After the Liberation, 1944–1949*, rev. ed. (London: Penguin, 2004), 206–7.

25   Jean Lacouture, *De Gaulle: The Ruler, 1945–1970* (New York: W.W. Norton, 1992), 64; Charles de Gaulle, *The Complete War Memoirs of Charles de Gaulle*, trans. Jonathan Griffin and Richard Howard (New York: Carroll & Graf, 1998), 910.

26   Lisle Rose, *Roots of Tragedy: The United States and the Struggle for Asia, 1945–1953* (Westport, Conn.: Greenwood, 1976), 51–52; Lacouture, *De Gaulle*, 64; De Gaulle, *War Memoirs*, 910–11.

27 Harold R. Isaacs, *No Peace for Asia* (New York: Macmillan, 1947), 232–34. On the extraordinary esteem in which Americans were held in Vietnam at the end of the war, see the 1981 interview with Herbert Bluechel, who served in Saigon at the time, WGBH Vietnam Collection, openvault.wgbh.org/catalog/org.wgbh .mla:Vietnam (last accessed on November 12, 2010). And see Bui Diem, *In the Jaws of History*, 34, 38.

28 Isaacs, *No Peace for Asia*, 233–34.

29 See the analysis in Paul Kattenburg, *The Vietnam Trauma in American Foreign Policy, 1945–75* (New Brunswick, N.J.: Transaction, 1980), 14.

30 Quoted in Ronald H. Spector, *In the Ruins of Empire: The Japanese Surrender and the Battle for Postwar Asia* (New York: Random House, 2007), 114.

31 Maclear, *Ten Thousand Day War*, 11.

32 Marr, *Vietnam 1945*, 488–89.

33 Ibid., 491, 492.

34 Bui Diem, *In the Jaws of History*, 39; Patti, *Why Viet Nam?*, 284; Phuong and Mazingarbe, *Ao Dai*, 54–55.

35 Duong Van Mai Elliott, *The Sacred Willow: Four Generations in the Life of a Vietnamese Family* (New York: Oxford University Press, 2000), 131.

36 Duiker, *Ho Chi Minh*, 327–28; Jacques Dalloz, *The War in Indo-China, 1945–1954* (New York: Barnes & Noble, 1990), 56.

37 David G. Marr, "Creating Defense Capacity in Vietnam, 1945–1947," in Mark Atwood Lawrence and Fredrik Logevall, eds., *The First Vietnam War: Colonial Conflict and Cold War Crisis* (Cambridge, Mass.: Harvard University Press, 2007), 88.

38 Duiker, *Ho Chi Minh*, 329; Ellen J. Hammer, *The Struggle for Indochina, 1940–1955* (Stanford, Calif.: Stanford University Press, 1955), 133.

39 David W. P. Elliott, *The Vietnamese War: Revolution and Social Change in the Mekong Delta, 1930–1975* (Armonk, N.Y.: M.E. Sharpe, 2007), chap. 4; Hammer, *Struggle for Indochina*, 106; Frances FitzGerald, *Fire in the Lake: The Vietnamese and the Americans in Vietnam* (Boston: Little, Brown, 1972), 71–74.

40 Norman Sherry, *The Life of Graham Greene*, vol. 2: *1939–1955* (New York: Viking, 1995), 365.

41 Quoted in Andrew Forbes, "Graham Greene's Saigon Revisited," *CPAmedia.com*, www.cpamedia.com/articles/20051020_01/ (last accessed on July 20, 2010).

42 Buttinger, *Dragon Embattled*, 218; Robert Shaplen, *The Lost Revolution: The U.S. in Vietnam, 1946–1966* (New York: Harper & Row, 1966), 6; Huynh Van Thieng interview, 1981, WGBH Vietnam Collection, openvault.wgbh.org/catalog/org.wgbh .mla:Vietnam (last accessed on November 24, 2010).

43 Peter Dennis, *Troubled Days of Peace: Mountbatten and South East Asia Command, 1945–1946* (New York: St. Martin's, 1987), 40.

44 M. E. Dening to FO, September 10, 1945, WO203, TNA; M. E. Dening to FO, September 25, 1945, FO 371/46308, TNA. British thinking in this period is examined in Mark Atwood Lawrence, "Forging the Great Combination: Britain and the Indochina Problem, 1945–1950," in Lawrence and Logevall, eds., *First Vietnam War*, 111–17; and in Peter Neville, *Britain in Vietnam: Prelude to Disaster, 1945–1946* (London: Routledge, 2007).

45 John Saville, *The Politics of Continuity: British Foreign Policy and the Labour Government, 1945–46* (London: Verso, 1993), 177–78; John Springhall, "Kicking Out the Viet Minh: How Britain Allowed France to Reoccupy South Indochina, 1945–46," *Journal of Contemporary History* 40 (2005), 128. A sympathetic assessment of

the thinking of Gracey and his officers is in Peter M. Dunn, *The First Vietnam War* (New York: St. Martin's, 1985), esp. 169–72, 186–88.

46 J. F. Cairns, *The Eagle and the Lotus: Western Intervention in Vietnam, 1847–1968* (Melbourne, Australia: Lansdowne Press, 1969), 29. See also the thoughtful examination of Gracey's mission in Neville, *Britain in Vietnam*.

47 John Keay, *Empire's End: A History of the Far East from High Colonialism to Hong Kong* (New York: Scribner, 1997), 278; Saigon Control Commission, "Political Report, 13th September, 1945, to 9th October, 1945," Gracey 4/8, Liddell Hart Centre for Military Archives, King's College London, UK.

48 Germaine Krull, "Diary of Saigon, following the Allied occupation in September 1945," WOS Special File, Record Group 59, Lot File 59 D 190, Box 9, NARA.

49 Marr, *Vietnam 1945,* 541; Springhall, "Kicking Out the Viet Minh," 122.

50 On the importance of this period in terms of what comes later, see Vo Nguyen Giap, *Chien Dau trong vong vay* (Hanoi: Nha Xuat Ban Quan Doi Nhan Dan [People's Army of Vietnam Publishing House], 1995), 22–23; and Vo Nguyen Giap, *Mémoires 1946–1954,* vol. 1: *La résistance encerclée* (Fontenay-sous-Bois: Anako, 2003–4), 27.

51 Harold Isaacs, "Indo-China: A Fight for Freedom," *New Republic,* February 3, 1947.

52 One Viet Minh sympathizer, interviewed many years later, expressed great affection for Dewey. See Huynh Van Thieng interview.

53 George Wickes, "Saigon 1945," unpublished ms. in author's possession, p. 6; Bluechel interview; Karnow, *Vietnam,* 151; Rose, *Roots of Tragedy,* 61.

54 Dixee R. Bartholomew-Feis, *The OSS and Ho Chi Minh: Unexpected Allies in the War Against Japan* (Lawrence: University Press of Kansas, 2006), 288–99. For speculation as to what may have occurred to Dewey's body, see Spector, *In the Ruins of Empire,* 131.

55 *NYT,* October 1, 1945; Mark Atwood Lawrence, *Assuming the Burden: Europe and the American Commitment to War in Vietnam* (Berkeley: University of California Press, 2005), 149; Saigon Control Commission, "Political Report."

56 Christopher E. Goscha, "Belated Asian Allies: The Technical and Military Contributions of Japanese Deserters (1945–50)," in Marilyn B. Young and Robert Buzzanco, eds., *A Companion to the Vietnam War* (London: Blackwell, 2002), 37–64; John T. McAlister, Jr., *Viet Nam: The Origins of Revolution* (Princeton, N.J.: Center for International Studies, Princeton University, 1969), 212; Lawrence, *Assuming the Burden,* 150.

57 Wickes, "Saigon 1945," 11–12. I'm grateful to Mr. Wickes for sharing this memoir with me.

58 Anthony Clayton, *The Wars of French Decolonization* (London: Longman, 1994), 127; J. Davidson, *Indo-China: Signposts in the Storm* (Hong Kong: Longman, 1979), 42.

59 Marr, *Vietnam 1945,* 1.

CHAPTER 5: *The Warrior Monk*

1 A superb, deeply researched study of the period covered in this chapter and the next is Stein Tønnesson, *Vietnam 1946: How the War Began* (Berkeley: University of California Press, 2009).

2 D'Argenlieu's devotion to de Gaulle is a theme in his posthumously published account, *Chronique d'Indochine 1945–1947* (Paris: Albin Michel, 1985). A trenchant

biographical summary produced in the British Foreign Office can be found in FO 371/46307, TNA.

3 Ellen J. Hammer, *The Struggle for Indochina, 1940–1955* (Stanford, Calif.: Stanford University Press, 1955), 122.

4 Bernard Fall, *The Two Viet-Nams: A Political and Military Analysis* (New York: Praeger, 1964), 72.

5 Philippe Devillers, *Histoire du Viêt-Nam de 1940 à 1952* (Paris: Éditions du Seuil, 1952), 195; Joseph Buttinger, *Vietnam: A Dragon Embattled,* vol. 1: *From Colonialism to the Vietminh* (New York: Praeger, 1967), 233.

6 François Guillemot, "Viêt Nam 1945–1946: L'élimination de l'opposition nationaliste et anticolonialiste dans le Nord: À coeur de la fracture vietnamienne," in Christopher E. Goscha and Benoît de Tréglodé, eds., *Le Viêt Nam depuis 1945: États, contestations et constructions du passé* (Paris: Les Indes savantes, 2004); David G. Marr, *Vietnam 1945: The Quest for Power* (Berkeley: University of California Press, 1995), 550.

7 Marr, *Vietnam 1945,* 551; Cecil. B. Currey, *Victory at Any Cost: The Genius of Viet Nam's Gen. Vo Nguyen Giap* (Dulles, Va.: Potomac, 2005), 106.

8 David G. Marr, "Creating Defense Capacity in Vietnam, 1945–1947," in Mark Atwood Lawrence and Fredrik Logevall, eds., *The First Vietnam War: Colonial Conflict and Cold War Crisis* (Cambridge, Mass.: Harvard University Press, 2007), 74–104; William J. Duiker, *Ho Chi Minh: A Life* (New York: Hyperion, 2000), 346.

9 Duiker, *Ho Chi Minh,* 347; Peter G. MacDonald, *Giap: The Victor in Vietnam* (New York: W.W. Norton, 1993), 69. On the extraordinary efforts made to secure weapons and ammunition in this period, see also Nguyen Thi Dinh interview, 1981, WGBH Vietnam Collection, openvault.wgbh.org/catalog/org.wgbh.mla:Vietnam (last accessed on October 15, 2010).

10 Stanley Karnow, *Vietnam: A History,* 2nd ed. (New York: Penguin, 1997), 168; Ilya V. Gaiduk, *Confronting Vietnam: Soviet Policy Toward the Indochina Conflict, 1954–1963* (Stanford, Calif.: Stanford University Press, 2003), 3.

11 Jean Sainteny, *Histoire d'une paix manquée, Indochine 1945–1947* (Paris: Amiot-Dumont, 1953), 166; Charles Fenn, *Ho Chi Minh: A Biographical Introduction* (New York: Charles Scribner's Sons, 1973), 94–95; Jean Sainteny, *Ho Chi Minh and His Vietnam: A Personal Memoir* (Chicago: Cowles, 1972), 51ff.

12 Robert Shaplen, *The Lost Revolution: The U.S. in Vietnam, 1946–1966* (New York: Harper & Row, 1966), 43. Pignon's memoirs, unfinished at the time of his death, were completed and published by a team led by his widow. See Elise Pignon et al., *Léon Pignon: Une vie au service des peuples d'Outre-Mer* (Paris: Academie des Sciences d'Outre-Mer, 1988). Pignon's role in French Indochina policy is also the subject of Daniel Varga, "La politique française en Indochine (1947–50): Histoire d'une décolonisation manqué," thèse de doctorat, Université d'Aix-Marseille I, 2004.

13 Frédéric Turpin, *De Gaulle, les gaullistes et l'Indochine 1940–1956* (Paris: Les Indes savantes, 2005), 183–90; Duiker, *Ho Chi Minh,* 355.

14 On this point, see Gilbert Bodinier and Philippe Duplay, "Montrer sa force et négocier," in Guy Pedroncini and Philippe Duplay, eds., *Leclerc et l'Indochine 1945–1947* (Paris: Albin Michel, 1992), 181–82; and Tønnesson, *Vietnam 1946,* 161, 351n54.

15 Devillers, *Histoire du Viêt-Nam,* 176; Fall, *Two Viet-Nams,* 107.

16 Leclerc to Juin and d'Argenlieu, February 14, 1946, Tel. 933, AOM; reprinted in Gilbert Bodinier, ed., *1945–1946. Le retour de la France en Indochine. Textes et documents* (Vincennes: Service historique de l'armée de terre, 1987), 208–9;

D'Argenlieu to Sainteny, February 20, 1946, F60 C3024, AN; Mark Atwood Lawrence, *Assuming the Burden: Europe and the American Commitment to War in Vietnam* (Berkley: University of California Press, 2005), 128. See also Martin Shipway, *The Road to War: France and Vietnam, 1944–1947* (Providence, R.I.: Berghahn, 1996), 167–68.

17 Operation Bentré is well described and analyzed in Tønnesson, *Vietnam 1946*, 42–49. See also Turpin, *De Gaulle, les gaullistes et l'Indochine*, 195–215.

18 Peter Worthing, *Revolution and Occupation: China and the Vietnamese August Revolution of 1945* (Berkeley: China Research Monograph, Institute of East Asian Studies, 2001), 120–24, 135–69; Stein Tønnesson, "La paix imposée par la Chine: L'accord franco-vietnamien du 6 mars 1946," in Charles-Robert Ageron and Philippe Devillers, eds., *Les guerres d'Indochine de 1945 à 1975* (Paris: Institut d'histoire du temps présent, 1996). On the important role played by the Chinese, see also Lin Hua, *Chiang Kai-shek, de Gaulle contre Hô Chi Minh: Viêt-nam 1945–1946* (Paris: Éditions L'Harmattan, 1994); and Laurent Cesari, *L'Indochine en guerres 1945–1993* (Paris: Belin, 1995), 42–43.

19 Lawrence, *Assuming the Burden*, 128. For Giap's defense of the March 6 deal, see Devillers, *Histoire du Viêt-Nam*, 229–31. In official Vietnamese historiography, the agreement is seen as having been necessary to keep Vietnam from having to fight two adversaries simultaneously. Nguyen Khac Vien, *Vietnam: A Long History* (Hanoi: Gioi, 1999), 251.

20 Quoted in Michael Maclear, *The Ten Thousand Day War* (New York: Avon, 1982), 18. See also Sainteny, *Ho Chi Minh and His Vietnam*, 59–64.

21 George Wickes, "Hanoi 1946," unpublished ms. in author's possession, pp. 4–5; Saigon to FO, April 11, 1946, FO 959/7, TNA.

22 A point made well in Buttinger, *Dragon Embattled*, 373. For d'Argenlieu's retrospective view of the agreement, see his *Chronique d'Indochine*, chap. 7.

23 Lawrence, *Assuming the Burden*, 124–26. Lawrence argues for a somewhat greater range of opinion in French thinking in this period than I would.

24 On the intricacies of French party politics in the early years of the war, see Martin Thomas, "French Imperial Reconstruction and the Development of the Indochina War, 1945–50," in Lawrence and Logevall, eds., *First Vietnam War*; and R.E.M. Irving, *The First Indochina War: French and American Policy, 1945–1954* (London: Croom Helm, 1975), 1–77.

25 Devillers, *Histoire du Viêt-Nam*, 242; Shipway, *Road to War*, 179–81; Tønnesson, *Vietnam 1946*, 62.

26 For the admiral's recapitulation of the Dalat talks, see his memorandum, April 26, 1946, F60 C3024, AN. See also Buttinger, *Dragon Embattled*, 247.

27 Devillers, *Histoire du Viêt-Nam*, 324.

28 David Schoenbrun, *As France Goes* (New York: Atheneum, 1968), 231; Duiker, *Ho Chi Minh*, 370.

29 Robert Shaplen, *Lost Revolution*, 47.

30 Jacques Dumaine, *Quai d'Orsay: 1945–1951* (Paris: Julliard, 1955), 103, quoted in Pierre Brocheux, *Ho Chi Minh: A Biography* (New York: Cambridge University Press, 2007), 121.

31 *NYT,* July 6, 1946.

32 Leclerc to Schumann, June 8, 1946, printed in Georgette Elgey, *Histoire de la IVème République*, vol. 1: *La République des illusions 1945–1951* (Paris: Fayard, 1965), 161.

33 Bui Diem with David Chanoff, *In the Jaws of History* (Boston: Houghton Mifflin, 1987), 44; Anthony Clayton, *The Wars of French Decolonization* (London: Longman, 1994), 131ff.

34 For Bidault's background and rise to power, see Jacques Dalloz, *Georges Bidault: Biographie politique* (Paris: Éditions L'Harmattan, 1992).

35 *Vietnam: A Television History*, episode 1: "Roots of a War," PBS, transcript.

36 Quoted in David Halberstam, *Ho* (New York: McGraw-Hill, 1987), 89.

37 Alexander Werth, *France 1940–1955* (New York: Henry Holt, 1956), 335–36; Jean Lacouture, *Leon Blum* (New York: Holmes & Meier, 1982), 532.

38 Werth, *France 1940–1955*, 336; Buttinger, *Dragon Embattled*, 252; D'Argenlieu, *Chronique d'Indochine*, 302–16. A solid account of the Fontainebleau talks is Shipway, *Road to War*, chap. 8.

39 Schoenbrun, *As France Goes*, 232–35; Sainteny, *Ho Chi Minh and His Vietnam*, 87.

40 Sainteny, *Histoire d'une paix manqué*, 209ff; Raoul Salan, *Mémoires: Fin d'un empire*, vol. 1: *Le sens d'un engagement juin 1899–septembre 1946* (Paris: Presses de la Cité, 1970), 404.

41 Duiker, *Ho Chi Minh*, 380; Buttinger, *Dragon Embattled*, 253; Lacouture, *Blum*, 532; *Newsweek*, September 30, 1946.

42 James P. Harrison, *Endless War: Vietnam's Struggle for Independence* (New York: Columbia University Press, 1989), 109.

43 Nhat Ky Hanh Trinh cua Ho Chu tich, "Bon thang sang Phap" [Travel notebook of President Ho: Four months in France], in *Toan Tap*, 4, pp. 323–411, as quoted in Brocheaux, *Ho Chi Minh*, 122.

CHAPTER 6: *The Spark*

1 Unbeknownst to Ho, the French secret services successfully infiltrated his cabin on the ship, outwitting his guards and photographing many of his private papers while he ate lunch. Due to a technical glitch, however, the film could not be developed. Paul Aussaresse, *Pour la France, Services spéciaux 1942–1954* (Paris: Éditions du Rocher, 2001), 175.

2 Bui Diem with David Chanoff, *In the Jaws of History* (Boston: Houghton Mifflin, 1987), 13. Biographies of Giap include Tran Trong Trung, *Tong tu lenh Vo Nguyen Giap* (Hanoi: NXB Chinh Tri Quoc Gia, 2006); Cecil B. Currey, *Victory at Any Cost: The Genius of Viet Nam's Gen. Vo Nguyen Giap* (Dulles, Va.: Potomac, 2005). Giap's most recent multivolume memoirs should also be consulted.

3 A. J. Langguth, *Our Vietnam: The War, 1954–1975* (New York: Simon & Schuster, 2000), 52.

4 Currey, *Victory at Any Cost*, 49–52.

5 Stein Tønnesson, *Vietnam 1946: How the War Began* (Berkeley: University of California Press, 2009), 28.

6 Edgar O'Ballance, *The Indo-China War, 1945–1954* (London: Faber & Faber, 1964), 66–67.

7 *NYT*, August 6, 1946.

8 Martin Windrow, *The Last Valley: Dien Bien Phu and the French Defeat in Vietnam* (Cambridge, Mass.: Da Capo, 2004), 89; Bui Diem, *In the Jaws of History*, 46–49.

9 O'Ballance, *Indo-China War*, 71–72; Saigon to FO, October 15, 1946, FO 959/11, TNA.

10 Christopher E. Goscha, "A 'Popular' Side of the Vietnamese Army: General

Nguyên Bình and the Early War in the South (1910–1951)," in Christopher E. Goscha and Benoît de Tréglodé, eds., *Naissance d'un état-parti: Le Viêt Nam depuis 1945* (Paris: Les Indes savantes, 2004), 325–54.

11 Instructions to Nam Bo from the Minister of Propaganda (Tran Huy Lieu), early September 1946, appendix to a memo from d'Argenlieu to the session of the COMININDO on November 23, 1946, F60 C3024, AN.

12 Tønnesson, *Vietnam 1946,* 76–77; Philippe Devillers, *Histoire du Viêt-Nam de 1940 à 1952* (Paris: Éditions du Seuil, 1952), 318.

13 Haussaire to COMININDO No. 1800F, November 10, 1946, Tel. 938, Archives nationales d'outre-mer (hereafter AOM); David G. Marr, *Vietnamese Anticolonialism, 1885–1925* (Berkeley: University of California Press, 1971), 39; Tønnesson, *Vietnam 1946,* 104.

14 Martin Shipway, *The Road to War: France and Vietnam, 1944–1947* (Providence, R.I.: Berghahn, 1996), 235; Mark Atwood Lawrence, *Assuming the Burden: Europe and the American Commitment to War in Vietnam* (Berkeley: University of California Press, 2005), 153.

15 Paul Mus, *Viêt-Nam: Sociologie d'une guerre* (Paris: Éditions du Seuil, 1952), 73.

16 Frédéric Turpin, *De Gaulle, les gaullistes et l'Indochine 1940–1956* (Paris: Les Indes savantes, 2005), 602–24; Tønnesson, *Vietnam 1946,* 107–8. For Valluy's retrospective view of Haiphong's strategic importance, see *La Revue des deux mondes,* December 1, 1967, 364ff.

17 Tønnesson, *Vietnam 1946,* 108.

18 Printed in Gilbert Bodinier, ed., *1945–1946. Le retour de la France en Indochine. Textes et documents* (Vincennes: Service historique de l'armée de terre, 1987), 315–17. See also Philippe Devillers, *Paris-Saigon-Hanoi: Les archives de la guerre, 1944–1947* (Paris: Gallimard/Julliard, 1988), 240–41.

19 Pignon to COMININDO, November 19, 1946, vol. 255, no. 4145/CAAP3, Série Asie-Océanie 1944–49, MAE.

20 Tønnesson, *Vietnam 1946,* 120.

21 General Morlière, "Rapport sur les événements politiques et militaires en Indochine du Nord, au cours du dernier trimestre 1946," January 10, 1947, printed in Georges Chaffard, *Les deux guerres du Viêt-nam de Valluy à Westmoreland* (Paris: La Table Ronde, 1969), 36–58; Devillers, *Histoire du Viêt-Nam,* 332ff. For a Vietnamese version of events, see Vo Nguyen Giap, *Unforgettable Days* (Hanoi: Foreign Languages Publishing House, 1975), 373.

22 Devillers, *Histoire du Viêt-Nam,* 335; Shipway, *Road to War,* 243.

23 *La Revue des deux mondes,* December 15, 1967, p. 510; Devillers, *Histoire du Viêt-Nam,* 339. For Martin quote, see *Vietnam: A Television History,* episode 1: "Roots of a War," PBS, transcript. For the varying estimates on the number of Vietnamese killed, see Tønnesson, *Vietnam 1946,* 133–35. Tønnesson concludes that the number must be in the thousands, and that most of the dead were civilians.

24 Shipway, *Road to War,* 245.

25 Stanley Karnow, *Vietnam: A History,* 2nd ed. (New York: Penguin, 1997), 172; Ellen J. Hammer, *The Struggle for Indochina, 1940–1955* (Stanford, Calif.: Stanford University Press, 1955), 185.

26 Hanoi to FO, December 9, 1946, 959/11, TNA.

27 William J. Duiker, *U.S. Containment Policy and the Conflict in Indochina* (Stanford, Calif.: Stanford University Press, 1994), 45–46. In early December, Moffat told a British official that Communism would in all likelihood increase in Vietnam as a result of the French actions there. D'Argenlieu, he added, had become much

more reactionary and imperialistic and had gone back on agreements. D'Argenlieu, for his part, told the British ambassador in Paris that the root of the trouble in Vietnam was Communism. FO to Saigon, December 4, 1946, FO 959/14, TNA.

28 David Halberstam, *The Best and the Brightest* (New York: Random House, 1972), 85.

29 Duong Van Mai Elliott, *The Sacred Willow: Four Generations in the Life of a Vietnamese Family* (New York: Oxford University Press, 2000), 135; Hanoi to FO, December 9, 1946, FO 959/11, TNA.

30 Tønnesson, *Vietnam 1946*, 195–98.

31 *NYT*, December 21, 1946; Shipway, *Road to War*, 262.

32 Elliott, *Sacred Willow*, 138–39.

33 Ibid., 141.

34 On the difficulty of pinpointing a start date, see Alain Ruscio, *La guerre "française" d'Indochine, 1945–1954* (Paris: Les Indes Savantes, 1992), 92.

35 The French determination to reoccupy Tonkin, through war with the DRV if necessary, is powerfully demonstrated in the works by Turpin, Tønnesson, and Devillers cited above. D'Argenlieu quoted in *Le Monde*, December 27, 1946.

36 On December 24, *L'Humanité* voiced support for diplomacy, but only if conditions had been met: "Negotiations as soon as peace and order have been reestablished."

37 Shipway, *Road to War*, 250, 259–65; Hammer, *Struggle for Indochina*, 190; Joseph Buttinger, *Vietnam: A Dragon Embattled*, vol. 1: *From Colonialism to the Viet Minh* (New York: Praeger, 1967), 279.

38 Martin Thomas, "French Imperial Reconstruction and the Development of the Indochina War, 1945–1950," in Mark Atwood Lawrence and Fredrik Logevall, *The First Vietnam War: Colonial Conflict and Cold War Crisis* (Cambridge, Mass.: Harvard University Press, 2007), 134. On the (noncolonial) success of French diplomacy after 1945, see William I. Hitchcock, *France Restored: Cold War Diplomacy and the Quest for Leadership in Europe, 1944–1954* (Chapel Hill: University of North Carolina Press, 1998). On the MRP's foreign policy more broadly, an excellent study is John W. Young, *France, the Cold War, and the Western Alliance, 1944–1949: French Foreign Policy and Postwar Europe* (Leicester, U.K.: Leicester University Press, 1990).

39 Roure quoted in Tønnesson, *Vietnam 1946*, 142.

40 Turpin, *De Gaulle, les gaullistes et l'Indochine 1940–1956*, esp. 219–325. De Gaulle quoted in *Le Monde*, August 26, 1946.

41 D'Argenlieu, *Chronique d'Indochine*, 370; Devillers, *Paris-Saigon-Hanoi*, 311.

CHAPTER 7: *War Without Fronts*

1 *NYT*, February 8, 1947.

2 Yves Gras, *Histoire de la guerre d'Indochine* (Paris: Plon, 1979), 162–67; Phillip B. Davidson, *Vietnam at War: The History, 1946–1975* (New York: Oxford University Press, 1991), 47. See also *La Revue des deux mondes*, December 1, 1967.

3 See, e.g., Douglas Porch, *The French Foreign Legion: A Complete History of the Legendary Fighting Force* (New York: HarperCollins, 1991).

4 Henry Ainley, *In Order to Die* (London: Burke, 1955), 13–14.

5 Seymour Topping, *Journey Between Two Chinas* (New York: Harper & Row, 1972), 119.

6 Moutet quoted in *Le Monde*, January 2 and January 5, 1947.

7 Gras, *Histoire de la guerre d'Indochine*, 175–77.

8 Vo Nguyen Giap, *Memoirs of War: The Road to Dien Bien Phu* (Hanoi: Gioi, 2004), 21.

9 Truong Chinh, *The Resistance Will Win* (Hanoi: Foreign Languages Publishing House, 1960 ed.). See also William J. Duiker, *The Communist Road to Power in Vietnam* (Boulder, Colo.: Westview, 1996), 135.

10 Vo Nguyen Giap, "Notre guerre de libération—stratégie et tactique," April 3, 1947, French translation in TFIN 2ᵉ Bureau BR No. 2788/2, June 11, 1947, CP 128, AOM. See also Vo Nguyen Giap, *Mémoires 1946–1954,* vol. 1: *La résistance encerclée* (Fontenay-sous-Bois: Anako, 2003–4), 37–39; and Vo Nguyen Giap, *Unforgettable Days* (Hanoi: Foreign Languages Publishing House, 1975), 409.

11 Martin Windrow, *The Last Valley: Dien Bien Phu and the French Defeat in Vietnam* (Cambridge, Mass.: Da Capo, 2004), 93.

12 Bernard B. Fall, "The Anatomy of Insurgency in Indochina, 1946–54," delivered on April 22, 1965, at the the National War College, Washington, D.C. A copy is in Box P-1, series 1.5, Papers and Reports by Dr. Fall, Bernard Fall Collection, JFKL.

13 An excellent description of the difficulties experienced by the French in this regard is in Windrow, *Last Valley,* 97–100.

14 Ibid., 96–97.

15 British Military Liaison Report, July 11, 1947, FO 474/1, TNA.

16 Windrow, *Last Valley,* 104.

17 Ibid., 99; Joseph Buttinger, *Vietnam: A Dragon Embattled,* vol. 2: *Vietnam at War* (New York: Praeger, 1967), 739–40; George Armstrong Kelly, *Lost Soldiers: The French Army and Empire in Crisis* (Cambridge, Mass.: MIT Press, 1965), 47.

18 Buttinger, *Dragon Embattled,* 737–38.

19 Le Ly Hayslip, *When Heaven and Earth Changed Places* (New York: Doubleday, 1989), 4.

20 Memorandum RM-5721-PR. *A Translation from the French: Lessons of the War in Indochina,* trans. V. J. Croizat (Santa Monica, Calif.: Rand Corporation, 1967), 2:56–57.

21 Joseph Buttinger, *Vietnam: A Political History* (New York: Praeger, 1968), 285; *NYT,* January 19, 1947; Singapore to FO, January 30, 1947, CAB 121/742, TNA.

22 See Paris to FO, April 8, 1947, FO 471/1, TNA; David Drake, "*Les Temps modernes* and the French War in Indochina," *Journal of European Studies* 28 (March–June 1998): 25–41.

23 Martin Thomas, "French Imperial Reconstruction and the Development of the Indochina War, 1945–1950," in Mark Atwood Lawrence and Fredrik Logevall, *The First Vietnam War: Colonial Conflict and Cold War Crisis* (Cambridge, Mass.: Harvard University Press, 2007), 139.

24 *Journal Officiel,* Assemblée Nationale, March 18, 1947, pp. 879–82; Mark Atwood Lawrence, *Assuming the Burden: Europe and the American Commitment to War in Vietnam* (Berkeley: University of California Press, 2005), 156–59; Thomas, "French Imperial Reconstruction," 140–41.

25 Cooper to Atlee, April 1, 1947, FO 474/1, TNA; Ellen J. Hammer, *The Struggle for Indochina, 1940–1955* (Stanford, Calif.: Stanford University Press, 1955), 197.

26 Lawrence, *Assuming the Burden,* 160; William I. Hitchcock, *France Restored: Cold War Diplomacy and the Quest for Leadership in Europe, 1944–1954* (Chapel Hill: University of North Carolina Press, 1998).

27 Lawrence, *Assuming the Burden,* 170–71; Paris to FO, April 1, 1947, FO 474/1, TNA.

28 A corrective is Lawrence, *Assuming the Burden.*

29 Quoted in Robert L. Beisner, *Dean Acheson: A Life in the Cold War* (New York: Oxford University Press, 2006), 60.

30 Walter Lippmann, *The Cold War: A Study in U.S. Foreign Policy* (New York: Harper & Row, 1947).

31 Eric Hobsbawm, *Age of Extremes: The Short Twentieth Century, 1914–1991* (London: Michael Joseph, 1994), 236–37.

32 Philippe Devillers, *Vietnam and France* (Paris: Comité d'études des problemes du Pacifique, distributed by Institute of Pacific Relations, 1950), 2.

33 Lawrence, *Assuming the Burden*, 172ff.

34 Marshall to Caffery, February 3, 1947, *Pentagon Papers. United States–Vietnam Relations, 1945–1967: Study Prepared by the Department of Defense* (Washington, D.C.: Government Printing Office, 1971), 8:98–99.

35 Jean Chauvel, "L'Indochine," February 10, 1947, Bidault Papers, File 128, Archives nationales, Paris (hereafter AN); Lawrence, *Assuming the Burden*, 181.

CHAPTER 8: *"If I Accepted These Terms I'd Be a Coward"*

1 Bollaert was not actually Ramadier's first choice to take over as high commissioner. Several weeks before, Ramadier had offered the post to General Leclerc and had attempted to sweeten the offer by granting him broad new powers. Leclerc declined, influenced perhaps by the cautionary words of Charles de Gaulle. "They want to use you," de Gaulle warned him. "You don't know politics. . . . They will make you take the responsibility for abandoning Indochina. . . . They will make you the instrument of capitulation." Philippe Devillers, *Histoire du Viêt-Nam de 1940 à 1952* (Paris: Éditions du Seuil, 1952), 397.

2 Coste-Floret quoted in *Combat*, May 14, 1947. See also Robert Shaplen, *The Lost Revolution: The U.S. in Vietnam, 1946–1966* (New York: Harper & Row, 1966), 58.

3 See the essays in David Chandler and Christopher E. Goscha, eds., *L'espace d'un regard : Paul Mus et l'Asie* (Paris: Les Indes savantes, 2006); Paul Mus, *Le déstin de l'Union Française de l'Indochine à l'Afrique* (Paris: Éditions du Seuil, 1954); John T. McAlister, Jr., and Paul Mus, *The Vietnamese and Their Revolution* (New York: Harper & Row, 1970), 7–8. For Mus's own description of his childhood, see Paul Mus, *L'angle de l'Asie*, ed. Serge Thion (Paris: Hermann, 1977), 214–15. Mus was an inspiration for Frances FitzGerald's classic work *Fire in the Lake: The Vietnamese and the Americans in Vietnam* (Boston: Little, Brown, 1972). She dedicated the book to the memory of Mus.

4 Douglas Porch, *The French Foreign Legion: A Complete History of the Legendary Fighting Force* (New York: HarperCollins, 1991), 527; Phillip B. Davidson, *Vietnam at War: The History, 1946–1975* (New York: Oxford University Press, 1991), 47–49.

5 Quoted in Susan Bayly, "Conceptualizing Resistance and Revolution in Vietnam: Paul Mus' Understanding of Colonialism in Crisis," *Journal of Vietnamese Studies* 4 (Winter 2009): 196.

6 David Chandler, "Paul Mus (1902–1969): A Biographical Sketch," *Journal of Vietnamese Studies* 4 (Winter 2009), 174; Paul Mus, *Viêt-Nam: Sociologie d'une guerre* (Paris: Éditions du Seuil, 1952), 312, 372; Paul Mus, *Ho Chi Minh, le Vietnam et l'Asie* (Paris: Éditions du Seuil, 1971), 79. See also Devillers, *Histoire du Viêt-Nam*, 404. Some accounts have the encounter occurring on May 11.

7 The book was never translated, but a useful compendium of Mus's ideas is McAlister and Mus, *The Vietnamese and Their Revolution*.

8 Christopher E. Goscha, "French Lessons from Indochina: Paul Mus and the American Debate over the Legitimacy of the Vietnam War," unpublished paper in author's possession.

9 Mark Philip Bradley, *Imagining Vietnam and America: The Making of Postcolonial Vietnam, 1919–1950* (Chapel Hill: University of North Carolina Press, 2000), 148–76; Christopher E. Goscha, "Le contexte asiatique de la guerre franco-vietnamienne: Réseaux, relations et économie," Ph.D. dissertation, École pratique des hautes études/Sorbonne, 2001, 563–99; Christopher E. Goscha, "Courting Diplomatic Disaster? The Difficult Integration of Vietnam into the Internationalist Communist Movement (1945–1950)," *Journal of Vietnamese Studies* 1 (February 2006): 59–103.

10 Bradley, *Imagining Vietnam and America,* 148–50; Tuong Vu, "From Cheering to Volunteering: Vietnamese Communists and the Coming of the Cold War," in Christopher E. Goscha and Christian F. Ostermann, eds., *Connecting Histories: Decolonization and the Cold War in Southeast Asia, 1945–1962* (Washington, D.C.: Woodrow Wilson Center Press, 2009), 184.

11 Bradley, *Imagining Vietnam and America,* 148–50.

12 Benoît de Tréglodé, "Premiers contacts entre le Vietnam et l'Union soviétique (1947–1948)," *Approches-Asie,* no. 16 (1999): 125–35; Goscha, "Courting Diplomatic Disaster?"

13 Already in January 1947, Pignon began articulating this argument. See his memo quoted in Philippe Devillers, *Paris-Saigon-Hanoi: Les archives de la guerre, 1944–1947* (Paris: Gallimard/Julliard, 1988), 334.

14 Devillers, *Histoire du Viêt-Nam,* 397–98; Robert Shaplen, *Lost Revolution,* 62.

15 Lloyd C. Gardner, *Approaching Vietnam: From World War II Through Dienbienphu* (New York: W.W. Norton, 1989), 77; Martin Windrow, *The Last Valley: Dien Bien Phu and the French Defeat in Vietnam* (Cambridge, Mass.: Da Capo, 2004), 105.

16 For biographical details, see, e.g., Devillers, *Histoire du Viêt-Nam,* 61–64; George McTurnan Kahin, *Intervention: How America Became Involved in Vietnam* (New York: Alfred A. Knopf, 1986), 24–26.

17 Ellen J. Hammer, *The Struggle for Indochina, 1940–1955* (Stanford, Calif.: Stanford University Press, 1955), 211–12.

18 Discours prononcé par M. E. Bollaert, September 11, 1947, Record Group 59, 851G.00/9–1147, NARA.

19 Neil L. Jamieson, *Understanding Vietnam* (Berkeley: University of California Press, 1993), 212–13.

20 Christopher E. Goscha, "Intelligence in a Time of Decolonization: The Case of the Democratic Republic of Vietnam at War (1945–1950)," *Intelligence & National Security,* 22 (2007), 13.

21 Yves Gras, *Histoire de la guerre d'Indochine* (Paris: Plon, 1979), 190–97.

22 Bernard Fall, *Street Without Joy: Indochina at War, 1946–1954* (Harrisburg, Pa.: Stackpole Books, 1961), 30.

23 Stanley Karnow, *Vietnam: A History,* 2nd ed. (New York: Penguin, 1997), 189.

24 Martin Thomas, "French Imperial Reconstruction and the Development of the Indochina War, 1945–1950," in Mark Atwood Lawrence and Fredrik Logevall, *The First Vietnam War: Colonial Conflict and Cold War Crisis* (Cambridge, Mass.: Harvard University Press, 2007), 144–45.

25 Consul General–Hanoi to Saigon, June 7, 1948, FO 959/19, TNA.

26 Shaplen, *Lost Revolution,* 62.

27 Andrew Roth, "French Tactics in Indo-China," *New Republic,* February 28, 1948.

28 See Odd Arne Westad, *Decisive Encounters: The Chinese Civil War, 1946–1950* (Stanford, Calif.: Stanford University Press, 2003), chap. 6.

29 An archive-based study giving close attention to Pignon's role in Indochina is Daniel Varga, "La politique française en Indochine (1947–1950): Histoire d'une décolonisation manquée," doctoral thesis, Université Aix-Marseille, July 2004.

30 Mark Atwood Lawrence, *Assuming the Burden: Europe and the American Commitment to War in Vietnam* (Berkeley: University of California Press, 2005), 203.

31 Hanoi to FO, n.d., FO 371/41723; Windrow, *Last Valley,* 105.

32 "General Report for September," November 1, 1948, FO 959/21, TNA.

33 Consul General–Hanoi to Saigon, September 20, 1948, FO 959/20, TNA.

34 Lucien Bodard, *The Quicksand War: Prelude to Vietnam* (Boston: Little, Brown, 1967), 125–26.

35 John English, *Citizen of the World: The Life of Pierre Elliott Trudeau* (Toronto: Alfred A. Knopf Canada, 2006), 185–86.

36 Gras, *Histoire,* 224–26.

37 One sober-minded British report estimated in October 1948: "Apart from a number of towns and ports and precariously fluid lines of communication held by the French, 80 percent of the country is controlled by the rebels." "French Indo-China," October 23, 1948, FO 959/23, TNA. See also William J. Duiker, *U.S. Containment Policy and the Conflict in Indochina* (Stanford, Calif.: Stanford University Press, 1994), 68.

38 "General Report for December 1948," January 2, 1949, FO 959/32, TNA.

39 Philippe Devillers, *Histoire du Viêt-Nam de 1940 à 1952* (Paris: Éditions du Seuil, 1952), 442–43; Joseph Buttinger, *Vietnam: A Political History* (New York: Praeger, 1968), 308.

40 Saigon to FO, n.d., FO 959/45, TNA.

41 Lawrence, *Assuming the Burden,* 194–95; Karnow, *Vietnam,* 191.

42 Robert E. Herzstein, *Henry R. Luce, Time, and the American Crusade in Asia* (New York: Cambridge University Press, 2005), xiii, 140, 157; *Time,* October 10, 1949. A superb biography of Luce is Alan Brinkley, *The Publisher: Henry Luce and His American Century* (New York: Alfred A. Knopf, 2010). On Luce's fervent anti-Communism throughout the period, and how it shaped his publications, see ibid., chap. 11–12. On intellectuals in the Luce empire, see the nuanced study by Robert Vanderlan, *Intellectuals Incorporated: Politics, Art, and Ideas Inside Henry Luce's Media Empire* (Philadelphia: University of Pennsylvania Press, 2010).

CHAPTER 9: *"The Center of the Cold War"*

1 Dean Acheson, *Present at the Creation: My Years in the State Department* (New York: W.W. Norton, 1969), 674.

2 Walter Isaacson and Evan Thomas, *The Wise Men: Six Friends and the World They Made* (New York: Simon & Schuster, 1986), 22.

3 James Reston, *Deadline: A Memoir* (New York: Random House, 1991), 144; Mark Atwood Lawrence, *Assuming the Burden: Europe and the American Commitment to War in Vietnam* (Berkeley: University of California Press, 2005), 225.

4 Neil Sheehan, *A Bright Shining Lie: John Paul Vann and America in Vietnam* (New York: Random House, 1988), 169.

5 Robert L. Beisner, *Dean Acheson: A Life in the Cold War* (New York: Oxford University Press, 2006), 268–69; James Chace, *Acheson: The Secretary of State Who*

Created the American World (New York: Simon & Schuster, 1998), 264; Robert M. Blum, *Drawing the Line: The Origin of American Containment Policy in East Asia* (New York: W.W. Norton, 1982), 115.

6 Chace, *Acheson*, 266; Lawrence, *Assuming the Burden*, 225.

7 Ronald McGlothlen, *Controlling the Waves: Dean Acheson and U.S. Foreign Policy in Asia* (New York: W.W. Norton, 1993), 181.

8 Blum, *Drawing the Line*, 120.

9 Michael Schaller, "Securing the Great Ascent: Occupied Japan and the Origins of Containment in Southeast Asia," *Journal of American History* 69 (September 1982), 392–413; Andrew J. Rotter, *The Path to Vietnam: Origins of the American Commitment to Southeast Asia* (Ithaca, N.Y.: Cornell University Press, 1987); McGlothlen, *Controlling the Waves*, 191–201.

10 *The Pentagon Papers: The Defense Department History of Decisionmaking on Vietnam*, Senator Gravel edition (Boston: Beacon Press, 1971), 1:82.

11 George C. Herring, *America's Longest War: The United States and Vietnam, 1950–1975*, 4th ed. (New York: McGraw-Hill, 2002), 16.

12 Chace, *Acheson*, 227–28, 430; Sam Tanenhaus, *Whitaker Chambers: A Biography* (New York: Random House, 1997), 437–38; Richard Nixon, *RN: The Memoirs of Richard Nixon* (New York: Grosset and Dunlap, 1978), 110.

13 On the thinking of Viet Minh leaders in this period with respect to the Cold War and the DRV's place within it, see Tuong Vu, "From Cheering to Volunteering: Vietnamese Communists and the Coming of the Cold War," in Christopher E. Goscha and Christian F. Ostermann, eds., *Connecting Histories: Decolonization and the Cold War in Southeast Asia, 1945–1962* (Washington, D.C.: Woodrow Wilson Center Press, 2009), 188–93.

14 Translation of captured document dated January 14, 1948, quoted in Christopher E. Goscha, "Courting Diplomatic Disaster? The Difficult Integration of Vietnam into the Internationalist Communist Movement (1945–1950)," *Journal of Vietnamese Studies* 1 (February 2006), 83.

15 Ibid. On Ho Chi Minh's reluctance to tie the Viet Minh to the Communist bloc, see Christoph Giebel, *Imagined Ancestries of Vietnamese Communism: Ton Duc Thang and the Politics of History and Memory* (Seattle: University of Washington Press, 2004).

16 János Radványi, *Delusion and Reality: Gambits, Hoaxes, and Diplomatic One-Upmanship in Vietnam* (South Bend, Ind.: Gateway Editions, 1978), 4; Goscha, "Courting Diplomatic Disaster?," 84; Ilya Gaiduk, "Soviet Cold War Strategy and Prospects of Revolution in South and Southeast Asia," in Goscha and Ostermann, *Connecting Histories*, 123–36.

17 Chen Jian, *Mao's China and the Cold War* (Chapel Hill: University of North Carolina Press, 2001), 50; Odd Arne Westad, ed., *Brothers in Arms: The Rise and Fall of the Sino-Soviet Alliance, 1945–1963* (Stanford, Calif.: Stanford University Press, 1998), 63.

18 William J. Duiker, *Ho Chi Minh: A Life* (New York: Hyperion, 2000), 418–19; Qiang Zhai, "Transplanting the Chinese Model: Chinese Military Advisers and the First Vietnam War, 1950–1954," *Journal of Military History* 57, no. 4 (October 1993): 689–715.

19 Quoted in Philip Short, *Mao: A Life* (New York: Henry Holt, 1999), 425.

20 Ibid., 424.

21 Vo Nguyen Giap, *Memoirs of War: The Road to Dien Bien Phu* (Hanoi: Gioi, 2004), 12–13; Duiker, *Ho Chi Minh*, 421.

22 Chen Jian, *Mao's China*, 122–23.

23 Qiang Zhai, "Transplanting the Chinese Model," 695.

24 Duiker, *Ho Chi Minh*, 416; Luu Doan Huynh interview with author, Hanoi, January 2003.

25 Robert J. McMahon, *The Limits of Empire: The United States and Southeast Asia Since World War II* (New York: Columbia University Press, 1999), 40.

26 Paris to Washington, February 13, 1950, File 257, Asie/Indochine, MAE.

27 See the analysis in Pignon to Paris, January 24, 1950, Série XIV, SLOTFOM, no. 16/ps/cab], Fonds Haut-Commissariat de France en Indochine, Dépôt des Archives d'Outre-Mer, Aix-en-Provence. I thank Mark Lawrence for making this document available to me.

28 Ronald H. Spector, *Advice and Support: The Early Years of the U.S. Army in Vietnam, 1941–1960* (Washington, D.C.: Center for Military History, 1985), 108.

29 *NYT*, March 9, 1950; Paris to FO, 5/9/50, FO 959/43, TNA; Spector, *Advice and Support*, 108.

30 Chace, *Acheson*, 267.

31 Herring, *America's Longest War*, 25; William J. Duiker, *U.S. Containment Policy and the Conflict in Indochina* (Stanford, Calif.: Stanford University Press, 1994), 96–97.

32 *Washington Post*, April 4, 1950.

33 Seymour Topping, *Journey Between Two Chinas* (New York: Harper & Row, 1972), 111.

34 "The Cold War's Center," *New Republic*, April 24, 1950.

35 Quoted in Christopher E. Goscha, "The 'Two Vietnams' and the Advent of the Cold War: 1950 and Asian Shifts in the International System," in Goscha and Ostermann, *Connecting Histories*, 214–15.

36 Chen Jian, *Mao's China*, 124–25.

37 Saigon to FO, April 8, 1950, FO 371/83648, TNA.

38 Norman Sherry, *The Life of Graham Greene*, vol. 2: *1939–1955* (New York: Viking, 1995), 361.

39 Alexander Werth, *France 1940–1955* (New York: Henry Holt, 1956), 455; Martin Windrow, *The Last Valley: Dien Bien Phu and the French Defeat in Vietnam* (Cambridge, Mass.: Da Capo, 2004), 107.

40 Yves Gras, *Histoire de la guerre d'Indochine* (Paris: Plon, 1979), 275–79.

CHAPTER 10: *Attack on the RC4*

1 Edgar O'Ballance, *The Indo-China War, 1945–1954* (London: Faber & Faber, 1964), 110; Lucien Bodard, *The Quicksand War: Prelude to Vietnam* (Boston: Little, Brown, 1967), 253; and Dang Van Viet, *Highway 4: The Border Campaign (1947–1950)* (Hanoi: Foreign Languages Publishing House, 1990), 120–23. For a firsthand French account of the border campaign of 1950, see Charles-Henry de Pirey, *La Route Morte: RC4–1950* (Paris: Indo Éditions, 2002). See also Serge Desbois, *Le rendez-vous manqué: Des colonnes Charton et Le Page, Indochine–RC4–1950* (Paris: Indo Éditions, 2003); and Erwan Bergot, *La bataille de Dong Khê: La tragédie de la R.C. 4: Indochine 1950* (Paris: Presses de la Cité, 1987).

2 Ronald H. Spector, *Advice and Support: The Early Years of the U.S. Army in Vietnam, 1941–1960* (Washington, D.C.: Center for Military History, 1985), 124; George W. Allen, *None So Blind: A Personal Account of the Intelligence Failure in Vietnam* (Chicago: Ivan R. Dee, 2001), 37–38.

3 O'Ballance, *Indo-China War,* 113.

4 Bodard, *Quicksand War,* 261–62.

5 Chen Jian, *Mao's China and the Cold War* (Chapel Hill: University of North Carolina Press, 2001), 125.

6 Chen Jian, *Mao's China,* 126; Bodard, *Quicksand War,* 245. See also Greg Lockhart, *Nation in Arms: The Origins of the People's Army of Vietnam* (Wellington, N.Z.: Allen & Unwin, 1989), 225–26.

7 Yves Gras, *Histoire de la guerre d'Indochine* (Paris: Plon, 1979), 317; Lockhart, *Nation in Arms,* 229.

8 Douglas Porch, *The French Foreign Legion: A Complete History of the Legendary Fighting Force* (New York: HarperCollins, 1991), 521; O'Ballance, *Indo-China War,* 113.

9 Joint Intelligence Committee Report, March 15, 1950, CAB 158/9; November 1, 1950, CAB 158/11, TNA.

10 Phillip B. Davidson, *Vietnam at War: The History, 1946–1975* (New York: Oxford University Press, 1991), 71–72. Lucien Bodard makes much of these French successes in the first half of 1950. See his *Quicksand War,* 188–220. Nguyen Binh, criticized by some DRV officials for his tactics, was recalled to the north for consultations and training. While crossing northeastern Cambodia in 1951, he was killed by French forces under Jacques Hogard. His remains were returned to Vietnam in 2000.

11 Vo Nguyen Giap, *Memoirs of War: The Road to Dien Bien Phu* (Hanoi: Gioi, 2004), 38–56; Porch, *French Foreign Legion,* 521.

12 Lucien Bodard, *La guerre d'Indochine* (Paris: Gallimard, 1965), 3:96–377; Gras, *Histoire de la guerre d'Indochine,* 323–54; Le Page quoted in Bodard, *Quicksand War,* 278.

13 Porch, *French Foreign Legion,* 523; Cecil B. Currey, *Victory at Any Cost: The Genius of Viet Nam's Gen. Vo Nguyen Giap* (Dulles, Va.: Potomac, 2005), 169.

14 Quoted in Bodard, *Quicksand War,* 282.

15 Legionnaire quoted in Porch, *French Foreign Legion,* 523; Marc Dem, *Mourir pour Cao Bang* (Paris: Éditions Albin Michel, 1978).

16 Giap, *Road to Dien Bien Phu,* 82–84.

17 Desbois, *Le rendez-vous manqué,* 110–15; Porch, *French Foreign Legion,* 524–25.

18 Dang Van Viet, *Highway 4,* 151.

19 See the documents in FO 959/45, TNA; Bodard, *Quicksand War,* 291–92. For the recollections of the two French principals, see Pierre Charton, *RC 4, Indochine 1950: La tragédie de l'évacuation de Cao Bang* (Paris: S.P.L., 1975); and Marcel Le Page, *Cao-Bang: La tragique épopée de la colunne Le Page* (Paris: Nouvelles éditions latines, 1981).

20 Bernard Fall, *Street Without Joy: Indochina at War 1946–1954* (Harrisburg, Pa.: Stackpole Books, 1961), 33; Giap, *Road to Dien Bien Phu,* 108.

21 Hanoi to FO, November 15, 1950, FO 959/48, TNA.

22 Christopher E. Goscha, "Soigner la guerre *moi,*" unpublished paper in the author's possession. I'm grateful to Chris Goscha for allowing me to cite this material.

23 O'Ballance, *Indo-China War,* 116.

24 See, e.g., Giap, *Road to Dien Bien Phu,* 53, 59. Chen Geng, for his part, in his diary referred to Giap as "slippery and not very upright and honest" and expressed surprise that the Vietnamese were not always accepting of his critiques. Qiang Zhai, *China and the Vietnam Wars, 1950–1975* (Chapel Hill: University of North Carolina Press, 2000), 64.

25 "Report on Thai Binh operation," November 24, 1950, FO 959/48, TNA.

26 Vo Nguyen Giap acknowledges the food problem in his valuable *Road to Dien Bien Phu,* 4.

27 Martin Thomas, "French Imperial Reconstruction and the Development of the Indochina War," in Mark Atwood Lawrence and Fredrik Logevall, eds., *The First Vietnam War: Colonial Conflict and Cold War Crisis* (Cambridge, Mass.: Harvard University Press, 2007), 147–51.

28 Pierre Mendès France, *Oeuvres complètes,* vol. 2: *Une politique de l'économie 1943–1954* (Paris: Gallimard, 1985), 297–307; Eric Roussel, *Pierre Mendès France* (Paris: Gallimard, 2007), 196–97. On the broader economic impact of the war in France in this period, see Hugues Tertrais, *La piastre et le fusil: Le coût de la guerre d'Indochine 1945–1954* (Paris: Comité pour l'histoire économique et financière de la France, 2002), 90–102.

29 Spector, *Advice and Support,* 131–34.

30 Not all French analysts were sanguine, however. Outgoing high commissioner Léon Pignon anticipated much later Franco-American friction by accusing U.S. officials of playing a "double game": To the French they lamented the lack of Vietnamese unity, while to Vietnamese they said the French were to blame. Kathryn C. Statler, *Replacing France: The Origins of American Intervention in Vietnam* (Lexington: University Press of Kentucky, 2007), 32.

31 Ibid., 25–28; Spector, *Advice and Support,* 123.

32 Spector, *Advice and Support,* 127; "Monthly Report," November 28, 1950, FO 959/57, TNA.

33 Lloyd C. Gardner, *Approaching Vietnam: From World War II Through Dienbienphu* (New York: W.W. Norton, 1989), 104.

34 Ngo Van Chieu, *Journal d'un combattant Viêt-minh* (Paris: Éditions du Seuil, 1955), 128–29, 140–41, quoted in Lockhart, *Nation in Arms,* 237.

CHAPTER 11: *King Jean*

1 Quoted in Guy Salisbury-Jones, *So Full a Glory: A Biography of Marshal de Lattre de Tassigny* (London: Weidenfeld & Nicolson, 1954), 247.

2 Ibid.

3 Anthony Clayton, *Three Marshals of France: Leadership After Trauma* (London: Brassey's, 1992), 149. Several of Bernard's letters home are printed in a posthumously published collection of documents, Jean de Lattre de Tassigny, *La ferveur et le sacrifice: Indochine 1951,* ed. Jean-Luc Barré (Paris: Plon, 1988), 47–50.

4 Lucien Bodard, *The Quicksand War: Prelude to Vietnam* (Boston: Little, Brown, 1967), 351.

5 *Time,* September 24, 1951; Clayton, *Three Marshals of France,* 22–34.

6 *NYT,* August 26, 1951; *Time,* September 24, 1951.

7 Quoted in Salisbury-Jones, *So Full a Glory,* 246. Salisbury-Jones is highly laudatory, as is Pierre Darcourt, *De Lattre au Viet-Nam: Une année de victoires* (Paris: La table ronde, 1965). For de Lattre's own posthumously published views, see de Lattre, *La ferveur et le sacrifice.*

8 Robert Shaplen, *The Lost Revolution: The U.S. in Vietnam, 1946–1966* (New York: Harper & Row, 1966), 80; *NYT,* August 26, 1951.

9 Gullion quoted in Norman Sherry, *The Life of Graham Greene,* vol. 2: *1939–1955* (New York: Viking, 1995), 361. See also Bernard Destremau, *Jean de Lattre de Tassigny* (Paris: Flammarion, 1999), 504–8.

10 *Time,* September 24, 1951; Salisbury-Jones, *So Full a Glory,* 248.

11 *Time,* September 24, 1951.

12 Rapport a Jean Letourneau, ministre des états associés, January 1, 1951, printed in de Lattre, *La ferveur et le sacrifice,* 91–96; Clayton, *Three Marshals of France,* 150–51.

13 See Hugues Tertrais, *La piastre et le fusil: Le coût de la guerre d'Indochine 1945–1954* (Paris: Comité pour l'histoire économique et financière de la France, 2002), 103–8.

14 Clayton, *Three Marshals of France,* 151.

15 The name comes from naphthenic and palmitic acids, two chemicals used in the manufacturing process. When a napalm canister hits a target, it explodes, sucking up the available oxygen and engulfing the target area in flames and thick smoke. De Lattre first used napalm in a skirmish near Tien Yen on December 22. The important effects of de Lattre's wide use of napalm are emphasized by Luu Doan Huynh, interview by author, Hanoi, January 2003.

16 Quoted in *Le Monde,* December 5, 1952.

17 William J. Duiker, *The Communist Road to Power in Vietnam* (Boulder, Colo.: Westview, 1996), 154–55.

18 Bernard Fall, *Street Without Joy: Indochina at War 1946–1954* (Harrisburg, Pa.: Stackpole, 1961), 37–38.

19 Ngo Van Chieu, *Journal d'un combattant Viet-Minh* (Paris: Éditions du Seuil, 1954), as quoted in Bernard Fall, *Street Without Joy,* 39. See also lettre au Colonel Vanuxem, January 16, 1951, printed in de Lattre, *La ferveur et le sacrifice,* 107–8.

20 *NYT,* January 24, 1951; Saigon to FO, January 23, 1951, FO 959/107, TNA.

21 Fall, *Street Without Joy,* 41–43; Ronald H. Spector, *Advice and Support: The Early Years of the U.S. Army in Vietnam, 1941–1960* (Washington, D.C.: Center for Military History, 1985), 137; Darcourt, *De Lattre au Viet-nam,* 88–103. For Giap's view of these events, see his *Memoirs of War: The Road to Dien Bien Phu* (Hanoi: Gioi, 2004), 170–97.

22 De Lattre, *La ferveur et le sacrifice,* 273-74; Edgar O'Ballance, *The Indo-China War, 1945–1954* (London: Faber & Faber, 1964), 134; Martin Windrow, *The Last Valley: Dien Bien Phu and the French Defeat in Vietnam* (Cambridge, Mass.: Da Capo, 2004), 114–15.

23 Duiker, *Communist Road,* 157; Cecil B. Currey, *Victory at Any Cost: The Genius of Viet Nam's Gen. Vo Nguyen Giap* (Dulles, Va.: Potomac, 2005), 174; Douglas Pike, "General Vo Nguyen Giap—Man on the Spot," typescript (in author's possession), May 1968, 12; Tran Trong Trung oral history, Hanoi, June 12, 2007 (courtesy of Merle Pribbenow).

24 Quoted in Howard R. Simpson, *Tiger in the Barbed Wire: An American in Vietnam, 1952–1991* (Washington, D.C.: Brassey's, 1992), 12. See also Greg Lockhart, *Nation in Arms: The Origins of the People's Army of Vietnam* (Wellington, N.Z.: Allen & Unwin, 1989), 241.

25 *Time,* September 24, 1951.

26 Salisbury-Jones, *So Full a Glory,* 260.

27 De Lattre, *La ferveur et le sacrifice,* 255–59; Salisbury-Jones, *So Full a Glory,* 260–61; Destremau, *De Lattre,* 521–23; *Time,* June 11, 1951.

28 Office of the Military Attaché, British Legation-Saigon, Report No. 3, August 9, 1951, FO 959/104, TNA.

29 Quoted in Salisbury-Jones, *So Full a Glory,* 263–64.

30 See his caustic comments as reported in Saigon to FO, June 29, 1951, FO 959/109, TNA.

31 Quoted in Marilyn B. Young, "'The Same Struggle for Liberty': Korea and Vietnam," in Mark Atwood Lawrence and Fredrik Logevall, eds., *The First Vietnam War: Colonial Conflict and Cold War Crisis* (Cambridge, Mass.: Harvard University Press, 2007), 342n22. See also *The Pentagon Papers: The Defense Department History of Decisionmaking on Vietnam,* Senator Gravel edition (Boston: Beacon Press, 1971), 1:67.

32 See Graham Greene, *Ways of Escape* (New York: Simon & Schuster, 1980), 164–65.

33 Saigon to FO, July 10, 1951, FO 371/92453, TNA.

34 Shaplen, *Lost Revolution,* 81. A draft of the address is printed in de Lattre, *La ferveur et le sacrifice,* 281–91.

35 MDAP Monthly Report, October 1951, G-3 091 Indochina, Record Group 319, NARA.

36 De Lattre's suspicions of U.S. intentions are a theme in his letters and telegrams of the period. See, e.g., Télégramme a Jean Letourneau, April 16, 1951, printed in de Lattre, *La ferveur et le sacrifice,* 228–30. See also Saigon to FO, April 28, 1951, FO 959/109, TNA; Heath to Sec. State, June 14, 1951, *FRUS, 1950, East Asia and the Pacific,* VI, 1:425ff.

37 Young, "Same Struggle for Liberty," 203; Kathryn C. Statler, *Replacing France: The Origins of American Intervention in Vietnam* (Lexington: University Press of Kentucky, 2007), 42–43.

38 Acheson to Heath, July 13, 1951, *FRUS, 1950, East Asia and the Pacific,* VI, 1:453.

39 Discours-d'inauguration de la salle de lecture des services américans d'information, July 23, 1951, printed in de Lattre, *La ferveur et le sacrifice,* 312–17; Saigon to FO, July 28, 1951, FO 959/109, TNA.

40 Hanoi to Saigon, July 30, 1951, FO 959/109, TNA.

41 Paris to FO, January 19, 1952, FO 959/126, TNA. See also Salisbury-Jones, *So Full a Glory,* 266.

42 See Paris to London, September 5, 1951, FO 959/109, TNA.

43 *Time,* September 24, 1951; Destremau, *De Lattre,* 531–38.

44 Jean de Lattre de Tassigny, "Indochine 1951: Ma Mission aux Etats-Unis," *La revue deux mondes,* December 1951, 387–89.

45 *NYT,* September 15, 1951; Spector, *Advice and Support,* 143.

46 Record of Meeting, September 20, 1951, *FRUS, 1951, Asia and the Pacific,* VI, 1:517–21.

47 *Washington Post,* September 21, 1951; Alan Brinkley, *The Publisher: Henry Luce and His American Century* (New York: Alfred A. Knopf, 2010), 377; Robert E. Herzstein, *Henry R. Luce, Time, and the American Crusade in Asia* (New York: Cambridge University Press, 2005), 168. The National Press Club remarks are printed in de Lattre, *La ferveur et le sacrifice,* 345–52.

48 *Washington Post,* September 18, 1951.

49 *NYT,* September 24, 1951. For de Lattre's assessment of the trip, see his report in *La ferveur et le sacrifice,* 354–62.

50 Spector, *Advice and Support,* 146.

51 Quoted in Salisbury-Jones, *So Full a Glory,* 269. Collins's private evaluation, in a memo to the Joint Chiefs of Staff, was also effusive in its praise of the general and his accomplishments. "I was greatly impressed by what I saw," Collins wrote. "Unless the Chinese Communists, perhaps under the guise of volunteers, enter Indo-China, the French and Vietnam forces should be able to hold Indo-China indefinitely." "Memorandum for the Joint Chiefs of Staff," November 13, 1951, Box 23, Collins Papers, Eisenhower Library.

52 Geoffrey Perret, *Jack: A Life Like No Other* (New York, Random House, 2001), 169; Robert Dallek, *An Unfinished Life: John F. Kennedy, 1917–1963* (Boston: Little, Brown, 2003), 168; Robert Mann, *A Grand Delusion: America's Descent into Vietnam* (New York: Basic, 2001), 85.

53 Mann, *A Grand Delusion,* 86.

54 *NYT,* January 8, 1951; Saigon to FO, November 8, 1951, FO 959/107, TNA. The author of this cable, British minister H. A. Graves, speculated that the suicide was not intentional; rather, the grenade got tangled in the assassin's clothing and went off prematurely.

55 Military Attaché, British Legation, to Minister, August 9, 1951, FO 959/107, TNA.

56 Yves Gras, *Histoire de la guerre d'Indochine* (Paris: Plon, 1979), 424–28.

57 See the accounts in Fall, *Street Without Joy,* 48–60; and O'Ballance, *Indo-China War,* 159–66.

58 Greene, *Ways of Escape,* 164.

59 Edward Rice-Maximin, *Accommodation and Resistance: The French Left, Indochina and the Cold War* (Westport, Conn.: Greenwood, 1986), 113; Clayton, *Three Marshals of France,* 163.

60 Paris to FO, January 19, 1952, FO 959/126, TNA.

CHAPTER 12: *The Quiet Englishman*

1 *NYT,* January 10, 1952.

2 *Life,* January 28, 1952.

3 Saigon to Washington, January 10, 1952, "Indo-China: Internal Affairs: 1950–54," Central Files, NARA.

4 Saigon to FO, February 29, 1952, FO 474/6, TNA. On Thé's background and rise, see Sergei Blagov, *Honest Mistakes: The Life and Death of Trình Minh Thê (1922–1955), South Vietnam's Alternative Leader* (Huntington, N.Y.: Nova Science, 2001), 27–30.

5 Graham Greene, *Ways of Escape* (New York: Simon & Schuster, 1980), 161.

6 Ibid., 146; Richard Greene, ed., *Graham Greene: A Life in Letters* (Toronto: Alfred A. Knopf Canada, 2007), 182, 187–88.

7 Tom Curry, "Graham Greene's Vietnam—The Quiet American," Literary Traveler (www.literarytraveler.com/authors/graham_greenes_vietnam.aspx). Last accessed April 20, 2009. Wartime Saigon in this period is described in David Lan Pham, *Two Hamlets in Nam Bo: Memoirs of Life in Vietnam* (Jefferson, N.C.: McFarland, 2000), chap. 4.

8 Journalist Seymour Topping of the Associated Press would later claim that he and his wife introduced Greene to the opium dens. Seymour Topping, *Journey Between Two Chinas* (New York: Harper & Row, 1972), 110–11.

9 Andrew Forbes, "Graham Greene's Saigon Revisited," CPAMedia, www.cpamedia .com/culture/graham_greene_saigon/ (last accessed on April 18, 2009); Michael Shelden, *Graham Greene: The Enemy Within* (New York: Random House, 1994), 322; Howard Simpson, *Tiger in the Barbed Wire: An American in Vietnam, 1952–1991* (Washington, D.C.: Brassey's, 1992), 12.

10 Quoted in Norman Sherry, *The Life of Graham Greene,* vol. 2: *1939–1955* (New York: Viking, 1995), 401.

11 *Time,* October 29, 1951.

12 Letter of November 16, 1951, in Greene, *Graham Greene,* 193. See also Graham

Greene diary entry for November 13, 1951, Box 1, Graham Greene Papers, George-town University Library (hereafter GU).

13 Graham Greene, *The Quiet American* (New York: Viking, 1956), 142.

14 Ibid., 43; Greene diary entry for December 16, 1957, Box 1, Greene Papers, GU. See also Sherry, *Life of Graham Greene,* 2:395–96.

15 Greene diary entry for February 2, 1952, Box 1, Greene Papers, GU; Joseph Buttinger, *Vietnam: A Dragon Embattled,* vol. 2: *Vietnam at War* (New York: Prae-ger, 1967), 782–83; Greene, *Ways of Escape,* 170.

16 See Sherry, *Life of Graham Greene,* 2:417–20; W. J. West, *The Quest for Graham Greene* (New York: St. Martin's, 1998), 157–58; Greene, *Ways of Escape,* 169–79.

17 Greene, *Quiet American,* 124.

18 Sol Sanders, "Viet Nam *Has* a Third Force," *New Republic,* July 30, 1951. See also the even earlier article by Edwin Halsey, "The Third Force," *Integrity* 5 (May 1951): 33–39.

19 Shelden, *Graham Greene,* 327; Graham Greene, "Indo-China: France's Crown of Thorns," *Paris Match,* July 12, 1952, reprinted in Graham Greene, *Reflections,* ed. Judith Adamson (New York: Reinhardt, 1990), 129–47.

20 Greene, "Indo-China," 146.

21 Letter to Catherine Walston, November 21, 1951, Box 12, Catherine Walston–Graham Greene Papers, GU; Greene, *Ways of Escape,* 125–27; Sherry, *Life of Gra-ham Greene,* 2:481–88.

22 Lucien Bodard, "L'appel aux américains," *L'Express,* 1967, as quoted in Sherry, *Life of Graham Greene,* 2:482. See also letter to Catherine Walston, December 11, 1951, Box 13, Walston–Greene Papers, GU.

23 Thomas A. Bass, *The Spy Who Loved Us: The Vietnam War and Pham Xuan An's Dangerous Game* (New York: Public Affairs, 2009), 54–55. An's remarkable life story is also detailed in Larry Berman, *Perfect Spy: The Incredible Double Life of Pham Xuan An* (New York: Smithsonian Books, 2007).

24 "Narrative of Lt. Col. A. G. Trevor-Wilson," n.d., Peter Dunn Collection, Vir-tual Vietnam Archive, Texas Tech University, Lubbock, Tex.; Shelden, *Graham Greene,* 328–30.

25 Sherry, *Life of Graham Greene,* 2:437–46; Judith Adamson, *Graham Greene, the Dangerous Edge: Where Art and Politics Meet* (New York: St. Martin's, 1990), 131–32.

26 Greene, *Quiet American,* 16–17, 29; H. Arthur Scott Trask, "The Quiet American: Graham Greene's Brilliant Novel Shines as a New Film," www.lewrockwell.com/ orig/trask2.html (last accessed May 2, 2009).

27 Greene, *Ways of Escape,* 171; Sherry, *Life of Graham Greene,* 2:430.

28 Heath to State, February 14, 1952, as quoted in Sherry, *Life of Graham Greene,* 2:432.

29 Saigon to FO, February 29, 1952, FO 474/6, TNA.

30 Jean Lartéguy, *Soldats perdus et fous de dieu: Indochine 1945–1955* (Paris: Presses de la cité, 1986), 179–81; Nhi Lang, *Phong Trao Khang Chien Trinh Minh Thé* (Boulder, Colo.: Lion Press, 1989), 107–9.

31 Sherry, *Life of Graham Greene,* 2:434.

32 Jonathan Nashel, *Edward Lansdale's Cold War* (Amherst: University of Massachu-setts Press, 2005), 156–57.

33 David Lan Pham, *Two Hamlets in Nam Bo,* 77, 90.

34 Simpson, *Tiger in the Barbed Wire,* 4–5, 8.

35 Ibid., 30–31.

36 Ibid., 32.

37 Ibid., 84, 105.

38 Ibid., 34; Paris to FO, December 31, 1951, FO 474/5, TNA.

39 Quoted in Sherry, *Life of Graham Greene*, 2:441.

CHAPTER 13: *The Turning Point That Didn't Turn*

1 Marc Trachtenberg, *A Constructed Peace: The Making of the European Settlement, 1945–1963* (Princeton, N.J.: Princeton University Press, 1999), 110–25; Laurent Cesari, "The Declining Value of Indochina: France and the Economics of Empire, 1950–1955," in Mark Atwood Lawrence and Fredrik Logevall, eds., *The First Vietnam War: Colonial Conflict and Cold War Crisis* (Cambridge, Mass.: Harvard University Press, 2007), 181–88.

2 Robert J. McMahon, *The Limits of Empire: The United States and Southeast Asia Since World War II* (New York: Columbia University Press, 1999), 61.

3 *NYT*, June 8, 1952.

4 Cited in Alexander Werth, "Indo-China: The French Must Choose," *Nation*, January 26, 1952.

5 "Critical Developments in French Policy Toward Indochina," January 10, 1952, CIA Office of National Estimates, www.faqs.org/cia/docs/127/0001167457/critical-developments-in-french-policy-toward-indochina.html (last accessed on September 19, 2010).

6 Werth, "Indo-China," 77.

7 *Le Monde*, January 16, 1952.

8 *The Joint Chiefs of Staff and the First Indochina War, 1947–1954* (Washington, D.C.: Office of Joint History, Office of the Chairman of the Joint Chiefs of Staff, 2004), 240; Ronald H. Spector, *Advice and Support: The Early Years of the U.S. Army in Vietnam, 1941–1960* (Washington, D.C.: Center for Military History, 1985), 152; "Military Situation in Indo-China," February 5, 1952, FO 371/101069, TNA.

9 Memo of Conversation, March 21, 1952, *FRUS, 1952–1954, Indochina*, XIII, 1:75–77; Edward Rice-Maximin, *Accommodation and Resistance: The French Left, Indochina and the Cold War* (Westport, Conn.: Greenwood, 1986), 117; Lloyd C. Gardner, *Approaching Vietnam: From World War II Through Dienbienphu* (New York: W.W. Norton, 1989), 119.

10 Gardner, *Approaching Vietnam*, 118.

11 Melvyn P. Leffler, "Negotiating from Strength: Acheson, the Russians, and American Power," in Douglas Brinkley, ed., *Dean Acheson and the Making of American Foreign Policy* (New York: St. Martin's, 1993), 176–210.

12 See Fredrik Logevall, "Bernath Lecture: A Critique of Containment," *Diplomatic History* (September 2004); and Campbell Craig and Fredrik Logevall, *America's Cold War: The Politics of Insecurity* (Cambridge, Mass.: Belknap Press/Harvard University Press, 2009), chap. 3.

13 Rosemary Foot, *The Wrong War: American Policy and the Dimensions of the Korean Conflict, 1950–1953* (Ithaca, N.Y.: Cornell University Press, 1985); Foot, *A Substitute for Victory: The Politics of Peacemaking at the Korean Armistice Talks* (Ithaca, N.Y.: Cornell University Press, 1990), x–xi, 158. See also Bruce Cumings's monumental study, *The Origins of the Korean War*, vol. 2: *The Roaring of the Cataract* (Princeton, N.J.: Princeton University Press, 1990), chap. 3.

14 June 14, 1952, *FRUS, 1952–1954, Indochina*, XIII, 1:183–87; June 16, 1952, *FRUS, 1952–1954, Indochina*, XIII, 1:189–95; June 17, 1952, *FRUS, 1952–1954, Indochina*, XIII, 1:197–202; Irwin Wall, *The United States and the Making of Postwar France, 1945–1954* (New York: Cambridge University Press, 1991), 248.

15 NSC-124/2, June 25, 1952, *United States–Vietnam Relations 1945–1967: Study Prepared by the Department of Defense* (Washington, D.C.: Government Printing Office, 1971), 8:531–34.

16 For Salan's own description of this period, see his *Mémoires: Fin d'un empire*, vol. 2: *Le Viêt-minh mon adversaire* (Paris: Presses de la cité, 1971). For his interwar experiences in Indochina, see volume 1.

17 De Gaulle quoted in Alistair Horne, *A Savage War of Peace: Algeria, 1954–1962* (New York: NYRB Classics, 2006), 180.

18 *Time*, August 4, 1952.

19 Martin Windrow, *The Last Valley: Dien Bien Phu and the French Defeat in Vietnam* (Cambridge, Mass.: Da Capo, 2004), 119.

20 Edgar O'Ballance, *The Indo-China War, 1945–1954* (London: Faber & Faber, 1964), 171; Chen Jian, *Mao's China and the Cold War* (Chapel Hill: University of North Carolina Press, 2001), 129.

21 Chen Jian, *Mao's China*, 130–31.

22 Quoted in Bernard Fall, *Street Without Joy: Indochina at War 1946–1954* (Harrisburg, Pa.: Stackpole Books, 1961), 65.

23 Yves Gras, *Histoire de la guerre d'Indochine* (Paris: Plon, 1979), 474–79; Phillip B. Davidson, *Vietnam at War: The History, 1946–1975* (New York: Oxford University Press, 1991), 141.

24 Windrow, *Last Valley*, 121; *Time*, November 3, 1952. A classic account of the Bigeard battalion's rearguard action is in Fall, *Street Without Joy*, 66–76.

25 *Newsweek*, November 3, 1952.

26 *Time*, November 3, 1952.

27 Vo Nguyen Giap, *Mémoires, 1946–1954*, vol. 2: *Le chemin menant à Diên Biên Phu* (Fontenay-sous-Bois: Anako, 2004), 261–76; Windrow, *Last Valley*, 124.

28 Gras, *Histoire de la guerre d'Indochine*, 479–82; David T. Zabecki, "Operation Lorraine: Costly French Failure," *Vietnam* (December 2001), 18–25, 57; Salan, *Le Viêt-minh mon adversaire*, 337–40.

29 Quoted in Joseph Starobin, *Eyewitness in Indo-China* (New York: Cameron & Kahn, 1954), 67.

30 "Back to the Jungle," *Images of War* 4, no. 51 (n.d.).

31 Ibid.; Windrow, *Last Valley*, 120–22.

32 Starobin, *Eyewitness in Indo-China*, 73.

33 Jacques Favreau and Nicolas Dufour, *Nasan: La victoire oubliée* (Paris: Economica, 1999).

34 Gras, *Histoire de la guerre d'Indochine*, 483–88; O'Ballance, *Indo-China War*, 184–86; Favreau and Dufour, *Nasan*.

35 *Time*, January 12, 1953; *Time*, January 5, 1953.

36 William J. Duiker, *Ho Chi Minh: A Life* (New York: Hyperion, 2000), 442–43.

37 Duong Van Mai Elliott, *The Sacred Willow: Four Generations in the Life of a Vietnamese Family* (New York: Oxford University Press, 2000), 229–30.

38 Ibid., 230.

39 Duiker, *Ho Chi Minh*, 444. For a description of an indoctrination session, see Xuan Phuong and Danièle Mazingarbe, *Ao Dai: My War, My Country, My Vietnam* (Great Neck, N.Y.: EMQUAD, 2004), 128–29.

40 *Time,* January 12, 1953.

41 "A Translation from the French: Lessons of the War in Indochina, Volume 2," trans. V. J. Croizat (Santa Monica, Calif.: Rand Corporation, 1967), 112. See also David W. P. Elliott, *The Vietnamese War: Revolution and Social Change in the Mekong Delta, 1930–1975* (Armonk, N.Y.: M.E. Sharpe, 2007), 71–75.

CHAPTER 14: *Eisenhower in Charge*

1 Richard H. Immerman, *John Foster Dulles: Piety, Pragmatism, and Power in U.S. Foreign Policy* (Wilmington, Del.: Scholarly Resources, 1998), 43; David M. Oshinsky, *A Conspiracy So Immense: The World of Joe McCarthy* (New York: Oxford University Press, 2005), 197–202.

2 Stephen E. Ambrose, *Nixon,* vol. 1: *The Education of a Politician, 1913–1962* (New York: Simon & Schuster, 1987), 298.

3 See Chester Pach, "Introduction," in Kathryn C. Statler and Andrew L. Johns, *The Eisenhower Administration, the Third World, and the Globalization of the Cold War* (Lanham, Md.: Rowman & Littlefield, 2006); and Kenneth Osgood, *Total Cold War: Eisenhower's Secret Propaganda Battle at Home and Abroad* (Lawrence: University Press of Kansas, 2006), 7, 372n9.

4 Eisenhower quoted in Walter LaFeber, *The American Age: United States Foreign Policy at Home and Abroad, 1750 to the Present* (New York: W.W. Norton, 1994), 2:537. Dulles's mother quoted in David Halberstam, *The Fifties* (New York: Villard, 1993), 393.

5 Immerman, *John Foster Dulles,* chap. 1.

6 Halberstam, *Fifties,* 392; Peter Grose, *Gentleman Spy: The Life of Allen Dulles* (Boston: Houghton Mifflin, 1994), 333; Harold Macmillan, *The Macmillan Diaries: The Cabinet Years, 1950–1957,* ed. Peter Catterall (London: Macmillan, 2003), 230.

7 Niebuhr is quoted in Halberstam, *Fifties,* 389.

8 Quoted in Robert Divine, *Eisenhower and the Cold War* (New York: Oxford University Press, 1981), 21.

9 Elizabeth N. Saunders, *Leaders at War: How Presidents Shape Military Interventions* (Ithaca, N.Y.: Cornell University Press, 2011), 56–57.

10 Richard H. Immerman, "Prologue: Perceptions by the United States of Its Interests in Indochina," in Lawrence S. Kaplan, Denise Artaud, and Mark Rubin, eds., *Dien Bien Phu and the Crisis of Franco-American Relations, 1954–1955* (Wilmington, Del.: Scholarly Resources, 1990), 12–13.

11 Diary, as quoted in James R. Arnold, *The First Domino: Eisenhower, the Military, and America's Intervention in Vietnam* (New York: William Morrow, 1991), 74.

12 Lodge diary, November 16, 1951, Papers of Henry Cabot Lodge, Jr., Massachusetts Historical Society, Boston, Mass. I'm grateful to Zachary Matusheski for drawing this item to my attention.

13 Arnold, *First Domino,* 83. See also John Foster Dulles, *War or Peace* (New York: Macmillan, 1950), 231.

14 Quoted in Lloyd C. Gardner, *Approaching Vietnam: From World War II Through Dienbienphu* (New York: W.W. Norton, 1989), 135.

15 Harry S. Truman, *Memoirs by Harry S. Truman,* vol. 2: *Years of Trial and Hope, 1946–1952* (Garden City, N.Y.: Doubleday, 1956), 519; Heath to Sec. State, February 4, 1953, in *FRUS, 1952–1954, Indochina,* XIII, 1:378–81.

16 *Public Papers of the Presidents: Dwight D. Eisenhower* (Washington, D.C.: Govern-

ment Printing Office, 1960), 16; Robert J. McMahon, *The Limits of Empire: The United States and Southeast Asia Since World War II* (New York: Columbia University Press, 1999), 63; *NYT,* January 28, 1953.

17 Carl W. McCardle oral history (OH-116), by John Luter, August 29, 1967, Dwight D. Eisenhower Presidential Library, Abilene, Kan.; Memcon, January 28, 1953, *FRUS, 1952-1954, Indochina,* XIII, 1:362; Memcon, March 24, 1953, *FRUS, 1952-1954, Indochina,* XIII, 1:419-20.

18 Ronald H. Spector, *Advice and Support: The Early Years of the U.S. Army in Vietnam, 1941-1960* (Washington, D.C.: Center for Military History, 1985), 167-68.

19 The War Office warned: "The fall of Indo-China to Communism, inevitably spreading to Siam and Burma, would give the enemy great influence elsewhere in Asia owing to their control of the vital rice supply ultimately making the defence of Malaya extremely difficult." War Office, "Cabinet Policy in South East Asia, Memorandum by the Secretary of State for War," November 52, DEFE 13/2/8, TNA. On the Indochina-Malaya connection, see also, e.g., Macmillan, *Macmillan Diaries,* 228.

20 "Relations franco-américaines," January 21, 1953, 457 AP 44, Dossier 2, Papiers Georges Bidault, AN; Irwin Wall, *The United States and the Making of Postwar France, 1945-1954* (New York: Cambridge University Press, 1991), 250; Kathryn C. Statler, *Replacing France: The Origins of American Intervention in Vietnam* (Lexington: University Press of Kentucky, 2007), 62-63.

21 George W. Allen, *None So Blind: A Personal Account of the Intelligence Failure in Vietnam* (Chicago: Ivan R. Dee, 2001), 46.

22 JCS memo to Wilson, April 21, 1953, in *FRUS, 1952-1954, Indochina,* XIII, 1:493-95; Arthur Radford, *From Pearl Harbor to Vietnam: The Memoirs of Admiral Arthur W. Radford,* ed. Stephen Jurika (Stanford, Calif.: Hoover Institution Press, 1980), 362. See also Spector, *Advice and Support,* 170-71; and Dwight D. Eisenhower, *Mandate for Change: 1953-1956* (Garden City, N.Y.: Doubleday, 1963), 168.

23 Arnold, *First Domino,* 114.

24 Memo of discussion, NSC, April 28, 1953, in *FRUS, 1952-1954, Indochina,* XIII, 1:516-19; Eisenhower to Dillon, May 6, 1953, International File: France, 1953 (3), Box 10, Eisenhower Library.

25 Vincent Auriol, *Journal du Septennat, 1947-1954,* vol. 7: *1953-1954* (Paris: Armand Colin, 1971), 220.

26 Dillon Memorandum, April 9, 1953, Ann Whitman File, Box 1, Dulles-Herter Series, Eisenhower Library; SecState to Paris, May 6, 1953, *FRUS, 1952-1954, Indochina,* XIII, 1:550-51. See also ibid., 561-62.

27 Memo of discussion, NSC, April 28, 1953, in *FRUS, 1952-1954, Indochina,* XIII, 1:516-19; Memo of discussion, NSC, May 6, 1953, in *FRUS, 1952-1954, Indochina,* XIII, 1:546-49.

28 Douglas Porch, *The French Secret Services: A History of French Intelligence from the Dreyfus Affair to the Gulf War* (New York: Farrar, Straus & Giroux, 1995), 323-24.

29 See, e.g., *L'Observateur,* May 8, 1953; Jacques Despuech, *Le trafic des piastres* (Paris: Deux Rives, 1953). And see Hugues Tertrais, *La piastre et le fusil: Le coût de la guerre d'Indochine 1945-1954* (Paris: Comité pour l'histoire économique et financière de la France, 2002), 133-50.

30 Ellen J. Hammer, *The Struggle for Indochina, 1940-1955* (Stanford, Calif.: Stanford University Press, 1955), 300-1; *NYT,* May 20, 1953.

31 CIA Office of National Estimates, "Staff Memorandum No. 349: French Political Developments," April 30, 1953, NSC Staff Papers, Box 12, PSB Central Files,
Eisenhower Library.

32 State Department memcon, "Metropolitan French Opinions and Attitudes on Indochina War," May 4, 1953, NSC Staff Papers, Box 12, PSB Central Files, Eisenhower Library. The poll results were not published in the paper until early the
following year. Declared the headline: *"65% de Francais souhaiterait le retrait des
troupes ou une négociation." Le Monde,* February 24, 1954. On the growing conviction in French official circles in this period that the war was ruining France economically, see Tertrais, *La piastre et le fusil.*

33 Paris to FO, May 30, 1953, FO 371/106752, TNA.

34 Both books were published in 1952.

35 The *Paris-Presse* article is described in *NYT,* May 9, 1953. As the year progressed,
Le Monde contained more and more articles critical of the war. A Gaullist deputy
complained in a letter in the paper: "Indochina resembles a ship without a captain. . . . We cannot continue to bog ourselves down in a war without end without
a goal." M. Raymond Dronne, "Pour quoi nous combattons," *Le Monde,* May 9,
1953.

36 "La France peut supporter la vérité," *L'Express,* May 16, 1953; Edward Rice-
Maximin, *Accommodation and Resistance: The French Left, Indochina and the Cold
War* (Westport, Conn.: Greenwood, 1986), 136.

37 Letourneau quoted in Jacques Dalloz, *The War in Indo-China, 1945–1954* (New
York: Barnes & Noble, 1990), 163. Dillon comment in Paris to SecState, July 2,
1953, in *FRUS, 1952–1954, Indochina,* XIII, 1:631–32.

38 Paris to SecState, June 17, 1953, *FRUS, 1952–1954, Indochina,* XIII, 1:610–12.

CHAPTER 15: *Navarre's American Plan*

1 Jules Roy, *The Battle of Dienbienphu,* trans. Robert Baldick (New York: Harper &
Row, 1965), 7; Stanley Karnow, *Vietnam: A History* (New York: Viking, 1983), 204.

2 Navarre was aware of the grumbling. He later wrote that "nothing in my career prepared me for this post. I had never served in the Far East and knew of the Indochina
problem only what every more or less well-informed Frenchman knew." Henri Navarre, *Agonie de l'Indochine* (Paris: Plon, 1956), 2.

3 According to French figures (as given to the British), "total French Union and National" forces in May 1953, when Navarre took command, were: regular armies,
316,438; air forces, 11,394; navies, 10,890; army suppletifs (auxiliaries), 104,113;
paramilitary, 75,380; interpreters, etc., 5,468; for a total of 523,683. "Appendix
B," May 4, 1953, FO 371/106777, TNA. Viet Minh assessments of enemy strength
in this period are similar. See Vo Nguyen Giap, *Dien Bien Phu: Rendezvous with
History* (Hanoi: Gioi, 2004), 9.

4 Roy, *Battle of Dienbienphu,* 12.

5 Navarre is quoted in *Time,* June 29, 1953, and in James Cable, *The Geneva Conference of 1954 on Indochina* (London: Macmillan, 1986), 22. For Navarre's reaction
to being asked to take the Indochina appointment, see his *Agonie de l'Indochine,*
1–3. For his awareness of the size of the task, see p. 67.

6 Pierre Rocolle, *Pourquoi Dien Bien Phu?* (Paris: Flammarion, 1968), 21; Paul Ély,
L'Indochine dans la tourmente (Paris: Plon, 1964), 25.

7 David Halberstam, *The Fifties* (New York: Villard, 1993), 400.

8 George W. Allen, *None So Blind: A Personal Account of the Intelligence Failure in Vietnam* (Chicago: Ivan R. Dee, 2001), 46–47; Ronald H. Spector, *Advice and Support: The Early Years of the U.S. Army in Vietnam, 1941–1960* (Washington, D.C.: Center for Military History, 1985), 175; Hugues Tertrais, "Stratégie et decisions," in Pierre Journoud and Hugues Tertrais, eds., *1954–2004: La bataille de Dien Bien Phu, entre histoire et mémoire* (Paris: Société française d'histoire d'outre-mer, 2004), 30–31; Pierre Journoud and Hugues Tertrais, *Paroles de Dien Bien Phu: Les survivants témoignent* (Paris: Tallandier, 2004), 46–51.

9 Navarre, *Agonie de l'Indochine,* 28. And see here Ambassador Heath's comments, in *FRUS, 1952–1954, Indochina,* XIII, 1:628. He cabled Washington: "Navarre's principles reflect . . . O'Daniel's impact here."

10 O'Daniel to Radford, June 30, 1953, *FRUS, 1952–1954, Indochina,* XIII, 1:625; Spector, *Advice and Support,* 175. Navarre returned to Paris to present the plan at a meeting of the National Defense Committee on July 24, where it won endorsement. See Rocolle, *Pourquoi Dien Bien Phu?,* 51–53. On O'Daniel's insistence on the need for a greater application of military force, see also Saigon to FO, July 2, 1953, FO 371/106761, TNA.

11 Bernard B. Fall, "Post-Mortems on Dien Bien Phu: Review Article," *Far Eastern Survey* 27, no. 10 (October 1958): 156.

12 Memcon, July 12, 1953, *FRUS, 1952–1954, Indochina,* XIII, 1:656–67.

13 "Note générale sur la politique française en Indochine," July 21, 1953, Box 31, René Mayer Papers, Series 363AP, AN.

14 Paris to FO, August 11, 1953, FO 474/7, TNA; Kathryn C. Statler, *Replacing France: The Origins of American Intervention in Vietnam* (Lexington: University Press of Kentucky, 2007), 73.

15 Quoted in Dorothy Fall, *Bernard Fall: Memories of a Soldier-Scholar* (Washington, D.C.: Potomac, 2006), 55–81.

16 Bernard Fall, *Street Without Joy: Indochina at War 1946–1954* (Harrisburg, Pa.: Stackpole Books, 1961), 255–56. See also Fall, *Bernard Fall,* 55–81.

17 Fall, *Bernard Fall,* 67.

18 Bernard B. Fall, "Insurgency Indicators," *Military Review* 46 (April 1966), 4.

19 Fall, *Bernard Fall,* 67–70.

20 "Appendix D," April 11, 1953, FO 371/106775, TNA.

21 Quoted in *Newsweek,* April 20, 1953.

22 Dennis Duncan, "The Year of the Snake," *Life,* August 3, 1953. On the subsequent dispute, see Bonnet to Bidault, July 24, 1953, Dossier 1, AN 457 AP 52, AN; and Saigon cables 391 and 461 in Record Group 59, 751 G.00/9–353, 9–1653, NARA; and C. D. Jackson daily summary, August 5, 1953, Box 68, C. D. Jackson Papers, Eisenhower Library. See also James Waite, "The End of the First Indochina War: An International History," Ph.D. dissertation, Ohio University, 2005, 98–99.

23 Robert E. Herzstein, *Henry R. Luce, Time, and the American Crusade in Asia* (New York: Cambridge University Press, 2005), 183–84.

24 On the gap between the information the Luce magazines received and their published version of events, see ibid., 182–83.

25 *Time,* September 28, 1953.

26 See, for example, the editorials on March 28, 1953, June 5, 1953, and October 2, 1953, and the interpretive articles by reporter Hanson W. Baldwin.

27 *United States-Vietnam Relations 1945–1967: Study Prepared by the Department of Defense* (Washington, D.C.: Government Printing Office, 1971), 9:46.

28 *The Pentagon Papers: The Defense Department History of Decisionmaking on Vietnam*, Senator Gravel edition (Boston: Beacon Press, 1971), 1:591–92.

29 Washington to FO, August 1953, FO 371/103497.

30 Paris to State, July 22, 1953, *FRUS, 1952–1954, Indochina*, XIII, 1:695. And see Spector, *Advice and Support*, 176.

31 Knowland press conference, September 16, 1953, "1953 Far East trip," Series 364, Box 3, Nixon Pre-Presidential Papers, NARA–Laguna Niguel.

32 Don Oberdorfer, *Senator Mansfield: The Extraordinary Life of a Great American Statesman and Diplomat* (Washington, D.C.: Smithsonian, 2003), 110–11; *NYT*, February 21, 1953. The senator was quoted in a front-page story concerning the prospect of increased U.S. aid to the war effort. The kicker under the headline read: "Mansfield Cites Urgency."

33 Oberdorfer, *Senator Mansfield*, 117; Edward Miller, "Vision, Power and Agency: The Ascent of Ngô Đình Diêm, 1945–54," *Journal of Southeast Asian Studies* 35 (October 2004): 446–47.

34 Warner quoted in Oberdorfer, *Senator Mansfield*, 112.

35 Mansfield, "Indochina," report prepared for the Senate Foreign Relations Committee of a mission to Vietnam, Cambodia, and Laos (Washington, D.C.: Government Printing Office, 1953). See also Robert Mann, *A Grand Delusion: America's Descent into Vietnam* (New York: Basic, 2001), 120–21.

36 *Time*, August 10, 1953.

37 Bui Diem with David Chanoff, *In the Jaws of History* (Boston: Houghton Mifflin, 1987), 79.

38 Ibid., 79–80; Bao Dai, *Le dragon d'Annam* (Paris: Plon, 1980), 315.

39 Saigon to State, October 17, 1953, *FRUS, 1952–1954, Indochina*, XIII, 1:828–30; Saigon to State, October 18, 1953, *FRUS, 1952–1954, Indochina*, XIII, 1:834–36.

40 *Newsweek*, November 2, 1953; Jacques Dalloz, *The War in Indo-China, 1945–1954* (New York: Barnes & Noble, 1990), 166.

41 *Time*, November 9, 1953; Paris to FO, October 2, 1953, FO 371/106770, TNA.

42 Saigon to FO, November 10, 1953, FO 474/7, TNA.

43 Ibid.; Richard Nixon, *RN: The Memoirs of Richard Nixon* (New York: Grosset & Dunlap, 1978), 122; "Conversations of Vice President Nixon with *Bao Dai*," "1953 Far Eastern Trip," Series 366, Box 2, Nixon Pre-Presidential Papers, NARA–Laguna Niguel.

44 Nixon, *RN*, 122–25.

45 Nixon speech in Hanoi, November 3, 1953, "1953 Far Eastern Trip," Series 366, Box 2, Nixon Pre-Presidential Papers, NARA–Laguna Niguel; Saigon to FO, November 10, 1953, FO 474/7, TNA.

46 Saigon to FO, November 10, 1953, FO 474/7, TNA.

47 Memcon, NSC meeting, December 24, 1953, Box 5, Ann Whitman File, NSC Series, Eisenhower Library.

48 "Vice President Nixon's Report to Department Officers on His Trip to the Near and Far East," January 8, 1954, Box 69, NSC Staff Papers, OCB Central File Series, Eisenhower Library.

49 Ibid.

CHAPTER 16: *Arena of the Gods*

1 Bernard B. Fall, *Hell in a Very Small Place: The Siege of Dien Bien Phu* (Philadelphia: Lippincott, 1966), 22–23.

2   Raoul Salan, *Mémoires: Fin d'un empire*, vol. 2: *Le Viêt-minh mon adversaire* (Paris: Presses de la cité, 1971), 417.

3   For an interpretation that emphasizes the importance of opium in French decision making, see Douglas Porch, *The French Secret Services: A History of French Intelligence from the Dreyfus Affair to the Gulf War* (New York: Farrar, Straus & Giroux, 1995), 319–38.

4   In 1955, following bitter charges and countercharges by Navarre and Cogny in the press, there would be an official government commission of inquiry into Dien Bien Phu, chaired by General Georges Catroux. Top commanders testified, as did colonels and unit commanders. Pierre Pellissier, *Diên Biên Phu: 20 novembre 1953– 7 mai 1954* (Paris: Perrin, 2004), 548–68.

5   "Comité de defense nationale du 24 juillet 1953; Extrait du process verbal no. 821/ CND du 18 septembre 1953," 10 H 179, Service historique de l'armée de terre. See also Joseph Laniel, *Le drame indochinois* (Paris: Plon, 1957), 20–22; Pierre Charpy, " 'Pourquoi je ne me suis pas suicidé,' par le général Navarre, responsable de Dien Bien Phu," *Nouveau Candide,* October 17, 1963; Général René Cogny, "La libre confession du général Cogny," *L'Express,* November 21, 1963; and *L'Express,* December 6, 1963.

6   Georges Catroux, *Deux actes du drame indochinois* (Paris: Plon, 1959), 168–69; Alphonse Juin, *Le Viêt Minh, mon adversaire* (Paris: Plon, 1956), 237. The text of the treaty is in Press and Information Division, French Embassy, Washington, D.C., *Indochinese Affairs* 1 (February 1954): 25–28.

7   Georges Boudarel and Francois Caviglioli, "Comment Giap a faille perdre la bataille de Dien Bien Phu," *Nouvel Observateur,* April 8, 1983. I thank Chris Goscha for drawing this illuminating article to my attention.

8   Henri Navarre, *Agonie de l'Indochine* (Paris: Plon, 1956), 121.

9   On Paris being informed of the operation after the event, see Laniel, *Le drame indochinois*, 36. On the November 20 operation, see also Pierre Journoud and Hugues Tertrais, *Paroles de Dien Bien Phu: Les survivants témoignent* (Paris: Tallandier, 2004), 67–74.

10 Chen Jian, *Mao's China and the Cold War* (Chapel Hill: University of North Carolina Press, 2001), 132; William J. Duiker, *Ho Chi Minh: A Life* (New York: Hyperion, 2000), 448.

11 These figures from BMA Saigon to War Office, June 7, 1953, FO 371/106748, TNA. See also Taquey to Craig, May 14, 1953, Box 12, NSC Staff Papers, PSB Central Files, Eisenhower Library.

12 Dang Huu Loc (Military History Institute of Vietnam chief editor), *Lich Su Quan Doi Nhan Dan Viet Nam* [History of the People's Army of Vietnam], 4th printing, with additions and corrections (Hanoi: People's Army Publishing House, 1994), 387. See also Cao Pha, *Nhung Ky Uc Khong Bao Gio Quen* [Memories I Will Never Forget] (Hanoi: People's Army Publishing House, 2006), 84–86. I thank Merle Pribbenow for his translations. See also Vo Nguyen Giap, *Dien Bien Phu: Rendezvous with History* (Hanoi: Gioi, 2004), 13–26.

13 Le Kinh Lich (chief editor), *Tran Danh Ba Muoi Nam: Ky Su Lich Su, Tap 1* [The Thirty Year Battle: A Historical Report, vol. 1] (People's Army Publishing House, 1995), 593. I thank Merle Pribbenow for his translation. See also Trinh Vuong Hong, "Dien Bien Phu: A Historical Inevitability," in *Dien Bien Phu: History, Impressions, Memoirs* (Hanoi: Gioi, 2004), 49.

14 *Tran Danh Ba Muoi Nam,* 593.

15 See here also Vu Quang Hien, *Tim hieu chu truong doi ngoai cua Dang thoi ky*

1945–1954 (Hanoi: Nha xuat ban Chinh tri quoc gia, 2005), 169–701; Pierre Asselin, "The DRVN and the 1954 Geneva Conference: New Evidence and Perspectives from Vietnam," unpublished paper in author's possession, p. 5.

16 *Tran Danh Ba Muoi Nam,* 593.

17 Bernard B. Fall, "Indochina: The Last of the War," *Military Review,* December 1956; Pierre Rocolle, *Pourquoi Dien Bien Phu?* (Paris: Flammarion, 1968), 169–76.

18 *Lich Su Quan Doi Nhan Dan Viet Nam,* 393.

19 "Dinh Cao Chien Cong Tinh Bao Thoi Chong Phat" [The Peak of Intelligence Success During the Resistance War Against the French], *Quan Doi Nhan Dan* [People's Army], October 21, 2005, at www.quandoinhandan.org.vn/sknc/?id= 1587&subject=8, last accessed June 5, 2009. I thank Merle Pribbenow for drawing this article to my attention and for his translation.

20 Rocolle, *Pourquoi Dien Bien Phu?,* 206; Martin Windrow, *The Last Valley: Dien Bien Phu and the French Defeat in Vietnam* (Cambridge, Mass.: Da Capo, 2004), 257.

21 Jules Roy, *La bataille de Diên Biên Phu* (Paris: René Julliard, 1963), 83–86.

22 Windrow, *Last Valley,* 258–59.

23 George W. Allen, *None So Blind: A Personal Account of the Intelligence Failure in Vietnam* (Chicago: Ivan R. Dee, 2001), 51–52.

24 Chen Jian, *Mao's China,* 133–34. Chen maintains that the Chinese played a determining role in the decision.

25 *Quan Doi Nhan Dan* [People's Army] newspaper supplement, "Su Kien va Nhan Chung" [Events and Witnesses], Special issue no. 1 commemorating the fiftieth anniversary of the Battle of Dien Bien Phu, June 12, 1953. I thank Merle Pribbenow for providing me with a translated version of this article.

26 Ibid.; Giap, *Rendezvous with History,* 47–48.

27 *Lich Su Quan Doi Nhan Dan Viet Nam,* 1:387–95; Christopher E. Goscha, "Building Force: Asian Origins of Vietnamese Military Science (1950–54)," *Journal of Southeast Asian Studies* 34 (2003): 556.

28 Ilya V. Gaiduk, *Confronting Vietnam: Soviet Policy Toward the Indochina Conflict, 1954–1963* (Stanford, Calif.: Stanford University Press, 2003), 14; Duiker, *Ho Chi Minh,* 449.

29 See Chen, *Mao's China,* 167–70.

30 Ho Chi Minh, *Toan Tap I,* no. 6, pp. 494–96, as cited in Duiker, *Ho Chi Minh,* 451.

31 Party studies quoted in Pierre Asselin, "The DRVN and the 1954 Geneva Conference: New Evidence and Perspectives from Vietnam," unpublished paper, in author's possession.

32 Quoted in Allan W. Cameron, ed., *Viet-Nam Crisis: A Documentary History,* 2 vols. (Ithaca, N.Y.: Cornell University Press, 1971), 1:217–18. See also Vu Quang Hien, *Tim hieu chu truong doi ngoai,* 171.

33 Ho Chi Minh, *Selected Works,* 4 vols. (Hanoi: Foreign Languages Publishing House, 1961–1962), 3:408–10; Pellissier, *Diên Biên Phu,* 116–17; James Cable, *The Geneva Conference of 1954 on Indochina* (London: Macmillan, 1986), 35.

34 Ho Chi Minh, "Report to the Assembly of the DRV," December 1–4, 1953, in *Ho Chi Minh on Revolution: Selected Writings, 1920–1966,* ed. Bernard B. Fall (New York: Praeger, 1967), 258–69.

35 General Hoang Van Thai, *Tran Danh Ba Muoi Nam,* 730.

36 Ho Chi Minh, *Selected Works,* 3:431.

37 Edward Rice-Maximin, *Accommodation and Resistance: The French Left, Indochina and the Cold War* (Westport, Conn.: Greenwood, 1986), 139.

38 Cable, *Geneva Conference*, 35.

39 *Le Monde*, December 1, 1953.

40 Cable, *Geneva Conference*, 36; Jean Lacouture, *Pierre Mendès France*, trans. George Holock (New York: Holmes & Meier, 1984), 200.

41 "Situation en Indochine de 1 au 9 Décembre 1953," F60 3038, AN. Tam is quoted in *Le Monde*, December 4, 1953, as cited in Waite, "End of the First Indochina War," 73.

42 C.D. Jackson notes, "Bermuda Commentary," December 1953, Box 68, C.D. Jackson Papers, Eisenhower Library.

43 Ibid.; Sir Evelyn Shuckburgh diary, as quoted in Cable, *Geneva Conference*, 37.

44 Lord Moran, *Winston Churchill: The Struggle for Survival 1940–1965* (London: Constable, 1966), 503–12; Cable, *Geneva Conference*, 37; David Carlton, *Anthony Eden: A Biography* (New York: HarperCollins, 1986), 335–37; John Colville, *The Fringes of Power: Downing Street Diaries, 1939–1955* (London: Hodder & Stoughton, 1985), 643.

45 See Memcon, December 4, 1953, *FRUS, 1952–1954, Western European Security*, V:1739.

46 Colville, *Fringes of Power*, 683, as quoted in Kevin Ruane, "Anthony Eden, British Diplomacy, and the Origins of the Geneva Conference of 1954," *Historical Journal* 37 (1994): 155.

47 Dulles to Acting SecState, December 7, 1953, *FRUS, 1952–1954, Indochina*, XIII, 1:901–2; Eden minute to Churchill, December 7, 1953, FO 371/105574, TNA.

48 Excerpt of communiqué, December 7, 1953, *FRUS, 1952–1954, Indochina*, XIII, 1:901n2.

CHAPTER 17: *"We Have the Impression They Are Going to Attack Tonight"*

1 Martin Windrow, *The Last Valley: Dien Bien Phu and the French Defeat in Vietnam* (Cambridge, Mass.: Da Capo, 2004), 320.

2 Bernard B. Fall, *Hell in a Very Small Place: The Siege of Dien Bien Phu* (Philadelphia: Lippincott, 1966), 72. See also Vo Nguyen Giap, *Dien Bien Phu: Rendezvous with History* (Hanoi: Gioi, 2004), 48–51.

3 Pierre Rocolle, *Pourquoi Dien Bien Phu?* (Paris: Flammarion, 1968), 225–26.

4 Jules Roy, *La bataille de Diên Biên Phu* (Paris: René Julliard, 1963), 89.

5 Ibid., 81–82; Pierre Pellissier, *Diên Biên Phu: 20 novembre 1953–7 mai 1954* (Paris: Perrin, 2004), 118–20; Fall, *Hell in a Very Small Place*, 54–56.

6 Pellissier, *Diên Biên Phu*, 124–28; Howard R. Simpson, *Dien Bien Phu: The Epic Battle America Forgot* (Washington, D.C.: Brassey's, 1994), 25.

7 Fall, *Hell in a Very Small Place*, 88–90; Roy, *Bataille de Diên Biên Phu*, 98.

8 Simpson, *Dien Bien Phu*, 36–38.

9 Roy, *Bataille de Diên Biên Phu*, 111–13.

10 Howard R. Simpson, *Tiger in the Barbed Wire: An American in Vietnam, 1952–1991* (Washington, D.C.: Brassey's, 1991), 102.

11 Quoted in Simpson, *Dien Bien Phu*, 40.

12 George Ball, "Cutting Our Losses in Vietnam," June 28, 1965, *FRUS, 1964–1968*, III: 222.

13 Saigon to FO, December 31, 1953, FO 371/106779, TNA.

14 *Lich su Dang Cong san Viet Nam* [A History of the Vietnamese Communist Party] (Hanoi: Su that, 1984), 691, as quoted in William J. Duiker, *Ho Chi Minh: A Life* (New York: Hyperion, 2000), 453.

15 Georges Boudarel and Francois Caviglioli, "Comment Giap a faille perdre la bataille de Diên Biên Phu," *Nouvel Observateur,* April 8, 1983, 97; Giap, *Rendezvous with History,* 86–92.

16 Vo Nguyen Giap, with Huu Mai, *Dien Bien Phu: Diem Hen Lich Su* [Dien Bien Phu: A Historic Meeting Place] (Hanoi: People's Army Publishing House, 2001), 93–94 (I thank Merle Pribbenow for his translation); Christopher J. Goscha, "Building Force: Asian Origins of Vietnamese Military Science (1950–54)," *Journal of Southeast Asian Studies* 34 (2003): 556.

17 Boudarel and Caviglioli, "Comment Giap a faille perdre," 97.

18 Ibid.; Qiang Zhai, *China and the Vietnam Wars, 1950–1975* (Chapel Hill: University of North Carolina Press, 2000), 38, 45–46.

19 Windrow, *Last Valley,* 266.

20 Simpson, *Dien Bien Phu,* 34.

21 Vo Nguyen Giap, *Dien Bien Phu: Diem Hen,* 183. I thank Merle Pribbenow for his translation. See also Dinh Van Ty, "The Brigade of Iron Horses," *Vietnamese Studies* 43 (1976).

22 Tran Do, *Stories of Dien Bien Phu* (Hanoi, 1963), 30–37.

23 Boudarel and Caviglioli, "Comment Giap a faille perdre," 99.

24 Ibid.

25 Roy, *Bataille de Diên Biên Phu,* 134–35. See also Pierre Journoud and Hugues Tertrais, *Paroles de Dien Bien Phu: Les survivants témoignent* (Paris: Tallandier, 2004), 104–5.

26 Fall, *Hell in a Very Small Place,* 104.

27 Saigon to SecState, January 3, 1954, *FRUS, 1952–1954, Indochina,* XIII, 1:937–38; Navarre to Monsieur le Secrétaire d'Etat à la Présidence du Conseil, chargé des relations avec les Etats Associés, January 1, 1954, Dossier IV, DPMP, Indochine, Institut Pierre Mendès France (hereafter IPMF); Rocolle, *Pourquoi Dien Bien Phu?,* 243.

28 Bernard B. Fall, "Post-Mortems on Dien Bien Phu: Review Article," *Far Eastern Survey* 27, no. 10 (October 1958).

29 For a lengthy description of such incidents, see Hanoi (Fish) to FO, February 8, 1954, FO 371/112024, TNA.

30 On Atlante, see Phillip B. Davidson, *Vietnam at War: The History, 1946–1975* (New York: Oxford University Press, 1991), 204–13; Fall, *Hell in a Very Small Place,* 45–49; Michel Grintchenko, *Atlante-Aréthuse: Une opération de pacification en Indochine* (Paris: Economica, 2001).

31 Ted Morgan, *Valley of Death: The Tragedy at Dien Bien Phu That Led America into the Vietnam War* (New York: Random House, 2010), 241.

32 Roy, *Bataille de Diên Biên Phu,* 151–54; Boudarel and Caviglioli, "Comment Giap a faille perdre," 90.

33 Vo Nguyen Giap, *The Most Difficult Decision: Dien Bien Phu: And Other Writings* (Hanoi: Giao, 1992), 21; Goscha, "Building Force," 557; Hoang Minh Phuong, "Ve mot cuon sach xuat ban o Trung Quoc viet ve Dien Bien Phu," *Xu'a va Nay* 3 (1994): 14.

34 See here the analysis in Goscha, "Building Force," 557. See also Bui Tin, *Following Ho Chi Minh: The Memoirs of a North Vietnamese Colonel* (Honolulu: University of Hawaii Press, 1995), 20–21; and Giap, *Dien Bien Phu: Diem Hen,* 103.

35 Giap, *Rendezvous with History,* 107–8.

36 Pellissier, *Diên Biên Phu*, 198–207; Giap, *Rendezvous with History*, 108; Boudarel and Caviglioli, "Comment Giap a faille perdre," 90; Ngo Dang Tri, "Le service logistique du Vietnam dans la bataille de Dien Bien Phu," in Pierre Journoud and Hugues Tertrais, eds., *1954–2004: La bataille de Dien Bien Phu, entre histoire et mémoire* (Paris: Société française d'histoire d'outre-mer, 2004), 121.

37 Giap, "Most Difficult Decision," 23–27; Bui Tin, *Following Ho Chi Minh*, 20.

38 Vo Nguyen Giap, *People's War, People's Army: The Viet Cong Insurrection Manual for Underdeveloped Countries* (Hanoi: Foreign Languages Publishing House, 1961), 170.

CHAPTER 18: *"Vietnam Is a Part of the World"*

1 Ho Chi Minh, "Report to the Assembly of the DRV," December 1–4, 1953, in *Ho Chi Minh on Revolution: Selected Writings, 1920–1966,* ed. Bernard B. Fall (New York: Praeger, 1967), 258–69.

2 Pierre Asselin, "The DRVN and the 1954 Geneva Conference: New Evidence and Perspectives from Vietnam," unpublished paper in author's possession; Truong Chinh, "Making Great Efforts to Smash the French and U.S. Imperialists' Schemes for Intensifying the War of Aggression," February 22, 1954, unpublished document in author's possession.

3 NSC 5405, January 16, 1954, *FRUS, 1952–1954, Indochina,* XIII, 1:971–76.

4 Memorandum of discussion, 179th meeting of the NSC, January 8, 1954, *FRUS, 1952–1954, Indochina,* XIII, 1:947–54.

5 Richard Immerman, "Between the Unattainable and the Unacceptable: Eisenhower and Dienbienphu," in Richard A. Melanson and David Mayers, eds., *Reevaluating Eisenhower: American Foreign Policy in the 1950s* (Urbana: University of Illinois Press, 1987), 124–25. The other members of the committee were Deputy Secretary of Defense Robert Kyes, special assistant to the president C. D. Jackson, Admiral Radford, and CIA director Allen Dulles.

6 For the early experience of these mechanics, see Robert K. Scudder, "Tonkin Taxi: Hanoi to Saigon and All the Stops in Between," *Friends Journal* 29 (Winter 2006–7), 8–14.

7 James C. Hagerty diary entry for February 7, 1954, Eisenhower Library.

8 Eden to Cabinet, November 24, 1953, CAB 129 64, TNA; Eden to Churchill, November 25, 1953, FO 800/784/95, TNA.

9 Lloyd note, August 23, 1953, FO 371/103518, TNA.

10 E. J. Kahn, Jr., *The China Hands: America's Foreign Service Officers and What Befell Them* (New York: Viking, 1975); and Robert P. Newman, *Owen Lattimore and the "Loss" of China* (Berkeley: University of California Press, 1992).

11 Paul Wright memorandum, August 22, 1953, FO 371/103518, TNA.

12 Lloyd note, August 23, 1953, FO 371/103518, TNA.

13 Paul Wright memorandum, August 22, 1953, FO 371/103518, TNA.

14 Robert Rhodes James, *Anthony Eden: A Biography* (New York: McGraw-Hill, 1987), 158. See also Dominic Sandbrook, *Never Had It So Good: A History of Britain from Suez to the Beatles,* vol. 1: *1956–1963* (Boston: Little, Brown, 2005), 7–8.

15 Eden to Cabinet, November 24, 1953, CAB 129 64, TNA. See here the fine analysis in Kevin Ruane, "Anthony Eden, British Diplomacy, and the Origins of the Geneva Conference of 1954," *Historical Journal* 37, no. 1 (1994): 156–57.

16 Rhodes James, *Eden,* 374–75.

17 Anthony Eden, *Full Circle: The Memoirs of Anthony Eden* (Boston: Houghton Mifflin, 1960), 87.

18 Quoted in Philippe Devillers and Jean Lacouture, *End of a War: Indochina, 1954* (New York: Praeger, 1969), 55. See also Pierre Grosser, "La France et l'Indochine (1953–1956): Une 'carte de visite' en 'peau de chagrin'" [France and Indochina (1953–1956): A Visitor's Pass to the Land of Sorrow], doctoral dissertation, Institut d'études politiques de Paris, September 2002, 483–500.

19 For the consensus in French officialdom that the United States was firmly committed to keeping the war going, see Le Général des Corps d'Armée Valluy à Monsieur le Général d'Armée Chef d'Etat-major Général des Forces Armées, February 4, 1954, Dossier 295, Indochine, Asie-Océanie 1944–1955, MAE.

20 André Siegfried, *L'Année Politique 1954* (Paris: Presses universitaires de France, 1955), 511–16.

21 C. L. Sulzberger, *A Long Row of Candles: Memoirs and Diaries, 1934–1954* (New York: Macmillan, 1969), 949.

22 Churchill to Eden, February 8, 1954, PREM 11/648. Churchill wrote: "I think that you are quite right to try your Far East meeting. It is important to keep parleys afloat."

23 David Dutton, *Anthony Eden: A Life and Reputation* (London: Hodder Arnold, 1997), 474.

24 A portion of the communiqué is printed in *FRUS, 1952–1954, The Geneva Conference*, XVI:415.

25 Quoted in David Carlton, *Anthony Eden: A Biography* (New York: HarperCollins, 1986), 339. The delegate in question was Livingston Merchant.

26 Dulles to Eisenhower, February 6, 1954, *FRUS, 1952–1954, Indochina*, XIII, 1:1021.

27 Memo of discussion, 186th NSC meeting, February 26, 1953, *FRUS, 1952–1954, Indochina*, XIII, 1:1080–81; Lawrence S. Kaplan, "NATO and French Indochina," in Lawrence S. Kaplan, Denise Artaud, and Mark Rubin, eds., *Dien Bien Phu and the Crisis of Franco-American Relations, 1954–1955* (Wilmington, Del.: Scholarly Resources, 1990), 239.

28 W. D. Allen note, February 24, 1954, FO 371/112047, TNA.

29 Georges Bidault, *D'une résistance à l'autre* (Paris: Les Presses du siècle, 1965), 193; James Cable, *The Geneva Conference of 1954 on Indochina* (London: Macmillan, 1986), 43.

30 Here, as so often on the subject of domestic politics and its impact on U.S. foreign policy, foreign observations are especially astute. Wrote a sympathetic Evelyn Shuckburgh in his diary on February 11: "American public opinion might easily turn on him for agreeing too readily to sit down with the Chinese Communists." Evelyn Shuckburgh, *Descent to Suez: Diaries, 1951–1956* (New York: W.W. Norton, 1987), 133.

31 William C. Gibbons, *The U.S. Government and the Vietnam War: Executive and Legislative Roles and Relationships* (Princeton, N.J.: Princeton University Press, 1986), 1:165–66; "Report on Berlin," February 24, 1954, quoted in Robert F. Randle, *Geneva 1954: The Settlement of the Indo-Chinese War* (Princeton, N.J.: Princeton University Press, 1969), 40–41.

32 Dulles to State, February 18, 1954, *FRUS, 1952–1954, Indochina*, XIII, 1:1057.

33 Pierre Pellissier, *Diên Biên Phu: 20 novembre 1953–7 mai 1954* (Paris: Perrin, 2004), 231–32; and James R. Arnold, *The First Domino: Eisenhower, the Military, and America's Intervention in Vietnam* (New York: William Morrow, 1991), 146–47.

34 Conversation tenue, Comité de défense nationale, March 11, 1954, vol. 297, Série Asie-Océanie 1944–1955, Sous-série Indochine, MAE; Pellissier, *Diên Biên Phu,* 243–45; Joseph Laniel, *Le drame indochinois* (Paris: Plon, 1957), 16–17; Pierre Grosser, "La France et l'Indochine," 624–37.

35 Devillers and Lacouture, *End of a War,* 62–66; Yves Gras, *Histoire de la guerre d'Indochine* (Paris: Plon, 1979), 541–42; Laniel, *Le drame indochinois,* 79–80.

36 On the urgent need to improve the performance of the VNA, see Général C. Blanc, "Situation d'ensemble," February 8, 1954, Dossier IV, DPMF Indochine, Institut Pierre Mendès France, Paris.

37 Laniel, *Le drame indochinois,* 82.

38 Jean Lacouture, *Pierre Mendès France,* trans. George Holock (New York: Holmes & Meier, 1984), 201.

39 Text in India, *Parliamentary Debates, Official Report, House of the People,* Part 2, 6th Session, vol. 1, no. 6 (February 22, 1954), cols. 415–16.

40 Pierre Rocolle, *Pourquoi Dien Bien Phu?* (Paris: Flammarion, 1968), 327, as cited in Martin Windrow, *The Last Valley: Dien Bien Phu and the French Defeat in Vietnam* (Cambridge, Mass.: Da Capo, 2004), 363.

41 General O'Daniel, "Report on the U.S. Special Mission to Indochina," February 5, 1954, Box 1, George Kahin Collection on the Origins of the Vietnam War, Carl A. Kroch Rare and Manuscript Collections, Cornell University.

42 Saigon to State, February 9, 1954, *FRUS, 1952–1954, Indochina,* XIII, 1:1026, 1065–66; *Time,* March 1, 1954.

43 Quoted in Jules Roy, *The Battle of Dienbienphu,* trans. Robert Baldick (New York: Harper & Row, 1965; reprint Carroll & Graf, 1984), 144. See also Robert Guillain, *Diên-Biên-Phu: La fin des illusions [Notes d'Indochine, février–juillet 1954]* (Paris: Arléa, 2004).

44 Graham Greene diary entry for January 5, 1954, Box 1, Greene Papers, GU; Graham Greene, *Ways of Escape* (New York: Simon & Schuster, 1980), 189. Greene's article appeared in two installments in the newspaper, on March 21 and March 28.

45 On Viet Minh gains in the south in early 1954, see David W. P. Elliott, *The Vietnamese War: Revolution and Social Change in the Mekong Delta, 1930–1975* (Armonk, N.Y.: M.E. Sharpe, 2007), 80–82.

46 Bernard B. Fall, "Solution in Indo-China: Cease-Fire, Negotiate," *Nation,* March 6, 1954. On February 20, Bao Dai startled the U.S. and British ambassadors by suggesting seriously that the best solution to the "pourriture" in the delta would be to remove all, or nearly all, its residents and transport them to southern Annam. After this exodus, the army could then launch an all-out bombardment of the barren zone. Saigon to FO, February 25, 1954, FO 371/112024, TNA.

47 Fall, "Solution in Indo-China."

48 A superb treatment of these early days in the battle remains Rocolle, *Pourquoi Dien Bien Phu?,* 343–90. See also Pierre Journoud and Hugues Tertrais, *Paroles de Dien Bien Phu: Les survivants témoignent* (Paris: Tallandier, 2004), 111–31. For the harrowing first hours, see Erwan Bergot, *Les 170 jours de Diên Biên Phû* (Paris: Presses de la cité, 1979), 85–98.

49 Gaucher letter quoted in Ted Morgan, *Valley of Death: The Tragedy at Dien Bien Phu That Led America into the Vietnam War* (New York: Random House, 2010), 256.

50 Howard R. Simpson, *Dien Bien Phu: The Epic Battle America Forgot* (Washington, D.C.: Brassey's, 1994), 53–54.

51 Ibid., 63.

52 *Lich Su Bo Doi Dac Cong, Tap Mot* [History of the Sapper Forces, Volume I] (Hanoi:

People's Army Publishing House, 1987), 68–70; Hanoi to FO, February 17, 1954, FO 371/112024, TNA. See also John Prados, "Mechanics at the Edge of War," *VVA Veteran* 22, no. 8 (August 2002); Simpson, *Dien Bien Phu,* 64–65.

53 Edgar O'Ballance, *The Indo-China War, 1945–1954* (London: Faber & Faber, 1964), 218.

54 Quoted in Roy, *Battle of Dienbienphu,* 167.

55 Phillip B. Davidson, *Vietnam at War: The History, 1946–1975* (New York: Oxford University Press, 1991), 236.

56 Roy, *Battle of Dienbienphu,* 172.

57 Bernard B. Fall, *Street Without Joy: Indochina at War 1946–1954* (reprint ed., Mechanicsburg, Pa.: Stackpole, 1994), 321.

58 Bernard B. Fall, *Hell in a Very Small Place: The Siege of Dien Bien Phu* (Philadelphia: Lippincott, 1966), 156.

59 Pellissier, *Diên Biên Phu,* 268–72.

60 Paul Grauwin, *J'étais médecin à Dien-Bien-Phu* (Paris: France-Empire, 1954). A shorter English translation is *Doctor at Dienbienphu* (New York: John Day, 1955).

61 Simpson, *Dien Bien Phu,* 89.

62 Navarre pour Ministre Etats Associés, March 23, 1954, Dossier I 457 AP 53, Conférence de Genève, AN.

63 Devillers and Lacouture, *End of a War,* 72.

64 Comité de défense nationale to Schumann, March 11, 1954, vol. 297, Série Asie-Océanie 1944–1955, Sous-série Indochine, MAE.

CHAPTER 19: *America Wants In*

1 Memo of discussion, 189th NSC meeting, March 18, 1954, *FRUS, 1952–1954, Indochina,* XIII, 1:1132–33.

2 Memo of conversation, March 19, 1954, *FRUS, 1952–1954, Indochina,* XIII, 1:1133–34; Comité de défense nationale to Schumann, March 11, 1954, vol. 297, Série Asie-Océanie 1944–1955, Sous-série Indochine, MAE.

3 Télégram a l'arrivée, March 24, 1954, vol. 297, Série Asie-Océanie 1944–1955, Sous-série Indochine, MAE; Memo for the record, March 21, 1954, *FRUS, 1952–1954, Indochina,* XIII, 1:1137–40; *NYT,* March 23, 1954; Paul Ely, *Mémoires: L'Indochine dans la tourmente* (Paris: Plon, 1964), 59–60.

4 Conversation tenue, March 23, 1954, vol. 297, Série Asie-Océanie 1944–1955, Sous-série Indochine, MAE; Ely, *Mémoires,* 65–67.

5 Memo of conversation with the president, March 24, 1954, *FRUS, 1952–1954, Indochina,* XIII, 1:1150; Dulles-Radford telcon, March 25, 1954, Box 2, Telephone Calls Series, John Foster Dulles Papers, Eisenhower Library.

6 Ely, *Mémoires,* 67–83; Bonnet to Paris, March 24 and 25, 1954, vol. 297, Série Asie-Océanie 1944–1955, Sous-série Indochine, MAE; Arthur Radford, *From Pearl Harbor to Vietnam: The Memoirs of Admiral Arthur W. Radford,* ed. Stephen Jurika (Stanford, Calif.: Hoover Institution Press, 1980), 391–401; Joseph Laniel, *Le drame indochinois* (Paris: Plon, 1957), 83–88; Kathryn C. Statler, *Replacing France: The Origins of American Intervention in Vietnam* (Lexington: University Press of Kentucky, 2007), 89; George C. Herring and Richard H. Immerman, "Eisenhower, Dulles, and Dienbienphu: 'The Day We Didn't Go to War' Revisited," *Journal of American History* 71 (September 1984), 347–48.

7 Richard H. Immerman, "Between the Unattainable and the Unacceptable: Eisen-

hower and Dienbienphu," in Richard A. Melanson and David Mayers, eds., *Re-evaluating Eisenhower: American Foreign Policy in the 1950s* (Urbana: University of Illinois Press, 1987), 131.

8 On Vulture, see John Prados, *Operation Vulture* (New York: ibooks, 2002).

9 Memo of discussion, 190th meeting of the NSC, March 25, 1954, *FRUS, 1952–1954, Indochina*, XIII, 1:1163–68.

10 Reported in Washington to FO, April 1, 1954, FO 371/112050, TNA.

11 *NYT*, March 28, 1954.

12 *NYT*, March 28, 1954; Richard Rovere, "Letter from Washington," *New Yorker*, April 17, 1954, pp.71–72.

13 Quoted in Richard Nixon, *RN: The Memoirs of Richard Nixon* (New York: Grosset & Dunlap, 1978), 151.

14 Prados, *Operation Vulture*, 112.

15 The speech is reproduced in *U.S. News & World Report*, April 9, 1954.

16 Robert Bowie, quoted in Immerman, "Between the Unattainable and the Unacceptable," 132.

17 *Wall Street Journal*, March 30, 1954; *U.S. News & World Report*, April 9, 1954; *New Republic*, April 12, 1954; *NYT*, March 30, 1954.

18 Melanie Billings-Yun, *Decision Against War: Eisenhower and Dienbienphu, 1954* (New York: Columbia University Press, 1988), 66; Robert Mann, *A Grand Delusion: America's Descent into Vietnam* (New York: Basic, 2001), 142.

19 Ronald H. Spector, *Advice and Support: The Early Years of the U.S. Army in Vietnam, 1941–1960* (Washington, D.C.: Center for Military History, 1985), 202. See also Robert Buzzanco, *Masters of War: Military Dissent and Politics in the Vietnam Era* (New York: Cambridge University Press, 1997), 42; and Ridgway's memo to the JCS, April 6, 1954, Folder 17, Box 37, Ridgway Papers, U.S. Army Heritage and Education Center, Carlisle, Pa. I thank the center's reference historian, Arthur Bergeron, for making this document available to me.

20 George W. Allen, *None So Blind: A Personal Account of the Intelligence Failure in Vietnam* (Chicago: Ivan R. Dee, 2001), 65.

21 Quoted in Mann, *Grand Delusion*, 143.

22 James C. Hagerty diary entry for April 1, 1954, Eisenhower Library.

23 The 1964 Gulf of Tonkin Resolution requested by Lyndon Johnson, by contrast, was more far-reaching. It did not "authorize" action by the president and was carefully crafted so as to avoid any suggestion that he needed congressional authorization; indeed, it sought to put lawmakers on record as agreeing that he had that power as commander in chief. The 1964 resolution thus stated that Congress "approves and supports the determination of the President, as Commander in Chief, to take all necessary measures to repel any armed attack against the forces of the United States and to prevent further aggression." The 1954 draft resolution had a termination date of June 30, 1955; the Gulf of Tonkin resolution had no fixed end date.

24 Memo of conversation with the president, April 2, 1954, *FRUS, 1952–1954, Indochina*, XIII, 1:1210–11. The draft resolution is on pp. 1211–12. See also Lloyd C. Gardner, *Approaching Vietnam: From World War II Through Dienbienphu* (New York: W.W. Norton, 1989), 205.

25 There is no indication that the FBI investigation came to anything. On June 18, 1954, *U.S. News & World Report* published an article under the title "Did U.S. Almost Get Into War?" For evidence that this article was planted by the administration and represented an official response to Roberts's *Washington Post* story, see

Dulles-McCardle telcon, July 23, 1954, Dulles Telcons 3, Dulles Papers, Eisenhower Library.

26 Chalmers M. Roberts, "The Day We Didn't Go to War," *Reporter* 11 (September 14, 1954): 31–35. Roberts's account draws mostly on interviews with several of the participants as well as McCormack's "copious notes," which he let the reporter see. The article has been seen as suspect by some historians for its heavy reliance on the recollections of Democrats with a possible interest in tarnishing the administration, but in fact it largely accords on the main issues with the only other record of the meeting, a brief memo Dulles wrote for his files. See Dulles memorandum for the file, April 5, 1954, *FRUS, 1952–1954, Indochina*, XIII, 1:1224–25. And see also Chalmers M. Roberts, *First Rough Draft: A Journalist's Journal of Our Times* (New York: Praeger, 1973), 114–15; and William C. Gibbons, *The U.S. Government and the Vietnam War: Executive and Legislative Roles and Relationships, Part I: 1945–1960* (Princeton, N.J.: Princeton University Press, 1986), 191–95. Roberts's initial article is in *Washington Post*, June 7, 1954. The account here relies on all these sources.

27 Dulles memcon with congressional leaders, April 5, 1954, Chronological Series, April 1954, Dulles Papers, Eisenhower Library; Billings-Yun, *Decision Against War*, 91–92.

28 Dulles-Eisenhower telcon, April 3, 1954, Dulles Papers, Eisenhower Library.

29 Memo of conversation, April 3, 1954, *FRUS, 1952–1954, Indochina*, XIII, 1:1225–29.

30 High Commissioner in Auckland to Colonial Office, April 7, 1954, FO 371/112051, TNA; Munro to Auckland, April 6, 1954, FO 371/112052, TNA; Gardner, *Approaching Vietnam*, 207–8. The passage from which Dulles read is in Winston Churchill, *The Gathering Storm* (Boston: Houghton Mifflin, 1948), 78–79.

31 James Waite, "Contesting the Right Decision: New Zealand, the Commonwealth, and the New Look," *Diplomatic History* 30 (November 2006): 908; Washington to FO, April 5, 1954 FO 371/112050, TNA.

32 Editorial note, *FRUS, 1952–1954, Indochina*, XIII, 1:1236; Sherman Adams, *Firsthand Report: The Story of the Eisenhower Administration* (New York: Harper & Bros., 1961), 122.

33 See, e.g., Billings-Yun, *Decision Against War* and especially Gareth Porter, *Perils of Dominance: Imbalance of Power and the Road to War in Vietnam* (Berkeley: University of California Press, 2005), 70–71. For the problem with claims that Eisenhower was deliberately setting forth conditions for intervention that he knew could not be fulfilled, see William J. Duiker, *U.S. Containment Policy and the Conflict in Indochina* (Stanford, Calif.: Stanford University Press, 1994), 190–91.

34 See, e.g., Prados, *Operation Vulture*; Gibbons, *U.S. Government*, 178.

35 A point made in Duiker, *U.S. Containment*, 161.

36 Ely, *Mémoires*, 76–78, 83–85; Philippe Devillers and Jean Lacouture, *End of a War: Indochina, 1954* (New York: Praeger, 1969), 75–76; Paris to FO, April 10, 1954, FO 371/112104, TNA.

37 Jean Pouget, *Nous e'tions à Dien-Bien-Phu* (Paris: Presses de la cité, 1964), 280; Laniel, *Le drame indochinois*, 83–86; Henri Navarre, *Agonie de l'Indochine* (Paris: Plon, 1956), 242–43.

38 Devillers and Lacouture, *End of a War*, 76–77. See also the revealing summary in Paris to FO, April 10, 1954, FO 371/112104, TNA.

39 Paris to State, April 5, 1954, *FRUS, 1952–1954, Indochina*, XIII, 1:1236–38; Devillers and Lacouture, *End of a War*, 77; Laniel, *Le drame indochinois*, 83–86.

40 James R. Arnold, *The First Domino: Eisenhower, the Military, and America's Intervention in Vietnam* (New York: William Morrow, 1991), 169.

41 State to London, April 4, 1954, *FRUS, 1952–1954, Indochina,* XIII, 1:1238–40.

42 Kevin Ruane, personal correspondence with the author, November 18, 2010. Might Eisenhower have inserted "appreciable" precisely in order to generate a negative British reply? Conceivably yes, but unlikely; it seems too clever by half. See also note 31 above.

43 White House to Dulles, April 5, 1954, *FRUS, 1952–1954, Indochina,* XIII, 1:1238n2.

44 Eisenhower-Dulles telcon, April 5, 1954, DDE Phone Calls, Eisenhower Library; Dulles to Dillon, April 4, 1954, *FRUS, 1952–1954, Indochina,* XIII, 1:1242.

45 Paris to State, April 5, 1954, *FRUS, 1952–1954, Indochina,* XIII, 1:1242–43.

46 Ibid., 1:1248–49.

47 Mann, *Grand Delusion,* 153.

48 Immerman, "Between the Unattainable and the Unacceptable," 137.

49 Presidential press conference, April 7, 1954, *Public Papers of Eisenhower,* 2:382–84; George C. Herring and Richard H. Immerman, "Eisenhower, Dulles, and Dienbienphu," 355. *The New York Times* liked the metaphor and the sentiment behind it: See the editorial on April 8, 1954.

50 Dulles-Wiley telcon, April 7, 1954, Box 2, Telephone Calls Series, John Foster Dulles Papers, Eisenhower Library.

51 Immerman, "Between the Unattainable and the Unacceptable," 138.

CHAPTER 20: *Dulles Versus Eden*

1 This remark is sometimes attributed to Eisenhower.

2 Martin Gilbert, *Never Despair: Winston S. Churchill, 1945–1965* (Boston: Houghton Mifflin, 1988), 959–60.

3 Diary entry, March 26, 1954, Evelyn Shuckburgh, *Descent to Suez: Diaries, 1951–1956* (New York: W.W. Norton, 1987), 155–56.

4 Lloyd C. Gardner, *Approaching Vietnam: From World War II Through Dienbienphu* (New York: W.W. Norton, 1989), 188–91, 215; and Roy Jenkins, *Churchill: A Biography* (New York: Farrar, Straus & Giroux, 2001), 876. Jenkins, a parliamentarian at the time, was present in the Commons that day. "The scene remains etched in my memory," he wrote.

5 Geoffrey Warner, "Britain and the Crisis over Dien Bien Phu, April 1954: The Failure of United Action," in Lawrence S. Kaplan, Denise Artaud, and Mark Rubin, eds., *Dien Bien Phu and the Crisis of Franco-American Relations, 1954–1955* (Wilmington, Del.: Scholarly Resources, 1990), 65–66; Anthony Eden, *Full Circle: The Memoirs of Anthony Eden* (Boston: Houghton Mifflin, 1960), 104–5.

6 Strong memo, April 12, 1954, PREM 11/645, TNA; Confidential Annex to COS 42nd meeting, Item 2, April 10, 1954, FO 371/112053, TNA; Warner, "Britain and the Crisis over Dien Bien Phu," 66–67. Eden's Australian counterpart, R. G. Casey, felt the same. See R. G. Casey diary entry for April 12, 1954, 34–M1153, National Archives of Australia (hereafter NAA).

7 Shuckburgh diary entry for April 8, 1954, quoted in James Cable, *The Geneva Conference of 1954 on Indochina* (London: Macmillan, 1986), 55.

8 Cable, *Geneva Conference,* 56.

9 Record of conversation, April 11, 1954, FO 371/112054; Memcon, April 11, 1954, *FRUS, 1952–1954, Indochina,* XIII, 1:1307–9. See also Eden, *Full Circle,* 107–8.

10 Ibid.

11 Walton Butterworth, Oral History Interview, Dulles Papers, Mudd Library, Princeton University, quoted in Gardner, *Approaching Vietnam*, 221–22.

12 Record of conversation, April 12, 1954, FO 371/112054, TNA; Memcon, April 12, 1954, *FRUS, 1952–1954, Indochina*, XIII, 1:1319–20.

13 Diary entry, April 12, 1954, Shuckburgh, *Descent to Suez*, 164. Robertson's Zhou comment is in Robert E. Herzstein, *Henry R. Luce, Time, and the American Crusade in Asia* (New York: Cambridge University Press, 2005), 173.

14 Memcon, April 13, 1954, *FRUS, 1952–1954, Indochina*, XIII, 1:1321–23; diary entry, April 13, 1954, Shuckburgh, *Descent to Suez*, 164.

15 Gardner, *Approaching Vietnam*, 221; Eden minute, March 26, 1954, FO 371/112048, TNA. See also his comment in the margin of W. D. Allen to I. Kirkpatrick, March 23, 1954, FO 371/112048, TNA.

16 Philippe Devillers and Jean Lacouture, *End of a War: Indochina, 1954* (New York: Praeger, 1969), 87–88. For Bidault's cynical view of United Action, see Ministère des Affaires Étrangère, "Note," April 7, 1954, Dossier 2 457 AP 52, Archives Nationale.

17 FO to Washington, April 15, 1954, FO 371/112053, TNA; Cable, *Geneva Conference*, 58.

18 FO to Washington, April 17, 1954, and April 18, 1954, FO 371/112053, TNA; Cable, *Geneva Conference*, 58–59; Eden, *Full Circle*, 99.

19 FO to Washington, April 19, 1954, FO 371/112053, TNA.

20 See the analysis in Warner, "Britain and the Crisis over Dien Bien Phu," 69–70; and David Dutton, *Anthony Eden: A Life and Reputation* (London: Hodder Arnold, 1997), 343.

21 Townsend Hoopes, *The Devil and John Foster Dulles* (Boston: Little, Brown, 1973), 216. See also Douglas Dillon oral history, Dulles Oral History Project, Princeton University.

22 Diary entry for April 15, 1954, in Shuckburgh, *Descent to Suez*, 166; Cable, *Geneva Conference*, 60.

23 Cable, *Geneva Conference*, 59.

24 *U.S. News & World Report*, April 30, 1954; *NYT*, April 17, 1954.

25 *Washington Post*, April 20, 1954; *Wall Street Journal*, April 19, 1954; *NYT*, April 20, 1954.

26 Richard Nixon, *RN: The Memoirs of Richard Nixon* (New York: Grosset & Dunlap, 1978), 151–52; Nixon interview, Dulles Oral History Project, Princeton University; Arthur Radford, *From Pearl Harbor to Vietnam: The Memoirs of Admiral Arthur W. Radford*, ed. Stephen Jurika (Stanford, Calif.: Hoover Institution Press, 1980), 405.

27 Nixon never regretted his stance. In his 1985 book *No More Vietnams*, he wrote that not intervening at Dien Bien Phu was "the first critical mistake" the United States made in Vietnam. "By standing aside as our ally went down to defeat, the United States lost its last chance to stop the expansion of communism in Southeast Asia at little cost to itself." Richard M. Nixon, *No More Vietnams* (New York: Arbor House, 1985), 31.

28 JFD-Nixon telcon, April 19, 1954, JFD Phone Calls, Eisenhower Library; Eisenhower-Nixon telcon, April 19, 1954, Box 5, DDE Diary, Ann Whitman File, Eisenhower Library; *Wall Street Journal*, April 19, 1954.

29 *Wall Street Journal*, April 19, 1954; *NYT*, April 19, 1954.

30 See also, e.g., *Washington Post*, April 20, 1954; *U.S. News & World Report*, April 30, 1954. The latter declared approvingly: "The White House, despite dip-

lomatic denials, has not closed the door to the use of troops if the alternative is Communist domination of Southeast Asia."

31 Robert F. Randle, *Geneva 1954: The Settlement of the Indo Chinese War* (Princeton, N.J.: Princeton University Press, 1969), 92; Herbert S. Parmet, *Richard Nixon and His America* (Boston: Little, Brown, 1990), 318–19.

32 James C. Hagerty diary entry for April 24, 1954, Eisenhower Library.

33 C. L. Sulzberger, *A Long Row of Candles: Memoirs and Diaries, 1934–1954* (New York: Macmillan, 1969), 836–37; C. L. Sulzberger, "Foreign Affairs: The Day It All Began," *NYT,* January 11, 1967.

34 "Rapport Navarre," April 21, 1954, 74 AP 39, Paul Reynaud Papers, Archives Nationale; Laurent Cesari and Jacques de Folin, "Military Necessity, Political Impossibility: The French Viewpoint on Operation *Vautour,*" in Kaplan, Artaud, and Rubin, *Dien Bien Phu,* 112–13.

35 Eden to FO, April 24, 1954, FO 371/112055, TNA; Dulles to Eisenhower, April 22, 1954, *FRUS, 1952–1954, Indochina,* XIII, 1:1361–62.

36 Dulles to Eisenhower, April 22, 1954, *FRUS, 1952–1954, Indochina,* XIII, 1:1361–62.

37 See, e.g., diary entry for April 22, 1954, Shuckburgh, *Descent to Suez,* 169; Cable, *Geneva Conference,* 61.

38 Diary entry for April 22, 1954, Shuckburgh, *Descent to Suez,* 169.

39 Georges Bidault, *Resistance: The Political Autobiography of Georges Bidault,* trans. Marianne Sinclair (New York: Praeger, 1968), 196.

40 Jean Chauvel, *Commentaire: De Berne à Paris, 1952–1962* (Paris: Fayard, 1973), 3:45–46; Georges Bidault, *D'une résistance à l'autre* (Paris: Presses de siècle, 1965), 198; Cesari and de Folin, "Military Necessity," 113. See also J. R. Tournoux, *Secrets d'état* (Paris: Plon, 1960), 48–49; and Roscoe Drummond and Gaston Coblentz, *Duel at the Brink* (New York: Doubleday, 1960), 121–22.

41 See MacArthur to Dulles, April 7, 1954, *FRUS, 1952–1954, Indochina,* XIII, 1:1270–72.

42 Cutler memo, April 30, 1954, *FRUS, 1952–1954, Indochina,* XIII, 1:1445–48; John Prados, *Operation Vulture* (New York: ibooks, 2002), 213; William J. Duiker, *U.S. Containment Policy and the Conflict in Indochina* (Stanford, Calif.: Stanford University Press, 1994), 167.

43 Gardner, *Approaching Vietnam,* 236, emphasis added.

44 Navarre to Ely, April 22, 1954, 1 K 233 (35), Ely Papers, Service historique de l'armée de terre; Ely's diary, April 23, 1954, 1 K 233 (19), Ely Papers, Service historique de l'armée de terre; Cesari and de Folin, "Military Necessity," 113–14.

45 Eden, *Full Circle,* 102; diary entry for April 24, 1954, Shuckburgh, *Descent to Suez,* 171.

46 Dulles to Eisenhower, April 23, 1954, *FRUS, 1952–1954, Indochina,* XIII, 1:1374. A few hours before sending this cable, Dulles told Australia's Casey that France was "in the death throes of her existence as a great power." Casey diary entry for April 23, 1954, 34–M1153, NAA.

47 Eisenhower-Smith telcon, April 24, 1954, Box 5, DDE diary, Ann Whitman File, Eisenhower Library.

48 Press Secretary Hagerty wrote that day in his diary that the option of using carrier-based aircraft "to support French troops at Dien Bien Phu" remained alive. Hagerty diary, April 24, 1954, Eisenhower Library.

49 This formulation from Gardner, *Approaching Vietnam,* 237.

50 Eden, *Full Circle,* 114–15; Iveragh McDonald, *A Man of the Times: Talks and Trav-*

els in a Disrupted World (London, 1976), 137, as quoted in David Carlton, *Anthony Eden: A Biography* (New York: HarperCollins, 1986), 345–46.

51 Dulles to Smith, April 24, 1954, *FRUS, 1952–1954, Indochina*, XIII, 1:1398–99; Eden to FO, April 24, 1954, FO 371/112056, TNA; Casey diary entry for April 26, 1954, 34–M1153, NAA; Eden, *Full Circle*, 116; Hoopes, *Devil and John Foster Dulles*, 217.

52 Eden to FO, April 24, 1954, FO 371/112056, TNA.

53 Diary entry for April 24, 1954, Shuckburgh, *Descent to Suez*, 172.

54 Shuckburgh, *Descent to Suez*, 173; Eden, *Full Circle*, 117.

55 "Indochina," April 27, 1954, CAB 129/68, TNA; entry for April 25, Harold Macmillan, *The Macmillan Diaries: The Cabinet Years, 1950–1957*, ed. Peter Catterall (London: Macmillan, 2003), 309.

56 Record of conversation at dinner, April 26, 1954, FO 371/112057, TNA. See also Chester L. Cooper, *In the Shadows of History: Fifty Years Behind the Scenes of Cold War Diplomacy* (Amherst, N.Y.: Prometheus, 2005), 123–24.

57 RN dictabelts, VP diary, April 29, 1954, Nixon Library, Yorba Linda, Calif.

58 Record of conversation at dinner, April 26, 1954, FO 371/112057, TNA.

59 Carl W. McCardle to Dulles, April 30, 1954, Box 2, General Correspondence and Memoranda Series, Dulles Papers, Eisenhower Library; diary entry for April 24, 1954, Shuckburgh, *Descent to Suez*, 172.

60 Dwight D. Eisenhower diary, April 27, 1954, diary series, "April 1954," Ann Whitman File, Eisenhower Library; Eisenhower to Hazlett, April 27, 1954, Ann Whitman File, Eisenhower Library.

61 *U.S. News & World Report*, April 30, 1954.

62 RN dictabelts, VP diary, April 29, 1954, Nixon Library, Yorba Linda, Calif.

CHAPTER 21: *Valley of Tears*

1 The climax at Dien Bien Phu has received a great deal of scrutiny over the past six decades, albeit in relatively few English-language accounts in recent years. Particularly useful accounts include Pierre Rocolle, *Pourquoi Dien Bien Phu?* (Paris: Flammarion, 1968); Martin Windrow, *The Last Valley: Dien Bien Phu and the French Defeat in Vietnam* (Cambridge, Mass.: Da Capo, 2004); Bernard B. Fall, *Hell in a Very Small Place: The Siege of Dien Bien Phu* (Philadelphia: Lippincott, 1966); Jules Roy, *The Battle of Dienbienphu*, trans. Robert Baldick (New York: Harper & Row, 1965; reprint Carroll & Graf, 1984); Pierre Pellissier, *Diên Biên Phu: 20 novembre 1953–7 mai 1954* (Paris: Perrin, 2004); Ted Morgan, *Valley of Death: The Tragedy at Dien Bien Phu That Led America into the Vietnam War* (New York: Random House, 2010); and Pierre Journoud and Hugues Tertrais, *Paroles de Dien Bien Phu: Les survivants témoignent* (Paris: Tallandier, 2004).

2 Howard R. Simpson, *Dien Bien Phu: The Epic Battle America Forgot* (Washington, D.C.: Brassey's, 1994), 138. See also Paul Grauwin, *J'étais médecin à Dien-Bien-Phu* (Paris: France-Empire, 1954), chaps. 10–11.

3 Morgan, *Valley of Death*, 504.

4 Simpson, *Dien Bien Phu*, 137; Marcel-Maurice Bigeard, *Pour une parcelle de gloire* (Paris: Plon, 1975), 176–79.

5 Navarre's grim perspective is in Navarre à Monsieur le Ministre des Etats Associés, May 6, 1954, Dossier 1, 457 AP 53, Conférence de Genève, Archives Nationale.

6 John Keegan, *Dien Bien Phu* (New York: Ballantine, 1974), 126.

7 Quoted in Simpson, *Dien Bien Phu*, 122; Fall, *Hell in a Very Small Place*, 341.

8 Fall, *Hell in a Very Small Place*, 237, 266.

9 Windrow, *Last Valley*, 538; Roy, *Battle of Dienbienphu*, 226–67.

10 Ton That Tung, *Reminiscences of a Vietnamese Surgeon* (Hanoi: Foreign Languages Publishing House, 1980), 47.

11 Nguyen Thi Ngoc Toan oral history, Hanoi, June 11, 2007. I thank interviewer Merle Pribbenow for making this oral history available to me.

12 The resolution of the Politburo, April 19, 1954, Archives of the Ministry of National Defense, Document 173, sheets 49–51, Central Department, as cited in Vo Nguyen Giap, *Memoirs of War: The Road to Dien Bien Phu* (Hanoi: Gioi, 2004), 114; Fall, *Hell in a Very Small Place*, 341–42; and Carlyle Thayer, *War by Other Means: National Liberation and Revolution in Viet Nam, 1954–1960* (Sydney: Allen & Unwin, 1989), 3–5.

13 Giap, *Road to Dien Bien Phu*, 114.

14 Truong Huyen Chi and Marc Jason Gilbert, "Voices of Dien Bien Phu," unpublished paper in author's possession. I'm grateful to Marc Gilbert for making this manuscript available to me.

15 Rocolle, *Pourquoi Dien Bien Phu?*, 484; Fall, *Hell in a Very Small Place*, 340.

16 Truong Chinh quoted in Pierre Asselin, "The DRVN and the 1954 Geneva Conference," unpublished conference paper, in the author's possession, 25.

17 Documents quoted in Asselin, "DRVN and Geneva Conference," 29.

18 Zhou quoted in Chen Jian, "China and the Indochina Settlement at the Geneva Conference of 1954," in Mark Atwood Lawrence and Fredrik Logevall, eds., *The First Vietnam War: Colonial Conflict and Cold War Crisis* (Cambridge, Mass.: Harvard University Press, 2007), 242.

19 Ilya V. Gaiduk, *Confronting Vietnam: Soviet Policy Toward the Indochina Conflict, 1954–1963* (Stanford, Calif.: Stanford University Press, 2003), 18. See also Mari Olsen, *Soviet-Vietnam Relations and the Role of China, 1949–1964: Changing Alliances* (London: Routledge, 2006), 32–34.

20 Gaiduk, *Confronting Vietnam*, 18; Zhou Enlai to Ho Chi Minh, telegram, March 11, 1954, in Cold War International History Project binder; Chen Jian, "China and Indochina Settlement," 244–45.

21 Quoted in Nguyen Vu Tung, "The Road to Geneva: How the DRV Changed Its Positions," unpublished paper (Cold War International History Project) in author's possession.

22 Qiang Zhai, *China and the Vietnam Wars, 1950–1975* (Chapel Hill: University of North Carolina Press, 2000), 51.

23 Chen Jian, "China and the Indochina Settlement," 245; Trinh Quang Thanh, interview by author, Hanoi, January 2003.

24 Zhai, *China and the Vietnam Wars*, 51–53. For an account of the Moscow meetings based on Russian documents, see Gaiduk, *Confronting Vietnam*, 22–24.

25 Zhai, *China and the Vietnam Wars*, 48.

26 Fall, *Hell in a Very Small Place*, 354; Erwan Bergot, *Les 170 jours de Diên Biên Phu* (Paris: Presses de la cité, 1979), 267–69.

27 Fall, *Hell in a Very Small Place*, 354.

28 Simpson, *Dien Bien Phu*, 151.

29 Ibid., 151–52, slightly edited by author.

30 Fall, *Hell in a Very Small Place*, 360–61.

31 Ibid., 371–72.

32 Windrow, *Last Valley*, 597; Fall, *Hell in a Very Small Place*, 373–74.

33 Simpson, *Dien Bien Phu*, 158.

34 In 1997, an American MIA team investigating an unrelated case found a C-119 propeller near Ban Sot, Laos, and a photo analyst spotted possible graves in aerial photos. Excavation in 2002 uncovered remains that turned out to be McGovern's; the CIA arranged for his nephew to fly to Hickam Air Force Base, near Honolulu, to escort the remains home to New Jersey. Buford's remains have not been found, making him one of thirty-five civilians among more than seventeen hundred Americans still unaccounted for in Indochina.

35 Quoted in Roy, *Battle of Dienbienphu*, 264.

36 Keegan, *Dien Bien Phu*, 141.

37 Captain Le Damany, quoted in Windrow, *Last Valley*, 601.

38 Rocolle, *Pourquoi Dien Bien Phu?*, 530–31; Windrow, *Last Valley*, 602–3; Roy, *Battle of Dienbienphu*, 268.

39 Roy, *Battle of Dienbienphu*, 268.

40 Rocolle, *Pourquoi Dien Bien Phu?*, 538.

41 Bernard B. Fall, "Dien Bien Phu: Battle to Remember," *NYT Magazine*, May 3, 1964. Whether the white flag flew at Dien Bien Phu has long been a source of controversy. Castries's use of the past tense *wanted* could support the argument that he did at some point raise the flag.

42 Quoted in Fall, *Hell in a Very Small Place*, 415–16.

43 Ibid.; Roy, *Battle of Dienbienphu*, 286. Herriott quoted in *Time*, May 17, 1954.

44 Quotes are from *Time*, May 17, 1954.

45 Quoted in Michael Maclear, *The Ten Thousand Day War* (New York: Avon, 1982), 46. See also Robert Guillain, *Diên-Biên-Phu: La fin des illusions [Notes d'Indochine, février–juillet 1954]* (Paris: Arléa, 2004), 163–69.

46 *Newsweek*, May 17, 1954.

47 The army's figure is 10,061 prisoners, broken down as follows: 2,257 French; 932 Moroccans; 804 Algerians; 221 Africans; 2,262 legionnaires; and 3,585 Vietnamese and others, such as Tai. Morgan, *Valley of Death*, 559.

48 Windrow, *Last Valley*, 638–39.

49 See, e.g., Pierre Journoud and Hugues Tertrais, *Paroles de Dien Bien Phu*, chap. 4; Fall, *Hell in a Very Small Place*, 432–47; Robert Bonnafous, *Les Prisonniers de guerre du corps expéditionnaire français en Extrême Orient dans les camps Viêt minh (1945–1954)* (Montpellier: Université Paul Valéry, 1985).

50 Douglas Porch, *The French Foreign Legion: A Complete History of the Legendary Fighting Force* (New York: HarperCollins, 1991), 561–62; Bernard B. Fall, *Street Without Joy: Indochina at War 1946–1954* (reprint ed., Mechanicsburg, Pa.: Stackpole, 1994), 301–2.

51 Jean-Louis Rondy, "Les méthodes Viet-Minh de lavage de cerveau," *Revue historiques des armées* 4 (1989), 74–81.

52 Bernard B. Fall, "Communist POW Treatment in Indochina," *Military Review* (December 1958): 6.

53 Windrow, *Last Valley*, 647; Rocolle, *Pourquoi Dien Bien Phu?*, 548–49; René Bail, *L'enfer de Diên Biên Phu, novembre 1953–mai 1954* (Bayeux: Éditions Heimdal, 2001), 158.

54 Christopher E. Goscha, "The Body Under Siege," unpublished book chapter, in author's possession. General de Castries was told in captivity that the Viet Minh casualties at Dien Bien Phu totaled thirty thousand.

55 Keegan, *Dien Bien Phu*, 153–54.

56 Bernard B. Fall, "Post-Mortems on Dien Bien Phu: Review Article," *Far Eastern Survey* 27, no. 10 (October 1958): 158; Keegan, *Dien Bien Phu, 154.*

CHAPTER 22: *With Friends Like These*

1 Philippe Devillers and Jean Lacouture, *End of a War: Indochina, 1954* (New York: Praeger, 1969), 122.

2 *NYT,* April 25, 1954.

3 Devillers and Lacouture, *End of a War,* 123.

4 Quoted in James Cable, *The Geneva Conference of 1954 on Indochina* (London: Macmillan, 1986), 65.

5 VP diary, RN dictabelt, April 29, 1954, Nixon Presidential Library, Yorba Linda, Calif.; NSC meeting of April 29, 1954, *FRUS, 1952–1954, Indochina,* XIII, 2:1431–35.

6 *New York Herald Tribune,* April 29, 1954; *Washington Post,* May 5, 1954; *Newsweek,* May 14, 1954.

7 Chester L. Cooper, *In the Shadows of History: Fifty Years Behind the Scenes of Cold War Diplomacy* (Amherst, N.Y.: Prometheus, 2005), 118.

8 The question of whether this encounter in fact took place has long been controversial. But several members of the American delegation claimed to witness it personally. See Cooper, *In the Shadows of History,* 113.

9 Cooper, *In the Shadows of History,* 117. Cooper's earlier book appeared in 1970 under the title *The Lost Crusade: America in Vietnam* (New York: Dodd, Mead, 1970). In this first book, he says that he and the Chinese did not exchange any words in the elevator, but merely smiled and then laughed (77).

10 Diary entry, April 26, 1954, Evelyn Shuckburgh, *Descent to Suez: Diaries, 1951–1956* (New York: W.W. Norton, 1987), 177.

11 Diary entry, April 30, 1954, ibid., 183–85; Matthew Jones, "The Geneva Conference of 1954: New Perspectives and Evidence on British Policy and Anglo-American Relations," unpublished paper in author's possession.

12 Geneva to FO, May 2, 1954, FO 371/104840; diary entry, May 2, 1954, Shuckburgh, *Descent to Suez,* 186. See also Eden, "Discussions on the Situation in South-East Asia, March 29–May 22," June 11, 1954, PREM 11/649, TNA.

13 Geoffrey Warner, "From Geneva to Manila: British Policy Toward Indochina and SEATO, May–September 1954," in Lawrence S. Kaplan, Denise Artaud, and Mark Rubin, eds., *Dien Bien Phu and the Crisis of Franco-American Relations, 1954–1955* (Wilmington, Del.: Scholarly Resources, 1990), 150.

14 Moran Diaries, entry for May 4, 1954 from Lord Moran, *Churchill: The Struggle for Survival, 1940–1965* (London: Constable, 1966), 573. Said Churchill a few weeks later: "What [Dulles] says counts for absolutely nothing here and the more he says it the more harmless he becomes." Churchill to Eden, June 16, 1954, PREM 11/666.

15 Jean Chauvel, *Commentaire: De Berne à Paris, 1952–1962* (Paris: Fayard, 1973), 3: 56, as quoted in Cable, *Geneva Conference,* 71.

16 Reading letter to Lloyd, May 14, 1954, SELO 5/15, Selwyn Lloyd Papers, Churchill College, Cambridge. Said one British cable: "Robertson, as we all know, is mad." Paris to FO, May 3, 1954, FO 371/112058, TNA. See also Donald Maitland, *Diverse Times, Sundry Places* (Brighton, U.K.: Alpha Press, 1996), 74.

17 Eden diary entry for May 3, 1954, AP20/1/30, Anthony Eden Papers, University of Birmingham (hereafter UB); Cable, *Geneva Conference,* 70. For Smith's low opinion of Dulles, see Tim Weiner, *Legacy of Ashes: The History of the CIA* (New York:

Doubleday, 2007), 79. Donald Maitland, who accompanied Eden to the airport to see off Dulles, recalled that Eden railed against the American en route to the airport. "I had no idea he was capable of such venom." Maitland, *Diverse Times,* 74.

18 Devillers and Lacouture, *End of a War,* 151–52. The text of Bidault's speech is in *Le Monde,* May 11, 1954.

19 See Zhou Enlai to Mao Zedong and others, "Regarding the Situation of the First Plenary Session," May 9, 1954, Record no. 206-Y0049, PRC Diplomatic Archives, Beijing; and Central Committee to Zhou Enlai, May 9, 1954, Record no. 206-Y0049, PRC Diplomatic Archives, Beijing. I'm grateful to Chen Jian for making these documents available to me, and for his translation.

20 "Indochine, Propositions faire par le Délégation de la République du Viêt-Nam," May 10, 1954, Box X, Indochine, Institut Pierre Mendès France (hereafter IPMF), Paris.

21 See Tahourdin and Allen, "Record of a talk with a member of the Soviet delegation," May 1, 1954, FO 371/112060, TNA.

22 De Brébisson memorandum, June 17, 1954, cited in Edouard Frédéric-Dupont, *Mission de la France en Asie* (Paris: Éditions France-Empire, 1956), 172–73.

23 Pierre Asselin, "The DRVN and the 1954 Geneva Conference: New Evidence and Perspectives from Vietnam," unpublished paper in author's possession; Zhou Enlai to Mao Zedong and others, "Regarding the Situation of the First Plenary Session," May 9, 1954, Record no. 206-Y0049, PRC Diplomatic Archives, Beijing.

24 Third Plenary Session on Indochina, Geneva, May 12, 1954, *FRUS, 1952–1954, The Geneva Conference,* XVI, 780–83.

25 "Notes made by Mr. MacArthur for his own information, following a meeting between the Secretary and Mr. Allen Dulles," May 14, 1954, *FRUS, 1952–1954, Indochina,* XIII, 2:1562–64; Eden to FO, May 15, 1954, FO 371/112065.

26 Bidault à MAE, May 11, 1954, Dossier IV, Conférence de la Genève 26 avril–17 juin, 457 AP 55, AN; "Décision prise en Comité de Défense Nationale le 15 May 1954," Dossier IV, DPMF, Indochine, IPMF; Jacques Dalloz, *Georges Bidault: Biographie politique* (Paris: Éditions L'Harmattan, 1993), 367–68.

27 "Memcon: French Military Briefing, Indochina," May 11, 1954, Box 49, CF 312, Record Group 59, NARA.

28 Guillermaz quoted in James Waite, "The End of the First Indochina War," Ph.D. dissertation, Ohio University, 2005, pp. 225–26; Eden to FO, May 11, 1954, FO 371/112063, TNA; Chiefs of Staff Committee, "Confidential Annex," May 12, 1954, FO 371/112064, TNA.

29 *Le Monde,* May 7, 1954.

30 See, e.g., the material in *FRUS, 1952–1954, Indochina,* XIII, 2:1534–36, 1566–68, 1574–75, 1586–90, 1618–20; Paris to FO, May 16, 1954, FO 371/112065, TNA.

31 Eden to FO, May 1954, FO 371/112065, TNA; Eden to FO, May 16, 1954, FO 371/112066, TNA.

32 Spender to Tange, May 21, 1954, A5462/1, pt. 3, CRS National Archives of Australia; and Webb to Holland, May 20, 1954, EA1, 316/4/1, pt.7, CRS Archives of New Zealand.

33 Dulles to Rusk, May 24, 1954, Box 8, "General Foreign Policy Matters (3)," White House Memoranda Series, Dulles Papers, Eisenhower Library. I thank Matthew Jones for drawing this document to my attention. No June meeting devoted to this topic appears to have taken place.

34 Devillers and Lacouture, *End of a War,* 201–2, 232.

35 Quoted in William J. Duiker, *U.S. Containment Policy and the Conflict in Indochina* (Stanford, Calif.: Stanford University Press, 1994), 176–77.

36 *U.S. News & World Report,* May 29, 1954; *Time,* May 31, 1954.

37 Geneva to FO, May 29, 1954, FO 371/112068, TNA; Geneva to State (Dulles), May 30, 1954, *FRUS, 1952–1954, The Geneva Conference,* XVI:974–78; Eden diary, May 29, 1954, AP20/17/231, UB; Cooper, *Lost Crusade,* 85.

38 Smith to Dulles, May 30, 1954, Box 9, Indochina May 1953–May 1954 (1), Dulles Papers, Eisenhower Library. This portion of the cable is excised from the version printed in *FRUS.* I thank Matthew Jones for bringing this version to my attention.

39 Paris to FO, May 29, 1954, FO 371/112089, TNA; Geneva to FO (for Churchill), May 30, 1954, FO 371/112089, TNA.

40 Eden to FO, June 1, 1954, FO 371/112089, TNA; Eden diary, May 30, 1954, AP20/17/231, UB; Eden diary, June 1, 1954, AP20/17/231, UB.

41 Geneva to State, June 2, 1954, *FRUS, 1952–1954, The Geneva Conference,* XVI:1005–8.

42 Hiroyuki Umetsu, "Australia's Response to the Indochina Crisis of 1954 Amidst the Anglo-American Confrontation," *Australian Journal of Politics and History* 52, no. 3 (2006), esp. 406–14; Casey quote is on p. 414. See also Gregory Pemberton, "Australia, the United States, and the Indo-China Crises of 1954," *Diplomatic History* 13 (Winter 1989): 45–66.

43 Umetsu, "Australia's Response," 414.

44 Ibid.; Memcon, June 4, 1954, *FRUS, 1952–1954, East Asia and the Pacific,* XII, 1:537–39; Washington to FO, June 3, 1954, FO 371/112089, TNA.

45 Pierre Pellissier, *Diên Biên Phu: 20 novembre 1953–7 mai 1954* (Paris: Perrin, 2004), 459–68; Devillers and Lacouture, *End of a War,* 181–83.

46 "Fiche sur la Conférence à cinq de Washington sur le Sud-Est Asiatique," Indochine 295, Asie-Océanie 1944–1955, MAE; British Joint Staff Mission (DC) to MOD, June 7, 1954, FO 371/112070, TNA; "Report of the Five Power Military Conference of June 1954, Pentagon, June 11, 1954," FO 371/111866, TNA. The French delegation's statements are in Enclosure C, Annexes 2 and 3.

47 Robert Buzzanco, "Prologue to Tragedy: U.S. Military Opposition to Intervention in Vietnam, 1950–1954," *Diplomatic History* 17 (Spring 1993): 201–22. Ridgway is quoted in David L. Anderson, *Trapped by Success: The Eisenhower Administration and Vietnam, 1953–1961* (New York: Columbia University Press, 1991), 29.

48 Cabinet minutes, June 5, 1954, CAB 128/27, TNA; Eden diary, June 6, 1954, AP20/17/231, UB.

49 June 16, 1954, *FRUS, 1952–1954, Indochina,* XIII, 2:1711–13.

50 R. G. Casey diary entry for June 13, 1954, 34–M1153, NAA.

51 SecState to Paris, June 14, 1954, in *FRUS, 1952–1954, Indochina,* XVI:1147.

52 NSC meeting notes, June 15, 1954, *FRUS, 1952–1954, Indochina,* XIII, 2:1693–94.

53 Wrote Robert McClintock, the counselor at the U.S. embassy, already in mid-May: "Much as I oppose partition in Vietnam, I would rather resort to that desperate recourse, retaining, above all, important air-base at Tourane, than to contemplate ramparts of sand in Cambodia and Laos." Saigon to State, May 13, 1954, *FRUS, 1952–1954, Indochina,* XIII, 2:1552–53.

54 Memo of discussion, NSC meeting, June 17, 1954, *FRUS, 1952–1954, Indochina,* XIII, 2:1713–18.

55 Geneva (Eden) to FO, June 12, 1954, FO 371/112089, TNA; Dwight D. Eisen-

hower, *Mandate for Change: The White House Years, 1953–1956* (Garden City, N.Y.: Doubleday, 1963), 366.

CHAPTER 23: *"We Must Go Fast"*

1 Quoted in Philippe Devillers and Jean Lacouture, *End of a War: Indochina, 1954* (New York: Praeger, 1969), 246. See also Eric Roussel, *Pierre Mendès France* (Paris: Gallimard, 2007), 226; and Jean Lacouture, *Pierre Mendès France*, trans. George Holock (New York: Holmes & Meier, 1984), 213.

2 The economics of the war are ably handled in Hugues Tertrais, *La piastre et le fusil: Le coût de la guerre d'Indochine 1945–1954* (Paris: Comité pour l'histoire économique et financière de la France, 2002).

3 Devillers and Lacouture, *End of a War,* 246.

4 Robert O. Paxton, "Mr. France," *New York Review of Books,* June 13, 1985.

5 Quoted in Lacouture, *Pierre Mendès France,* 205.

6 See, e.g., "Entretien de Bidault et Chou En Lai," June 8, 1954, Indochine, Box V, Oc, IPMF.

7 For Bidault's bitter and resentful recollection of this period, see Georges Bidault, *Resistance: The Political Autobiography of Georges Bidault,* trans. Marianne Sinclair (New York: Praeger, 1968), chap. 10.

8 Aron quoted in Lacouture, *Pierre Mendès France,* 217.

9 "Extract from Minute #6 of the Plenum Conference of the Central Committee of the Communist Party of the Soviet Union, Conference June 24, 1954," Molotov's report to CPSU Central Committee on the Geneva Conference, Harvard Project on Cold War Studies Online Archive, www.fas.harvard.edu/~hpcws/documents.htm; Geneva (Eden) to FO, June 19, 1954, FO 371/112074, TNA.

10 Geneva (Eden) to FO, June 16, 1954, FO 371/112073, TNA; Eden diary, entry for June 16, 1954, AP20/17/231, Eden Papers, UB; Zhou Enlai to Mao Zedong and the CCP Central Committee, June 19, 1954, in Xiong Huayuan, *Zhou Enlai chudeng shijie wutai* [Zhou Enlai's Debut on the World Scene] (Beijing: Zhongyang wenxian, 1998), 98. Translated for me by Chen Jian.

11 Lacouture, *Pierre Mendès France,* 220. On the Chinese playing the lead role among the two Communist giants, see also Mari Olsen, *Soviet-Vietnam Relations and the Role of China, 1949–1964: Changing Alliances* (London: Routledge, 2006), 40.

12 Eden diary, entry for June 18, 1954, AP20/17/231, Eden Papers, UB.

13 Zhou Enlai to Mao Zedong and the CCP Central Committee, June 19, 1954, in Xiong Huayuan, *Zhou Enlai chudeng shijie wutai,* 98; Chen Jian, "China and the Indochina Settlement at the Geneva Conference of 1954," in Mark Atwood Lawrence and Fredrik Logevall, eds., *The First Vietnam War: Colonial Conflict and Cold War Crisis* (Cambridge, Mass.: Harvard University Press, 2007), 251–52; François Joyaux, *La Chine et le règlement du premier conflit d'Indochine, Genève 1954* (Paris: Publications de la Sorbonne, 1979), 227–31.

14 Quoted in Christopher E. Goscha, "Geneva 1954 and the 'Deinternationalization' of the Vietnamese Idea of Indochina," unpublished paper in author's possession.

15 Goscha, "Geneva 1954"; Joyaux, *La Chine et le règlement du premier conflit d'Indochine*; Gilles Boquérat, "India's Commitment to Peaceful Coexistence and the Settlement of the Indochina War," *Cold War History* 5 (May 2005): 211–34.

16 Chen Jian, "China and the Indochina Settlement," 251–52.

17 William J. Duiker, *U.S. Containment Policy and the Conflict in Indochina* (Stanford, Calif.: Stanford University Press, 1994), 182–83. Little evidence has emerged

to support this Vietnamese claim, but it's hardly implausible; in later years, the PRC would often indicate a determination to preserve Chinese influence in Laos and Cambodia, and after Saigon's collapse in 1975, Beijing intervened openly on the side of Pol Pot to thwart the establishment of a Hanoi-dominated "special relationship" among the three Indochinese states.

18 Geneva to Ottawa, June 21, 1954, CAB 12/69, TNA; James Cable, *The Geneva Conference of 1954 on Indochina* (London: Macmillan, 1986), 104.

19 Lacouture, *Pierre Mendès France,* 220.

20 Geneva to MAE, "Entrevue Mendès-France–Chou En Lai à Berne," June 23, 1954, Dossier V, DPMF Indochine, IPMF; Roussel, *Pierre Mendès France,* 238–40. The Chinese record of the meeting is now also available: Minutes of Zhou Enlau's meeting with Pierre Mendès France, June 23, 1954, Record no. 206-Y0007, Chinese Foreign Ministry Archives, Beijing (hereafter CFMA). I thank Chen Jian for making this document available to me.

21 "Réunion du 24 juin 1954 chez le Président Mendès France," June 24, 1954, Dossier V, DPMF, Indochine, IPMF.

22 Quoted in Devillers and Lacouture, *End of a War,* 257.

23 "Réunion du 24 juin 1954 chez le Président Mendès France," June 24, 1954, Dossier V, DPMF Indochine, IPMF.

24 Edward Miller, "Vision, Power and Agency: The Ascent of Ngô Dình Diêm, 1945–54," *Journal of Southeast Asian Studies* 35 (October 2004): 433–58; and Philip E. Catton, *Diem's Final Failure: Prelude to America's War in Vietnam* (Lawrence: University Press of Kansas, 2002), 5–7. Mansfield later denied that Diem's Catholic faith affected his own estimate of Diem's ability. See Don Oberdorfer, *Senator Mansfield: The Extraordinary Life of a Great American Statesman and Diplomat* (Washington, D.C.: Smithsonian, 2003), 118. See also Wilson D. Miscamble, "Francis Cardinal Spellman and 'Spellman's War,'" in David L. Anderson, ed., *The Human Tradition in the Vietnam Era* (Wilmington, Del.: Scholarly Resources, 2000), 3–22.

25 Edward Lansdale, who as we shall see became a key adviser to the regime later that summer, had never heard of him when he departed for Saigon in the late spring of 1954. Edward G. Lansdale interview, 1979, WGBH Vietnam Collection, openvault.wgbh.org/catalog/org.wgbh.mla:Vietnam (last accessed on October 25, 2010).

26 Miller, "Vision, Power and Agency."

27 Bao Dai, *Le dragon d'Annam* (Paris: Plon, 1980), 328. See also the recollections of Chester Cooper, who was part of the U.S. delegation at Geneva. Cooper, *The Lost Crusade: America in Vietnam* (New York: Dodd, Mead, 1970), 126–27; and Cooper, *In the Shadows of History: Fifty Years Behind the Scenes of Cold War Diplomacy* (Amherst, N.Y.: Prometheus, 2005), 120. According to R. G. Casey, Bao Dai pleaded for U.S. support when he met with Dulles in Paris on April 24. R. G. Casey diary entry for April 26, 1954, 34–M1153, NAA.

28 Quoted in Seth Jacobs, *America's Miracle Man in Vietnam: Ngo Dinh Diem, Religion, Race, and U.S. Intervention in Southeast Asia, 1950–1957* (Durham, N.C.: Duke University Press, 2005), 54.

29 Cooper, *Lost Crusade,* 124; Paris to State, May 24, 1954, *FRUS, 1952–1954, Indochina,* XIII 2:1608–9; Saigon to State, July 4, 1954, *FRUS, 1952–1954, Indochina,* XIII, 2:1782–84.

30 Paris to State, May 24, 1954, *FRUS, 1952–1954, Indochina,* XIII, 2:1609.

31 Stelle to Bowie, June 24, 1954, *FRUS, 1952–1954, Indochina,* XIII, 2:1741–43.

32 Quoted in Duiker, *U.S. Containment,* 185.

33 Churchill to Eisenhower, June 21, 1954, PREM 11/649, TNA.

34 Hagerty diary entries for June 23, June 24, and June 28, as cited in George C. Herring, *America's Longest War: The United States and Vietnam, 1950–1975,* 4th ed. (New York: McGraw-Hill, 2002), 47–48.

35 Editorial Note, *FRUS, 1952–1954, Indochina,* XIII, 2:1751.

36 "The US Government/HMG would be willing to respect an agreement which: (1) preserves the integrity of Laos and Cambodia and assures the withdrawal of Viet Minh forces therefrom; (2) preserves at least the southern half of Vietnam, and if possible an enclave in the Delta; in this connection we would be unwilling to see the line of division of responsibility drawn further south than a line running generally west of Dong Hoi; (3) does not impose on Laos, Cambodia or retained Vietnam any restrictions materially impairing their capacity to maintain stable non-Communist regimes; and especially restrictions on their right to maintain adequate forces for internal security; to import arms and to employ foreign advisers; (4) does not contain political provisions which would risk loss of retained area to communist control; (5) does not exclude the possibility of the ultimate unification of Vietnam by peaceful means; (6) provides for the peaceful and humane transfer, under international supervision of those people desiring to be moved from one zone to another of Vietnam; and (7) provides effective machinery for international supervision of the agreement." See "The Secretary of State to Embassy in France," June 29, 1954, *FRUS, 1952–1954, Indochina,* XIII, 2:1757–58; "The Ambassador in France (Dillon) to the Department of State," June 30, 1954, *FRUS, 1952–1954, Indochina,* XIII, 2:1768–69.

37 Chauvel (Geneva) to PMF, July 1, 1954, Dossier V, DPMF Indochine, IPMF.

38 Paris to FO, June 30, 1954, FO 371/112075, TNA; Chauvel (Geneva) to PMF, June 29, 1954, Dossier V, DPMF Indochine, IPMF.

CHAPTER 24: *"I Have Seen Destiny Bend to That Will"*

1 Jawaharlal Nehru, *Selected Works of Jawaharlal Nehru,* 2nd series, vol. 26: *June 1, 1954–September 30, 1954* (New Delhi: Oxford University Press, 2001), 371–72; Outward Telegram from Commonwealth Relations Office, June 30, 1954, PREM 11/64, TNA; *The Pentagon Papers: The Defense Department History of Decision-making on Vietnam,* Senator Gravel edition (Boston: Beacon Press, 1971), 1:148.

2 Philippe Devillers and Jean Lacouture, *End of a War: Indochina, 1954* (New York: Praeger, 1969), 260–62.

3 Chen Jian, "China and the Indochina Settlement at the Geneva Conference of 1954," in Mark Atwood Lawrence and Fredrik Logevall, eds., *The First Vietnam War: Colonial Conflict and Cold War Crisis* (Cambridge, Mass.: Harvard University Press, 2007), 254–57; Pierre Asselin, "The Democratic Republic of Vietnam and the 1954 Geneva Conference: A Revisionist Critique," *Cold War History* 11:2 (May 2011), 169–70. See also Christopher Goscha, "Geneva 1954 and the 'Deinternationalization' of the Vietnamese Idea of Indochina," unpublished paper in author's possession. And see the Ministry of Foreign Affairs' internal study, *Dau Tranh Ngoai Giao trong Cach Mang Dan Toc Dan Chu Nhan Dan (1945–1954)* [The Diplomatic Struggle as Part of the People's National Democratic Revolution, 1945–1954] (Hanoi, Bo Ngoai Giao, 1976), 2:41. Translated by Merle Pribbenow.

4 Chen Jian, "China and the Indochina Settlement," 257–58.

5 All quotes from the Central Committee's Sixth Plenum are from Nguyen Vu Tung, "The Road to Geneva: How the DRV Changed Its Positions," unpublished paper (Cold War International History Project) in author's possession, 22–24; Asselin, "Democratic Republic of Vietnam," 171–73.

6 Nguyen, "The Road to Geneva," 25–26; *Dau Tranh Ngoai Giao trong Cach Mang Dan Toc Dan Chu Nhan Dan*, 43; Asselin, "Democratic Republic of Vietnam," 171.

7 Goscha, "Geneva 1954 and the 'Deinternationalization' of the Vietnamese Idea of Indochina," excerpts cited in *Dau Tranh Ngoai Giao trong Cach Mang Dan Toc Dan Chu Nhan Dan*, 119.

8 Mao quoted in Chen Jian, "China and the Indochina Settlement," 258.

9 Trinh Quang Thanh, interview by author, Hanoi, January 2003.

10 Paris to Washington, July 9, 1954, Dossier V, DPMF Indochine, IPMF.

11 Hagerty diary entry, July 6, 1954, Box 1, George Kahin Collection on the Origins of the Vietnam War, Division of Rare and Manuscript Collections, Cornell University Library; Editorial Note, *FRUS, 1952–1954, Indochina*, XIII, 2:1803; William J. Duiker, *U.S. Containment Policy and the Conflict in Indochina* (Stanford, Calif.: Stanford University Press, 1994), 188.

12 Hagerty diary entry, July 8, 1954, Box 1, Kahin Collection, Division of Rare and Manuscript Collections, Cornell University; State to Paris, July 10, 1954, *FRUS, 1952–1954, Indochina*, XIII, 2:1807–10.

13 Jean Lacouture, *Pierre Mendès France*, trans. George Holock (New York : Holmes & Meier, 1984), 226–27; "Réunion des trois ministres des affaires étrangères," July 13, 1954, Dossier V, DPMF Indochine, IPMF; Washington to Paris, July 12, 1954, Dossier V, DPMF Indochine, IPMF; M. Roux, "Position américaine à Genève," July 13, 1954, Dossier V, DPMF Indochine, IPMF.

14 Paris to FO, July 14, 1954, PREM 11/646, TNA; "Memo of Discussion at 206th Meeting of the National Security Council," July 15, 1954, *FRUS, 1952–1954, Indochina*, XIII, 2:1834–40.

15 Eden to FO, July 15, 1954, FO 371/112078, TNA; James Cable, *The Geneva Conference of 1954 on Indochina* (London: Macmillan, 1986), 116.

16 Chester L. Cooper, *The Lost Crusade: America in Vietnam* (New York: Dodd, Mead, 1970), 97.

17 Eden to FO (for PM), July 18, 1954, FO 371/112079, TNA.

18 The developments on July 20 are well handled in a number of studies. See, e.g., Devillers and Lacouture, *End of a War*, 290–313; Lacouture, *Pierre Mendès France*, 234–39; Cable, *Geneva Conference*, 120–23; Eric Roussel, *Pierre Mendès France* (Paris : Gallimard, 2007), chap. 14.

19 Minutes of meeting between Zhou Enlai and Cambodian delegation, July 20, 1954, Record No. 206-Y0008, CFMA. Translated by Chen Jian.

20 Molotov quoted in Lacouture, *Pierre Mendès France*, 237.

21 See *FRUS, 1952–1954, The Geneva Conference*, XVI, 1479.

22 Quoted in *Newsweek*, August 2, 1954.

23 For the full text of the Franco–Viet Minh agreement and the Final Declaration, and the verbatim record of the final plenary session, see Allan W. Cameron, ed., *Viet-Nam Crisis: A Documentary History* (Ithaca, N.Y.: Cornell University Press, 1971), 1:288–308.

24 U.S. delegation to State, July 19, 1954, *FRUS, 1952–1954, The Geneva Conference*, XVI, 1500.

25 Quoted in David Schoenbrun, *As France Goes* (New York: Atheneum, 1968), 122–23.

26 Michel Bodin, *La France et ses soldats, Indochine, 1945–1954* (Paris: Éditions L'Harmattan, 1996), 7; Bodin, *Dictionnaire de la guerre d'Indochine, 1945–1954* (Paris: Economica, 2004), 214.

27 Saigon to MAE, July 10, 1954, Dossier V, DPMF Indochine, IPMF; Saigon to MAE, July 18, 1954, Dossier V, DPMF Indochine, IPMF.

28 Quoted in Devillers and Lacouture, *End of a War*, 309. The VNA's role and performance in the final months of the war is examined in Michel Bodin, "L'armée nationale du Vietnam à fin du conflit (1953–1954)," in Pierre Journoud and Hugues Tertrais, eds., *1954–2004: La Bataille de Dien Bien Phu, entre histoire et mémoire* (Paris: Publications de la Société française d'histoire d'outre-mer, 2004), 89–101. The 800 figure is from *Newsweek*, August 23, 1954.

29 See, e.g., George C. Herring, *America's Longest War: The United States and Vietnam, 1950–1975*, 4th ed. (New York: McGraw-Hill, 2002), 48; Duiker, *U.S. Containment*, 183.

30 See here, e.g., Zhou Enlai's comments to Eden on July 13, as recorded in Minutes of meeting between Zhou Enlai and Anthony Eden, July 13, 1954, Record No. 206-Y0006, CFMA. Translated by Chen Jian.

31 Chester L. Cooper, *In the Shadows of History: Fifty Years Behind the Scenes of Cold War Diplomacy* (Amherst, N.Y.: Prometheus, 2005), 126.

32 Zhou's "servant mentality" vis-à-vis Mao is a theme in Gao Wenqian, *Zhou Enlai: The Last Perfect Revolutionary: A Biography* (New York: Public Affairs, 2009). On Mao's strategy at Geneva, see also Yang Kuisong, "Changes in Mao Zedong's Attitude toward the Indochina War, 1949–1973," Cold War International History Project Working Paper no. 34 (Washington, D.C.: Woodrow Wilson International Center for Scholars, 2002), 6–11.

33 Quoted in Stanley Karnow, *Vietnam: A History* (New York: Viking, 1983), 220. This point was also emphasized by Trinh Quang Thanh, interviewed by author, Hanoi, January 2003.

34 I'm grateful to Geoffrey Warner for sharing his views on this point. And see here also Asselin, "Democratic Republic of Vietnam."

35 Dwight D. Eisenhower, *Mandate for Change: The White House Years, 1953–1956* (Garden City, N.Y.: Doubleday, 1963), 362.

36 Mendès-France, "Entrevue Mendès-France–Chou En Lai à Berne," June 23, 1954, 71–77, IPMF.

37 Casey and Chauvel quoted in Cable, *Geneva Conference*, 88, 134.

38 Anthony Eden, *Full Circle: The Memoirs of Anthony Eden* (Boston: Houghton Mifflin, 1960), 144.

39 *Le Figaro*, July 21, 1954.

40 The press conference is excerpted in *FRUS, 1952–1954, The Geneva Conference*, XVI, 1503.

41 Cooper, *Lost Crusade*, 99–100; Eisenhower-Dulles telcon, July 20, 1954, Box 4, Diary Series, Eisenhower Library.

42 Eden and Chauvel are quoted in Devillers and Lacouture, *End of a War*, 313.

CHAPTER 25: *"We Have No Other Choice but to Win Here"*

1 Quoted in *Newsweek*, October 18, 1954. See also Donald Lancaster, *The Emancipation of French Indochina* (London: Oxford University Press, 1961), 359–67.

2 Quoted in *NYT*, October 11, 1954.

3 Jawaharlal Nehru, *Selected Works of Jawaharlal Nehru,* 2nd. series, ed. Ravinder Kumar and H. Y. Prasad (New York: Oxford University Press, 2002), 27:21ff.

4 Luu Doan Huynh, interview by author, Hanoi, January 2003.

5 Neither the Democratic Republic of Vietnam nor its successor, the Socialist Republic of Vietnam, has ever published casualty figures for their armed forces in the years 1945–54. The French have estimated a total of 500,000 Vietnamese killed during the war, including civilians. The figure here is an estimate drawn from various sources, including Stein Tønnesson, *Vietnam 1946: How the War Began* (Berkeley: University of California Press, 2009), 1; and Michael Clodfelter, *Warfare and Armed Conflicts: A Statistical Reference to Casualty and Other Figures, 1618–1991,* vol. 2: *1900–1991* (Jefferson, N.C.: McFarland & Company, 1992), 1122.

6 *Lich Su Bien Nien Xu Uy Nam Bo va Trung Uong Cuc Mien Nam (1954–1975)* [Historical Chronicle of the Cochin China Party Committee and the Central Office for South Vietnam (1954–1975)] (Hanoi: National Political Publishing House, 2002), 33–47. Translated by Merle Pribbenow.

7 Sainteny to Paris, October 21, 1954, Dossier VII, DPMF Indochine, IPMF; Marcel Duval, "L'Avenir des Intérêts Français en Indochine," *France-Indochine* (December 1954), 236.

8 Philippe Devillers and Jean Lacouture, *End of a War: Indochina, 1954* (New York: Praeger, 1969), 355; Pierre Grosser, "La France et l'Indochine (1953–1956): Une 'carte de visite' en 'peau de chagrin' [France and Indochina (1953–1956): Visitor's Pass to the Land of Sorrow], doctoral dissertation, Institut d'études politiques de Paris, September 2002, 1253–54.

9 MAE to Washington, August 13, 1954, Dossier V, DPMF Indochine, IPMF; Claude Cheysson to PMF, "Note pour le Président," August 12, 1954, Dossier VII, DPMF Indochine, IPMF; Baudet to MAE, August 13, 1954, Indochine, vol. 157, Asie, 1944–1955, MAE.

10 Duval, "L'Avenir des Intérêts Français en Indochine," 239; "Projet d'instructions à M. Sainteny," September 1954, Dossier VI, DPMF Indochine, IPMF; Grosser, "La France et l'Indochine," 1258.

11 Note du Ministre des Etats Associés, September 30, 1954, *Documents diplomatiques français, 1954 (21 juillet–31 décembre),* 489–92. See also Paul Ely, *L'Indochine dans la tourmente* (Paris: Plon, 1964), 246–49; and Laurent Cesari, "The Declining Value of Indochina: France and the Economics of Empire, 1950–1955," in Mark Atwood Lawrence and Fredrik Logevall, eds., *The First Vietnam War: Colonial Conflict and Cold War Crisis* (Cambridge, Mass.: Harvard University Press, 2007), 193–94.

12 The Dulles press conference is reprinted in *Department of State Bulletin,* August 2, 1954.

13 Dulles is quoted in George McTurnan Kahin, *Intervention: How America Became Involved in Vietnam* (New York: Alfred A. Knopf, 1986), 75.

14 NSC, "Review of U.S. Policy in the Far East," August 1954, *Pentagon Papers. United States-Vietnam Relations, 1945–1967: Study Prepared by the Department of Defense* (Washington, D.C.: Government Printing Office, 1971), 10:731–41.

15 Saigon to MAE, July 10, 1954, Dossier V, DPMF Indochine, IPMF. See also Frances FitzGerald, *Fire in the Lake: The Vietnamese and the Americans in Vietnam* (Boston: Little, Brown, 1972), 97.

16 Two important studies are Edward Miller, "Grand Designs: Vision, Power, and Na-

tion Building in America's Alliance with Ngo Dinh Diem, 1954–1960," Ph.D. dissertation, Harvard University, 2004; and Jessica M. Chapman, "Debating the Will of Heaven: South Vietnamese Politics and Nationalism in International Perspective, 1953–56," Ph.D. dissertation, University of California–Santa Barbara, 2006.

17 Thomas L. Ahearn, Jr., *CIA and the House of Ngo: Covert Action in South Vietnam, 1954–63* (Washington, D.C.: Center for the Study of Intelligence, Central Intelligence Agency, 2000), 31. At another point in these weeks Harwood put it more starkly: The "task is hopeless, but [the] effort must be made." Thomas L. Ahearn, Jr., *CIA and Rural Pacification in South Vietnam* (Washington, D.C.: Center for the Study of Intelligence, Central Intelligence Agency, 2001), 2.

18 On the sects' origins and their roles, see Jayne Susan Werner, *Peasant Politics and Religious Sectarianism: Peasant and Priest in the Cao Dai in Viet Nam* (New Haven, Conn.: Yale University Southeast Asia Studies, 1981); Frances R. Hill, "Millenarian Machines in South Vietnam," *Comparative Studies in Society and History* 13 (July 1971): 325–50; Hue-Tam Ho Tai, *Millenarianism and Peasant Politics in Vietnam* (Boston: Harvard University Press, 1983); Bernard B. Fall, "The Political-Religious Sects of Viet-Nam," *Pacific Affairs* 28 (September 1955): 235–53.

19 Don Oberdorfer, *Senator Mansfield: The Extraordinary Life of a Great American Statesman and Diplomat* (Washington, D.C.: Smithsonian, 2003), 120–21. On Diem and relations with the U.S., see Seth Jacobs, *America's Miracle Man in Vietnam: Ngo Dinh Diem, Religion, Race, and U.S. Intervention in Southeast Asia, 1950–1957* (Durham, N.C.: Duke University Press, 2005); Chapman, "Debating the Will of Heaven"; Miller, "Grand Designs"; David L. Anderson, *Trapped by Success: The Eisenhower Administration and Vietnam, 1953–1961* (New York: Columbia University Press, 1991).

20 Mike Mansfield, "Indochina," report prepared for the Senate Foreign Relations Committee of a mission to Vietnam, Cambodia, and Laos (Washington, D.C.: Government Printing Office, 1953), 14–15.

21 Oberdorfer, *Senator Mansfield*, 128; Memcon, Dulles and La Chambre, September 6, 1954, *FRUS, 1952–1954, Indochina*, XIII, 2:2007–10.

22 Oberdorfer, *Senator Mansfield*, 128.

23 Summary minutes of State Department meeting, September 25, 1954, *FRUS, 1952–1954, Indochina*, XIII, 2:2069.

24 George C. Herring, *America's Longest War: The United States and Vietnam, 1950–1975*, 4th ed. (New York: McGraw-Hill, 2002), 57.

25 Barbara W. Tuchman, *The March of Folly: From Troy to Vietnam* (New York: Alfred A. Knopf, 1984), 270.

26 Ronald H. Spector, *Advice and Support: The Early Years of the U.S. Army in Vietnam, 1941–1960* (Washington, D.C.: Center for Military History, 1985), 228–30.

27 The letter is reprinted in Marvin E. Gettleman et al., eds., *Vietnam and America: A Documented History* (New York: Grove, 1995), 113–14.

28 *NYT*, October 25, 1954.

29 "Compte rendu de la conversation entre M. Mendès France, M. Dulles, et M. Eden," October 23, 1954, Dossier V, DPMF Indochine, IPMF; Memcon, Dulles and PMF, October 24, 1954, *FRUS, 1952–1954, Indochina*, XIII, 2:2198–99; Grosser, "La France et l'Indochine," 1282–85.

30 Eden quoted in Arthur Combs, "The Path Not Taken: The British Alternative to U.S. Policy in Vietnam, 1954–1956," *Diplomatic History* 19 (Winter 1995): 51. A few weeks later, when Mendès France visited Washington, he reiterated the

pledge. "Compte rendu de la conversation entre M. Mendès France, M. Dulles, et M. Eden," November 18–19, 1954, Dossier V, DPMF Indochine, IPMF.

31 Edwin E. Moïse, "Land Reform and Land Reform Errors in North Vietnam," *Pacific Affairs* 49, no. 1 (Spring 1976): 70–92; and Moïse, *Land Reform in China and North Vietnam* (Chapel Hill: University of North Carolina Press, 1983), 178–268. See also Pierre Brocheux, *Ho Chi Minh: A Biography* (New York: Cambridge University Press, 2007), 152–60.

32 Quoted in Hy Van Luong, *Revolution in the Village: Tradition and Transformation in North Vietnam, 1925–1988* (Honolulu: University of Hawaii Press, 1992), 190. Another firsthand account is Xuan Phuong and Danièle Mazingarbe, *Ao Dai: My War, My Country, My Vietnam* (Great Neck, N.Y.: EMQUAD, 2004), 162–86.

33 Moïse, "Land Reform and Errors in North Vietnam," 73–78; Mark Philip Bradley, *Vietnam at War* (Oxford, U.K.: Oxford University Press, 2009), 70.

34 Ho quotes are from Brocheux, *Ho Chi Minh*, 158.

35 William J. Duiker, *Ho Chi Minh: A Life* (New York: Hyperion, 2000), 486–88.

36 A key study of Franco-American relations concerning Vietnam in this period is Kathryn C. Statler, *Replacing France: The Origins of American Intervention in Vietnam* (Lexington: University Press of Kentucky, 2007), chap. 4. French policy is also closely examined in Pierre Grosser's massive study, "La France et l'Indochine," 1253–1342.

37 Chester L. Cooper, *The Lost Crusade: America in Vietnam* (New York: Dodd, Mead, 1970), 129.

38 Stanley Karnow, *In Our Image: America's Empire in the Philippines* (New York: Random House, 1989), 15.

39 A fine study is Jonathan Nashel, *Edward Lansdale's Cold War* (Amherst: University of Massachusetts Press, 2005). Also useful is a highly sympathetic account by a former aide, Rufus Phillips, *Why Vietnam Matters: An Eyewitness Account of Lessons Not Learned* (Annapolis, Md.: Naval Institute Press, 2008). See also Ahearn, *CIA and the House of Ngo*; and Cecil B. Currey, *Edward Lansdale: The Unquiet American* (Boston: Houghton Mifflin, 1988). Lansdale's own recollections are in Edward Lansdale, *In the Midst of Wars: An American's Mission to Southeast Asia* (New York: Fordham University Press, 1991). The Dulles quotes are in Nashel, *Landsdale's Cold War*, 1.

40 Phillips, *Why Vietnam Matters*, 14–15; J. Lawton Collins interview, 1981, WGBH Vietnam Collection, openvault.wgbh.org/catalog/org.wgbh.mla:Vietnam (last accessed on November 18, 2010).

41 Peter Schmid, "Free Indo-China Fights Against *Time*," *Commentary*, January 1955, 28, quoted in Cooper, *Lost Crusade*, 136.

42 Peter Hansen, "Bac Di Cu: Catholic Refugees from the North of Vietnam, and their Role in the Southern Republic, 1954–59," *Journal of Vietnamese Studies* 4 (Fall 2009): 173–211.

43 Nashel, *Lansdale's Cold War*, 60–61. On the exodus not being spontaneous, see Cooper, *Lost Crusade*, 130.

44 Howard R. Simpson, *Tiger in the Barbed Wire: An American in Vietnam, 1952–1991* (Washington, D.C.: Brassey's, 1992), 127.

45 Stump quoted in Spector, *Advice and Support*, 231.

46 For Collins's recollection of the appointment, see J. Lawton Collins, *Lightning Joe: An Autobiography* (Baton Rouge: Louisiana State University Press, 1979), 378.

47 Ely to Paris, November 6, 1954, Dossier VII, DPMF Indochine, IPMF; Paul Ely,

L'Indochine dans la tourmente (Paris: Plon, 1964), 168; Spector, *Advice and Support,* 236–37; Collins interview, WGBH. Collins quoted in Ellen J. Hammer, *A Death in November: America in Vietnam, 1963* (New York: Dutton, 1987), 71.

48 Ely cited in Collins to Dulles, November 10, 1954, Box 25, Collins Papers, Eisenhower Library; Collins to Dulles, November 13, 1954, Box 25, Collins Papers; Oberdorfer, *Senator Mansfield,* 132–33. Ely's low opinion of Diem at year's end is described in C. Cheysson, "Opinion du General Ely sur le Viet-nam," December 28, 1954, Dossier IX, DPMF Indochine, IPDF.

49 Memo of conversation with Mansfield, December 7, 1954, *FRUS, 1952–1954, Indochina,* XIII, 2:2350–52; Oberdorfer, *Senator Mansfield,* 133.

50 Memo from Lansdale to Collins, January 3, 1955, *FRUS, 1955–1957, Vietnam,* I:3–4; Edward G. Lansdale interview, 1979, WGBH Vietnam Collection, openvault .wgbh.org/catalog/org.wgbh.mla:Vietnam (last accessed on November 20, 2010).

51 Memo from Collins to Dulles, January 20, 1955, *FRUS, 1955–1957, Vietnam,* I: 56–57.

52 A detailed summary of CIP is in Kahin, *Intervention,* 85–88. See also Anderson, *Trapped by Success,* 155–57.

53 Seth Jacobs, *Cold War Mandarin: Ngo Dinh Diem and the Origins of America's War in Vietnam, 1950–1963* (Lanham, Md.: Rowman & Littlefield, 2006), 69.

54 The best study of the sect crisis is Jessica M. Chapman, "The Sect Crisis of 1955 and the American Decision for Diem," *Journal of Vietnamese Studies* 5 (Winter 2010): 37–85. See also Chapman, "Debating the Will of Heaven," chap. 3.

55 Currey, *Edward Lansdale,* 172–73. Lansdale, *In the Midst of Wars,* 251; Collins to State, March 15, 1955, *FRUS, 1955–1957, Vietnam,* I:125. For more on the amounts involved, see Chargé in Vietnam (Kidder) to Department of State, February 8, 1955, *FRUS, 1955–1957, Vietnam,* I:79–80; Miller, "Grand Designs," 162–63.

56 Chapman, "Sect Crisis," 45–46.

57 Ely diary cited in Grosser, "La France et l'Indochine," 1564. See also Ely to M. Laforest, April 6, 1955, *Documents diplomatiques français* (hereafter *DDF*), 1955, Vol. 1, Document 178, 410–14; and Ely to M. Laforest, March 31, 1955, *DDF,* Document 162, 364–77.

58 Collins to State, March 31, 1955, *FRUS, 1955–1957, Vietnam,* I:168–71; telcon, Eisenhower and Dulles, April 1, 1955, *FRUS, 1955–1957, Vietnam,* I:175–76; Mansfield, memo for files, April 1, 1955, *FRUS, 1955–1957, Vietnam,* I:176–77.

59 Dulles to Collins, April 4, 1955, *FRUS, 1955–1957, Vietnam,* I:196–97; Oberdorfer, *Senator Mansfield,* 135–36. On the last point, see Grosser, "La France et l'Indochine," 1532.

60 Collins interview, WGBH; *NYT,* April 18, 1955.

61 Dulles to Dillon, April 27, 1955, *FRUS, 1955–1957, Vietnam,* I:297–98.

62 Anderson, *Trapped by Success,* 111–13; Ahearn, *CIA and Rural Pacification in South Vietnam,* 12.

63 *NYT,* April 30, 1955; *Washington Post,* May 2, 1955; Jacobs, *Cold War Mandarin,* 77.

64 *Life,* May 16, 1955; *U.S. News & World Report,* May 13, 1955, as cited in Jacobs, *Cold War Mandarin,* 77; Larry Berman, *Perfect Spy: The Incredible Double Life of Pham Xan An* (New York: Smithsonian Books, 2007), 79

65 *NYT,* May 7, 1955.

66 George W. Allen, *None So Blind: A Personal Account of the Intelligence Failure in Vietnam* (Chicago: Ivan R. Dee, 2001), 84. See also Paul Kattenburg interview, 1981,

WGBH Vietnam Collection, openvault.wgbh.org/catalog/org.wgbh.mla:Vietnam (last accessed on November 18, 2010). His book is *The Vietnam Trauma in American Foreign Policy, 1945–1975* (New Brunswick, N.J.: Transaction, 1980).

67 Simpson, *Tiger in the Barbed Wire*, 152.

CHAPTER 26: *Miracle Man*

1 Quoted in Philippe Devillers, "The Struggle for the Unification of Vietnam," *China Quarterly* 9 (January–March 1962): 8.

2 Bernard B. Fall, *The Two Viet-Nams: A Political and Military Analysis* (New York: Praeger, 1964), 319–20.

3 Chester L. Cooper, *The Lost Crusade: America in Vietnam* (New York: Dodd, Mead, 1970), 148.

4 O'Neill to Macmillan, "Elections in Vietnam," November 1, 1955, FO 371/106778, TNA.

5 J. E. Cable, "Elections in Vietnam," January 11, 1955, FO 371/117115, TNA.

6 U.S. Policy on All-Vietnam Elections, NSC report, May 17, 1955, *FRUS, 1955–1957, Vietnam,* I:410–12.

7 John Prados, *Vietnam: The History of an Unwinnable War, 1945–1975* (Lawrence: University Press of Kansas, 2009), 51.

8 Mari Olsen, *Soviet-Vietnam Relations and the Role of China, 1949–1964: Changing Alliances* (London: Routledge, 2006), chap. 4.

9 Ilya V. Gaiduk, *Confronting Vietnam: Soviet Policy Toward the Indochina Conflict, 1954–1963* (Stanford, Calif.: Stanford University Press, 2003), 61.

10 Military History Institute of Vietnam, *Victory in Vietnam: The Official History of the People's Army of Vietnam, 1954–1975,* trans. Merle Pribbenow (Lawrence: University Press of Kansas, 2002), 18.

11 Ho is quoted in William J. Duiker, *Ho Chi Minh: A Life* (New York: Hyperion, 2000), 474.

12 Seth Jacobs, *Cold War Mandarin: Ngo Dinh Diem and the Origins of America's War in Vietnam, 1950–1963* (Lanham, Md.: Rowman & Littlefield, 2006), 89–90.

13 Jessica M. Chapman, "Staging Democracy: South Vietnam's 1955 Referendum to Depose Bao Dai," *Diplomatic History* 30, no. 4 (September 2006): 671–703.

14 Cooper, *Lost Crusade,* 151–52.

15 Seth Jacobs, *America's Miracle Man in Vietnam: Ngo Dinh Diem, Religion, Race, and U.S. Intervention in Southeast Asia, 1950–1957* (Durham, N.C.: Duke University Press, 2005), 37.

16 Edward Miller, "The Diplomacy of Personalism: Civilization, Culture, and the Cold War in the Foreign Policy of Ngo Dinh Diem," in Christopher E. Goscha and Christian F. Ostermann, eds., *Connecting Histories: Decolonization and the Cold War in Southeast Asia, 1945–1962* (Washington, D.C.: Woodrow Wilson Center Press, 2009), 376–402; Philip E. Catton, *Diem's Final Failure: Prelude to America's War in Vietnam* (Lawrence: University Press of Kansas, 2002), 44.

17 Neil Sheehan, *A Bright Shining Lie: John Paul Vann and America in Vietnam* (New York: Random House, 1988), 138. See also Edward G. Lansdale interview, 1979, WGBH Vietnam Collection, openvault.wgbh.org/catalog/org.wgbh.mla:Vietnam (last accessed on November 22, 2010). And see the insightful analysis of Lansdale's role in 1954–55 in Larry Berman, *Perfect Spy: The Incredible Double Life of Pham Xuan An* (New York: Smithsonian Books, 2007), 70–81.

18 Howard R. Simpson, *Tiger in the Barbed Wire: An American in Vietnam, 1952–*

1991 (Washington, D.C.: Brassey's, 1992), 172. See also Frances FitzGerald, *Fire in the Lake: The Vietnamese and the Americans in Vietnam* (Boston: Little, Brown, 1972), 98.

19 Joseph G. Morgan, *The Vietnam Lobby: The American Friends of Vietnam, 1955–1975* (Chapel Hill: University of North Carolina Press, 1997).

20 On modernization and postwar U.S. foreign policy, see, e.g., Michael E. Latham, *The Right Kind of Revolution: Modernization, Development, and U.S. Foreign Policy from the Cold War to the Present* (Ithaca, N.Y.: Cornell University Press, 2011); David Ekbladh, *The Great American Mission: Modernization and the Construction of an American World Order* (Princeton, N.J.: Princeton University Press, 2009); and Nils Gilman, *Mandarins of the Future: Modernization Theory in Cold War America* (Baltimore: Johns Hopkins University Press, 2004).

21 Jonathan Nashel, *Edward Lansdale's Cold War* (Amherst: University of Massachusetts Press, 2005), 54.

22 Ibid., 137.

23 *Times Literary Supplement,* December 9, 1955; *Manchester Guardian,* December 6, 1955. The other reviews are quoted in Norman Sherry, *The Life of Graham Greene,* vol. 2: *1939–1955* (New York: Viking, 1995), 472.

24 A. J. Liebling, "A Talkative Something-or-Other," *New Yorker,* April 7, 1956, reprinted in John Clark Pratt, ed., *The Quiet American: Text and Criticism* (New York: Penguin, 1996), 347–55. Curiously, the *Newsweek* review appeared on January 2, 1956, three months before the book was published in the United States.

25 Graham Greene, *The Quiet American* (New York: Viking, 1956), 156.

26 Ibid., 87.

27 Richard West, "Graham Greene and 'The Quiet American,'" *New York Review of Books,* May 16, 1991. A perceptive scholarly assessment of the novel in the context of subsequent U.S. involvement is Stephen J. Whitfield, "Limited Engagement: *The Quiet American* as History," *Journal of American Studies* 30 (1996): 65–86.

28 See Pico Iyer, "The Disquieting Resonance of 'The Quiet American,'" NPR *All Things Considered,* April 21, 2008, www.npr.org/templates/story/story.php ?storyId=89542461 (last accessed on November 7, 2010).

29 Graham Greene, "Last Act in Indo-China," *New Republic,* May 9 and 16, 1954.

30 Reinhardt quoted in David L. Anderson, *Trapped by Success: The Eisenhower Administration and Vietnam, 1953–1961* (New York: Columbia University Press, 1991), 133. See also FitzGerald, *Fire in the Lake,* 112–13.

31 Jacobs, *Cold War Mandarin,* 102; Morgan, *Vietnam Lobby.*

32 Robert E. Herzstein, *Henry R. Luce, Time, and the American Crusade in Asia* (New York: Cambridge University Press, 2005), 204–5.

33 *Pentagon Papers. United States–Vietnam Relations, 1945–1967: Study Prepared by the Department of Defense* (Washington, D.C.: Government Printing Office, 1971), 2: part IV, A.5, tab 1, p. 31. See also Jacobs, *America's Miracle Man,* 241–45.

34 Morgenthau quoted in Morgan, *Vietnam Lobby,* 41.

35 An excellent biography is James T. Fisher, *Dr. America: The Lives of Thomas A. Dooley, 1927–1961* (Amherst: University of Massachusetts Press, 1997).

36 Ibid., chap. 3; Jacobs, *America's Miracle Man,* chap. 4; Lansdale interview, WGBH.

37 Quoted in Jacobs, *Cold War Mandarin,* 49.

38 Jacobs, *Cold War Mandarin,* 50. See also the interview with Daniel Redmond, who worked with Dooley in Vietnam, in Christian G. Appy, *Patriots: The Vietnam War Remembered from All Sides* (New York: Viking, 2003), 42–44.

39 David L. Anderson, *Trapped by Success,* 133.

40 James R. Arnold, *The First Domino: Eisenhower, the Military, and America's Intervention in Vietnam* (New York: William Morrow, 1991), 306.

41 See Ronald H. Spector, *Advice and Support: The Early Years of the U.S. Army in Vietnam, 1941–1960* (Washington, D.C.: Center for Military History, 1985), 278–82.

42 Quoted in Spector, *Advice and Support,* 274.

43 Ibid., 275–76.

44 Defense Information Relating to the U.S. Aid Program in Vietnam, April 13, 1956, in *FRUS, 1955–1957, Vietnam,* I:673. An insightful history of the ARVN is Robert K. Brigham, *ARVN: Life and Death in the South Vietnamese Army* (Lawrence: University Press of Kansas, 2006).

45 Arnold, *First Domino,* 318–19.

CHAPTER 27: *Things Fall Apart*

1 *Journal d'Extrême-Orient,* quoted in *NYT,* May 5, 1957. The shooter, Ha Minh Tri (alias Phan Van Dien), later admitted being a member of a Cao Dai dissident group, but a DRV document asserts that he was acting on orders of southern Communist leaders under Le Duan. The document also says he had a female accomplice who escaped capture. *Lich Su Bien Nien Xu Uy Nam Bo va Trung Uong Cuc Mien Nam (1954–1975)* [Historical Chronicle of the Cochin China Party Committee and the Central Office for South Vietnam, 1954–1975] (Hanoi: National Political Publishing House, 2002), 134. Translated by Merle Pribbenow.

2 *NYT,* May, 9, 1957.

3 Quoted in Seth Jacobs, *America's Miracle Man in Vietnam: Ngo Dinh Diem, Religion, Race, and U.S. Intervention in Southeast Asia, 1950–1957* (Durham, N.C.: Duke University Press, 2005), 254.

4 *NYT,* May 7, 1957; *St. Petersburg Times,* May 9, 1957; *Washington Evening Star,* May 9, 1957; *Boston Globe,* May 6, 1957, as quoted in Seth Jacobs, *Cold War Mandarin: Ngo Dinh Diem and the Origins of America's War in Vietnam, 1950–1963* (Lanham: Md.: Rowman & Littlefield, 2006), 103; *Washington Post,* May 8, 1957. "Sharkskin suit" is quoted in James R. Arnold, *The First Domino: Eisenhower, the Military, and America's Intervention in Vietnam* (New York: William Morrow, 1991), 328.

5 Quoted in "Diem's Success Story," *New Republic,* May 6, 1957.

6 "President's Toast to Diem," May 9, 1957, Box 2, International Meeting Series: Diem Visit, Ann Whitman File, Eisenhower Library.

7 *NYT,* May 14, 1957.

8 Diem's dinner remarks quoted in Seth Jacobs, *Cold War Mandarin,* 103.

9 Joseph G. Morgan, *The Vietnam Lobby: The American Friends of Vietnam, 1955–1975* (Chapel Hill: University of North Carolina Press, 1997), 51; Jacobs, *America's Miracle Man in Vietnam,* 259–60.

10 Arnold, *First Domino,* 324.

11 John Osborne, "The Tough Miracle Man of Vietnam," *Life,* May 13, 1957.

12 Durbrow to State, May 2, 1957, *FRUS, 1955–1957, Vietnam,* I:787–88; Thomas L. Ahearn, Jr., *CIA and the House of Ngo: Covert Action in South Vietnam, 1954–63* (Washington, D.C.: Center for the Study of Intelligence, Central Intelligence Agency, 2000), chap. 8.

13 Gregory A. Olson, *Mansfield and Vietnam: A Study in Rhetorical Adaptation* (East Lansing: Michigan State University Press, 1995), 76; Chester L. Cooper, *The Lost Crusade: America in Vietnam* (New York: Dodd, Mead, 1970), 153.

14 John Ernst, *Forging a Fateful Alliance: Michigan State University and the Vietnam War* (East Lansing: Michigan State University Press, 1998); James M. Carter, *Inventing Vietnam: The United States and State Building, 1954–1968* (New York: Cambridge University Press, 2008), chap. 3.

15 Graham Greene, *Ways of Escape* (New York: Simon & Schuster, 1980), 17; Graham Greene, *Yours, Etc.: Letters to the Press,* ed. Christopher Hawtree (New York: Viking, 1989), as quoted in Graham Greene, *The Quiet American,* Viking Critical Edition, ed. John Clark Pratt (New York: Penguin, 1996), 310–12.

16 Lansdale letters to Diem, October 28, 1957, and to General John O'Daniel, October 28, 1957, quoted in Pratt, ed., *Quiet American,* 307–9.

17 "Statement of General John W. O'Daniel, Chairman of the American Friends of Vietnam, in Regard to the World Premiere of the Motion Picture 'The Quiet American,'" (n.d.), Douglas Pike Collection, Virtual Vietnam Archive, Texas Tech University, Lubbock. See also Morgan, *Vietnam Lobby,* 52.

18 Bernard B. Fall, "Danger Signs," *Nation,* May 31, 1958.

19 Robert Scheer, *How the United States Got Involved in Vietnam* (Santa Barbara, Calif.: Center for the Study of Democratic Institutions, 1965), 53.

20 Philip E. Catton, *Diem's Final Failure: Prelude to America's War in Vietnam* (Lawrence: University Press of Kansas, 2002), 65.

21 Robert L. Sansom, *The Economics of Insurgency in the Mekong Delta of Vietnam* (Cambridge, Mass.: MIT Press, 1970), 58; Robert Scigliano, *South Vietnam: Nation Under Stress* (Boston: Houghton Mifflin, 1963), 121–22. For the experience in one province in the Mekong Delta, see Jeffrey Race, *War Comes to Long An: Revolutionary Conflict in a Vietnamese Province* (Berkeley: University of California Press, 1972). On Ladejinsky, see David A. Biggs, *Quagmire: Nation-Building and Nature in the Mekong Delta* (Seattle: University of Washington Press, 2010), 158–61.

22 Several attacks are described in *Mien Dong Nam Bo Khang Chien (1945–1975), Tap II* [The Resistance War in Eastern Cochin China (1945–1975), Volume 2] (Hanoi: People's Army Publishing House, 1993), 60–63. Translated by Merle Pribbenow.

23 A superb treatment of the origins of the insurgency, focusing in particular on My Tho province, is David W. P. Elliott, *The Vietnamese War: Revolution and Social Change in the Mekong Delta, 1930–1975* (Armonk, N.Y.: M.E. Sharpe, 2007), chap. 6. See also Ta Xuan Linh, "How Armed Struggle Began in South Vietnam," *Vietnam Courier,* no. 22 (March 1974). The discussions within the southern revolutionary leadership are described in *Lich Su Bien Nien Xu Uy Nam Bo va Trung Uong Cuc Mien Nam (1954–1975)* [Historical Chronicle of the Cochin China Party Committee and the Central Office for South Vietnam (1954–1975)] (Hanoi: National Political Publishing House, 2002), 129–39. Translated by Merle Pribbenow.

24 Dorothy Fall, *Bernard Fall: Memories of a Soldier-Scholar* (Washington, D.C.: Potomac, 2006), 109.

25 Fall described this 1957 visit, and his broader conclusion about the village chief assassinations, in an unpublished paper, "The Anatomy of Insurgency in Indochina, 1946–64," delivered on March 20, 1964, at the Industrial College of the Armed Forces in Washington, D.C. A copy is in Box P-1, Series 1.5, "Papers and Reports by Dr. Fall," Bernard Fall Collection, JFKL.

26 Ibid., 122.

27 Durbrow to State, December 5, 1957, *FRUS, 1955–1957, Vietnam,* I:869–84.

28 Quoted in David L. Anderson, *Trapped by Success: The Eisenhower Administration and Vietnam, 1953–1961* (New York: Columbia University Press, 1991), 185–86. On CIA misgivings, see Thomas L. Ahearn, Jr., *CIA and Rural Pacification in South Vietnam* (Washington, D.C.: Center for the Study of Intelligence, Central Intelligence Agency, 2001), 21–22, 27.

29 Mao quoted in Odd Arne Westad, *Brothers in Arms: The Rise and Fall of the Sino-Soviet Alliance, 1945–1963* (Stanford, Calif.: Stanford University Press, 1998), 20.

30 Eisenhower to Diem, May 23, 1958, *FRUS, 1958–1960, Vietnam,* I:39–40.

31 Quoted in Ronald H. Spector, *Advice and Support: The Early Years of the U.S. Army in Vietnam, 1941–1960* (Washington, D.C.: Center for Military History, 1985), 325.

32 George McTurnan Kahin, *Intervention: How America Became Involved in Vietnam* (New York: Alfred A. Knopf, 1986), 101; Scigliano, *South Vietnam,* 158.

33 Mari Olsen, *Soviet-Vietnam Relations and the Role of China, 1949–1964: Changing Alliances* (London: Routledge, 2006), chap. 5; *Cuoc Khang Chien Chong My Cuu Nuoc 1954–1975* [The Anti-U.S. War of National Salvation, 1954–1975] (Hanoi: Quan doi Nhan den, 1980), 35; Paul Kattenburg interview, 1981, WGBH Vietnam Collection, openvault.wgbh.org/catalog/org.wgbh.mla:Vietnam (last accessed on November 18, 2010).

34 *Mien Dong Nam Bo Khang Chien,* 30–68.

35 Carlyle A. Thayer, *War by Other Means: National Liberation and Revolution in Viet-Nam, 1954–1960* (Sydney: Allen & Unwin, 1989), 92; A. J. Langguth, *Our Vietnam: The War, 1954–1975* (New York: Simon & Schuster, 2000), 100. See also Christopher E. Goscha and Stein Tønnesson, "Le Duan and the Break with China," in Priscilla Roberts, ed., *Behind the Bamboo Curtain: China, Vietnam, and the World Beyond Asia* (Stanford, Calif.: Stanford University Press, 2006), 455–57.

36 *Van Kien Dang, Toan Tap, 20, 1959* [Collected Party Documents, Volume 20, 1959] (Hanoi: National Political Publishing House, 2002), 2–55, translated by Merle Pribbenow; Military History Institute of Vietnam, *Victory in Vietnam: The Official History of the People's Army of Vietnam, 1954–1975,* trans. Merle Pribbenow (Lawrence: University Press of Kansas, 2002), 49–50.

37 William J. Duiker, *Sacred War: Nationalism and Revolution in a Divided Vietnam* (New York: McGraw-Hill, 1995), 120–21; *Cuoc Khang Chien Chong My Cuu Nuoc 1954–1975,* 49–50; *Lich Su Bien Nien Xu Uy Nam Bo va Trung Uong Cuc Mien Nam,* 179–84. There is confusion in the documentation about whether the decisions made at the Fifteenth Plenum were formalized then, in January 1959, or after another meeting in May, when another, similar "Resolution 15" was debated and adopted. Most likely the later meeting, which occurred after Ho Chi Minh traveled to the USSR and China to consult with Hanoi's principal allies, ratified the earlier decision. Thayer, *War by Other Means,* 185.

38 Military History Institute of Vietnam, *Victory in Vietnam,* 51–53.

39 Elliott, *Vietnamese War,* 119.

40 Cited in David Chanoff and Doan Van Toai, *Vietnam: A Portrait of Its People at War* (London: I. B. Tauris, 1996), 151–53. See also William J. Duiker, *Ho Chi Minh: A Life* (New York: Hyperion, 2000), 517–18.

41 *Cuoc Khang Chien Chong My Cuu Nuoc 1954–1975,* 81; Mark Moyar, *Triumph Forsaken: The Vietnam War, 1954–1965* (New York: Cambridge University Press, 2006), 81–91. On the founding of the NLF, a classic account is Frances FitzGerald, *Fire in the Lake: The Vietnamese and the Americans in Vietnam* (Boston:

Little, Brown, 1972), chap. 4. And see Robert K. Brigham, *Guerrilla Diplomacy: The NLF's Foreign Relations and the Viet Nam War* (Ithaca, N.Y.: Cornell University Press, 1999), chap. 1; Douglas Pike, *Viet Cong: The Organization and Techniques of the National Liberation Front of South Vietnam* (Cambridge, Mass.: MIT Press, 1966); and Joseph J. Zasloff, *Political Motivation of the Viet Cong: The Vietminh Regroupees* (Santa Monica, Calif.: Rand Corporation, 1975).

42 John Prados, *Vietnam: The History of an Unwinnable War, 1945–1975* (Lawrence: University Press of Kansas, 2009), 71; William S. Turley, *The Second Indochina War: A Short Political and Military History, 1954–1975* (Boulder: Westview Press, 1986), 44.

43 Elliott, *Vietnamese War,* 102–3; Kahin, *Intervention,* 97–98; *The Pentagon Papers: The Defense Department History of Decisionmaking on Vietnam,* Senator Gravel edition (Boston: Beacon Press, 1971), 1:252; Pham Thanh Gion interview, 1981, WGBH Vietnam Collection, openvault.wgbh.org/catalog/org.wgbh.mla:Vietnam (last accessed on November 2, 2010).

44 Quoted in Elliott, *Vietnamese War,* 103.

45 *Pentagon Papers* (Gravel) 1:312. On the agrovilles and their development, see, e.g., Catton, *Diem's Final Failure,* chap. 3; and Biggs, *Quagmire,* 188–93. A more or less contemporaneous account is Joseph J. Zasloff, "Rural Resettlement in Vietnam: The Agroville Program," *Pacific Affairs* 35 (1962–63).

46 Elliott, *Vietnamese War,* 127, 103. See also FitzGerald, *Fire in the Lake,* 194–95; and David Hunt, *Vietnam's Southern Revolution: From Peasant Insurrection to Total War* (Amherst: University of Massachusetts Press, 2008), chap. 3.

47 Nguyen Thi Dinh interview, 1981, WGBH Vietnam Collection, openvault.wgbh .org/catalog/org.wgbh.mla:Vietnam (last accessed on November 22, 2010).

48 Mrs. Nguyen Thi Dinh, *No Other Road to Take,* translated by Mai V. Elliott (Ithaca, N.Y.: Cornell Southeast Asia Program Publications, 1976); Nguyen Thi Dinh interview, 1981, WGBH Vietnam Collection, openvault.wgbh.org/catalog/org.wgbh .mla:Vietnam (last accessed on November 22, 2010).

49 Dinh, *No Other Road,* 69–70.

50 Arnold, *First Domino,* 342; *NYT,* July 7, 1959, as quoted in Moyar, *Triumph Forsaken,* 81.

51 Bernard B. Fall, *The Two Viet-Nams: A Political and Military Analysis* (New York: Praeger, 1964), 327–28.

52 Operations Coordinating Board Report, January 7, 1959, Box 25, NSC 5809 Policy Paper Subseries, Eisenhower Library.

53 Catton, *Diem's Final Failure,* 48–50. On Diem's conception of democracy, see also FitzGerald, *Fire in the Lake,* 109–11.

54 Nhu quoted in Catton, *Diem's Final Failure,* 29.

55 Diem quoted in James Fisher, "'A World Made Safe for Diversity': The Vietnam Lobby and the Politics of Pluralism, 1945–1963," in Christian Appy, ed., *Cold War Constructions: The Political Culture of United States Imperialism, 1945–1966* (Amherst: University of Massachusetts Press, 2000), 229.

56 Ahearn, *CIA and Rural Pacification in South Vietnam,* 31. The intelligence agent quoted in Barbara W. Tuchman, *The March of Folly: From Troy to Vietnam* (New York: Alfred A. Knopf, 1984), 280.

57 Spector, *Advice and Support,* 371; William J. Duiker, *U.S. Containment Policy and the Conflict in Indochina* (Stanford, Calif.: Stanford University Press, 1994), 241. On Diem continuing to frame the problem in military terms, even as Williams fi-

nally appeared to concede that the political dimension also mattered, see Ahearn, *CIA and the House of Ngo,* 136.

58 *Time,* July 20, 1959; Spector, *Advice and Support,* 329; *Mien Dong Nam Bo Khang Chien,* 70–71. See also *Houston Post,* July 8, 1984; and *USA Today,* July 8, 2009.

59 *People,* July 9, 1984.

60 Ibid.

61 Stanley Karnow, *Vietnam: A History* (New York: Viking, 1983), 10–11. Due to his name being misspelled as "Ovnard," Ovnand's name was later added to the Wall a second time, at Panel 7E, Row 46. A case for the first American to be killed in South Vietnam could also be made for Captain Harry Griffith Cramer, Jr., who died in an explosion of uncertain cause near Nha Trang in October 1957. His name was added to the Wall in 1983 and appears on panel 01E, Row 78. Another candidate is Air Force T-Sgt. Richard B. Fitzgibbon, Jr., killed on June 8, 1956. His name, added in 1999, appears on Panel 52E, Row 21.

62 Spector, *Advice and Support,* 329.

63 *Time,* July 20, 1959; Karnow, *Vietnam,* 10–11.

EPILOGUE: *Different Dreams, Same Footsteps*

1 Quoted in Barbara W. Tuchman, *The March of Folly: From Troy to Vietnam* (New York: Alfred A. Knopf, 1984), 283. Paul Kattenburg, in 1961 a State Department specialist on Vietnam, would later write of this period: "Policy-planning exercises never defined vital interest positions themselves, but always assumed them." Paul Kattenburg, *The Vietnam Trauma in American Foreign Policy, 1945–75* (New Brunswick, N.J.: Transaction, 1980), 101–2.

2 Robert Dallek, *An Unfinished Life: John F. Kennedy, 1917–1963* (Boston: Little, Brown, 2003), 166–67; and *The Pentagon Papers: The Defense Department History of Decisionmaking on Vietnam,* Senator Gravel edition (Boston: Beacon Press, 1971), 1:72.

3 Quoted in Christopher Matthews, *Kennedy and Nixon: The Rivalry That Shaped Postwar America* (New York: Simon & Schuster, 1996), 118.

4 Arthur M. Schlesinger, Jr., *A Thousand Days* (Boston: Little, Brown, 1965), 505, 547.

5 Christian G. Appy, *Patriots: The Vietnam War Remembered from All Sides* (New York: Viking, 2003), 66–67.

6 *NYT,* February 25, 1962, reprinted in *Reporting Vietnam, Part 1: American Journalism 1959–1975* (New York: Library of America, 1998), 11–17.

7 Lorenz M. Lüthi, *The Sino-Soviet Split: Cold War in the Communist World* (Princeton, N.J.: Princeton University Press, 2008); Sergey Radchenko, *Two Suns in the Heavens: The Sino-Soviet Struggle for Supremacy, 1962–67* (Washington, D.C.: Woodrow Wilson Center Press, 2009). The JCS memo is quoted in Seymour Topping, *Journey Between Two Chinas* (New York: Harper & Row, 1972), 178.

8 The literature on the 1961–65 period is very large. See, e.g., David Halberstam, *The Best and the Brightest* (New York: Random House, 1972); Fredrik Logevall, *Choosing War: The Lost Chance for Peace and the Escalation of War in Vietnam* (Berkeley: University of California Press, 1999); David Kaiser, *American Tragedy: Kennedy, Johnson, and the Origins of the Vietnam War* (Cambridge, Mass.: Harvard University Press, 2000); Gordon Goldstein, *Lessons in Disaster: McGeorge Bundy and the Path to War in Vietnam* (New York: Times Books, 2008); Andrew

Preston, *The War Council: McGeorge Bundy, the NSC, and Vietnam* (Cambridge, Mass.: Harvard University Press, 2006).

9 White letter quoted in Michael E. Latham, *The Right Kind of Revolution: Modernization, Development, and U.S. Foreign Policy from the Cold War to the Present* (Ithaca, N.Y.: Cornell University Press, 2011), 136.

10 Lansdale speech, "Soldiers and the People," August 30, 1962, Box 7, #239, Lansdale Papers, Hoover Institution on War, Revolution, and Peace. On another occasion, Lansdale argued that the preferred way to get rid of the Viet Cong in one particular area was to use "human defoliation" in the hardwood forests: Instead of using chemical defoliants, officials should award a timber concession to a Taiwanese firm that would arm its workers. "They might very well have to fight to get to the trees so they would clean up the Viet Cong along the way," Lansdale reasoned. The scheme was quietly filed. Jonathan Nashel, *Edward Lansdale's Cold War* (Amherst: University of Massachusetts Press, 2005), 66.

11 Richard Stubbs, *Hearts and Minds in Guerrilla Warfare: The Malayan Emergency, 1948–1960* (Singapore: Oxford University Press, 1989); Susan L. Carruthers, *Winning Hearts and Minds: British Governments, the Media, and Colonial Counter-Insurgency, 1944–1960* (Leicester, U.K.: Leicester University Press, 1998); Michael Osborne, *Strategic Hamlets in Vietnam* (Ithaca, N.Y.: Cornell University Press, 1965).

12 David Halberstam, "The Americanization of Vietnam," *Playboy*, January 1970, as quoted in Nashel, *Edward Lansdale's Cold War*, 151.

13 For counterfactual assessments regarding what a surviving Kennedy might have done in Vietnam, see, e.g., Logevall, *Choosing War*, 395–400; and James G. Blight, Janet M. Lang, and David A. Welch, *Vietnam If Kennedy Had Lived: Virtual JFK* (Lanham, Md.: Rowman & Littlefield, 2009). For the argument (which I find unpersuasive) that Kennedy had initiated a withdrawal at the time of his death, see James Galbraith, "Exit Strategy," *Boston Review*, January–February 2004, 29–34; and Gareth Porter, *Perils of Dominance: Imbalance of Power and the Road to War in Vietnam* (Berkeley: University of California Press, 2005), 165–79.

14 LBJ-Bundy telcon, September 8, 1964, in Michael Beschloss, ed., *Reaching for Glory: Lyndon Johnson's Secret White House Tapes, 1964–1965* (New York: Simon & Schuster, 2001), 35–36; LBJ-Russell telcon, March 6, 1965, ibid., 210–13.

15 On Kennedy and Johnson's options in 1963–65, see Logevall, *Choosing War.*

16 On this vulnerability and its influence on foreign policy in the Cold War as a whole, see Campbell Craig and Fredrik Logevall, *America's Cold War: The Politics of Insecurity* (Cambridge, Mass.: Belknap Press/Harvard University Press, 2009).

17 Ho is quoted in William J. Duiker, *Ho Chi Minh: A Life* (New York: Hyperion, 2000), 535.

18 O.A. Westad, Chen Jian, Stein Tønnesson, Nguyen Vu Tung, and James G. Hershberg, eds., "77 Conversations Between Chinese and Foreign Leaders on the Wars in Vietnam," Cold War International History Project Working Paper, 1998, pp. 83–84.

19 Duiker, *Ho Chi Minh*, 548.

20 David Schoenbrun, *As France Goes* (New York: Atheneum, 1968), 232–35.

21 Alain Peyrefitte, *C'était de Gaulle: La France reprend sa place dans la monde* (Paris: Fayard, 1997), 501; Paris to State, May 5, 1965, Box 171, National Security File, Country File, France, Lyndon Baines Johnson Library. On French policy in this period, see Pierre Journoud, *De Gaulle et le Vietnam, 1945–1969* (Paris: Éditions Tallandier, 2011), chap. 4.

22 Bernard B. Fall, "The War in Vietnam," *Current* (December 1965), 9–10. Emphasis in original. See also Christopher E. Goscha, "'Sorry About That . . .': Bernard Fall, the Vietnam War, and the Impact of a French Intellectual in the U.S.," in Christopher E. Goscha and Maurice Vaïsse, eds., *La Guerre du Vietnam et l'Europe (1963–1973)* (Paris: LGDJ, 2003), 363–82.

23 The literature on counterinsurgency has grown enormously in the years since 9/11 and the interventions in Afghanistan and Iraq. See, e.g., David Kilcullen, *The Accidental Guerrilla: Fighting Small Wars in the Midst of a Big One* (New York: Oxford University Press, 2009); John A. Nagl, *Counterinsurgency Lessons from Malaya and Vietnam: Learning to Eat Soup with a Knife* (New York: Praeger, 2002); Gian P. Gentile, "A (Slightly) Better War: A Narrative and Its Defects," *World Affairs* (Summer 2008); Edward Luttwak, "Dead End: Counterinsurgency Warfare as Military Malpractice," *Harper's* (February 2007); and *The U.S. Army/Marine Corps Counterinsurgency Field Manual* (Chicago: University of Chicago Press, 2005). See also Jeffrey Record, *Beating Goliath: Why Insurgencies Win* (Washington, D.C.: Potomac Books, 2007); and Andrew J. Bacevich, *Washington Rules: America's Path to Permanent War* (New York: Metropolitan, 2010), chap. 5.

24 Quoted in David Halberstam, *Ho* (New York: McGraw-Hill, 1987), 106. On Fall and his experience, see Dorothy Fall, *Bernard Fall: Memories of a Soldier-Scholar* (Washington, D.C.: Potomac, 2006). In early 1966, the Harvard historian John K. Fairbank would put it slightly differently: "On the long thin coast of Vietnam, we are sleeping in the same bed the French slept in even though we dream different dreams." *New York Review of Books,* February 17, 1966.

FURTHER READING

Although the literature on the period covered in this book pales in size next to that detailing the years of heavy U.S. military involvement (1961–73), interested readers can find numerous studies that shed light on key parts of the story—and that were exceptionally helpful to me. Here follows a selected list of English-language works I utilized. For additional published sources, please see the endnotes.

Ahearn, Thomas L., Jr. *CIA and the House of Ngo: Covert Action in South Vietnam, 1954–63.* Washington, D.C.: Center for the Study of Intelligence, Central Intelligence Agency, 2000.

Allen, George W. *None So Blind: A Personal Account of the Intelligence Failure in Vietnam.* Chicago: Ivan R. Dee, 2001.

Anderson, David L. *Trapped by Success: The Eisenhower Administration and Vietnam, 1953–1961.* New York: Columbia University Press, 1991.

Appy, Christian G. *Patriots: The Vietnam War Remembered from All Sides.* New York: Viking, 2003.

Arnold, James R. *The First Domino: Eisenhower, the Military, and America's Intervention in Vietnam.* New York: William Morrow, 1991.

Asselin, Pierre. "The Democratic Republic of Vietnam and the 1954 Geneva Conference: A Revisionist Critique." *Cold War History* 11:2 (May 2011).

Bartholomew-Feis, Dixee R. *The OSS and Ho Chi Minh: Unexpected Allies in the War Against Japan.* Lawrence: University Press of Kansas, 2006.

Berman, Larry. *Perfect Spy: The Incredible Double Life of Pham Xuan An.* New York: Smithsonian Books, 2007.

Bidault, Georges. *Resistance: The Political Autobiography of Georges Bidault.* Translated by Marianne Sinclair. New York: Praeger, 1968.

Billings-Yun, Melanie. *Decision Against War: Eisenhower and Dienbienphu, 1954.* New York: Columbia University Press, 1988.

Bodard, Lucien. *The Quicksand War: Prelude to Vietnam.* Boston: Little, Brown, 1967.

Bradley, Mark Philip. *Imagining Vietnam and America: The Making of Postcolonial Vietnam, 1919–1950.* Chapel Hill: University of North Carolina Press, 2000.

Brocheux, Pierre. *Ho Chi Minh: A Biography.* New York: Cambridge University Press, 2007.

———— and Daniel Hémery. *Indochina: An Ambiguous Colonization, 1858–1954.* Translated by Ly Lan Dill-Klein et al. Berkeley: University of California Press, 2009.

Bui Diem with David Chanoff. *In the Jaws of History.* Boston: Houghton Mifflin, 1987.

Bui Tin. *Following Ho Chi Minh: The Memoirs of a North Vietnamese Colonel.* Honolulu: University of Hawaii Press, 1995.

Buttinger, Joseph. *Vietnam: A Dragon Embattled.* 2 vols. New York: Praeger, 1967.

Cable, James. *The Geneva Conference of 1954 on Indochina.* London: Macmillan, 1986.

Catton, Philip E. *Diem's Final Failure: Prelude to America's War in Vietnam.* Lawrence: University Press of Kansas, 2002.

Chen Jian. *Mao's China and the Cold War.* Chapel Hill: University of North Carolina Press, 2001.

Cooper, Chester L. *In the Shadows of History: Fifty Years Behind the Scenes of Cold War Diplomacy.* Amherst, N.Y.: Prometheus, 2005.

_____. *The Lost Crusade: America in Vietnam.* New York: Dodd, Mead, 1970.

Currey, Cecil B. *Victory at Any Cost: The Genius of Viet Nam's Gen. Vo Nguyen Giap.* Dulles, Va.: Potomac, 2005.

Dalloz, Jacques. *The War in Indo-China, 1945–1954.* New York: Barnes & Noble, 1990.

Davidson, Phillip B. *Vietnam at War: The History, 1946–1975.* New York: Oxford University Press, 1991.

Devillers, Philippe and Jean Lacouture. *End of a War: Indochina, 1954.* New York: Praeger, 1969.

Dreifort, John E. *Myopic Grandeur: The Ambivalence of French Foreign Policy toward the Far East, 1919–1945.* Kent, Oh.: Kent State University Press, 1991.

Duiker, William J. *Ho Chi Minh: A Life.* New York: Hyperion, 2000.

_____. *U.S. Containment Policy and the Conflict in Indochina.* Stanford, Calif.: Stanford University Press, 1994.

Eden, Anthony. *Full Circle: The Memoirs of Anthony Eden.* Boston: Houghton Mifflin, 1960.

Elliott, David W. P. *The Vietnamese War: Revolution and Social Change in the Mekong Delta, 1930–1975.* Armonk, N.Y.: M.E. Sharpe, 2007.

Elliott, Duong Van Mai. *The Sacred Willow: Four Generations in the Life of a Vietnamese Family.* New York: Oxford University Press, 2000.

Fall, Bernard B. *Hell in a Very Small Place: The Siege of Dien Bien Phu.* Philadelphia: Lippincott, 1966.

_____, ed. *Ho Chi Minh on Revolution: Selected Writings 1920–1966.* New York: Praeger, 1967.

_____. *Street Without Joy: Indochina at War 1946–1954.* Harrisburg, Pa.: Stackpole Books, 1961.

_____. *The Two Viet-Nams: A Political and Military Analysis.* New York: Praeger, 1964.

Fall, Dorothy. *Bernard Fall: Memories of a Soldier-Scholar.* Washington, D.C.: Potomac, 2006.

FitzGerald, Frances. *Fire in the Lake: The Vietnamese and the Americans in Vietnam.* Boston: Little, Brown, 1972.

Gaiduk, Ilya V. *Confronting Vietnam: Soviet Policy Toward the Indochina Conflict, 1954–1963.* Stanford, Calif.: Stanford University Press, 2003.

Gardner, Lloyd C. *Approaching Vietnam: From World War II Through Dienbienphu.* New York: W.W. Norton, 1989.

Goscha, Christopher E. "Courting Diplomatic Disaster? The Difficult Integration of Vietnam into the Internationalist Communist Movement (1945–1950)." *Journal of Vietnamese Studies* 1 (February 2006).

Goscha, Christopher E. and Christian F. Ostermann, eds. *Connecting Histories: Decolonization and the Cold War in Southeast Asia, 1945–1962.* Washington, D.C.: Woodrow Wilson Center Press, 2009.

Greene, Graham. *The Quiet American.* New York: Viking, 1956.

_____. *Ways of Escape.* New York: Simon & Schuster, 1980.

Halberstam, David. *The Best and the Brightest.* New York: Random House, 1972.

Hammer, Ellen J. *The Struggle for Indochina, 1940–1955.* Stanford, Calif.: Stanford University Press, 1955.

Herring, George C. *America's Longest War: The United States and Vietnam, 1950–1975,* 4th ed. New York: McGraw-Hill, 2002.

_____ and Richard H. Immerman. "Eisenhower, Dulles, and Dienbienphu: 'The Day We Didn't Go to War' Revisited." *Journal of American History* 71 (September 1984).

Herzstein, Robert E. *Henry R. Luce, Time, and the American Crusade in Asia.* New York: Cambridge University Press, 2005.

Hess, Gary. *The United States' Emergence as a Southeast Asian Power, 1940–1950.* New York: Columbia University Press, 1987.

Immerman, Richard. "Between the Unattainable and the Unacceptable: Eisenhower and Dienbienphu." In *Reevaluating Eisenhower: American Foreign Policy in the 1950s,* edited by Richard A. Melanson and David Mayers. Urbana: University of Illinois Press, 1987.

Jackson, Julian. *France: The Dark Years, 1940–1944.* Oxford, U.K.: Oxford University Press, 2001.

Jacobs, Seth. *America's Miracle Man in Vietnam: Ngo Dinh Diem, Religion, Race, and U.S. Intervention in Southeast Asia, 1950–1957.* Durham, N.C.: Duke University Press, 2005.

Jennings, Eric. *Vichy in the Tropics: Pétain's National Revolution in Madagascar, Guadeloupe, and Indochina, 1940–1944.* Stanford, Calif.: Stanford University Press, 2004.

Kahin, George McTurnan. *Intervention: How America Became Involved in Vietnam.* New York: Alfred A. Knopf, 1986.

Kaplan, Lawrence S., Denise Artaud, and Mark Rubin, eds. *Dien Bien Phu and the Crisis of Franco-American Relations, 1954–1955.* Wilmington, Del.: Scholarly Resources, 1990.

Karnow, Stanley. *Vietnam: A History,* 2nd ed. New York: Penguin, 1997.

Kattenburg, Paul. *The Vietnam Trauma in American Foreign Policy, 1945–75.* New Brunswick, N.J.: Transaction, 1980.

Kimball, Warren F. *The Juggler: Franklin Roosevelt as Wartime Statesman.* Princeton, N.J.: Princeton University Press, 1991.

Lacouture, Jean. *Pierre Mendès France.* Translated by George Holock. New York: Holmes & Meier, 1984.

LaFeber, Walter. "Roosevelt, Churchill, and Indochina: 1942–1945." *American Historical Review* 80 (December 1975).

Langguth, A.J. *Our Vietnam: The War, 1954–1975.* New York: Simon & Schuster, 2000.

Lawrence, Mark Atwood. *Assuming the Burden: Europe and the American Commitment to War in Vietnam.* Berkeley: University of California Press, 2005.

_____ and Fredrik Logevall, eds. *The First Vietnam War: Colonial Conflict and Cold War Crisis.* Cambridge, Mass.: Harvard University Press, 2007.

Logevall, Fredrik. *Choosing War: The Lost Chance for Peace and the Escalation of War in Vietnam.* Berkeley: University of California Press, 1999.

Mann, Robert. *A Grand Delusion: America's Descent into Vietnam.* New York: Basic, 2001.

Marr, David G. *Vietnam 1945: The Quest for Power.* Berkeley: University of California Press, 1995.

_____. *Vietnamese Anticolonialism, 1885–1925.* Berkeley: University of California Press, 1971.

McAlister, John T., Jr., and Paul Mus. *The Vietnamese and Their Revolution.* New York: Harper & Row, 1970.

Miller, Edward. "Vision, Power and Agency: The Ascent of Ngô Dình Diêm, 1945–54." *Journal of Southeast Asian Studies* 35 (October 2004).

Morgan, Ted. *Valley of Death: The Tragedy at Dien Bien Phu That Led America into the Vietnam War*. New York: Random House, 2010.

Moyar, Mark. *Triumph Forsaken: The Vietnam War, 1954–1965*. New York: Cambridge University Press, 2006.

Nashel, Jonathan. *Edward Lansdale's Cold War*. Amherst: University of Massachusetts Press, 2005.

O'Ballance, Edgar. *The Indo-China War, 1945–1954*. London: Faber & Faber, 1964.

Oberdorfer, Don. *Senator Mansfield: The Extraordinary Life of a Great American Statesman and Diplomat*. Washington, D.C.: Smithsonian, 2003.

Patti, Archimedes L. A. *Why Viet Nam? Prelude to America's Albatross*. Berkeley: University of California Press, 1981.

Porch, Douglas. *The French Foreign Legion: A Complete History of the Legendary Fighting Force*. New York: HarperCollins, 1991.

Prados, John. *Operation Vulture*. New York: ibooks, 2002.

Quinn-Judge, Sophie. *Ho Chi Minh: The Missing Years 1919–1941*. Berkeley: University of California Press, 2003.

Rotter, Andrew J. *The Path to Vietnam: Origins of the American Commitment to Southeast Asia*. Ithaca, N.Y.: Cornell University Press, 1987.

Roy, Jules. *The Battle of Dienbienphu*. Translated by Robert Baldick. New York: Harper & Row, 1965.

Ruane, Kevin. "Anthony Eden, British Diplomacy, and the Origins of the Geneva Conference of 1954." *Historical Journal* 37 (1994).

Sainteny, Jean. *Ho Chi Minh and His Vietnam: A Personal Memoir*. Chicago: Cowles, 1972.

Schoenbrun, David. *As France Goes*. New York: Atheneum, 1968.

Shaplen, Robert. *The Lost Revolution: The U.S. in Vietnam, 1946–1966*. New York: Harper & Row, 1966.

Sheehan, Neil. *A Bright Shining Lie: John Paul Vann and America in Vietnam*. New York: Random House, 1988.

Sherry, Norman. *The Life of Graham Greene*, vol. 2: *1939–1955*. New York: Viking, 1995.

Shipway, Martin. *The Road to War: France and Vietnam, 1944–1947*. Providence, R.I.: Berghahn, 1996.

Shuckburgh, Evelyn. *Descent to Suez: Diaries, 1951–1956*. New York: W.W. Norton, 1987.

Simpson, Howard R. *Dien Bien Phu: The Epic Battle America Forgot*. Washington, D.C.: Brassey's, 1994.

————. *Tiger in the Barbed Wire: An American in Vietnam, 1952–1991*. Washington, D.C.: Brassey's, 1992.

Spector, Ronald H. *Advice and Support: The Early Years of the U.S. Army in Vietnam, 1941–1960*. Washington, D.C.: Center for Military History, 1985.

————. *In the Ruins of Empire: The Japanese Surrender and the Battle for Postwar Asia*. New York: Random House, 2007.

Statler, Kathryn C. *Replacing France: The Origins of American Intervention in Vietnam*. Lexington: University Press of Kentucky, 2007.

Thayer, Carlyle. *War by Other Means: National Liberation and Revolution in Viet Nam, 1954–1960*. Sydney: Allen & Unwin, 1989.

Thomas, Martin. *The French Empire at War, 1940–1945*. Manchester, U.K.: Manchester University Press, 2007.

Thorne, Christopher G. *Allies of a Kind: The United States, Britain, and the War Against Japan*. London: Hamish Hamilton, 1978.

Tønnesson, Stein. *The Vietnamese Revolution of 1945: Roosevelt, Ho Chi Minh and de Gaulle in a World at War.* London: Sage, 1991.

_____. *Vietnam 1946: How the War Began.* Berkeley: University of California Press, 2009.

Vo Nguyen Giap. *Dien Bien Phu: Rendezvous with History.* Hanoi: Gioi, 2004.

_____. *Memoirs of War: The Road to Dien Bien Phu.* Hanoi: Gioi, 2004.

_____. *Unforgettable Days.* Hanoi: Foreign Languages Publishing House, 1975.

Windrow, Martin. *The Last Valley: Dien Bien Phu and the French Defeat in Vietnam.* Cambridge, Mass.: Da Capo, 2004.

Young, Marilyn B. *The Vietnam Wars, 1945–1990.* New York: HarperCollins, 1991.

Zinoman, Peter. *The Colonial Bastille: A History of Imprisonment in Vietnam, 1862–1940.* Berkeley: University of California Press, 2001.

PHOTO CREDITS

INDEX

Page numbers of photographs and maps appear in italics.